# IMPORTANT:

## HERE IS YOUR REGISTRATION CODE TO ACCESS
## YOUR PREMIUM McGRAW-HILL ONLINE RESOURCES.

For key premium online resources you need THIS CODE to gain access. Once the code is entered, you will be able to use the Web resources for the length of your course.

If your course is using **WebCT** or **Blackboard**, you'll be able to use this code to access the McGraw-Hill content within your instructor's online course.

Access is provided if you have purchased a new book. If the registration code is missing from this book, the registration screen on our Website, and within your WebCT or Blackboard course, will tell you how to obtain your new code.

## Registering for McGraw-Hill Online Resources

TO gain access to your McGraw-Hill web resources simply follow the steps below:

(1) USE YOUR WEB BROWSER TO GO TO: **www.mhhe.com/bordens6**

(2) CLICK ON **FIRST TIME USER**.

(3) ENTER THE REGISTRATION CODE* PRINTED ON THE TEAR-OFF BOOKMARK ON THE RIGHT.

(4) AFTER YOU HAVE ENTERED YOUR REGISTRATION CODE, CLICK **REGISTER**.

(5) FOLLOW THE INSTRUCTIONS TO SET-UP YOUR PERSONAL UserID AND PASSWORD.

(6) WRITE YOUR UserID AND PASSWORD DOWN FOR FUTURE REFERENCE. KEEP IT IN A SAFE PLACE.

**TO GAIN ACCESS** to the McGraw-Hill content in your instructor's **WebCT** or **Blackboard** course simply log in to the course with the UserID and Password provided by your instructor. Enter the registration code exactly as it appears in the box to the right when prompted by the system. You will only need to use the code the first time you click on McGraw-Hill content.

Thank you, and welcome to your McGraw-Hill Online Resources!

0-07-297571-7  T/A  BORDENS/ABBOTT,  RESEARCH DESIGN AND METHODS, 6/E

# Research and Design Methods

## A Process Approach

### SIXTH EDITION

Kenneth S. Bordens

Bruce B. Abbott

*Indiana University—Perdue University, Fort Wayne*

Boston   Burr Ridge, IL   Dubuque, IA   Madison, WI   New York
San Francisco   St. Louis   Bangkok   Bogotá   Caracas   Kuala Lumpur
Lisbon   London   Madrid   Mexico City   Milan   Montreal   New Delhi
Santiago   Seoul   Singapore   Sydney   Taipei   Toronto

RESEARCH DESIGN AND METHODS: A PROCESS APPROACH
Published by McGraw-Hill, a business unit of The McGraw-Hill Companies, Inc., 1221 Avenue of the Americas,
New York, NY 10020. Copyright © 2005, 2002, 1999, 1996, 1991, 1988 by The McGraw-Hill Companies, Inc.
All rights reserved. No part of this publication may be reproduced or distributed in any form or by any means, or
stored in a database or retrieval system, without the prior written consent of The McGraw-Hill Companies, Inc.,
including, but not limited to, in any network or other electronic storage or transmission, or broadcast for distance learning.

Some ancillaries, including electronic and print components, may not be available to customers outside the
United States.

This book is printed on acid-free paper.

2  3  4  5  6  7  8  9  0  FGR/FGR  0  9  8  7  6  5  4

ISBN 0 07 288764 8

Publisher:   *Stephen Rutter*
Senior sponsoring editor:   *John T. Wannemacher*
Marketing manager:   *Melissa S. Caughlin*
Senior media producer:   *Sean Crowley*
Project manager:   *Catherine R. Iammartino*
Lead production supervisor:   *Randy L. Hurst*
Designer:   *Cassandra J. Chu*
Media project manager:   *Kathleen Boylan*
Senior print supplement producer:   *Louis Swaim*
Art director:   *Jeanne Schreiber*
Cover design:   *Bill Stanton*
Cover art:   *©Photodisc*
Interior design:   *Glenda King*
Typeface:   *10/12 Goudy*
Compositor:   *Thompson Type*
Printer:   *Quebecor World Fairfield Inc.*

**Library of Congress Cataloging-in-Publication Data**
Bordens, Kenneth S.
    Research design and methods : a process approach / Kenneth S. Bordens, Bruce B. Abbott.—6th ed.
    p. cm.
    Includes bibliographical references and index.
    ISBN 0-07-288764-8 (hardcover : alk. paper)
    1. Psychology—Research—Textbooks. 2. Psychology—Research—Methodology—Textbooks. I. Abbott, Bruce
B. II. Title.
BF76.5.B67 2005
150'.72—dc22        2004045911

www.mhhe.com

*To the memory of*
*Dr. Daniel P. Murphy,*
*colleague, friend, and teacher*

# CONTENTS

# PREFACE

It has been 16 years since the publication of the first edition of *Research Design and Methods: A Process Approach* (1988). The sixth edition represents a continuing evolution of the text to better meet the needs of students and instructors. With each new edition, our goal has been to provide students and instructors with a book that accurately reflects the research process.

We have retained the basic theme of taking students through the entire research process, from getting and developing a research idea, to designing and conducting a study, through analyzing and reporting data. Our goal continues to be presenting students with information on the numerous decisions they must make when designing and conducting research and how early decisions affect how data are collected, analyzed and interpreted later in the research process. We also wanted to reinforce the need to treat research subjects ethically and show how requirements of ethical treatments interface with research needs. The text is still organized to follow the sequence of steps involved in actually designing and conducting research. We worked to present the material in a friendly, easy-to-read style, with plenty of examples to clarify crucial concepts.

On the basis of the response to the earlier editions of this text, we think we have achieved many of these goals. We have preserved all of these elements in the sixth edition. We have remained true to our goal to provide students with a realistic view of how research is done, written in an engaging and interesting style. We have retained the basic focus on the research process, from developing ideas, to doing a literature search and evaluating research, to developing a research design and conducting the research, through analyzing and reporting results. However, based on feedback from students and reviewers, we have made some changes, described below, that we hope will further improve the book.

## CHANGES IN THE SIXTH EDITION

Several important changes have been made to the sixth edition that distinguish it from earlier editions. Although the basic structure and organization of the book remain the same, changes have been made to each chapter. First, each chapter now begins with an outline of the chapter and includes a set of Review Questions following the Chapter Summary. The outline should help students by giving a preview of the main topics covered in each chapter. The Review Questions will help students focus on the major issues covered in each chapter. Additionally, many of the research examples throughout the text have been updated.

In addition to the changes common to all chapters, the following changes have been made to individual chapters.

## CHAPTER 1

1. A new opening vignette focusing on a case involving the effects of violent video games on aggressive behavior (replacing the old vignette and research example). This example is carried through the chapter where appropriate.
2. A new section has been added on "Why You Should Care About Learning about Research."

## CHAPTER 2

1. The section on getting and developing ideas for research has been updated and refined to provide a clearer presentation of how research ideas are developed.
2. The major section on theory has been rewritten to more clearly focus on the role of theory in science.
3. New examples have been added relating to behavioral science, replacing many of the examples from other sciences that were included in earlier editions.
4. The sections on developing theories have been eliminated.

## CHAPTER 3

1. The chapter has been updated to conform with the latest version of *PsycINFO*.
2. A new section on using *PsycARTICLES* has been added.
3. A new section added on Internet-based search engines (e.g. JESTOR, ISI Web of Science).
4. The section on fraud in science has been updated and expanded.
5. A new figure showing the process of how a manuscript is reviewed and published has been added.

## CHAPTER 4

1. A new research example of a correlational study (replacing the old one) is tied to the opening vignette and research example in Chapter 1.
2. A new research example of an experiment (replacing the old one) is tied to the opening vignette and research example in Chapter 1.
3. The section discussing threats to internal validity has been expanded to include concrete examples.
4. A table summarizing threats to external validity has been added.

## CHAPTER 5

1. New, up-to-date examples replace many older examples.
2. There is a newly organized and expanded section on the reliability of a measure.
3. The section on scales of measurement has been expanded and clarified.
4. A section on Q-sort methodology has been added.
5. The material on experimenter bias has been expanded and includes a new example from the research literature.

## CHAPTER 6

1. The section on sampling in Internet research has been expanded to include recent research in the area.
2. The American Psychological Association Ethical guidelines section has been updated reflecting the latest (2002) version of the guidelines.
3. The Department of Health and Human Services Ethical guidelines section has been updated reflecting the latest (2001) version of the guidelines.
4. Information on changing attitudes about using animals in research has been added.
5. An update to the controversy surrounding using animals in research has been added.

## CHAPTER 7

1. A new, updated example of observational research has been added.
2. A new section on using Intraclass Correlation to measure inter-rater reliability has been added.
3. A new example of a case history using a classic study from the history of psychology has been added (replacing the old one).
4. An example of archival research has been added.
5. A new example of content analysis has been added (replacing the old one).

## CHAPTER 8

1. A new example of a survey replaces the old one. This new example is carried through appropriate sections of the chapter.
2. The chapter has been revised to reflect Dillman's updated approach to survey design and execution (replaces information based on Dillman's earlier work).
3. The section on writing questionnaire items has been extensively revised and simplified. A table of question–writing flaws has been added and largely replaces the previous in-text list of writing flaws.
4. A discussion of the "navigational path" of a questionnaire has been added.
5. The section on "nonresponse bias" in mail surveys has been updated.
6. The section on Internet surveys has been updated and expanded.
7. The section on telephone surveys has been trimmed down

## CHAPTER 9

1. The section on making treatment order an independent variable has been rewritten and shortened to improve clarity.
2. In the section on interactions in factorial designs, a paragraph has been added to define the simple effects of each factor.

## CHAPTER 10

1. Under nested designs, a paragraph has been added describing the advantages and disadvantages of nested designs, relative to factorial designs. Portions of this section have been rewritten to improve clarity.
2. A paragraph has been added to the section on adding a covariate to an experimental design, in order to clarify the nature of a covariate.
3. The initial description of a quasi-independent variable now includes a brief concrete example to clarify the concept.
4. An example has been added to the discussion of pretest-posttest designs to illustrate a case in which a pretest may be needed to completely answer a research question.

## CHAPTER 11

1. To the section on the historical development of single-subject designs has been added a paragraph describing the introduction of the journal *Applied Behavior Analysis*.
2. The chapter now distinguished three categories of single-subject design by adding the category of "dynamic designs," which resemble baseline designs but employ a continuously varying independent variable and focus on observing a dynamically changing dependent variable rather than steady-state behavior.
3. The discussion of baseline designs has been reorganized and simplified to eliminate redundant discussions of the AB, ABA, and ABAB designs.
4. A new example has been provided illustrating the dynamic design.
5. The signal-detection example of a discrete-trials single-subject design has been rewritten and expanded to improve clarity.

## CHAPTER 12

1. The section on entering data on the computer has been updated to reflect the process on modern PC-based machines.
2. A clearer distinction between a histogram and bar graph has been made.
3. A clearer discussion and example of a bimodal distribution has been included

## CHAPTER 13

1. A new, updated example of the *t*-test replaces the old one.

2. A new, updated example of the two-factor ANOVA replaces the old one.
3. A discussion of the Wilcoxon Signed Ranks Test has been added.

## CHAPTER 14

1. The section on sample size needed for multiple regression has been updated.
2. A section on exploratory and confirmatory factor analysis has been added.
3. A new example of factor analysis replaces the old one.
4. A new example multiple regression replaces the old one.

## CHAPTER 15

1. The entire chapter has been revised to reflect the latest edition of the American Psychological Association's writing style.
2. The section on "typing" a manuscript has been updated to reflect the use of wordprocessors.

## CHANGES TO THE ANCILLARIES

The student study guide is now on CD-ROM and will be available at no additional cost to the student. The student study guide that accompanies the sixth edition has been updated to reflect the organizational and content changes made to the text. Each chapter now includes a list of key terms, practice questions (multiple-choice, fill-in, and essay) and hands-on exercises.

The instructor's manual remains largely unchanged, except for the fact that it is now completely on CD-ROM. Instructors may request a printed copy of the instructor's manual from the publisher. The instructor's manual still includes ideas for class exercises, many of which make use of the ever-expanding research methodology resources available on the Internet. The test bank has been updated to reflect changes in the new edition. And, once again we offer the test bank in computerized form for ease of exam preparation.

For this edition we have also developed a PowerPoint presentation for each chapter in the text. The PowerPoint presentations provide an overview of the key concepts and information in each chapter. The presentations are in a "generic format." That is, there is no animation or color scheme. Each instructor can generate his or her own personalized presentations by adding animation and a color scheme.

## ACKNOWLEDGMENTS

With each new edition the number of talented people to whom we owe a debt of thanks grows, although we can name only a relative few. The reviewers of the first edition helped to make is a success and pave the way for the second edition: Helen J. Crawford (University of Wyoming), Arthur D. Fiske (University of South Carolina), Daniel Leger (University of Nebraska), Beth A. Shapiro (Emory University), Michael S. Wolgarter (University of Richmond), Barbara Tabachnick (California State University, Northridge), and Elaine

Blakemore (Indiana University Purdue University Fort Wayne). The reviewers of the second edition showed us how we could improve the text in several areas: Carol Lawton (Indiana University Purdue University Fort Wayne), Patricia Phillips (Illinois State University), Daniel Leger (University of Nebraska), and Lori Temple-Colvet (University of Nevada, Las Vegas). The insightful comments and suggestions of the following reviewers helped to guide us through the third edition: Barry H. Cohen (New York University), George Mitchell (University of California, Davis), Charlotte Mandell (University of Massachusetts, Lowell), Beverly A. Goldfield (Rhode Island College), Particia Phillips (Mercer University), Charles Collyer (University of Rhode Island), Donald Leitner (Saint Joseph's University), Constance Jones (California State University, Fresno), Carol Lawton and Dennis Cannon (Indiana University Purdue University Fort Wayne), and Jonathan Tubman (Florida International University). To these names we add the reviewers of the fourth edition: Frank Haist (Georgia State University), Robert A. Hancock (Lincoln University), Christopher Leone (North Florida University), Scott M. Monroe (University of Oregon), and Blaine Peden (University of Wisconson). Fifth edition reviewers were Helen J. Crawford (Virginia Polytechnic Institute and State University), Dana L. Gross (Saint Olaf College), Margaret S. Jelinek Lewis (University of Idaho), and Scott Monroe (University of Oregon). For sixth edition, we add Gordon A. Allen (Miami University of Ohio), Martin Bink (University of North Texas), Elliot Bonam (Eastern Michigan University), Kathleen Donovan (University of Central Oklahoma), W. Jake Jacobs (University of Arizona), Matthew D. Johnson (Binghamton University), Jennifer Ann Morrow (Old Dominion University), and John P. Wilson (Cleveland State University). We thank each of them for their thoughtful and detailed comments. Our thanks go also to Franklin Graham, Sponsoring Editor at Mayfield Publishing Company, who nurtured the previous five editions of this text. To John Wannemacher, Sponsoring Editor at McGraw-Hill; and to Cathy Iammartino and the rest of the production staff at McGraw-Hill for their expert crafting of the final product.

We also extend our thanks to those students of ours who used the earlier editions and provided valuable feedback and suggestions on how to make the text better, and to everyone else we neglected to mention by name for their efforts.

Finally, to our success in this project we owe the continued support and encouragement of our wives, Stephanie Abbott and Ricky Bordens, and of our families. To them we owe a special thanks.

# 1

# Explaining Behavior

I n 2002, the U.S. District Court of Connecticut had to decide a
controversial case. In the case of *Andrea Wilson v. Midway Games,
Incorporated*, the court had to determine if the death of Wilson's 13-
year-old son, Noah, was related to the video game Mortal Kombat.
The circumstances leading up to the case were that Noah and his
friend (identified only as Yancy S.) had become addicted to the game,
in which players tried to kill each other in the most violent ways
imaginable. In the suit, Ms. Wilson maintained that the violent nature of the game and its addictive qualities caused Yancy S. to stab
her son Noah to death. She alleged that in killing Noah, Yancy had
used a maneuver that was very similar to one depicted in the game.
Andrea Wilson contended that the realistic, virtual-reality nature of
the game as well as its ability to immerse a child into its violent world
contributed to her son's death.

The heart of Andrea Wilson's complaint centered on two con-
tentions: first, that Midway, Inc., failed to warn potential players of the
game of its likely addictive effects, and second, that the game itself was
negligently designed . For its part, Midway, Inc., moved to dismiss Wilson's complaint on First Amendment (free speech) grounds. The court
ruled in Midway's favor, stating that the nature of the game protected
it under the First Amendment. However, the court went on to say this:

> Even accepting Wilson's allegations that Mortal Kombat caused
> violence and physical harm to be visited upon her son and de-
> spite the seemingly minimal utility of such depictions of violence,
> the First Amendment precludes Wilson's action for damages un-
> less Mortal Kombat's images or messages are "directed to inciting
> or producing imminent lawless action and [would be] likely to
> incite or produce such action."

The court found that this was not the case with Mortal Kombat
and issued a judgment in favor of Midway, Inc.

What makes this case so interesting is that it pits a legal question against a psychological one. The legal question surrounds a
company's liability in marketing a product that *may* cause a person

to do harm to another. The psychological question focuses on whether exposure to violent video games actually causes imitative violent behavior. Clearly, the court believed that this is possible. This case and the unfortunate killing of Noah Wilson reactivate a question that social scientists have been arguing over for years: the effects of media violence on aggressive behavior.

Several questions can be asked about the issues raised by this case. First and foremost is whether playing violent video games contributes to violent behavior. If so, then, second, are all violent video games equally likely to increase violence? Third, are all children affected equally by violent video games? These and similar questions can be directly addressed by scientific research. Psychological research on this issue has the potential to inform the courts about the relationship between media and real-world violence.

## FRAMING A PROBLEM IN SCIENTIFIC TERMS

Kelly (1963) characterizes each person as a scientist who develops a set of strategies for determining the causes of behavior observed. We humans are curious and like to have explanations for the things that happen to us and others. For example, after reading about the case of *Wilson v. Midway*, you probably began to think about other possible situational or personal factors that could have explained Yancy's behavior. Was he reared in an abusive home? Was he biologically predisposed to violence? Was he a normal kid who had his sense of reality warped by repeated exposure to a violent video game? Usually, the explanations we come up with are based on little information and mainly reflect personal opinions and biases. The everyday strategies we use to explain what we observe frequently lack the rigor to qualify as truly scientific approaches. In most cases, the explanations for everyday events are made on the spot, with little attention given to ensuring their accuracy. We simply develop an explanation and, satisfied with its plausibility, adopt it as correct. We do not consider exploring whether our explanation is correct or whether there might be other, better explanations.

If we do give more thought to our explanations, we often base our thinking on hearsay, conjecture, anecdotal evidence, or unverified sources of information. These revised explanations, even though they reduce transient curiosity, remain untested and are thus of questionable validity. For example, in the *Wilson* case, you might conclude that a child's worldview can be warped by overexposure to violent video games. To make matters worse, we have a tendency to look for information that will confirm our prior beliefs and assumptions and to ignore or downplay information that does not conform to those beliefs and assumptions. Thus, if you are satisfied that a child's worldview can be warped by video games, you may seek out information (e.g., magazine articles) that supports your point of view. The human tendency to seek out information that confirms what is already believed is known as the **confirmation bias**. At the same time, you may ignore information concerning the actual factors that contribute to the behavior.

Unfounded but commonly accepted explanations for behavior can have widespread consequences when the explanations become the basis for social policy. For example, segregation of Blacks in the South was based on stereotypes of assumed racial differences in intelligence and moral judgment. These beliefs sound ludicrous today and have failed to survive a scientific analysis. Such mistakes might have been avoided if lawmakers of the time had relied on objective information rather than on prejudice.

To avoid the trap of easy, untested explanations for behavior, we need to abandon the informal, unsystematic approach to explanation and adopt an approach that has proven its ability to find explanations of great power and generality. This approach, called the *scientific method*, and how you can apply it to answer questions about behavior are the central topics of this book.

This book is about the research process. In a broader sense, it is about the business of finding unambiguous explanations for behavior. This text describes how to develop scientifically testable research questions about behavior, how to develop and use acceptable methods of observation by using appropriate research designs, how to properly analyze and interpret the resulting data, and how to use these results to arrive at scientifically acceptable explanations.

## WHY SHOULD YOU CARE ABOUT LEARNING ABOUT RESEARCH?

Students sometimes express the sentiment that they think learning about research is a waste of time because they do not plan on a career in science. Although it is true that a strong background in science is essential if you plan to further your career in psychology after you graduate, it is also true that knowing about science is important even if you do *not* plan to become a researcher.

The layperson is bombarded by science every day. When you read about a "scientific" poll on a political issue, you are being exposed to science. When you hear about a new cure for a disease, you are being exposed to science. When you are persuaded to buy one product over another, you are being exposed to science. Science, on one level or another, permeates our everyday lives. In order to deal rationally with your world, you must be able to critically analyze the information thrown at you and be able to separate scientifically verified facts from unverified conjecture.

Another reason you should learn about research is so that you can critically analyze information on a variety of issues presented in the popular media. Often, television news programs present segments that *appear* scientific but on further scrutiny turn out to be flawed. One example was a segment on the ABC television news show *20/20* on sexual functions in women after a hysterectomy. In the segment, three women discussed their post-hysterectomy sexual dysfunction. One woman reported, "It got to the point where I couldn't have sex. I mean, it was so painful . . . we couldn't do it." The testimonials of the three patients were backed up by a number of medical experts who discussed the link between hysterectomy and sexual dysfunction.

Had you watched this segment and looked no further, you would have come away with the impression that post-hysterectomy sexual dysfunction is common. After all, all of the women interviewed experienced it and the experts supported them. However, your impression would not be correct. When we examine the research on post-hysterectomy sexual functioning, the picture is not nearly as clear as the one portrayed in the *20/20* segment. In fact, there are studies showing that after hysterectomy, women may report an *improvement* in sexual function (Rhodes, Kjerulff, Langenberg, & Guzinski, 1999). Other studies show that the type of hysterectomy a woman has makes a difference. If the surgery involves removing the cervix (a total hysterectomy), there is more sexual dysfunction after surgery than if the cervix is left intact (Saini, Kuczynski, Gretz, & Sills, 2002). Finally, the Boston University School of Medicine's Institute for Sexual Medicine reports that of 1,200 women seen at its Center for Sexual Medicine, very few women complained of post-hysterectomy sexual dysfunction (Goldstein, 2003).

So, whether you plan a career in research or not, it is to your benefit to learn how research is done. This will put you in a position to evaluate information you encounter that is supposedly based on "science." For example, we have heard much about the detrimental effects of exposure to secondhand smoke. Generally, we are led to believe that being around someone who smokes may be nearly as bad as smoking itself. This and other beliefs enter our consciousnesses and can shape personal opinion and public policy. (Recently, New York City banned smoking even in bars.) When confronted with a statement that links secondhand smoke with health hazards, you should ask yourself what the basis for the statement is. Is it based on conjecture, political expediency, or solid scientific evidence? In fact, if you were to look carefully at the real science on secondhand smoke, you would find that it is not the serious health hazard it is made out to be.

## EXPLORING THE CAUSES OF BEHAVIOR

Psychology is the science of human and animal behavior. The major goals of psychology (as in any other science) are to (1) build an organized body of knowledge about its subject matter and (2) to develop valid, reliable explanations for the phenomena within its domain. For example, psychologists interested in aggression and the media would build a storehouse of knowledge concerning how various types of media violence (e.g., movies, television shows, cartoons, or violent video games) affect aggressive behavior. If, for example, violent video games do increase aggression, the psychologist would seek to explain how this occurs.

How do you, as a scientist, go about adding to this storehouse of knowledge? The principal method for acquiring knowledge and uncovering causes of behavior is **research**. You identify a problem and then systematically set out to collect information about the problem and develop explanations.

Robert Cialdini (1994) offers a simple yet effective analogy to describe the process of studying behavior: He likens science to a hunting trip. Before you go out to "bag" your prey, you must first scout out the area within which you are going to hunt. On a hunting trip, scouting involves determining the type and number of prey available in an area. Cialdini suggests that in science "scouting" involves making systematic observations of naturally occurring behavior.

Sometimes scouting may not be necessary. Sometimes the prey falls right into your lap without you having to go out and find it. Cialdini tells a story of a young woman who was soliciting for a charity. Initially, Cialdini declined to give a donation. However, after the young woman told him that "even a penny would help," he found himself digging into his wallet. As he reflected on this experience, he got to wondering why he gave a donation after the "even a penny would help" statement. This led him to a series of studies on the dynamics of compliance. In a similar manner, as you read about the *Wilson* case, you might already have begun to wonder about the factors that contribute to the development of violent behavior. As we shall see in Chapter 2, "scouting" can involve considering many sources.

The second step Cialdini identifies is "trapping." After you have identified a problem that interests you, the next thing to do is to identify the factors that might affect the behavior you have scouted. Then, much like a hunter closing in on prey, you systematically study the phenomenon and identify the factors that are crucial to explaining that phenomenon. For example, after wondering whether violent video games cause aggressive behavior, you could set up an experiment to test this. You could have participants in one condition play a violent video game and participants in a second condition play a nonviolent video game. Later, you give participants from both groups an opportunity to behave aggressively. If more aggression is shown by the participants who played the violent game than those who played the nonviolent game, you have evidence for the effects of violent video games on aggressive behavior.

## EXPLAINING BEHAVIOR

We have noted that one goal of science is to develop explanations for behavior. This goal is shared by other disciplines as well. For example, historians may attempt to explain why Robert E. Lee ordered "Pickett's Charge" on the final day of the Battle of Gettysburg. Any explanation would be based on reading and interpreting historical documents and records. However, the explanations developed would not be considered scientific, because history is not a science in the true sense of the word.

What distinguishes science from nonscience (and pseudoscience)? The difference lies in the methods used to collect information and draw conclusions from it. An explanation developed from these methods is known as a **scientific explanation**. Scientific explanations differ from other types of explanations, such as those based on common sense or faith, in several important ways. Let's take a look at how scientific and nonscientific explanations differ.

### Scientific Explanations

Through the application of the scientific method and specific research designs, we attempt to develop scientific explanations for behavior. A scientific explanation for a phenomenon is a tentative explanation, based on objective observation and logic, that can be empirically tested.

Although other types of explanations exist, such as those based on common sense or faith, scientific explanations are the only kind accepted by scientists. Scientific explanations have a unique blend of characteristics that set them apart from other types. These are as follows:

*Scientific Explanations Are Empirical*   An explanation is *empirical* if it is based on the evidence of the senses. To qualify as scientific, an explanation must be based on objective and systematic observation, often carried out under carefully controlled conditions. The observable events and conditions referred to in the explanation must be capable of verification by others.

*Scientific Explanations Are Rational*   An explanation is *rational* if it follows the rules of logic and is consistent with known facts. If the explanation makes assumptions that are known to be false, commits logical errors in drawing conclusions from its assumptions, or is inconsistent with established fact, then it does not qualify as scientific.

*Scientific Explanations Are Testable*   A scientific explanation should either be verifiable through direct observation or lead to specific predictions about what should occur under conditions not yet observed. An explanation is *testable* if confidence in the explanation could be undermined by a failure to observe the predicted outcome. One should be able to imagine outcomes that would disprove the explanation.

*Scientific Explanations Are Parsimonious*   Often more than one explanation is offered for an observed behavior. When this occurs, scientists prefer the **parsimonious explanation**, the one that explains behavior with the fewest number of assumptions.

*Scientific Explanations Are General*   Scientists prefer explanations of broad explanatory power over those that "work" only within a limited set of circumstances.

*Scientific Explanations Are Tentative*   Scientists may have confidence in their explanations, but they are nevertheless willing to entertain the possibility that the explanation is faulty. This attitude has been strengthened in this century by the realization that even Newton's conception of the universe, one of the most strongly supported views in scientific history, had to be replaced when new evidence showed that some of its predictions were wrong.

*Scientific Explanations Are Rigorously Evaluated*   This characteristic derives from the other characteristics just mentioned, but it is important enough to deserve its own place in our list. Scientific explanations are constantly evaluated for consistency with the evidence and with known principles, for parsimony, and for generality. Attempts are made to extend the scope of the explanation to cover broader areas and to include more factors. As plausible alternatives appear, these are pitted against the old explanations in a continual battle for the "survival of the fittest." In this way, even accepted explanations may be overthrown in favor of views that are more general, more parsimonious, or more consistent with observation.

## Commonsense versus Scientific Explanations

During the course of everyday experience, we develop explanations of the events we see going on around us. Largely, these explanations are based on the limited information available from the observed event and what our previous experience has told us is true. These rather loose explanations can be classified as **commonsense explanations** because they are based on our own sense of what is true about the world around us. Of course, scientific explanations and commonsense explanations share something in common: They both start with an observation of events in the real world. However, the two types of explanations differ in the level of proof required to support the explanation. Commonsense explanations tend to be accepted at face value, whereas scientific explanations are subjected to rigorous research scrutiny.

Take the case of Andrea Wilson, who, as we described earlier, sued the producer of a computer-based game because she believed that the game had caused her son's friend to kill her son in the course of acting out a violent scene from the game. That the game could cause a player to mistake reality for fantasy might seem to be a viable explanation of why Yancy behaved as he did. Although this explanation may be intuitively appealing, several factors disqualify it as a scientific explanation.

First, the "fantasy" explanation was not based on careful, systematic observation. Instead, it was based on what people *believe* to be true of the effect of playing such violent and addictive games. Consequently, the explanation may have been derived from biased, incomplete, or limited evidence (if from any evidence at all). Second, it was not examined to determine its consistency with other available observations. For example, other observations might have revealed that even with highly addicted players, most do not attempt to act out game scenarios in real life as a result. Third, no effort was made to evaluate it against plausible alternative explanations. For example, Yancy may have been prone to violence to begin with and only used the game as a source of inspiration for his vicious attack on Noah. Fourth, no predictions were derived from the explanation and tested. Fifth, no attempt was made to determine how well the explanation accounted for similar behavior in a variety of other circumstances. The explanation was accepted simply because it appeared to make sense of Yancy's behavior and was consistent with preexisting beliefs about the influence of games with violent content.

Because commonsense explanations are not rigorously evaluated, they are likely to be incomplete, inconsistent with other evidence, lacking in generality, and probably wrong. This is certainly the case with the "fantasy" explanation. Most individuals who have become addicted to such games have not displayed any tendency to carry out attacks on others as a result. Other factors must also contribute.

Although commonsense explanations may "feel right" and give us a sense that we understand a behavior, they may lack the power to apply across a variety of apparently similar situations. To see how commonsense explanations may fail to provide a truly general account of behavior, consider the following event.

Late in December 1903, a fire started in the crowded Iroquois Theater of Chicago, and 602 people lost their lives. Of interest to psychologists is not the fact that 602 people died, per se, but rather the circumstances that led to many of the deaths. Many of the victims were not directly killed by the fire. Rather, they were trampled to death in the panic that ensued in the first few minutes after the fire started. In his classic book *Social Psychology*, Brown (1965) reproduced an account of the event provided by Eddie Foy, a famous comedian of the time. According to Foy's account,

> it was inside the house that the greatest loss of life occurred, especially on the stairways leading down from the second balcony. Here most of the dead were

trampled or smothered. . . . In places on the stairways, particularly where a turn caused a jam, bodies were piled seven or eight deep. (Brown, 1965, p. 715)

As a student of psychology, you may already be formulating explanations of why normally rational human beings would behave mindlessly in this situation. Clearly, many lives would have been saved had the patrons of the Iroquois Theater filed out in an orderly fashion. How would you explain the tragedy?

A logical and "obvious" answer is that the patrons believed their lives to be in danger and wanted to leave the theater as quickly as possible. In this view, the panic inside the theater was motivated by a desire to survive.

Notice that the explanation at this point is probably adequate to explain the crowd behavior under the specific conditions inside the theater and perhaps to explain the same behavior under other life-threatening conditions. However, the explanation is probably too situation-specific to serve as a general scientific explanation of irrational crowd behavior. It cannot explain, for example, the following incident.

On December 10, 1979, a crowd of young people lined up outside a Cincinnati arena to wait for the doors to open for a concert by a then-popular rock group called the Who. As the doors opened, the crowd surged ahead. Eleven people were trampled to death even though the conditions were certainly less than life-threatening. In fact, the identifiable reward in this situation was obtaining a good seat at an open-seating concert.

Clearly, the explanation for irrational crowd behavior at the Chicago Theater cannot be applied to the Cincinnati tragedy. People were not going to die if they failed to get desirable seats at the concert. What seemed a reasonable explanation for irrational crowd behavior in the Iroquois Theater case must be discarded here.

You must look for common elements to explain such similar, yet diverse, events. In both situations, the available rewards were perceived to be limited. A powerful reward (avoiding pain and death) in the Iroquois Theater undoubtedly was perceived as attainable only for a brief time. Similarly, in Cincinnati the perceived reward (a seat close to the stage), although not essential for survival, was also available for a limited time only. In both cases, apparently irrational behavior resulted as large numbers of people individually attempted to maximize the probability of obtaining the reward.

The new tentative explanation for the irrational behavior now centers on the perceived availability of rewards, rather than situation-specific variables. This new tentative explanation has been tested in research and has received some support.

As these examples illustrate, simple commonsense explanations may not apply beyond the specific situations that spawned them. The scientist interested in irrational crowd behavior would look for a more general concept (such as perceived availability of rewards) to explain observed behavior. That is not to say that simple, obvious explanations are always incorrect. However, when you are looking for an explanation that transcends situation-specific variables, you often must look beyond simple, commonsense explanations.

## Belief-Based versus Scientific Explanations

Explanations for behavior often arise not from common sense or scientific observation but from individuals or groups who (through indoctrination, upbringing, or personal need) have accepted on faith the truth of their beliefs. You may agree or disagree with those beliefs, but you should be aware that explanations offered by science and **belief-based explanations** are fundamentally different.

Explanations based on belief are accepted because they come from a trusted source or appear to be consistent with the larger framework of belief. No evidence is required. If evidence suggests that the explanation is incorrect, then the evidence is discarded or reinterpreted to make it appear consistent with the belief. For example, certain religions hold that Earth was created only a few thousand years ago. The discovery of fossilized remains of dinosaurs and other creatures (apparently millions of years old) challenged this belief. To explain the existence of these remains, people defending the belief suggest that fossils are actually natural rock formations that resemble bones or that the fossils are the remains of the victims of the Great Flood. Thus, rather than calling the belief into question, apparently contrary evidence is interpreted to appear consistent with the belief.

This willingness to apply a different post hoc (after-the-fact) explanation to reconcile the observations with belief leads to an unparsimonious patchwork quilt of explanations that lack generality, fail to produce testable predictions about future findings, and often require that one assume the common occurrence of highly unlikely events. Scientific explanations of the same phenomena, in contrast, logically organize the observed facts by means of a few parsimonious assumptions and lead to testable predictions.

Nowhere is the contrast between these two approaches more striking than in the current debate between evolutionary biologists and the so-called creation scientists, whose explanation for fossils was just described. To take one example, consider the recent discoveries based on gene sequencing, which reveal the degree of genetic similarity among various species. These observations and some simple assumptions about the rate of mutation in the genetic material allowed biologists to develop "family trees" indicating how long ago the various species separated from one another. The trees drawn up from the gene-sequencing data agree amazingly well with, and to a large degree were predicted by, the trees assembled from the fossil record. In contrast, because creationists assume that all animals alive today have always had their current form and that fossils represent the remains of animals killed in the Great Flood, their view could not have predicted relationships found in the genetic material. Instead, they must invent yet another post hoc explanation to make these new findings appear consistent with their beliefs.

In addition to the differences described thus far, scientific and belief-based explanations also differ in tentativeness. Whereas explanations based on belief are assumed to be true, scientific explanations are accepted because they are consistent with existing objective evidence and have survived rigorous testing against plausible alternatives. Scientists accept the possibility that better explanations may turn up or that new tests may show that the current explanation is inadequate.

Scientific explanations also differ from belief-based explanations in the subject areas for which explanations are offered. Whereas explanations based on belief may seek to answer virtually any question, scientific explanations are limited to addressing those questions that can be answered by means of objective observations. For example, what happens to a person after death and why suffering exists in the world are explained by religion, but such questions remain outside the realm of scientific explanation. No objective tests or observations can be performed to answer these questions within the confines of the scientific method. Science offers no explanation for such questions, and you must rely on faith or belief for answers. However, for questions that can be settled on the basis of objective observation, scientific explanations generally have provided more satisfactory and useful accounts of behavior than those provided by a priori belief.

## WHEN SCIENTIFIC EXPLANATIONS FAIL

Scientific explanation is preferable to other kinds of explanation when scientific methods can be applied. Using a scientific approach maximizes the chances of discovering the best explanation for an observed behavioral phenomenon. Despite the application of the most rigorous scientific methods, instances do occur in which the explanation offered by a scientist is not valid. Scientific explanations are sometimes flawed. Understanding some of the pitfalls inherent to developing scientific explanations will help you avoid arriving at flawed or incorrect explanations for behavior.

### Failures Due to Faulty Inference

Explanations may fail because developing them involves an inference process. We make observations and then infer the causes for the observed behavior. This inference process always involves the danger of incorrectly inferring the underlying mechanisms that control behavior.

The problem of faulty inference is illustrated in a satirical book by David Macaulay (1979) called *Motel of the Mysteries*. In this book, a scientist (Howard Carson) uncovers the remnants of our civilization 5,000 years from now. Carson unearths a motel and begins the task of explaining what our civilization was like, based on the artifacts found in the motel.

Among the items unearthed were various bathroom plumbing devices: a plunger, a showerhead, and a spout. These items were assumed by Carson to be musical instruments. The archaeologist describes the items as follows:

> The two trumpets [the showerhead and spout] . . . were found attached to the wall of the inner chamber at the end of the sarcophagus. They were both coated with a silver substance similar to that used on the ornamental pieces of the metal animals. Music was played by forcing water from the sacred spring through the trumpets under great pressure. Pitch was controlled by a large silver handle marked HC. . . . The [other] instrument [the plunger] is probably of the percussion family, but as yet the method of playing it remains a mystery. It is, however, beautifully crafted of wood and rubber. (1979, p. 68)

By hypothesizing that various plumbing devices served as ceremonial musical instruments, Macaulay's archaeologist has reached a number of inaccurate conclusions. Although the *Motel of the Mysteries* example is pure fiction, real-life examples of inference gone wrong abound in science, and psychology is no exception. R. E. Fancher (1985) described the following example in his book *The Intelligence Men: Makers of the IQ Controversy*. During World War I, the U.S. Army administered group intelligence tests under the direction of Robert Yerkes. More than 1.75 million men had taken either the Alpha or Beta version of the test by the end of the war and provided an excellent statistical sample from which conclusions could be drawn about the abilities of U.S. men of that era.

The results were shocking. Analysis of the data revealed that the average army recruit had a mental age of 13 years—3 years below the "average adult" mental age of 16 and only 1 year above the upper limit for moronity. Fancher described Yerkes's interpretation as follows:

> Rather than interpreting his results to mean that there was something wrong with the standard, or that the army scores had been artificially depressed by . . . the failure to re-test most low Alpha scorers on Beta, as was supposed to have been the case, Yerkes asserted that the "native intelligence" of the average recruit was shockingly low. The tests, he said, were "originally intended, and now definitely known, to measure native intellectual ability. They are to some extent influenced by educational requirement, but in the main the soldier's inborn intelligence and not the accidents of environment determined his mental rating or grade." Accordingly, a very substantial proportion of the soldiers in the U.S. Army were actually morons. (1985, p. 127)

In fact, Yerkes's assertions about the tests were not in any sense established, and indeed the data provided evidence against Yerkes's conclusion. For example, poorly educated recruits from rural areas scored lower than their better-educated city cousins. Yerkes's tests had failed to consider the differences in educational opportunities among recruits. As a result, Yerkes and his followers inappropriately concluded that the average intellectual ability of Americans was deteriorating.

In the Yerkes example, faulty conclusions were drawn because the conclusions were based on unfounded assumptions concerning the ability of the tests to unambiguously measure intelligence. The researchers failed to consider possible *alternative explanations* for observed effects. Although the intelligence of U.S. Army recruits may in fact have been distressingly low, an alternative explanation centering on environmental factors such as educational level would have been equally plausible. These two rival explanations (real decline in intelligence versus lack of educational experience) should have been subjected to the proper tests to determine which was more plausible. Later, this book discusses how developing, testing, and eliminating such rival hypotheses are crucial elements of the scientific method.

## Pseudoexplanations

Failing to consider alternative explanations is not the only danger waiting to befall the unwary scientist. In formulating valid scientific explanations for behavioral events, it is important to avoid the trap of **pseudoexplanation**. In seeking to provide explanations for behavior, psychologists sometimes offer positions, theories, and explanations that do nothing more than provide an alternative label for the behavioral event. One notorious example was the attempt to explain aggression with the concept of an instinct. According to this position, people (and animals) behave aggressively because of an aggressive instinct. Although this explanation may have intuitive appeal, it does not serve as a valid scientific explanation.

Figure 1–1 illustrates the problem with such an explanation. Notice that the observed behavior (aggression) is used to prove the existence of the aggressive instinct. The concept of instinct is then used to explain the aggressive behavior.

This form of reasoning is called a **circular explanation** or **tautology**. It does not provide a true explanation but rather merely provides another label (instinct) for a class of observed behavior (aggression). Animals are aggressive because they have aggressive instincts. How do we know they have aggressive instincts? Because they are aggressive! Thus all we are saying is that animals are aggressive because of a tendency to behave aggressively. Obviously, this is not an explanation.

You might expect only novice behavioral scientists to be prone to using pseudo-explanations. However, even professional behavioral scientists have proposed "explanations" for behavioral phenomena that are really pseudoexplanations. In a 1970 article, Martin Seligman proposed a continuum of preparedness to help explain why an animal can learn some associations easily (such as between taste and illness) and other associations only with great difficulty (such as between taste and electric shock).

According to Seligman's analysis, the animal may be biologically prepared to learn some associations (those learned quickly) and contraprepared to learn others (those learned slowly, if at all). Thus, some animals may have difficulty acquiring an association between taste and shock because they are contraprepared by evolution to associate the two.

As with the use of instinct to explain aggression, the continuum-of-preparedness notion seems intuitively correct. Indeed, it does serve as a potentially valid explanation for the observed differences in learning rates. But it does not qualify as a true explanation as it is stated. Refer back to Figure 1–1 and substitute "quickly or slowly acquired association" for "aggressive behavior" and "continuum of preparedness" for "aggressive instinct." As presently stated, the continuum-of-preparedness explanation is circular: Animals learn a particular association with difficulty because they are contraprepared to learn it. How do you know they are contraprepared? You know because they have difficulty learning.

How can you avoid falling into the trap of proposing and accepting pseudoexplanations? When evaluating a proposed explanation, ask yourself whether or not the researcher has provided *independent measures* of the behavior of interest (such as difficulty learning an association) *and* the proposed explanatory concept (such as the continuum of preparedness). For example, if you could find an independent measure of preparedness that does *not* involve the animal's ability to form an association, then the explanation in terms of preparedness would qualify as a true explanation. If you can determine the animal's preparedness only by observing its ability to form a particular association, the proposed explanation is circular. Rather than explaining the differing rates of learning, the statement actually serves only to define the types of preparedness.

Developing independent measures for the explanatory concept and the behavior to be explained may not be easy. For example, in the continuum-of-preparedness case, it may take some creative thought to develop a measure of preparedness that is independent of the observed behavior. The same is true for the concept of an instinct.

As these examples have illustrated, even scientific explanations may fail. However, you should not conclude that such explanations are no better than those derived from other sources. Living, behaving organisms are complex systems whose observable

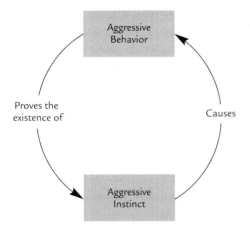

**FIGURE 1–1**   A Circular Explanation. The observed behavior is "explained" by a concept, but the behavior itself is used as proof of the existence of the explanatory concept.

workings provide only clues to their inner processes. Given the available evidence, you make your best guess. It should not be surprising that these guesses are often wrong. As these conjectures are evaluated against new evidence, even the failures serve to rule out plausible alternatives and to prepare the way for better guesses. As a result, science has a strong tendency to converge on valid explanations as research progresses. Such progress in understanding is a hallmark of the scientific method.

## METHODS OF INQUIRY

Before a scientist can offer valid and general explanations for behavior, he or she must gather information about the behavior of interest. Knowledge about behavior can be acquired by several methods, including the method of authority, the rational method, and the scientific method.

### The Method of Authority

After reading about the Iroquois Theater tragedy, you might make a trip to your local public or university library or call your former social psychology professor in search of information to help explain the irrational behavior inside the theater. When you use expert sources (whether books or people), you are using the **method of authority**. Using the method of authority involves consulting some source you consider authoritative on the issue in question (for example, consulting books, television, religious leaders, scientists).

Although useful in the early stages of acquiring knowledge, the method of authority does not always provide valid answers to questions about behavior for at least two reasons. First, the source you consult may not be truly authoritative. Some people (such as Lucy in the *Peanuts* comic strip) are more than willing to give you their "expert" opinions on any topic, no matter how little they actually know about it (writers are no exception). Second, sources often are biased by a particular point of view. A sociologist may offer a different explanation for the Iroquois Theater tragedy from the one offered by a behaviorally oriented psychologist. For these reasons, the method of authority by itself is not adequate for producing reliable explanations.

Although the method of authority is not the final word in the search for explanations of behavior, the method does play an important role in the acquisition of scientific knowledge. Information you obtain from authorities on a topic can familiarize you with the problem, the available evidence, and the proposed explanations. With this information you could generate new ideas about causes of behavior. However, these ideas must then be subjected to rigorous scientific scrutiny rather than being accepted at face value.

## The Rational Method

René Descartes proposed in the 17th century that valid conclusions about the universe could be drawn through the use of pure reason, a doctrine called *rationalism*. This proposal was quite revolutionary at the time, because most scholars of the day relied heavily on the method of authority to answer questions. Descartes's method began with skepticism, a willingness to doubt the truth of every belief. Descartes noted, as an example, that it was even possible to doubt the existence of the universe. What you perceive, he reasoned, could be an illusion. Could you prove otherwise?

After establishing doubt, Descartes moved to the next stage of his method: the search for "self-evident truths," statements that *must* be true because to assume otherwise would contradict logic. Descartes reasoned that if the universe around him did not really exist, then perhaps he himself also did not exist. It was immediately obvious to Descartes that this idea contradicted logic—it was self-evidently true that if he did not exist, he certainly could not be thinking about the question of his own existence. And it was just as self-evidently true that he was indeed thinking.

These two self-evident truths can be used as assumptions from which deductive logic will yield a firm conclusion:

Assumption 1: Something that thinks must exist.

Assumption 2: I am thinking.

Conclusion: I exist.

Using only his powers of reasoning, Descartes had identified two statements whose truth logically cannot be doubted, and from them he was able to deduce a conclusion that is equally bulletproof. It is bulletproof because, if the assumptions are true and you make no logical errors, deduction guarantees the truth of the conclusion. By the way, this particular example of the use of his method was immortalized by Descartes in the declaration "*Cogito, ergo sum*" (Latin for "I think, therefore I am"). If you've heard that phrase before and wondered what it meant, now you know.

Descartes's method came to be called the **rational method**, because it depends on logical reasoning rather than on authority or the evidence of one's senses. Although the method satisfied Descartes, we must approach "knowledge" acquired in this way with caution. The power of the rational method lies in logically deduced conclusions from self-evident truths. Unfortunately, precious few self-evident truths can serve as assumptions in a logical system. If one (or both) of the assumptions used in the deduction process is incorrect, the logically deduced conclusion will be invalid.

Because of its shortcomings, the rational method is not used to develop scientific explanations. However, it still plays an important role in science. The tentative ideas that we form about the relationship between variables are often deduced from earlier assumptions. For example, having learned that fleeing from a fire or trying to get into a crowded arena causes irrational behavior, we may deduce that "perceived availability of reinforcers" (escaping death or getting a front-row seat) is responsible for such behavior. Rather than accepting such a deduction as correct, however, the scientist puts the deduction to empirical test.

## The Scientific Method

Braithwaite (1953) proposed that the function of a science is to "establish general laws covering the behavior of the empirical events with which the science in question is concerned" (p. 1). According to Braithwaite, a science should allow us to fuse together information concerning separately occurring events and to make reliable predictions about future, unknown events. One goal of psychology is to establish general laws of behavior that help explain and predict behavioral events that occur in a variety of situations.

Although explanations for behavior and general laws cannot be adequately formulated by relying solely on authoritative sources and using deductive reasoning, these methods (when combined with other features) form the basis for the most powerful approach to knowledge yet developed: the **scientific method**. This method comprises a series of four cyclical steps that you can repeatedly execute as you pursue the solution to a scientific problem (Yaremko, Harari, Harrison, & Lynn, 1982, p. 212). These steps are (1) observing a phenomenon, (2) formulating tentative explanations or statements of cause and effect, (3) further observing or experimenting (or both) to rule out alternative explanations, and (4) refining and retesting the explanations.

*Observing a Phenomenon* The starting point for using the scientific method is to observe the behavior of interest. This first step is essentially what Cialdini (1994) called "scouting," in which some behavior or event catches your attention. These preliminary observations of behavior and of potential causes for that behavior can take a variety of forms. In the case of the effects of violent video games, you might have read about Andrea Wilson's case and begun to wonder if violent video games could cause violent behavior. Your curiosity might have been further piqued when the topic of media effects on violencewas discussed in one of your classes or when you read about media violence in a magazine or book. Or you might even have known someone who had a child who appeared to be affected by playing violent video games. In any of these cases, your curiosity might be energized so that you begin to formulate hypotheses about what factors affect the behavior you have observed.

Through the process of observation, you identify variables that appear to have an important influence on behavior. A **variable** is any characteristic or quantity that can take on two or more values. For example, the amount of violence in a video game is a variable. The amount of violence can vary from very low to very high. Remember that in order for something to be considered a variable, it must be capable of taking on *at least* two values. A characteristic or quantity that takes on only one value is known as a *constant*.

*Formulating Tentative Explanations*    After identifying an interesting phenomenon to study, your next step is to develop one or more tentative explanations that seem consistent with your observations. In science these tentative explanations often include a statement of the relationship between two or more variables. That is, you tentatively state the nature of the relationship between variables that you expect to uncover with your research. The tentative statement you offer concerning the relationship between your variables of interest is called a **hypothesis**. It is important that any hypothesis you develop be testable with empirical research.

As an example of formulating a hypothesis, consider the issue of the relationship between playing violent video games and aggressive behavior. After your preliminary observations, you might formulate the following hypothesis:

> A person is more likely to be aggressive after playing a violent video game than after playing a nonviolent video game.

Notice that the hypothesis links two variables (the violent content of a video game and aggressive behavior) by a statement indicating the expected relationship between them. In this case, the relationship expected is that playing violent video games will increase the likelihood of behaving aggressively. Research hypotheses often take the form of a statement of how changes in the value of one variable (playing violent or nonviolent video games) will affect the value of the other variable (aggressive behavior).

*Further Observing and Experimenting*    When Cialdini (1994) talked about "trapping" effects, he was referring to the process of designing empirical research studies to isolate the relationship between the variables chosen for study. Up to the point of developing a hypothesis, the scientific method does not differ markedly from other methods of acquiring knowledge. At this point, all you have done is to identify a problem to study and develop a hypothesis based on some initial observation. The scientific method, however, does not stop here. The third step in the scientific method marks the point at which the scientific method differs from other methods of inquiry. Unlike the other methods of inquiry, the scientific method demands that further observations be carried out to test the validity of any hypotheses you develop. In other words, "a-trapping we shall go."

What exactly is meant by "making further observations"? The answer to this question is what the scientific method is all about. After formulating your hypothesis, you design a research study to test the relationship you proposed. This study can take a variety of forms. It could be a *correlational study*, in which you simply measure two or more variables and look for a relationship between them (see Chapter 4); a *quasi-experimental study*, in which you take advantage of some naturally occurring event or preexisting conditions; or an *experiment*, in which you systematically manipulate a variable and look for changes in the value of another that occur as a result (see Chapters 8–10).

In this case, you decide to design an experiment in which you systematically manipulate the amount violence in a video game and observe whether different levels of violence in the video game produce different rates of aggressive behavior.

*Refining and Retesting Explanations*    The final step in the scientific method is the process of refinement and retesting. As an example of this process, imagine that you found that violent video games increase aggressive behavior. Having obtained this result, you would probably want to explore the phenomenon further: Would the realism of a video game matter? A refined research hypothesis might take the following form:

> Realistic violent video games are more likely to result in increased aggression than unrealistic violent video games.

This process of generating new, more specific, hypotheses in the light of previous results illustrates the *refinement process*. Often, confirming a hypothesis with a research study leads to other hypotheses that expand on the relationships discovered, explore the limits of the phenomenon under study, or explore the causes for the relationship observed.

As you become more familiar with the process of conducting research, you will find that not all research studies produce affirmative results. That is, sometimes your research does not confirm your hypothesis. What do you do then? In some cases you might completely discard your original hypothesis. In other cases, however, you might revise and retest your hypothesis. In the latter instance you are using a strategy known as *retesting*. Keep in mind that any revised or refined hypothesis must be tested as rigorously as was the original hypothesis.

The scientific method requires a great deal of time making careful observations. Sometimes your observations don't confirm your hypothesis. Is the scientific method worth all the extra effort? In fact, the ability to discover that a relationship does *not* exist makes the scientific method the powerful tool that it is. By repeatedly checking and rechecking hypotheses in the ruthless arena of empirical testing, the scientist learns which ideas are worthy and which belong on the trash heap. No other method incorporates such a powerful check on the validity of its conclusions.

## The Scientific Method at Work: Playing Violent Video Games

Throughout this chapter we've used the question of the effect of exposure to violent video games on aggressive behavior to illustrate hypothetically how you might go about developing, testing, and refining a research hypothesis. As you might have suspected, the question has actually been the subject of scientific research, and we thought it might be helpful for you to see how an actual research study on this topic was carried out. The study we chose for our example was conducted by Craig Anderson and Karen Dill (2000).

Anderson and Dill had male and female participants play either a violent video game or a nonviolent video game. Participants were told that they were participating in a study on how people acquired learning skills. In fact, they were taking part in an experiment on the relationship between playing violent video games and aggression. During the first laboratory session, participants played either the violent or nonviolent video game for 30 minutes in two 15 minute blocks. After the first block, participants answered some questions designed to assess how the participants were feeling (e.g., angry or happy). After the second block, participants completed a reaction time test that involved the participant reading aloud words that appeared on a computer screen. Some of the words were aggression-related (e.g., murder), whereas others were not (e.g., consider).

One week later, participants returned to the laboratory for a second session. Participants played the same video game they had played the week before. Participants then played a competitive reaction time game, supposedly with another research participant. Unbeknownst to the participants, they were actually playing a game that was preprogrammed into a computer. On each trial during the game a tone would be sounded and the participants were told to press a button on the mouse as fast as they could. Participants were told that if they pressed the button faster than their "opponent" they would have "won" that trial. If not, they would have "lost." Each time the participant won, he or she would then deliver a noise blast to the "opponent." If the participant lost, he or she would receive a noise blast. The game was programmed so that participants won on 13 trials and lost on 12. Participants were told that they would be delivering a noise blast to their "opponent" each time the opponent "lost" in the game. The participants were told that they would choose the volume of the noise blast and could control the duration of the noise blast by holding down a key on the computer's keyboard. The main measure of aggression was the duration of the noise delivered after win and lose trials.

The results showed that playing a violent video game did not significantly affect the duration of the noise blast delivered after a "win" trial. However, females delivered longer noise blasts after a win (M = 6.89 seconds) than males (M = 6.65 seconds). The results also showed that playing a violent video game significantly affected the duration of the noise blast delivered after a "lose" trial. Those playing the violent video game delivered longer noise blasts (M = 6.81 seconds) than those playing the nonviolent video game (M = 6.65 seconds). Once again, females delivered longer noise blasts than males. So, after being provoked by the "opponent's" noise blast, participants delivered longer noise blasts in return after playing the violent video game than after playing the nonviolent video game.

### The Scientific Method as an Attitude

The scientific method is not just a means of acquiring knowledge; it is also a way of thinking and viewing the world. An individual who subscribes to the scientific method approaches a problem by carefully defining its parameters, seeking out relevant information, and subjecting proposed solutions to rigorous testing. Similarly, the scientific view of the world causes a person to be skeptical about what he or she reads or hears in the popular media. As noted earlier, having a scientific outlook leads a person to question the validity of provocative statements made in the media and to find out what scientific studies say on those statements. In short, an individual with a scientific outlook does not accept everything on face value.

Remember, however, that the scientific method is not the only way of approaching a problem. Some problems (philosophical, ethical, or religious) may not lend themselves to exploration with the scientific method. In those cases other methods of inquiry may be more useful.

## TRANSLATING THE SCIENTIFIC METHOD INTO PRACTICE: THE RESEARCH PROCESS

The scientific method provides the general framework within which scientists operate. However, to test hypotheses, the inherent logic of the scientific method must be translated into a workable research study. It is important to recognize that the scientific method provides the rules within which information is acquired. Working within those rules, you must decide on the particular technique that best tests your hypothesis.

## Method versus Technique

Once you have chosen the scientific method as your means of inquiry, you must make some decisions about how you are going to gather information about the behavior of interest. A variety of techniques are available for any given research hypothesis. For example, if you are interested in studying the relationship between violent television programs and children's violent behavior, you have several techniques at your disposal. You might choose to send parents a questionnaire to indicate how much violent television the children watch and relate that information to observed aggressive behavior. Or you might choose to expose different groups of children to television shows that vary in their levels of violence and then evaluate aggressive behavior in free-play situations.

## Basic and Applied Research

The science of psychology encompasses scientists working in a variety of areas to gain knowledge that helps explain behavior. As a science, psychology systematically approaches the study of behavior by following the scientific method. Observations are carefully planned, with consideration being given to such problems as defining the questions to be answered, specifying what behaviors will be observed and how they will be measured, and determining what steps will be taken to ensure that the observer's expectations do not contaminate the observations.

The science of psychology is highly diverse. Consequently, the goals established by scientists working within the field may vary according to the nature of the research problem being considered. For example, the goal of some scientists is to discover general laws that explain particular classes of behaviors. In the course of developing those laws, psychologists study behavior in specific situations and attempt to isolate the variables controlling behavior. Other scientists within the field are more interested in tackling practical problems than in finding general laws. For example, they might be interested in determining which of several therapy techniques is best to treat severe phobias.

An important distinction has been made between basic research and applied research along the lines just presented.

*Basic Research*    **Basic research** is conducted to investigate issues relevant to the confirmation or disconfirmation of theoretical or empirical positions. The major goal of basic research is to acquire general information about a phenomenon, with little emphasis placed on applications to real-world examples of the phenomenon (Yaremko et al., 1982). For example, research on the memory process may be conducted to test the efficacy of interference as a viable theory of forgetting. The researcher would be interested in discovering something about the forgetting process while testing the validity of a theoretical position. Of less immediate interest would be the application of results to forgetting in a real-world situation.

*Applied Research*    The focus of **applied research** is somewhat different. Your concern is to investigate a problem based in the real world. Although you may still work from a theory when formulating your hypotheses, your primary goal is to generate information that can be applied directly to a real-world problem. A study by James Ogloff and Neil Vidmar (1994) on pretrial publicity would be best classified as applied research. It informs us about a very real problem facing the court system. The results of studies such as Ogloff and Vidmar's can help trial and appeals court judges make decisions concerning limitations placed on jury exposure to pretrial publicity. Further examples of applied research can be found in the areas of clinical, environmental, and industrial psychology (among others).

*Overlap between Basic and Applied Research*    In many instances, the distinction between applied and basic research is not clear. Some research areas have both an applied and basic flavor. As an example, consider the work of Elizabeth Loftus (1979) on the psychology of the eyewitness. Loftus has extensively studied the factors that affect the ability of an eyewitness to accurately perceive, remember, and recall a criminal event. Her research certainly fits the mold of applied research. Her results have some implications for theory in the psychology of memory, so they also fit the mold of basic research. In fact, many of Loftus's findings can be organized within existing theories of memory.

Even applied research is not independent of theories and other research in psychology. The defining quality of applied research is that the researcher attempts to conduct a study whose results can be applied directly to a real-world event. To accomplish this task, you must choose a research strategy that maximizes the applicability of findings.

## The Steps of the Research Process

Scientists in the field of psychology adhere to the scientific method as the principal method for acquiring information about behavior. This is true whether the psychologist is a "clinical psychologist" evaluating the effectiveness of a new therapy technique or an "experimental psychologist" investigating the variables that affect memory. Of course, researchers in psychology adopt a wide variety of techniques in their quest for scientific knowledge.

From the inception of a research idea to the final report of results, the research process has several crucial steps. These steps are outlined in Figure 1–2. At each step you must make one or more important decisions that will influence the direction of your research. Let's explore each of these steps and some of the decisions you must make.

*Developing a Research Idea and Hypothesis*    The first step in the research process is to identify an issue you want to study. There are many sources of research ideas (observing everyday behavior or reading scientific journals, for example). Once you have identified a behavior to study, you must then state a research question in terms that will allow others to test it empirically. Many students of research have trouble at this point. Students seem to have little trouble identifying interesting, broadly defined behaviors to study (for example, "I want to study memory"), but they have trouble isolating crucial variables that need to be explored.

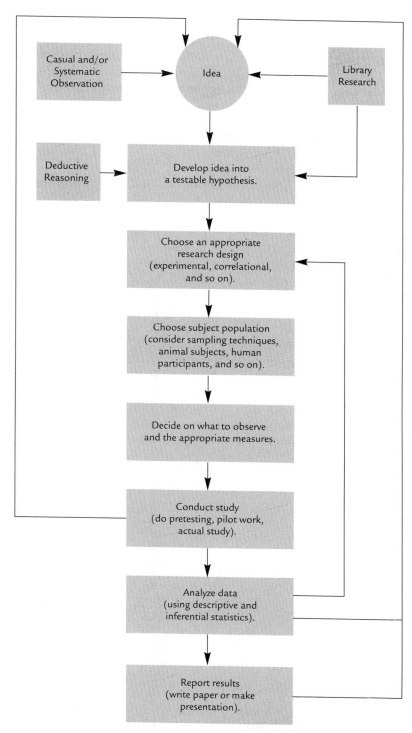

**FIGURE 1–2**    The Research Process. Arrows show the sequence of steps, along with feedback.

To rationally apply the scientific method, you must be able to state clearly the relationships you expect to emerge in a research study. In other words, you must be able to formulate a precise, testable hypothesis. As noted in Figure 1–2, hypothesis development involves **deductive reasoning**, which involves deriving a specific hypothesis (in this case) from general ideas. For example, during your literature review you may have come across a theory about how memory operates. Using the general ideas developed in a theory, you may logically deduce that one variable (for example, meaningfulness of the information to be learned) causes changes in a second (amount remembered). The specific statement connecting these two variables is your hypothesis.

***Choosing a Research Design***    Once you have narrowed your research question and developed a testable hypothesis, you must next decide on a design or plan of attack for your research. As discussed in later chapters, a variety of options are available. For example, you must decide whether to do a correlational study (measure two or more variables and look for relationships among them) or an experimental study (manipulate a variable and look for concomitant changes in a second). Other important decisions at this point include where to conduct your study (in the laboratory or in the field) and how you are going to measure the behavior of interest.

With the preliminary decisions out of the way, you must consider a host of practical issues (equipment needs, preparation of materials, and so on). You might find it necessary to conduct a miniature version of your study, called a **pilot study**, to be sure your chosen procedures and materials work the way you think they will.

***Choosing Subjects***    Once you have designed your study and tested your procedures and materials, you need to decide whether to use human participants or animal subjects. You must decide how to obtain your subjects and how they will be handled in your study. You also must be concerned with treating your subjects in an ethical manner.

***Deciding on What to Observe and Appropriate Measures***    Your next step is to decide exactly what it is you want to observe, which will be determined by the topic or issue you have chosen to investigate. For example, if you were interested in the issue of the impact of media violence on children's aggression, you might interview parents who have noticed an increase in aggression after their children play violent video games. Or you might design an experiment similar to Anderson and Dill's (2000) experiment to test the conditions under which violent video games cause aggression. After choosing what to observe, you must next decide on the most appropriate way to measure the behavior of interest. For example, should you use the same measure that Anderson and Dill used, or should you develop a new one?

***Conducting Your Study***    Now you actually have your participants take part in your study. You observe and measure their behavior. Data are formally recorded for later analysis.

***Analyzing Your Results***    After you have collected your data, you must summarize and analyze them. The analysis process involves a number of decisions. You can analyze your data in several ways, and some types of data are better analyzed with one method than another. In most cases, you will probably calculate some descriptive statistics that provide a "nutshell" description of your data (such as averages and standard deviations) and inferential statistics that assess the reliability of your data (such as a *t test*).

*Reporting Your Results*    After analyzing your data, you are nearing the final steps in the research process. You are now ready to prepare a report of your research. If your results were reliable and sufficiently important, you may want to publish them. Consequently, you would prepare a formal paper, usually in American Psychological Association (APA) style, and submit it to a journal for review. You also might decide to present your paper at a scientific meeting, in which case you prepare a brief abstract of your research for review.

*Starting the Whole Process Over Again*    Your final report of your research is usually not the final step in your research. You may have achieved closure on (finished and analyzed) one research project. However, the results from your first study may raise more questions. These questions often serve as the seeds for a new study. In fact, you may want to replicate an interesting finding within the context of a new study. This possibility is represented in Figure 1–2 by the arrow connecting "Report results" with "Idea."

## SUMMARY

Although we are constantly trying to explain the behavior we see around us, commonsense explanations of behavior often are too simplistic and situation-specific and are frequently based on hearsay, conjecture, anecdote, or other unreliable sources. Scientific explanations are based on carefully made observations of behavior, rigorously tested against alternative explanations, and developed to provide the most general account that is applicable over a variety of situations. For these reasons, scientific explanations tend to be more valid and general than those provided by common sense.

The goal of the science of psychology is to build an organized body of knowledge about its subject matter and to develop explanations for phenomena within its domain. The principal method used to achieve these goals is research. Research involves three steps: identifying a phenomenon to study, discovering information about that phenomenon, and developing explanations for the phenomenon. A useful analogy is to think of science as a hunting trip. First, you scout where you are going to hunt for prey (analogous to identifying a phenomenon to study). Second, you go hunting to trap your prey (analogous to discovering information and developing explanations).

Explanations for behavior also are provided by beliefs. Explanations provided by belief differ from scientific explanations in that they are considered absolutely true, whereas scientific explanations are always considered tentative. Consequently, when evidence conflicts with an explanation based on belief, the evidence is questioned. When evidence conflicts with a scientific explanation, the explanation is questioned. Although beliefs can provide answers to virtually any question, the scientific method can address only those questions that can be answered through observation.

Even explanations that sound scientific may fail because relationships are often inferred from observable events. The danger always exists that inferences are incorrect, despite being based on empirical data. An explanation also may fail if you do not use independent measures of the explanatory concept and the behavior to be explained. In such cases, you have a pseudoexplanation, which is only a new label for behavior.

There are many ways to acquire knowledge about behavior. With the method of authority, you acquire information from sources that you perceive to be expert on your topic of interest and use the information to develop an explanation for behavior. With the rational method, you deduce explanations from other sources of information. Although the method of authority and the rational method play important roles in the early stages of science, they are not acceptable methods for acquiring scientific knowledge. The scientific method is the only method accepted for the acquisition of scientific knowledge.

The four major steps of the scientific method are observation of a phenomenon, formation of tentative explanations or statements of cause and effect, further observation or experimentation to rule out alternative explanations (or both), and retesting and refinement of the explanations. The scientific method is also an attitude or a way of viewing the world. The scientist frames problems in terms of the scientific method.

The scientific method is translated into action by the research process. When performing research, you first choose a technique. Regardless of the technique chosen, research must follow the guidelines of the scientific method. The science of psychology is highly complex and diverse, and the goals of research vary from individual to individual. Some researchers, who are mainly interested in solving real-world problems, conduct applied research. Other scientists, mainly interested in evaluating theoretical problems, conduct basic research. Even though basic and applied research are different to some extent, considerable overlap does exist. Some basic research problems have real-world applications, and some applied problems have some basic research undertones.

The research process involves a sequence of steps. At each step, important decisions affect the course of research and how you analyze and interpret data. The steps in the research process are (1) develop a research idea into a testable hypothesis, (2) choose a research design, (3) choose a subject or participant population, (4) decide on what to observe and appropriate measures, (5) obtain subjects or participants for the study and conduct the study, (6) analyze results, and (7) report results. Often the results of research raise a host of new research ideas, which starts the whole research process over again.

## REVIEW QUESTIONS

1. How are problems framed in research terms?
2. What is the confirmation bias, and what are its implications for understanding behavior?
3. Why should you care about learning about research, even if you are not planning a career in research?

4. What are the two steps suggested by Cialdini (1994) for exploring the causes of behavior, and how do they relate to explaining behavior?
5. What are the main characteristics of scientific explanations? Describe each.
6. How do scientific and commonsense explanations differ?
7. How do belief-based and scientific explanations differ?
8. What kinds of questions do scientists refrain from investigating? Why do scientists refrain from studying these issues?
9. How can faulty inference invalidate a scientific explanation?
10. What are pseudoexplanations, and how do you avoid them?
11. What are the defining characteristics and weaknesses of the method of authority and the rational method?
12. What is the scientific method, and why is it preferred in science?
13. What is meant by the statement that the scientific method is an attitude (explain)?
14. How do method and technique differ?
15. How do basic and applied research differ and how are they similar?
16. What are the steps involved in the research process, and how are they applied to answering research questions?

## KEY TERMS

| | |
|---|---|
| confirmation bias | method of authority |
| research | rational method |
| scientific explanation | scientific method |
| parsimonious explanation | variable |
| commonsense explanation | hypothesis |
| belief-based explanation | basic research |
| pseudoexplanation | applied research |
| circular explanation | deductive reasoning |
| tautology | pilot study |

# 2 CHAPTER

## Developing Ideas for Research and Evaluating Theories of Behavior

As a student who is just becoming acquainted with the research process, you are probably wondering just how to come up with good ideas for research. It may seem to you that by this point in the history of psychology, every interesting research question must already have been asked and answered. Or perhaps you do have some rather general idea of a topic you'd like to explore but don't know how to convert that idea into something specific that you could actually carry out. However, once you learn how to go about it, finding a research topic and developing it into an executable project becomes relatively easy—you just have to know where and how to look. In fact, you may be surprised to find that your biggest problem is deciding which of several interesting research ideas you should pursue first. To help you reach that point, in the first part of this chapter we identify a number of sources of research ideas and offer some guidelines for developing good research questions.

Although finding and developing a research idea is usually the first step in the research process, the ultimate goal of that process, as noted in Chapter 1, is to develop valid explanations for behavior. These explanations may be limited in scope (e.g., an explanation of why a certain autistic child keeps banging his head against the wall) or comprehensive (e.g., a system that explains the fundamental mechanisms of learning). Of course, any single study will have only a limited purpose, such as to test a particular hypothesis, to identify how certain variables are related, or simply to describe what behaviors occur under given conditions. Yet each properly conceived and executed study contributes new information—perhaps, for example, by identifying new behavioral phenomena for which explanations will be needed or by ruling out certain alternative hypotheses. Ultimately, this information shapes the formulation of new explanations or tests the adequacy of existing ones.

In this chapter we pursue two separate, but related topics. First, we explore how to get research ideas and how they can be developed into viable, testable research questions. Second, we discuss the roles that theory, theory testing, and theory evaluation play in the research process.

## SOURCES OF RESEARCH IDEAS

The sources of research ideas are virtually endless. However, they can be seen as falling into three broad categories: experience, theory, and applied issues.

### Experience

Your everyday experience and observations of what goes on around you can serve as a rich source of research ideas. Some of these observations may be unsystematic and informal. For example, after reading a newspaper article about a convicted murderer being executed, you may begin to wonder about the reasons why a jury sentenced him to death in the first place. Did race play a role? Did the makeup of the jury play a role? General questions like these can be translated into viable research questions. Other observations may be more systematic and formal. For example, after reading a journal article for a class, you may begin to formulate a set of questions raised by the article. These too could serve as the foundation of a viable research study.

*Unsystematic Observation*    One of the most potent sources of research ideas is curiosity about the causes or determinants of commonplace, everyday behavior. You make a helpful suggestion to a friend, and she angrily rebukes you. Why? Perhaps she just found out she did not get the job she was hoping for. Is this the cause, or is it something else? Or you study all week for an important exam, and the test results show you did very well. Although initially you feel good, the emotion soon passes, and you find yourself falling into a deep depression. What caused this paradoxical result? Such observations can provide the basis for a research project.

Casual observation of animal behavior also can lead to research ideas. Behaviors such as starlings staging a mass attack on a soaring hawk, a squirrel dropping an acorn on your head, or the antics of a pet all raise questions about the conditions that trigger and direct them—questions that can be the basis of a research idea. For example, Niko Tinbergen's well-known research on territorial defense and courtship behavior in the three-spined stickleback (a minnow-sized fish that inhabits European streams) began when Tinbergen happened to observe some odd behavior in a small group of sticklebacks he kept in an aquarium near a window. One day as a Dutch mail truck passed by the window, Tinbergen watched in astonishment as the male sticklebacks rushed to the surface of the water nearest the window in an apparent attempt to attack the red truck and drive it away. Because mail trucks are not normally a part of a stickleback's environment, Tinbergen wondered whether the red coloration of the males' underbellies might provide the natural trigger that elicited attack by other males, and *that* led to a carefully designed research project aimed at answering the question. (See Chapter 4 for more information about this research.)

Unsystematic observation sometimes is a good way to discover a general research idea. Given your casual observations, you may decide to study a particular issue. For example, your questions about the juries in death penalty cases may lead you to some general questions about the factors affecting death penalty decisions. You may decide to focus your research on one or two variables that you believe are strongly associated with those decisions. You could, for example, focus your research on the defendant's age and the type of evidence (e.g., factual versus emotional).

You also can get research ideas just by paying attention in your classes. In many classes, your professors undoubtedly use research examples to illustrate points. As you listen to or read about these research examples, you may be able to think of some interesting research questions. For example, you might ask whether the research results just presented apply equally to men and women or to Western as well as non-Western cultures. With a little follow-up digging through published research, you may find that many questions surrounding gender and culture remain wide open.

It is important to remember that casual observations (from a scientific perspective) represent only the starting point. You still must transform your casual observations into a form that can be tested empirically. Rarely will you be able to infer the causes of observed behavior from your casual observations. Such inferences can only be derived from a careful and systematic study of the behavior of interest.

**Systematic Observation**    There are many ways that systematic observation can lead to research ideas. One source is focused observation of real-world behavior. As an example, consider the work of Jean Piaget. Piaget developed the most comprehensive theory of cognitive development in existence. You may not know, however, what led up to Piaget's grand theory. As a young boy, Piaget was a keen observer of the world around him. For example, at age 10 he came across an albino sparrow in a park. He made careful observations of the sparrow and eventually published a one-page paper, his first scientific publication. His keen eye for observation would serve him well later in life. Piaget spent many an hour observing the behavior of his own children at home and other children on playgrounds. These observations helped lay the foundation for his theory.

It is important to note that Piaget did not make his observations in a vacuum. Instead, he approached a situation with some ideas in mind about the nature of children's thought processes. As he observed children's behavior, he began developing hypotheses that he later tested in a more systematic way.

A second valuable source of systematic observation is published research reports. Instead of observing behavior firsthand, you read about other firsthand observations from researchers. Published research offers an almost limitless source of systematic observations of both human and animal behavior made under well-defined conditions. Although such research answers many questions, it typically raises more than it answers. Are the results reliable? Would the same thing happen if participants with different characteristics were used? What is the shape of the function relating the variables under study? Would you obtain the same results if the dependent measure were defined differently? These questions and others like them provide a rich source of research ideas.

Here is a good example of how this works. In my (Bordens) social psychology class, students read an article by H. Andrew Sagar and Janet Schofield originally published in the *Journal of Personality and Social Psychology* (1980). The article reports an experiment conducted by Sagar and Schofield on how behavior of Black and White children is perceived. In their experiment 40 Black and 40 White children were shown an artist's rendering of four different situations depicting two children (e.g., one child poking another in a classroom). Each picture was accompanied by an oral description. The oral description for the "poking" picture was as follows:

Mark was sitting at his desk, working on his social studies assignment, when David started poking him in the back with the eraser end of his pencil. Mark just kept on working, David kept poking him for a while, and then he finally stopped. (Sagar & Schofield, 1980, p. 593)

There were four versions of each situation in which the race of the child engaging in the behavior (Black or White) and the race of the victim (Black or White) were manipulated. For example, in one version David (the "actor") was Black and Mark (the victim) was White. In another version, Mark was Black and David was White. Participants rated the degree to which several adjectives describing the actor's behavior applied to the situation (e.g., playful, mean, friendly, threatening). The results showed that the actor's behavior was rated as more threatening and mean when the actor was Black than when the actor was White. So the same behavior is rated differently depending upon the race of the actor.

In and of itself, this finding is interesting. However, just as interesting is the number of questions this study raises that could serve as the foundation for further experiments. For example, in discussions of this article, students invariably bring up a wide variety of issues that I always suggest could be studied empirically. For example, students often ask if the results are the same for male and female children. Since Sagar and Schofield did not include participant gender as a variable, we have no way of knowing. It is an open question. Another question that comes up concerns whether the results would be the same if the actor were representative of another ethnic or racial group (e.g., Asian or Hispanic). Once again, Sagar and Schofield did not evaluate this, so we don't know. Finally, students note that the study was published in 1980. They wonder if the results are still valid today. Unfortunately, nobody has ever replicated Sagar and Schofield's study. So, once again, we just don't know. All of these issues, as well as a myriad of others, could be used to develop research ideas leading to a number of studies.

Another potent source of research ideas is your own previous or ongoing research. Unexpected observations made during the course of a project (for example, a result that contradicts expectations) or the need to test the generality of a finding can be the basis for further research. As you examine your data, you may see unexpected relationships or trends emerging. These trends may be interesting enough to warrant a new study.

For example, my (Bordens) research colleague and I conducted an experiment on the effect of the number of plaintiffs in a civil trial on damage awards. In our original experiment (Horowitz & Bordens, 1988), we found that as the size of the plaintiff population increased so did damage awards. This finding then led us to wonder what the critical number of plaintiffs in a trial was. That is, at what number of plaintiffs do you reach the maximum effect on damage awards? We then developed and conducted follow-up experiments addressing this question. We found that the critical number of plaintiffs was four. In this example, we found something interesting (increasing the size of the plaintiff population leads to higher damage awards), which led to another interesting question (what is the critical number?). In the same way, you can get research ideas from your own research.

It is important to note that this particular source of research ideas usually is not immediately available to the scientific community. Other researchers may not become aware of these unexpected trends until you publish or present your research findings. Consequently, you and your close colleagues may be the only ones who can benefit from this potentially rich source of research ideas.

Finally, you may be able to get some research ideas by perusing research projects being run on the Internet. At any time there are several different psychological research projects being conducted there. These include nonexperimental studies (surveys), as well as experimental studies. You can access these research projects through the Yahoo! search engine. First, click on "Science," then "Psychology," and finally "Tests and Experiments." You will find a listing of the research projects currently being run on the Internet. If you wish, you can participate.

One study being run during the fall of 2003 involved the evaluation of the performances of several stand-up comics. Short video clips of 10 comics were presented and the participant was asked to evaluate each comic on a number of dimensions (e.g., was the comedian funny, interesting, attractive, etc.). As you participate in this or another study, some research ideas may begin to develop. For example, in the comedian study, you may wonder if the race or gender of the comic is an important factor in how a comedian is evaluated. Or you might focus on the style of the comedian (animated versus static) or the subject matter of the comedy. All of these could serve as variables that could be investigated in a study.

## Theory

A **theory** is a set of assumptions about the causes of behavior and rules that specify how those causes act. Designed to account for known relationships among given variables and behavior, theories generate new research questions through deductive reasoning. We explore the finer points of scientific theories later in this chapter. For now, we focus on how research ideas can be generated based on theory.

Theories can lead to the development of research questions in two ways. First, a theory allows you to predict the behavior expected under new combinations of variables. For example, *terror management theory* (Solomon, Greenberg, & Pysczynski, 1991) suggests that human beings acknowledge that they live in an uncertain, often unpredictable world and that our existence could end at any moment. According to the theory, when we become aware of this, we get scared and experience "terror." The theory also predicts that we develop a variety of strategies to cope with our mortality as a way of managing the terror. The theory predicts that cultures provide "terror shields" that buffer us against sources of terror, most notably our own mortality. One such terror shield may be romantic relationships (Florian, Mikulincer, & Harschberger, 2002). In fact, Florian et al. conducted a series of experiments that looked at romantic relationships from a terror management perspective. Let's see how this all worked.

As noted above, terror management theory predicts that cultures provide us with buffers against the knowledge of our own mortality. Florian et al. hypothesized that close romantic relationships serve as one such buffer against terror. They note that for decades psychologists have known that close relationships serve a variety of emotional needs for individuals. Florian et al. suggested that one such emotional need served by these relationships is the management of mortality-related terror. They focused on one important component of relationships: relationship commitment.

Commitment is our motivation to maintain a close relationship over time and is associated with a myriad of positive relationship outcomes (e.g., communication, positive conflict resolution). Florian et al. believe that commitment is also an important factor in buffering against terror. Specifically, they predicted that "if relationship commitment acts as a death-anxiety buffer, one could expect that exposing persons to a mortality salience induction would increase their feelings of relationship commitment" (p. 531). In other words, if you get people thinking about their own mortality, relationship commitment should increase.

Before we examine Florian et al.'s study and results, let's pause and review how their research idea flowed from a theory. Florian et al. started with three postulates from terror management theory: that each of us is mortal, that individuals are scared (terrorized) by knowledge of their own mortality, and that individuals will find culturally relevant ways of managing terror. They reasoned that one important cultural institution is the close interpersonal relationship. Further, they reasoned that this cultural institution could be one buffer (among many) against terror. So, based on terror management theory, they developed the research hypothesis quoted above. This hypothesis, as you can see, flows directly from the predictions of terror management theory. Now back to the study . . .

In their first experiment, 49 males and 49 females participated. Participants completed several measures, including items concerning their own mortality. The wording of the questions about mortality was manipulated to create three "mortality priming" conditions. In the first condition ("mortality salience"), participants answered questions that clearly pointed to the participant's mortality (e.g., "What do you think happens to you as you physically die and once you are physically dead?"). Participants in a second condition ("mortality neutral") answered questions in which "watching television" replaced mortality. In the third condition ("physical pain"), the questions asked about the participants' dealing with intense physical pain. After a filler task (a questionnaire on leisure activities), participants completed a measure of relationship commitment.

The results were consistent with the predictions from terror management theory. As shown in Figure 2–1, participants showed more relationship commitment in the "mortality salience" condition than in either of the other two conditions. This finding supports the predictions derived from terror management theory.

The second way that theory can generate research ideas arises when two or more alternative theories account for the same initial observations. This situation may provide a fascinating opportunity to pit the different interpretations against one another. If the alternatives are rigorously specified and mutually exclusive, they may lead to different predictions about what will be observed under a new set of conditions. In this case, a single experiment or observation may be enough to provide strong support for one alternative over another.

One example of this source for research ideas is the different accounts for attitude change provided by cognitive dissonance theory (Festinger, 1957) and self-perception theory (Bem, 1972). Cognitive dissonance theory maintains that when there is inconsistency between our attitudes and our behavior, a negative motivational state called *cognitive dissonance* arises. Because this is a negative state, dissonance theory states that an individual will be motivated to reduce or eliminate it

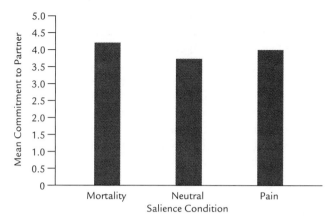

**FIGURE 2-1**    Results from Florian et al. (2002) showing the relationship between the salience condition and mean commitment to one's romantic partner.

through attitude or behavior change. The linchpin of dissonance theory is the arousal of cognitive dissonance. It is a necessary precondition for attitude change. Without dissonance, no attitude change should occur.

In contrast, self-perception theory states that dissonance is not necessary for attitude change. Instead, the theory states that we learn about our motives by observing and evaluating our own behavior. In short the theory maintains that we observe our own behavior and then assume that our attitudes must be consistent with that behavior. So, if we behave in a manner that is inconsistent with an attitude, we change the attitude so that it is consistent with our self-observed behavior. Attitude change comes about because we *reason* that we have a particular attitude that is consistent with our behavior and not because we are motivated to reduce cognitive dissonance.

Here we have an example of two theories designed to account for the same behavior. Which one is correct? This is where research comes in. The question of when, or if, either or both theories account for behavior is an empirical one. When researchers addressed this question they found that both theories were valid. There are situations in which dissonance is clearly aroused and it motivates attitude change. There are other situations in which we undergo attitude change without dissonance arousal. Situations like this provide a fruitful source of research ideas.

## Applied Issues

Often research ideas arise from the need to solve practical problems. Chapter 1 distinguished between basic and applied research. Applied research is problem oriented, whereas basic research is aimed toward building basic knowledge about phenomena. Applied research might be designed, for example, to find effective ways to get people to engage in "safe sex." In an age where sexually transmitted diseases, most notably AIDS, can cause serious long-term illness or death, this problem has become a central issue for health researchers. One safe sex strategy often pointed to is condom use. Despite the fact that people know about the benefits of condom use, the number of AIDS cases worldwide continues to climb: Between 1985 and 1999 the rate of AIDS infection among adult and adolescent women grew from 7 percent to 23 percent (CDC, 2000). However, research has shown consistently that merely disseminating information about safe sex (e.g., condom use) does not effectively increase the rate of practicing safe sex. Other strategies need to be found.

One such alternative strategy was investigated by Suzanne Thompson, Diana Kyle, Joye Swain, Craig Thomas, and Shelley Vrungos (2002). Thompson et al. randomly assigned male and female participants to one of two condom-use intervention conditions. In one condition (labeled the DCC condition), participants watched a standard AIDS information videotape that included information about HIV, technical information on using condoms, and a scene depicting a person being informed that he was HIV-positive. There was nothing in the videotape concerning one's *personal vulnerability* to HIV infection. In the second condition (labeled the IU condition), participants completed three tasks. The first task asked participants to write about a personal sexual experience in which they did not use a condom (or if they had no such encounter, to write about one of an acquaintance). For the second task, participants were given a set of 12 black-and-white photographs accompanied by a biographical sketch of the person depicted. The biographical sketch included factual information about the person's sexual history. Participants were asked to indicate which of the people depicted were HIV-positive and which were HIV-negative (in fact, five were HIV-positive and seven were HIV-negative). The third task had participants list reasons why condoms should be used to prevent the spread of AIDS and then write a persuasive appeal for high school and college students advocating the use of condoms. The tasks in this condition were intended to increase participants' perception of personal vulnerability to HIV infection and condom use.

The main measures were an immediate measure of intention to use condoms and perception of risk of contracting AIDS and a follow-up measure three months later on actual condom use. The results showed that participants in the IU condition indicated a greater intention to use condoms and felt that they were at higher personal risk of contracting AIDS on the immediate measures than participants in the DCC condition. Results from the three-month follow-up revealed that a higher percentage of participants in the IU condition (65 percent) reported using condoms than participants in the DCC condition (37 percent).

A wealth of other practical problems lend themselves to similar research solutions. Finding an effective diet that people will follow might require a systematic evaluation of several proposed diets to identify those characteristics of a diet plan that lead to success. Applied research also might identify the most effective therapy for depression or develop a work environment that leads to the highest levels of productivity and job satisfaction. As with theories, you might find that a single study is not adequate to solve a problem, or, during the course of applied research, you might find that new ideas come to mind. Hence, even applied research can raise new questions that suggest more research. In any event, a need to solve a practical problem can be a rich source of research ideas.

## DEVELOPING GOOD RESEARCH QUESTIONS

Having a good idea for research is not enough. You must translate that idea into good research questions. This section describes how to identify good research questions and suggests what kinds of questions are likely to be important.

### Asking Answerable Questions

Whatever the source of your research ideas, you must be able to frame them in terms of specific questions that can be answered through application of the scientific method. After you have decided on a general topic, you must then narrow that topic to a testable hypothesis. This means that you must develop your research idea into a specific set of predictions about the relationships among variables. In addition, your ideas must be testable.

### Asking the Right Questions

The first step in developing a workable research project is to ask the kind of question that can be answered by using the scientific method. Not all questions can. Here are a few questions that cannot be answered by scientific means: Does God exist? Why is there suffering in the world? Are there human abilities that cannot be measured? How many angels can stand on the head of a pin? Is abortion moral or immoral?

These questions are not answerable by scientific means because the answers cannot be obtained through objective observation. To be objective, an observation must be made under precisely defined conditions, must be reproducible when those same conditions are present again, and must be confirmable by others. Questions that can be answered by objective observation are called **empirical questions**. Here are some examples of empirical questions: Do a criminal defendant's personality characteristics affect a jury's decision? Does a deprived early environment result in lower intelligence? Is punishment an effective tool in socializing children? All these questions can be answered through appropriately designed and executed research. Unlike the first set of questions, the second set identifies variables that can be defined in terms of observable characteristics.

Some questions seem to be empirical but are formulated too broadly to make appropriate observations. Consider the following example of such a question: Do children raised in a permissive atmosphere lack self-discipline as adults? Before this question can be answered, a number of preliminary questions must be addressed. What exactly is a permissive atmosphere? How is it to be measured? Precisely what does it mean to lack self-discipline, and how do we determine when self-discipline is present or absent? Until you can specify exactly what these terms mean and how to measure the variables they represent, you cannot answer the original question.

Defining a variable in terms of the operations required to measure it entails creating an **operational definition** of that variable. Defining variables operationally allows you to measure precisely the variables you include in your study and to determine whether a relationship exists between them. For example, you could operationally define "permissive parenting" in terms of the frequency that parents discipline their children for bad behavior. You could operationally define "lack of self-discipline" as an adult as the number of reprimands a person receives at work for late or sloppy work. You then conduct a study to see if increased parental permissiveness is related to adult self-discipline in the hypothesized way.

Although defining variables operationally is generally a good thing, there is a downside. Operational definitions restrict the generality of answers obtained. Permissive parenting, for example, is no longer addressed in general, but rather as particular behaviors defined as permissive. Self-discipline is no longer addressed in general, but rather in the context of specific behaviors said to indicate self-discipline. Other ways of measuring the two variables may yield a different answer to the question. Nevertheless, without using operational definitions, the question cannot be answered meaningfully.

To summarize, to conduct meaningful research you must choose a question that can be answered through scientific means. You must then operationally define your variables carefully so that you are working with precise definitions. When you have formulated your empirically testable question, you then proceed to the next step in the research process.

## Asking Important Questions

Developing answerable questions is not enough. They also should be important questions. Researching a question imposes demands on a researcher's time, financial resources, and the institution's available space. Researching a question makes demands on the available population of human participants or animal subjects. These resources should not be expended to answer trivial questions. Whether a question is important is often difficult to determine. Some valuable information occasionally has been obtained in the course of answering an apparently mundane question. Some questions that at one time seemed terribly important to answer now appear trivial. However, some rough guidelines will help in identifying important questions.

A question is probably important if answering it will clarify relationships among variables known to affect the behavioral system under study. For example, knowing that memory tends to deteriorate with time since learning, you would want to establish the rate of deterioration as a function of time. You would want to identify how the amount of initial practice, overlearning, previous learning, activity during the retention interval, and other such factors interact to determine the rate of forgetting under specified conditions.

A question is probably important if the answer can support only one of several competing hypotheses or theoretical views. Developing and testing such questions is at the heart of the scientific method. The answers to such questions allow you to "home in" on a proper interpretation of the data. (This technique is discussed later in this chapter.) On the negative side, if the theories under test are later discarded, research designed to test the theories may become irrelevant unless the findings demonstrate clearly interpretable empirical relationships that must be accounted for by theory.

A question is probably important if its answer leads to obvious practical application. (However, the lack of obvious practical application does *not* render the question automatically unimportant!) Much research has been conducted to identify working conditions that maximize productivity and job satisfaction or to screen drugs for potential effectiveness in controlling psychosis. Few would argue that the answers to these problems are unimportant.

In contrast, a question is probably unimportant if its answer is already firmly established. "Firmly established" means that the results have been replicated (duplicated) by different scientists and that the scientists agree that the finding does occur under the stated conditions. Unless serious deficiencies are identified in the methods used to establish those answers, performing the research again is likely to be a waste of time.

A question is probably unimportant if the variables under scrutiny are known to have small effects on the behavior of interest and if these effects are of no theoretical interest. A question is also probably unimportant if there is no a priori reason to believe the variables in question are causally related. Research aimed at determining whether the temperature of a room affects memory recall for faces may turn out to have surprising and useful results. However, without a reason to expect a relationship, such research would amount to a fishing expedition that would be unlikely to pay off. The time would be better spent pursuing more promising leads.

When you have identified your research idea, the next step is to develop it to the point at which you can specify testable hypotheses and define the specific methods to be used to test these hypotheses. This step is accomplished by identifying and familiarizing yourself with research already conducted in your area of interest and is called "reviewing the literature." We show you how to go about reviewing the literature and evaluating research reports in Chapter 3. Next, however, we explore scientific theories and how they relate to the world of research

## SCIENTIFIC THEORIES

Defining what a theory is has always been hazardous, because the term is so often used in a variety of contexts. For example, a detective in a mystery novel is said to develop a "theory" of who committed a crime. In this context, the word *theory* is used as a synonym for *hypothesis*. That is, the detective has an idea about who is guilty, an idea that he or she will then test. The word also has been used to describe ideas that are developed about unverifiable events. For example, many ideas exist about how the miracles recounted in the Bible actually occurred. In this context, a "theory" is used to provide the final explanation for a phenomenon. Finally, the term often is applied in our everyday lives. How often have you said, "I have a theory about how that happened"?

As used in science, the term *theory* means something more than it does in everyday usage. A **scientific theory** is one that goes beyond the level of a simple hypothesis, deals with potentially verifiable phenomena, and is highly ordered and structured. This discussion adopts and extends the definition of theory provided by Martin (1985): A theory is a partially verified statement of a scientific relationship that cannot be directly observed. If the theory is stated formally, this statement consists of a set of interrelated propositions (and corollaries to those propositions) that attempt to specify the relationship between a variable (or set of variables) and some behavior. Not all scientific theories are expressed this way, but most could be.

A good example of a psychological theory with a clearly defined set of propositions and corollaries is "equity theory" (Walster, Walster, & Berscheid, 1978). Equity theory was developed to explain how individuals behave when placed in an interpersonal exchange situation, such as employer–employee relations or friendships. Table 2–1

---

**TABLE 2–1   Propositions and Corollaries of Equity Theory**

---

1. In an interpersonal relationship, a person will try to maximize his or her outcomes (where outcome = rewards − costs).

   *Corollary:* As long as a person believes that he or she can maximize outcomes by behaving equitably, he or she will. If a person believes that inequitable behavior is more likely to maximize outcomes, inequitable behavior will be used.

2a. By developing systems whereby resources can be equitably distributed among members, groups can maximize the probability of equitable behavior among their members.

2b. A group will reward members who behave equitably toward others and punish those who do not.

3. Inequitable relationships are stressful for those within them. The greater the inequity, the greater the distress.

4. A person in an inequitable relationship will take steps to reduce the distress aroused by restoring equity. The more distress felt, the harder the person will try to restore equity.

---

SOURCE: Based on Walster, Walster, & Berscheid, 1978.

---

presents the major propositions of equity theory and one corollary (other corollaries are outlined by Walster et al.). Notice that the first set of propositions makes a general statement about how interpersonal exchanges are perceived. The later propositions and corollaries specify how a set of variables (such as inputs and outputs) should affect the perception of equity within a relationship.

A deeper exploration of the definition of *theory* shows that a scientific theory has several important characteristics. First, a scientific theory describes a scientific relationship—one established through observation and logic—that indicates how variables interact within the system to which the theory applies.

Second, the described relationship cannot be observed directly. Its existence must be *inferred* from the data. (If you could observe the relationship directly, there would be no need for a theory.) Third, the statement is only partially verified. This means that the theory has passed some tests but that not all relevant tests have been conducted.

Colloquial use of the term *theory* leads to confusion over what a theory really is. Confusion also can be found within the scientific community over the term. Even in scientific writing, "theory," "hypothesis," "law," and "model" are often used interchangeably. Nevertheless, these terms can be distinguished, as described in the next sections.

## Theory versus Hypothesis

Students often confuse *theory* with *hypothesis*, and even professionals sometimes use these terms interchangeably. However, as usually defined, theories are more complex than hypotheses. For example, if you observe that more crime occurs during the period of full moon than during other times of the month, you might hypothesize that the observed relationship is caused by the illumination that the moon provides for nighttime burglary. You could then test this hypothesis by comparing crime rates during periods of full moon that were clear with crime rates during periods of full moon that were cloudy.

In contrast to the simple one-variable account provided by this hypothesis, a theory would account for changes in crime rate by specifying the action and interaction of a *system* of variables. Because of the complexity of the system involved, no single observation could substantiate the theory in its entirety.

### Theory versus Law

A theory that has been substantially verified is sometimes called a **law**. However, most laws do not derive from theories in this way. Laws are usually empirically verified, quantitative relationships between two or more variables, and thus are not normally subject to the disconfirmation that theories are. For example, E. L. Thorndike's *law of effect* states that any behavior followed by a satisfying state of affairs will be repeated. This law derives from Thorndike's research using kittens in a puzzle box. The kitten was placed in the puzzle box and if it made the necessary response, the box opened and the kitten received a small piece of fish. Thorndike noticed that on successive trials, the kitten's behavior became more efficient. At first the kitten's random explorations of the puzzle box produced the desired response by accident. Eventually, the kitten learned to make the response as soon as it was placed in the puzzle box. The law of effect was not derived from a theory, but rather from Thorndike's empirical observations.

Sometimes laws idealize real-world relationships; for example, Boyle's law, which relates change in temperature to change in pressure of a confined ideal gas. Because there are no ideal gases, the relationship described by Boyle's law is not directly observable. However, as a description of the behavior of real gases, it holds well enough for most purposes. To an approximation, it represents a verified empirical relationship and is thus unlikely to be overthrown.

Such empirical laws are not theories grown solid through verification. They are relationships that must be explained by theory. For example, a theory relating to Thorndike's law of effect would specify the psychological and perhaps the physiological mechanisms underlying the learning process.

### Theory versus Model

Like *theory*, the term **model** can refer to a range of concepts. In some cases, it is simply used as a synonym for *theory*. However, in most cases *model* refers to a specific implementation of a more general theoretical view. For example, the Rescorla–Wagner model of classical conditioning formalizes a more general associative theory of conditioning (Rescorla & Wagner, 1972). This model specifies how the associative strength of a conditional stimulus (CS) is to be calculated following each of a series of trials in which the CS is presented alone or in conjunction with other stimuli. Where the general associative theory simply states that the strength of the stimulus will increase each time the CS is paired with an unconditional stimulus (US), the Rescorla–Wagner model supplies a set of assumptions that mathematically specify how characteristics of the stimuli interact on each trial.

Rescorla and Wagner made it clear when they presented their model that the assumptions were simply starting points. For example, they assumed that the associative strength of a compound stimulus (two or more stimuli presented together) would equal the sum of the strengths of the individual stimuli. If the learning curves resulting from this assumption proved not to fit the curves obtained from experiment, then the assumption would be modified.

Rescorla and Wagner could have chosen to try several rules for combining stimulus strengths. Each variation would represent a somewhat different model of classical conditioning, although all would derive from a common associative view of the conditioning process.

In a related sense, a model can represent an application of a general theory to a specific situation. In the case of the Rescorla–Wagner model, the assumptions of the model can be applied to generate predictions for reinforcement of a simple CS, for reinforcement of a compound CS, for inhibitory conditioning, for extinction, and for discrimination learning (to name a few). The assumptions of the model remain the same across all these cases, but the set of equations required to make the predictions changes from case to case. You might then say that each set of equations represents a different model: a model of simple conditioning, a model of compound conditioning, a model of differential conditioning, and so on. However, all the models would share the same assumptions of the Rescorla–Wagner model of conditioning.

This chapter uses the term *model* in all the ways just discussed. At times, a model will simply be a theory. At other times a model will be a specific version of a less well-specified theory or a particular application of a theory to a specific situation. The context will tell you which meaning applies.

*Computer Modeling*    Theories in psychology most commonly take the form of a set of verbal statements that describe their basic assumptions and the ways in which the various entities of the theory interact to produce behavior. Unfortunately, predictions based on such theories must be derived by verbally tracing a chain of events from a set of initial conditions to the ultimate result, a difficult process to carry out successfully in an even moderately complex theory and one that may be impossible if the theory involves entities that mutually influence one another. Because of these difficulties, scientists may at times disagree about what a given theory predicts under given circumstances.

One way to avoid such problems is to cast specific implementations of the theory in the form of a *computer model*. A computer model is a set of program statements that define the variables to be considered and the ways in which their values will change over the course of time or trials. The process of creating a model forces you to be specific: to state precisely what variables are involved, their initial values or states, and how the variables interact. Developing a computer model offers several advantages:

1. The attempt to build a computer model may reveal inconsistencies, unspoken assumptions, or other defects in the theory and thus can help bring to light problems in the theory that otherwise might go unnoticed.

2. Having a computer model eliminates ambiguity; you can determine exactly what the model assumes by examining the code.

3. A properly implemented computer model will show what is to be expected under specified conditions. These predictions may be difficult or impossible to derive correctly by verbally tracing out the implications of the theory.

4. The behavior of the model under simulated conditions can be compared with the behavior of real people or animals under actual conditions to determine whether the model behaves realistically. Discrepancies reveal where the model has problems and may suggest how the model can be improved.

5. Competing theories can be evaluated by building computer models based on each and then determining which model does a better job of accounting for observed phenomena.

An interesting example of computer modeling is provided by Josef Nerb and Hans Spada (2001). Nerb and Spada were interested in explaining the relationship between cognitive, emotional, and behavioral responses to environmental disasters. More specifically, they were interested in investigating the relationship between media portrayals of single-event environmental disasters and cognitive, emotional, and behavioral responses to them. They developed a computer model called "Intuitive Thinking in Environmental Risk Appraisal," or ITERA for short. The ITERA model was designed to make predictions about the cognitive appraisals made about environmental disasters as well as the emotions and behavioral tendencies generated in response to the disasters. By inputting data into the model relating to several variables, predictions about cognitive, emotional, and behavioral outcomes can be made. Those predictions could then be tested empirically to verify the validity of the computer model.

Let's see how the model works. Nerb and Spada extracted crucial pieces of information from media reports of environmental disasters that related to elements of the ITERA model. This information was systematically varied and entered as variables into the model. For example, one piece of information referred to damage done by the disaster. This was entered into the model as either "given," "not given," or "unknown." The same protocol was followed for other variables (e.g., extent to which the events surrounding the disaster were controllable). By systematically entering one or more variables into the model, predictions about cognitive, emotional, and behavioral responses can be made. For example, the computer model predicts that if controllability information is entered indicating that the events leading to the disaster were controllable, anger should be a stronger emotion than sadness and boycott behavior should be preferred over providing help. In contrast, the model predicts that if the disaster was uncontrollable, the dominant emotion should be sadness and the dominant behavioral tendency would be to offer help.

Nerb and Spada tested this prediction in an experiment in which participants read a fictitious, but realistic newspaper account of a tanker running aground in the North Sea, spilling oil into the sea. There were three versions of the newspaper article. In one version, participants were told that "the tanker did not fulfill safety guidelines, and the damage could have been avoided." In a second version, participants read that "the tanker did fulfill safety guidelines, and the damage could not have been avoided." In the third condition, no information was provided about safety guidelines or whether the damage could have been avoided. The results from the experiment were compared to the predictions made by the ITERA computer model. Nerb and Spada found that the model correctly predicted emotional and behavioral outcomes for the controllable condition (safety guidelines not followed and the damage could have been avoided). Consistent with the model's prediction, the dominant emotion reported by participants was anger and the favored behavioral response was a boycott. However, the model did not correctly predict outcomes for an uncontrollable event (guidelines followed and damage was unavoidable). In this condition sadness and helping did not dominate.

## Mechanistic versus Functional Explanations

Theories provide explanations for observed phenomena, but not all explanations are alike. When evaluating a theory, you should carefully note whether the explanations provided are mechanistic or functional. A **mechanistic explanation** describes the mechanism (physical components) and the chain of cause and effect through which conditions act on the mechanism to produce its behavior; it describes *how* something works. In contrast, a **functional explanation** describes an attribute of something (such as physical attractiveness) in terms of its function, that is, what it does (for example, signaling reproductive health, according to evolutionary psychologists); it describes *why* the attribute or system exists. To clarify this distinction, consider the notion of motivated reasoning, which involves goals and motives influencing one's reasoning process (Kunda, 1990). Kunda describes the mechanisms involved in motivated reasoning (e.g., optimistic reasoning) by pointing to the idea that individuals using motivated reasoning come up with a set of reasonable justifications for their conclusions. So a person may convince herself that the chance of surviving breast cancer is excellent. However, she also must develop justifications for her optimism (e.g., that she is a strong person, that she will adhere to her treatment schedule rigorously). Contrast this with the more functional explanation for optimism provided by Shelly Taylor (1989). Taylor explains optimism in terms of its function of helping a person get better faster.

Mechanistic explanations tell you how a system works without necessarily telling you why it does what it does; functional explanations refer to the purpose or goal of a given attribute or system without describing how those purposes or goals are achieved. A full understanding requires both types of explanation.

Although you can usually determine a mechanism's function once you know how it works, the converse is not true. Knowing what a system does gives only hints as to the underlying mechanism through which its functions are carried out. Consider, for example, the buttons on your television's remote control. You can quickly determine their functions by trying them out—this one turns on the power, that one changes the volume, the next one changes the channel. However, without some knowledge of electronics, you may have no idea whatever how this or that button accomplishes its function, and even with that knowledge there may be dozens of different circuits (mechanisms) that can do the job. Knowing *what* a button does in no way tells you *how* it does it.

Given the choice between a mechanistic explanation and a functional one, you should prefer the mechanistic one. Unfortunately, arriving at the correct mechanism underlying a given bit of human or animal behavior may not be possible given our current understanding of the brain. For example, we currently have no firm idea how memories are stored in the brain and subsequently accessed (although there has been plenty of speculation). Yet we do have a fair understanding of many functional properties of the brain mechanism or mechanisms involved. Given this knowledge, it is possible to construct a theory of, say, choice among alternatives not currently present that simply *assumes* a memory with certain properties without getting into the details of mechanism.

## TYPES OF THEORY

Theories may be classified in several ways. This section classifies theories along three dimensions: (1) quantitative or qualitative aspect, (2) level of description, and (3) scope (or domain) of the theory.

### Quantitative versus Qualitative Theory

The first dimension along which a theory can be classified is whether the theory is quantitative or qualitative. Some theories are expressed in mathematical terms, whereas others are stated in verbal terms. The next sections describe these two types of theories.

*Quantitative Theory*    A **quantitative theory** is expressed in mathematical terms. It specifies the variables and constants with which it deals numerically and relates the numerical states of these variables and constants to one another. Given specific numerical inputs, the quantitative theory generates specific numerical outputs. The relationships thus described then can be tested by setting up the specified conditions and observing whether the outputs take on the specified values (within the error of measurement).

A good example of a quantitative theory in psychology is information integration theory developed by Norman Anderson (1968). Anderson's theory attempts to explain how diverse sources of information are integrated into an overall impression. The theory proposes that each item of information used in an impression formation task is assigned both a weight and scale value. The weights and scale values are then combined according to the following formula:

$$J = \frac{\Sigma\,(w_i x s_i)}{\Sigma\,w_i}$$

where $w_i$ is the weight assigned to each item of information and $s_i$ is the scale value assigned to each item of information. According to this theory, your final judgment ($J$) about a stimulus (for example, whether you describe a person as warm or cold, caring or uncaring, honest or dishonest) will be the result of a mathematical combination of the weights and scale values assigned to each piece of information.

*Qualitative Theory*    A **qualitative theory** is any theory that is not quantitative. Qualitative theories tend to be stated in verbal, rather than mathematical, terms.

These theories state which variables are important and, loosely, how those variables interact.

The relationships described by qualitative theories may be quantitative, but, if so, the quantities will be measured on no higher than an ordinal scale. For example, a theory of drug addiction may state that craving for the drug will increase with the time since the last administration and that this craving will be intensified by emotional stress. Note that the predictions of the theory specify only ordinal relationships. They state that craving will be greater under some conditions than under others, but they do not state by how much.

A good example of a qualitative theory in psychology is a theory of language acquisition by Noam Chomsky (1965). This theory states that a child acquires language by analyzing the language that he or she hears. The language heard by the child is processed, according to Chomsky, and the rules of language are extracted. The child then formulates hypotheses about how language works and then tests those hypotheses against reality. No attempt is made in the theory to quantify the parameters of language acquisition. Instead, the theory specifies verbally the important variables that contribute to language acquisition.

## Descriptive, Analogical, and Fundamental Theories

The second dimension along which theories may be categorized is according to the level of description the theory provides. Recall from Chapter 1 that two goals of science are to describe and explain phenomena within its domain. A theory may address itself to the first goal (description), whereas another may address itself to the second (explanation). So some theories are primarily designed to describe a phenomenon, whereas others attempt to explain relationships among variables that control a phenomenon. The following sections describe theories that deal with phenomena at different levels.

*Descriptive Theories*    At the lowest level, a theory may simply describe how certain variables are related without providing an explanation for that relationship. A theory that merely describes a relationship is termed a **descriptive theory**.

An example of a descriptive theory is Wilhelm Wundt's systematic theory of the structure of consciousness. Wundt, as you probably know, is credited with being the founder of scientific psychology. His empirical and theoretical work centered on describing the structure of consciousness. Wundt maintained that consciousness was made up of *psychical elements* (sensations, feelings, and volition). He stated that all examples of consciousness are made up of these three basic building blocks. When the psychical elements combined, they formed *psychical compounds*. Wundt focused on describing the structure of consciousness and how complex conscious events could be broken down into their component parts.

Most descriptive theories are simply proposed generalizations from observation. For example, arousal theory states that task performance increases with arousal up to some optimal arousal value, then deteriorates with further increases in arousal. The proposed relationship thus follows an inverted U-shaped function. Arousal and task performance are both classes of variables that can be operationally defined a number of ways. Arousal and task performance are general concepts rather than specific variables. The proposed relationship is thus not directly observable but must be inferred from observation of many specific variables representative of each concept. Note also that the theory describes the relationship but offers no real explanation for it.

A potential trap you can fall into when constructing a descriptive theory is to think you have explained a phenomenon when you have only given it a name. This problem became particularly acute during the heyday of "Functionalism" (an early school of psychological thought focusing on the functions that consciousness played in helping individuals adapt), when nearly every animal behavior was being "explained" as the product of an instinct. For example, if a female mouse took care of her newborn offspring, it was because she had a "mothering instinct." But how do you know that the mouse had a mothering instinct? You know simply because she took care of her offspring. The concept of mothering instinct as used here is nothing more than a name for the observed behaviors. It says only that the mouse mothered because she had a tendency to mother.

*Analogical Theories*    At the next level is an **analogical theory**, which explains a relationship through analogy. Such theories borrow from well-understood models (usually of physical systems) by suggesting that the system to be explained behaves in a fashion similar to that described by the well-understood model.

To develop an analogical theory, you equate each variable in the physical system with a variable in the behavioral system to be modeled. You then plug in values for the new variables and apply the rules of the original theory in order to generate predictions.

An example of an analogical theory was provided by Konrad Lorenz in 1950. Lorenz wanted to explain some relationships he had observed between the occurrence of a specific behavioral pattern (called a *fixed action pattern*, or FAP), a triggering stimulus (called a *sign* or *releaser stimulus*), and the time since last occurrence of the FAP. For example, chickens scan the ground and then direct pecks at any seeds they find there. Here the visual characteristics of the seeds act as a releaser stimulus, and the directed pecking at the seeds is the FAP. Lorenz had observed that the FAP could be elicited more easily by a sign stimulus as the time increased since the last appearance of the FAP. In fact, with enough time, the behavior became so primed that it sometimes occurred in the absence of any identifiable sign stimulus. However, if the behavior had just occurred, the sign stimulus usually was unable to elicit the FAP again.

Let's return to the chicken example. Chickens at first peck only at seeds. With increasing hunger, however, they begin to peck at pencil marks on a paper and other such stimuli that only remotely resemble seeds. With further deprivation, they even peck at a blank paper.

To explain this relationship, Lorenz imagined that the motivation to perform the FAP was like the pressure of water at the bottom of a tank that was being continuously filled (see Figure 2–2). As time went on, the water in the tank became deeper and the pressure greater. Lorenz pictured a pressure-sensitive valve at the bottom of the tank. This valve could be opened by depressing a lever, but the pressure required to open it became less as the pressure inside the tank rose. In Lorenz's conception, the lever was normally "pressed" by the appearance of the sign stimulus.

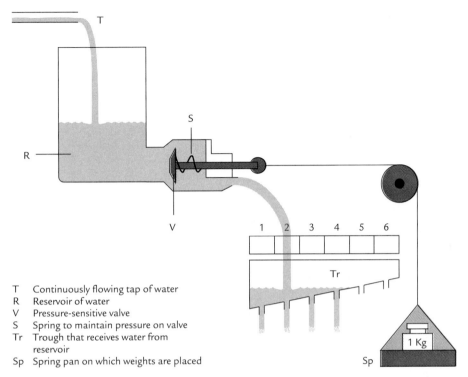

T    Continuously flowing tap of water
R    Reservoir of water
V    Pressure-sensitive valve
S    Spring to maintain pressure on valve
Tr   Trough that receives water from
     reservoir
Sp   Spring pan on which weights are placed

**FIGURE 2–2**   Lorenz's Hydraulic Model of Motivation.
(Source: Lorenz, 1950; legend adapted from Dewsbury, 1978; reprinted with permission.)

Notice the analogies in Lorenz's model. Motivation to perform the FAP is analogous to water pressure. Engaging in the FAP is analogous to water rushing out the open valve. And perception of the sign stimulus is analogous to pressing the lever to open the valve.

Now put the model into action. Motivation to perform the FAP builds as time passes (the tank fills). If a sign stimulus appears after the tank has partially filled, the valve opens and the FAP occurs. However, if the sign stimulus does not occur for a long time, the tank overfills and the pressure triggers the valve to open spontaneously (the FAP occurs without the sign stimulus). Finally, if the FAP has just occurred (the valve has just opened), there is no motivation to perform the FAP (the tank is empty) and the sign stimulus is ineffective. The model thus nicely accounts for the observed facts.

Lorenz's hydraulic model of motivation eventually gave way to more sophisticated theories when new data revealed its limitations. In general, analogical theories can only be pushed so far. At some point the analogy breaks down. After all, motivation is *not* quite the same thing as water pressure in a tank and may vary in ways quite unexpected for water pressure. Nevertheless, analogical theories can provide conceptual organization for the data and may predict relationships that otherwise would be unexpected.

*Fundamental Theories*    At the highest level are theories created to explain phenomena within a particular area of research. These theories do not depend on analogy to provide their basic structures. Instead, they propose a new structure that directly relates the variables and constants of the system. This structure includes entities and processes not directly observable but invented to account for the observed relationships. Thus, these entities and processes go beyond descriptive theories, which simply describe relationships among observable variables. Because these theories have no accepted name, we'll call this type of theory a **fundamental theory** to distinguish them from the more superficial descriptive and analogical types. Such theories seek to model an underlying reality that produces the observed relationships among variables. In this sense, they propose a more fundamental description of reality than the analogical theory.

Although psychological theories abound, fundamental theories are disturbingly rare in psychology. Part of the reason for this rarity is that psychology is still a relatively new science, but this is probably only a small part. Mostly this rarity is because of the complexity of the system being studied and because of the extreme difficulty in controlling the relevant variables well enough to clearly reveal the true relationships among them (or even to measure them properly). The physicist can expect every electron to behave exactly like every other. The psychologist cannot even hope that his or her subjects will be this interchangeable. Nevertheless, some attempts at fundamental theorizing have been made. One of the most famous fundamental theories is the *cognitive dissonance theory* proposed by Festinger (1957).

As we noted earlier in this chapter, dissonance is the fundamental process in cognitive dissonance theory. According to the theory, whenever two (or more) attitudes or behaviors are inconsistent, a negative psychological state called *cognitive dissonance* is aroused. The arousal of dissonance motivates the individual to reduce dissonance. This can be done by changing behavior or by changing attitudes. Festinger's theory thus described how dissonance leads to behavioral or attitude change.

Another example of fundamental theory in psychology is the scalar timing theory proposed by John Gibbon (1977) to account for the patterns of responding that develop under various schedules of reinforcement. The central idea of Gibbon's theory is that well-trained subjects are able to estimate time to reinforcement by means of a "scalar timing" process. With scalar timing, the subject is able to adjust to changes in the time constant of a schedule by simply rescaling the estimated time distribution to fit the new constant. Estimates of time to reinforcement (together with the size and attractiveness of the reinforcer) determine the "expectancy" of reward, which in turn determines the probability of a response through a well-defined mechanism. Gibbon described how the assumption of scalar timing produces a better fit to data from a variety of paradigms than do other assumptions (such as timing based on a Poisson process).

## Domain of a Theory

The third dimension along which theories differ is **domain** or *scope*. This dimension concerns the range of situations to which the theory may be legitimately applied. A theory with a wide scope can be applied to a wider range of situations than can a theory with a more limited scope.

Gibbon's scalar timing theory is an example of a theory with a relatively limited scope. It provided an explanation for behavioral patterns that emerge under a wide variety of reinforcement schedules, but it did not attempt to account for other factors that could affect behavior. Cognitive consistency theory, such as Festinger's (1957) theory of cognitive dissonance, is an example of a theory with a wider scope. It has been applied beyond attitude change (for which it was developed) to help explain motivational processes in other contexts.

The chances of dealing adequately with a range of phenomena are better for a small area of behavior than they are for a large area. On the negative side, however, concepts invented to deal with one area may have no relationship to those invented to deal with others, even though the behaviors may be mediated by partly overlapping (or even identical) mechanisms.

## ROLES OF THEORY IN SCIENCE

Theories have several roles to play in science. These roles include providing an understanding of the phenomena for which they account, providing a basis for prediction, and guiding the direction of research.

### Understanding

At the highest level, theories represent a particular way to understand the phenomena with which they deal. To the degree that a theory models an underlying reality, this understanding can be deep and powerful. For example, Jean Piaget's (1952) theory of development provided a deep insight into the thought processes of children and helped us better understand how these processes changed with age and experience. Piaget provided a broad description of the behaviors that are characteristic of children at various ages. Within the theory, he also proposed mechanisms (organization, adaptation, and equilibration) to explain why development takes place.

### Prediction

Even when theories do not provide a fundamental insight into the mechanisms of a behaving system (as descriptive theories do not), they at least can provide a way to predict the behavior of the system under different values of its controlling variables. The descriptive theory will specify which variables need to be considered and how they interact to determine the behavior to be explained. If it is a good theory, the predictions will match the empirical outcome with a reasonable degree of precision.

A good example of how a theory can generate testable predictions comes from *social impact theory* proposed by Bibb Latané (1981). Social impact theory is intended to explain the process of social influence (e.g., conformity and obedience). According to the theory, the amount of influence obtained is dependent upon the interaction of three factors: The strength of an influence source ($S$), the immediacy of an influence source ($I$), and the number of influence sources ($N$). The relationship between influence and these three variables is summed up with this simple formula:

$$\text{Influence} = \int (S \times I \times N)$$

One prediction made by the theory is that the relationship between the number of sources and the amount of influence obtained is nonlinear. That is, after a certain number of sources, influence should not increase significantly and should "level off." The prediction made from social impact theory is consistent with the results obtained from empirical research findings on the relationship between the size of a majority and conformity.

## Organizing and Interpreting Research Results

A theory can provide a sound framework for organizing and interpreting research results. For example, the results of an experiment designed to test Piaget's theory will be organized within the existing structure of confirmatory and disconfirmatory results. This organization is preferable to having a loose conglomeration of results on a topic.

In addition to being organized by theory, research results can be interpreted in the light of a theory. This is true even if your research was not specifically designed to test a particular theory. For example, results of a study of decision making may be interpreted in the light of cognitive dissonance theory, even though you did not specifically set out to test dissonance theory.

## Generating Research

Finally, theories are valuable because they often provide ideas for new research. This is known as the *heuristic value* of a theory. The heuristic value of a theory is often independent of its validity. A theory can have heuristic value despite the fact that it is not supported by empirical research. Such a theory may implicate certain variables in a particular phenomenon, variables that had not been previously suspected of being important. Researchers may then design experiments or collect observations to examine the role of these variables. Often such variables turn out to be significant, although the theory that emphasized them eventually may be proven wrong.

A theory specifies the variables that need to be examined and the conditions under which they are to be observed and may even state how they are to be measured. It provides a framework within which certain research questions make sense and others become irrelevant or even nonsensical. Franz Gall's phrenology provides an example of how a theory guides research and determines which questions will be considered important. Gall was a nineteenth-century surgeon who became convinced that a person's abilities, traits, and personality were determined by specific areas of the cerebral cortex. If a part of the brain were highly developed, Gall believed, a person would have a higher degree of the particular trait or ability associated with that area than if that same part of the brain was less highly developed. In addition, Gall reasoned, the more highly developed area would require more volume of cortex. Consequently, the part of the skull covering this area would bulge outward and create a "bump" on the person's head (Fancher, 1979).

In the context of Gall's theory, the important research problems were to identify which parts of the cortex represented which traits or abilities and to relate individual differences in the topography of the skull (its characteristic bumps and valleys) to personality variables. Special instruments were developed to measure the skull. Thousands of hours were devoted to making measurements and collecting profiles of mental abilities and personality traits.

Phrenology never gained acceptance within the scientific community and was severely damaged by evidence (provided by Pierre Flourens and other Gall contemporaries) showing rather conclusively that at least some of the brain areas identified as the seat of a particular trait had entirely different functions (Fancher, 1979). With the discrediting of phrenology, interest in measuring the skull and in correlating these measurements with traits and abilities went with it.

Phrenology provided a framework for research within which certain problems and questions became important. When this view was displaced, much of the work conducted under it became irrelevant. This loss of relevance is a serious concern. If data collected under a particular theory become worthless when the theory dies, then researchers working within a particular framework face the possibility that the gold they mine will turn to dross in the future.

This possibility has led some researchers to suggest that perhaps theories should be avoided, at least in the early stages of research. Speaking at a time when the Hull–Spence learning theory was still a force within the psychology of learning, B. F. Skinner (1949) asked in his presidential address to the Midwestern Psychological Association, "Are theories of learning necessary?" In this address, Skinner disputed the claim that theories are necessary to organize and guide research. Research should be guided, Skinner said, not by theory but by the search for functional relationships and for orderly changes in data that follow the manipulation of effective independent variables. Such clearly established relationships have enduring value. These relationships become the data with which any adequate theory must deal.

Skinner's point has a great deal of merit, and it is discussed later in this chapter. However, for now you should not get the idea that theory is useless or, even worse, wasteful. Even theories that are eventually overthrown do provide a standard against which to judge new developments. New developments that do not fit the existing theory become anomalies, and anomalies generate further research in an effort to show that they result from measurement error or some other problem unrelated to the content of the theory. The accumulation of serious anomalies can destroy a theory. In the process, however, the intense focus on the problem areas may bring new insights and rapid progress within the field. Because anomalies are unexpected findings, they exist only in the context of expectation—expectation provided by theory. Thus, even in failing, a theory can have heuristic value.

## CHARACTERISTICS OF A GOOD THEORY

In the history of psychology, many theories have been advanced to explain behavioral phenomena. Some of these theories have stood the test of time, whereas others have fallen by the wayside. Whether or not a theory endures depends on several factors, including the following.

## Ability to Account for Data

To be of any value, a theory must account for most of the existing data within its domain. Note that the amount of data is "most" rather than "all" because at least some of the data may, in fact, be unreliable. A theory can be excused for failing to account for erroneous data. However, a theory that fails to account for well-established facts within its domain is in serious trouble. The phrase "within its domain" is crucial. If the theory is designed to explain the habituation of responses, it can hardly be criticized for its failure to account for schizophrenia. Such an account clearly would be beyond the scope of the theory.

## Explanatory Relevance

A theory also must meet the criterion of *explanatory relevance* (Hempel, 1966). That is, the explanation for a phenomenon provided by a theory must offer good grounds for believing that the phenomenon would occur under the specified conditions. If a theory meets this criterion, you should find yourself saying, "Ah, but of course! That was indeed to be expected under the circumstances!" (Hempel, 1966). If someone were to suggest that the rough sleep you had last night was caused by the color of your socks, you would probably reject this theory on the grounds that it lacks explanatory relevance. There is simply no good reason to believe that wearing a particular color of socks would affect your sleep. To be adequate, the theory must define some logical link between socks and sleep.

## Testability

Another condition that a good theory must meet is *testability*. A theory is testable if it is capable of failing some empirical test. That is, the theory specifies outcomes under particular conditions, and if these outcomes do not occur, then the theory is rejected.

The criterion of testability is a major problem for many aspects of Freud's psychodynamic theory of personality. Freud's theory provides explanations for a number of personality traits and disorders, but it is too complex and loosely specified to make specific, testable predictions. For example, if a person is observed to be stingy and obstinate, Freudian theory points to unsuccessful resolution of the anal stage of psychosexual development. Yet diametrically opposite traits also can be accounted for with the same explanation. There is no mechanism within the theory to specify which will develop in any particular case. When a theory can provide a seemingly reasonable explanation no matter what the outcome of an observation, you are probably dealing with an untestable theory.

## Prediction of Novel Events

A good theory should predict new phenomena. Within its domain, a good theory should predict phenomena beyond those for which the theory was originally designed. Strictly speaking, such predicted phenomena do not have to be new in the sense of not yet observed. Rather, they must be new in the sense that they were not taken into account in the formulation of the theory.

As an example, consider Einstein's theory of relativity. This theory accounted for the same data and produced the same predictions for a wide range of phenomena as did Newtonian mechanics. However, Einstein's theory went beyond Newton's to predict new phenomena not expected to occur from Newton's point of view. One implication of the relativistic view was that if two totally accurate clocks were set to the same time, and one of the clocks was shot into orbit while the other remained on Earth, then the clock in orbit would appear to lose time relative to the one on Earth. This experiment was actually conducted using superaccurate atomic clocks, and the predicted loss of time was, in fact, detected.

## Parsimony

The medieval English philosopher William of Ockham popularized an important principle stated by Aristotle. Aristotle's principle states, "Entities must not be multiplied beyond what is necessary" (http://2Think.org). Ockham's refinement of this principle is now called *Occam's Razor* and states that a problem should be stated in the simplest possible terms and explained with the fewest postulates possible. Today we know this as the *law of parsimony*. Simply put, a theory should account for phenomena within its domain in the simplest terms possible and with the fewest assumptions. If there are two competing theories concerning a behavior, the one that explains the behavior in the simplest terms is preferred under the law of parsimony.

Many theories in psychology fit this requirement very well. Modern theories of memory, attribution processes, development, and motivation all adhere to this principle. However, the history of science in general, and psychology in particular, is littered with theories that were crushed under their own weight of complexity.

For example, the collapse of interest in the Hull–Spence model of learning occurred primarily because the theory had been modified so many times to account for anomalous data (and had in the process gained so many ad hoc assumptions) that it was no longer parsimonious. Researchers could not bring themselves to believe that learning could be *that* complicated.

## STRATEGIES FOR TESTING THEORIES

A major theme developed in the preceding sections is that a good scientific theory must be testable with empirical methods. In fact, the final step in the business of theory construction is to subject the propositions of your theory to rigorous empirical scrutiny.

A theory is usually tested by identifying implications of the theory for a specific situation not yet examined, then setting up the situation and observing whether the predicted effects occur. If the predicted effects are observed, the theory is said to be supported by the results, and your confidence in the theory increases. If the predicted effects do not occur, then the theory is not supported and your confidence in it weakens.

When you test the implications of a theory in this way, you are following what is called a **confirmational strategy** (that is, a strategy of looking for confirmation of the theory's predictions). A positive outcome supports the theory.

Looking for confirmation is an important part of theory testing, but it does have an important limitation. Although the theory must find confirmation if it is to survive (too many failures would kill it), you can find confirmation until doomsday and the theory may still be wrong.

Spurious confirmations are particularly likely to happen when the prediction only loosely specifies an outcome. For example, in an experiment with two groups, if a theory predicts that Group A will score higher on the dependent measure than Group B, only three outcomes are possible at this level of precision: A may be greater than B, B may be greater than A, or A and B may be equal. Thus, the theory has about a one-in-three chance of being supported by a lucky coincidence.

Such coincidental support becomes less likely as the predictions of the theory become more precise. For example, if the theory predicts that Group A will score 25, plus or minus 2, points higher than Group B, it is fairly unlikely that a difference in this direction and within this range will occur by coincidence. Because of this relationship, confirmation of a theory's predictions has a much greater impact on your confidence in the theory when the predictions are precisely stated than when they are loosely stated.

*Following a Disconfirmational Strategy*   Even when a theory's predictions are relatively precise, many alternative theories could potentially be constructed that would make the same predictions within the stated margin of error. Because of this fact, following a confirmational strategy is not enough. To test a theory requires more than simply finding out if its predictions are confirmed. You also must determine whether outcomes *not* expected, according to the theory, do or do not occur.

This strategy follows this form: If A is true (the theory is correct), then B will not be true (a certain outcome will not occur); thus, if B is true (the outcome does happen), then A is false (the theory is erroneous). Because a positive result will *disconfirm* (rather than confirm) the prediction, this way of testing a theory is called a **disconfirmational strategy**.

## USING CONFIRMATIONAL AND DISCONFIRMATIONAL STRATEGIES TOGETHER

Adequately testing a theory requires using both confirmational and disconfirmational strategies. Usually you will pursue a confirmational strategy when a theory is fresh and relatively untested. The object during this phase of testing is to determine whether the theory is able to predict or explain the phenomena within its domain with reasonable precision.

If the theory survives these tests, you will eventually want to pursue a disconfirmational strategy. The objective during this phase of testing is to determine whether outcomes that are unexpected from the point of view of the theory nevertheless happen. If unexpected outcomes do occur, it means that the theory is, at best, incomplete. It will have to be developed further so that it can account for the previously unexpected outcome, or it will have to be replaced by a better theory.

## Using Strong Inference

The usual picture of progress in science is that theories are subjected to testing and then gradually modified as the need arises. The theory evolves through a succession of tests and modifications until it can handle all extant data with a high degree of precision. This view of science has been challenged by Thomas Kuhn (1970). According to Kuhn, the history of science reveals that most theories continue to be defended and elaborated by their supporters even after convincing evidence to the contrary has been amassed. People who have spent their professional careers developing a theoretical view have too much invested to give up the view. When a more adequate view appears, the supporters of the old view find ways to rationalize the failures of their view and the successes of the new one. Kuhn concluded that the new view takes hold only after the supporters of the old view actually die off or retire from the profession. Then a new generation of researchers without investment in either theory objectively evaluates the evidence and makes its choice.

Commitment to a theoretical position well beyond the point at which it is objectively no longer viable is wasteful of time, money, and talent. Years may be spent evaluating and defending a view, with nothing to show for the investment. According to John Platt (1964), this trap can be avoided. Platt stated that the way to progress in science is to develop several alternative explanations for a phenomenon. Each of these alternatives should give rise to testable predictions. To test the alternatives, you try to devise experiments whose outcomes can support only one or a few alternatives while ruling out the others.

When the initial experiment has been conducted, some of the alternatives will have been ruled out. You then design the next experiment to decide among the remaining alternatives. You continue this process until only one alternative remains. Platt called this process **strong inference**.

Strong inference can work only if the alternative explanations generate well-defined predictions. In biochemistry (the field that Platt uses to exemplify the method), strong inference is a viable procedure because of the degree of control scientists have over variables and the precision of their measures. The procedure tends to break down when the necessary degree of control is absent (so that the data become equivocal) or when the alternatives do not specify outcomes with sufficient precision to discriminate them. Unfortunately, in most areas of psychology, the degree of control is not sufficient, and the theories (usually loosely stated verbalizations) generally predict little more than the fact that one group mean will be different from another.

Nevertheless, Platt's approach can often be applied to test specific assumptions within the context of a particular view. In this case, applying strong inference means developing alternative models of the theory and then identifying areas in which clear differences emerge in predicted outcomes. The appropriate test then can be performed to decide which assumptions to discard and which to submit to further testing.

If several theories have been applied to the same set of phenomena, and if these theories have been specified in sufficient detail to make predictions possible, you also may be able to use the method of strong inference if the theories make opposing predictions for a particular situation. The outcome of the experiment, if it is clear, will lend support to one or more of the theories while damaging others. This procedure is much more efficient than separately testing each theory, and you should adopt it wherever possible.

You now should have clear ideas about how to recognize, develop, and test adequate theories. However, an important question remains to be addressed: Should research be directed primarily toward testing theories or toward discovering empirical relationships?

## THEORY-DRIVEN VERSUS DATA-DRIVEN RESEARCH

At one time in the not-too-distant history of psychology, research efforts in one field centered on developing a theory of learning. This theory would organize and explain data obtained from many experiments involving white laboratory rats running down straight alleys, learning discrimination tasks, and finding their ways through mazes. Ultimately, this was to be a mathematical theory, complete with equations relating theoretical entities to each other and to observable variables.

The task of developing such a theory was taken up by Clark Hull at Iowa State University and by Hull's student, Kenneth Spence. Hull's approach to theory development was to follow the "hypothetico-deductive method," which consisted of adopting specific assumptions about the processes involved in learning, deriving predictions, submitting these predictions to experimental test, and then (as required) modifying one or more assumptions in the light of new evidence. Applied at a time when very few data were, in fact, available, the method was remarkably successful in producing an account that handled the relevant observations. This initial success galvanized researchers in the field, and soon it seemed that nearly everyone was conducting experiments to test the Hull–Spence theory.

The new data quickly revealed discrepancies between prediction and outcome. Some researchers, such as Edwin Tolman, rejected some of the key assumptions of the Hull–Spence theory and proposed alternative views. However, they were never able to develop their positions completely enough to provide a really viable theory of equivalent scope and testability. Besides, every time Tolman and others would find an outcome incompatible with the Hull–Spence view, Hull and Spence would find a way to modify the theory in such a way that it would now account for the new data. The theory evolved with each new challenge.

These were exciting times for researchers in the field of learning. The development of a truly powerful, grand theory of learning seemed just around the corner. Then, gradually, things began to come apart. Hull died in 1952. Even before his death, discontent was beginning to set in, and even the continued efforts of Spence were not enough to hold researchers' interest in the theory.

Interest in the Hull–Spence theory collapsed for a number of reasons. Probably the most significant reason was that it had simply become too complex, with too many assumptions and too many variables whose values had to be extracted from the very data the theory was meant to explain. Like the Ptolemaic theory of planetary motion, the system could predict nearly any observation (after the fact) once the right constants were plugged in—but it had lost much of its true predictive power, its parsimony, and its elegance.

With the loss of interest in the Hull–Spence theory went the relevance of much of the research that had been conducted to test it. Particularly vulnerable were those experiments that manipulated some set of variables in a complex fashion in order to check on some implication of the theory. These experiments demonstrated no clear functional relationship among simple variables, and the results were therefore of little interest except within the context of the theory. Viewed outside this context, the research seemed a waste of time and effort.

It was a tough lesson for many researchers. Much of the time and effort spent theorizing, tracing implications of the theory, developing experimental tests, and conducting observations was lost. This experience raises several questions concerning the use of theory in psychology. Should you attempt to develop theories? If you should develop theories, at what point should you begin? Should you focus your research efforts on testing the theories you do develop?

The answer to the first question is definitely yes, you should attempt to develop theories. The history of science is littered with failed theories: the Ptolemaic system of astronomy, the phlogiston theory of heat, Gall's phrenology—the list goes on. In each case, much of the theorizing and testing became irrelevant when the theory was discarded. However, in each case, the attempt to grapple with the observations (particularly the anomalous ones) eventually led to the development of a more adequate theory. In this sense, the earlier efforts were not wasted.

Furthermore, it is the business of science to organize the available observations and to provide a framework within which the observations can be understood. At some point, theories must be developed if psychology is to progress.

The real question is not whether you should develop theories, but when. The major problem with the Hull–Spence theory is probably that it was premature. The attempt was made to develop a theory of broad scope before there was an adequate empirical database on which to formulate it. As a result, the requirements of the theory were not sufficiently constrained. The assumptions had to be repeatedly modified as new data became available, making some tests obsolete even before they could be published.

To avoid this problem, a theory that is more than a simple hypothesis should await the development of an adequate observational base. A sufficient number of well-established phenomena and functional relationships should be available to guide theory development and demonstrate the power of the resulting formulation.

The third question asked to what extent you should focus your research efforts on testing the theories you do develop. There is no general agreement on the answer to this question. For one side of the issue, consider the letter written to *Science* by Bernard Forscher (1963) entitled "Chaos in the Brickyard."

Forscher's letter presented an allegory in which scientists were compared to builders of brick edifices. The bricks were facts (observations) and the edifices were theories. According to the story Forscher developed, at one time the builders made their own bricks. This was a slow process, and the demand for bricks was always ahead of the supply. Still, the bricks were made to order, guided in their manufacture by a blueprint called a *theory* or *hypothesis*.

To speed the process, a new trade of brickmaking was developed, with the brickmakers producing bricks according to specifications given by the builders. With time, however, the brickmakers became obsessed with making bricks and began to create them without direction from the builders. When reminded that the goal was to create edifices, not bricks, the brickmakers replied that when enough bricks had been made, the builders could select the ones they needed.

Thus it came to pass that the land was flooded with bricks. For the builders, constructing an edifice became impossible. They had to examine hundreds of bricks to find a suitable one, and it was difficult to find a clear spot of ground on which to build. Worst of all, little effort was made to maintain the distinction between an edifice and a pile of bricks.

Forscher's message was that experimentation conducted without the guidance of theory produces a significant amount of irrelevant information that is likely to obscure the important observations. From the infinite number of potential observations you could make, you need to select just those observations that will contribute most to progress in understanding. Theory provides one rationale for making that selection.

However, theory does not provide the only guide to choosing what observations to make. Observation also can be guided by the systematic exploration of functional relationships within a well-defined domain. This empirical approach was forcefully defended by B. F. Skinner in his 1949 address to the Midwestern Psychological Association.

Much of the research conducted in psychology has followed this program. A systematic study of memory by Ebbinghaus (1885/1964), and the work that followed it, provides a case in point. Ebbinghaus invented a nearly meaningless unit to memorize (the CVC trigram) and several methods to measure the strength of memory for the CVCs. He then systematically explored the effects of many variables in a series of parametric experiments. These variables included the amount of practice, spacing of practice, length of the retention interval, and serial position of the CVC within the list. The resulting functional relationships between these variables and retention were subsequently shown to be highly reliable phenomena.

The data from such observations provide the reliable phenomena that any subsequently developed theory must explain. As Skinner and others have indicated, these data stand independent of any particular theoretical view. Thus, if an experiment is designed to clearly illuminate simple functional relationships among variables—even when the experiment is conducted mainly for the purpose of testing theory—then the data will retain their value even if the theory is later discarded. What conclusions can you draw from this discussion? First, the choice of observations to make can be guided both by theory and by a plan of systematic exploration. Second, guidance by theory is more likely to be of value when sufficient observations already have been conducted to construct a reasonably powerful theory. Third, even when theory testing is the major goal of the research, designing the study to illuminate simple functional relationships among the variables, if possible, ensures that the resulting observations will continue to have value beyond the usefulness of the theory.

Chapter 1 indicated that a science is an organized and systematic way of acquiring knowledge. Science is best advanced when results from research endeavors can be organized within some kind of framework. In many cases, results from both basic and applied research can be understood best when organized within a theory. Keep in mind, however, that not all research *must* be organized within a theoretical framework. Some purely applied research, for example, may best be organized with other research that also was geared toward the solution of a specific problem. Nevertheless, theory plays a central role in advancing science.

# SUMMARY

Sources of research ideas include unsystematic observation, systematic observation, theory, and the need to solve a practical problem. Unsystematic observation includes casual observation of both human and animal behavior. Systematic observation includes carefully planned personal observations, published research reports, and your own previous or ongoing research. Theory is a set of assumptions about the causes of a phenomenon and the rules that specify how causes act; predictions made by theory can provide testable research hypotheses.

Developing good research questions begins by asking questions that are answerable through objective observations. Such questions are said to be empirical. Before a question can be answered through objective observation, its terms must be supplied with operational definitions. An operational definition defines a variable in terms of the operations required to measure it. Operationally defined variables can be measured precisely but may lack generality.

Good research questions should address important issues. A research question is probably important if (1) answering it will clarify relationships among variables known to affect the behavioral system under study, (2) the answer can support only one of several competing hypotheses, or (3) the answer leads to obvious practical applications. A research question is probably unimportant if (1) its answer is already firmly established, (2) the variables under scrutiny are known to have small, theoretically uninteresting effects, or (3) there is no a priori reason to believe the variables in question are causally related.

Theory is a partially verified statement concerning the relationship among variables. A theory usually consists of a set of interrelated propositions and corollaries that specify how variables relate to the phenomena to be explained. Hypothesis, law, and model are all terms that are often used as synonyms for theory. There are, however, important differences among them. A hypothesis is a specific statement about a relationship that is subjected to direct empirical test. A law is a relationship that has received substantial support and is not usually subject to disconfirmation as theories are. A model is a specific implementation of a more general theoretical perspective. Models, therefore, usually have a more limited domain than do theories.

Computer models test the implications of a theory by encoding the theory as a series of program statements, supplying a set of initial conditions, and then observing how the model behaves. Such models remove ambiguity in the specific application of a theory and can reveal predictions of the theory that cannot be deduced by mere verbal reasoning. The behavior of the model under simulated conditions can be compared with the actual behavior of people or animals to determine whether the model behaves correctly, and alternative models can be compared to determine which does a better job of modeling actual behavior under given conditions.

Explanations provided by theories may be mechanistic or functional. Mechanistic explanations describe the physical components of a system and their connections (mechanism), whereas functional explanations describe only what the system does (function). Because function can be deduced from mechanism but mechanism cannot be uniquely deduced from function, you should prefer mechanistic theories over functional ones.

Theories vary along at least three dimensions. Some theories are quantitative in that they express relationships among variables in mathematical terms. Anderson's integration theory and the Rescorla–Wagner model of classical conditioning are examples of quantitative theories. Qualitative theories verbally express relationships among variables. No attempt is made to mathematically specify the nature of the relationships. Chomsky's theory of language acquisition is an example of a qualitative theory. Theories also differ according to level of analysis. At the lowest level, descriptive theories simply seek to describe a phenomenon. At the next level, analogical theories try to explain phenomena by drawing parallels between known systems and the phenomenon of interest. At the highest level, fundamental theories represent new ways of explaining a phenomenon. These theories tend to provide a more fundamental look at a phenomenon than do descriptive or analogical theories. Finally, theories differ according to domain. A theory with a large domain accounts for more phenomena than does a theory with a more limited domain.

Theories play an important role in science. They help us to better understand a phenomenon, allow us to predict relationships, help us to organize and interpret our data, and, in many cases, help generate new research. This latter role is often independent of the correctness of the theory. Some theories, even though they are not correct, have led to important research and new discoveries that greatly advance science.

A theory must meet certain criteria before it can be accepted as a good theory. A theory must be able to account for most of the data within its domain. A theory that does not do this is of little value. A good theory also must meet the criterion of explanatory relevance, which means that a theory must offer good grounds for believing that the phenomenon would occur under the specified conditions. An important criterion that any good theory must meet is that the theory be testable. The propositions stated in, and the predictions made by, a theory must be testable with empirical methods. Theories that are not testable, such as Freudian psychodynamics, cannot be classified as valid scientific theories. A theory also must be able to account for novel events within its domain. Finally, a good theory should be parsimonious. That is, it should explain a phenomenon with the fewest number of propositions possible.

Theories that are subjected to empirical tests can be confirmed or disconfirmed. Confirmation of a theory means that you have more confidence in the theory than before confirmation. Unfortunately, it is logically impossible to prove that a theory is absolutely correct. Theories that are disconfirmed may be modified or discarded entirely, although many disconfirmed theories are adhered to for a variety of reasons.

In the course of testing a theory, various strategies can be used. Strong inference involves developing testable alternative explanations for a phenomenon and subjecting them simultaneously to an empirical test. The empirical test should be one that will unambiguously show which alternative is best. One way to test a theory is to use a confirmational strategy. That is, you design tests that will confirm the predictions made by the theory under test. When predictions are confirmed, then your confidence in the theory increases. Unfortunately, you may find confirming evidence even though the theory is wrong. Another approach is to adopt a disconfirmational strategy. In this case, you look for evidence that does not support the predictions made by a theory. Often the best strategy to adopt is to use both confirmational and disconfirmational strategies together.

Finally, a controversy exists over the role a theory should play in driving research. Some scientists believe that research should be data driven, whereas others believe that research should be theory driven. Strong arguments have been made for each position, and no simple solution to the controversy exists.

## REVIEW QUESTIONS

1. How can experience help you come up with research ideas?
2. How can unsystematic observation help you develop research ideas?
3. How can systematic observation help you develop research ideas?
4. In what two ways can a theory help you develop research ideas?
5. How can applied issues suggest research ideas to you?
6. What are the characteristics of a "good research question"?
7. What is the definition of a scientific theory?
8. How does a theory differ from a hypothesis, a law, and a model?
9. What is a computer model, and what are the advantages of designing one?
10. How do mechanistic and functional theories differ? Which type is better and why?
11. What are the defining characteristics of quantitative and qualitative theories?
12. What is an analogical theory?
13. What is a fundamental theory?
14. How do descriptive, analogical, and fundamental theories differ? Which is preferred and why?
15. What roles do theories play in science (describe each role in detail)?
16. What are the defining characteristics of a "good theory" (describe each characteristic in detail)?
17. What is meant by confirmation and disconfirmation of a theory?
18. How are theories tested?
19. What is the difference between a confirmational and a disconfirmational strategy? How are they used to test a theory?
20. How do theory-driven research and data-driven research differ?
21. What are the relative advantages and disadvantages of theory-driven and data-driven research?

## KEY TERMS

theory  
empirical question  
operational definition  
scientific theory  
law  
model  
mechanistic explanation  
functional explanation  
quantitative theory  

qualitative theory  
descriptive theory  
analogical theory  
fundamental theory  
domain  
confirmational strategy  
disconfirmational strategy  
strong inference

# 3

# Reviewing the Scientific Literature

One of the most important preliminary steps in the research process is doing a thorough review of the scientific literature on the topic you have identified for study. This is true whether you begin only with a vague idea of a research project or with a well-developed research plan. In this chapter, we introduce you to the tools, techniques, and knowledge that will enable you to identify, read, and evaluate published information on your research topic. In addition, we discuss the process of scientific peer review and describe how this process affects the content and quality of published scientific findings.

## REASONS FOR REVIEWING THE LITERATURE

A **literature review** is the process of locating, obtaining, reading, and evaluating the research literature in your area of interest. There are several important reasons for conducting a literature review. Perhaps the most important reason is to avoid needless duplication of effort. No matter what topic you choose, chances are that someone has already done research on it. By becoming familiar with that area through a literature review, you can avoid "reinventing the wheel." Your specific research question may have already been addressed and answered. If so, then conducting your research as originally planned would be a waste of time. This does not mean, however, that you must start over from scratch. To the contrary, your literature review may reveal other questions (perhaps more interesting) that remain to be answered. By familiarizing yourself with existing research and theory in an area, you can revise your research project to explore some of these newly identified questions.

Another advantage to reviewing the literature applies to the design phase of your research. Designing a study involves several decisions as to what variables to include and how to measure them, what apparatus to use, what procedures to use, and so on. Published research provides you with a rich resource for addressing these important design questions. You may find, for example, that you can use established procedures and existing materials. Or your review of the literature may show that existing methods are inadequate. You may have to develop your own methods to suit your research needs.

Yet another advantage is that a review of the literature keeps you up to date on current empirical or theoretical controversies in a particular research area. As science progresses, new ideas develop concerning age-old behavioral issues. For example, a debate is under way concerning the motives for altruistic behavior. Some argue that altruism is motivated by empathy (a concern for the victim) and others by egoism (self-satisfaction). Such controversies not only provide a rich source of research ideas but also give direction to specific research hypotheses and designs.

## SOURCES OF RESEARCH INFORMATION

Sources of information about a topic range in quality from the high levels found in the scholarly books and journals of a discipline down to the supermarket tabloids of the sensationalist press. Although information presented in the tabloids may arouse your curiosity and suggest a topic for scientific research, you cannot count on that information to be accurate or even true. Popular writing such as that found in magazines such as *Newsweek* may provide more reliable information that has been gleaned from scientific sources, but the information presented generally lacks the detail that would allow you to determine much beyond the major conclusions offered. More substantive writing aimed at a better-educated reader generally provides more details about the methods used to gather the information but still omits important details and may not mention alternative interpretations or other evidence for or against the conclusions presented. Only scholarly sources can be counted on to provide the level of detail and thoroughness needed for a competent scientific review. Table 3–1, which is based on an analysis provided by the Cornell University Library (2000), identifies four types of periodicals and compares them on a number of important features. You can use this table to determine whether a given publication is scholarly or not.

Sources of research findings include books, scholarly journals, conventions and professional meetings, and others, such as personal communications and certain pages on the World Wide Web. Here are a few things you should know about these sources.

### Primary versus Secondary Sources

Sources containing research information can be classified according to whether a source is primary or secondary. A **primary source** is one containing the full research report, including all details necessary to duplicate the study. A primary source includes descriptions of the rationale of the study, its subjects, apparatus, procedure, results, and references. A **secondary source** is one that summarizes information from primary sources (such as presenting the basic findings). Secondary sources of research include review papers and theoretical articles that briefly describe studies and results, as well as descriptions of research found in textbooks, popular magazines, newspaper articles, television programs, films, or lectures. Another type of secondary source is a meta-analysis. In a meta-analysis, a researcher statistically combines or compares the

**TABLE 3–1  Comparison of Four Types of Published Periodicals**

| SCHOLARLY | SUBSTANTIVE NEWS/ GENERAL INTEREST | POPULAR | SENSATIONAL |
|---|---|---|---|
| Sober, serious look with graphs and tables | Attractive appearance, usually with photographs | Often have a slick, attractive appearance with many photographs | Often in newspaper format |
| Reference citations always provided | Sources are sometimes cited | Sources are rarely, if ever, cited | References to sources are often obscure |
| Written by a scholar in the field or someone who has done research in the field | Articles written by members of editorial staff, scholar, or free-lance writer | Written by a wide range of authors who may or may not have expertise in an area | Written by a variety of authors |
| Language of the discipline, assuming a scholarly background of the reader | Language geared to educated audience, but no specialty assumed | Written in simple language with short articles geared to audience with minimal education | Elementary, inflammatory language geared to a gullible audience |
| Report original research | Do not report original research, report on research in format geared to a general audience | Research may be mentioned, but it may come from an obscure source | Support may come from pseudoscientific sources |
| Many, but not all, published by professional organizations | Published by commercial publishers or individuals, but some from professional organizations | Published commercially with the intent to entertain the reader, sell products, or promote a viewpoint | Commercially published to arouse curiosity and play to popular superstition. Use flashy, astonishing headlines |
| Examples: *Journal of Personality and Social Psychology, Child Development, Journal of Experimental Psychology* | Examples: *National Geographic, Scientific American, New York Times, Christian Science Monitor* | Examples: *Time, U.S. News & World Report, Newsweek, Parents, Reader's Digest* | Examples: *National Enquirer, Globe, Star, Weekly World News* |

SOURCE of much of the information: Cornell University Library Web site.

results from research in a particular area to determine which of the variables studied are important contributors to behavior. Meta-analysis is discussed in Chapter 7.

The distinction between primary and secondary sources is important. Students often rely too heavily on secondary sources. One reason for this may be that it is a daunting task to read a primary source research report. The language can be technical and the statistical tests reported can be intimidating. However, with some experience and perseverance, you can get through and understand primary source materials.

Another reason that students may rely heavily on secondary sources is to "save time." Students reason, "After all, someone else has already read and summarized the research, so why not save time and use the summary?" This sounds good but can lead to trouble. The author of a secondary source may describe or interpret research results incorrectly or simply view data from a single (and perhaps narrow) theoretical perspective. Also, secondary sources do not usually present detailed descriptions of methods used in the cited studies. You must know the details of the methods used so you can evaluate the quality and the importance of the cited studies. The only way to obtain such detailed information is to read the primary source.

Heavy reliance on secondary sources can be dangerous. You cannot be sure that the information in a secondary source is complete and accurate. For example, Treadway and McCloskey (1987) found that many secondary sources had misrepresented the methods and results of a classic experiment conducted by Allport and Postman (1945). These representations led researchers and sometimes courts to draw incorrect inferences concerning the role of racial bias in eyewitness accuracy (Treadway & McCloskey, 1987). To avoid this trap, obtain and read the original report.

Secondary sources do have value, which lies in the summaries, presentations, and integrations of results from related research studies. The secondary source provides an excellent starting point for your literature search. However, it should not be considered a substitute for the primary source. An up-to-date review paper will include a reference section from which you can generate a list of primary sources.

An exception to the general rule concerning the use of secondary sources may be necessary if the primary source is not available. In this case you may wish to use a secondary source. If you must do so, always stay aware of the possible problems. If you do use a secondary source, cite *only* the secondary source in your research report.

To summarize, use secondary sources as a starting point in your literature search. Avoid overreliance on secondary sources and make every effort to obtain the primary sources of interest to you that have been cited in a secondary source. Only by reading the primary source can you critically evaluate a study and determine whether the reported results are reliable and important. Finally, do not rely on a single secondary source. The author of a review article may not have completely reviewed the literature. Always augment the information obtained from a secondary source with a thorough literature search of your own.

## Books

You are probably most familiar with general textbooks (such as those covering introductory psychology) or texts covering content areas (such as motivation and emotion, abnormal psychology, personality, or human learning and memory). More specialized professional texts present the results of programmatic research conducted by the author over a period of years. These specialized texts may cover research previously published in journals, as well as findings not presented elsewhere. Edited anthologies present a series of articles on related topics, each written by a different set of authors. Some anthologies are collections of articles previously published separately; others present articles written especially for the occasion. Either kind of text may present reviews of the literature, theoretical articles, articles dealing with methodological issues, or original research.

Anthologies are useful because they assemble papers the editor feels are important in a given area. However, be cautious when reading an anthology. The editor may be biased in judgment on which articles to include. Also, be sure to check the original publication date of articles in an anthology. Even if the publication date of the anthology is recent, it may contain outdated (sometimes classic) articles.

Texts or anthologies are most valuable in the early stages of the literature search. Often you can use the references from these books to track down relevant articles. Books (especially textbooks) may have to be treated as secondary sources. Whenever you use a textbook as a source, make an effort to obtain a copy of the original report.

The articles in an anthology may be original works and thus can be treated as primary sources—provided they have been reproduced exactly, not edited for the anthology. Be careful about relying on a chapter reproduced from a book. Isolating a single chapter from the original book can be misleading. In other chapters from the same book, the original author might elaborate on points made in the reproduced chapter. You could miss important points if you do not read the original work.

Whereas some books present original research, others provide only summaries. For example, if you were studying the development of intelligence, you could use Piaget's *The Origins of Intelligence in Children* (1952) as a good original source. However, a book such as *Piaget's Theory of Cognitive Development* by Wadsworth (1971)—a primer on Piaget's theory—should be treated as a secondary source in which you may find references for Piaget's original work.

Whatever route you choose, keep in mind one important factor. Even though you may have used an original work such as Piaget's, problems with using it as a principal source may still exist. Books (especially by noted authors) may not undergo as rigorous a review as works published in scientific journals. You cannot be assured of the quality of any original research reported in the book. Also, you would be well advised to seek out recent research on the issues covered in a book. Was Piaget correct when he speculated in his book about the origins of intelligence? Research published since his book came out may bear on this question. A review of the recent research would help you to evaluate Piaget's theory and contributions.

## Scholarly Journals

Although textbooks are valuable, the information they contain tends to be old. By the time a scientific finding makes its way into a text, it could already have been around for several years. For current research and theories regarding a subject, researchers turn to scholarly journals. Like popular magazines, journals appear periodically over the year in monthly, bimonthly, or quarterly issues. Some journals focus on detailed research reports (although occasionally a theoretical or methodological article may appear). These research reports are the most important primary sources. Other journals deal with reviews of the literature, issues in methodology, or theoretical views.

Table 3–2 provides a list of journals currently published by the American Psychological Association (APA), the American Psychological Society, and the Psychonomic Society. (The list is not complete. In addition to those listed, many journals are published by major textbook publishers. You become familiar with these by doing reviews of the literature.)

Keep in mind that not all journals are created equal. You must consider the source. When you submit your work to a **refereed journal**, it is usually reviewed by two (or more) reviewers. Other, **nonrefereed journals** do not have such a review procedure; the articles may be published in the order in which they were received or according to some fee that the author must pay. The review process is intended to ensure that high-quality articles appear in the journal. Although problems do occur with the review procedures (as discussed later in this chapter), you can have greater confidence in an article in a refereed journal than one in a nonrefereed journal.

A problem more likely to be encountered in a nonrefereed journal than in a refereed journal is that the information could be sketchy and incomplete (Mayo & LaFrance, 1977). If information is incomplete, you may not be able to identify the significance of the article. Rely more heavily on articles published in high-quality, refereed journals than on articles in lower-quality, nonrefereed journals.

There are several ways to assess the quality of a research journal. First, you can consult *Journals in Psychology*, published by the American Psychological Association. In this publication, journals are listed alphabetically, and information such as acceptance rates is given. Top journals in a field have low acceptance rates (15 percent or less), whereas lesser journals have higher acceptance rates. Second, you can consult the *Social Science Citations Index (SSCI)*. One section of this publication lists journals by category (for example, Psychology) and subcategory (for example, Social Psychology, Experimental Psychology, and so on). Journals are ranked within category by their *impact factor*, which is a measure of "the frequency with which the 'average article' in a journal [was] cited in a particular year . . ." (Institute for Scientific Information [ISI], 1988, p. 10A). Third, you can use the method of authority discussed in Chapter 1. Ask your professors which journals in their fields of specialty are of highest and lowest quality.

## Conventions and Professional Meetings

Books and journals are not the only sources of research findings, nor are they necessarily the most current. Behavioral scientists who want the most up-to-date information about research in their areas attend psychological conventions. If you attended one of these conventions, you would find a number of **paper sessions** covering different areas of research. Paper sessions are usually simultaneously conducted in different rooms and follow one another throughout the day (much as classes do on campus).

When you register at a convention, you receive a program listing the times and places for each session. Figure 3–1 shows a page from the program of the 2003 meeting of the Midwestern Psychological Association. Listed under the session shown are the

TABLE 3–2  **Journals Published by Major Psychological Organizations**

### JOURNALS OF THE AMERICAN PSYCHOLOGICAL ASSOCIATION

*American Journal of Orthopsychiatry*
*American Psychologist*
*Behavioral Neuroscience*
*Consulting Psychology Journal: Practice and Research*
*Cultural Diversity and Ethnic Minority Psychology*
*Developmental Psychology*
*Emotion*
*Experimental & Clinical Psychopharmacology*
*Group Dynamics: Theory, Research, and Practice*
*Health Psychology*
*History of Psychology*
*Journal of Abnormal Psychology*
*Journal of Applied Psychology*
*Journal of Comparative Psychology*
*Journal of Consulting and Clinical Psychology*
*Journal of Counseling Psychology*
*Journal of Educational Psychology*
*Journal of Occupational Health Psychology*
*Journal of Experimental Psychology: Animal Behavior Processes*
*Journal of Experimental Psychology: Applied*
*Journal of Experimental Psychology: General*
*Journal of Experimental Psychology: Human Perception and Performance*
*Journal of Experimental Psychology: Learning, Memory, and Cognition*
*Journal of Family Psychology*
*Journal of Personality and Social Psychology*
*Journal of Psychotherapy Integration*
*Neuropsychology*
*Prevention & Treatment*

times at which the papers will be presented, the titles of the papers, the names of the authors, and short abstracts of the papers. You can use the program to identify papers relevant to your research interests. Each participant at a paper session is allotted time to describe his or her most recent findings, and then usually has about five minutes to answer any questions from the audience.

Paper sessions are not the best way to convey details of methodology. The written report is far superior for that purpose. At a convention, the author of a paper typically

**TABLE 3–2  Journals Published by Major Psychological Organizations** *continued*

### JOURNALS OF THE AMERICAN PSYCHOLOGICAL ASSOCIATION

*Professional Psychology: Research and Practice*
*Psychoanalytic Psychology: A Journal of Theory, Practice, Research, and Criticism*
*Psychological Assessment*
*Psychological Bulletin*
*Psychological Methods*
*Psychological Review*
*Psychology and Aging*
*Psychology of Addictive Behaviors*
*Psychology of Men and Masculinity*
*Psychology, Public Policy, and Law*
*Psychotherapy: Theory, Research, Practice, Training*
*Rehabilitation Psychology*
*Review of General Psychology*

### JOURNALS OF THE AMERICAN PSYCHOLOGICAL SOCIETY

*Current Directions in Psychological Science*
*Psychological Science*
*Psychological Science in the Public Interest*

### JOURNALS OF THE PSYCHONOMIC SOCIETY

*Behavior Research Methods, Instruments, & Computers*
*Cognitive, Affective, & Behavioral Neuroscience*
*Learning & Behavior* (formerly *Animal Learning & Behavior*)
*Memory & Cognition*
*Perception & Psychophysics*
*Psychonomic Bulletin & Review*

has only 15 minutes to describe his or her research. In that short time, the author must often omit some details of methodology.

An increasingly popular format for convention presentations is the poster session. In this format, the presenter prepares a poster that is displayed on a bulletin board. The poster includes an introduction to the topic and method, results, discussion, and reference sections, and the presenter is usually there to discuss the research with you and answer any questions. This form allows the author to provide more details than would be practical in a paper session and allows you to speak directly to the researcher about the research. Many good research ideas can emerge from such encounters.

```
**************************************************
```
## FRIDAY MAY 9
```
**************************************************
```

### Applied Social Psychology

*Friday, 10:00-12:00 Upper Exhibit Hall*
ROBIN A. ANDERSON, St. Ambrose University Moderator

## APPLIED SOCIAL PSYCHOLOGY

**1**
**Toward Predicting the Good Judge: Three Proposed Underlying Moderators**
AMBER R. MCLARNEY, FRANK J. BERNIERI, MICHAEL FRANCESCHINI,
ANDREW BOUROSSA, & ARWA Y. SARTAWI, University of Toledo
amclarn@pop3.utoledo.edu
The general ability to read others has been debated. Three hypothesized moderators of
interpersonal perception accuracy were experimentally manipulated in this study: social
knowledge, the motivation to read others, and general cognitive ability. Each influenced
accuracy as predicted. These moderators should lead to a better understanding of "good
judge" research.

**2**
**Mock Jurors' Responsibility Judgments and Damage Awards Following the
Introduction of Judgmental Anchors**
ALLISON K. ALBRECHT & VERLIN B. HINSZ, North Dakota State University
Verlin.Hinsz@NDSU.NoDak.edu
We examine how low numerical anchors influence judgments of responsibility (0%) and
damage awards ($0) with jurors in a mock civil trial. We found decisions assimilated to
the anchors for damage awards. An indirect effect of the award anchor was also found
for the defendant's responsibility for the incident.

**3**
**Two Experiments, Web-based and Paper-based, on Racial Discrimination and the
McCleskey v. Kemp (1987) Case**
KRISTIN Y. TRIGG, Castleton State College
kristin.trigg@castleton.edu
The current 2 (defendant's race) x 2 (victim's race) x 2 (prior record) experimental study
was conducted over the Internet to determine whether laypersons would perceive if the
U.S. Supreme Court's dismissal of the McCleskey v. Kemp (1987) case reflected racial
discrimination.

**4**
**The Effect of Verbal Overshadowing and Biased Instructions on the Accuracy of
Eyewitness Identification**
ANDY BLACK, & DAVID C. MATZ, Augsburg College
matz@augsburg.edu
After viewing a videotape of a crime, participants were asked to identify the perpetrator
in a lineup. Some participants first engaged in verbal overshadowing and / or were given

**FIGURE 3–1**    An Excerpt from the Program for the 2003 Meeting of the Midwestern
Psychological Association, May 2003.

Attending a paper or poster session has two distinct advantages over reading a journal article. First, the information is from the very frontiers of research. The findings presented may not appear in print for many months (or even years), if ever. Attending a paper session exposes you to newly conducted research that might otherwise be unavailable to you. Second, it provides an opportunity to meet other researchers in your field and to discuss ideas, clarify methodology, or seek assistance. These contacts could prove valuable in the future.

One drawback to paper and poster sessions at a convention is that a convention can be expensive to attend. In most instances, conventions are located in cities other than where you live. This means you must pay for travel, lodging, and food. Fortunately, you can gain some of the benefits of going to a conference by obtaining a copy of the program. By reading the abstracts of the papers, you can identify those papers of interest and glean something of the findings. If you want more information, you can then write or call the author.

## Other Sources of Research Information

Personal replies to your inquiries fall under the heading of **personal communications** and are yet another source of research information. Projects completed under the auspices of a grant or agency often result in the production of a *technical report*, which can be obtained through the agency. In addition, dissertations and theses completed by graduate students as part of their degree requirements are placed on file in the libraries of the university at which the work was done. You can find abstracts describing these studies in *Dissertation Abstracts International*, a reference work found in most college libraries. For a fee, the abstracting service will send you a copy of the complete manuscript on paper or microfilm.

The Internet provides yet another source of research information. You can find journal articles, technical reports, original papers, and so on via an online search. For example, entering the keyword "helping behavior" in the Yahoo! search engine turned up several research papers maintained on the Missouri Western State College Web page. Such sources, although they may prove valuable when developing ideas for research, should be used with caution as they may not be refereed. However, the Internet also provides electronic versions of refereed professional journals. For example, *The Canadian Journal of Behavioral Science* provides an online electronic version of full articles. When judging the quality of the material you find on the Internet, use the same criteria discussed earlier (refereed versus nonrefereed, ISI ranking). Use caution if you cannot determine the quality of a resource found on the Internet.

The Internet also offers services that will allow you to search for and obtain full-text versions of articles from a variety of publications (some scholarly and some not). One such service is provided by EBSCO, which indexes articles in a variety of publications from 1990 to the present. You can search for literature by subject, journal, and a host of other categories. You also can limit your search to full-text articles from peer-reviewed journals. For example, a search for full-text articles on "altruism" (used as the keyword for the search) turned up 124 such articles in scholarly journals. Of course, many of the articles identified in such a search may not contain what you are looking for. You can specify additional criteria to further narrow your search. For example, replacing "altruism" with "altruism and empathy" reduced the number of articles found to seven. Once you have located the full-text articles that interest you, you can read them online and, if you wish, print them out.

You can gain access to EBSCO in a couple of ways. Check with your university library to determine whether it has a subscription to the service. Some states (e.g., Indiana) have contracts with EBSCO so that any resident of the state can access the databases for free. If you are not given free access, you can subscribe individually. See your librarian for information on subscribing to EBSCO.

## PERFORMING LIBRARY RESEARCH

With so many sources of research information to choose from, you may find yourself quickly overwhelmed if you do not adopt an efficient strategy for separating the wheat from the chaff. You need a method that quickly identifies articles relevant to your topic. Ideally, the method should identify all such articles, because the one you miss may be the one that duplicates exactly what you were planning to do. Fortunately, such a method exists.

### The Basic Strategy

Although a number of variations exist, the basic strategy is this: (1) Find a relevant research article (you can do this by consulting the reference sections of textbooks or other books or tracking down an article using a periodical index or computerized database); (2) use the reference section of the article you found to locate other articles (inspecting the titles of articles can give you some insight into the terminology used by researchers in an area); (3) repeat steps 1 and 2 for each relevant article identified until you can find no more; (4) use one of the many indexes available in your library (discussed in the next sections) to identify more recent articles; and (5) repeat the entire process as you find more and more recent articles.

*Research Tools*    The most fundamental library research tool for doing a literature search is an index or a searchable electronic database. Many libraries now subscribe to a number of electronic databases that allow you to quickly and easily search for information sources. One such database is **PsycINFO**. *PsycINFO* includes over 1,800 journals in 25 languages, as well as books, conference papers, and dissertations. The database covers materials published as far back as 1872 through the present. Another useful searchable database to which your library might subscribe is **PsycARTICLES**, which provides online access to journals published by the American Psychological Association (APA). Through *PsycARTICLES* you can obtain full-text copies of articles published in APA journals.

In addition to *PsycINFO* and *PsycARTICLES*, there are other electronic and hardcopy databases you can use. In the following sections, we explore some of the indexes and databases available to you. Although we can give you some basic information on how to use these sources, the best way to learn is through hands-on experience. Also, because space limitations prohibit an in-depth exploration of all resources, we focus on using *PsycINFO* to do literature searches.

## Using *PsycINFO*

In the past it was common to search for articles in psychological journals using the hardbound volumes of the **Psychological Abstracts**. This process was long, laborious, and fatiguing. Fortunately, the advent of computer technology has spared us much of this tedious work. Now you can use the computer and *PsycINFO* to rapidly and efficiently search for articles, books, and book chapters. Currently, *PsycINFO* indexes over 1,400 scientific journals and book chapters, dating back to 1887.

*Conducting a PsycINFO Search*   When conducting a computer search using *PsycINFO*, you enter a keyword or keywords, and the computer finds every instance in which those terms are used in citations contained in the *PsycINFO* database and adds those citations to your reference list. You can then mark those citations ("records") that you wish to keep and save them to your computer or print them. Additionally, you also can see how many times a given record was cited by others. By clicking on the "Cited by #" hyperlink, you can obtain a list of articles that cited a particular record.

Suppose you were interested in conducting a study on how college students perceive sexual harassment situations. You could use *PsycINFO* to search for relevant research by entering "sexual harassment" as a keyword. *PsycINFO* then searches the titles, abstracts, and descriptor lists (lists of descriptors found at the end of a *PsycINFO* entry) for instances of your keyword. When the search is complete, you can display the reference list generated. Figure 3–2 shows a reference citation generated using "sexual harassment" as a keyword.

The example record shown in Figure 3–2 includes several important pieces of information that are provided by default by *PsycINFO*. This information can help you determine if the article is what you are looking for. Along the left side of the record you will see a two-letter code in all capital letters (e.g., AN, AU, AF) representing a field on the record. Next to the two-letter code is a brief description of what the code means. Each field contains information that tells you something about the article and/or gives you a way to search further for documents. For example, the SO field gives you the bibliographic information for the source (e.g., journal, volume, pages). The AN, or accession number, is a number assigned to a particular source. If you write this number down, you can immediately get back to the source at a later date. You can use the various fields to customize a search. For example, maybe you want only journal articles about studies done with a certain population and published in a certain year.

Once you have obtained a general reference list, you can review it, mark the articles most relevant to your research project, print them, or save them to a computer disk. You can tailor your printed list by specifying which fields to include on the printout. For example, if you only wanted the bibliographic information, you would specify to print the fields TI, AU, and SO.

*Narrowing Your Search*   *PsycINFO* can save you a great deal of time by doing much of the tedious work of searching indexes for you. However, you may find that your search yields more citations than you can possibly look at. For example, using the keyword "sexual harassment" produced 1,399 citations. Many may not be relevant to

AU:    Author
       Maass, Anne; Cadinu, Mara; Guarnieri, Gaia; Grasselli, Annalisa
AF:    Author Affiliation
       U Padova, Dipartimento di Psicologia dello Sviluppo e della Socializzazione,
       Padova, Italy [Maass, Cadinu, Guarnieri, Grasselli]
EA:    Email Address
       [mailto:anne.maass@unipd.it]
CI:    Contact Individual
       Maass, Anne, U Padova, Dipartimento di Psicologia dello Sviluppo e della
       Socializzazione, Via Venezia 8, 35139, [mailto:anne.maas@unipd.it]
SO:    Source
       Journal of Personality & Social Psychology. Vol 85(5), Nov 2003, pp. 853-870
IP:    Information Provider
       [URL:http://www.apa.org/journals/psp.html]
IS:    ISSN
       0022-3514
PB:    Publisher
       US: American Psychological Assn, [URL:http://www.apa.org]
AB:    Abstract
       Two laboratory experiments investigated the hypothesis that threat to male iden-
       tity would increase the likelihood of gender harassment. In both experiments,
       using the computer harassment paradigm, male university students (N=80 in
       Experiment 1, N=90 in Experiment 2) were exposed to different types of identity
       threat (legitimacy threat and threat to group value in Experiment 1 and distinc-
       tiveness threat and prototypicality threat in Experiment 2) or to no threat and
       were then given the opportunity to send pornographic material to a virtual fe-
       male interaction partner. Results show that (a) participants harassed the female
       interaction partner more when they were exposed to a legitimacy, distinctiveness,
       or prototypicality threat than to no threat; (b) this was mainly true for highly
       identified males; and (c) harassment enhanced postexperimental gender identifi-
       cation. Results are interpreted as supporting a social identity account of gender
       harassment. (PsycINFO Database Record © 2003 APA, all rights reserved)
       (journal abstract)
LA:    Language
       English
PY:    Publication Year
       2003
DE:    Descriptors
       *Gender Identity; *Human Computer Interaction; *Sexual Harassment; *Social
       Identity; "Threat; Computers; Human Males; Pornography; Probability
ID:    Identifiers
       gender harassment; social identity threat; sexual harassment; male identity; like-
       lihood; computer harassment; pornographic material; gender identification
CL:    Classification
       3230 Behavior Disorders & Antisocial Behavior; 4000 Engineering & Environ-
       mental Psychology
NR:    Number of References
       67 reference(s) present, 67 reference(s) displayed
AN:    Accession Number
       2003-09138-006

**FIGURE 3–2**    Example of a *PsycINFO* Entry.

your interests. You probably don't want to wade through 1,399 abstracts to find the few that fit your needs. You must find a way to narrow your search.

One way to do this is to look over some of the citations provided by your first search, focusing on the identifiers (ID) and descriptors (DE) fields. These fields may give you some other terms you can enter along with your original keyword to narrow your search. For example, look at the identifiers and descriptors fields of the sample *PsycINFO* entry shown in Figure 3–2 and you will notice that "human males" is listed. Entering the keywords "sexual harassment" and "human males" pares your reference list down to 48 entries—a more manageable number to inspect.

Another way to narrow your search is to use the online version of **Thesaurus of Psychological Index Terms** (which also may be available in a hardbound copy). The thesaurus can be accessed from *PsycINFO* directly. For example, if you entered the term "sexual harassment," the thesaurus would provide information on other terms you can try during your search. It will provide you with terms that can help you narrow your search (by providing narrower keywords), broaden your search (by providing broader keywords), or expand your search using related terms.

*A Note of Caution about Using* PsycINFO   *PsycINFO* and other electronic database search systems can save you a considerable amount of time and effort. However, keep in mind certain limitations on using computerized search systems. A search is only as good as the keywords you enter. The computer is incredibly fast and obedient—and, unfortunately, pretty stupid. It will only do what you tell it to do. It cannot think for itself and figure out what you really want when you enter a keyword. It will find *every* reference that includes your keywords. You may find, much to your annoyance, that terms are used more broadly in the indexed material than you anticipated. Imagine, for example, that you are looking up a topic concerning elderly individuals and decide to use the keyword "aged" (as in age-ed). You are initially excited to find more than 200 articles using that term. Your excitement turns to irritation, however, when you discover that the majority of titles with "aged" refer to an age range (for example, "subjects *aged* 12–14 years"). If this happens, use the online thesaurus to help you identify a more useful keyword.

## Using *PsycARTICLES*

One disadvantage of *PsycINFO* is that you may not be able to obtain a full copy of an article you want to read. Such is not the case with *PsycARTICLES*. This database comprises 45 journals published by the American Psychological Association, including the *Journal of Personality and Social Psychology, Psychological Review, Developmental Psychology,* and the *Journal of Experimental Psychology.* Using the *PsycARTICLES* search engine, you can locate full versions of the journal articles that you want to read. For example, entering the keywords "prejudice" and "race" yielded 15 articles in several different journals. By clicking on one of the full-text options (html or pdf) the full article is displayed. You then can read the article online, print the article, or save the article to disk.

The advantages of using *PsycARTICLES* are obvious (ease of use, access to full articles). However, there are a couple of drawbacks. First, your literature search using

*PsycARTICLES* is limited to those journals published by the American Psychological Association. Although these are among the top journals in psychology, the list does not include many top-flight journals such as *Child Development, Personality and Social Psychology Bulletin,* or *Law and Human Behavior.* To access materials in journals not published by the American Psychological Association, you would have to use another search engine such as *PsycINFO.* A second drawback is that *PsycARTICLES* only includes volumes of journals dating back to 1988. If you need to find citations that are older than 1988, you will have to use another search engine.

## Other Computerized Databases

*PsycINFO* and *PsycARTICLES* are not the only electronic search resources available. Another search engine is *Ingenta* (formerly *Carl Uncover Database*). Entering the keywords "prejudice" and "race" turned up 71 references in a number of journals. *Ingenta* returns full reference citations for the articles found and access to the abstract (summary) of the article. There is, however, a charge for the full text of the article. An advantage of *Ingenta* is that you can access it directly from the Internet and do not need to go through a subscribing library. This database is a good alternative to *PsycINFO* if you do not have access to *PsycINFO* or it is temporarily unavailable at your library.

Another computerized database that you may find helpful is *JSTOR,* which comprises journals from a wide range of fields (e.g., sociology, philosophy, anthropology, and political science). A *JSTOR* search with the same keywords as used above (searching sociology, anthropology, and political science journals) uncovered over 200 reference citations. *JSTOR* provides access to abstracts and allows you to download a full version of an article free of charge in a number of different formats.

You may find that *JSTOR* is not the best search engine for specific topics in psychology. You will not get the same kind of comprehensive results that you will with *PsycINFO.* However, used as a supplement to other databases, *JSTOR* may turn up articles that give a different perspective on your topic. This may give you a broader perspective on your topic and also give you some ideas about research that needs to be done.

## General Internet Resources

Reference material also can be found by using one of the many Internet search engines (e.g., Yahoo!, AltaVista, Google). Entering the phrase "prejudice and race" into the Yahoo! search engine turned up a hodgepodge of links to related material. Some of the links led to apparently "scholarly" articles on the issues. One can find materials that appear to be scholarly works. For example, one link was to an essay on past and present racism and the African-American community. Others dealt with racism in historical context and compensation for victims of prejudice.

Using a general Internet search engine can turn up a treasure trove of information. However, you must be cautious when you consider using any materials found this way on the Internet. The fact of the matter is that anyone can publish anything he or she pleases on the Internet. Typically, materials do not undergo any kind of peer review. As a consequence, you cannot be sure that the information you are getting is valid, reliable, or objective. You should read such materials with a very critical eye. The Purdue University "OWL" Web site suggests that you find out about the author of the material, the affiliated institution, the timeliness of the material, the publisher (if any), the accuracy of the information, the goals of the Web site on which the information was found, and the reputation of the links that brought you to the information. Further information on evaluating Web-based information sources can be found on the Web site that accompanies this text.

## Computer-Searching for Books and Other Library Materials

Many libraries have installed computerized databases indexing the books and journals housed in the library. These systems are similar to *PsycINFO* and allow you to search for materials by author, title, subject, and keywords. The beauty of these modern systems is that you are not limited to searching your university library. You can easily gain access to other library databases via the Internet. For example, using the Yahoo! search engine, type in the search term "university libraries," and then click on "Academic Libraries." This will take you to a list of university libraries that you can search. Select the desired library and follow the instructions on how to use the library's database search system.

## Computers and Literature Reviews: A Closing Note

It is not possible to review all the possibilities that currently exist for computer-searching library materials. Availability of computer systems depends on the individual library. If you want to use a library's computerized search system, contact your local librarian. Most libraries with computer systems run special classes on how to perform computer searches.

## Using the *Psychological Abstracts*

Although *PsycINFO* has supplanted the hardbound edition of the *Psychological Abstracts* in many libraries (some libraries may no longer subscribe to the hardbound edition), there may come a time when you find it necessary to use the hardbound edition. Using the *Psychological Abstracts* will be necessary if your library does not have *PsycINFO* or if *PsycINFO* is unavailable because of technical problems. In any event, it is useful to know how to use the hardbound edition of the *Psychological Abstracts*.

Doing a manual search of the *Psychological Abstracts* for a particular topic involves looking up topics in the *Subject Index*. In this index you would find a long list of brief index entries. For example, if you looked up "sexual harassment," you would find a list of entries that briefly describe the subject of articles indexed under that keyword and provide an abstract number. You must search through this list, identify those articles that seem to fit your needs, and write down each abstract number. Next, you look up the abstract in the appropriate volume of the *Psychological Abstracts*. An abstract entry in the *Psychological Abstracts* includes a full bibliographical citation (title of the article, authors, journal, issue, volume, and pages) along with a summary (abstract) of the article. If you still think the article is what you are looking for, you write down the bibliographical information and find the article in the appropriate journal.

If you only have the name of the author of an article or of someone working in a field, you can use the *Author Index* of the *Psychological Abstracts* to find articles written by that person. The method we just described for using the *Subject Index* would then be applied to entries found in the *Author Index*.

## Citations Index

Other indexes you might find useful when trying to track down research sources include the *Science Citations Index* and *Social Science Citations Index*. Each of these has three separate indexes: the *Citation Index*, the *Source Index*, and the *Permuterm Subject Index*. The *Citation Index* is used when you want to find out what other, more recent articles have cited the article that you already have.

The *Source Index* is useful when you have very little information concerning an article. For example, imagine you have read an article about sexual harassment in *Time*. That article mentions a study you are interested in. Unfortunately, popular magazines such as *Time* do not provide a full reference, so all you have is the author's name and date of publication. Using the *Source Index*, you could track down the article (assuming it is in an indexed journal) and obtain the full reference.

The *Permuterm Subject Index* is similar to the *Psychological Abstracts Subject Index* in that you can look up a particular topic and find related articles. One advantage to using the *Permuterm Subject Index* is that it covers more journals than the *Psychological Abstracts*. You might consider using the *Permuterm Subject Index* in addition to PsycINFO or the *Psychological Abstracts*.

Another powerful search tool is *ISI Web of Science*. The *Web of Science* provides access to a wide range of scientific search tools including the *Science Citation Index Expanded, the Social Science Citation Index, and the Arts and Humanities Citation Index.* The service allows access to over 10,000 journals and allows a number of flexible search strategies. You should check with your college or university library to see if they have a subscription to this search tool.

## READING RESEARCH REPORTS

Let's say that your search of the literature has identified several potentially useful articles, including reviews, theoretical articles, and research reports. This section describes how to obtain copies of these materials, how to read the materials, and how to critically evaluate the research reports you obtain.

## Obtaining a Copy

After identifying relevant research reports, your next step is to obtain copies. Your library has a list of all periodicals (including scientific journals) found on its shelves or stored on microfilm. Where this list can be found depends on what resources your library has. Many libraries have this information on a computerized database, perhaps linked with the general database system that you would use to search for books. Libraries without computerized systems most likely have a *Serials Index* that includes the call number assigned to each journal. Use the call number to find the journal, just as you would to locate a book. If your library subscribes or has online access to the particular journal you are looking for, then all you need do is find the article on the shelf or download it from the online source. If your library does *not* subscribe to that journal, you may still be able to obtain a copy of the article you want by submitting a request for interlibrary loan (see your librarian for advice on how to do this). Getting articles via interlibrary loan has become faster with the advent of the Internet: Articles can be faxed or e-mailed to you. However, the library may not always use these electronic methods, and in some instances it can take several days or weeks to get your article via interlibrary loan. If you need the article right away, you might want to check first to see if the article is available online (e.g., through EBSCO or *PsycARTICLES*). If so, you can simply download it and print it out.

If you do find the article in the library, quickly scan it to determine if it is indeed relevant to your research. If so, copy the article for future reference (libraries have photocopiers available). Making a copy is legal, even if the article is copyrighted, as long as the copy is for personal use in your research. Having your own copy will simplify the job of keeping track of important details. You can underline and make marginal notes right on the copy. If you become concerned about some point you had not paid much attention to in your original reading, you can reread your copy.

## Reading the Research Report

Assume you have obtained a copy of a research report. Knowing what you will find in it can save you time in locating specific kinds of information. The information contained in the report reflects the purposes for which it was written. These purposes include (1) to argue the need for doing the research, (2) to show how the research addresses that need, (3) to clearly describe the methods used so that others can duplicate them, (4) to present the findings of the research, and (5) to integrate the findings with previous knowledge, including previous research findings and theories.

Consider the components of a typical research report and how they fulfill these purposes. Although the format of an article may vary from journal to journal, most research articles include the standard sections shown in Table 3–3. Sometimes sections are combined (e.g., Results and Discussion) or a section is added (e.g., Design). Generally, however, research articles in psychological journals follow the outline shown in Table 3–3.

## Reading the Literature Critically

When reading a journal article, think of yourself as a consumer of research. Apply the same skills to deciding whether you are going to "buy" a piece of research as you would when deciding whether to buy any other product. Critically reading and analyzing research literature (or any source of information for that matter) involves two steps: an initial appraisal and a careful analysis of content (Cornell University Library, 2000).

The *initial* appraisal involves evaluating the following (Cornell University Library, 2000): the author, date of publication, edition or revision, publisher, and title of the journal. When evaluating the author, you should look at his or her credentials, including institutional affiliation and past experience in the area. It is important to consider the author and the author's institutional affiliation because not all research findings are reported in scholarly journals. Some research is disseminated through "research centers" and other organizations. By evaluating the author and the institution,

| TABLE 3–3 | Parts of an APA-Style Article |
| --- | --- |
| Abstract | |
| Introduction | |
| Method | |
|     Participants or subjects | |
|     Apparatus or materials | |
|     Procedure | |
| Results | |
| Discussion | |
| References | |

you can make an assessment of any potential biases. For example, a study that comes from an organization with a political agenda may not present facts in a correct or unbiased fashion. The main author of a research report from such an organization might not even be academically qualified or trained to conduct research and correctly interpret findings. One way you can check on the author is to see if the author's work has been cited by others in the same area. Important works by respected authors are often cited by other researchers.

Look at the date of the publication to see if the source is current or potentially out of date. In some areas (e.g., neuroscience), new discoveries are made almost daily and may make older research out of date and obsolete. Try to find the most up-to-date sources you can. When evaluating a book, determine if the copy you have is the most recent edition. If it is not, find the most recent edition, because it will have been updated with the most current information available at the date of publication. Also, note the publisher for both books and journals. Some books are published by companies (sometimes called "vanity presses") that require authors to pay for publication of their works. Books published in this way may not undergo a careful scholarly review prior to publication. Generally, books published by university publishers will be scholarly, as will books published by well-recognized publishing houses (e.g., Lawrence Erlbaum Associates). Although this is no guarantee of quality, a book from a reputable publisher will usually be of high quality. The same goes for journals. As indicated earlier, some journals are peer reviewed and some are not. Try to use peer-reviewed journals whenever possible. Finally, look at the title of the publication you are thinking of using. This will help you determine if the publication is scholarly or not. There is no hard and fast rule of thumb to tell you if a publication is scholarly. Use the guidelines in Table 3–1 to determine the nature of the publication.

Evaluating the content of an article published in a scholarly psychological journal involves a careful reading and analysis of the different parts of the article (outlined in Table 3–3). In the next sections we explore how to critically analyze each section of an APA-style journal article.

*Evaluating the Introduction*    When reading the introduction to a paper, determine whether or not the author has adequately reviewed the relevant literature. Were any important papers neglected? Does the author support any assertions with reference citations? In addition, ask yourself,

1. Has the author correctly represented the results from previous research? Sometimes when authors summarize previous research, they make errors or select only findings consistent with their ideas. Also, as already noted, authors may have a theoretical orientation that may bias their summary of existing research findings. If you are suspicious, look up the original sources and evaluate them for yourself. Also, you should determine if the author has cited the most up-to-date materials. Reliance on older material may not give you an accurate picture of the current research or theory in an area.

2. Does the author clearly state the purposes of the study and the nature of the problem under study?

3. Do the hypotheses logically follow from the discussion in the introduction?

4. Are the hypotheses clearly stated and, more important, are they testable?

*Evaluating the Method Section*    The method section describes precisely how the study was carried out. You might think of this section as a "cookbook" or a set of directions for conducting the study. It usually contains subsections including *participants* or *subjects* (describing the nature of the subject sample used), *materials* or *apparatus* (describing any equipment or other materials used), and *procedure* (describing precisely how the study was carried out). When reading the method section of an article, evaluate the following:

1. Who served as participants in the study? How were the participants selected (randomly, through a subject pool, etc.)? Were the participants all of one race, gender, or ethnic background? If so, this could limit the generality of the results (the degree to which the results apply beyond the parameters of the study). For example, if only male participants were used, a legitimate question is whether the results would apply as well to females. Also, look at the size of the sample. Were enough participants included to allow an adequate test of any hypotheses stated in the introduction?

2. Does the design of the study allow an adequate test of the hypotheses stated in the introduction? For example, do the variables included allow an adequate test of the hypotheses? Is information provided about the reliability and validity of any measures used?

3. Are there any flaws in materials or procedures used that might affect the validity of the study? A good way to assess this is to outline the design of the study and evaluate it against the stated purpose of the study.

*Evaluating the Results Section*    The results section presents the data of the study, usually in summary form (such as means, standard deviations, correlations, and so on), along with the results from any statistical tests applied to the data (for example, a *t* test or analysis of variance). When evaluating the results section, look for the following:

1. Which effects are statistically significant? Note which effects were significant and whether those effects are consistent with the hypotheses stated in the introduction.

2. Are the differences reported large or small? Look at the means (or other measures of center) being compared and note how much difference emerged. You may find that although an effect is significant, it is small.

3. Were the appropriate statistics used?

4. Do the text, tables, and figures match? Sometimes errors occur in the preparation of tables and figures, so be sure to check for accuracy. Also, check to see if the author's description of the relationships depicted in any tables or figures matches what is shown.

If statistics are not reported, determine whether the author has correctly described the relationships among the variables and has indicated how reliability was assessed.

*Evaluating the Discussion Section*     In the discussion section, you will find the author's interpretations of the results reported. The discussion section usually begins with a summary of the major findings of the study, followed by the author's interpretations of the data and a synthesis of the findings with previous research and theory. You also may find a discussion of any limitations of the study. When evaluating the discussion section, here are a few things to look for:

1. Do the author's conclusions follow from the results reported? Sometimes authors overstep the bounds of the results and draw unwarranted conclusions.

2. Does the author offer speculations concerning the results? In the discussion section, the author is free to speculate on the meaning of the results and on any applications. Carefully evaluate the discussion section and separate author speculations from conclusions supported directly by the results. Evaluate whether the author strays too far from the data when speculating about the implications of the results.

3. How well do the findings of the study mesh with previous research and existing theory? Are the results consistent with previous research, or are they unique? If the study is the only one that has found a certain effect (if other research has failed to find the effect or found just the opposite effect), be skeptical about the results.

4. Does the author point the way to directions for future research in the area? That is, does the author indicate other variables that might affect the behavior studied and suggest new studies to test the effects of these variables?

*References*     The final section of an article is usually the reference section (a few articles include appendixes as well) in which the author lists all the references cited in the body of the paper. Complete references are provided. You can use these to find other research on your topic.

# FACTORS AFFECTING THE QUALITY
# OF A SOURCE OF RESEARCH INFORMATION

One thing to keep in mind when selecting a source of information about a particular area of research is that not all books, journals, or convention presentations are created equal. Some sources of information publish original research, whereas others may only summarize the findings of a study. The criteria that journals use for acceptance of a manuscript determine which manuscripts will be accepted or rejected for publication, leading potentially to a bias in the content of the journal. Additionally, although most publications use a peer-review process to ensure the quality of the works published, some do not. In this section, we explore these issues and show how they relate to your literature review.

## Publication Practices

When you conduct a literature review, one question should come to mind in considering a research area as a whole: Do the articles you are reading provide a fair and accurate picture of the state of the research in the field? Figure 3–3 shows the general process that a manuscript undergoes when submitted for publication. Although it is true that journals generally provide a good comprehensive view of the research within their scope, there may be research that never makes it into the hallowed pages of scientific journals because of the publication practices adopted by scholarly journals.

When a manuscript is submitted for consideration to a scholarly journal, editors and reviewers guide their evaluations of the manuscript by a set of largely unwritten rules. These include whether the results reported meet conventionally accepted levels of statistical significance, whether the findings are consistent with other findings in the area, and the significance of the contribution of the research to the area. The policies adopted by the current editor also could affect the chances of a manuscript being accepted for publication. We examine these publication practices and their possible effects on the published literature next.

## Statistical Significance

Data collected in psychological research are usually subjected to a statistical analysis in order to determine the probability that chance and chance alone would have resulted in effects as large as or larger than those actually observed. If this probability is sufficiently low (e.g., less than .05, or 1 chance in 20), it is deemed unlikely that chance alone was responsible for the observed effect, and the effect is said to be *statistically significant*. (See Chapter 13 for a more detailed discussion of statistical significance testing.) The criterion probability used to determine statistical significance, called *alpha*, determines how often effects that are actually just chance differences end up being declared statistically significant. Thus, if alpha is .05, this will happen, on average, 5 times in 100 tests. In most journals, editors are reluctant to accept papers in which results fail to achieve the accepted minimum alpha level of .05. The reason, of course, is that such results stand a relatively high chance of being attributable to random factors rather than to the variable whose possible effect was being assessed in the

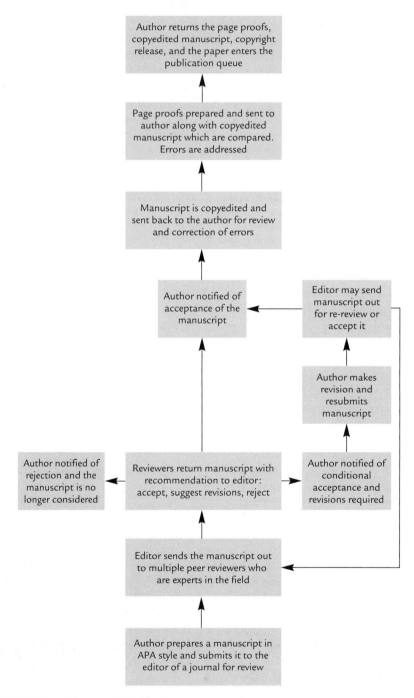

**FIGURE 3–3**  Diagram of the editorial review process

study. Researchers are aware of the requirement for statistical significance and, therefore, usually do not report the results of studies that fail to meet it.

If the investigator is convinced that an effect is there, despite the lack of statistical significance, he or she may elect to repeat the study while using better controls or different parameters. Nothing is inherently wrong with such a strategy. If the effect is there, better control over extraneous variables and selection of more favorable parameters are likely to reveal it. If the effect is *not* there, however, repeated attempts to demonstrate the effect eventually lead to obtaining statistically significant results by chance. Through probability pyramiding (see Chapter 13), the likelihood that this will happen is much greater than the stated alpha level would suggest.

The failures to obtain significant results generally wind up in someone's file drawer, forgotten and buried. In most cases, only those attempts that were successful in obtaining significant results are submitted for publication. Yet, because of probability pyramiding, the published results are more likely to have been significant because of chance than the stated alpha would lead us to believe. This effect is known as the **file drawer phenomenon** (Rosenthal, 1979, 1984). To the extent that the file drawer phenomenon operates, published findings as a group may be less reliable than they seem. Later, this chapter shows you how to estimate the magnitude of the file drawer phenomenon.

The problem of negative findings is serious. The failure to obtain an expected relationship can be as important for understanding and for advancement of theory as confirmation. Yet this information is difficult to disseminate to the scientific community. Laboratories may independently and needlessly duplicate each other's negative findings simply because they are unaware of each other's negative results.

## Consistency with Previous Knowledge

Another criterion used to assess a research paper's acceptability is the consistency of its findings with previous knowledge. Most findings are expected to build on the existing structure of knowledge in the field: to add new information, to demonstrate the applicability of known principles in new areas, and to show the limits of conditions within which a phenomenon holds. Findings that do not make sense within the currently accepted framework are suspect.

When the currently accepted framework has deep support, then such anomalous findings call into question the study that generated them, rather than the framework itself. Reviewers and editors are likely to give the paper an especially critical appraisal in an attempt to identify faults in the logic and implementation of the design that may have led to the anomalous results. Ultimately, some reason may be found for rejecting the paper.

An excellent example in which this process operated was the initial work by Garcia and Koelling (1966) on learned taste aversions. Garcia and Koelling exposed thirsty rats to a solution of water that had been given a flavor unfamiliar to the rats. Some of the rats were then injected with lithium chloride, and the rest of the group was given a placebo injection of saline solution. The rats injected with lithium chloride became ill from the injection about six hours later. The rats were allowed to recover and then were given a choice between drinking plain water or the flavored water. Rats injected with the saline solution showed no preference between the two, but rats injected with lithium chloride avoided the novel flavor.

From this evidence, Garcia and Koelling concluded that the rats injected with lithium chloride had formed, in a single "trial," an association between the novel flavor and the illness. In other words, classical conditioning had occurred between a conditioned stimulus (the flavor) and an unconditioned stimulus (the illness) across a six-hour interstimulus interval.

This was a striking finding. Classical conditioning had been extensively researched by Pavlov and others. It was well known that interstimulus intervals beyond a few *minutes* were completely ineffective in establishing a conditioned response, even when hundreds of trials were conducted. To reviewers and editors looking at Garcia and Koelling's manuscript, something was fishy. Garcia and Koelling's finding was a fluke, or some unreported aspect of methodology was introducing a confounding factor. The results simply couldn't be correct. The paper was repeatedly rejected by reviewers.

It was not until others heard of Garcia and Koelling's findings "through the grapevine" and successfully replicated their results that the phenomenon of learned taste aversions gained credibility among reviewers. Only then did papers on the topic begin to be accepted in the established refereed journals. Once accepted, Garcia and Koelling's discovery and other similarly anomalous findings became the basis for new theories concerning the nature and limits of laws of learning (such as Seligman & Hager, 1972). Hence, in refusing to publish Garcia and Koelling's findings, reviewers and editors delayed progress, but ultimately the new findings surfaced to challenge established thinking.

Editors and reviewers are thus in a tough position. To function effectively, they must be conservative in accepting papers that report anomalous findings. Yet they must be open-minded enough to avoid simply assuming that such findings *must* result from methodological flaws. Later this chapter examines just how successful editors and reviewers have been at maintaining this balance.

## Significance of the Contribution

When determining whether to accept or reject a paper for publication, editors and reviewers must assess the degree to which the findings described in the paper contribute to the advancement of knowledge. At one time, papers were considered acceptable even if they reported only a single experiment involving simply an experimental and a control group. A researcher could publish a number of papers in a relatively short time, but each contributed little new information.

Today, journals usually insist that a paper report a series of experiments or at least a parametric study involving several levels of two or more variables. For example, a paper might report a first experiment that demonstrates a relationship between two variables. Several follow-up experiments might then appear that trace the effective range of the independent variable and test various alternative explanations for the relationship. Such a paper provides a fair amount of information about the phenomenon under investigation and, in pursuing the phenomenon through several experiments, also demonstrates the phenomenon's reliability through immediate systematic replication.

Although these are important advantages, insisting on multiple experiments or studies within a paper also can have a negative side. Although the study provides more information, the information contained in the study cannot see the light of day until the entire series of experiments or observations has been completed. The resulting paper is more time-consuming to review and evaluate. Reviewers have more opportunities to find defects that may require modification of the manuscript. The result is delay in getting what may be an important finding out to the scientific community.

## Editorial Policy

Editorial policy is yet another factor that can influence what appears in journals. Frequently, an area of research becomes "hot," resulting in a flood of articles in the area. Researchers latch onto a particular research area (e.g., eyewitness identification, day care in early infancy) and investigate it, sometimes to the exclusion of other important research areas. When this happens, a journal editor may take steps to ensure that more variety appears in a journal. For example, research on eyewitness identification has been a hot topic for the past several years. Interest reached its peak in the 1980s, and the premier journal in the area, *Law and Human Behavior*, published a large number of articles on this topic—perhaps too large a number. In 1986 Michael Saks took over as editor of the journal. He made it clear that he was going to give preference to manuscripts dealing with issues other than eyewitness identification.

Editorial policy also can show itself if the editor enters an unintended bias into the review system. The editor is the one who decides whether a paper will be sent out for review and ultimately if it will be published. If the editor has a bias, say toward a particular theory, that editor may be unwilling to publish articles that do not support that theory. We discuss this issue in the next section.

## Peer Review

Some sources of information (including books, journal articles, and convention proceedings) use a **peer-review** process. This means that the materials to be published or presented are reviewed by experts in the area that the material covers. These experts will receive a copy of the materials and do a thorough review of the content. They will then recommend to the editor of the journal whether to accept (either outright or with revisions) or reject the manuscript.

Although peer review is a time-honored tradition in science as a way to ensure quality, it is far from perfect. Just because something is published in a refereed journal does not mean that it is a sound or important piece of research. Conversely, you may find some gems in nonrefereed journals. The reason for this seeming lack of consistency has to do with problems in the peer review process.

*Problems with Peer Review*   As we noted, when you send a manuscript to a refereed journal, the editor will send your manuscript to expert reviewers (usually two) who will carefully evaluate your paper. In some cases, peer review is anonymous, and in others it is not. Individual journals determine their peer-review policies and some choose to use anonymous peer review. Anonymous peer review might be necessary, but it does have its problems. Although you hope that your colleagues in research are honest and fair in their appraisals of your work, someone with a personal dislike for you or your ideas could sabotage your efforts. Even in the absence of malice, the reviewer may judge your manuscript unfairly because of a lack of knowledge, a bias against your general approach to research, or misreading.

The extent to which such factors operate within the peer-review system has been the subject of research and debate over the past three decades. For example, Mahoney (1977) investigated the influence of several properties of a research manuscript on its acceptance for publication by reviewers. With the approval of the editor, Mahoney sent manuscripts describing a fictitious experiment to 75 reviewers working for the *Journal of Applied Behavior Analysis*. Five randomly constituted groups of reviewers received different versions of the manuscript that varied according to their results and interpretations of those results. Mahoney found that the paper was consistently rated higher if its results supported the reviewer's theoretical bias and lower if they did not. How the results were interpreted had little impact. Similarly, the recommendation to accept or reject the paper for publication was strongly influenced by the direction of the data. If the data supported the reviewer's theoretical leanings, the reviewer usually recommended acceptance. If the data argued against those leanings, the reviewer usually recommended rejection or major revision.

Mahoney's findings showed that results favorable or unfavorable to the reviewer's point of view affect how the reviewer receives the manuscript. If the results are favorable, the reviewer is likely to believe that the results are valid and that the methodology was adequate. If the results are unfavorable, however, the reviewer is likely to believe that the study must be defective. The reviewer will search diligently for flaws in the design or execution of the study and use even minor problems as reasons for rejection.

Partly because of such sources of bias, estimates of interreviewer reliability in the social sciences have tended to be low. Fiske and Fogg (1990) examined 402 reviews of 153 papers and found almost no agreement among reviewers, not because the reviewers overtly disagreed but because the reviewers found different aspects of the papers to criticize. It was as if they had read different papers! Lindsey (1978), in his book *The Scientific Publication System in Social Science*, noted that empirical studies have consistently found reliabilities of around .25 (the correlation between reviewer judgments). Whether both reviewers will agree that your paper is publishable is thus very nearly a chance affair.

The unreliability of the peer-review system was highlighted by a study conducted by Peters and Ceci (1982). Peters and Ceci identified 12 *published* articles that had appeared in different major psychology journals. Each article was authored by at least one individual from a "prestige" institution and had appeared between 18 and 32 months earlier. The names of the original authors and their institutional affiliations were removed and replaced by fictitious names and affiliations. In addition, the titles, abstracts, and introductions were cosmetically altered (without changing the content) to reduce the chances that the articles would be recognized. Retyped as manuscripts, the articles were then resubmitted *to the same journals that had originally published them* (and in most cases, to the same editor).

The results were dramatic. Only 3 of the 12 articles were identified as resubmissions and rejected for this reason. The remaining 9 were undetected. Of those 9, 8 *were rejected for publication*. Even more amazing, in every case both reviewers agreed and the editor concurred.

Because the articles had appeared before, the reviewers might have rejected the papers because they remembered the earlier data (although not the articles themselves) and thus viewed the information they contained as contributing nothing new. If this were the case, however, no hint of this was given in the reasons cited by the reviewers. According to Peters and Ceci, the reasons given for rejecting the papers usually concerned major flaws in the methodology. Thus, papers that had already been accepted into the archival literature only months earlier were subsequently seen as too methodologically flawed to merit publication.

Peters and Ceci offered two possible reasons for the new attitude toward the papers. The change in authorship and affiliation from prestigious to unknown may have had a negative influence on the evaluation. Or, because of the approximately 80 percent rejection rate, peer review may have been so unreliable that the chances of getting positive evaluations were just too low to expect acceptance the second time. This latter view assumes that getting a positive evaluation is essentially a matter of chance for manuscripts that cannot be rejected out of hand for obvious fatal flaws. Whether either or both possibilities are true, the implication is that acceptance of your paper (given that it is reasonably good) depends to a large extent on factors that are not under your control.

Despite the problems associated with the peer-review process, it does work pretty well. Although peer review is no guarantee that all things published are of impeccable quality, it does provide a measure of confidence that what you read is valid and reliable.

## FRAUD AND THE ROLE OF VALUES IN THE RESEARCH PROCESS

In addition to the publication practices we just reviewed, there are two other factors that you should consider when determining the value of any published work. Odds are that most of the research you will encounter during a literature review will be the product of the work of honest and diligent scientists. Sometimes, however, for various reasons, scientists falsify or otherwise perpetrate research fraud. When this happens, it not only calls into question the validity of the individual scientist's results but also the credibility of science in general. On another level, research results can be influenced not so much by outright fraud as by the values and beliefs of the researcher. In this case, the researcher's values may bias a field of study, yielding results that may lack validity and generality. In this section, we explore how fraud and values affect the progress of science.

### Fraud in Research

The news seemed great for thousands of women diagnosed with breast cancer. Research had shown that for women in the early stages of breast cancer, an operation called a *lumpectomy* (in which the cancerous lump and some surrounding tissue are removed) was just as effective as the more common, and disfiguring, *mastectomy* (in which all or part of a woman's breast is removed, perhaps along with lymph glands).

The research clearly showed that for women in the early stages of breast cancer, survival rates for the two procedures were nearly identical.

This research imbued new confidence in cancer patients and physicians alike. Doctors began to recommend lumpectomy, and use of the procedure soared. However, in 1994 the optimism evaporated when Dr. Roger Poisson, a noted cancer researcher, admitted that he had falsified his data concerning clinical tests of the two surgical procedures. He had allowed women into his research who were in more advanced stages of cancer than were to be permitted in the study, and he had reported on the progress of women who had died. He kept two sets of files on his research, one false and one truthful.

As a result of Poisson's unethical conduct, confidence in the lumpectomy versus mastectomy research was shaken. It also called into question the honesty of the entire scientific community. The public could no longer be sure that the results coming out of research laboratories could be trusted.

The preceding example illustrates how the process of science can be subverted by a dishonest scientist. Expectations of a researcher also can affect the outcome of a study. The case of Poisson and the impact of researcher expectations reveal an important truth about research in the social and behavioral sciences: It is a very human affair. The research process benefits from all the good qualities of human researchers: ingenuity, dedication, hard work, a desire to discover the truth, and so on. However, as in any human endeavor, the more negative qualities of human researchers also may creep into the research process. Donning a lab coat does not guarantee that a person checks his or her ambitions, flaws, desires, and needs at the laboratory door (Broad & Wade, 1983).

*What Constitutes Fraud in Research?*    Fraud in research takes a variety of forms. Perhaps the most pernicious, albeit rare (Broad & Wade, 1983), form of research fraud is the outright fabrication of data. A scientist may fabricate an entire set of data based on an experiment that might never have been run or replace actual data with false data. Other forms of fraud in research include altering data to make them "look better" or fit with a theory, selecting only the best data for publication, and publishing stolen or plagiarized work (Broad & Wade, 1983). Altering or otherwise manipulating data in order to achieve statistical significance (for example, selectively dropping data from an analysis) also would constitute research fraud.

Broad and Wade also suggest that using the "least publishable unit" rule, which involves getting several small publications out of a single experiment (as opposed to publishing one large paper), might be considered dishonest. Research fraud can occur if scientists sabotage each other's work. Claiming credit for work done by others also could be considered fraud. If, for example, a student conceptualizes, designs, and carries out a study and a professor takes senior author status on the publication, that would be considered fraud. Finally, it is also dishonest to attach your name to research that you had little to do with, just to pad your résumé. Some articles may have as many as 10 or more authors. Each of the junior authors may have had some minor input (such as suggesting that Wistar rats be used rather than Long–Evans rats). However, that minor input does not warrant authorship credit.

*The Prevalence of Research Fraud*   At one time, the editor of *Science* stated that 99.9999 percent of scientific papers are truthful and accurate (Bell, 1992). Despite this optimism, other critics suggest that it is not possible to exactly quantify research fraud (Bell, 1992). For one thing, fraud may not be reported, even if it is detected. In Poisson's case, for example, some evidence exists that there was a suspicion of fraud as early as 1990. In addition, in one survey (cited in Bell, 1992), many researchers who suspected that a colleague was falsifying data did not report it. Another reason why fraud may go underreported is that the liabilities associated with "blowing the whistle" can be quite severe. Whistle-blowers typically are vilified, their credibility is called into question, and they may, perhaps, even be fired for "doing the right thing." Thus, the relatively few celebrated cases of fraud reported may be only the tip of the iceberg.

Regardless of how low the actual rate of fraud in science turns out to be, even a few cases can have a damaging effect on the credibility of science and scientists (Broad & Wade, 1983). Erosion of the credibility of science undermines the public's confidence in the results that flow from scientific research. In the long run, this works to the detriment of individuals and of society.

*Explanations for Research Fraud*   Why would a scientist perpetrate a fraud? There are many reasons. Fraud may be perpetrated for personal recognition. Publishing an article in a prestigious journal is a boost to one's self-esteem. Personal pressure for such self-esteem and recognition from others can motivate a person to falsify data or commit some other form of research fraud.

The pursuit of money is a major factor in fraudulent research (Bell, 1992). Doing research on a large scale takes quite a bit of money, and researchers are generally not wealthy and cannot fund their own research. Nor can financially strapped universities or hospitals provide the level of funding needed for many research projects. Consequently, researchers must look to funding agencies such as the National Science Foundation, the National Institute of Mental Health, or some other available funding source. The budgets for these agencies are typically limited with respect to the number of applications that can be accepted for funding. Consequently, competition for research funding becomes very intense. In addition, it is generally easier to obtain grant money if you have a good track record of publications. The pressure for obtaining scarce grant money can lead a person to falsify data in order to "produce" and be in a good position to get more funding. Moreover, at some universities, obtaining grants is used as an index of one's worth and may even be a requirement of retaining one's job. This can add additional pressure toward committing research fraud.

Another reason for fraud in research relates to the tenure process within the academic environment. A new faculty member usually has five years to "prove" himself or herself. During this five-year probationary period, the faculty member is expected to publish some given quantity of research articles. At high-power, research-oriented universities, the number of publications required may be large, creating a strong "publish or perish" atmosphere. This atmosphere seems to have grown stronger over the past 40 years. When James D. Watson (Nobel Prize winner with Francis Crick for his discovery of the DNA double helix) was a candidate for tenure and promotion at Harvard University in 1958, he had 18 publications. By 1982, 50 publications were required for the same promotion (Broad & Wade, 1983). This need to publish as many papers as possible in a relatively short period of time can lead to outright fraud and/or vita (résumé) padding using the least-publishable-unit rule.

Finally, fraud in research can arise from scientific "elitism" (Broad & Wade, 1983). Sometimes we see fraud committed by some of the biggest names in science.

*Dealing with Research Fraud*     Bell (1992) points out that science has three general methods for guarding against research fraud: the grant-review process, the peer review process for publication, and replication of results. Bell points out that, unfortunately, none of these is effective in detecting fraud. Editors may be disinclined to publish papers that are critical of other researchers, let alone that make accusations of fraud (Bell, 1992). In addition, replication of experiments is expensive and time-consuming and unlikely to occur across labs (Bell, 1992). Even if a finding cannot be replicated, that does not necessarily mean fraud has occurred.

One way to deal with research fraud is to train students in the ethics of the research process. Students should learn, early in their academic careers, that ethical research practice requires scientific integrity and that research fraud is unethical. Unfortunately, students are often not taught this lesson very well. Michael Kalichman and Paul Friedman (1992) conducted a survey of biomedical science trainees and found that only 24 percent indicated that they had received training in scientific ethics. Additionally, 15 percent said that they would be willing to alter or manipulate data in order to get a grant or a publication.

Jane Steinberg (2002) indicates that another safeguard against fraud is to make it clear to scientists and assistants that they will get caught if they commit scientific fraud. Steinberg suggests that researchers check data often and openly in front of those who collect and analyze the data. Questions should be asked about any suspicious marks on datasheets or changes/corrections made to the data.

Probably the best guard against fraud in science is to imbue researchers during the training process with the idea that ethical research means being honest. This process should begin as early as possible. Steinberg (2002) suggests that teaching about research fraud should begin in psychology students' research methods courses. She recommends that students be presented with cases of research fraud. Those cases should be discussed and evaluated carefully. Students should learn the implications of research fraud for researchers themselves, their field of study, and the credibility of science (Steinberg, 2002). The short-term consequences (loss of a job, expulsion from school, and so forth) and long-term consequences (harm to innocent individuals because of false results, damage to the credibility of science, and so forth) should be communicated clearly to researchers during their education and training.

Another strategy suggested by Steinberg (2002) is to contact research participants after they have participated in a study to see if they actually participated. Participants should be asked if they actually met with the person running the study, whether they met eligibility requirements, if they knew the person running the study beforehand, and if the study ran for the appropriate amount of time. Similar steps can be taken with animal subjects by carefully scrutinizing animal use records and laboratory notes (Steinberg, 2002).

When fraud does occur, scientists should be encouraged to blow the whistle when they have strong proof that fraud took place. The U.S. Office of Research Integrity

(2003) suggests that whistle-blowers are a crucial component in the fight against fraud in science. The Office recommends that before making an allegation of research fraud, the whistle-blower familiarize him- or herself with the policies of the institution, find out what to include in a report, and find out to whom the report should be given. The whistle-blower also should find out about protection against retaliation and about the role he or she will play after the report is made. The Office underscores the need for institutions to protect whistle-blowers from negative consequences. A survey commissioned by the Office of Research Integrity found that 30.9 percent of whistle-blowers studied reported no negative consequences for their actions. However, 27.9 percent reported at least one negative consequence and 41.2 percent reported multiple negative outcomes. Those negative outcomes included being pressured to drop the charges (42.6 percent), being hit with a countercomplaint (40 percent), being ostracized by coworkers (25 percent), or being fired (or not renewed, 23.6 percent). Thus, the climate for whistle-blowers is quite hostile. For example, Stephen Bruening based a recommendation that retarded children be treated with stimulants (most research and practice suggested using tranquilizers) on years of fraudulent data. Robert Sprague exposed Bruening's fraud and was subjected to pressure from members of the University of Pittsburgh administration not to pursue his allegations against Bruening. Sprague was even threatened with a lawsuit.

Finally, a researcher must determine whether fraud has actually occurred. In some cases, this may be relatively easy. If a scientist knows for a fact that a particular study reported in a journal was never done, fraud can be alleged with confidence. In other cases, fraud may be detected by noticing strange patterns in the data reported. This is essentially what happened in the case of Cyril Burt. Some researchers noted that some of Burt's correlations remained invariant from study to study, even though the numbers of participants on which the correlations were based changed. This, and the fact that an assistant Burt claimed helped him could not be found, served as the foundation of what seemed like a strong case against Burt based on circumstantial evidence. Burt's posthumous reputation has been ruined and his work discredited. However, Joynson (1989) has reevaluated the Burt case and has provided convincing alternative explanations for the oddities in Burt's data. Joynson maintains that Burt did not deliberately perpetrate a fraud on science and that Burt's name should be cleared. At this point, the jury is still out on Burt's conduct as to whether he committed outright fraud. Even if Burt did not commit fraud, he was willing to misrepresent his data and recycle old text (Butler & Petrulis, 1999). On the other hand, there are those who contend that the evidence shows that Burt was guilty of fraud beyond any reasonable doubt (Tucker, 1997).

## The Role of Values in Science

Fraud involves deliberately altering an experiment or results to produce a desired outcome. However, the validity of research also can be reduced inadvertently by allowing general cultural values, political agendas, and personal values of the researcher to influence the research process. Although we would like to think of research as "value free" and objective, some philosophers of science suggest that research cannot easily be separated from a set of values dominating a culture or a person (Longino, 1990).

Values can influence the course of scientific inquiry in several ways. Helen Longino (1990), for example, lists five nonmutually exclusive categories (p. 86):

1. *Practices.* Values can influence the practice of science, which affects the integrity of the knowledge gained by the scientific method.

2. *Questions.* Values can determine which questions are addressed and which are ignored about a given phenomenon.

3. *Data.* Values can affect how data are interpreted. Value-laden terms can affect how research data are described. Values also can determine which data are selected for analysis and the decision concerning which phenomena are to be studied in the first place.

4. *Specific Assumptions.* Values influence the basic assumptions that scientists make concerning the phenomena they study. This may cause a scientist to make inferences in specific areas of study.

5. *Global Assumptions.* Values can affect the nature of the global assumptions scientists make that can affect the nature and character of the research conducted in an entire area.

Similarly, David Myers (1999) has indicated three broad areas that combine some of Longino's categories. First, values can affect the topics that scientists choose to study and how they are studied. Second, values can affect how we interpret observations we make and results we uncover. Third, values can come into play when research findings are translated into statements of what "ought to be."

***How Values Influence What and How Scientists Study***    Cultural values can be seen operating on science. For example, in the United States, researchers interested in conformity effects have focused on the role of the majority in influencing the minority. This probably filters down from the American political system in which the "majority rules." In Europe, where there are parliamentary democracies, minority viewpoints are often taken into account when political coalitions are formed. As a consequence, much of the research on how a minority can influence a majority came out of European psychological laboratories.

Even within a culture, values can influence what we study. For example, feminist scholars point out that assumptions about gender can influence how research questions are formulated (Unger & Crawford, 1992). For example, research on the effects of early infant day care on children is usually couched in negative terms concerning how maternal employment may adversely affect a child's development. Rarely are such questions phrased in terms of the potential positive outcomes (Unger & Crawford, 1992).

Unger and Crawford (1992) also point out that gender may play a role in the manner in which research hypotheses are tested. They suggest, for example, that focusing on quantitative data (representing behavior with numerical values) may be biased against female research participants. They suggest that research also should be done that focuses on qualitative data. Such a focus would lead to a richer understanding of the motives underlying behavior. They also point out that research designs are not value neutral. Overreliance on rigid, laboratory experimentation, according to Unger and Crawford, divorces social behavior from its normal social context. They suggest using more field-oriented techniques. They do not advocate, however, abandoning experimental techniques.

*Interpreting Behavior*     Scientists do not merely "read" what is out there in nature. Rather, scientists interpret what they observe (Myers, 1999). One's personal biases and cultural values may exert a strong influence over how a particular behavior is interpreted. For example, a scientist who harbors a prejudice against Blacks may be more likely to label a Black child's behavior as aggressive than the same behavior committed by a White child. A conservative scientist may favor a biological explanation for aggression, whereas a more liberal one may favor a societal explanation. In both cases, the values of the researcher provide an overarching view of the world that biases his or her interpretations of a behavioral event.

*Moving from What Is to What Ought to Be*     Values also can creep into science when scientists go beyond describing and explaining relationships and begin to speculate on what ought to be (Myers, 1999). That is, scientists allow values to creep into the research process when they endeavor to define what is "right" or "normal" based on research findings. On another level, this influence of values also is seen when researchers conduct research to influence the course of political and social events. Some feminist scholars, for example, suggest that we not only should acknowledge that values enter into science but also that we should use them to evaluate all aspects of the research process (Unger, 1983). According to this view, science should be used to foster social change and challenge existing power structures (Peplau & Conrad, 1989).

Making sense of research requires that you be aware of the biases and other sources of error that afflict research. Given the ubiquitous nature of these sources, it is not surprising that research findings within a given area often appear contradictory.

## DEVELOPING HYPOTHESES

All the library research and critical reading you have done has now put you on the threshold of the next major step in the research process: developing your idea into a testable hypothesis. This hypothesis, as we pointed out in Chapter 1, will be a tentative statement relating two (or more) variables that you are interested in studying. Your hypothesis should flow logically from the sources of information used to develop your research question. That is, given what you already know from previous research (either your own or what you read in the journals), you should be able to make a tentative statement about how your variables of interest relate to one another.

Hypothesis development is an important step in the research process because it will drive your later decisions concerning the variables to be manipulated and measured in your study. Because a poorly conceptualized research hypothesis may lead to invalid results, take considerable care when stating your hypothesis.

As an example, imagine that your general research question centers on the relationship between aging and memory. You have spent several hours in the library using *PsycINFO* to find relevant research articles. You have found several articles showing that older adults show poorer memory performance on tasks such as learning nonsense syllables, learning lists of words, and recognizing pictures. However, you find very little on age differences in the ability to recall details of a complex event such as a crime. Based on what you found about age differences in memory from your literature review, you strongly suspect that older adults will not recall the details of a complex event as well as younger adults.

Thus far, you have a general research question that centers on age differences in the ability to recall details of a complex event. You have identified two variables to study: participant age and memory for a complex event. Your next step is to translate your suspicion about the relationship between these two variables into a testable research hypothesis. You might, for example, develop the following hypothesis:

> Older adults are expected to recall fewer details of a complex event correctly than younger adults.

Notice that you have taken the two variables from your general research question and have linked them with a specific statement concerning the expected relationship between them. This is the essence of distilling a general research question into a testable hypothesis.

Once you have developed your hypothesis, your next task is to decide how to test it. You must make a variety of important decisions concerning how to conduct your study. The next chapter explores the major issues you will face during the preliminary stages of planning your study.

## SUMMARY

After developing your research idea, you need to conduct a careful review of the literature in your area of interest. There are several reasons for conducting a careful literature review. It can prevent you from conducting a study that has already been done, identify questions that need to be answered, and help you get ideas for designing your study.

Research information can be found in several different types of sources. The best source of information is a scholarly source, such as a journal. This type of source centers on research and theory in a given area. Another source is a substantial publication containing information that rests on a solid base of research findings. A popular publication, intended for the general population, may have articles relevant to your topic of study. However, you will not find original sources or reference citations in these publications. Finally, a sensational publication is intended to arouse curiosity or emotion. Typically, information from such a source cannot be trusted.

Scholarly information can be found in books and journals, at conventions and meetings of professional associations, and through other sources such as the Internet. Books come in a variety of forms, including original works, anthologies, and textbooks. Some books contain original material, whereas others have secondhand material. Books are a useful source of information, but they may be unreviewed or out of date. Scholarly journals provide articles on current theory and research. Some journals are refereed (the articles undergo prepublication review), whereas others are nonrefereed (there is no prepublication review). Generally, articles in refereed journals are preferred over those in nonrefereed journals. The most up-to-date information is presented at professional conventions and meetings. You also can find research information on the Internet through sources such as EBSCO.

The basic strategy to follow in reviewing the literature is (1) find a relevant review article, (2) use the references in the article to find other relevant articles, and (3) use one of the many literature search tools to locate more recent articles. A number of research tools are available to help you, including *PsycINFO*, *PsycARTICLES*, *EBSCO*, and *Ingenta*.

Research reports follow a standard format that includes an abstract, introduction, method section, results section, discussion section, and references. Each section has a specific purpose. When you read a research report, read it critically, asking questions about the soundness of the reasoning in the introduction, the adequacy of the methods to test the hypothesis, and how well the data were analyzed and interpreted. A good rule of thumb to follow when reading critically is to be skeptical of everything you read.

Publication practices are one source of bias in scientific findings. Criteria for publication of a manuscript in a scientific journal include statistical significance of the results, consistency of results with previous findings, and editorial policy. Each of these can affect which manuscripts are eventually accepted for publication. The result is that published articles are only those that meet subjective, and somewhat strict, publication criteria.

The peer-review process is intended to ensure the quality of the product in scientific journals. Peer review involves an editor of a journal sending your manuscript to two (perhaps more) experts in your research field. The reviewers are expected to read your work and pass judgment. Unfortunately, peer reviewers are affected by personal bias. For example, reviewers are more likely to find fault with a manuscript if the reported results do not agree with their personal views on the issue studied.

Fraud in science is a problem that damages the credibility of science and its findings. Although it is rare, fraud does occur. Fraud comprises outright fabrication of data, altering data to look better, selecting only the best data for publication, using the least publishable rule, and taking credit for another's work. Motivation to commit fraud may stem from the desire to publish in prestigious journals, pressure to obtain scarce research funding, pressure to obtain publications necessary for tenure, and scientific elitism. The best way to deal with fraud in research is to train scientists so that they understand the importance of honesty in research.

Values also can enter the research process and affect the process of research, the types of questions asked, how data are interpreted, and the types of assumptions made about phenomena under study. Values also can enter into science when scientists translate their findings into what "ought to be." Although many scientists believe values should not be allowed to creep into research, others believe that values should be acknowledged and used to evaluate all aspects of science.

## REVIEW QUESTIONS

1. Why should you conduct a literature review before you begin to design your study?

2. What are the differences between the different types of periodicals, and on which should you rely most heavily (and why)?
3. What is the difference between a primary and a secondary source, and why should you not rely too heavily on secondary sources?
4. How do the major sources of research information differ? What are the advantages and disadvantages of each?
5. What is the difference between a nonrefereed and a refereed journal? Which is more trustworthy (and why)?
6. What is *PsycINFO* and how is it used to conduct a literature search?
7. How can you broaden or narrow a *PsycINFO* search?
8. What is *PsycARTICLES* and what are its advantages and disadvantages?
9. List and describe some of the "other" Internet-based tools for doing a literature search.
10. Why is it important to read a research report critically?
11. What initial appraisals should you make of an article you are going to read?
12. What should you look for in each section of an APA-style research article?
13. What are the factors that affect the quality of research published in journals (describe each)?
14. What constitutes research fraud and why does it occur?
15. How can research fraud be dealt with?
16. How do values affect the research process?
17. How do you develop hypotheses for research?

## KEY TERMS

| | |
|---|---|
| literature review | *PsycINFO* |
| primary source | *PsycARTICLES* |
| secondary source | *Psychological Abstracts* |
| refereed journal | *Thesaurus of Psychological Index Terms* |
| nonrefereed journal | file drawer phenomenon |
| paper session | peer review |
| personal communication | |

# 4

# Choosing a Research Design

A fter spending long hours reading and digesting the literature in a particular research area, you have isolated a behavior that needs further investigation. You have identified some
potentially important variables and probably have become familiar with the methods commonly used to measure that behavior. You may even have developed some possible explanations
for the relationships you have identified through your reading
and personal experience. You are now ready to choose a research
design that will allow you to evaluate the relationships you suspect exist.

    Choosing an appropriate research design is crucially important
to the success of your project. The decisions you make at this stage of
the research process do much to determine the quality of the conclusions you can draw from your research results. This chapter identifies
the problems you must face when choosing a research design, introduces the major types of research design, and describes how each type
attempts to solve (or at least cope with) these problems.

## FUNCTIONS OF A RESEARCH DESIGN

Scientific studies tend to focus on one or the other of two major
activities. The first activity consists of *exploratory data collection
and analysis*, which is aimed at classifying behaviors within a given
area of research, identifying potentially important variables, and
identifying relationships between those variables and the behaviors. Such exploration is typical of the early stages of research in
an area. The second activity, called *hypothesis testing*, consists of
evaluating potential explanations for the observed relationships.
Testable explanations allow you to predict what relationships
should and should not be observed if the explanation is correct.
Hypothesis testing usually begins after you have collected enough
information about the behavior to begin developing supportable
explanations.

## CAUSAL VERSUS CORRELATIONAL RELATIONSHIPS

The relationships you identify in these activities fall into two broad categories: causal and correlational. In a **causal relationship**, one variable directly or indirectly influences another. For example, if you accidentally drop a brick on your toe, the impact of the brick will probably set off a chain of events (stimulation of pain receptors in your toe, avalanche of neural impulses traveling up your leg to the spinal cord and from there to your brain, registration of pain in your brain, involuntary scream). Although there are several intervening steps between the impact of the brick on your toe and the scream, it would be proper in this case to conclude that dropping the brick on your toe *causes* you to scream. This is because it is possible to trace an unbroken chain of physical influence running from the initial event (impact of brick on toe) to final result (scream).

Causal relationships can be unidirectional, in which case variable A influences variable B but not vice versa. The impact of the brick (A) may produce a scream (B), but screaming (B) does not cause the impact of the brick on your toe (A). They also can be bidirectional, in which case each variable influences the other. Everything else being equal, reducing the amount of exercise a person gets leads to weight gain. And because of the increased effort involved, heavier people tend to exercise less. Thus, exercise influences body weight, and body weight influences exercise. Even more complex causal relationships exist, and teasing them out may require considerable ingenuity on the part of the investigator. In each case, however, one can identify a set of physical influences that tie the variables together.

Simply observing that changes in one variable tend to be associated with changes in another is not enough to establish that the relationship between them is a causal one. In a **correlational relationship**, changes in one variable accompany changes in another, but the proper tests have not been conducted to show that either variable actually influences the other. Thus, all that is known is that a relationship between them exists. When changes in one variable tend to be accompanied by specific changes in another, the two variables are said to *covary*. However, such covariation does not necessarily mean that either variable exerts an influence on the other (although it may). The number of baseball games and the number of mosquitoes tend to covary (both increase in the spring and decrease in the fall), yet you would not conclude that mosquitoes cause baseball games or vice versa.

When you first begin to develop explanations for a given behavior, knowledge of observed relationships can serve as an important guide, even though you may not yet know which relationships are causal. You simply make your best guess and then develop your explanation based on the causal relationships you think exist. The validity of your explanation will then depend in part on whether the proposed causal relationships turn out, on closer examination, to be in fact causal. Distinguishing between causal and correlational relationships is thus an important part of the research process, particularly in the hypothesis-testing phase.

Your ability to identify relationships and to distinguish causal from correlational relationships varies with the degree of control you have over the variables under study. The next sections describe two broad types of research design: correlational and experimental. Both approaches allow you to identify relationships among variables, but they differ in the degree of control exerted over variables and in the ability to identify causal relationships. We begin with correlational research.

## CORRELATIONAL RESEARCH

In **correlational research**, your main interest is to determine whether two (or more) variables covary, and, if so, to establish the directions, magnitudes, and forms of the observed relationships. The strategy involves developing measures of the variables of interest and collecting your data.

Correlational research belongs to a broader category called *nonexperimental* research, which also includes designs not specifically aimed at identifying relationships between variables. The latter type of research, for example, might seek to determine the average values and typical spread of scores on certain variables (for example, grade point average, SAT scores) in a given population (for example, applicants for admission to a particular university). Strictly speaking, such a study would be nonexperimental but not correlational. Our discussion here will focus on those nonexperimental methods used to identify and characterize relationships.

Correlational research involves observing the values of two or more variables and determining what relationships exist between them. In correlational research, you make no attempt to manipulate variables, but observe them "as is." For example, imagine that you wished to determine the nature of the relationship, if any, between pretest anxiety and test performance in introductory psychology students on campus. On test day, you have each student rate his or her own level of pretest anxiety and, after the test results are in, you determine the test performances of those same students. Your data consist of two scores for each student: self-rated anxiety level and test score. You analyze your data to determine the relationship (if any) between these variables. Note that both anxiety level and test score are simply observed as found in each student.

In some types of correlational research, you compare the average value of some variable across preformed groups of individuals, where membership in a group depends on characteristics or circumstances of the participant (such as political party affiliation, eye color, handedness, occupation, economic level, age). For example, you might compare Democrats to Republicans on attitudes toward education. Such a study would qualify as correlational research because group membership (whether Democrat or Republican) was determined by the participants' choice of party and was not in the hands of the researcher.

Establishing that a correlational relationship exists between two variables makes it possible to predict from the value of one variable the probable value of the other variable. For example, if you know that college grade point average (GPA) is correlated with Scholastic Assessment Test (SAT) scores, then you can use a student's SAT score to predict (within limits) the student's college GPA.

When you use correlational relationships for prediction, the variable used to predict is called the *predictor variable* and the variable whose value is being predicted is called the *criterion variable*. Whether the linkage between these variables is causal remains an open question.

## An Example of Correlational Research

In Chapter 1, we described how Andrea Wilson sued the maker of the popular video game Mortal Kombat after Wilson's son Noah was killed by his friend Yancy S. It was alleged that, when he committed the murder, Yancy was acting out a violent scene he had encountered previously in the game. But this allegation presupposes a direct, causal link between playing such graphically violent fantasy games and displaying aggressive behavior in real life. This hypothesis was tested in a correlational study by Craig Anderson and Karen Dill (2000).

Anderson and Dill recruited 227 introductory psychology students for the study and had them fill out a set of self-report questionnaires. The questionnaires assessed a variety of factors, including personality factors (irritability and trait aggression), delinquency (aggressive behavior and nonaggressive delinquency), severity of exposure to video game violence, time spent playing video games, perceived likelihood of being a victim of certain crimes, and feelings of safety. The resulting data were analyzed to determine what relationships existed among these variables.

Among other results, Anderson and Dill (2000) found that low exposure to video game violence was associated with relatively low levels of aggressive behavior and nonaggressive delinquency, regardless of the level of aggressive personality. In contrast, high exposure to video game violence was associated with relatively high levels of nonaggressive delinquency, but only for those scoring high in aggressive personality. (Figure 4–1 displays these results for aggressive behavior; results for nonaggressive delinquency were similar to these.)

Anderson and Dill concluded that "playing violent video games often may well cause increases in delinquent behaviors, both aggressive and nonaggressive." Furthermore, they noted that the positive association found between exposure to violent video games and aggressive personality was consistent with a developmental model in which exposure to violence in video games and other media contributes to the development of an aggressive personality.

*Assessing the Anderson and Dill Study*    What qualifies Anderson and Dill's study as a correlational study? In their study, aspects of the participants' personalities, their exposure to video games and to violent content in those video games, and self-reported levels of aggressive behavior and nonaggressive delinquency were all simply recorded as found. No attempt was made to manipulate variables in order to observe any potential effects of those variables.

## Causation and the Correlational Approach

Given Anderson and Dill's (2000) results, you might be tempted to conclude that exposure to violent video games *causes* aggressive behavior and nonaggressive delinquency. However, this conclusion that a causal relationship exists is inappropriate, even though the relationship appears compelling. Indeed, Anderson and Dill were quick to emphasize, quite properly, that "the correlational nature of [the study] means that causal statements are risky at best." Two obstacles stand in the way of drawing clear causal inferences from correlational data: the third-variable problem and the directionality problem.

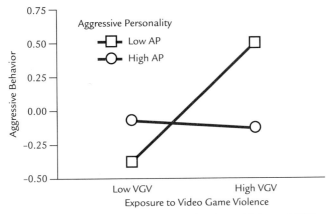

**FIGURE 4–1**    Effect of Exposure to Video Game Violence (VGV) on Aggressive Behavior as a Function of Aggressive Personality (AP).

*The Third-Variable Problem*    To establish a causal relationship between two variables, you must be able to demonstrate that variation in one of the observed variables could only be due to the influence of the other observed variable. In the example, you want to show that variation in the level of exposure to violent video games causes variation in the levels of aggressive behavior and nonaggressive delinquency. However, because the students (and not the researchers) chose how much exposure they received to violent video games, it is possible that the observed relationship between video game violence and aggressive or delinquent behaviors may actually be due to the influence of a third variable. A strong suspect in this case is the level of aggressive personality. Perhaps those who have more aggressive personalities are both more likely to enjoy playing violent video games *and* more likely to display aggressive behavior and nonaggressive delinquency. Degree of aggressive personality, then, and not the amount of exposure to violent video games, could be the real cause of differences in aggressive behavior and nonaggressive delinquency.

The possibility that correlational relationships may result from the action of an unobserved "third variable" is called the **third-variable problem**. This unobserved variable may influence both of the observed variables (e.g., exposure to video game violence and aggressive behavior), causing them to vary together even though no direct relationship exists between them. The two observed variables thus may be strongly correlated even though neither variable causes changes in the other.

To resolve the third-variable problem, you must examine the effects of each potential third variable to determine whether it does, in fact, account for the observed relationship. Techniques to evaluate and statistically control the effects of such variables are available (see Chapter 14).

*The Directionality Problem*    A second reason why it is hazardous to draw causal inferences from correlational data is that, even when a direct causal relationship exists, the direction of causality is sometimes difficult to determine. This difficulty is known as the **directionality problem**.

The directionality problem lurks in Anderson and Dill's finding of a positive relationship between level of aggression (as self-reported by the students in their questionnaires) and the amount of exposure to violent video games. You might be tempted to conclude that students become more aggressive from playing violent video games, but it seems just as reasonable to turn the causal arrow around. Perhaps finding gratification in aggressive behavior leads to a preference for playing violent video games.

## Why Use Correlational Research?

Given the problems of interpreting the results of correlational research, you may wonder why you would want to use this approach. However, correlational research has a variety of applications, and there are many reasons to consider using it. In this section, we discuss three situations in which a correlational approach makes good sense.

*Gathering Data in the Early Stages of Research*    During the initial, exploratory stage of a research project, the correlational approach's ability to identify potential causal relationships can provide a rich source of hypotheses that later may be tested experimentally. Consider the following example.

As noted in Chapter 2, Niko Tinbergen (1951) became interested in the behavior of the three-spined stickleback, a fish that inhabits the bottoms of sandy streams in Europe. Observing sticklebacks in their natural habitat, Tinbergen found that, during the spring, the male stickleback claims a small area of a stream bed and builds a cylindrically shaped nest at its center. At the same time, the male's underbelly changes from the usual dull color to a bright red, and the male begins to drive other males from the territory surrounding the nest. Female sticklebacks lack this coloration and are not driven away by the males.

These initial observations were purely correlational and as such do not allow one to draw firm conclusions with respect to cause and effect. The observations showed that the defending male's behavior toward an intruding stickleback is correlated with the intruder's physical characteristics, but which characteristics actually determine whether or not an attack will occur? Certainly many cues, such as the male's red coloration, his shape, or even perhaps his odor, could be responsible. However, these cues always appeared and disappeared together (along with the fish to which they belonged). So there was no way, through correlational study alone, to determine whether the red coloration was the actual cause of the defensive behavior or merely an ineffective correlate.

To disentangle these variables, Tinbergen turned to the experimental approach. He set up an artificial stream in his laboratory and brought in several male sticklebacks. The fish soon adapted to the new surroundings, setting up territories and building nests. Tinbergen then constructed a number of models designed to mimic several characteristics of male sticklebacks. These models ranged from one that faithfully duplicated the appearance (but not the smell) of a real stickleback to one that was just a gray disk (see Figure 4–2). Some of the models included red coloration, and some did not.

When the realistic model with a red underbelly was waved past a male stickleback in the artificial stream, the male immediately tried to drive it away. Odor obviously was not necessary to elicit defensive behavior. However, Tinbergen soon

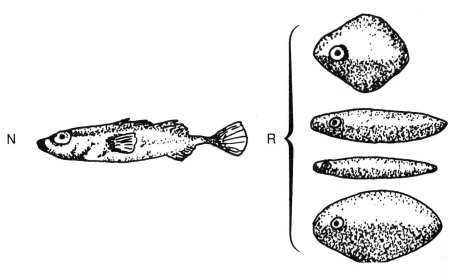

N                    R

**FIGURE 4–2**   Stimuli Used by Tinbergen to Follow Up on Initial Observations Made in the Field: N, neutral underbelly; R, red underbelly.
(SOURCE: Tinbergen, 1951. Reprinted with permission.)

discovered that almost any model with red color elicited the response. The only requirements were that the model include an eyespot near the top and that the red color appear below the eyespot.

By manipulating factors such as color and shape, Tinbergen was able to experimentally identify the factors that were necessary to elicit the behavior. The earlier, correlational research conducted in a naturalistic (and therefore poorly controlled) setting had paved the way for the more definitive research that followed.

*Inability to Manipulate Variables*   In an experimental design, variables are manipulated to determine their effects on other variables. A second reason for choosing a correlational design over an experimental one is that manipulating the variables of interest may be impossible or unethical (see Chapter 6 for a discussion of ethics). For example, imagine that you were interested in determining whether psychopathic personality develops when a child is raised by cold, uncaring parents. In order to establish a clear causal connection between the parents' behavior toward the child and psychopathic personality, you would have to conduct an experiment in which the parents' behavior was manipulated by assigning infants at random to be raised by either normal parents or cold, uncaring ones. Unfortunately, this experiment would be difficult to carry out (who would allow their child to participate in such an experiment?) and, because of its potential for inflicting serious harm on the child, unethical as well. In such cases, a correlational design may be the only practical and ethical option.

*Relating Naturally Occurring Variables*   A third situation in which a correlational research design may be chosen over an experimental design is one in which you want to see how naturally occurring variables relate in the real world. Such information can be used to make useful predictions, even if the reasons for the discovered relationships are not clear. High school grade point average, scores on the Scholastic Assessment Test (SAT), class rank, and scores on the Nelson–Denny reading comprehension test correlate well with each other and with performance in college. Knowledge of these relationships has been used to predict college success. Certain theoretical views also may lead to predictions about which real-world variables should be correlated with which. These predictions can be tested by using a correlational design.

## EXPERIMENTAL RESEARCH

Unlike correlational research, experimental research incorporates a high degree of control over the variables of your study. This control, if used properly, permits you to establish causal relationships among your variables. This section describes the defining characteristics of experimental research and explains how these characteristics enable us to identify causal relationships in data.

### Characteristics of Experimental Research

**Experimental research** has two defining characteristics: manipulation of an independent variable and control over extraneous variables. Be sure you understand these concepts, described as follows, because they are central to understanding experimental research.

*Manipulation of Independent Variables*    An **independent variable** is a variable whose values are chosen and set by the experimenter. (Another way to look at it is that the value of the independent variable is independent of the participant's behavior.) We call these set values the *levels* of the independent variable. For example, imagine you want to determine how sleep deprivation affects a person's ability to recall previously memorized material. To examine this relationship, you might assign participants to one of three groups defined by the number of hours of sleep deprivation: 0 hours (rested), 24 hours, and 48 hours. These three amounts would constitute the three levels of sleep deprivation, your independent variable.

To *manipulate* your independent variable, you must expose your participants to at least two levels of that variable. The specific conditions associated with each level are called the **treatments** of the experiment. Depending on the design of your experiment, the independent variable may be manipulated by exposing a different group of participants to each treatment or by exposing each participant to all the treatments in sequence. By manipulating the independent variable, you hope to show that changes in the level of the independent variable *cause* changes in the behavior being recorded.

The variable whose value you observe and record in experimental designs is called the **dependent variable** (or *dependent measure*). If a causal relationship exists, then the value of the dependent variable depends, at least to some extent, on the level of the independent variable. (Its value also depends on other factors, such as participant characteristics.) Another way to think about the dependent variable is that its value depends on the behavior of the participant, rather than being set by the experimenter.

Manipulating an independent variable can be as simple as exposing one group of participants to some treatment (distracting noises, for example) and another group of participants to the absence of the treatment. In this most basic of experimental designs, the group receiving the treatment is called the **experimental group** and the other group the **control group**. The control group is treated exactly like the experimental group except that it is not exposed to the experimental treatment. The performances of the two groups on the dependent measure are then compared to assess the effect of the independent variable.

Although all experiments present at least two levels of the independent variable, many do not include a no-treatment control group. A clinical study, for example, might compare a standard therapy with a new, experimental therapy of unknown effectiveness. Administering the standard therapy to the control group ensures that even the participants who do not receive the experimental treatment do not go untreated for their disorder. In both cases, the behavior of participants in the control group provides a baseline against which to compare the behavior of participants in the experimental group.

More complex experiments can be conducted using more levels of the independent variable, several independent variables, and several dependent variables. You also can choose to expose a single group, or even a single participant, to several levels of an independent variable.

*Control over Extraneous Variables*    The second characteristic of experimental research is control over extraneous variables. **Extraneous variables** are those that may affect the behavior you wish to investigate but that for the present experiment are not of interest. For example, you may be interested in determining how well a new anxiety therapy (experimental group), compared with an existing therapy (control group), affects test anxiety in anxious students. If some of your participants show up for the experiment drunk, their degree of intoxication becomes an extraneous variable. This would be especially problematic if more drunk students ended up in one group than in the other.

If allowed to vary on their own, extraneous variables can produce uncontrolled changes in the value of the dependent variable, with two rather nasty possible consequences. First, uncontrolled variability may make it difficult or impossible to detect any effects of the independent variable. (In our example, the effects of the therapy could be buried under the effects of the alcohol.) Second, uncontrolled variability may produce chance differences in behavior across the levels of the independent variable. These differences could make it appear as though the independent variable produced effects when it did not (the therapy would appear to work even though the real effect came from the alcohol). To identify clear causal relationships between your independent and dependent variables, you must control the effects of extraneous variables.

You have two ways to control these effects. The first way is simply to *hold extraneous variables constant*. If these variables do not vary over the course of your experiment, they cannot cause uncontrolled variation in your dependent variable. In the test anxiety experiment, for example, you might want to make sure that all your participants are sober (or at least intoxicated to the same degree). In fact, to the degree possible, you would want to make sure that all treatments are *exactly* alike, except for the level of the independent variable.

The second way to deal with extraneous variables is to *randomize their effects across treatments*. This technique deals with the effects of extraneous variables that cannot be held constant or, for reasons that will be explained later, should not be held constant. In an experiment assessing the effect of sleep deprivation on memory, for example, it may not be possible to ensure that all your participants have had identical amounts of sleep deprivation (some may have slept better than others the day before your experiment began) or that their recall abilities are equivalent. The idea is to distribute the effects of these differences across treatments in such a way that they tend to even out and thus cannot be mistaken for effects of the independent variable.

For statistical reasons, one of the better ways to accomplish this goal is to assign participants to treatments at random—by picking their names out of a hat, for example. This technique does not *guarantee* that the effects of extraneous variables will be distributed evenly across treatments, but it usually works reasonably well, and better yet, it allows you to use inferential statistics to evaluate the probability with which chance alone could have produced the observed differences. (We discuss the logic underlying inferential statistics in Chapter 13.) Other techniques to deal with uncontrolled extraneous variables are also available. We describe these in later chapters that cover specific design options.

However it is done, control over extraneous variables is crucial to establishing clear causal relationships between your variables. By controlling variables that might affect your dependent variable, you rule them out as possible alternative explanations for your results.

## An Example of Experimental Research

As an illustration of experimental research, consider a second study reported by Anderson and Dill (2000) examining the relationship between exposure to violent video games and aggressive behavior. (For clarity, we present a simplified version of the study's design.) As you read the description of this study, try to identify the features that qualify the study as a true experiment.

To determine whether exposure to violent video games fosters aggressive behavior, Anderson and Dill (2002) selected two video games (Castle Wolfenstein 3D and Myst) that differ in the level of violence depicted. Castle Wolfenstein 3D was selected for its "blatant violent content, realism, and human characters." Myst, in contrast, was specifically designed to be nonviolent and, like Castle Wolfenstein 3D, offers a 3D "walk through" environment. In pretesting, the two games produced similar ratings of difficulty, enjoyment, frustration, and action speed and similar levels of blood pressure and heart rate.

Participants (210 undergraduates) were randomly assigned *either* to an experimental group or to a control group. The experimental group spent several sessions playing the violent video game (Castle Wolfenstein 3D), whereas the control group spent the same number of sessions playing the nonviolent game (Myst). At certain points, the play was interrupted and participants' levels of aggressive behavior were assessed using a "competitive reaction-time task." In this task, the participants were led to believe that they were competing against a second participant seated in another room. The goal was to push a button faster than the opponent did, with the loser of each round receiving a loud blast of noise. Prior to each trial, the participant set the intensity and duration of the noise that would be delivered to the opponent. (These values were recorded for later analysis.) After each trial, the participant saw a display of the intensity and duration levels supposedly set by the opponent. Whether the participant won or lost and the levels of noise "set" by the nonexistent opponent were varied in an apparently random pattern.

Results indicated that, after losing a competitive reaction-time trial (and thus receiving a noise blast from the fictitious opponent), participants who had been playing the highly violent Castle Wolfenstein 3D game delivered significantly longer noise blasts to their opponents than participants who had been playing the nonviolent Myst game. Thus, after apparently losing a trial, those who had just been playing the violent video game tended to respond more violently (by administering a longer retaliatory blast of noise to their opponent) than those who had just been playing the nonviolent game.

**Assessing the Anderson and Dill Experiment**   Have you identified the features of the Anderson and Dill (2000) experiment that qualify it as a true experiment? If you have not done so yet, do it now, before you read the next paragraphs.

A crucial element of every true experiment is the manipulation of at least one independent variable. What is the independent variable in the Anderson and Dill study? If you said that the type of video game (violent or nonviolent) was the independent variable, you are correct. Note that the value of the independent variable to which a given participant was exposed (violent or nonviolent video game) was assigned by the experimenters; it was not chosen by the participant.

A second crucial element in an experiment is measuring a dependent variable. Can you identify the dependent variable in Anderson and Dill's experiment? If you said that the length of the noise blast delivered after a losing trial was the dependent variable, you were correct. Notice that Anderson and Dill were looking for changes in the value of the dependent variable relating to changes in the value of the independent variable.

A third crucial element of an experiment is control over extraneous variables. Were extraneous variables controlled in the Anderson and Dill experiment, and if so, how? The answer to the first part of this question is yes, and if you examine the design of the study carefully, you will see that extraneous variables were controlled using both methods described earlier. First, several extraneous variables were held constant across treatments. For example, the video games were carefully selected so that they were equally difficult and enjoyable, and produced comparable levels of frustration and action speed. And other than the game being played, both groups of participants received the same treatment. Second, the participants were assigned to their treatments at random, not according to some behavior or characteristic of the participants. This design ensured that any remaining uncontrolled differences in the participants would tend to be distributed evenly between the two treatments. As a result, the investigators could be reasonably sure that any differences found between treatments in the values of the dependent measures were caused by the difference in treatments, that is, by the difference in violent content between Castle Wolfenstein 3D and Myst.

## Strengths and Limitations of the Experimental Approach

The great strength of the experimental approach is its ability to identify and describe causal relationships. This ability is not shared by the correlational approach. Whereas the correlational approach can tell you only that changes in the value of one variable tend to accompany changes in the value of a second variable, the experimental approach can tell you whether changes in one variable (the independent variable) actually produced changes in the other (the dependent variable).

Despite its power to identify causal relationships, the experimental approach has limitations that restrict its use under certain conditions. The most serious limitation is that you cannot use the experimental method if you cannot manipulate your hypothesized causal variables. For example, studies of personality disorders must use correlational approaches to identify possible causal relationships. Exposing people to various nasty conditions in order to identify which of those conditions cause personality disorders is not ethical.

A second limitation of the experimental approach entails the tight control over extraneous factors required to clearly reveal the effects of the independent variable. Such control tends to reduce your ability to apply your findings to situations that differ from the conditions of your original experiment. A rather unpleasant trade-off exists in experimental research: As you increase the degree of control you exert over extraneous variables (and thus your ability to establish causal relationships), you decrease your ability to assess the generality of any relationships you uncover. For example, in the Anderson and Dill experiment, extraneous variables such as game difficulty and enjoyment were controlled. However, this control may limit the generality of their results, as it is possible that different results would be obtained using other games that are, for example, more difficult or less enjoyable. (We discuss the problem of generality more fully later in the chapter.)

## Experiments versus Demonstrations

One kind of research design resembles an experiment but lacks one of the crucial features of a true experiment, an independent variable. This design, called a **demonstration**, exposes a group of subjects to one (and only one) treatment condition. Remember, a true experiment requires exposing subjects to at least two treatments. Whereas a true experiment shows the effect of manipulating an independent variable, a demonstration simply shows what happens under a specified set of conditions. To conduct a demonstration, you simply expose a single group to a particular treatment and measure the resulting behavior.

Demonstrations can be useful because they show that, under such-and-such conditions, *this* happens and not *that*. However, demonstrations are not experiments and thus do not show causal relationships. This fact is sometimes overlooked, as the following example shows.

In his book *Subliminal Seduction* (1973), Wilson Bryan Key reported a study in which the participants looked at a Gilbey's Gin advertisement that allegedly had subliminal sexual messages embedded within it. The most prominent subliminal message was the word "SEX" spelled out in the bottom three ice cubes in the glass to the right of a bottle of gin (Key, 1973).

Key reported that the ad was tested "with over a thousand subjects" (the details of the study were not given). According to Key, 62 percent of the male and female participants reported feelings of sexual arousal in response to the ad. Key concluded that the subliminal messages led to sexual arousal. Key asserted that advertisers capitalize on these subliminal messages to get you to buy their products.

Now, are you convinced of the power of subliminal messages by this demonstration?

If you said you are not convinced, good for you! The fact that 62 percent of the participants reported arousal is *not* evidence that the subliminal messages caused the arousal, no matter how many participated. All you know from this demonstration is that under the conditions tested, the advertisement evoked reports of arousal in a fair proportion of the participants. You do not learn the cause.

In fact, several plausible alternatives can be offered to the explanation that the arousal was caused by subliminal perception. For example, an advertisement for alcohol may lead participants to recall how they feel when under the influence or may conjure up images of having fun at a party. As the demonstration was reported, you cannot tell which of the potential explanations is valid. What would you have to do to fully test whether subliminal messages (such as the ones in the Gilbey's Gin ad) actually lead to sexual arousal? Give this question some thought before continuing.

To test whether subliminal messages caused the arousal, you need to add a control group and randomly assign participants to groups. Participants in this control group would see the same Gilbey's Gin ad but without the subliminal messages. If 62 percent of the participants in the "subliminal" group were aroused, but only 10 percent in the control group were aroused, then you could reasonably conclude that the subliminal messages caused the arousal. A different conclusion would be drawn if 62 percent of the participants in *both* groups reported arousal. In this case, you would have to conclude that the subliminal messages were ineffective. The fact that the ad leads to reports of sexual arousal (as shown by the demonstration) would have to be explained by some other factor. By the way, most of the controlled, scientific research on subliminal perception shows little or no effect of subliminal messages on behavior.

## INTERNAL AND EXTERNAL VALIDITY

Whether the general design of your study will be experimental or correlational, you need to consider carefully two important but often conflicting attributes of any design: its internal and external validity. In this section we define these concepts and briefly discuss the factors you should consider relating to internal and external validity when choosing a research design.

### Internal Validity

Much of your research will be aimed at testing the hypotheses you developed long before you collected any data. The ability of your research design to adequately test your hypotheses is known as its **internal validity** (Campbell & Stanley, 1963). Essentially, internal validity is the ability of your design to test the hypothesis it was designed to test.

In an experiment, this means showing that variation in the independent variable caused the observed variation in the dependent variable. In a correlational study, it means showing that changes in the value of your criterion variable relate solely to changes in the value of your predictor variable and not to changes in other, extraneous variables that may have varied along with your predictor variable.

Internal validity is threatened to the extent that extraneous variables can provide alternative explanations for the findings of a study, or as Huck and Sandler (1979) called them, *rival hypotheses*. As an example, imagine that an instructor wants to know whether a new teaching method works better than the traditional method used with students in an introductory psychology course. The instructor decides to answer this question by teaching her morning section of introductory psychology using the new method and her afternoon section using the traditional method. Both sections will use the same text, cover the same material, and receive the same tests. The effectiveness of the two methods will be assessed by comparing the average scores achieved on the test by the two sections. Now, imagine that the instructor conducts the study and finds that the section receiving the new method receives a substantially higher average grade than the section receiving the traditional method. She concludes that the new method is definitely better for teaching introductory psychology. Is she justified in drawing this conclusion?

The answer, as you probably suspected, is no. Several rival hypotheses cannot be eliminated by the study, explanations at least as credible as the instructor's view that the new method was responsible for the observed improvement in average grade. Consider the following rival hypotheses:

1. The morning students did better because they were "fresher" than the afternoon students.

2. The morning students did better because their instructor was "fresher" in the morning than in the afternoon.

3. The instructor expected the new method to work better and thus was more enthusiastic when using the new method than when using the old one.

4. Students who registered for the morning class were more motivated to do well in the course than those who registered for the afternoon class.

These rival hypotheses do not exhaust the possibilities; perhaps you can think of others. Because the study was not designed to rule out these alternatives, there is no way to know whether the observed difference between the two sections in student performance was due to the difference in teaching methods, instructor enthusiasm, alertness of the students, or other factors whose levels differed across the sections. Whenever two or more variables combine in such a way that their effects cannot be separated, a **confounding** of those variables has occurred. In the teaching study, teaching method is confounded by all those variables just listed and more. Such a study lacks internal validity.

Confounding, although always a matter of concern, does not necessarily present a serious threat to internal validity. Confounding is less problematic when the confounding variable is known to have little or no effect on the dependent or criterion variable or when its known effect can be taken into account in the analysis. For example, in the teaching study, it may be possible to eliminate concern about the difference in class meeting times by comparing classes that meet at different times but use the same teaching method. Such data may show that meeting time has only a small effect that can be ignored. If meeting time had a larger effect, you could arrange your study of teaching method so that the effect of meeting time would tend to make the new teaching method appear worse than the standard one, thus biasing the results against your hypothesis. If your results still favored the new teaching method, that outcome would have occurred despite the confounding rather than because of it. Thus, a study may include confounding and still maintain a fair degree of internal validity, if the effects of the confounding variable in the situation under scrutiny are known.

This is fortunate, because it is often impossible to eliminate all sources of confounding in a study. For example, the instructor in our example might have attempted to eliminate confounding by having students randomly assigned to two sections meeting simultaneously. This would certainly eliminate those sources of confounding related to any difference in the time at which the sections met, but now it would be impossible for the instructor to teach both classes. If a second instructor is recruited to teach one of the sections using the standard method, this introduces a new source of confounding in that the two instructors may not be equivalent in a number of ways that could affect class performance. Often the best that can be done is to substitute what you believe to be less serious threats to internal validity for the more serious ones.

*Threats to Internal Validity*     Confounding variables occur in both experimental and correlational designs, but they are far more likely to be a problem in the latter, in which tight control over extraneous variables is usually lacking. Campbell and Stanley (1963) identified seven general sources of confounding that may affect internal validity: history, maturation, testing, instrumentation, statistical regression, biased selection of subjects, and experimental morality (see Table 4–1).

*History* may confound studies in which multiple observations are taken over time. Specific events may occur between observations that affect the results. For example, a study of the effectiveness of an advertising campaign against drunk driving might measure the number of arrests for drunk driving immediately before and after the campaign. If the police institute a crackdown on drunk driving at the same time that the advertisements air, this event will destroy the internal validity of your study.

*Maturation* refers to the effect of age or fatigue. Performance changes observed over time due to these factors may confound those due to the variables being studied. You might, for example, assess performance on a proofreading task before and after some experimental manipulation. Decreased performance on the second proofreading assessment may be due to fatigue rather than to any effect of your manipulation.

*Testing* effects occur when a pretest sensitizes participants to what you are investigating in your study. As a consequence, they may respond differently on a post-treatment measure than if no pretest were given. For example, if you measure participants' racial attitudes and then manipulate race in an experiment on person perception, participants may respond to the treatment differently than if no such pretest of racial attitudes was given.

In *instrumentation*, confounding may be introduced by unobserved changes in criteria used by observers or in instrument calibration. If observers change what

TABLE 4–1    **Factors Affecting Internal Validity**

| FACTOR | DESCRIPTION |
| --- | --- |
| History | Specific events other than the treatment occur between observations |
| Maturation | Performance changes due to age or fatigue confound the effect of the treatment |
| Testing | Testing prior to the treatment changes how subjects respond in post-treatment testing |
| Instrumentation | Unobserved changes in observer criteria or instrument calibration confound the effect of the treatment |
| Statistical regression | Subjects selected for treatment on the basis of their extreme scores tend to move closer to the mean on retesting |
| Biased selection of subjects | Groups of subjects exposed to different treatments are not equivalent prior to treatment |
| Experimental mortality | Differential loss of subjects from the groups of a study results in nonequivalent groups |

counts as "verbal aggression" when scoring behavior under two experimental conditions, any apparent difference between those conditions in verbal aggression could be due as much to the changed criterion as to any effect of the independent variable. Similarly, if an instrument used to record activity of rats in a cage becomes more (or less) sensitive over time, it becomes impossible to tell whether activity is really changing or just the ability of the instrument to detect activity.

*Statistical regression* threatens internal validity when participants have been selected based on extreme scores on some measure. When measured again, scores will tend to be closer to the average in the population. Thus, if students are targeted for a special reading program based on their unusually low reading test scores, they will tend to do better, on average, on retesting even if the reading program has no effect.

*Biased selection of subjects* threatens internal validity because subjects may differ initially in ways that affect their scores on the dependent measure. Any influence of the independent variable on scores cannot be separated from the effect of the preexisting bias. This problem typically arises when researchers use preexisting groups in their studies rather than assigning subjects to groups at random. For example, the effect of a program designed to improve worker job satisfaction might be evaluated by administering the program to workers at one factory (experimental group) and then comparing the level of job satisfaction of those workers to that of workers at another factory where the program was not given (control group). If workers given the job satisfaction program indicate more satisfaction with their jobs, is it due to the program or to preexisting differences between the two groups? There is no way to tell.

Finally, *experimental mortality* refers to the differential loss of participants from groups in a study. For example, imagine that some people drop out of a study because of frustration with the task. A group exposed to difficult conditions is more likely to lose its frustration-intolerant participants than one exposed to less difficult conditions. Any differences between the groups in performance may be due as much to the resulting difference in participants as to any difference in conditions.

*Enhancing Internal Validity*    The time to be concerned with internal validity is during the design phase of your study. During this phase, you should carefully plan which variables will be manipulated or observed and recorded, identify any plausible rival hypotheses not eliminated in your initial design, and redesign so as to eliminate those that seriously threaten internal validity. Discovering problems with internal validity after you have run your study is too late. A poorly designed study cannot be fixed later on.

## External Validity

A study has **external validity** to the degree that its results can be extended beyond the limited research setting and sample in which they were obtained. A common complaint about research using white rats or college students and conducted under the artificial conditions of the laboratory is that it may tell us little about how white rats and college sophomores (let alone animals or people in general) behave under the conditions imposed on them in the much richer arena of the real world.

The idea seems to be that all studies *should* be conducted in such a way that the findings can be generalized immediately to real-world situations and to larger populations. However, as Mook (1983) noted, it is a fallacy to assume "that the purpose of collecting data in the laboratory is to *predict real-life behavior in the real world*" (p. 381). Mook points out that much of the research conducted in the laboratory is designed to determine:

1. whether something *can* happen, rather than whether it typically *does* happen,

2. whether something we specify *ought* to happen (according to some hypothesis) under specific conditions in the lab *does* happen there under those conditions,

   or

3. what happens under conditions not encountered in the real world.

In each of these cases, the objective is to gain insight into the underlying mechanisms of behavior rather than to discover relationships that apply under normal conditions in the real world. It is this understanding that generalizes to everyday life, not the specific findings themselves.

*Threats to External Validity*    In Chapter 1, we distinguished between basic research, which is aimed at developing a better understanding of the underlying mechanisms of behavior, and applied research, which is aimed at developing information that can be directly applied to solve real-world problems. The question of external validity may be less relevant in basic research settings that seek theoretical reasons to determine what will happen under conditions not usually found in natural settings or that examine fundamental processes expected to operate under a wide variety of conditions. The degree of external validity of a study becomes more relevant when the findings are expected to be applied directly to real-world settings. In such studies, external validity is affected by several factors. Using highly controlled laboratory settings (as opposed to naturalistic settings) is one such factor. Data obtained from a tightly controlled laboratory may not generalize to more naturalistic situations in which behavior occurs. Other factors that affect external validity, as discussed by Campbell and Stanley (1963), are listed and briefly described in Table 4–2. Many of these threats to external validity are discussed in later chapters, along with the appropriate research design.

### Internal versus External Validity

Although you should strive to achieve a high degree of both internal and external validity in your research, in practice you will find that the steps you take to increase one type of validity tend to decrease the other. For example, a tightly controlled laboratory experiment affords you a relatively high degree of internal validity. Your findings, however, may not generalize to other samples and situations; thus, external validity may be reduced. Often the best you can do is reach a compromise on the relative amounts of internal and external validity in your research.

Whether internal or external validity is more important depends on your reasons for conducting the research. If you are most interested in testing a theoretical position (as is often the case in basic research), you might be more concerned with internal than external validity and hence conduct a tightly controlled laboratory experiment. However, if you are more concerned with applying your results to a real-world problem (as in applied research), you might take steps to increase the external validity while attempting to maintain a reasonable degree of internal validity. These issues need to be considered at the time you design your study.

As just mentioned, the setting in which you conduct your research strongly influences the internal and external validity of your results. The kinds of setting available and the issues you should consider when choosing a research setting are the topics we take up next.

## RESEARCH SETTINGS

In addition to deciding on the design of your research, you also must decide on the setting in which you conduct your research. Your choice of setting is affected by the potential costs of the setting, its convenience, ethical considerations, and the research question you are addressing.

The two research settings open for psychological research are the laboratory and the field. For this discussion, the term *laboratory* is used in a broad sense. A laboratory is any research setting that is artificial relative to the setting in which the behavior naturally occurs. This definition is not limited to a special room with special equipment for research. A laboratory can be a formal lab, but it also can be a classroom,

TABLE 4–2  Factors Affecting External Validity

| FACTOR | DESCRIPTION |
| --- | --- |
| Reactive testing | Occurs when a pretest affects participants' reaction to an experimental variable, making those participants' responses unrepresentative of the general population. |
| Interactions between participant selection biases and the independent variable | Effects observed may apply only to the participants included in the study, especially if they are a unique group (such as college sophomores rather than a cross section of adults). |
| Reactive effects of experimental arrangements | Refers to the effects of highly artificial experimental situations used in some research and the participant's knowledge that he or she is a research subject. |
| Multiple treatment interference | Occurs when participants are exposed to multiple experimental treatments in which exposure to early treatments affects responses to later treatments. |

a room in the library, or a room in the student union building. In contrast, the *field* is the setting in which the behavior under study naturally occurs.

Your decision concerning the setting for your research is an important one, so you must be familiar with the relative advantages and disadvantages of each.

## The Laboratory Setting

If you choose to conduct your research in a *laboratory setting*, you gain important control over the variables that could affect your results. The degree of control depends on the nature of the laboratory setting. For example, if you are interested in animal learning, you can structure the setting to eliminate virtually all extraneous variables that could affect the course of learning. This is what Ivan Pavlov did in his investigations of classical conditioning. Pavlov exposed dogs to his experimental conditions while the dogs stood in a sound-shielded room. The shielded room permitted Pavlov to investigate the impact of the experimental stimuli free from any interfering sounds. Like Pavlov, you can control important variables within the laboratory that could affect the outcome of your research.

Complete control over extraneous variables may not be possible in all laboratory settings. For example, if you were administering your study to a large group of students in a psychology class, you could not control all the variables as well as you might wish (students may arrive late or disruptions may occur in the hallway). For the most part, the laboratory affords more control over the research situation than does the field.

*Simulation: Re-creating the World in the Laboratory*   When you choose the laboratory as your research setting, you gain control over extraneous variables that could affect the value of your dependent variable. However, you make a trade-off when choosing the laboratory. Although you gain better control over variables, your results may lose some generality (the ability to apply your results beyond your specific laboratory conditions). If you are concerned with the ability to generalize your results, as well as with controlling extraneous variables, consider using a **simulation**. In a simulation, you attempt to re-create (as closely as possible) a real-world situation in the laboratory. Carefully designed and executed simulation may increase the generality of results. Because this strategy has been used with increasing frequency lately, a detailed discussion is in order.

*Why Simulate*    You may decide for a variety of reasons to simulate rather than conduct research in the real world. You may choose simulation because the behavior of interest could not be studied ethically in the real world. For example, Chapter 1 mentioned factors that control panic behavior. Re-creating a panic situation in order to study the ensuing behavior is unethical. If you were interested in studying how juries reach a decision, you could not eavesdrop on real juries. However, you could conduct a jury simulation study and analyze the deliberations of the simulated juries.

Often researchers choose to simulate for practical reasons. A simulation may be used because studying a behavior under its naturally occurring conditions is expensive and time-consuming. By simulating in the laboratory, the researcher also gains the advantage of retaining control over variables while studying the behavior under relatively realistic conditions.

*Designing a Simulation*    For a simulation to improve the generality of laboratory-based research, it must be properly designed. Observe the actual situation and study it carefully (Winkel & Sasanoff, 1970). Identify the crucial elements and then try to reproduce them in the laboratory. The more realistic the simulation, the greater are the chances that the results will be applicable to the simulated real-world phenomenon. As an example, suppose you were interested in studying the interpersonal relationships and dynamics that evolve in prisons. It might be difficult to conduct your study in an actual prison, so you might consider a simulation. In fact Haney, Banks, and Zimbardo (1973) did just that.

In their now-famous Stanford prison study, Haney et al. constructed a prison in the basement of the psychology building at Stanford University. Participants in the study were randomly assigned to be either prisoners or prison guards. Those participants assigned to be prisoners were "arrested" by the police, fingerprinted, and incarcerated in the simulated prison. Treatment of the prisoner-participants was like that of actual prisoners: They were issued numbers and drab uniforms and were assigned to cells. Prison guards were issued uniforms, badges, and nightsticks. Their instructions were to maintain order within the simulated prison.

The behavior of the participants within the simulated prison was observed by a team of social psychologists. Behavior within the simulated prison was similar to (though less extreme than) behavior in a real prison. Guards developed rigid and sometimes demeaning rules, and prisoners banded together in a hunger strike. In fact, the simulation was so real for the participants that the experiment had to be discontinued after only a few days.

*Realism*    Most researchers would agree that a simulation should be as realistic as possible (as was the case in the Stanford prison study). The physical reality created in the Stanford prison study probably helped participants become immersed in their roles. However, a simulation may not have to be highly realistic to adequately test a hypothesis. For example, many jury simulation studies do not re-create the physical setting of a courtroom. However, many of these studies are highly involving and compelling for the participants.

The importance of the "realism" of a simulation depends in part on the definition of realism you adopt. Aronson and Carlsmith (1968) distinguish between two types of realism: mundane and experimental. The term *mundane realism* refers to the degree to which a simulation mirrors the real-world event. In contrast, *experimental realism* refers to the degree to which the simulation psychologically involves the participants in the experiment.

Simulation has become an important issue in the area of social psychology and law. Many researchers have used simulation methods to study issues such as plea bargaining and jury decision making. A simulation in which a courtroom is realistically reconstructed in the laboratory could have high mundane realism. However, such high levels of mundane realism do not guarantee that the results of the study will be any more valid than those of the same study conducted in a more ordinary laboratory setting. Experimental realism is an important factor to be considered. An involving task in a laboratory with low mundane realism may produce more general results than a less involving task in a laboratory with high mundane realism.

A good illustration of the importance of experimental realism comes from a study by Wilson and Donnerstein (1977). These researchers reported that a crucial factor in the applicability of simulated jury research findings is whether or not the participant believes that his or her decision will have real consequences. As an independent variable, Wilson and Donnerstein varied whether or not participants believed that their decisions would have consequences. They found that when participants believed that their judgments had consequences, the defendant's character (a variable previously shown in other research to be an important factor in the decision process) was no longer important.

Leading the participant to believe that his or her decision has consequences beyond the advancement of science increases experimental realism and thus increases the generality of the results. You may be able to increase the generality of your results when designing simulation studies by taking steps to increase not only mundane realism but also experimental realism.

To summarize, the laboratory approach to research has the advantage of allowing you to control variables and thus to isolate the effects of the variables under study. However, in gaining such control over variables, you lose a degree of generality of results. Using simulations that are high in experimental realism may improve the ability to generalize laboratory results in the real world.

## The Field Setting

*Field research* is research conducted outside the laboratory in the participants' natural environment (the "field"). In this section, we briefly discuss conducting experiments in the field. However, most field research employs nonexperimental (correlational) methods such as naturalistic observation or survey designs. We discuss these nonexperimental methods in Chapters 7 and 8.

***The Field Experiment***    A field experiment is an experiment conducted in the participant's natural environment. In a field experiment (as in a laboratory experiment), you manipulate independent variables and measure a dependent variable. You decide which variables to manipulate, how to manipulate them, and when to manipulate them. Essentially, the field experiment has all the qualities of the laboratory experiment except that the research is conducted in the real world rather than in the artificial laboratory setting.

As an example, consider a field experiment conducted by Bernd Schmitt, Laurette Dube, and France Leclerc (1992) on reactions of individuals to those who cut into a waiting line. These researchers reasoned that waiting lines (e.g., a line of people waiting to purchase tickets to a concert) are rudimentary social systems that have rules governing them. One such rule is that everyone waits his or her turn. They expected that people waiting in line would be upset if someone cut into the line, especially if the reason for the intrusion was illegitimate.

Schmitt et al. conducted their field experiment in the Grand Central railroad station in New York City. Confederates working for the experimenters intruded on 123 waiting lines that had formed in front of a counter. The researchers varied whether intrusion was illegitimate or legitimate. In the illegitimate intrusion condition the confederate approached a person (the participant) who was already in line and said "Excuse me, I'd like to get in here" and then cut into line. In the legitimate condition, the intruder pretended to know another confederate who was in line in front of the participant and said "Hi, what are you doing here?" and then turned to the participant and said "Excuse me, I'd like to get in here." The participant's verbal, nonverbal, and emotional reactions to the intrusion were recorded by the confederate acting as the intruder.

The results showed that most participants waiting in line showed no reaction to the confederate's intrusion. However, among those who reacted, participants were more likely to react (nonverbally or verbally) when the intrusion was illegitimate (48%) than when it was legitimate (11.6%). In addition, participants appeared more emotionally upset when the intrusion was illegitimate than legitimate.

This field experiment has all the elements of a true experiment. An independent variable was systematically manipulated (illegitimate versus legitimate intrusion) and dependent variables were measured (e.g., the reaction of the participant in line). Hence causal inferences about helping behavior can be made from the observations.

***Advantages and Disadvantages of the Field Experiment***    As with the laboratory experiment, the field experiment has its advantages and disadvantages. Because the research is conducted in the real world, one important advantage is that the results can be easily generalized to the real world. An important disadvantage is that you have little control over potential confounding variables. In the Schmitt, Dube, and Leclerc field experiment, for example, the researchers could not control how many people were in line at any given time nor could they control the number of counters that were open. Each of these variables could affect the reaction of a person standing in line waiting to approach a counter. These sources of confounding can make interpreting results from field experiments hazardous.

## A Look Ahead

At this point, you have been introduced to the broad issues you should consider when choosing a research design, the basic design options available to you, and the strengths and weaknesses of each choice. Before you are ready to conduct your first study, you also will need to know how to measure your variables; what methods of observation are available; how to conduct systematic, reliable, and objective observations; how to choose participants and deal with them ethically; how to minimize participant and experimenter biases; and many other details concerning specific research designs. In the next chapter, we consider how to go about making systematic, scientifically valid observations.

## SUMMARY

Some of the most important decisions you will make about your research concern its basic design and the setting in which it will be conducted. Research designs serve one or both of two major functions: (1) exploratory data collection and analysis (to identify new phenomena and relationships) and (2) hypothesis testing (to check the adequacy of proposed explanations). In the latter case, it is particularly important to distinguish causal from correlational relationships between variables. The relationship is causal if one variable directly influences the other. The relationship is correlational if the two variables simply change values together (covary) and may or may not directly influence one another.

Two basic designs are available for determining relationships between variables: correlational designs and experimental designs. Correlational research involves collecting data on two or more variables across subjects or time periods. The states of the variables are simply observed or measured "as is" and not manipulated. Participants enter a correlational study already "assigned" to values of the variables of interest by nature or circumstances. Correlational designs can establish the existence of relationships between the observed variables and determine the direction of the relationships. However, two problems prevent such designs from determining whether the relationships are causal. The third-variable problem arises because of the possibility that a third, unmeasured variable influences both observed variables in such a way as to produce the correlation between them. The directionality problem arises because even if two variables are causally related, correlational designs cannot determine in which direction the causal arrow points.

Despite its limitations, correlational research is useful on several accounts. It provides a good method for identifying potential causal relationships during the early stages of a research project, can be used to identify relationships when the variables of interest cannot or should not be manipulated, and can show how variables relate to one another in the real world outside the laboratory. Such relationships can be used to make predictions even when the reasons for the correlation are unknown. A variable in a correlational relationship that is used to make predictions is termed a *predictor variable*, whereas a variable whose value is being predicted is termed a *criterion variable*.

Experimental designs provide strong control over variables and allow you to establish whether variables are causally related. The defining characteristics of experimental research are (1) manipulation of an independent variable and (2) control over extraneous variables. Independent variables are manipulated by exposing subjects to different values or levels and then assessing differences in the participants' behavior across the levels. The observed behavior constitutes the dependent variable of the study. Extraneous variables are controlled by holding them constant, if possible, or by randomizing their effects across the levels of the independent variable.

The simplest experimental designs involve two groups of participants. The experimental group receives the experimental treatment; the control group is treated identically except that it does not receive the treatment. More complex designs may include more levels of the independent variable, more independent variables, or more dependent variables.

Although experiments can identify causal relationships, in some situations they cannot or should not be used. Variables may be impossible to manipulate, or it may not be ethical to do so. In addition, tight control over extraneous variables may limit the generality of the results.

A demonstration is a type of nonexperimental design that resembles an experiment but lacks manipulation of an independent variable. It is useful for showing what sorts of behaviors occur under specific conditions, but it cannot identify relationships among variables.

Two important characteristics of any design are its internal and external validity. Internal validity is the ability of a design to test what it was intended to test. Results from designs low in internal validity are likely to be unreliable. A serious threat to internal validity comes from confounding. Confounding exists in a design when two variables are linked in such a way that the effects of one cannot be separated from the effects of the other. External validity is the ability of a design to produce results that apply beyond the sample and situation within which the data were collected. Results from designs low in external validity have little generality when applied directly to real-world situations. However, not all research is designed for such application; nonapplied studies need not possess high external validity.

After deciding on a research design, you must then decide on a setting for your research. You can conduct your research in the laboratory or in the field. The laboratory setting affords you almost total control over your variables. You can tightly control extraneous variables that might confound your results. Laboratory studies, however, tend to have a degree of artificiality. You cannot be sure the results you obtain in the laboratory apply to real-world behavior. Simulation is a technique in which you seek to recreate the setting in which the behavior naturally occurs. The success of your simulation depends on its realism, which is of two types. Mundane realism is the degree to which your simulation re-creates a real-world environment. Experimental realism concerns how involved in your study your participants become. High levels of mundane realism do not guarantee a valid simulation. Experimental realism is often more important.

Field research is conducted in your participants' natural environment. Although this setting allows you to generalize your results to the real world, you lose control over extraneous variables. Field experiments therefore tend to have high external validity but relatively low internal validity.

## REVIEW QUESTIONS

1. How are correlational and causal relationships similar, and how are they different?
2. What features of research allow you to draw causal inferences from your data?
3. What are the defining features of correlational research?
4. Why is it inappropriate to draw causal inferences from correlational data?
5. Under what conditions is correlational research preferred over experimental research?
6. What are the characteristics of experimental research?
7. What is the relationship between an independent and a dependent variable in an experiment?
8. How do extraneous variables affect your research?
9. What can be done to control extraneous variables?
10. How does a demonstration differ from a true experiment?
11. What is the value of doing a demonstration?
12. What is internal validity and why is it important?
13. What factors threaten internal validity?
14. How do confounding variables threaten internal validity, and how can they be avoided?
15. What is external validity, and when is it important to have high levels of external validity?
16. How do internal and external validity relate to one another?
17. What is a simulation, and why would you use one?
18. How does the realism of a simulation relate to the validity of the results obtained from a simulation?
19. What are the defining features of laboratory and field research?
20. What are the relative advantages and disadvantages of laboratory and field research?

## KEY TERMS

| | |
|---|---|
| causal relationship | experimental group |
| correlational relationship | control group |
| correlational research | extraneous variable |
| third-variable problem | demonstration |
| directionality problem | internal validity |
| experimental research | confounding |
| independent variable | external validity |
| treatment | simulation |
| dependent variable | |

# 5

**Deciding What to Observe**

**Choosing Specific Variables
for Your Study**

Research Tradition

Theory

Availability of New Techniques

Availability of Equipment

**Choosing Your Measures**

Reliability of a Measure

Accuracy of a Measure

Validity of a Measure

Acceptance as an Established
Measure

Scale of Measurement
of a Measure

Variables and Scales
of Measurement

Choosing a Scale of Measurement

Adequacy of a Dependent Measure

Tailoring Your Measures to Your
Research Participants

Types of Dependent Variables and
How to Use Them

**Choosing When to Observe**

**The Reactive Nature of
Psychological Measurement**

Reactivity in Research with Human
Participants

Demand Characteristics

Other Influences

The Role of the Experimenter

Reactivity in Research
with Animal Subjects

**Automating Your Experiments**

**Detecting and Correcting Problems**

Conducting a Pilot Study

Adding Manipulation Checks

# Making Systematic Observations

The everyday observations we make (the weather is hot and humid today; Martha is unusually grouchy; I'm feeling grouchy, too) are generally unsystematic, informal, and made haphazardly, without a plan. In contrast, scientific observations are systematic: What will be observed, how the observations will be made, and when the observations will be made are all carefully planned in advance of the actual observation.

Information recorded in this systematic way becomes the data of your study. Your conclusions come from these data, so it is important that you understand how your choice of variables to observe, methods of measurement, and conditions of observation affect the conclusions you can legitimately draw. This chapter provides the information you need to make these choices intelligently.

## DECIDING WHAT TO OBSERVE

Chapters 2, 3, and 4 discussed how to obtain and develop a research idea and how to select a general strategy to attack the questions your research idea raises. After you select a specific question to investigate, you must decide exactly what to observe. Most research situations offer many ways to address a single question.

As one example, assume you want to study the relationship between weather and mood. Your general research question involves how the weather relates to a person's mood. You must decide what specific observations to make. First, you must specify what you mean by "weather." "Weather" can be defined in terms of a number of specific variables such as barometric pressure, air temperature, humidity, amount of sunlight, and perhaps the type and amount of precipitation. You may want to measure and record all these variables, or you may want to define weather in terms of some combination of these variables. For example, you could dichotomize weather into two general categories: gloomy (cloudy or foggy, humid, low barometric pressure) and zesty (sunny, dry, high barometric pressure).

You also must decide how to index the moods of your participants. Again a number of possibilities exist. You may choose to have participants rate their own moods, perhaps by using the Mood Adjective Check List (Nowlis & Green, 1957, cited in Walster, Walster, & Berscheid, 1978); or you may decide to gauge the moods of your participants through observation of mood-related behaviors. In this example, you have translated your general research idea into action by selecting particular observations to make. Note that the same general variables (weather, mood) can be defined and measured in a number of ways. As discussed in Chapter 2, the specific way you choose to measure a variable becomes the *operational definition* of that variable within the context of your study. How you choose to operationalize a variable, and thus to observe and measure it, affects how you will later analyze your data and determines what conclusions you can draw from that analysis. So you should carefully consider what variables to observe and manipulate and how to operationally define them.

## CHOOSING SPECIFIC VARIABLES FOR YOUR STUDY

Assuming you have decided on a general research topic, a number of factors may influence your choice of specific variables to observe and manipulate. Some of them are research tradition, theory, availability of new techniques, and availability of equipment.

### Research Tradition

If your topic follows up on previous research in a particular area, the variables you choose to observe may be the same as those previously studied. In particular, you may choose to study the same dependent variables while manipulating new independent variables. For example, research on operant conditioning typically focuses on how various factors affect the rate of lever pressing (in rats) or key pecking (in pigeons). In experiments on cognitive processing, reaction times are frequently recorded in order to determine how long a hypothesized process requires to complete. Using these traditional measures allows you to compare the results of different manipulations across experiments.

### Theory

Your decision about what to observe may depend on a particular theoretical point of view. For example, you may choose to observe behaviors that are seen as important from a certain theoretical perspective. If these behaviors (or other variables) have been used in previous research, you probably should use the measures already developed for them. However, the theory may suggest looking at behaviors not previously observed, in which case you may need to develop your own measures.

### Availability of New Techniques

Sometimes a variable cannot be investigated because there is no suitable way to measure it. In this case, the development of new techniques may open the way to observation and experimentation. You may want to use the new measure simply to explore its potential for answering your research question. As an example, consider the development of positron emission tomography (PET), a technique allowing researchers to visualize the level of activity of parts of a person's brain. A scanner picks up positrons (positively charged electrical particles) emitted by radioactively labeled glucose, which is being absorbed by neurons of the cerebral cortex to fuel their metabolic activity. More active neurons absorb more glucose and therefore emit more positrons. A computer translates the rates of positron emission in various regions of the cortex into a color-coded image of the cortex on the computer's display screen. By keeping track of changes in the colors, an observer can determine the ongoing pattern of neural activity.

This technology has enabled researchers to observe which parts of the cortex are most active during a variety of cognitive tasks. For example, using PET technology, Hakan Fischer, Jesper Anderson, Thoms Furmark, Gustav Wik, and Mats Fredrikson (2002) found increased metabolic activity in the right medial gyrus of the prefrontal cortex when an individual was presented with a fear-inducing stimulus. No such activity was found when an individual was presented with a nonfear control stimulus. Thus, using PET scan technology, Fischer et al. were able to confirm the role of the prefrontal cortex in mediating fear responses.

### Availability of Equipment

You are always tempted to adopt measures for which you already are equipped. For example, if you have invested in an operant chamber equipped with a lever and feeder, you may find it easier to continue your studies of operant conditioning by using this equipment rather than starting from scratch. Perhaps this equipment makes it trivially easy to collect data on response frequency (number of lever presses per minute) but does not readily yield information about response duration (amount of time the lever is depressed) or response force (amount of pressure exerted on the lever). You may decide that measuring response frequency will be adequate to answer your research question, particularly if previous research has successfully used this measure.

If the chosen measures provide reasonable answers to your research questions, this decision is not wrong. Problems arise when the measure really is not appropriate or adequate for the question being investigated but is chosen anyway on the basis of mere convenience. If you have chosen a particular measure simply because it is readily available or convenient, you should ask yourself whether it really *is* the best measure for your question.

The decision of how to observe the behavior and other variables of your study requires that you select appropriate measures of these variables. The next section examines some issues you need to consider when choosing measures of your variables.

## CHOOSING YOUR MEASURES

Whether your research design is experimental or correlational, your study will involve measuring the values of those variables included in the design. Yet there are many ways in which a given variable can be measured, and some may prove better for your purposes than others. In this section we describe several important characteristics of a measure that you should consider before adopting it for your study, including its reliability, its accuracy, its validity, and the level of measurement it represents. We then discuss two additional factors that affect the adequacy of a dependent measure: its sensitivity and its susceptibility to range effects. Next, we take up the problem of tailoring your measures to your research participants. Measures must be adapted to the special situations posed, for example, by the testing of young children. Finally, we identify and describe several types of behavioral measure commonly used in psychological research.

## Reliability of a Measure

The **reliability** of a measure concerns its ability to produce similar results when repeated measurements are made under identical conditions. Imagine weighing yourself several times in quick succession using an ordinary bathroom scale. You expect to see the same body weight appear on the scale each time, but if the scale is cheap or worn, the numbers may vary by one or two pounds, or even worse. The more variability you observe, the less reliable is the measure. Procedures used to assess reliability differ depending on the type of measure, as discussed next.

*Reliability of a Physical Measure*   The reliability of measures of physical variables such as height and weight are assessed by repeatedly measuring a fixed quantity of the variable and using the observed variation in measured value to derive the *precision* of the measure, which represents the range of variation to be expected on repeated measurement. For example, the precision of weighings produced by a given bathroom scale might be reported as ±1.2 pounds. A more precise measurement has a smaller range of variation.

*Reliability of Population Estimates*   For measures of opinion, attitude, and similar psychological variables, in which the problem is to estimate the average value of the variable in a given population based on a sample drawn from that population, the precision of the estimate (its likely variation from sample to sample) is called the *margin of error*. The results of a poll of registered voters asking whether the voter favors or opposes stronger legislation on gun control might be reported as "41 percent favor stronger legislation, 54 percent against, and 5 percent are unsure, with a margin of error of ±3 percent."

*Reliability of Judgments or Ratings by Multiple Observers*   When the measure being made consists of judgments or ratings of multiple observers, you can establish the degree of agreement among observers by using a statistical measure of *interrater reliability*. We describe ways to assess interrater reliability in Chapter 6.

*Reliability of Psychological Tests or Measures*   Assessing the reliability of measures of psychological variables such as intelligence, introversion/extraversion, anxiety level, mood, and so on poses a special difficulty in that these variables tend to change naturally over time. By the time you repeat a measurement of mood or anxiety level, for example, the underlying quantity being measured in the individual may have changed. If so, the measure will appear to be unreliable even though the changes in measured value reflect real changes in the variable. In addition, for various reasons, it is often not possible to administer psychological assessment devices to the same individuals a sufficient number of times to determine the precision of the measure. Thus, an alternative strategy is needed for assessing the reliability of these measures.

The basic strategy for assessing the reliability of psychological measures is to administer the assessment twice to a large group of individuals and then determine the *correlation* (Pearson r) between the scores on the first and second administrations. The higher the correlation, the greater the reliability. A test is considered to have high reliability if r is 0.95 or higher. (See Chapter 12 for a discussion of the Pearson r statistic.)

You can choose among several methods for assessing the reliability of a psychological test, each with a different set of advantages and drawbacks. These include the test–retest, parallel forms, and split-half reliability assessments.

**Test–retest reliability** involves administering the same test twice, separated by a relatively long interval of time. Because the same test is used on each occasion, changes in scores on the test cannot be due to such factors as different wording of the questions or nonequivalent items. By the same token, however, participants may respond in the same way on repeated administration simply because they recall how they responded on first administration. If so, the test will appear to be more reliable than it actually is. Furthermore, participants may change between administrations of the test, leading to an artificially low reliability figure. For these reasons, the test–retest method is best for assessing stable characteristics of individuals such as intelligence. The variable being assessed by the test is unlikely to change much between administrations, and administrations can be spaced far enough apart that participants are unlikely to remember much about their previous responses to the test.

The problem of remembering previous responses can be avoided by assessing a **parallel-forms** (or *alternate-forms*) **reliability**. This is the same as a test–retest reliability, except that the form of the test used on first administration is replaced on second administration by a parallel form. A parallel form contains items supposedly "equivalent" to those found in the original form. These assess the same knowledge, skills, and so on but use somewhat different questions or problems, which eliminates the possibility that on second administration the person could simply recall his or her answer on the previous occasion. However, if the items of the parallel form are not really equivalent, differences in test performance due to this nonequivalence may reduce the apparent reliability of the test. In addition, the parallel-forms method still suffers from the possibility that the quantity measured may have changed since first administration, thus making the test appear less reliable than it really is.

You can avoid the problem caused by changes between administrations in the quantity being measured by choosing the **split-half reliability** method. Here, the two parallel forms of the test are intermingled in a single test and administered together in one sitting. The responses to the two forms are then separated and scored individually. Because both forms are administered simultaneously, the quantity being measured has no time to change. However, the need to use alternate forms in the two halves introduces the same problem found in the parallel-forms method, that of ensuring that the two forms are in fact equivalent.

These methods for assessing the reliability of a psychological test apply equally well to assessing the reliability of a questionnaire designed for distribution in a survey. For a discussion of these methods in the context of survey design, see Chapter 8.

## Accuracy of a Measure

The term **accuracy** describes a measure that produces results that agree with a known standard. For example, a bathroom scale is accurate if it indicates 50 pounds when a standard 50-pound weight is placed on it, 100 pounds when a standard 100-pound weight is placed on it, and so on. A thermometer calibrated in degrees Celsius is accurate if it reads 0 degrees when tested in a slurry of ice and 100 degrees when placed in boiling water (both tested under sea-level air pressure). A counter is accurate if the number of events counted equals the actual number of events that occurred.

Determining accuracy is hampered by lack of precision. Your measurement may not agree with the known standard each time you make it. However, the measurement may still be accurate in the sense that the value observed agrees with the standard *on average*. Thus, you can determine accuracy by measuring the standard a large number of times and computing the average; the measure is accurate if the average value equals the value of the standard.

Any difference between this average value and the standard value is termed *bias*. Bias can be overcome either by adjusting the measuring instrument to eliminate it or, if this is not possible, by mathematically removing the bias from the measured value.

Although a somewhat unreliable measure may be accurate *on average*, any *single* measurement in such a case will tend to deviate from the actual value by some amount. When a value is reported as being, for example, "accurate to within ±0.1 cm," this means that, in general, measured values will tend to be within 0.1 cm of the true value. Thus, the precision of the measure limits the accuracy (probable closeness to the true value) of a single measurement. However, the converse is not true. A measurement can be precise (repeatable within narrow limits) and yet wildly inaccurate. For example, a thermometer whose glass has slipped with respect to the scale behind it may yield the same value in ice water within ±0.1 degree C, yet give an average value of 23 degrees instead of the correct 0 degrees.

In psychological measurement, standards are rare, and, therefore, the accuracy of a measure cannot be assessed. This does not mean that you should ignore accuracy issues altogether. For example, no standard introvert exists against which to assess the accuracy of a measure of introversion/extraversion (a personality variable). In such cases, test scores may be "standardized" by statistical methods to have a specified average value in a given population and a specified amount of variability. An extensive discussion of these methods and other issues related to psychological testing can be found in Cohen and Swerdlik (2002).

## Validity of a Measure

In the previous chapter, we introduced the concepts of internal and external validity, which are attributes of a research design. In this section, we discuss other forms of validity that apply to measures. The **validity** of a *measure* is the extent to which it measures what you intend it to measure. Imagine, for example, that you decided you could "measure" a person's general intelligence by placing a tape measure around that person's skull at the level of the forehead, on the theory that larger skulls house larger brains, and that larger brains produce higher intelligence. Most of us would agree that the tape measure is a valid measure of *length*, but, used in this way, is it a valid measure of intelligence? This question was actually investigated. Near the end of the 19th century, the so-called science of phrenology enjoyed a brief popularity. Phrenologists believed that by carefully measuring the cranium of a person, they could learn something about that person's personality, aptitudes, and, yes, general intelligence. They were wrong. For one thing, the correlations between skull size, brain size, and intelligence are very small. In fact, the largest brain on record belonged to a mildly retarded person, and several of the leading thinkers of the day turned out to have disappointingly small brains. Thus, measures of brain size turned out not to be the most valid indicator of intelligence (Fancher, 1979).

You should be concerned about the validity of any measure, but in psychology the topic comes up most often when discussing tests designed to measure psychological attributes. In this context, several types of validity have been defined, each requiring a somewhat different operation to establish. Here we briefly discuss three: face validity, content validity, and criterion-related validity. For more information on test validity, see Chapter 8.

**Face validity** describes how well a measurement instrument (e.g., a test of intelligence) appears to measure (judging by its appearance) what it was designed to measure. For example, a test of mathematical ability would have face validity if it contained math problems. Face validity is a weak form of validity in that an instrument may lack face validity and yet, by other criteria, measure what it is intended to measure. Nevertheless, having good face validity may be important. If those who take the test do not perceive the test as valid, they may develop a negative attitude about its usefulness (Cohen & Swerdlik, 2002).

**Content validity** has to do with how adequately the content of a test samples the knowledge, skills, or behaviors that the test is intended to measure. For example, a final exam for a course would have content validity if it adequately sampled the material taught in the course. An employment test would have content validity if it adequately sampled from the larger set of job-related skills. Finally, a test designed to measure "assertiveness" would have content validity to the extent that it adequately sampled from the population of all behaviors that would be judged as "assertive" (Cohen & Swerdlik, 2002).

**Criterion-related validity** reflects how adequately a test score can be used to infer an individual's value on some "criterion" measure. To determine the test's criterion-related validity, you compare the values inferred from the test to the criterion values actually observed. Criterion-related validity includes two subtypes. You assess **concurrent validity** if the scores on your test and the criterion are collected at about the same time. For example, you might establish the concurrent validity of a new, 10-minute, paper-and-pencil test of intelligence by administering it and the Stanford–Binet (an established test of intelligence) at about the same time and demonstrating that the scores on the two tests correlated strongly. You assess **predictive validity** by comparing the scores on your test with the value of a criterion measure observed at a later time. A high correlation between these measures indicates good predictive validity. Predictive validity indicates the ability of a test to predict some future behavior. For example, the Scholastic Assessment Test (SAT), given in high school, does a good job of predicting future college performance (as shown by its high correlation with the latter) and thus has predictive validity.

Finally, **construct validity** applies when a test is designed to measure a "construct," which is a variable, not directly observable, that has been developed to explain behavior on the basis of some theory. Examples of constructs include such variables as "intelligence," "self-esteem," and "achievement motivation." To demonstrate the construct validity of a measure, you must demonstrate that those who score high or low on the measure behave as predicted by the theory. For example, those who receive low (high) scores on an intelligence test should behave the way people of low (high) intelligence would be expected to behave, as predicted by the theory of intelligence on which the construct was based.

Just as a measure can be reliable but inaccurate, it also can be reliable but invalid. The phrenologists we discussed earlier developed large calipers and other precision instruments to make the task of measurement reliable. By using these instruments properly, they were able to collect highly reliable measurements of cranial shapes and sizes. Unfortunately, the phrenologists chose to interpret these measurements as indicators of the magnitudes of various mental characteristics such as memory, personality, intelligence, and criminality. Of course, cranial size and shape actually provide no such information. Despite being highly reliable, the phrenologists' measures were not valid indicators of mental characteristics.

Although a measure can be reliable but invalid, the converse is not true. If a measure is unreliable, it is not a valid gauge of anything except the amount of random error in the measuring instrument.

## Acceptance as an Established Measure

In our weather and mood example, the Mood Adjective Check List was one possible measure of participants' moods. This established measure has been used in previous research. Using established measures is advantageous because the reliability and the validity of the measure are known.

Although you do not have to spend precious time validating an established measure, it may not be suitable for addressing your research questions. A case in which the established measure was *not* appropriate comes from the literature on jury decision making. Early research on the factors that affect jury decision making required participants to sentence a defendant (see Landy & Aronson, 1969, for example), and several subsequent studies also used this measure. Because jurors are not empowered to sentence a defendant (except in death penalty cases), the established measure lacked realism. Later research attempted to correct this problem by having participants evaluate the guilt of the defendant either on rating scales or as a dichotomous (two-value) guilty–not guilty verdict.

An alternative to using established measures is to develop your own. This alternative has the advantage of freeing you from previous dogma and theory. In fact, a successful new measure may shed new light on an old phenomenon. However, you should evaluate its reliability and validity. This may mean testing reliability and validity before you use your new measure in your research. Alternatively, you can use your measure in your research and demonstrate its reliability and validity based on your results. A danger with this latter strategy is that, if the measure has problems with reliability or validity, the results of your research will be questionable. Because demonstrating the validity, reliability, and accuracy of a new measure can be time-consuming and expensive, using measures that are already available (especially if you are new to a research area) is advisable.

## Scale of Measurement of a Measure

The phrase "scale of measurement" usually refers to the units in which a variable is measured: centimeters, seconds, IQ points, and so on. However, this phrase also can refer to the *type* of scale represented by a given set of units. Stevens (1946) identified four basic scales, which can be arranged in order of information provided about the values along the scale. These are the nominal, ordinal, interval, and ratio scales. Stevens argued that the type of scale along which a given variable is measured determines the kinds of statistical analyses that can be applied to the data. Because some kinds of statistical analysis are more informative and sensitive than others, it is important that you carefully consider the scale of measurement when evaluating the suitability of a given variable for your study. You should learn the characteristics of each scale and be able to identify the type of scale a given variable represents.

*Nominal Scales*   At the lowest level of measurement, a variable may simply define a set of cases or types that are qualitatively different. For example, sex may be male or female. According to one scheme, a person's personality may be classified as introverted or extraverted. Variables whose values differ in quality and not quantity are said to fall along a **nominal scale**. In a nominal scale, the values have different names (in fact, the term *nominal* refers to name), but no ordering of the values is implied. For example, to say that male is higher or lower in value than female makes no sense. They are simply different.

Sometimes the qualitative values of a nominal-scale variable are identified by numbers. For example, three candidates for political office—Smith, Jones, and Brown—might be assigned the numbers 0, 1, and 2, respectively. If the assignment of numbers to the different qualitative values is arbitrary and does not imply any quantitative ordering of the values, then the results of certain mathematical calculations on these numbers will be meaningless.

To see that this is true, imagine that you determine how many voters voted for Smith, for Jones, and for Brown in a recent election and identify each candidate by a number as indicated above. You compute the average vote, which turns out to be 1.5. What does it mean to say that the average vote was 1.5? Does it mean that the average voter favored a candidate who was halfway between Jones (candidate 1) and Brown (candidate 2)? That seems doubtful. Moreover, had you assigned different numbers to the three candidates (say, Brown = 0, Smith = 1, and Jones = 3), you would have obtained a different average.

Although it makes no sense to apply mathematical operations to nominal values (even when these values are represented by numbers), you *can* count the number of cases (observations) falling into each nominal category and apply mathematical operations to those counts. (Such counts fall along a ratio scale; see below.)

*Ordinal Scales*    At the next level of measurement are variables measured along an **ordinal scale**. The different values of a variable in an ordinal scale not only have different names (as in the nominal scale) but also can be ranked according to quantity. For example, a participant's self-esteem may be scored along an ordinal scale as low, moderate, or high. However, the distance between low and moderate, and between moderate and high, is not known. All you can say for sure is that moderate is greater than low and high is greater than moderate. Because you do not know the actual amount of difference between ordinal values, mathematical operations such as addition, subtraction, multiplication, and division, which assume that the quantitative distance between values is known, are likely to produce misleading results. For example, if three teams are ranked first, second, and third, the difference in ranking between first and second, and between second and third, are both 1.0. This implies that the teams are equally spaced in terms of performance. However, it may be the case that the first- and second-place teams are almost neck-and-neck, and both performing far above the third-place team.

*Interval and Ratio Scales*    If the spacing between values along the scale is known, then the scale is either an **interval scale** or a **ratio scale**. In either case, you know that one unit is larger or smaller than another, as well as by how much.

Ratio scales have a zero point that literally indicates the absence of the quantity being measured. Interval scales have a zero point that does not indicate the absence of the quantity. With interval scales the position of the zero point is established on the basis of convenience, but its position is purely arbitrary.

The Celsius scale for temperature is an interval scale. Its zero point does not really indicate the absence of all temperature. Zero on the Celsius scale is the temperature at which ice melts—a convenient, easy-to-determine value. Although this temperature may seem cold to you, things can get much colder. In contrast, the Kelvin scale for temperature is a ratio scale. Its zero point is the temperature at which all heat is absent. You simply can't get any colder.

In psychological research, when you measure the number of responses on a lever in an operant chamber, you are using a ratio scale. Zero responses means literally that there are no responses. Other examples of psychological research data measured on a ratio scale are the number of items recalled in a memory experiment, the number of errors made in a signal detection experiment, and the time required to respond in a reaction time experiment. Again, zero on these scales indicates an absence of the quantity measured. In contrast, if you have participants rate how much they like something on a scale from zero to 10, you are using an interval scale. In this case, a rating of zero does not necessarily mean the total absence of liking.

For practical purposes, an important difference between interval and ratio scales concerns the kinds of mathematical operations you can legitimately apply to the data. Both scales allow you to determine by how much the various data points *differ*. For example, if one participant makes 30 responses and a second makes 15 responses, you can confidently state that there is a 15-response difference between participants. If the data are measured on a ratio scale (as in this example), you can also correctly state that one participant made half as many responses as the other (that is, you can divide one quantity by the other to form a ratio). Making ratio comparisons makes little sense when data are scaled on an interval scale. Consider the IQ scale of intelligence, which is an interval scale. If one person has an IQ of 70 and another an IQ of 140, saying that the person with the 140 IQ is twice as intelligent as the person with the 70 IQ is nonsense. The reason is that even a person scoring zero on the test may have some degree of intelligence.

## Variables and Scales of Measurement

The four basic scales of measurement identified by Stevens help to clarify the level of information conveyed by the numbers that result from measuring some variable. However, they should be viewed only as rough guides to aid in thinking about the numbers. Not all measures fall precisely into one or the other scale category; for example, many psychological measures do not seem to fall along a scale of precisely equal intervals, as required of an interval-scale measure, yet the distances between values along the scale are known with greater precision than would be implied by the mere rank ordering of an ordinal scale. Researchers usually analyze such measures as if they had full interval-scale properties. Furthermore, it is possible to construct alternatives or additions to the basic scales. For example, Mosteller and Tukey (1977) offered an alternative classification that included seven categories: amounts, counts, counted fractions (ratios with a fixed base, such as "eight out of ten doctors"), names (categories with no particular order), ranks, grades (categories with a natural order), and balances. This scheme is based on the nature of the values rather than on what logical or mathematical operations legitimately can be performed on them.

Despite these caveats, Stevens' four basic scales do at least highlight the information content of a set of numbers representing some particular variable as measured. In the next section we discuss several factors you should consider when deciding on a scale of measurement to adopt for some variable to be included in your study.

## Choosing a Scale of Measurement

You should consider at least three factors when choosing a scale of measurement for a given variable: the information yielded, the statistical measures you would like to apply to the data, and, if you expect to apply your results directly to natural settings, the ecological validity of the measure.

*Information Yielded*    One way to think about the four scales of measurement described is in terms of the amount of information each provides. The nominal scale provides the least amount of information: All you know is that the values differ in *quality*. The ordinal scale adds crude information about *quantity* (you can rank the order of the values). The interval scale refines the measurement of quantity by indicating how much the values *differ*. Finally, the ratio scale indicates precisely how much of the quantity exists. When possible, you should adopt the scale that provides the most information.

*Statistical Tests*    As noted, Stevens (1946) argued that the basic scale of measurement of a variable determines the kinds of statistics that can be applied to the analysis of your data. Typically, the statistics that are used for nominal and ordinal data are less powerful (i.e., less sensitive to relationships among variables) than are the statistics used for interval or ratio data (see Chapter 13 for a more detailed discussion of the power of a statistical test). On a practical level, this means that you are less likely to detect a significant relationship among variables when using a nominal or an ordinal scale of measurement.

Many statisticians now believe that this view is overly restrictive. They suggest that the numbers resulting from measurement are just numbers and that a statistical analysis does not "care" how the numbers were derived or where they came from (for example, see Velleman & Wilkinson, 1993). To illustrate this viewpoint, Lord (1953) told a story about football jerseys being sold to the football team on campus. Each jersey displayed a number. When used to identify which jersey belongs to whom, the numbers serve only as names; they might just as well be letters when used for this purpose, and thus they represent a nominal scale of measurement. However, according to the story, after quite a number of jerseys had been sold, the members of the freshman team became quite unhappy when the sophomore team began laughing at them because the freshman players' jerseys all had low numbers. The freshman players suspected that a trick was being played on them, so they asked a statistician to investigate. The statistician immediately computed the mean (average) jersey number for the freshman players for all the jerseys that had been in the store's original inventory. The freshman students were indeed getting more than their fair share of low numbers and the probability that this was a chance event was so low as to be, for all practical intents, zero.

To compute the means, the statistician used the jersey numbers as quantities along an interval scale of measurement, as if larger numbers indicated larger "amounts" of some variable. Indeed, both freshmen and sophomores were behaving as if the numbers represented something like social status, with low numbers corresponding to low status and high numbers corresponding to high status. In fact, the analysis in terms of means was meant to discover whether the jersey numbers were systematically assigned according to class rank, rather than being arbitrarily assigned substitutes for the player's names, as would normally be the case for nominally scaled values.

As Lord's story makes clear, the scale of measurement that applies to a number depends on how the number is to be interpreted. However, in most cases, you know when designing the study how you would like to go about analyzing the data and therefore what assumptions the data will have to meet when you apply those analyses to them. For example, computing means of numbers representing a set of three or more nominal-scale categories would make no sense, because the values of those means would change depending on which numbers were used to identify which categories.

*Ecological Validity*    The discussion thus far would indicate that you should use ratio or interval scales whenever possible in order to maximize the amount of information contained in the data. However, your research question may limit your choice of a measurement scale. If you are planning to conduct applied research, for example, you may be forced to use a certain scale, even if that scale is one of the less informative ones. Consider the following example.

One author of this book (Bordens, 1984) conducted a study of the factors that influence the decision to accept a plea bargain. In this study, participants were told to play the role of either an innocent or a guilty defendant. They then were given information concerning the likelihood of conviction at trial and the sentences that would be received on conviction at trial or after a plea bargain.

In this situation the most realistic dependent measure is a simple "acceptance–rejection" of the plea bargain. Real defendants in plea bargaining must make such a choice, so a dichotomous accept–reject measure was used, even though it employs a less informative (dichotomous) scale of measurement (nominal). Sometimes you must compromise your desire for a sensitive measurement scale so that you will have an ecologically valid dependent measure (Neisser, 1976). A dependent measure has *ecological validity* if it reflects what people must do in real-life situations.

Adopting a more limited (nominal, ordinal, dichotomous) scale for your measure (even if it results in an ecologically valid measure) has two problems: The amount of information is limited, and the statistical tests that can be applied are less powerful. If you need to adopt a more limited measure to preserve ecological validity, you may be able to circumvent the limitations of scale by using special techniques.

One technique is to include an interval or ratio scale in your study along with your nominal or ordinal measure. Before you analyze your data, you can create a *composite scale* from these measures. A composite scale is one that combines the features of more than one scale.

In the plea-bargaining study, Bordens (1984) included both a nominal dichotomous accept–reject measure and an interval scale (participants rated how firm their decisions were on a scale ranging from 0 to 10). A composite scale was created from these two scales by adding 11 points to the firmness score of participants who rejected the plea bargain and subtracting from 10 the firmness scores of participants who accepted the plea bargain. The resulting scale (0–21) provided a continuous measure of degree of firmness of a participant's decision to accept or reject a plea bargain (0 was *firmly accept* and 21 was *firmly reject* the plea bargain). The composite scale was reported along with the dichotomous accept–reject measure. The composite scale revealed some subtle effects of the independent variables that were not apparent with the dichotomous measure.

Another strategy you can use when you feel that a dichotomous scale is important is to arrange an interval scale so that a dichotomous decision is also required. For example, Horowitz, Bordens, and Feldman (1980) developed a scale that preserved some of the qualities of an interval scale while yielding dichotomous data. To assess the guilt or innocence of a defendant in a simulated criminal trial, Horowitz et al. used the six-point, bracketed scale illustrated in Figure 5–1. Notice that points one through three are bracketed as a not-guilty verdict, whereas points four through six are bracketed as a guilty verdict. The points on the scale were labeled so that participants could also rate the degree to which the evidence proved either guilt or innocence. This scale forced participants to decide that the defendant was either guilty or innocent while yielding a more sensitive measure of the effects of the independent variables.

## Adequacy of a Dependent Measure

You might find that a carefully planned dependent measure looks better on paper than it works in practice. Two potential problems involve the sensitivity of the dependent measure and range effects.

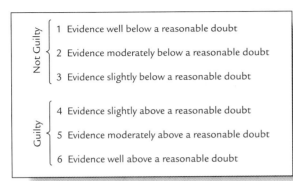

**FIGURE 5-1** A Bracketed Six-Point Scale.
SOURCE: Based on Horowitz, Bordens, & Feldman, 1980.

*Sensitivity of the Dependent Measure*    Some measures of a dependent variable may be insensitive to the effect of a manipulation, while, under the same conditions, other measures definitely show an effect, as was clearly demonstrated to one author of this book (Abbott) in a study designed to investigate the role of the cerebral cortex in the expression of fear. Normal laboratory rats and rats whose cortexes had been surgically removed immediately after birth were exposed to three brief (0.5-second), relatively mild foot shocks in an operant chamber and then observed there for several minutes. During the observation period, fear of the chamber cues was assessed by recording the number of 2-second intervals during which the rats "froze" (remained immobile). The normal rats froze during most of the observation period (as is typical), but no freezing was observed in the decorticate rats.

If only observations of freezing had been collected, the experimenter would have concluded from these data that the shocks had absolutely *no* effect on the behaviors of the decorticate rats. However, unsystematic observations made during the course of the experiment revealed that, far from being unaffected by the shock, the behaviors of the decorticate rats changed radically. Even with almost no freezing, exploratory activity (which had been going on strongly prior to shock) all but ceased following the shocks and was replaced by a tentative stretch-and-quickly-withdraw behavior. Although frequently observed prior to shock, standing on the hind legs alone was all but absent following shock.

Unfortunately, these behaviors were not carefully defined and systematically recorded. The experimenter could refer only to impressions of behavioral change rather than to hard data. To determine the precise effect of the shocks on decorticate behaviors, the experiment must be run again, with the dichotomously scaled freezing measure replaced by a ratio-scaled continuous measure of behavioral activity, and the incidence of other behaviors (such as standing) must be recorded.

In this case, the measure of freezing was insensitive to the subtle changes in behavior brought about by the independent variable. This was the case despite the fact that the measure had proven effective in other experiments. Unsystematic observations carried out during the course of the experiment can provide a useful check on the adequacy of your measure and may reveal defects, as they did here. Although you may have to redesign and rerun your study, your understanding of the phenomenon under investigation will benefit.

*Range Effects*    In addition to worrying about the sensitivity of your dependent variable, you also need to be concerned with what are commonly called **range effects**. Range effects occur when the values of a variable have an upper or lower limit, which is encountered during the course of the observation. Range effects come in two types: *floor effects* and *ceiling effects*. As you might expect from the names, floor effects occur when the variable reaches its lowest possible value, whereas ceiling effects occur when the variable reaches its highest possible value.

The problems that range effects can cause are subtle and pernicious (harmful). They are subtle in that you don't always know that you have encountered them. Range effects are pernicious in that their consequences are hard to deal with after the fact and may require a redesign of the study. Consider the following example.

Assume you have decided to study the effect of retention interval on memory for fruit and vegetable words (you happen to be fond of salads). You settle on a set of retention intervals that span 10–100 minutes in 10-minute increments, and you decide to measure retention by having participants attempt to pick out the correct word from a list of 10 items. The retention score for each participant is the percentage of correct choices in 10 trials.

You vary the retention interval across trials and get a retention score for each interval. To your surprise, you find absolutely no effect of retention interval. Averaged across participants, retention is about 95 percent at each interval!

Fortunately, you are aware of the potential for range effects in your data and stop to examine the scores more closely before concluding that retention interval has no effect on memory for fruit and vegetable words. Looking at the scores of each participant, you realize that 19 out of 20 participants have scored perfectly at every interval. Could the retention task be too easy?

It is possible that differences in retention might have been detected if the task were more demanding. Perhaps there *is* an effect of retention interval on memory. In this case, however, even at the longest interval, memory was still good enough to score 100 percent correct on the retention task. Because 100 percent was the upper limit of your measure, showing any better retention at shorter intervals was impossible. You have encountered a ceiling effect.

Range effects affect your data in two distinct ways: First, by limiting the values of your highest (or lowest) data points, the range effect decreases the differences between your treatment means. The apparent effects of your independent variables are lessened, perhaps to the extent that no statistically reliable differences will surface between them. Second, the variability of scores within the affected treatments is reduced. Because many commonly used inferential statistics estimate variability due to random causes from the variability of scores within the treatments, these statistics tend to give misleading results. In this case, they will usually underestimate the probability of the observed differences in treatments arising through chance alone. (See Chapter 13 for a discussion of inferential statistics and how they work.)

Because range effects distort your data both in central tendency and in variability, do your best to avoid them. Often previous research provides a guide, but on some occasions you may need to determine appropriate methods by trial and error.

## Tailoring Your Measures to Your Research Participants

As another aspect to designing appropriate measures, you must consider the capabilities of your research participants. If you are working with young children or mentally impaired adults, you must tailor your measure to their level of understanding. It makes little sense to use a complicated rating scale with complex instructions if your participants have limited mental capacities.

One way to tailor the dependent measure to your participants is to represent your measures graphically. For example, instead of using a rating scale to measure a preference among young children (perhaps for a toy), you could use a more concrete measure. The child could be asked to give you a number of blocks, blow up a balloon, or vary the space between two objects to indicate the degree of preference. Another technique used with children is to adapt rating scales to a visual format. For example, a scale for children to rate pain they are experiencing uses a series of six cartoon faces with varying expressions (Wong & Baker, 1988). Children point to the face that best reflects the amount of pain they are experiencing. This scale is shown in Figure 5–2. Cartoon faces could also be used to represent the points on a rating scale. Creative measurement techniques also may be needed when dealing with intellectually impaired or very old adults.

Some good examples of creative measurement techniques are those developed to study infant development. With preverbal infants, you have the problem that the participants of your study cannot understand verbal instructions or respond to measures as would an older child or an adult. Consequently, researchers of infant behavior have developed techniques to indirectly test the capabilities of the infant. Popular techniques used with preverbal infants include habituation, preference testing, and discrimination learning. The *habituation technique* capitalizes on the fact that even infants get bored with repeatedly presented stimuli. For example, in a study of the ability to discriminate shapes, you might repeatedly present the infant with a square until the infant no longer looks at the stimulus. You would then present a new stimulus (a circle). If the infant looked at the circle, you could infer that the infant could tell the difference between the two stimuli.

Alternatively, you could investigate the same problem with the *preference technique*. Here you present the two stimuli simultaneously. If the infant looks at one stimulus more than the other, you can infer that the infant can distinguish them.

In *discrimination learning*, you attempt to train different behaviors to the different stimuli (for example, suck when a square is present, but not a circle). Differential rates of responding suggest the capacity to discriminate.

The need to tailor a measure to your participants is not limited to children and impaired adults. Even adults of normal intelligence may have difficulty responding to your measures. Remember that your participants are probably naive to the research jargon with which you are familiar. For example, they may not understand what you mean when you say that increasing numbers on a scale represent an increase in whatever is being studied. Whenever you suspect that your participants may misunderstand how to use the measure, make a special effort to clearly describe it. For example, Figure 5–3 shows how a scale from 0 to 10 can be graphically presented. Notice how the arrow increases in width as the numbers increase. Such a visual presentation may help participants understand that a 7 means they feel more strongly and a 4 less so.

FIGURE 5–2   The Wong-Baker Faces Pain Rating Scale.
SOURCE: http://www.intelihealth.com/IH/ihtIH/WSIHW000/29721/32087.html#wong, Reprinted with permission.

Regardless of the measure chosen, pretest it to ensure that it is appropriate for your participants. During the pretest, you may find that your measure must be modified to fit the needs of your research. Such modifications can then be made before you invest large amounts of time and effort in your actual study.

## Types of Dependent Variables and How to Use Them

Now that we have covered some of the basics of measurement and scaling, we can examine the types of dependent variables in psychological research and their uses. The following sections describe three types of dependent measures: behavioral measures, physiological measures, and self-report measures.

*Behavioral Measures*    Although the number of dependent variables is potentially vast, those used in behavioral research do tend to fall into a few basic categories. One type of dependent measure is a **behavioral measure**. When using a behavioral measure, you record the actual behavior of your subjects. In a study of helping behavior, for example, you might expose participants to different treatments (such as having a male or a female experimenter drop some packages) and then take note of the behavior of your participants (such as whether or not a participant helps).

One behavioral measure is the *frequency* of responding. To determine the frequency of a behavior, you count the number of occurrences over some specified period. For example, Goldiamond (1965) calculated the frequency of stuttering in a behavior modification study. Participants read pages of text, and Goldiamond counted the instances of stuttering across successive pages. Goldiamond found that the rate of stuttering declined during periods in which stuttering was punished with bursts of loud noise. Frequency counts also can be made over successive time periods.

Another behavioral measure is *latency*. Here you measure the amount of time it takes for subjects to respond to some stimulus. In the helping experiment just described, you could have measured how long it took participants to offer help in addition to whether or not participants helped. Any measure of reaction time is a latency measure.

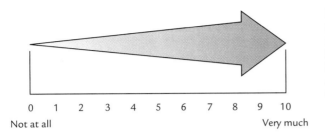

**FIGURE 5–3**  How to Format a Rating Scale to Reinforce the Idea That Increasing Numbers Represent an Increasing Amount of Some Characteristic.

In some types of research, *number of errors* might be an appropriate behavioral measure, which can be used with a well-defined "correct" response. Learning experiments often record number of errors as a function of the number of learning trials.

Behavioral measures are fine indicators of overt behavior. However, with a behavioral measure, you may not be able to collect data dealing with the underlying causes for behavior. To gain insight into the factors that underlie behavior, you often must follow up behavioral measures with other measures.

*Physiological Measures*    A second type of dependent variable is a **physiological measure**. This type of measure typically requires special equipment designed to monitor the participant's bodily functions. Such measures include heart rate, respiration rate, electrical activity of the brain, galvanic skin resistance, and blood pressure.

A good example of the application of physiological measures is found in research on sleep. Participants come to the sleep laboratory, and physiological responses such as brain activity (EEG), heart rate, respiration rate, and eye movements are recorded. This research has shown that the activities of the brain and body change cyclically over the course of a night's sleep.

Modern brain imaging techniques such as PET (positron emission tomography) and fMRI (functional magnetic resonance imaging) have opened a new window into the dynamic activity of the brain during various kinds of mental tasks and have highlighted differences in brain functioning between normal individuals and those diagnosed with mental disorders such as schizophrenia.

The physiological measures just described are all noninvasive—the participant is not harmed in any way when they are used. Some measures are invasive and are used with animals. For example, a physiological psychologist may implant an electrode into a rat's brain in order to record the activity of particular brain cells while the animal learns to perform a new behavior. Changes in brain cell activity during learning constitute the dependent variable.

Physiological measures provide you with fairly accurate information about the state of arousal within the participant's body. A drawback to this type of measure is that you often must infer psychological states from physiological states. As noted in Chapter 1, whenever you make inferences, you run the risk of drawing incorrect conclusions.

*Self-Report Measures*    A third method commonly used to assess behavior is the **self-report measure**. Self-report measures take a variety of forms. One common form is the *rating scale*. In a study of jury decision making, for example, participants could rate the degree of guilt on a scale ranging from 0 to 10. A popular method in attitude assessment is *Likert scaling*. Participants are provided with statements (for example, "Nuclear power plants are dangerous") and are asked to indicate the degree to which they agree or disagree with the statement on a five-point scale ranging from 1 (*strongly disagree*) to 5 (*strongly agree*). (See Chapter 8 for more information on rating scales.)

Rating scales are but one method of quantifying a dependent variable. Another method is **Q-sort methodology**. Q-sort methodology is a qualitative measurement technique that involves establishing evaluative categories and sorting items into those categories. The method, pioneered by William Stephenson in 1935, is a technique for exploring subjectivity in a wide variety of situations (Brown, 1996). For example, if you were interested in having participants evaluate poems using different literary styles, you could have participants read short poems printed on index cards and then sort them into seven evaluative categories: dislike very much, dislike somewhat, dislike slightly, neutral, like slightly, like somewhat, and like very much. This process is repeated with a number of participants. The data from each participant can be analyzed to determine if any significant patterns exist (e.g., a general liking for Haiku and a general disliking for blank verse). This can be accomplished with specialized Q-sort correlational and factor analytic techniques (see Brown, 1996, for an example). Q-sort data also can be entered into a standard analysis of variance to explore main effects and interactions among variables.

Self-report measures are highly versatile and relatively easy to use. You can ask participants to evaluate how they are feeling at the present time. In the jury decision example, participants would be providing an evaluation of the defendant's guilt immediately after exposure to a trial. In other cases, you may ask participants to reflect on past experiences and evaluate those experiences. This is referred to as a *retrospective verbal report* (Sheridan, 1979). In still other cases, you may ask for a *prospective verbal report* (Sheridan, 1979). Here you would ask participants to speculate on how they would react in a certain future situation.

Although self-reports are popular and relatively easy to use, they do suffer from reliability and validity problems. When using the retrospective verbal report, you must be aware of the possibility that the measure is somewhat invalid. You cannot really be sure that the participant is giving an accurate assessment of prior behaviors. The participant may be giving you a report or reconstruction of how he or she felt about the behavior you are studying rather than a true account of what happened. The report provided by the participant could be clouded by events that intervened between the original event and the present report. Validity is lowered to the extent that this report is at variance with the actual behavior. Similarly, prospective verbal reports require a participant to speculate about future behavior. In this case, you cannot be sure what the participant says he or she will do is what he or she actually does. For these reasons, a self-report measure should be used along with another measure whenever possible.

Another problem with self-report measures is that you cannot be sure that participants are telling the truth. Participants have a tendency to project themselves in a socially desirable manner. In a study of racial prejudice using a Likert scaling technique, for example, participants may not be willing to admit that they have prejudicial attitudes. In fact, research in social psychology has found that self-reports of attitudes (especially on sensitive topics) often do not accurately reflect actual attitudes. You can detect responses that project social desirability by including questions that, if the participant agrees (or disagrees) with them, indicate self-effacement (such as "I have never had a bad thought about a member of a racial minority"). If a participant says he or she has *never* had such a thought, he or she is probably responding in a socially desirable way.

## CHOOSING WHEN TO OBSERVE

After you have chosen what to observe and how to measure it, you need to decide when you will make your observations. If you are performing laboratory research, experimental sessions generally are *when* you would observe. However, even within experimental sessions, you must still decide when observations are to be made.

As with the other aspects of your design, *when* you observe may be determined by established practices. For example, if previous research has proven the adequacy of a time-sampling procedure (you make observations at 10-minute intervals during the session), then making continuous observations may be safely abandoned in favor of the less demanding technique.

Your decision of when to observe may have to take into account the resources you have at your disposal, particularly if the required observations must be made frequently or over long periods of time. For example, in the "freezing" experiment described earlier, an enormous amount of time would be required to code freezing behavior across consecutive two-second intervals of time during an experimental session that lasted five hours, especially if a large number of subjects were to be observed. In such cases, you may be able to adopt a sampling strategy and make occasional observations at randomly chosen intervals during the session. Averaged over a number of subjects, such observations could provide a representative picture of changes across time.

An even better solution than the sampling strategy is to automate the observations. For example, Robert Leaton and George Borszcz of Dartmouth College described a way to automatically record the freezing behavior of rats (Leaton & Borszcz, 1985). They suspended the observation chamber between stiff springs. A bar magnet affixed to the chamber moved slightly up or down whenever the rat made the slightest move, generating an electric current in a coil of wire through which the magnet passed. When the rat froze, movement ceased and the current disappeared. A microcomputer counted the passing intervals of time and scored each interval for the presence or absence of movement. With the apparatus used by Leaton and Borszcz, it was possible to continuously observe the freezing behavior during sessions of any desired length.

Of course, it is important to show that any device provides a good measure of the variable before you adopt the measure. One good measure of success is the degree to which the new measurements agree with measurements done "the old-fashioned way." In the case of the automated freezing measure, Leaton and Borszcz demonstrated that the automatic readings correlate highly with personal observations. Techniques for automating your experiment are discussed in more detail later in the chapter.

## THE REACTIVE NATURE
## OF PSYCHOLOGICAL MEASUREMENT

One advantage that physicists and chemists have over psychologists when it comes to conducting research is that the "subjects" of physical and chemical experiments (for example, balls rolling down inclined planes) pay absolutely no attention to the fact that they are participants in an experiment. They behave as they ordinarily do in nature. The subjects (rats, pigeons) and participants (college students) of psychological research do pay attention to their status as such and may modify their behavior as a result of their perceptions. This "reactive" nature of subjects and participants must be considered when designing and assessing psychological research. This section describes the kinds of reactions, the situations that sometimes give rise to them, and the things you can do to minimize (or at least assess) their impact on your data. A discussion of research with human participants begins this section, followed by a discussion of research with animal subjects.

### Reactivity in Research with Human Participants

Assume for the moment that you have defined your population of participants and are now ready to acquire your participants and to run your experiment. You plan to have volunteers sign up and come to your laboratory for your experiment. What can you expect from these creatures that we call human participants?

One thing to realize is that the psychological experiment is a social situation. You as the experimenter, by definition, are in a position of power over the participant. Your participant enters this situation with a social history that may affect how he or she responds to your manipulations. Assuming that the participant is a passive recipient of your experimental manipulations is a mistake. The participant is a living, thinking human being who will generate personal interpretations of your experiment and perhaps guide behavior based on these interpretations. In short, the participant is a reactive creature. The behavior you observe in your participants may not be representative of normal behavior, simply because you are making observations.

To help you understand the reactions of research participants to your experiment, imagine that you have volunteered for a psychological experiment for the first time. You are a first-year student enrolled in introductory psychology who has had a little experience with psychological research. As you sit waiting to be called for the experiment, you imagine what the experiment will be like. Perhaps you have just talked about Milgram's obedience research in your psychology class and are wondering if you are going to be given electric shocks or if the researcher is going to be honest with you. You wonder if you are going to be told the experiment is about one thing when it is actually about something else.

At last the experimenter comes out of the laboratory and says she is ready for you. You are led into a room with a white tile floor, white walls, a stainless steel sink in the corner, some ominous-looking equipment in another corner, and rather harsh fluorescent lighting. The experimenter apologizes for the cold surroundings and says she is a graduate student and had to settle for one of the animal labs to run her master's thesis research. (Do you believe her?) You take a look around the room and muster enough courage to ask whether you are going to be shocked. The experimenter chuckles and assures you that the experiment deals with memory for abstract pictures. She then begins to read you the instructions. At that moment, some workers begin to hammer out in the hall. (Is this part of the experiment?) Again the experimenter apologizes. She explains that they are installing a new air-conditioning system in that wing of the building. You think you detect a hint of a smile on her face. You don't believe her. You have decided that the experimenter is really trying to test how well you can perform a memory task under distracting conditions. You decide to "show the experimenter" that you can do well despite her obvious attempt to trick you. The experimenter runs you through the experiment. Of course, you try your hardest to get all the items right.

After you have completed the memory test, the experimenter asks you whether you have any questions. You smugly tell her that you saw through her obvious deception and worked even harder to get the items correct. After all, you weren't born yesterday! To this the experimenter incredulously assures you the noise was not part of the experiment and tells you she will have to throw out your data. The experiment has been set back an entire day.

## Demand Characteristics

Consider the psychological experiment in the light of this example. As stated, the human participant in a psychological experiment does not passively respond to what you may expose him or her to. On entering the laboratory, your participant probably assesses you and the laboratory (Adair, 1973). Given these assessments, the participant begins to draw inferences concerning what the experiment is about.

The cues provided by the researcher and the context that communicate to the participant the purpose of the study (or the expected responses of the participant) are referred to as **demand characteristics**. Participants gain information about the experiment from these demand characteristics. Unfortunately for you, the participant may be paying attention to cues that are irrelevant to the experiment at hand (as happened in the previous example when you believed the noise created by the work crew was related to the experiment). With the information obtained from the demand characteristics, the participant begins to formulate hypotheses about the nature of the experiment (such as "The experiment is measuring my ability to perform under adverse conditions") and begins to behave in a manner consistent with those hypotheses. Problems occur when the participant's hypotheses differ from the intended purpose of the experiment. Adair (1973) refers to this class of demand characteristic as "performance cues."

A second source of demand characteristics centers around the participant. According to Adair (1973), a class of demand characteristics known as **role attitude cues** may signal the participant that a change in the participant's attitude is needed to conform with his or her new role as a research participant (Adair, 1973, p. 24). Further, Adair points out that participants enter experiments with preexisting attitudes that dispose them to react in either a positive or negative way to the experimental manipulations. Through various demand characteristics, the experiment can cause the participant to change his or her attitudes (Adair, 1973, p. 26). Adair lists the following three categories of predisposing attitudes of participants: the cooperative attitude, the defensive or apprehensive attitude, and the negative attitude.

The cooperative attitude is characterized by a strong desire to please the experimenter. According to Adair, volunteering for an experiment "seals a contract between the experimenter and the participant, fostering cooperative behavior" (p. 26). Reasons for the cooperative attitude include a desire to help science, a desire to please the experimenter, a desire to perform as well as possible, and a desire to be positively evaluated by others.

Several demonstrations of the impact of this positive attitude on the outcome of an experiment have been made. For example, Orne (1962) demonstrated that participants will engage in a boring, repetitive task for hours to please the experimenter. Participants were provided 2,000 sheets of paper (on which were columns of numbers to add) and a stack of index cards (on which instructions were printed). They were instructed to select the first card (which told the participants to add the numbers on the page) and then to select the next card. The next card told the participants to tear the completed sheet into pieces (not less than 32), then select another sheet and add the numbers. The cycle of adding numbers and tearing sheets continued for as long as a participant was willing to go on.

If you were a participant in this experiment, what would you do? You may have said, "I'd do it for a few times and then quit." In fact, quite the opposite happened: Participants continued to do the task for hours. Evidently, participants perceived the test as one of endurance. The participants' cooperative attitude in this example interacted with the demand characteristics to produce some rather bizarre behavior. This "good participant" effect was also shown in an experiment by Goldstein, Rosnow, Goodstadt, and Suls (1972).

Some participants enter the laboratory worried about what will happen to them. One of us (Bordens) was conducting an experiment on jury decision making, and several participants, on entering the lab, asked if they were going to be shocked. This apprehension may stem from the participants' perception of the experimenter as someone who will be evaluating the participants' behavior (Adair, 1973). The apprehensive attitude also has been shown to affect the research outcome, especially in the areas of compliance and attitude change (Adair, 1973).

Some participants come to the laboratory with a negative attitude. Even though most participants are either positive or defensive (Adair, 1973), some participants come to the lab to try to ruin the experiment. This attitude was most prevalent when participants were *required* to serve in experiments. Required participation made many participants angry. The present rules against forced participation may reduce the frequency of negative attitudes. However, you cannot rule out the possibility that some participants will be highly negative toward the experiment and experimenter.

## Other Influences

In addition to demand characteristics and participants' attitudes, evidence also indicates that events outside the laboratory can affect research. For example, Greene and Loftus (1984) conducted an experiment on jury decision making in which eyewitness testimony was being studied. Around the time the experiment was conducted and in the same city, a celebrated case of mistaken identification was being unmasked. Knowledge of that case was reflected in the data. Participants generally were more skeptical of the eyewitness in the study after finding out about the case than they were before. However, after a while, the impact of the case diminished and the responses returned to "normal."

The moral to this story is that participants are not passive responders to the experiment. The experiment is a social situation in which the interaction between participant attitudes and the experimental context may affect the outcome of the experiment. As a researcher, you must be aware of demand characteristics and take steps to avoid them, or at least to assess their impact. As with other participant-related problems, demand characteristics, participant attitudes, previous research experience, and exposure to everyday life can affect both internal and external validity.

## The Role of the Experimenter

The participant is not the only potential source of bias in the psychological experiment. The experimenter can sometimes unintentionally affect the outcome of the experiment. Assume you are running your first experiment, an experiment of your own design. Because you are a student, you will be testing your own participants.

You are sitting alone in your laboratory awaiting the arrival of your first participant. You have butterflies in your stomach and are a bit apprehensive about how you will perform in the experiment. The experiment is important to you, because it is required for a class you need for graduation. At last your first participant arrives and you usher him into your laboratory. You begin to read your instructions (which you feel are well written) to your participant and are puzzled to see that your participant is obviously not understanding the instructions. However, you press on.

Your experiment deals with the ability of people to recall certain words embedded within the context of other words. You want to show that interference will occur when the words are embedded in a context of other similar words. You are going to read a list of words to your participant and then give a recall test. In the high-similarity condition, you unconsciously read the words at a faster rate than in the low-similarity condition. You notice later that your collected data consistently confirm your pre-experimental hypothesis.

Now, analyze what has happened. You wrote your instructions believing your participants would be able to understand them. As it turns out, the instructions were less clear than you thought. The problem here was that you assumed too much about the ability of your participants to understand the instructions. This may happen because you are used to talking to other psychology majors or professors familiar with the jargon of your discipline. The participants may not have that advantage. One thing that you could do to detect this problem is to pretest the instructions.

*Experimenter Bias*  In the classic 1960s sitcom *Mr. Ed*, Wilbur Post owned a horse named Ed with a special talent. Ed could talk. In each episode, Ed's antics created some interesting problems for Wilbur. Over a half century before *Mr. Ed* hit the airwaves, another horse, named Hans, created a sensation in the entertainment world in Europe. Hans, it seemed, could solve simple mathematical problems. His owner, Wilhelm Von Osten, took great pains to teach Hans to solve the problems and then took Hans on the road to entertain people. Von Osten would show Hans a card with a math problem (e.g., an addition problem), and Hans would begin clopping out the answer with his hoof. Hans would stop clopping his hoof when the correct answer was reached. Audiences were astounded and for two years Hans earned Von Osten a nice living.

Not everyone was taken with Hans' mathematical prowess. A scientist named Oskar Pfungst doubted that Hans was able to solve math problems. Instead, he believed that Hans was picking up subtle cues from Von Osten. So Pfungst designed a series of tests to see if Hans had the miraculous abilities claimed. In one test, Von Osten showed Hans a card with a problem. The catch was that Von Osten did not know what the problem was. In this and similar tests in which Von Osten was not allowed to see the problem being put to the horse, Pfungst found that Hans could not solve the problems. Pfungst believed that Hans was reading his trainer's behavior, looking for cues to signal when he should stop clopping his hoof. In fact, Pfungst found that as Hans began clopping, Von Osten would unconsciously tense up, which showed in his body position and facial expressions. As Hans reached the correct answer, Von Osten would unconsciously relax, signaling Hans that the correct answer had been reached (Wozniak, 1999). In cases where Von Osten did not know what problem Hans was to solve, Von Osten could not provide Hans with the unconscious signals and Hans' performance deteriorated.

At this point you may be asking yourself: What does this have to do with my research? I don't plan on dragging a horse around to entertain people. The answer to your question is simple. The "Clever Hans phenomenon" poses a potential threat to the validity of your research. Let's take a look at a modern-day research example to see how this might work.

There is a phenomenon known as *facilitated communication*, which involves a "facilitator" physically helping an impaired person communicate by touching letters on a screen. The facilitator supports the impaired person's hand while the person guides his finger to a symbol on a screen (Montee, Miltenberger, & Wittrock, 1995). Supposedly, this technique allows the impaired person to communicate with others in ways and at levels previously believed to be impossible. But is facilitated communication a real phenomenon or another example of the Clever Hans phenomenon? Let's find out.

Barbara Montee, Raymond Miltenberger, and David Wittrock (1995) conducted an experiment to test the validity of facilitated communication. Seven client–facilitator dyads participated in this experiment. The experiment was conducted in the client–facilitator pairs' normal setting (e.g., day care center) at the usual time of day. The pairs completed several facilitated communication tasks involving describing an activity or naming a picture. The independent variable was the information provided to the facilitators prior to the facilitated communication session. In one condition (the known condition), the facilitator was informed about the activity the client had engaged in or the picture the client had been shown. In another condition (the unknown condition), the facilitator was not informed about the activity or picture. In the final condition (the false feedback condition), the facilitator was given incorrect information about the activity or picture. The dependent variable was whether, using facilitated communication, the client correctly described the activity or named the picture.

The results from this experiment were rather dramatic and are shown in Table 5–1. As you can see, the client's ability to describe the activity or name the picture

**TABLE 5–1** Mean Number of Correct Responses Made in the Montee, Miltenberger, and Wittrock (1995) Experiment on Facilitated Communication

| | INFORMATION CONDITION | | |
| --- | --- | --- | --- |
| *Task* | *Known* | *Unknown* | *False* |
| Picture naming | 75 | 0 | 1.8 |
| Activity identification | 87 | 0 | 0 |

was almost totally dependent upon whether the facilitator had accurate information about the nature of the activity or picture. Just as Hans could not solve his math problems when Von Osten did not know the answer, so the clients in this experiment were not able to respond correctly unless the facilitators knew the answers.

In both the Clever Hans and facilitated communication situations, there was a common problem known as **experimenter bias** (Rosenthal, 1976). Experimenter bias creeps in when the behavior of the experimenter influences the results of the experiment. This influence serves to confound the effect of your independent variable, making it impossible to determine which of the two was responsible for any observed differences in performance on the dependent measure. Experimenter bias flows from at least two sources: expectancy effects and treating various experimental groups differently to produce results consistent with the preexperimental hypotheses.

When an experimenter develops preconceived ideas about the capacities of the participants, **expectancy effects** emerge. For example, if you believe your participants are incapable of learning, you may treat them in such a way as to have that expectation fulfilled. Rosenthal (1976) reports a perception experiment in which the independent variable was the information provided to students acting as experimenters. Some students were told that, according to previous ratings, their participants should perform well. Others were told that the participants would probably perform poorly. The student experimenters also were told they would be paid twice as much if the results confirmed the prior expectations. Rosenthal reports that establishing the expectancy led to different behavior on the part of the participants in the two experimental groups. Rosenthal points out that such expectancy effects may be a problem, not only in experimental research but also in survey research and clinical studies. In the previous hypothetical example, you (as the experimenter) read the list of words to participants differently, depending on the condition to which they were assigned. If the experimenter knows what the hypotheses of the experiment are, he or she may possibly behave in a manner that leads participants into certain behaviors to confirm the hypotheses. Keep in mind that this could be quite unintentional. When running your own research, you may have a vested interest in the outcome of the study, particularly if you have developed a hypothesis that predicts a certain result. Consequently, your expectations may subtly influence the participants in the different groups.

These two sources of experimenter bias threaten both internal and external validity. If your behavior becomes a source of systematic bias or error, then you cannot be sure the independent variable caused the observed changes in the dependent variable. External validity is threatened because the data obtained may be idiosyncratic to your particular influence.

Because experimenter bias can pose such a serious threat to internal and external validity, you must take steps to reduce the bias. You can do this by using a *blind technique*; in a blind technique the experimenter and/or the subject is blind to (not aware of) what behavior is expected or what, if any, treatment the subject has been exposed to. In a **single-blind** experiment, the experimenter does not know to which experimental condition a subject has been assigned. For example, in an experiment on the effects of children watching violent television on aggression, some children could be randomly assigned to watch violent cartoons, and others assigned to watch nonviolent cartoons. The measure of aggression could be the number of aggressive acts a child engages in during freeplay on the playground. In a single-blind experiment, the observers watching the children do not know the condition to which the children were assigned.

In some research situations, a **double-blind** technique is appropriate. Neither the experimenter nor the participants know at the time of testing which treatments the participants are receiving. If you were interested in testing the effects of a particular drug on learning abilities, for example, you would give some participants the active drug and some a placebo (perhaps an injection of saline solution). The participants would not know which treatment was being administered, thus reducing the possibility that the participants' expectations about the drug would affect the results. Furthermore, you would have an assistant mix the drugs and label them arbitrarily with some code, such as "A" and "B." As the experimenter, you would not be told which was the active drug and which was the placebo until after the experiment was completed and the data were analyzed. Thus, neither you nor the participant would know at the time of testing which treatment the participant was receiving. Neither your nor the participants' expectations could systematically bias the results. This is the essence of the double-blind procedure.

Another method for reducing experimenter bias is to *automate* the experiment as much as possible. In a memory experiment, you could present your stimulus items with a slide projector connected to an electronic timer. The interstimulus interval would be held constant, avoiding the possibility that you might present the stimuli more rapidly to one group than to the other. You also could automate the instructions by having a videotaped version of the instructions that would simply be turned on by the person conducting the experimental session. All participants would thus be exposed to the same instructions. Automation is more fully discussed later in this chapter.

Other potential sources of experimenter bias include the sex, personality, and previous experience of the experimenter. It is beyond the scope of this book to explore all the potential experimenter effects. See *Experimenter Effects in Behavioral Research* (Rosenthal, 1976) for a complete treatment of this topic.

## Reactivity in Research with Animal Subjects

The section on using human participants in research pointed out that the behavior of participants can be affected by the behavior of the experimenter and by demand characteristics. Similar effects can be found with animal subjects. For example, Rosenthal (1976) reported research in which experimenter expectancy effects influenced the rate of learning of animals in a maze-learning experiment. Participants serving as experimenters were told that the rats they would be teaching to run a maze were either very bright (would learn the maze quickly with few errors) or very dull (would have trouble learning the maze). The animals were actually assigned at random to the experimenters. Rosenthal found that the animals in the "bright" condition learned more quickly than the animals in the "dull" condition. The differing expectations of the student experimenters led them to treat their rats differently, and these differences in treatment led to changes in the behaviors of the rats.

Use blind techniques to avoid these and other sources of experimenter bias in animal research. For example, in a study in which a drug is to be administered, the person making the observations of the animal's behavior should not know which subjects received the drug and which received the placebo.

Remember that demand characteristics are cues that subjects use to guide behavior within an experiment. Although animals will not be sensitive to "demand characteristics" in the same way as are human participants, some features of your experiment may inadvertently affect your subject's behavior. For example, you may be interested in how a rat's learning capacity is affected by receiving electric shocks just before the opportunity to work for food. If you do not clean the experimental chamber thoroughly after each animal is tested, the animals may respond to the odor cues from the previous animal. These odor cues may affect the current animal's behavior differently, depending on whether or not the previous animal had received a shock. You must remember that, much like the human participants, the animal subject is an active processor of information. Your animals sense cues that are not intended to be a part of the experiment and may behave accordingly. Ultimately, the internal validity of your experiment may be threatened by the effects of these cues.

## AUTOMATING YOUR EXPERIMENTS

Psychological research presents many opportunities for outside, uncontrolled variables to affect your results. Automation can help to eliminate experimenter effects and increase the precision of your measures.

In addition, automation can save time. Automated equipment allows you to run subjects even if you cannot be present. This is most useful in animal research in which subjects can be left unattended in the testing apparatus. In this case, you simply start the testing program and then return at the end of the session to record the data and return the subjects to their home cages.

Automation has other advantages as well. Automated measurements tend to be more accurate and less variable, as they are not subject to the vagaries of human judgment. An automated system is not likely to miss an important event because it was daydreaming at the moment or distracted by an aching back. Nor is such a system likely to misperceive what actually happened because of expectations about what will happen (eliminating this source of experimenter bias).

Conversely, automation can cause you to miss important details. The changes in behavior shown by the nonfreezing decorticate rats might not have been detected had the automated freezing measure of Leaton and Borszcz been in use. Even when all your measurements are automated, you should observe your subjects occasionally. What you learn from these observations may provide fruitful explanations for changes seen in your automated variables and may provide you with new ideas to test.

Techniques for automation include the use of videotaped instructions, timers to control the duration that a stimulus is present and to time interstimulus intervals, and computers to control an experiment. Because the computer has become almost a standard piece of laboratory equipment, a brief discussion of its components and their uses is in order.

Relatively inexpensive personal computers can be programmed and outfitted with the hardware and software needed to fully automate your experiment. For example, a computer could be programmed to control complex schedules of reinforcement in an animal learning experiment. Computers can be used to control research conducted with humans as well as animals. For example, you could program your computer to present stimuli to be used in research areas such as human learning and memory, perception, developmental psychology, and decision making.

If you use computers to conduct your research, remember that the computer performs many of the more tedious tasks involved in your research quickly and accurately but always does what you tell it to do (even if you make a mistake). Your automated experiment will only be as good as your program. Whether you use commercially available software or programs you write yourself, you must be intimately familiar with the commercial software or with the computer language you will be using and know how to interface your computer with your equipment.

## DETECTING AND CORRECTING PROBLEMS

No matter how carefully you plan your study, problems almost inevitably crop up when you begin to execute it. Two methods you can use to minimize these problems and ensure the usefulness of the data you collect are conducting a pilot study and adding manipulation checks.

### Conducting a Pilot Study

A pilot study establishes procedures and parameters. Frequently it is a study that began life as a serious piece of research but "went wrong" somewhere along the way. The decorticate rat study became a pilot study for this reason. However, many pilot studies are designed from the ground up as pilot studies, intended to provide useful information that can be used when the "real" study gets under way.

Pilot studies can save tremendous amounts of time and money if done properly. Perhaps you intend to conduct a large study involving several hundred participants in order to determine which of two methods of teaching works best in introductory psychology. As part of the study, you intend to hand out a large questionnaire to the students in several introductory psychology classes. Conducting a small pilot study (in which you hand out the questionnaire to students in only a couple of classes) may turn up inadequacies in your formulation of questions, inadequacies that lead to confusion or misinterpretation. Finding these problems *before* you train instructors in the two teaching methods, have them teach a full term, and then collect the questionnaires from 2,000 students is certainly preferable to finding the problems afterward.

Pilot studies can help you to clarify instructions, determine appropriate levels of independent variables (to avoid range effects), determine the reliability and validity of your observational methods, and work the bugs out of your procedures. They also can give you practice in conducting your study so that you make fewer mistakes when you "do it for real." For these reasons, pilot studies are often valuable.

You should also be aware of some negative aspects of pilot studies. Pilot studies require time to conduct (even if less than that of the formal study) and may entail some expenditure of supplies. Where animals are involved, their use for pilot work may be questioned by the local animal care and use committee (particularly if the procedures involve surgery, stressful stimulation, or deprivation). In these cases, you may want to use the best available information to determine procedures and to try to "get it right" the first time around. Then only if you guess wrong will the study become a pilot study.

## Adding Manipulation Checks

In addition to the dependent measures of the behavior under study, you should include **manipulation checks**. Manipulation checks simply test whether or not your independent variables had the intended effects on your participants. They allow you to determine if the participants in your study perceived your experiment in the manner in which you intended. For example, if you were investigating the impact of a person's attractiveness on how his or her work is evaluated, you might have participants evaluate an essay attributed to either an attractive or unattractive author. This could be done by attaching a photograph of an attractive or unattractive person to an author profile accompanying the essay. As a manipulation check, you could have participants rate the attractiveness of the author on a rating scale.

Manipulation checks also provide you with information that may be useful later when attempting to interpret your data. If your experiment yielded results you did not expect, it may be that participants interpreted your independent variable differently from the way you thought they would. Without manipulation checks, you may not be able to properly interpret surprising effects. Manipulation checks may permit you to determine why an independent variable failed to produce an effect. Perhaps you did not effectively manipulate your independent variable. Again, manipulation checks provide information on this.

A set of measures closely related to manipulation checks are those asking participants to report their perceptions of the entire experiment. Factors to be evaluated might include their perceptions of the experimenter, what they believed to be the true purpose of the experiment, the impact of any deception, and any other factors you think are important. Like manipulation checks, these measures help you to interpret your results and help you establish the generality of your data. If you find that participants perceived your experiment as you intended, you are in a better position to argue that your results are valid and perhaps apply beyond the laboratory.

## SUMMARY

In contrast to casual, everyday observations, scientific observations are systematic. Systematic observation involves making decisions about what, how, and when to make observations. Observations of behavior are made under controlled conditions using operational definitions of the variables of interest.

When choosing variables for your study, you should be guided in your choice by research tradition in the area of study, theory, the availability of new techniques or measures, and the limits imposed by the equipment available to you. In addition, you need to be concerned with the characteristics of the measure, including its reliability, its validity, and the level of measurement it represents. A measure is reliable to the extent that repeated measurements of the same quantity yield similar values. For measures of physical variables, reliability is indexed by the precision of the measure, and for population estimates, by the margin of error. The reliability of the judgments of multiple observers is indexed by a statistical measure of interrater reliability. The reliability of psychological tests can be determined in a variety of ways, yielding test–retest, parallel forms, or split-half reliabilities. A measure is accurate if the numbers it yields agree with a known standard. Accuracy is not a characteristic of most psychological measures as there are no agreed-upon standards for them. A measure is valid to the extent that it measures what it is intended to measure. Several types of validity assessment exist for psychological tests, including face validity, content validity, construct validity, and criterion-related validity. The latter takes two forms, called concurrent validity and predictive validity.

One aspect of systematic observation is developing dependent measures. Your data can be scaled along one of four scales of measurement: nominal, ordinal, interval, and ratio. Nominal and ordinal scales provide less information than do interval and ratio scales, so use an interval or ratio scale whenever possible. You will not be able to use an interval or ratio scale in all cases because some research questions demand that a nominal or ordinal scale be used. Your choice of measurement scale should be guided by the needs of your research question. When a less informational scale must be used to preserve ecological validity, you can preserve information by creating a composite scale from a nominal and interval scale. This will help you to "recover" information not yielded by a nominal scale. Beyond choosing a scale of measurement, you must also decide how to design and collect your dependent measures. Your measures must be appropriate for your subject population. Consequently, you may have to be creative when you design your measures. You may count number of responses, which is a ratio scale. You can use interval scales in a variety of research applications. You must decide how to format these scales, how to present them to subjects, and how to develop clear and concise instructions for their uses.

In some research, your measure of behavior may be limited by range effects. That is, there may be an upper and lower limit imposed on your measure by the behavior of interest. For example, rats can run just so fast in a maze. Range effects become a problem when the behavior quickly reaches its upper or lower limit. In such cases you may not detect a difference between two groups because of ceiling or floor effects. It is a good idea to conduct pilot studies to test your measures before investing the time and energy in your study. During the pilot study, you may find that your measures need to be modified.

Observation in psychological research differs from observation in other sciences because the psychologist deals with living organisms. The participants in an experiment are reactive; they may respond to more in the experimental situation than the manipulated variables. Participants bring to the experiment unique histories and attitudes that may affect the outcome of your experiment.

Demand characteristics can be a problem in behavioral research. Participants pick up on cues from the experimenter and research context. These cues may affect the participant's behavior. Furthermore, the experimenter must be careful not to inadvertently affect the participants. Experimenter effects can be avoided by using blind techniques or automating your experiment or both. Automation can be done by videotaping instructions or applying computers to control your experiment or both.

## REVIEW QUESTIONS

1. What factors should you consider when deciding what to observe in a study?
2. What is the reliability of a measure?
3. How does the concept of reliability apply to different types of measures?
4. What is meant by the accuracy of a measure?
5. How do the reliability and accuracy of a measure affect the generality of the results of a study?
6. What is the validity of a measure?
7. What are the ways you can assess the validity of a measure?
8. What is the relationship between the reliability and validity of a measure?
9. What are the defining characteristics of Stevens' four scales of measurement? Do all measures fall neatly into one of the four categories?
10. What factors affect your choice of a scale of measurement?
11. What is ecological validity, and why should you be concerned about it?
12. What is meant by the adequacy of a dependent measure?
13. What is meant by the sensitivity of a dependent measure, and why should you be concerned about it?
14. What are range effects, and why should you be concerned about them?
15. When should you consider tailoring your dependent measures to the needs of your research participants?
16. How can you tailor your dependent measures (give examples)?
17. What are defining characteristics of the three types of dependent variables? What are the advantages and disadvantages of each?
18. What is Q-sort methodology and when is it used?
19. How can the act of measurement affect your subjects' responses?
20. What are role attitude cues, and how might they affect the results of your study?
21. What are demand characteristics, and how can they affect the results of your study?
22. What is experimenter bias, and how can it affect the results of your study?
23. What measures can be taken to deal with reactivity in research?
24. What is a pilot study, and why should you conduct one?
25. What are manipulation checks, and why should you include them in your study?

## KEY TERMS

| | |
|---|---|
| reliability | interval scale |
| test–retest reliability | ratio scale |
| parallel-forms reliability | range effects |
| split-half reliability | behavioral measure |
| accuracy | physiological measure |
| validity | self-report measure |
| face validity | Q-sort methodology |
| content validity | demand characteristics |
| criterion-related validity | role attitude cues |
| concurrent validity | experimenter bias |
| predictive validity | expectancy effects |
| construct validity | single-blind |
| nominal scale | double-blind |
| ordinal scale | manipulation checks |

6

# Choosing and Using Subjects: Pragmatic and Ethical Issues

So far in the research process you have made several important decisions. You have decided on a topic for your research and have taken an amorphous, broad idea and honed it into a tight, testable research hypothesis. You also have made some important decisions about the nature of the research design you will use, the variables you want to manipulate and measure, and how to manipulate and measure those variables. Your next decision involves who will participate in your research study.

You may have noticed in previous chapters that when discussing those who serve in psychological research, we have referred to humans as *participants* and to animals as *subjects*. We have also used the term *subjects* when the discussion could apply to either humans or nonhumans (for example, between-subjects design). These conventions were adopted by the American Psychological Association (2001) and have been followed throughout this book in order to be consistent with APA usage.

A number of important questions must be addressed when choosing subjects for psychological research. Should you use human participants or animal subjects? How will you acquire your sample? What ethical guidelines must you follow when using human participants or animal subjects? If you choose human participants, what is your sample going to look like (age, race, gender, ethnicity, and so on)? If you choose to use animals, where do you get them? What are the implications of choosing one species or strain of a species over another? We explore these and other questions in this chapter. The principles discussed in this chapter apply equally to experimental and nonexperimental research. However, there are additional subject-related issues to consider if your study uses survey methodology. We discuss these issues in Chapter 8, along with other issues concerning survey research methodology.

## GENERAL CONSIDERATIONS

As we have already noted, choosing and using subjects in psychological research requires you to confront several important questions

155

and make several important decisions. Some of those decisions may be driven by the nature of your research. For example, if you are experimentally investigating the effects of brain lesions on learning abilities, you must use animal subjects. If you are interested in the dynamics of obedience to authority figures, you must use human participants. However, many research areas can be investigated using either animals or humans (such as operant conditioning, memory, or perception). In these cases, your choice of animals versus humans may depend on the needs of your particular experiment. However, regardless of whether you choose humans or animals, you must consider issues such as ethics, how the subjects will react to your experimental procedure, and the degree of generality of your results.

## Populations and Samples

Imagine that you are interested in investigating the effect of three teaching techniques on how well eighth graders learn mathematics. Would it be feasible to include *every* eighth grader in the world in your experiment? Obviously not, but what are the alternatives? You may have thought to yourself, "I will have to choose *some* eighth graders for the experiment." If this is what you thought, you are considering an important distinction in research methodology: populations versus samples.

In the hypothetical experiment, you could not hope to include all eighth graders. "All eighth graders" constitutes the **population** under study. Because it is usually not possible to study an entire population, you must be content to study a **sample** of that population. Figure 6–1 illustrates the relationship between populations and samples. A sample is a small subgroup chosen from the larger population.

Often researchers find it necessary to define a subpopulation for study. In your imaginary study, cost or other factors may limit you to studying a certain region of the country. Your subpopulation might consist of eighth graders from a particular city, town, or district. Furthermore, you might limit yourself to studying certain eighth-grade classes (especially if the school district is too large to allow you to study every class). In this case, you are further dividing your subpopulation. In effect, rather than studying an entire population, you are studying only a small segment of that population.

A population can be defined in many ways. For example, if you were interested in how prejudiced attitudes develop in young children, you could define the population as those children enrolled in day care centers and early elementary school grades. If you were interested in jury decision making, you could define the population as registered voters who are eligible for jury duty. In any case, you may need to limit the nature of the subject population and sample because of special needs of the research.

## Sampling and Generalization

An important goal of many research studies is to apply the results, which are based on a sample of individuals, to the larger population from which the individuals were drawn. You do not want the results from your study of the three teaching techniques to apply only to those eighth graders who participated in the study. Rather, you want your results to apply to all eighth graders. The ability to apply findings from a sample to a larger population is known as **generalization**. In Chapter 4 we noted that studies whose findings can be applied across a variety of research settings and subject popu-

Population

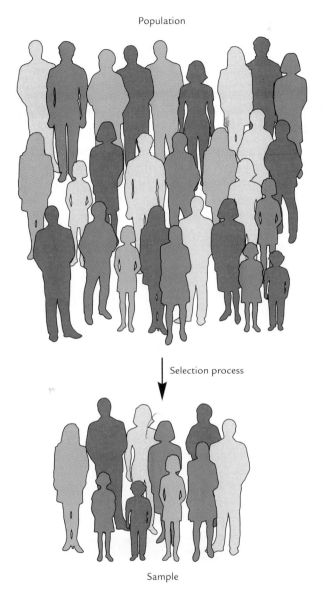

Selection process

Sample

**FIGURE 6–1**   Relationship between Population and Sample. A sample is a subset of individuals selected from a larger population.

lations possess a high degree of *external validity*. Thus, the ability to generalize findings to a larger population contributes to the external validity of a study.

   If the results of a study are to generalize to the intended population, you must be careful when you select your sample. The optimal procedure is to identify the population and then draw a **random sample** of individuals from that population. In a random sample, every person in the population must have an equal chance of being chosen for the study. (Chapter 8 discusses various methods that can be used to acquire a random sample.) A true random sample allows for the highest level of generality from research to real life.

Unfortunately, having a random sample of individuals from the population is an ideal that is rarely met in psychological research. In practice, most psychological studies use a **nonrandom sample**, usually of individuals from a highly specialized subpopulation—college students. In fact, McNemar (1946) characterized psychology as the "science of college sophomores." A more recent study (Higbee, Millard, & Folkman, 1982) reported that a majority of studies in social psychology published in the 1970s still relied on college students for participants, and there is little to suggest that this practice has changed since then.

College students are used so often because most psychological research is conducted by college professors, for whom such students form a readily available pool of potential research participants. In fact, many psychology departments set up *subject pools*, usually consisting of introductory psychology students, to provide participants for psychological studies. They are essentially a captive pool of individuals that can be tapped easily. Sampling from a relatively small subject pool is much easier than drawing a random sample from the general population and greatly reduces the time and financial costs of doing research. However, using such a nonrandom sample has a downside. If you choose to use college students in order to save time, effort, and money, you may be sacrificing the generality of your results, and the study will have less external validity. College students differ from the noncollege population in a number of ways (such as in age or socioeconomic status). These differences may limit your ability to apply your results to the larger population beyond college. You may be limited to generalizing only to other college students.

Research on the issue of student versus nonstudent participants has produced mixed results. A few studies (such as Feild & Barnett, 1978) have found differences between college and noncollege participants. In contrast, Tanford (1984) reported a jury simulation study in which student participants did not differ significantly from "real jurors" on most of the measures included in the study. Given these inconsistent findings, the true impact of using students as participants is difficult to assess. You should recognize the possible limitations on the generality of results from using students as participants.

Studies being conducted on the Internet provide further examples of nonrandom sampling. Participants are self-selected volunteers who participate by filling out Web-page questionnaires, actively engaging in experimental activities available on the Web, and so on. The samples for these studies comprise individuals who know how to use computers, have access to them, know enough about the Internet to stumble into or otherwise find the studies, and volunteer to participate in them—characteristics that may not be true of many people in the general population. However, proponents of Internet-based research argue that similar problems exist when using traditional subject pools such as those from which college students are drawn. Proponents of Internet research suggest that proper participant recruitment techniques (using postings to various news groups, discussion groups, list servers, and Web sites) is analogous to posting sign-up sheets for a study being offered to members of a traditional subject pool. Proponents argue that proper recruitment techniques actually may lead to a broader range of participants geographically and demographically than do traditional subject pools.

So where do things stand on the Internet sampling issue? John Krantz and Reeshad Dalal (2000) suggest that there are two ways to establish the validity of Web-based research. First, results from studies (surveys and experiments) done on the Web can be compared to parallel studies done using more traditional methods. Second, results from Web-based research can be evaluated to see if they conform with theoretical predictions. Krantz and Dalal conclude that, for the most part, research (survey and experimental studies) conducted via the Internet produce results that are highly similar to the results from research done with more conventional methods. A recent study supports this conclusion. Giuseppe Riva, Tiziana Teruzszi, and Luigi Anolli (2003) compared the results from an attitude survey administered via the Internet with the same survey administered using a paper-and-pencil format. They found no major differences between the two methods. They conclude that, given careful attention to sampling, reliability, and validity issues, the Internet can produce results that mirror those from traditional surveys.

Although there are striking parallels between the results of Internet and non-Internet studies, this does not mean that all Web-based findings match findings using other methods (Krantz & Dalal, 2000). What the research in this area does suggest, however, is that the Internet provides a powerful tool for researchers that may have fewer liabilities than critics allege.

Nonrandom sampling is not restricted to research using human participants. In fact, it is almost standard procedure for research using animal subjects. Laboratory animals are usually ordered for a given study from a single supplier and typically consist of animals of the same species, strain, sex, and age (indeed, many of them may be littermates). A group of 30 female Sprague–Dawley laboratory rats, all 90 days old and obtained from the same supplier, can hardly be considered a random sample of all female laboratory rats, let alone rats in general. In some cases, even supposedly minor differences in strain have been found to alter the results. For example, Helmstetter and Fanselow (1987) showed that the opiate blocker naloxone was effective in suppressing conditioned analgesia (reduced sensitivity to pain) under certain conditions in the Long–Evans strain of laboratory rat but not in the Sprague–Dawley strain. Those who believed that their research on the effects of this drug would generalize from the strain of rat they had selected for testing to laboratory rats in general turned out to be mistaken. However, this problem may be mitigated somewhat if different laboratories attempt to follow up on initial reports but employ animals of different species, strain, sex, or age, or even similar animals from a different supplier. If the original findings are restricted to a given species, strain, sex, age, or supplier, they will fail to replicate in laboratories in which these factors differ. In fact, Helmstetter and Fanselow's study was prompted by such a replication failure.

Factors other than the nature of the sample that affect the degree of generality of your results include how realistic the research setting is and how independent variables are manipulated. Other sampling considerations most relevant to nonexperimental research are discussed in Chapters 7 and 8.

## Is Random Sampling Always Necessary?

The highest level of generality will flow from research using a true random sample. However, is it necessary for all kinds of research to have high levels of generality (external validity)? As we noted in Chapter 4, perhaps not. Random sampling is especially necessary when you want to apply your findings directly to a population (Mook, 1983; Stanovich, 1986). Political polls, for example, have such a requirement. Pollsters want to accurately predict the percentage of voters who will vote for candidate A or B. That is, pollsters try to predict a specific behavior (for example, voting) in a specific set of circumstances (Stanovich, 1986). Mook, however, suggests that most research in psychology does not have a specific-to-specific application. In fact, the goal of most psychological research is to predict from the general level (for example, a theory) to the specific (specific behavior; Stanovich, 1986). Most findings from psychological research are applied *indirectly* through theories and models (Stanovich, 1986). According to Stanovich, many applications of psychological research operate indirectly through the impact of their theories, thus making random samples less of a concern.

## CONSIDERATIONS WHEN USING HUMAN PARTICIPANTS

Assume for the moment that you have developed a testable hypothesis, have selected your population for study, and are now ready to start recruiting participants. Before you can run your study, you should be aware of the ethical guidelines, established by the American Psychological Association (APA) and the U.S. Department of Health and Human Services (HHS), that you must follow. The next section addresses these ethical principles.

### Ethical Research Practice

In 1954, W. Edgar Vinacke wrote a letter to the editor of the *American Psychologist* (the official journal of the APA) lambasting psychologists for lack of concern over the welfare of their research participants. In his letter, Vinacke pointed out that the psychological researcher frequently misinforms participants or exposes them to painful or embarrassing conditions, often without revealing the nature and purpose of the study.

Although Vinacke's concerns were well founded and represented some of the earliest criticisms of research practice among psychologists, the concern over ethical treatment of research participants predates Vinacke's letter by several years. The APA established a committee in 1938 to consider the issue of ethics within psychological research (Schuler, 1982). The current concern over ethical treatment of research participants can be traced to the post–World War II Nuremberg war crimes trials. Many of the ethical principles eventually adopted by the APA in 1951 are rooted in what is now called the Nuremberg Code.

### Nazi War Crimes and the Nuremberg Code

In the years before World War II, when the Nazis were first assuming and consolidating power in Germany, several anti-Jewish laws were passed (laws preventing Jews from holding civil service jobs, shopping in non-Jewish stores, and so forth). Through shrewd propaganda, the Nazis were able to identify in the public mind (albeit incorrectly) the Jews with the ills that befell the German people in the post–World War I era. As a consequence of these laws, concentration camps were eventually established to which Jews were deported. Many of these concentration camps served as slave labor camps. Others (Auschwitz, Treblinka, and Sobibor) had another purpose: to carry out Hitler's "final solution of the Jewish problem." The principal reason for the existence of this latter group of concentration camps was the systematic extermination of human beings.

At some of these extermination camps (for example, Auschwitz), a variety of "medical" experiments were conducted on the doomed inmates. For example, an SS doctor at Auschwitz selected inmates for either immediate extermination or incarceration in the camp. Some of those who were spared (most notably twins) served as participants in a variety of experiments. Some of the experiments were carried out in the name of eugenics and were aimed at proving the existence of a master race or "improving" the genetic stock of such a race. Mass sterilization procedures (without anesthesia) were tried out on inmates in an attempt to find the most efficient way to reduce the population of "inferior races."

Other experiments were carried out for the German military. For example, inmates were placed in decompression chambers to see how long it would take them to die under high-altitude conditions or were immersed in near-freezing water to see how long a pilot could survive in the water before rescue (research carried out for the German Air Force). Bones were broken and rebroken to see how many times they could be broken before healing was not possible. The list of these sadistic "experiments" goes on and on.

In all the experiments conducted at concentration camps, the inmates were unwilling participants. After the war, when the Nazi atrocities came to light, some of those responsible were tried for their crimes at the Nuremberg trials. Out of these trials came the Nuremberg Code, which laid the groundwork for many of the current ethical standards for psychological and medical research. The 10 major principles set forth in the Nuremberg Code (Katz, 1972, pp. 305–306) are listed in Table 6–1.

Note that Point 1 requires that participation in research be voluntary and that the participant has the right to know about the nature, purposes, and duration of the research. In addition, Points 2 and 3 suggest that frivolous research is unethical. Scientists should not subject people to experimental manipulations if there is another way to acquire the same information, and a firm scientific base must exist for the experiment. Points 4, 5, 6, 7, and 8 place the responsibility on the researcher to ensure that participants are not exposed to potentially harmful research practices. Finally, Points 9 and 10 require that research be terminated by either the participant or experimenter if it becomes obvious to either that continuation of the experiment would be, for any reason, impossible. These factors were embodied in the ethical standards adopted by the APA and the HHS.

## APA Ethical Guidelines

The APA began preparing its ethical guidelines in 1947. Complaints from members of the APA served as the impetus for looking into the establishment of ethical guidelines for researchers. The first ethical code of the APA was accepted in 1953 (Schuler, 1982).

**TABLE 6–1   Ten Points of the Nuremberg Code**

1. Participation of subjects must be totally voluntary and the subject should have the capacity to give consent to participate. Further, the subject should be fully informed of the purposes, nature, and duration of the experiment.

2. The research should yield results that are useful to society and that cannot be obtained in any other way.

3. The research should have a sound footing in animal research and be based on the natural history of the problem under study.

4. Steps should be taken in the research to avoid unnecessary physical or psychological harm to subjects.

5. Research should not be conduced if there is reason to believe that death or disability will occur to the subjects.

6. The risk involved in the research should be proportioned to the benefits to be obtained from the results.

7. Proper plans should be made and facilities provided to protect the subject against harm.

8. Research should be conducted by highly qualified scientists only.

9. The subject should have the freedom to withdraw from the experiment at any time if he (or she) has reached the conclusion that continuing in the experiment is not possible.

10. The researcher must be prepared to discontinue the experiment if it becomes evident to the researcher that continuing the research will be harmful to the subjects.

SOURCE: Based on Katz, 1972, pp. 305–306.

Since their original publication in 1953, the APA guidelines have been revised several times, most recently in 2002, which took effect in June 2003. Table 6–2 presents the most recent version of the guidelines for using human participants in research. Note the similarities between the Nuremberg Code and the present APA guidelines.

The APA (1973) also has established a set of ethical guidelines for research in which children are used as participants. If you are going to use children as participants, you should familiarize yourself with those guidelines.

The period spanning the early 1940s through the late 1950s was one in which researchers became increasingly concerned with the ethical treatment of research participants. This was true for researchers in psychology as well as in the medical profession. Unfortunately, a greater sensitivity about ethics and the newly drafted guidelines did not ensure that research was carried out in an ethical manner, as the next example clearly shows.

The director of medicine at the Jewish Chronic Disease Hospital in Brooklyn, New York, approved the injection of live cancer cells into two chronically ill patients

**TABLE 6–2    Summary of the 2002 APA Ethical Principles That Apply to Human Research Participants**

1. Research proposals submitted to Institutional Review Boards shall contain accurate information. Upon approval researchers shall conduct their research within the approved protocol.

2. When informed consent is required, informed consent shall include: (1) the purpose of the research, expected duration, and procedures; (2) their right to decline to participate and to withdraw from the research once participation has begun; (3) the foreseeable consequences of declining or withdrawing; (4) reasonably foreseeable factors that may be expected to influence their willingness to participate such as potential risks, discomfort, or adverse effects; (5) any prospective research benefits; (6) limits of confidentiality; (7) incentives for participation; and (8) whom to contact for questions about the research and research participants' rights. They provide opportunity for the prospective participants to ask questions and receive answers.

3. When intervention research is conducted that includes experimental treatments, participants shall be informed at the outset of the research of (1) the experimental nature of the treatment; (2) the services that will or will not be available to the control group(s) if appropriate; (3) the means by which assignment to treatment and control groups will be made; (4) available treatment alternatives if an individual does not wish to participate in the research or wishes to withdraw once a study has begun; and (5) compensation for or monetary costs of participating including, if appropriate, whether reimbursement from the participant or a third-party payor will be sought.

4. Informed consent shall be obtained when voices or images are recorded as data unless (1) the research consists solely of naturalistic observations in public places, and it is not anticipated that the recording will be used in a manner that could cause personal identification or harm, or (2) the research design includes deception, and consent for the use of the recording is obtained during debriefing.

5. When psychologists conduct research with clients/patients, students, or subordinates as participants, psychologists take steps to protect the prospective participants from adverse consequences of declining or withdrawing from participation. When research participation is a course requirement or an opportunity for extra credit, the prospective participant is given the choice of equitable alternative activities.

6. Informed consent may be dispensed with only (1) where research would not reasonably be assumed to create distress or harm and involves (a) the study of normal educational practices, curricula, or classroom management methods conducted in educational settings; (b) only anonymous questionnaires, naturalistic observations, or archival research for which disclosure of responses would not place participants at risk of criminal or civil liability or damage their financial standing, employability, or reputation, and confidentiality is protected; or (c) the study of factors related to job or organization effectiveness conducted in organizational settings for which there is no risk to participants' employability, and confidentiality is

continues

TABLE 6–2    **Summary of the 2002 APA Ethical Principles That Apply to Human Research Participants** *continued*

protected or (2) where otherwise permitted by law or federal or institutional regulations.

7. Psychologists make reasonable efforts to avoid offering excessive or inappropriate financial or other inducements for research participation when such inducements are likely to coerce participation. When offering professional services as an inducement for research participation, psychologists clarify the nature of the services, as well as the risks, obligations, and limitations.

8. Deception in research shall be used only if they have determined that the use of deceptive techniques is justified by the study's significant prospective scientific, educational, or applied value and that effective nondeceptive alternative procedures are not feasible. Deception is not used if the research is reasonably expected to cause physical pain or several emotional distress. Psychologists explain any deception that is an integral feature of the design and conduct of an experiment to participants as early as is feasible, preferably at the conclusion of their participation, but no later than at the conclusion of the data collection, and permit participants to withdraw their data.

9. (a) Participants shall be offered a prompt opportunity to obtain appropriate information about the nature, results, and conclusions of the research, and they take reasonable steps to correct any misconceptions that participants may have of which the psychologists are aware. (b) If scientific or humane values justify delaying or withholding this information, psychologists take reasonable measures to reduce the risk of harm. (c) When psychologists become aware that research procedures have harmed a participant, they take reasonable steps to minimize the harm.

SOURCE: APA, 2002.

in July 1963. The patients were unaware of the procedure, which was designed to test the ability of the patients' bodies to reject foreign cells (Katz, 1972). Predictably, the discovery of this ethical violation of the patients' rights raised quite a controversy.

## Government Regulations

As a result of abuses similar to the Jewish Chronic Disease Hospital case, the U.S. government addressed the issue of ethical treatment of human participants in research. The result of this involvement was the establishment of the HHS guidelines for the "protection of human subjects" (U.S. Department of Health and Human Services, 2001). The key points of these guidelines, which apply to government agencies and any institution receiving government funds, are summarized in Table 6–3.

The guidelines established by the HHS are much more complex than the brief overview presented in Table 6–3. Familiarize yourself with the full set of HHS guidelines and APA code of ethics before you conduct your research.

There are also guidelines that apply to using children as research participants. The U.S. Department of Health and Human Services (2001) regulations for research with human participants states that unless the research involving children is exempt

**TABLE 6-3   Summary of the 2001 Department of Health and Human Services Guidelines for the use of Human Research Participants**

1. All research with human participants is subject to the DHHS guidelines except (a) research conducted in established, commonly accepted educational settings involving normal educational practices; (b) research using standard educational tests, surveys, interviews, or observation of behavior as long as participants cannot be identified or where disclosure of information can make a participant liable under criminal or civil law; (c) research using standard educational tests, surveys, interviews, or observation of behavior as long as participants are not elected or appointed officials, or candidates for public office, or if federal law requires a person's identity to remain confidential; (d) research involving existing data, documents, or records as long as participants cannot be identified; (e) research conducted by or with approval of Agency heads involving public benefit programs, gaining access to public benefit programs, or changes in such programs; and (f) taste and food quality and consumer acceptance studies as long as the food has no harmful additives and levels of chemicals are at or below federal limits.

2. Research that does not fall into one of the above categories must be reviewed by an institutional review board (IRB). The IRB shall ensure that proposed research meets all of the requirements set forth in the DHHS guidelines. The IRB has the power to approve, require modifications to, or disapprove research proposals.

3. Approval of a research proposal by the IRB shall be granted if (a) risks to participants are minimized; (b) risks to participants are reasonable in relation to the benefits to the participants, and the knowledge that is reasonably expected to result from a study; (c) participant selection is equitable; (d) necessary informed consent is obtained; (e) when appropriate, provisions are made to monitor the data collected to ensure the safety of participants; and (f) when appropriate, provisions are made to protect a participant's identity and maintain the confidentiality of data.

4. Additional safeguards must be enacted when participant populations are vulnerable to influence or coercion (e.g., children, prisoners, pregnant women, mentally disabled individuals, or economically or educationally disadvantaged individuals).

SOURCE: U.S. Department of Health and Human Services, 2001.

under the code, the assent of the child must be obtained. This means that the child must be informed about the study and must give his or her permission for participation. If the child is not old enough to give such assent, then permission must be obtained from one or both parents. Permission from one parent is sufficient if the research poses no more than minimal risk or has a direct potential benefit to the child participant. Permission from both parents is required if there is greater than minimal risk and there is no direct benefit to the child participant.

The federal regulations covering the use of human research participants and the APA code of ethics are both intended to safeguard the health and welfare of child research participants. However, ethical issues arise even in cases in which all regulations and codes are followed. Take the case of memory implantation research conducted with children. In a typical experiment, an event that never happened will be implanted in a child's memory. The purpose of this type of research is to discover the extent to which memories can be implanted in childhood. Douglas Herrmann and Carol Yoder (1998) have raised some serious ethical issues concerning this type of research. They point out that children and adults may respond very differently to the deception involved in implanted memory research. They argue further that children may not fully understand the nature of the deception being used and may be participating only under parental permission. Herrmann and Yoder suggest that at the time parental permission is sought, it is not possible to fully inform parents of the potential risks because those risks are not fully understood. They called upon researchers in this area to rethink the ethics of the implanted memory procedure with children.

On the other side of the argument, Stephen Ceci, Maggie Bruck, and Elizabeth Loftus (1998), while agreeing that it is important to protect the welfare of child participants, stated that Herrmann and Yoder's concerns about memory implantation research are not logical because many of the risks they talked about were either inflated or nonexistent. In addition, one must also balance the potential risk to the individual child against the potential benefits that come from systematic research (Ornstein & Gordon, 1998). However, Ornstein and Gordon point out that it is essential for researchers to follow up with parents to make sure that child participants do not experience negative side effects because of their participation in a memory implantation study. They also suggest that careful screening of children (for psychopathology and self-esteem) be conducted before allowing a child to participate.

As you can see, issues surrounding using children as research participants are complex. There is no simple answer to the question of whether children should be allowed to participate in psychological experiments. Certainly, it is important to protect the welfare of children who take part in research. However, discontinuing an important line of research with potential benefits to society would be throwing the baby out with the bathwater.

## Ethical Guidelines, Your Research, and the IRB

Now that you are familiar with the ethical principles for research with human participants, you can begin to think about obtaining subjects and running your study. Can you now proceed with your research? In days gone by, you could have done just that. Presently, however, you may be required to have your research reviewed by an **institutional review board (IRB)**. If you are affiliated with any institution that receives federal funding, you will be required to have your research screened for ethical treatment of participants before you can begin to conduct your research. The role of the IRB is to ensure that you adhere to established ethical guidelines.

Submitting your research to the IRB for review involves drafting a proposal. The form of that proposal varies from institution to institution. However, an IRB requires certain items of information to evaluate your proposal. Information will be needed concerning how participants will be acquired, procedures for obtaining informed consent, experimental procedures, potential risks to the participants, and plans for following up your research with reports to participants. Depending on the nature of your research, you may be required to submit a draft of an "informed consent form" outlining to your participants the nature of the study. The sample informed consent form shown in Figure 6–2 illustrates an informed consent form that conforms to rules established by Purdue University. Each institution, however, may have additional requirements for what must be included in an informed consent form. Additionally, requirements for informed consent forms may change frequently within an institution. Before using any consent form, you should consult your IRB and ensure that your form complies with its requirements.

One final note on the role of the IRB is in order. You may see these preliminary steps as unnecessary and, at times, a bother. After all, aren't you (the researcher) competent to determine whether participants are being treated ethically? Although you may be qualified to evaluate the ethics of your experiment, you still have a vested interest in your research. Such a vested interest may blind you to some ethical implications of your research.

The IRB is important because it allows a group of individuals who do not have a vested interest in the research to screen your study. The IRB review and approval provides protection for both you and the sponsoring institution. If you choose to ignore the recommendations of the IRB, you may be assuming legal liability for any harm that comes to people as a result of participation in your research. In the long run, the extra time and effort needed to prepare the IRB proposal is in the best interests of the sponsoring institution, the participant, and you.

One factor that both the IRB and the researcher must assess is the risk–benefit ratio of doing research. Research may involve some degree of risk to participants ranging from minimal to very high. This risk might involve psychological and/or physical harm to the participants. For example, a participant in an experiment on the effects of stress on learning might be subjected to stimuli that create high levels of stress. It is possible the participants might be harmed psychologically by such high levels of stress. The researcher and the IRB must determine if the benefits of the research (for example, new techniques for handling stress discovered, new knowledge about the effects of stress, and so forth) outweigh the potential risks to the participant. In the event that high-risk research is approved by the IRB, the researcher will be required to take steps to deal with any harmful side effects of participation in such research. For example, you may have to provide participants with the opportunity to speak to a counselor if they have an adverse reaction to your study.

## ACQUIRING HUMAN PARTICIPANTS FOR RESEARCH

Whether your research is experimental or nonexperimental, you must consider three factors when acquiring participants for your research. First, you must consider the setting in which your research will take place. Second, you must consider any special needs of your particular research. Third, you must consider any institutional, departmental, and ethical policies and guidelines governing the use of participants in research.

### The Research Setting

Chapter 4 distinguished between laboratory and field research. In field research, you conduct your research in the participant's natural environment, whereas in laboratory

## RATING CHILDREN'S TOYS
### Dr. Elizabeth Smith,
### Indiana University–Purdue University Fort Wayne
### Department of Psychology

**Purpose of Research**

The purpose of this project is to rate toys on a number of different characteristics.

**Specific Procedures to Be Used**

You will be shown pictures of 15 children's toys and asked to rate each toy on 26 scales.

**Duration of Participation**

It will take about 2 minutes to rate each toy on all the scales. The entire project will take about 40 to 50 minutes to complete.

**Benefits to the Individual**

This project will help us to learn more about the characteristics of children's toys, and how toys might influence children's development. You will gain an understanding of how knowledge is gathered in psychological research, and you will receive credit toward the PSY 120 research requirement.

**Risks to the Individual**

The risks associated with your participation in this project should be no greater than those encountered under normal daily activities.

**Confidentiality**

Your privacy will be protected by the researchers throughout the study. Your name will not be associated with the answers that you give. Only a code number will be used to identify the data, and this code number will not appear on any sheet with your name. Since you are participating in a group session, to protect everyone's confidentiality, we ask you to sit separated from other participants, and that you not examine their responses. While we do everything possible to protect the confidentiality of your responses, we cannot guarantee that other participants in your session will protect your confidentiality.

**Voluntary Nature of Participation**

You do not have to participate in this research project. If you do agree to participate, you can withdraw participation at any time without penalty.

**Human Subject Statement**

If you have any questions about this research project, contact Dr. Elizabeth Smith, (260) 555-5555. If there are concerns about the treatment of research participants, contact the Committee on the Use of Human Research Subjects at Purdue University, 1071 HOVD Room 307, West Lafayette, IN 47907-1071. The phone number for the Committee's secretary is (765) 555-5942. The email address is irb@purdue.edu.

I HAVE HAD THE OPPORTUNITY TO READ THIS CONSENT FORM, ASK QUESTIONS ABOUT THE RESEARCH PROJECT AND AM PREPARED TO PARTICIPATE IN THIS PROJECT.

_____    _____
Participant's Signature                                          Date

_____
Participant's Name

_____    _____
Researcher's Signature (Elizabeth Smith)                    Date

**FIGURE 6-2**    Sample Informed Consent Form.

research, your participants are brought into a laboratory environment of your creation. Acquiring participants for laboratory research differs from acquiring subjects for field research.

*Laboratory Research*   If you choose to conduct your research in a laboratory setting, there are two principal ways of acquiring participants. First, you can solicit volunteers from whatever participant population is available. For example, you could recruit participants from your university library or lounge area. These participants would participate on a purely voluntary basis. As we indicate later in this chapter, voluntary participation has both positive and negative consequences for your research. Second, you can make use of a subject pool if one exists. People in the subject pool may be required to participate in a certain number of studies (with an alternative to the research option provided). If you adopt this strategy, you must make sure your recruitment procedures do not put pressure on participants to participate or coerce them in any way. Even when using a subject pool, participation in a research study must be voluntary.

*Field Research*   Field research requires you to select your participants while they are in their natural environment. How you acquire your participants for field research depends on the nature of your research. For example, if you are conducting a survey, you would use one of the survey sampling techniques discussed in Chapter 8 to acquire a sample of participants. Essentially, these techniques involve selecting a participant from a population, contacting that person, and having him or her complete your questionnaire.

If you were running a field experiment, you could use one of two methods for acquiring participants, again depending on the nature and needs of your research. Some field experiments are actually carried out much like laboratory experiments except that you take your "show" (equipment, assistants, measuring devices, and so forth) on the road and set up in the participant's natural environment. For example, Friedrich and Stein (1973) conducted a field experiment in a day care center on the effect of watching violent television on children's aggression.

In this experiment, the researchers randomly assigned participants to different television "diets" and later observed them during free-play situations for instances of aggressive behavior. In this type of field experiment, the researchers maintain about as much control over participant selection and assignment as they would if the experiment were conducted in the laboratory. However, the researchers are at the mercy of whoever happens to be at the day care center on days on which manipulations are introduced and measurements made. Thus, with field research, you have less control over participants than in the laboratory.

In another type of field experiment, you set up a situation and wait for participants to happen along. For example, if you were interested in conducting a field experiment on helping behavior, you might have a well-dressed or poorly dressed confederate (someone working for you) slumped over on a street corner and count the number of passers-by who stop to help. In this case, you have less control over who participates in your research.

## The Needs of Your Research

Special needs of your research may affect how you acquire participants. In some cases, you may have to screen potential participants for certain characteristics (such as gender, age, or personality characteristics). For example, in a jury study, you might screen participants for their level of authoritarianism and include only authoritarians in your research. If this is the case, you must first pretest participants using some measure of authoritarianism and recruit only those who fall into the category you want. Bear in mind that doing this affects the external validity of your findings. The results you obtain with participants who score high in authoritarianism may not apply to those who show lower levels of authoritarianism.

As another example, you may need children of certain ages for a developmental study of intelligence. Acquiring a sample of children for your research is a bit more involved than acquiring a sample of adults. You must obtain permission from the child's parent or guardian, as well as from the child him- or herself. In practice, some parents may not want their children to participate. This again raises issues of external validity. Your sample of children of parents who agree to allow participation may differ from the general population of children.

## Institutional Policies and Ethical Guidelines

Institutions have their own rules concerning how human participants can be recruited and used in research. Although these rules must conform to relevant ethical codes and laws, there is considerable latitude when it comes to setting up subject pools. During the planning stages of your research, you should familiarize yourself with the federal and state laws concerning research using human participants, as well as the policies of the institution in which you are conducting your research.

## VOLUNTARY PARTICIPATION AND VALIDITY

Ethical treatment of participants mandates that they be informed of the nature, purpose, and requirements of your study and be given the opportunity to decline participation. There are undoubtedly differences between individuals who choose to participate in research and those who do not. Because a sample made up entirely of volunteers is biased, the validity of your experiment may be affected; this is known as the **volunteer bias**. As Schuler (1982) pointed out, ethical requirements sometimes act in direct opposition to the methodological requirements of good research.

There are two assumptions inherent in the previous discussion: (1) that volunteers differ in meaningful ways from nonvolunteers and (2) that the differences between volunteers and nonvolunteers affect the external validity of your research.

## Factors That Affect the Decision to Volunteer

There are two categories of factors that affect a prospective participant's decision to volunteer. These are characteristics of the participant that either increase or decrease the likelihood that he or she will volunteer and situational factors. We explore each of these next.

TABLE 6–4  **Characteristics of People Who Volunteer for Research**

## MAXIMUM CONFIDENCE

1. Volunteers tend to be more highly educated than nonvolunteers.
2. Volunteers tend to come from a higher social class than nonvolunteers.
3. Volunteers are of higher intelligence in general, but not when volunteering for atypical research (such as hypnosis, sex research).
4. Volunteers have a higher need for approval than nonvolunteers.
5. Volunteers are more social than nonvolunteers.

## CONSIDERABLE CONFIDENCE

1. Volunteers are more "arousal seeking" than nonvolunteers (especially when the research involves stress).
2. People who volunteer for sex research are more unconventional than nonvolunteers.
3. Females are more likely to volunteer than males, except where the research involves physical or emotional stress.
4. Volunteers are less authoritarian than nonvolunteers.
5. Jews are more likely to volunteer than Protestants; however, Protestants are more likely to volunteer than Catholics.
6. Volunteers have a tendency to be less conforming than nonvolunteers, except where the volunteers are female and the research is clinically oriented.

SOURCE: Adapted from Rosenthal & Rosnow, 1975.

*Participant-Related Characteristics*  Rosenthal and Rosnow (1975) provided the most comprehensive study of the characteristics of the volunteer subject in their book *The Volunteer Subject.* Table 6–4 lists several characteristics that, according to Rosenthal and Rosnow, distinguish volunteers from nonvolunteers. Associated with each characteristic is the degree of confidence Rosenthal and Rosnow believe you can have in the validity of each attribute.

In some cases, no clear, simple effect of a variable is apparent on whether or not a person will volunteer for behavioral research. For example, Rosenthal and Rosnow pointed out that firstborns may respond more frequently than later-borns to an "intimate" recruitment style for an experiment dealing with group dynamics. Later-borns may respond more frequently than firstborns to a request for participants for an experiment involving stress. Similarly, a sociable person may be more likely to volunteer for an experiment that is "sociable" in nature and less likely to volunteer for an experiment in which there is little or no contact with others. Also, volunteers may show better adjustment than nonvolunteers in experiments that require self-disclosure.

In addition, other research suggests that volunteers also may be more field dependent (rely heavily on environmental cues) than are nonvolunteers (Cooperman, 1980) and willing to endure higher levels of stress in an experiment (Saunders, 1980).

Thus, participant characteristics separate the person who volunteers from the person who does not.

*Situational Factors*     In addition to participant characteristics, situational factors also may affect a person's decision to volunteer for behavioral research. According to Rosenthal and Rosnow, you can have "maximum confidence" in the conclusion that people who are more interested in the topic being researched and who have expectations of being favorably evaluated will be more likely to volunteer for a particular research study. You can have "considerable confidence" that if potential participants perceive the research as being important, feel guilty about not participating, and are offered incentives to participate, they will be more likely to volunteer. Other factors that have less impact on the decision include personal characteristics of the person recruiting the participants, the amount of stress inherent in the experiment, and the degree to which participants feel that volunteering is the "normative, expected, appropriate thing to do" (Rosenthal & Rosnow, 1975, p. 119). Finally, you can have only "minimum confidence" that a personal acquaintance with the recruiter or public commitment to volunteering will affect the rate of volunteering.

As with the participant-related factors, the operation of the situational factors may be complex. For example, people are generally less disposed to volunteer for experiments that involve stress or aversive situations. According to Rosenthal and Rosnow, the personal characteristics of the potential participant and the nature of the incentives offered may mediate the decision to volunteer for this type of research. Also, stable personal characteristics may mediate the impact of offering material rewards for participation in research.

The general conclusion from the research of Rosenthal and Rosnow is that several participant-related and situational characteristics affect an individual's decision about volunteering for a particular research study. Such a decision may be influenced by a variety of factors that interact with one another. In any case, it is apparent that volunteering is not a simple random process. Certain types of people are disposed to volunteer generally, and for certain specific types of research. The next question is whether or not this volunteer bias affects the outcome of an experiment.

## Volunteerism and Internal Validity

Ideally, you want to establish that variation in your independent variable *causes* observed variation in your dependent variable. However, variables related to voluntary participation may, quite subtly, cause variation in your dependent variable. If you conclude that the variation in your independent variable caused the observed effects, you may be mistaken. Thus, volunteerism may affect "inferred causality" (Rosenthal & Rosnow, 1975), which closely relates to internal validity.

Rosenthal and Rosnow conducted a series of experiments investigating the impact of volunteering on inferred causality within the context of an attitude change experiment. In the first experiment, 42 undergraduate women (20 of whom had previously indicated their willingness to volunteer for a study) were given an attitude questionnaire concerning fraternities on college campuses. A week later, the experimenters randomly assigned some participants to a profraternity communication, others to an antifraternity communication, and still others to no persuasive communication. The participants were then given a measure of their attitudes toward fraternities.

Although the persuasive communication changed attitudes more than the other types, the volunteers were more affected by the antifraternity communication than were nonvolunteers, as shown in Figure 6–3. A tentative explanation offered by Rosenthal and Rosnow for this effect centered on the higher need for approval among volunteers than nonvolunteers. Volunteers tended to see the experimenter as being antifraternity (although only slightly). Apparently, the volunteers were more motivated to please the experimenter than were the nonvolunteers. The desire to please the experimenter, not the content of the persuasive measure, may have caused the observed attitude change. The results of this experiment show that variables relating to voluntary participation may cloud any causal inferences you draw about the relationship between your independent and dependent variables. Rosenthal and Rosnow (1975, p. 155) concluded that "subjects' reactions to a persuasive communication can be largely predicted from their original willingness to participate in the research." According to Rosenthal and Rosnow, the volunteers' predisposition to comply with demand characteristics of the experiment indicates that volunteerism serves as a "motivation mediator" and may affect the internal validity of an experiment.

## Volunteerism and External Validity

Ideally, we would like the results of any research we conduct to generalize beyond our research sample. Volunteerism may affect our ability to thus generalize. It may be that any results you find apply only to participants with the characteristics of the volunteers you used in your research. Thus volunteerism may affect external validity as well as internal validity.

To see how volunteerism affects the external validity of a study, consider an experiment conducted by Horowitz (1969). This study investigated the relationship between the level of fear aroused by a persuasive communication and attitude change. Horowitz examined the impact of fear arousal, along with a second variable: whether participants were volunteers or not. Participants in a "high-fear" group were exposed to a persuasive communication that pointed out the dangers of drug abuse (participants read a pamphlet and saw a film). The high-fear communication presented graphic descriptions of drug abuse. Participants in the low-fear group only read the pamphlet (they did not see the film), and the graphic references to dire consequences of drug abuse were eliminated. Attitudes were measured on a postexperimental questionnaire.

As shown in Figure 6–4, the high-fear communication affected volunteers and nonvolunteers differently. The volunteers showed more attitude change in response to the high-fear communication than did the nonvolunteers. However, little difference emerged between volunteers and nonvolunteers in the low-fear condition. Thus the relationship between fear arousal and attitude change was different for volunteer and nonvolunteer participants. These results suggest that using volunteer participants in an attitude change experiment may produce results that do not generalize to the general population. Arnett and Rikli (1981) confirm this problem of external validity in a different research context (motor behavior).

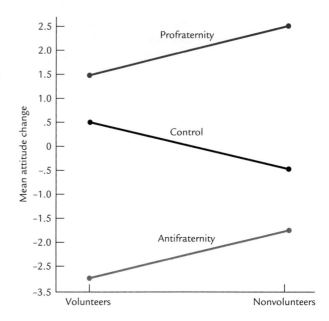

**FIGURE 6–3** Attitude Change as a Function of Type of Message and Volunteerism.
SOURCE: Based on data from Rosenthal & Rosnow, 1975.

## Remedies for Volunteerism

Are there any remedies for the "volunteerism" problem? Rosenthal and Rosnow (1975, pp. 198–199) listed the following things you can do to reduce the bias inherent in the recruitment of volunteers:

1. Make the appeal for participants as interesting as possible, keeping in mind the nature of the target population.

2. Make the appeal as nonthreatening as possible so that potential volunteers will not be "put off" by unwarranted fears of unfavorable evaluation.

3. Explicitly state the theoretical and practical importance of the research for which volunteering is requested.

4. Explicitly state in what way the target population is particularly relevant to the research being conducted and the responsibility of the potential volunteers to participate in research that has potential for benefiting others.

5. When possible, potential volunteers should be offered not only pay for participation but also small courtesy gifts simply for taking the time to consider whether they will want to participate.

6. Have the request for volunteering made by a person of status as high as possible, and preferably by a woman.

7. When possible, avoid research tasks that may be psychologically or biologically stressful.

8. When possible, communicate the normative nature of the volunteering response.

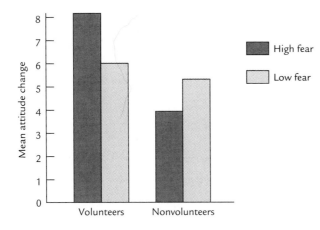

**FIGURE 6–4**    Attitude Change as a Function of Fear Arousal and Volunteerism.
SOURCE: Based on an experiment by Horowitz, 1969.

9. After a target population has been defined, an effort should be made to have someone known to that population make an appeal for volunteers. The request for volunteers itself may be more successful if a personalized appeal is made.

10. In situations in which volunteering is regarded by the target population as normative, conditions of public commitment to volunteer may be more successful. If nonvolunteering is regarded as normative, conditions of private commitment may be more successful.

## RESEARCH USING DECEPTION

In most cases, psychological research involves fully informing participants of the purposes and nature of an experiment. Participants in research on basic processes such as perception and memory are usually informed beforehand of what the experiment will involve. However, in some cases full disclosure of the nature and purpose of your study would invalidate your research findings. When you either actively mislead participants or purposely withhold information from the participant, you are using **deception**. Although the use of deception in research declined (Sieber, Iannuzzo, & Rodriguez, 1995) between 1969 and 1995, it is still used for some research applications. In the sections that follow we shall discuss how deception is used, its effects on research participants, and possible remedies to the problems inherent in using deception in research.

### Types of Research Deception

Deception may take a variety of forms. Arellano-Galdamas (1972, cited in Schuler, 1982) distinguished between active and passive deception. Active deception includes the following behavior (Schuler, 1982, p. 79):

1. Misrepresenting the purposes of the research.

2. Making false statements as to the identity of the researcher.

3.   Making false promises to the participants.

4.   Violating a promise to keep the participant anonymous.

5.   Providing misleading explanations of equipment and procedures.

6.   Using pseudosubjects (people who pose as participants but work for the experimenter).

7.   Making false diagnoses and other reports.

8.   Using false interaction.

9.   Using placebos and secret administration of drugs.

10.  Providing misleading settings for the investigations and corresponding behavior by the experimenter.

Passive forms of deception include (Schuler, 1982, p. 79)

1. Unrecognized conditioning.

2. Provocation and secret recording of negatively evaluated behavior.

3. Concealed observation.

4. Unrecognized participant observation.

5. Use of projective techniques and other personality tests.

## Problems Involved in Using Deception

Although deception is a popular research tactic (especially in social psychology), some researchers consider it inappropriate (Kelman, 1967). In fact, deception does pose a number of problems for both the participant and experimenter. For example, research suggests that once participants are deceived, they may react differently from nondeceived participants in a subsequent experiment (Silverman, Shulman, & Weisenthal, 1970).

Another problem with deception is that the participant in a deception experiment has been exposed to an elaborate hoax. The participant may feel duped by the experimenter and consequently experience a loss of self-esteem or develop negative attitudes toward research. According to Holmes (1976a), the researcher's responsibility is to "dehoax" the participant after the experiment.

Yet another problem may arise from deception research if, during the course of the experiment, participants find out something disturbing about themselves. Holmes (1976b) maintained that the researcher has the responsibility to desensitize participants concerning their own behaviors.

Stanley Milgram's (1963, 1974) classic obedience research illustrates these problems of deception research. Briefly, Milgram led participants to believe they were participating in an experiment investigating the effects of punishment on learning. The participant was told to deliver an electric shock to the "learner" each time the learner made an error. The shock intensity was to be increased following each delivery of shock. In reality, the assignment of individuals to the role of "teacher" or "learner" was prearranged (the "learner" was a confederate of the researcher), and no real shocks were being delivered by the participants. The true purpose of the research was to test the participant's obedience to an authority figure (the experimenter) who insisted that the participant continue with the procedure whenever the participant protested.

Milgram's research relied heavily on deception. Participants were deceived into believing that the experiment was about learning and that they were actually delivering painful electric shocks to another person. The problem of hoaxing is evident in this experiment. Participants also were induced to behave in a highly unacceptable manner. The participant may have found out that he or she was "the type of person who would intentionally hurt another," an obvious threat to the participant's self-concept. To be fair, Milgram did extensively debrief his participants to help reduce the impact of the experimental manipulations. (Debriefing is discussed later in the chapter.) However, some social psychologists (for example, Baumrind, 1964) maintain that the experiment was still unethical.

Ethical treatment of participants requires that participants be informed of the nature and purpose of the research before they participate. Does deception on the part of the researcher constitute unethical behavior? According to the APA ethical principles (2002), deception only may be used if the experimenter can justify the use of deception based on the study's scientific, educational, or applied value; if alternative procedures that do not use deception are not available; and if the participants are provided with an explanation for the deception as soon as possible. The APA code of ethics thus allows researchers to use deception, but only under restricted conditions.

If you were in a deception experiment, how do you think you would feel about the deception? Unfortunately, there is not much research on how research participants respond to being deceived. In one experiment by Nicholas Epley and Chuck Huff (1998), participants served in a replication of a deception experiment. During the first experimental session, participants completed several tasks, including completion of a self-efficacy scale and a task requiring them to read short essays and answer questions about them. Half of the participants were given positive feedback about their performance on the essay task and half were given negative feedback. At the end of the first session, half of the participants received full debriefing that explained the deception (false feedback). The remaining participants were partially debriefed, not including a description of the deception. In two subsequent sessions, participants completed several measures, some of which were the same measures completed in the first session.

Epley and Huff found that participants generally reported positive reactions to being in the experiment, regardless of whether they received full or partial debriefing. However, participants who were fully debriefed indicated greater suspicion concerning future experiments than those who were only partially debriefed. The suspicion over future research persisted and actually gained strength over three months. Generally, participants did not have strong negative reactions to being in a deception experiment. Apparently, deception is not as costly and negative to research participants as previously believed (Epley & Huff, 1998).

## Solutions to the Problem of Deception

Obviously, deception may result in ethical and practical problems for your research. To avoid these problems, researchers have suggested some solutions. These range from eliminating deception completely and substituting an alternative method called *role playing* to retaining deception but adopting methods to soften its impact.

*Role Playing*    As an alternative to deception, critics have suggested using **role playing**. In role playing, participants are fully informed about the nature of the research and are asked to act as though they were subjected to a particular treatment condition. The technique thus relies on a participant's ability to assume and play out a given role.

Some studies demonstrate that participants *can* become immersed in a role and act accordingly. The famous Stanford prison study is one such example. In that study, participants were randomly assigned to the role of either prisoners or guards in a simulated prison. Observations were made of the interactions between the "guards" and their "prisoners" (Haney, Banks, & Zimbardo, 1973). Participants were able to play out their roles even though they were fully aware of the experimental nature of the situation. Similarly, Janis and Mann (1965) directly tested the impact of emotional role playing by having participants assume the role of a dying cancer patient. Other, non-role-playing participants did not assume the role but were exposed to the same information as the role-playing participants. Participants in the role-playing condition showed more attitudinal and behavioral changes than participants in the non-role-playing control group.

Participants are thus *capable* of assuming a role. The next question is whether the data obtained from role-playing participants are equivalent to the data generated from deception methods.

Opponents of role playing have likened the practice of role playing to "the days of prescientific techniques when intuition and consensus took the place of data" (Freedman, 1969, p. 100). They contend that participants fully informed of the nature and purposes of research will produce results qualitatively different from those produced from uninformed participants.

Resnick and Schwartz (1973) provided support for this view. In a simple verbal conditioning experiment (statements that use "I" or "we" were reinforced), some participants were fully informed of the reinforcement manipulation, whereas others were not. The results showed that the uninformed participants displayed the usual learning curve (using more "I–we" statements in the reinforcement condition). In contrast, the fully informed volunteers showed a decline in the rate of "I–we" statements. Thus, informed and uninformed participants behaved differently. Other research (Horowitz & Rothschild, 1970) has provided additional evidence that role-playing techniques are not equivalent to deception methods.

The use of deception raises questions of both ethics and sound methodology. Role playing has not been the panacea for the problems of deception research. For this reason, deception continues to be used in psychological research (most often in social psychological research). Given that you may decide to use deception in your research, are there any steps you can take to deal with the ethical questions about deception and reduce the impact of deception on participants? The answer to this question is a qualified yes.

*Obtaining Prior Consent to Be Deceived*    Campbell (1969) suggested that participants in a subject pool be told at the beginning of the semester that some experiments in which they may participate might involve deception. They could be provided with an explanation of the need for deception at that time. Gamson, Fireman, and Rytina (1982) devised an additional ingenious method for the securing of informed consent to be deceived. Participants were contacted and asked to indicate the types of research in which they would be willing to participate. Included in the list was research in which the participants were not fully informed. With this strategy, you might choose only those participants who agree to be deceived. Of course, choosing only the agreeable participants may contribute to sampling error and affect external validity.

*Debriefing*    Even if you are able to quell your conscience about the ethical aspects of deception by obtaining prior consent to deceive, you are still obligated to your participants to inform them of the deception as soon as possible after the research. A technique commonly used to do this is **debriefing**.

During a debriefing session, you inform your participants about the nature of the deception used and why the deception was necessary. Because knowledge of having been deceived may lead to bad feelings on the part of the participant, one goal of the debriefing session should be to restore the participant's trust and self-esteem. You want the participant to leave the experiment feeling good about the research experience and less suspicious of other research.

Research shows that debriefing has become more frequent in research (Ullman & Jackson, 1982). Ullman and Jackson showed that only 12 percent of studies published in two major social psychology journals reported using debriefing in 1964. In contrast, 47 percent were found to have used debriefing in 1980. Clearly, researchers are becoming sensitive to the problems of deception research and have begun to use debriefing more.

But is debriefing effective? Research on this issue has yielded conflicting results. Walster, Berscheid, Abrahams, and Aronson (1967) found that the effects of deception persisted even after debriefing. In contrast, Smith and Richardson (1983) reported that debriefing was successful in removing negative feelings about deception research. They concluded that effective debriefing not only can reverse the ill effects of deception but also can help to make participants who felt harmed by research become more positive about the research experience.

A possible resolution to this conflict in results emerges from an evaluation of different debriefing techniques. Smith and Richardson pointed out that "effective" debriefing can reverse the negative feelings associated with deception. But what constitutes "effective" debriefing?

An answer to this question can be found in a study reported by Ross, Lepper, and Hubbard (1975). This study found that the effects of false feedback about task performance persevered beyond debriefing. When participants were presented with "outcome" debriefing (which merely pointed out the deception and justified it), the effects of deception persevered. In contrast, if participants were told that sometimes the effects of experimental manipulations persist after the experiment is over, the debriefing was more successful.

Although no easy answers to the problems generated by using deception can be found, some insight on how to soften the effects of deceptive strategies might help solve the problems. First, carefully consider the ethical implications of deception before using it. You, the researcher, are ultimately responsible for treating your participants ethically. If deception is necessary, you should take steps both to dehoax and to desensitize participants through debriefing (Holmes, 1976a, b). The debriefing session should be conducted as soon as possible after the experimental manipulations and should include

1. A full disclosure of the purposes of the experiment.

2. A complete description of the deception used and a thorough explanation of why the deception was necessary.

3. A discussion of the problem of perseverance of the effects of the experimental manipulations.

4. A convincing argument for the necessity of the deception. You also should convince the participant that the research is scientifically important and has potential applications.

During debriefing, be as sincere with the participants as possible. The participant has already been "duped" in your experiment. The last thing the participant needs is an experimenter who behaves in a condescending manner during debriefing (Aronson & Carlsmith, 1968). Despite the deception used, make the participant recognize that he or she was an important part of the research.

One final question about debriefing: Will the participant believe your debriefing? That is, will the person who has already been deceived believe the experimenter's assertions made during debriefing? Holmes (1976a) pointed out that there is no guarantee that the participants will believe the experimenter during debriefing. According to Holmes, participants may feel they are being set up for another deception. The researcher may need to take some drastic measures to ensure that the participant leaves the experiment believing the debriefing. Holmes suggested the following options:

1. Use demonstrations for the participant. For example, the participant could be shown that the experimenter never saw the participant's actual responses (this would be effective when false feedback is given) or that the equipment used to monitor the participant was bogus.

2. Allow the participants to observe a subsequent experimental session showing another participant receiving the deception.

3. Give participants an active role in the research. For example, the participant could serve as a confederate in a subsequent experimental session.

Complete and honest debriefing is designed to make the participant feel more comfortable about deceptive research practices. Whereas this goal may be accomplished to some degree, the integrity of your research may be compromised. If your participants tell other prospective participants about your experiment (especially in cases in which deception is used), subsequent data may be invalid. Consequently, asking participants not to discuss with anyone else the nature of your experiment is a good idea. Point out to the participants that any disclosure of the deception or any other information about your experiment will invalidate your results. Your goal should be to have your participant understand and agree that not disclosing information about your experiment is important.

Note that debriefing is not used exclusively for research using deception. In fact, it is good, ethical research practice to debrief participants after *any* experiment. During such a debriefing session, the participants should be given a full explanation of the methods used in the experiment, the purpose of the experiment, and any results available. Of course, participants also should be given honest answers to any questions they may have.

How do participants respond to being in research and debriefing? A survey of research participants by Janet Brody, John Gluck, and Alfredo Aragon (2000) found that only 32 percent of research participants surveyed found their research experience completely positive. Additionally, they found that research participants reported that the debriefing that they received varied in quality, quantity, and format. Only 40 percent of respondents said that their debriefing experience was positive. However, survey respondents reported the most positive debriefing experiences when they were given a thorough explanation of the study in which they had participated and when they were given a detailed account of how the research is broadly relevant. The biggest complaint that respondents (28.8 percent) had about debriefing was that the debriefing was unclear or that insufficient information was provided.

To summarize, deception raises serious questions about ethical treatment of participants in psychological research. In the absence of alternative techniques, you may find yourself in the position of having to use deception. Strive to maintain the dignity of the participant by using effective debriefing techniques. However, do not be lulled into believing you can use ethically questionable research techniques just because debriefing is used (Schuler, 1982).

## CONSIDERATIONS WHEN USING ANIMALS AS SUBJECTS IN RESEARCH

Psychological research is not limited to research with human participants. There is a rich history of using animals as research subjects dating back to the turn of the 20th century. Generally, there is considerable support among psychologists for using animals as subjects in research (Plous, 1996). Plous reports that 80 percent of respondents to a survey expressed either strong support or just support for using animals in research. Support for animal research was strongest for research that did not involve the animals suffering pain or death, even if it were described as having scientific merit and institutional support. Interestingly, respondents were more accepting of animal research involving pain or death for rats or pigeons than for primates or dogs.

The final section of this chapter considers some relevant factors if you decide to use animals as your research subjects.

### Contributions of Research Using Animal Subjects

Animal research has played a prominent role in the development of theories in psychology and in the solution of applied problems. For example, Pavlov discovered the principles of classical conditioning by using animal subjects (dogs). Thorndike laid the groundwork for modern operant conditioning by using cats as subjects. B. F. Skinner developed the principles of modern operant conditioning by using rats and pigeons as subjects.

Snowdon (1983) pointed out several areas in which research using animal subjects has contributed significantly to knowledge about behavior. For example, animal research has helped explain the variability in behavior across species. This is important because understanding the variability across animal species may help explain the variability in behavior across humans. Also, research using animals has led to the development of animal models of human psychopathology. Such models may help explain the causes of human mental illness and facilitate the development of effective treatments. Animal research also has contributed significantly to explaining how the brain works and how basic psychological processes (such as learning and memory) operate.

## Choosing Which Animal to Use

Animals used in psychological research include (but are not limited to) chimpanzees and gorillas (language acquisition research), monkeys (research on attachment formation), cats (learning, memory, physiology), dogs (learning, memory), fish (learning), pigeons (learning), and rats and mice (learning, memory, physiology). Of these, the laboratory rat and the pigeon are by far the most popular. The choice of which animal to use depends on several factors. Certain research questions may mandate the use of a particular species of animal. For example, you would probably use chimpanzees or gorillas if you were interested in investigating the nature of language and cognition in nonhuman subjects. In addition, using the same type of animal used in a previous experiment allows you to relate your findings to those previously obtained without having to worry about generalizing across animals.

Your choice of animals also will depend in part on the facilities at your particular institution. Many institutions are not equipped to handle primates or, for that matter, any large animal. You may be limited to using smaller animals such as rats, mice, or birds. Even if you do have the facilities to support the larger animals, your choice may be limited by the availability of certain animals (chimpanzees and monkeys are difficult to obtain). Finally, cost also may be a factor. For example, a cat may cost around $125 and a monkey about $600. Contrast that cost to around $10 for a laboratory rat.

## Why Use Animals?

You might choose to use animals in your research for many reasons. One reason is that some procedures can be used on animals that cannot be used on humans. Research investigating how different parts of the brain influence behavior often uses surgical techniques such as lesions, ablation, and cannula surgery. These procedures obviously cannot be conducted on humans.

As an example, suppose you were interested in studying how lesions to the hypothalamus affect motivation. You probably would not find many humans willing to volunteer for research that involves destroying a part of the brain! Animal subjects are the only available choice for research of this type. Similarly, even if there are areas of research that can be studied with humans (such as examining the effects of stress on learning), you may not be able to expose humans to extremely high levels of an independent variable. Again, animals would be the choice for subjects in research in which the independent variable cannot be manipulated adequately within the guidelines for the ethical treatment of human participants.

In addition to these reasons for choosing animals, animals allow you greater control over environmental conditions (both within the experiment and in the living conditions of the animal). Such control may be necessary to ensure internal validity. By controlling the environment, you can eliminate extraneous, possibly confounding, variables. By using animals, you also have control over the genetic or biological characteristics of your subjects. If you wanted to replicate an experiment that used Long–Evans rats, you could acquire your animals from the same source that supplied them to the author of the original study. Finally, animal subjects are convenient.

## How to Acquire Animals for Research

After you have decided to use animals and have chosen which animals you are going to use, your next step is to acquire the animals. Two methods for acquiring animals are acceptable. First, your institution may maintain a breeding colony. Second, you may use one of the many reliable and reputable breeding farms that specialize in raising animals for research.

Each method has advantages and disadvantages. The on-site colony is convenient, but the usefulness of these animals may be limited. The conditions under which they were bred and housed may cause them to react in idiosyncratic ways to experimental manipulations. Thus, you cannot be sure that the results you produce with on-site animals will be the same as the results that would be obtained had you used animals from a breeding farm.

One advantage to using animals from a breeding farm is that you can be reasonably sure of the history of the animals. These farms specialize in breeding animals for research purposes. The animals are bred and housed under controlled conditions, ensuring a degree of uniformity across the animals. However, animals of the same strain obtained from different breeding farms may differ significantly. For example, Sprague–Dawley rats obtained from different breeders may differ in subtle characteristics, such as reactivity to stimuli. These differences may affect the results of some experiments.

## Ethical Considerations

One advantage of using animals in research is that you can carry out manipulations that are not ethically permissible with human participants. Does this mean that if you use animals in your research you have a free hand to do anything you please? The answer is no. If you use animals in research, you are bound by a code of ethics, just as when you use human participants. This ethical code specifies how animals may be treated, housed, and disposed of after use (see Table 6–5). The U.S. Public Health Service has endorsed a set of principles for the care and use of animals that is strikingly similar to the APA's ethical principles. Table 6–6 reprints these "U.S. Government Principles for the Utilization and Care of Vertebrate Animals Used in Testing, Research, and Training."

These tables make clear that if you use animals in your research, you must follow all applicable laws and closely supervise all procedures involving animals, including procedures carried out by laboratory assistants. They also make clear your responsibility

**TABLE 6–5   2002 APA Ethical Code for the Care and Use of Animal Subjects**

1. Psychologists acquire, care for, use, and dispose of animals in compliance with current federal, state, and local laws and regulations, and with professional standards.

2. Psychologists trained in research methods and experienced in the care of laboratory animals supervise all procedures involving animals and are responsible for ensuring appropriate consideration of their comfort, health, and humane treatment.

3. Psychologists ensure that all individuals under their supervision who are using animals have received instruction in research methods and in the care, maintenance, and handling of the species being used, to the extent appropriate to their role.

4. Psychologists make reasonable efforts to minimize the discomfort, infection, illness, and pain of animal subjects.

5. Psychologists use a procedure subjecting animals to pain, stress, or privation only when an alternative procedure is unavailable and the goal is justified by its prospective scientific, educational, or applied value.

6. Psychologists perform surgical procedures under appropriate anesthesia and follow techniques to avoid infection and minimize pain during and after surgery.

7. When it is appropriate that an animal's life be terminated, psychologists proceed rapidly, with an effort to minimize pain and in accordance with accepted procedures.

SOURCE: APA, 2002.

to minimize discomfort, illness, and pain of the animals and to use painful procedures only if alternatives are not available.

Just as proposals for research using human participants must be reviewed and approved by an institutional review board before the research can be conducted, so proposals for research using animal subjects must be reviewed and approved by an **institutional animal care and use committee (IACUC)**. According to the *Guide for the Care and Use of Laboratory Animals* (National Research Council, 1996, p. 9):

Committee membership should include the following:

- A doctor of veterinary medicine, who is certified . . . or has training or experience in laboratory animal science and medicine or in the use of the species in question

- At least one practicing scientist experienced in research involving animals

- At least one public member to represent general community interests in the proper care and use of animals. Public members should not be laboratory-animal users, be affiliated with the institution, or be members of the immediate family of a person who is affiliated with the institution.

---

**TABLE 6–6   U.S. Government Principles for the Utilization and Care of Vertebrate Animals Used in Testing, Research, and Training**

---

The development of knowledge necessary for the improvement of the health and well-being of humans as well as other animals requires *in vivo* experimentation with a wide variety of animal species. Whenever U.S. Government agencies develop requirements for testing, research, or training procedures involving the use of vertebrate animals, the following principles shall be considered; and whenever these agencies actually perform or sponsor such procedures, the responsible Institutional Official shall ensure that these principles are adhered to:

I.  The transportation, care, and use of animals should be in accordance with the Animal Welfare Act (7 U.S.C. 2131 et seq.) and other applicable Federal laws, guidelines, and policies.

II. Procedures involving animals should be designed and performed with due consideration of their relevance to human or animal health, the advancement of knowledge, or the good of society.

III. The animals selected for a procedure should be of an appropriate species and quality and the minimum number required to obtain valid results. Methods such as mathematical models, computer simulation, and *in vitro* biological systems should be considered.

IV. Proper use of animals, including the avoidance or minimization of discomfort, distress, and pain when consistent with sound scientific practices, is imperative. Unless the contrary is established, investigators should consider that procedures that cause pain or distress in human beings may cause pain or distress in other animals.

---

**continues**

---

In practice such committees are usually larger than this minimum; in colleges and universities, it is common to find representatives from departments that do *not* use animals in their research or teaching, as well as from those that do, and at least one student representative. The Purdue Animal Care and Use Committee (PACUC) at Purdue University comprises more than 30 members and has a full-time staff, including specialists in laboratory animal science and veterinary medicine.

The use of animal subjects for research or teaching is regulated by the federal government, which mandates oversight by the IACUC and by the U.S. Department of Agriculture, as well as by various state and local agencies. The strict requirements for institutional care and use of animals under federal jurisdiction are given in the *Guide for the Care and Use of Laboratory Animals* (1996), published by the National Research Council.

Before you begin conducting your research using animal subjects, you should familiarize yourself with the principles for the care and use of animals and design your research accordingly. Before you can conduct your study, you will have to submit a research protocol to your IACUC describing what animals you plan to use in your research and how and justifying your decisions concerning the species and number of

**TABLE 6-6    U.S. Government Principles for the Utilization and Care of Vertebrate Animals Used in Testing, Research, and Training** *continued*

V. Procedures with animals that may cause more than momentary or slight pain or distress should be performed with appropriate sedation, analgesia, or anesthesia. Surgical or other painful procedures should not be performed on unanesthetized animals paralyzed by chemical agents.

VI. Animals that would otherwise suffer severe or chronic pain or distress that cannot be relieved should be painlessly killed at the end of the procedure or, if appropriate, during the procedure.

VII. The living conditions of animals should be appropriate for their species and contribute to their health and comfort. Normally, the housing, feeding, and care of all animals used for biomedical purposes must be directed by a veterinarian or other scientist trained and experienced in the proper care, handling, and use of the species being maintained or studied. In any case, veterinary care shall be provided as indicated.

VIII. Investigators and other personnel shall be appropriately qualified and experienced for conducting procedures on living animals. Adequate arrangements shall be made for their in-service training, including the proper and humane care and use of laboratory animals.

IX. Where exceptions are required in relation to the provisions of these Principles, the decisions should not rest with the investigators directly concerned but should be made, with due regard to Principle II, by an appropriate review group such as an institutional animal care and use committee. Such exceptions should not be made solely for the purposes of teaching or demonstration.

animals to be used and specifics of your procedure. Only when your protocol has been formally approved by the IACUC will you be permitted to obtain your animals.

Finally, keep in mind that ethical treatment of animals is in your best interest as a researcher. Ample evidence shows that mistreatment of animals (such as rough handling or housing them under stressful conditions) leads to physiological changes (for example, housing animals under crowded conditions leads to changes in the adrenal glands). These physiological changes may interact with your experimental manipulations, perhaps damaging the external validity of your results. Proper care and handling of your subjects helps you to obtain reliable and generalizable results. Thus, it is to your benefit to treat animals properly.

## Should the Research Be Done?

Even though a study is designed to conform to ethical standards for the use of animal subjects—giving proper care and housing, avoiding unnecessary pain or hardship, and so on—this does not automatically mean that the study should be done. Your decision to go ahead with the study should be based on a critical evaluation of the cost of the study to the subjects weighed against its potential benefits, otherwise known as the *cost–benefit ratio*. Cost to the subjects includes such factors as the stressfulness of the procedures and the likely degree of discomfort or suffering the subjects may experience as a result of the study's procedures. The potential benefits of the study include the study's possible contribution to knowledge about the determinants of behavior, its ability to discriminate among competing theoretical views, or its possible applied value in the real world.

Conducting an unbiased evaluation is not easy. Having designed the study, you have a certain vested interest in carrying it out and must guard against this bias. Yet if you reject a study because its potential findings do not have obvious practical application, you may be tossing out research that would have provided key insights necessary for the development of such applications. The history of science is littered with research findings whose immense value was not recognized at the time they were announced.

Despite these difficulties, in most cases it is possible to come up with a reasonable assessment of the potential cost–benefit ratio of your study. For example, imagine you have designed a study to evaluate the antianxiety effect of a certain drug (para-methyl-doublefloop). You have no particular reason to believe that it has any effect on anxiety; in fact, its chemical structure argues against such an effect. However, you have a sample of the drug, and you're curious. Your subjects (rats) will have to endure a procedure involving water deprivation and exposure to foot shock in order for you to assess the effect of the drug. Given that the cost in stress and discomfort to the rats is not balanced against any credible rationale for conducting the study, you should shelve the study.

## Generality of Animal Research Data

One criticism of animal research is that the results may not generalize to humans or even to other animal species. This criticism has at its core a basic assumption: All psychological research must be applicable to humans. However, psychology is not concerned only with human behavior. Many research psychologists are interested in exploring the parameters of animal behavior, with little or no eye toward making statements about human behavior.

Much animal research, in fact, does generalize to humans. The basic laws of classical and operant conditioning, which were discovered through animal research, have been found to apply to human behavior. Figure 6–5 shows a comparison between two extinction curves. Panel (a) shows a typical extinction curve generated by an animal in an operant chamber after reinforcement of a response has been withdrawn. Panel (b) shows the extinction curve generated when a parent stops reinforcing a child's crying at bedtime (Williams, 1959). Notice the similarities. Other examples also can be cited. The effects of alcohol on prenatal development have been studied extensively with rats and mice. The pattern of malformations found in the animal research is highly similar to the pattern observed in the offspring of alcoholic mothers.

Although results from animal studies often do generalize to humans, such generalization should always be done with caution, as the following example illustrates. In the 1950s, many pregnant women (mainly in Sweden) took the drug thalidomide to help reduce morning sickness. Some of the mothers who took thalidomide gave birth to

**FIGURE 6–5**
Comparison of Extinction
Curves: (a) a rat's lever-
pressing behavior and (b)
a child's crying at
bedtime.
SOURCE: Panel b from
Williams, 1959, p. 269;
reprinted with permission.

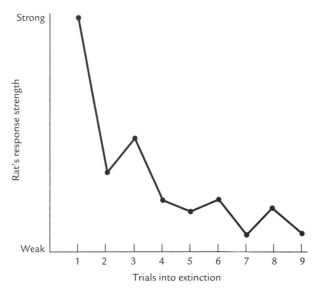

(a)

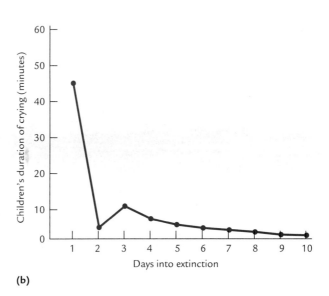

(b)

children with a gross physical defect called *phocomelia*. A child with this defect might
be born without legs and have feet attached directly to the lower body. Tests were conducted on rats to determine whether thalidomide was the cause for the malformations.
No abnormalities were found among the rats. However, the malformations were found
when animals more closely related to humans (monkeys) were used.

Of course, whether results obtained with animal subjects can be applied to humans is an empirical question that can be answered through further research. If the
findings do have relevance to human behavior, then so much the better. Even if they

do not, we gain a better understanding of the factors that differentiate humans from other animals and of the limits to our behavioral laws.

## The Animal Rights Movement

Concern for how animals are treated is not new. Organizations such as the Humane Society and the Society for the Prevention of Cruelty to Animals (SPCA) have existed for many years. The concern over treatment of animals in a variety of areas (farming, research, and so forth) has become more visible. People have begun to seriously question the use of animals in research. Many people have taken the position that the role of the animal in research should be reduced. Some have even advocated completely banning the use of animals as subjects in research.

The degree of reduction being advocated varies from a total ban on using animals to simply ensuring that researchers treat their animals ethically. The remainder of this chapter is devoted to exploring the issues surrounding the arguments made against using animals in research. The intention of this discussion is to present the arguments made by both sides and then analyze them critically. The final judgment about the role of animals in research is left to you.

Singer (1975), in a book devoted exclusively to the treatment of animals, raised several objections to using animals in a variety of capacities (from research subjects to food). This discussion is limited to the issue of using animals in research. Singer maintained that animals should not be used in research that causes them to suffer. Singer argued that it is "species-ist" (setting our own species above other animal species) to use animals in research that would not be done with human subjects. Singer further argued that "most animal studies published are trivial anyway" (p. 227). To support his point, Singer provided a litany of research examples that subjected animals to sometimes painful procedures. According to Singer, the suffering of the animals was not justified given the trivial nature of the research question and results. Consider an example that Singer provided (a critical analysis of Singer's assertions follows):

> . . . P. [Badia], S. Culbertson, and J. Harsh of Bowling Green State University, Ohio, tested whether a signal warning the rats when they were going to receive an electric shock made a difference to the severity of punishment. They used ten rats. Electric current was again delivered to the rats' feet through a grid on the floor. The test sessions were six hours long and frequent shock was "at all times unavoidable and inescapable." The rats could press either of two levers within the test chamber in order to receive warning of a coming shock. The experimenters concluded that rats preferred to be warned of a shock even when the warning signal led to a longer and stronger punishment. (p. 35)

In 1990, Singer published a revised edition of his book in which he had this to say about the research of Badia and his colleagues:

> In 1984 the same research was still being carried out. Because someone had suggested that the previous experiment could have been "methodologically unsound," P. Badia, this time with B. Abbott of Indiana University, placed ten rats in electrified chambers, subjecting them again to six-hour shock sessions. . . . The experimenters found, once again, that the rats preferred shock that was signaled, even if it resulted in their receiving more shocks. (1990, p. 48)

These and several other summaries like them are included in Singer's book to point out the trivial nature of the research results obtained at the expense of animal suffering. If you had read only Singer's book, you would probably come away with the feeling that "everyone already knows that rats will prefer a warning." Singer can be criticized on at least two grounds concerning the brief research summaries.

First, each of the summaries referred to research that was taken out of the theoretical, empirical, or applied context in which the research was originally conducted. By isolating a study from its scientific context, Singer made the research appear trivial. You could take just about any piece of research and trivialize it by removing it from its context. In fact, Badia's studies (summarized in the preceding excerpts) provided important information about how organisms react to stress. To gain a full understanding of the purposes of research, you *must* read the original paper (as pointed out in Chapter 2). In the introduction to the paper, the author will surely provide the theoretical context and potential importance of the research.

Second, Singer leaves the strong impression that each study of a series merely replicates the ones before it, without contributing anything new to our understanding of the phenomenon under investigation or to its generality across different procedures and contexts. For example, in the paragraph just quoted reviewing the follow-up study by Badia and Abbott (1984), Singer begins by asserting that "the *same* research was still being conducted" (emphasis ours). In fact, scientific understanding of a phenomenon typically progresses by the gradual elimination of rival explanations over a long series of experiments designed for that purpose and by demonstrations that a phenomenon is not an artifact of a particular method of study.

Third, Singer's presentation of the research strongly suggested that the research was unnecessary because the findings were already obvious and known. Singer committed what social psychologists call the "I-knew-it-all-along phenomenon" (Myers, 1996). The "I-knew-it-all-along phenomenon" refers to the fact that when you hear about some research results you have the tendency to believe that you already knew that the reported relationship exists. Several researchers (Slovic & Fischoff, 1977; Wood, 1979) have shown that when individuals are asked to predict the outcome of research *before* they hear the results, they fail. However, when the results are known, they are not surprised. You can demonstrate this for yourself with the following experiment, suggested by Bolt and Myers (1983).

Choose 10 participants for this demonstration. Provide half of them with the following statement:

Social psychologists have found that the adage "Out of sight, out of mind" is valid.

Provide the other half with this statement:

Social psychologists have found that the adage "Absence makes the heart grow fonder" is valid.

Ask participants to indicate whether they are surprised by the finding. You should find that your participants are not surprised by the finding reported to them. Next, have participants write a brief paragraph explaining why they believe the statement to be true. You should find that, in addition to believing that the statement is true, participants will be able to justify the reported finding.

The point of this exercise is that when you are told about the results of research, they often seem obvious. Singer played on this tendency (probably inadvertently) when he presented results from animal studies and then implied that "we knew it all along." In fact, before the research was done, we probably did *not* know it all along. The research reported by Singer made valuable contributions to science. Taking it out of context and suggesting that the results were obvious leads to the illusion that the research was trivial.

Not all the points made by Singer are invalid. In fact, researchers should treat their animals in a humane fashion. However, you must consider the cost–benefit ratio when evaluating animal research. Is the cost to the subject outweighed by the benefits of the research? Some people within the animal rights movement place a high value on the cost factor and a low value on the benefit factor. You must consider the benefits of the research that you plan to do on several levels: theoretical, empirical, and applied. In many cases, the benefits derived from the research outweigh the costs to the subjects.

Although controversy over the use of animals in research still exists, the issue may be cooling down. A study by Plous (1998) compared attitude changes of animal rights activists between 1990 and 1996. Plous reports that in 1990 a majority of animal rights activists believed that using animals in research was the most important issue facing the animal rights movement. A similar survey of activists done in 1996 revealed that a majority of activists believed that the use of animals in agriculture was the number-one issue facing the animal rights movement. Further, respondents to the 1996 survey advocated less radical methods for dealing with animals used in research. For example, fewer respondents (compared to the 1990 survey) advocated break-ins at laboratories using animals as a method of controlling the use of animals in research. In fact, most respondents in 1996 advocated more dialogue between activists and animal researchers. Common ground may yet be found.

## ALTERNATIVES TO ANIMALS IN RESEARCH: *IN VITRO* METHODS AND COMPUTER SIMULATION

Animal rights activists point out that viable alternatives to using living animals in research (known as *in vivo* methods) exist, two of which are *in vitro* methods and computer simulations. These methods are more applicable to biological and medical research than to behavioral research. *In vitro* (which means "in glass") methods substitute isolated living tissue cultures for whole, living animals. Experiments using this method have been performed to test the toxicity and mutagenicity of various chemicals and drugs on living tissue. *Computer simulations* also have been suggested as an alternative to using living organisms in research. In a computer simulation study, a mathematical model of the process to be simulated is programmed into the computer. Parameters and data concerning variables fed into a computer then indicate what patterns of behavior would develop according to the model.

Several problems with *in vitro* and computer simulation methods preclude them from being substitutes for psychological research on living organisms. In drug studies, for example, *in vitro* methods may be adequate in the early stages of testing. However, the only way to determine the drug's effects on behavior is to test the drug on living, behaving animals. At present, the behavioral or psychological effects of these chemical agents cannot be predicted by the reactions of tissue samples or the results of computer simulations. Behavioral systems are simply too complex for that. Would you feel confident taking a new tranquilizer that had only been tested on tissues in a petri dish?

The effects of environmental variables and manipulations of the brain also cannot be studied using *in vitro* methods. It is necessary to have a living organism. For example, if you were interested in determining how a particular part of the brain affects aggression, you would not be able to study this problem with an *in vitro* method. You would need an intact organism (such as a rat) in order to systematically manipulate the brain and observe behavioral changes.

A different problem arises with computer simulation. You need enough information to write the simulation, and this information can only be obtained by observing and testing live, intact animals. Even when a model has been developed, behavioral research on animals is necessary to determine whether the model correctly predicts behavior. Far from eliminating the need for animals in behavioral research, developing and testing computer simulations actually increases this need.

In short, there are really no viable alternatives to using animals in behavioral research. Ultimately, it is up to you to be sure the techniques you use do not cause the animals undue suffering. Always be aware of your responsibility to treat your animal subjects ethically and humanely.

## SUMMARY

You need to decide on your subject population when you decide to conduct research. Two choices available in behavioral research are human participants and animal subjects. Your decision about which to use depends on your research question and any special needs of your research.

Using participants or subjects involves selecting an appropriate population of individuals. Because you cannot test every individual in the population (especially when that population is very large), you must select a sample of individuals for inclusion in your study. One goal of your study should be to generalize from your sample to the larger population. This is only possible if the characteristics of your sample match closely the characteristics of the population. Much research in psychology has used college students as the subject sample. Whether the results from such research generalize to the wider population is a subject of debate among researchers.

Precisely how you acquire human participants for your research depends on two factors: the policies of the institution at which the research is being conducted and the nature of the research strategy. Some institutions have subject pools consisting of a population of individuals (such as introductory psychology students) who are available as participants. Participants in this pool may be offered extra credit or other incentives for their voluntary participation in research. If no subject pool exists, you will have to recruit participants on your own. Acquiring participants for laboratory research can be done through a subject pool. However, participants for field research cannot be acquired that way.

You must consider the ethics of your research when human participants are chosen for study. Concern over the ethical treatment of participants can be traced back to the Nuremberg trials after World War II. During those trials medical experiments conducted on inmates in concentration camps came to light. Because of the treatment of individuals in those experiments, the Nuremberg Code was developed to govern experiments with humans. The APA developed a code of ethics for treatment of human participants in research that is based on the Nuremberg Code. Ethical treatment of participants in an experiment requires voluntary participation, informed consent, the right to withdraw, the right to obtain results, and the right to confidentiality (among others).

Sometimes ethical treatment of participants comes into conflict with research methodology. The requirement of voluntary participation and full disclosure of the methods of your research may lead to problems. For example, individuals who volunteer have been found to differ from nonvolunteers in several ways. This volunteer bias represents a threat to both internal and external validity. It can be counteracted to some extent by careful participant recruitment procedures. In cases in which you must use a deceptive technique, take special care to ensure that your participants leave your experiment in the proper frame of mind. You can accomplish this through effective debriefing techniques. At all times, however, you must remain cognizant of the ethical problems with deception even if debriefing is used.

A large amount of psychological research uses animal subjects. Animals are preferred to humans in situations in which experimental manipulations are unethical for use with humans. However, if you use animal subjects, you are still bound by an ethical code. Animals must be treated humanely. It is to your advantage to treat your animals ethically, because research shows that mistreated animals may yield data that are invalid.

Alternatives to using animals in research have been proposed, including the use of *in vitro* testing and computer simulation. These alternatives, unfortunately, are not viable for behavioral research, in which the goal is to understand the influences of variables on the behavior of the intact, living animals.

## REVIEW QUESTIONS

1. What factors affect your decision to use human participants or animal subjects in research?
2. What is a population, and how does it relate to a sample?
3. What is a sample, and how is one used in research?
4. What is random sampling, and how does it relate to the generality of your research?
5. What is nonrandom sampling, and how does it relate to the generality of your research?
6. Under what conditions is random sampling preferred over nonrandom sampling?
7. Why did the APA code of research ethics evolve?
8. What are the historical roots of the APA code of research ethics?
9. What are the main points of the APA code of research ethics?

10. What role does an institutional review board (IRB) play in the research process?
11. How can ethical requirements affect how you conduct your research and the conclusions you draw from your research?
12. How does the nature of your research affect how you acquire your human research participants?
13. How does the requirement for voluntary participation affect the validity of your research?
14. How do participant characteristics and situational factors relate to one's decision to volunteer for research?
15. How does volunteerism affect the internal and external validity of your research?
16. What steps can you take to reduce the effect of volunteerism on your research?
17. What is deception in research, and when is it allowed to be used?
18. What effect does deception have on research participants, and how can the effects be reduced?
19. What are the advantages and disadvantages of the techniques used to reduce the impact of deception?
20. Why would you consider using animals as research subjects?
21. What factors affect your decision about which animals to use in your research, and how can those animals be obtained?
22. What are the ethical guidelines that you must follow when using animal subjects?
23. Must the results from animal research generalize to humans (why or why not)?
24. What arguments have been raised by animal rights activists concerning the use of animals in research, and how have scientists countered them?
25. What are the alternatives to using animals in research, and what are the advantages and disadvantages of each?

## KEY TERMS

| | |
|---|---|
| population | volunteer bias |
| sample | deception |
| generalization | role playing |
| random sample | debriefing |
| nonrandom sample | institutional animal care and use |
| institutional review board (IRB) | committee (IACUC) |

# Using Nonexperimental Research

In Chapter 4 we distinguished between correlational research (which involves observing variables as they exist in nature) and experimental research (which involves manipulating variables and observing how those manipulations affect other variables). In this chapter, we introduce you to several nonexperimental (correlational) research designs and to observational techniques often associated with them. As you read about the observational techniques, bear in mind that many of them also can be used when conducting experimental research.

## CONDUCTING OBSERVATIONAL RESEARCH

Although all research is observational (in the sense that variables are observed and recorded), the observational research designs described in this chapter are purely observational in two senses: (1) They are correlational designs and thus do not involve manipulation of variables, and (2) all use trained researchers to observe subjects' behaviors. This section describes how to make and assess behavioral observations. Before we look at the "nuts and bolts" of observational research, let's take a look at an example of observational research.

### Is a Dog Really a Human's Best Friend?

One adage that most of us learned as we grew up was that a dog was "man's best friend." Many dog owners would heartily agree that they have a special relationship with their pets. However, is there really a special quality to the human–dog relationship that places it in the category of a true emotional attachment? Emanuela Prato-Previde, Deborah Custance, Caterina Spiezio, and Francesca Sabatini (2003) conducted an observational study to investigate the nature of the human–dog relationship.

Prato-Previde et al. (2003) used the Ainsworth Strange Situation Test to evaluate the human–dog relationship. This test, when done with human children and their primary caregivers, involves a sequence of observations made of a child's behavior under varying conditions. For example, a mother and her toddler are left alone in an unfamiliar room and the toddler's behavior is observed. Will the child stay close to the mother or explore the room? Children who have a secure attachment to their primary caregiver usually show a willingness to explore the environment after a short time at their mother's side. The securely attached child will interact with a stranger who comes into the room. If the mother leaves the room, the securely attached child may show some distress but can be calmed down and will have a positive reaction when the mother returns. The child's exploratory behavior, reaction to a stranger, and behavior upon separation and upon reunification are behavioral indexes of attachment.

In Prato-Previde's (2003) study, 38 dog owner–dog dyads were observed in a strange-situation test environment. In the preexperimental phase, the owner and his or her dog were escorted to a waiting room where the owner filled out a questionnaire. Following this initial phase were eight experimental episodes that composed the strange-situation test. Table 7–1 shows what these episodes were.

The behaviors of the humans and the dog were videotaped for analysis. The dog's behavior was evaluated by two trained observers for its willingness to explore the unfamiliar room, reactions to an unfamiliar human, behavior upon separation from the owner, and behavior upon reunification with the owner. Prato-Previde et al. (2003) found that the dogs engaged in more exploratory behavior when the owner was present in the room than when the owner was absent. However, the dogs did not display behavior typical of a true "attachment" in the presence of the stranger. The dogs did not use their owners as a "secure base" (i.e., staying by the owner's side when a stranger entered the room and then gradually approaching the stranger). Prato-Previde et al. concluded that there is certainly evidence of a strong affectionate relationship between humans and dogs, but that the relationship is not the same as a true attachment.

Now that you have seen how an observational study works, we can turn to the mechanics of performing observational research. The first step is to develop behavioral categories.

## Developing Behavioral Categories

Behavioral categories (also referred to as *coding schemes* or in animal research as *ethograms*) include both the general and specific classes of behavior you are interested in observing. Each category must be operationally defined. For example, Prato-Previde et al. (2003) defined two of the behavioral categories for their study of human–dog attachment as follows:

Exploration:  "Activity directed toward physical aspects of the environment, including sniffing, close visual inspection, distal visual inspection, and genital oral examination, such as licking" (p. 234).

Vocalizing:  "Any kind of vocalization, i.e., barking, growling, howling, whining" (p. 235).

Developing behavioral categories can be a simple or formidable task. Recording physical characteristics of the subject is a relatively simple affair. However, when recording social behaviors, defining behavioral categories becomes more difficult.

**TABLE 7–1  Episodes Used by Prato-Previde et al. (2003) in Their Observational Study of Human–Dog Attachment**

| EPISODE | EPISODE TITLE | EPISODE DESCRIPTION |
|---|---|---|
| 1 | Dog and owner | Owner fills out questionnaire and interacts with dog only if specifically approached by the dog. |
| 2 | Owner, dog, and stranger | Stranger enters the room and sits quietly across the room. At end of the episode, the owner leaves the room. |
| 3 | Stranger and dog | Stranger and dog are alone in the room. The stranger attempts to play with the dog or soothe it if it is distressed. |
| 4 | Owner and dog: First reunion | Owner returns to the room and the stranger leaves. |
| 5 | Dog alone | Owner leaves the room, leaving the dog alone in the room. |
| 6 | Stranger and dog | Stranger enters the room and attempts to interact with the dog. At the end of the episode, the stranger leaves. |
| 7 | Owner and dog: Second reunion | The owner returns to the room. At the end of the episode, the owner leaves but leaves his or her shoes and an article of clothing on the chair. |
| 8 | Dog and objects | The dog is left alone in the room with the objects. The owner returns at the end of the episode. |

This is because coding "socially based" behaviors may involve cultural traditions that are not agreed on (for example, coding certain speech as "obscene"—Bakeman & Gottman, 1989).

Your behavioral categories operationally define what behaviors should be recorded during observation periods. Define your categories clearly. Your observers should not be left wondering what category a particular behavior falls into. Ill-defined and ambiguous categories lead to recording errors and results that are difficult to interpret.

To develop clear, well-defined categories, begin with a clear idea about the goals of your study. Clearly defined hypotheses help narrow your behavioral categories to those that are central to your research questions. Also, keep your behavioral categories as simple as possible (Bakeman & Gottman, 1989) and stay focused on your research objectives. Avoid the temptation to accomplish too much within a single study.

One way to develop behavioral categories is to make informal, preliminary observations of your subjects under the conditions that will prevail during your study. During these preliminary observation periods, become familiar with the behaviors exhibited by your subjects and construct as complete a list of them as you can. Later you can condense these behaviors into fewer categories, if necessary. Another way to develop behavioral categories is to conduct a literature search to determine how other researchers in your field define behavioral categories in research situations similar to your own. You might even find an article in which the researchers used categories that are nearly perfect for your study. Adapting someone else's categories for your own use is an acceptable practice. In fact, standardizing on categories used in previous research will enhance the comparability of your data with data previously reported.

Even if you do find an article with what appear to be the "perfect categories," make some preliminary observations to be sure the categories fit your research needs. Take the time necessary to develop your categories carefully. In the long run, it is easier to adjust things before you begin your study than to worry about how to analyze data that were collected using poorly defined categories.

## Quantifying Behavior in an Observational Study

As with any other type of measure, direct behavioral observation requires that you develop ways to quantify the behaviors under observation. Methods used to quantify behavior in observational studies include the frequency method, the duration method, and the intervals method (Badia & Runyon, 1982).

**Frequency Method**    With the *frequency method*, you record the number of times a particular behavior occurs within a time period. This number is the frequency of the behavior. For example, Prato-Previde et al. (2003) counted the number of vocalizations each dog made within each episode.

**Duration Method**    With the *duration method*, your interest is in how long a particular behavior lasts. For example, you could record the duration of each aggressive act displayed by children during free play. In their dog study, Prato-Previde et al. (2003) recorded how long a dog greeted a human (in seconds) before it displayed another behavior.

The duration method can be used along with the frequency method. In this case, you record both the frequency of occurrence of a behavior and its duration.

**Intervals Method**    With the *intervals method*, you divide your observation period into discrete time intervals and then record whether a behavior occurs within each interval. For example, you might record whether an aggressive act occurs during successive two-minute time periods. Ideally, your intervals should be short enough that only one instance of a behavior can occur during an interval.

## Recording Single Events or Behavior Sequences

Researchers doing observational studies have long recorded single events occurring within some identifiable observation period. Bakeman and Gottman (1989) advocated looking at *behavior sequences* rather than at isolated behavioral events. As an example, consider an observational study of language development in which you record the number of times a parent uses language to correct a child's behavior. Although such data may be informative, a better strategy might be to record those same behaviors sequentially, noting which instances of language use normally follow one another. For example, is a harsh reprimand more likely to follow destructive behavior than nondestructive behavior? Recording such behavior sequences provides a more complete picture of complex social behaviors and the transitions between them.

Although recording behavior sequences requires more effort than recording single events, the richness of the resulting data may be well worth the effort. You can find more information about this method in Bakeman and Gottman, *Observing Interaction: An Introduction to Sequential Analysis* (1989).

## Coping with Complexity

When you have defined your behavioral categories and settled on a method of quantifying behavior, you next must decide how to make your observations. Defining discrete time intervals during which to record behavior is easy enough, but actually recording the observations may be another matter. Take the example of observing the free-play behavior of preschool children.

Assume that you have clearly defined your behavioral categories and have decided to use the frequency method to quantify behavior. On Monday at 8 A.M. you arrive at the preschool classroom at which you intend to make your observations. Fourteen children are in the class. You sit in an observation room equipped with a one-way mirror and begin to observe the children in the classroom on the other side of the mirror. It doesn't take you long to realize that something is wrong. Your participants are running around in small groups, scurrying hither and yon. You cannot possibly observe all the children at once. Dejectedly, you leave the preschool and return home to try to work out an effective observation strategy.

This vignette illustrates an important fact about behavioral observation: Having clearly defined behavioral categories and adequate quantification methods does not guarantee that your observational techniques will work. Naturally occurring behavior is often complex and fast paced. To make effective observations, you may need to use special techniques to deal with the rate at which the behaviors you wish to observe occur.

One solution to the problem is to sample the behaviors under observation rather than attempt to record every occurrence. Three sampling techniques to choose from are time sampling, individual sampling, and event sampling (Conrad & Maul, 1981).

*Time Sampling*   With time sampling, you scan the group for a specific period of time (for example, 30 seconds) and then record the observed behaviors for the next period (for example, another 30 seconds). You alternate between periods of observation and recording as long as necessary. Time sampling is most appropriate when behavior occurs continuously rather than in short bursts spaced over time and when you are observing large groups of subjects engaged in complex interactions. Prato-Previde et al. (2003) used time sampling in their study of human–dog attachments. For behavior categories for which duration was not critical (e.g., exploration), each dog's behavior was observed for several five-second intervals.

*Individual Sampling*    With individual sampling, you select a single subject for observation over a given time period (for example, 10 minutes) and record his or her behavior. Over successive time periods, you repeat your observations for the other individuals in the observed group. Individual sampling is most appropriate when you want to preserve the organization of an individual's behavior over time rather than simply noting how often particular behaviors occur.

*Event Sampling*    In event sampling, you observe only one behavior (for example, sharing behavior) and record all instances of that behavior. Event sampling is most useful when you can clearly define one behavior as more important than others and focus on that one behavior.

*Recording*    You also could use recording devices to make a permanent record of behavior for later analysis, as Prato-Previde et al. (2003) did in their study. They installed two video cameras in the unfamiliar room to record the dog's behavior on tape. Recording equipment has several advantages. First, because you have a permanent record, you can review your subjects' behavior several times, perhaps picking up nuances of behavior that would have been missed in a single, live observation. Second, you can have multiple observers watch the tape independently and then compare their evaluations of behavior. (Although you can use multiple observers for live observations, it may be disruptive to your subjects to have several observers watching.) Finally, you may be able to hide a camera more easily than you can hide yourself. The hidden camera may be less disruptive to your subjects' behavior than an observer.

Recording behavior on tape does not eliminate the need to classify the behaviors and to measure such aspects of the behaviors as frequencies and durations. Whether you perform these activities "live" or work from a recording, you will need a system for coding these characteristics.

One option is to develop a paper-and-pencil coding form similar to the one shown in Figure 7–1. Your observers would use the form to record the behaviors they see. Another option is to have observers speak into a handheld tape recorder.

Which of these two options you should choose depends on the nature of your study and limitations inherent in the situation. Paper-and-pencil coding sheets can be used in just about any situation. They are quiet and, if properly constructed, efficient. They do have a few drawbacks, however. If you are requiring your observers to make extensive notes (not just checking behavioral categories), the task may become too complex and time-consuming, especially if behaviors occur in rapid succession. In such cases, you might consider having your observers use tape recorders instead of paper-and-pencil coding forms. The main advantage with this technique is that your observers will probably be able to speak into the recorder faster than they could make written notes. They also can keep their eyes on the subjects *while* making their notes. A disadvantage is that observers speaking into a recorder may disturb your subjects. Consequently, this technique should only be used when your observers are out of earshot of your subjects.

## Establishing the Reliability of Your Observations

Assume that by now you have adequately defined the behavior you want to observe, developed a coding sheet, and worked out how you are going to observe behavior.

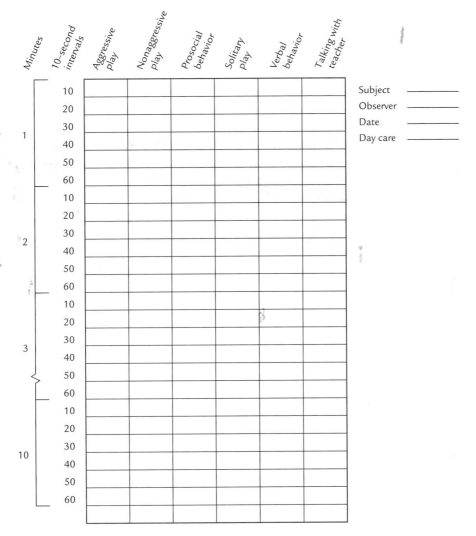

**FIGURE 7-1**    Example of a Paper-and-Pencil Coding Sheet for an Observational Study.

You go into the field and begin making your observations. You come back with reams of data-coding sheets in hand and begin to summarize and interpret your data. You have apparently covered every possible base, and believe that your observations accurately portray the observed behavior. But do they? Your observations may not be as accurate as you think. Your personal biases and expectations may have affected how you recorded the behavior observed. As with any measurement technique, when you conduct direct behavioral observations, you should make an effort to establish the reliability of your observations.

If you were the only observer, you could not firmly establish the reliability of your observations. To avoid the problem of single-observer idiosyncrasies, you should use multiple observers. This practice is generally preferred over single-observer methods.

If you decide to use multiple observers, you face the possibility that your observers will not agree on how to code behavior. Theoretically, if you use well-trained observers and well-defined behavior categories, there should be a minimum of disagreement. However, disagreement is likely to arise despite your best efforts. Observers invariably differ in how they see and interpret behavior. Disagreement also may arise if your behavioral categories are not clearly defined. Because disagreement is likely to occur to one degree or another, you must establish **interrater reliability**, which provides an empirical index of observer agreement.

Bakeman and Gottman (1989) pointed out that there are three reasons to check for interrater reliability. First, establishing interrater reliability helps ensure that your observers are accurate and that your procedures can be easily reproduced. Second, you can check to see that your observers meet some standard you have established. Third, any problems detected can be corrected with additional training.

*Percent Agreement*    The simplest way to assess interrater reliability is to evaluate *percent agreement.* This method involves counting the number of times your observers agreed and dividing this number by the total number of observations. Specifically, you calculate percent agreement according to the following formula:

$$\frac{\text{Total number of agreements}}{\text{Total number of observations}} \times 100$$

For example, if your observers agreed on 8 of 10 observations, then the percent agreement would be

$$\frac{8}{10} \times 100 = 80\%$$

Of course, you want your percent agreement to be as high as possible, approaching 100 percent. However, for most applications, a percent agreement around 70 percent is acceptable.

Although percent agreement is a simple way to assess interrater reliability, the technique has drawbacks. First, if you define agreement as an exact match between observations, then percent agreement *underestimates* interrater agreement (Mitchell, 1979). This problem can be reduced somewhat by using a looser definition of agreement. Second, percent agreement gives you only a raw estimate of agreement. Some agreement between observers is to be expected based on chance alone. Percent agreement makes no provision for determining whether the amount of agreement observed is real or due to chance (Mitchell, 1979). Third, behaviors that occur with very high or low frequency may have extremely high levels of chance agreement. In those cases, percent agreement *overestimates* interrater agreement (Mitchell, 1979).

*Cohen's Kappa*    A more popular method of assessing interrater reliability than percent agreement is **Cohen's Kappa**. Unlike percent agreement, Cohen's Kappa allows you to evaluate the possibility that the amount of agreement observed between observers is due to chance (via a statistical test; see Bakeman & Gottman, 1989). To use this method, you need to determine (1) the proportion of actual agreement between observers (actual agreement) and (2) the proportion of agreement you would expect by chance (expected agreement). Use these two values in the following formula (Bakeman & Gottman, 1989):

$$K = \frac{P_o - P_c}{1 - P_c}$$

where $P_o$ is the observed proportion of actual agreement and $P_c$ is the chance proportion of expected agreement.

Suppose you conducted a study of the relationship between the number of hours an infant spends in day care and later attachment security. As your measure of attachment security, you have two observers watch a mother and her child for a 20-minute period. The coding scheme here is simple. All your observers are required to do is code the child's behavior as indicative of either a "secure attachment" or an "insecure attachment" within each of 20 one-minute observation periods. Sample coding sheets are shown in Figure 7–2. A "1" in a cell indicates that the behavior of the subject fell into that category.

The first step in computing Cohen's Kappa is to tabulate in a *confusion matrix* the frequencies of agreements and disagreements between observers (Bakeman & Gottman, 1989), as shown in Figure 7–3. The numbers on the diagonal (red line in the figure) represent agreements, and the numbers off the diagonal represent disagreements. The numbers along the right edge and bottom of the matrix represent the row and column totals and the total number of observations.

The next step is to compute the value of Cohen's Kappa (K). First, determine the proportion of actual agreement by summing the values along the diagonal and dividing by the total number of observations:

$$P_o = \frac{16 + 3}{20} = .95$$

Next, find the proportion of expected agreement by multiplying corresponding row and column totals and dividing by the number of observations squared (Bakeman & Gottman, 1989):

$$P_c = \frac{(17 \times 16) + (3 \times 4)}{20^2} = .71$$

Finally, enter these numbers into the formula for Cohen's Kappa:

$$K = \frac{.95 - .71}{1 - .71} = .83$$

At this point you have computed a reliability score of .83. What does this number mean? Is this good or bad? According to Bakeman and Gottman (1989), any value of .7 or greater indicates acceptable reliability.

*Pearson's Product–Moment Correlation* Pearson's product–moment correlation coefficient, or Pearson r (see Chapter 12), provides a convenient alternative to Cohen's Kappa for measuring interrater agreement. Table 7–2 shows the frequency of aggressive

| Observation period | Observer 1 Secure | Observer 1 Insecure | Observer 2 Secure | Observer 2 Insecure |
|---|---|---|---|---|
| 1 | / |  | / |  |
| 2 | / |  | / |  |
| 3 | / |  | / |  |
| 4 | / |  | / |  |
| 5 |  | / |  | / |
| 6 | / |  | / |  |
| 7 | / |  |  | / |
| 8 |  | / |  | / |
| 9 |  | / |  | / |
| 10 | / |  | / |  |
| 11 | / |  | / |  |
| 12 | / |  | / |  |
| 13 | / |  | / |  |
| 14 | / |  | / |  |
| 15 | / |  | / |  |
| 16 | / |  | / |  |
| 17 | / |  | / |  |
| 18 | / |  | / |  |
| 19 | / |  | / |  |
| 20 | / |  | / |  |

**FIGURE 7–2**    Sample Coding Sheets for Two Observers Counting "Secure" and "Insecure" Behavior Instances.

behavior among members of a hypothetical monkey colony over five two-minute observation periods as coded by two observers. If your observers agree, Pearson $r$ will be strong and positive. For example, Pearson $r$ for the data shown in Table 7–2 is .90 This strong correlation (the maximum possible is 1.00) indicates substantial agreement. After calculating Pearson $r$, you can easily determine its statistical significance (see Chapter 12), an advantage over Cohen's Kappa.

You must be cautious when using Pearson $r$ to assess interrater agreement. Two sets of numbers can be highly correlated even when observers disagree markedly. This situation occurs when the *magnitudes* of the recorded scores increase and decrease similarly across observations by the two observers but differ in absolute value. For example, assume Observer 1 recorded 1, 2, 3, 4, and 5, and Observer 2 recorded 6, 7, 8, 9, and 10 over the same intervals. These numbers are perfectly correlated ($r = 1.00$), yet the two observers never agreed on the actual numbers to record. You can check for this problem by comparing the means and standard deviations of the two sets of scores. If they are similar and Pearson $r$ is high, you can safely assume that your observers agree.

*Intraclass Correlation (ICC)*    The **intraclass correlation coefficient ($r_I$)** can be used when your observations are scaled on an interval or ratio scale of measurement.

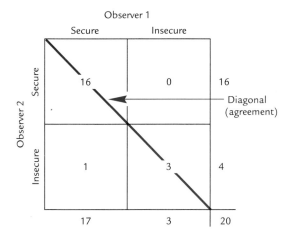

**FIGURE 7-3**   Sample Confusion Matrix.

For example, if you have observers count the frequency of aggressive behavior, ICC would be a good way to assess interrater reliability. ICC uses an analysis-of-variance approach to assess reliability. To conduct an ICC, you construct a two-way table in which the columns represent observers' ratings (one column for each observer) and the rows represent participants (each row has the data from one participant), as shown in Table 7–3. The formula for calculating $r_I$ uses the mean squares (MS) components from the analysis of variance: the mean square within subjects ($MS_W$) and mean square between subjects ($MS_B$). The formula used to calculate $r_I$ suggested by Shrout and Fleiss (1979) is

$$r_I = \frac{(MS_B - MS_W)}{(MS_B + (k-1)(MS_W))}$$

where $k$ is the number of raters. For the data shown in Table 7–3, we have

$$r_I = \frac{(14.6056 - .3833)}{[14.6056 + (2-1)(.3833)]} = .9488$$

   Intraclass correlation analysis is a flexible, powerful tool for evaluating interrater reliability. The interested reader should refer to Shrout and Fleiss (1979) and McGraw and Wong (1996) for an in-depth discussion of intraclass correlation.

***Dealing with Data from Multiple Observers***   When multiple observers disagree, what should you do? If you have a high level of agreement, you can average across observers. For example, in Table 7–2, you can average across observers within each observation period to get a mean, or X [for the first period, X = (6 + 7)/2 = 6.5], and then obtain an overall average across observation periods. This gives you the average aggression shown during the observation period.

   Another common method is to have observers meet and resolve any discrepancies. This method is practical when the behavior being coded has been recorded and can be reviewed. Yet another method is to designate one of the observers as the "main observer" and the other as the "secondary observer." Make this designation before

TABLE 7–2    **Hypothetical Monkey Aggression Data Collected by Two Observers**

| Observation Period | FREQUENCY OF AGGRESSIVE BEHAVIOR | |
|---|---|---|
| | Observer 1 | Observer 2 |
| One | 6 | 7 |
| Two | 2 | 4 |
| Three | 1 | 0 |
| Four | 5 | 7 |
| Five | 3 | 2 |

you begin your observations. The observations from the "main observer" then serve as the numbers used in any data analyses. The observations from the "secondary observer" are used only to establish reliability.

### Sources of Bias in Observational Research

Because observational research is a human endeavor, a degree of bias may contaminate the observations. One source of bias that can easily be avoided is *observer bias*. Observer bias occurs when your observers know the goals of a study or the hypotheses being tested and their observations are influenced by this information. For example, suppose you have hypothesized that more interpersonal aggression will be shown by males than by females and that you have told your observers of this hypothesis. Suppose that your observers see a male child roughly take a toy away from another child and later see a female child do the same. Because of observer bias, your observers may code the male child's behavior, but not the female child's behavior, as aggressive. This is the same problem discussed in Chapter 5 as experimenter bias, and the solution is the same: Use a *blind observer*. A blind observer is one who is unaware of the hypotheses under test. (For more details about blind techniques, see Chapter 5.)

Another source of bias in observational research arises when observers interpret what they see rather than simply record behavior. We have all seen nature specials on television in which a researcher is observing animals in the wild (chimpanzees, for example). Too often those researchers infer intentions behind the behaviors they observe. When one chimp prods another with a stick, for example, the behavior may be recorded as a "playful, mischievous attack."

The problem with such inferences is that we simply do not know whether they are correct. We tend to read into the behaviors of animals the motivations and emotions we ourselves would likely experience in similar situations. However, the animal's motivations and emotions may, in fact, be very different from ours. Stick to what is immediately apparent from the observation. If you have preserved the actual behavior in your records rather than your interpretation of the behavior, you can always

TABLE 7–3  **Hypothetical Data for an Example of an Intraclass Correlation Coefficient to Test Interrater Reliability**

| PARTICIPANT | RATER 1 | RATER 2 |
| --- | --- | --- |
| 1 | 8.00 | 10.00 |
| 2 | 6.00 | 5.00 |
| 3 | 2.00 | 2.00 |
| 4 | 7.00 | 7.00 |
| 5 | 5.00 | 5.00 |
| 6 | 9.00 | 9.00 |
| 7 | 1.00 | 1.00 |
| 8 | 6.00 | 6.00 |
| 9 | 7.00 | 8.00 |
| 10 | 8.00 | 7.00 |

provide an interpretation later. If new evidence suggests a different interpretation, you will have the original behavioral observations available to reinterpret.

When your subjects are people, you should still do your best to record behaviors rather than your interpretations of those behaviors. Piaget showed that inferences concerning the motivation and knowledge of children are often wrong, and the same is probably true of inferences about adults. Once again, if your data preserve the behavior rather than your interpretations of the behavior, you can always reinterpret your data later if this is required by new evidence.

Now that you know how to go about developing and using direct behavioral measures, it is time to become familiar with several nonexperimental approaches to data collection.

## QUALITATIVE APPROACHES

Counting and otherwise quantifying behavior is not the only approach one can take when conducting research. In some instances you might consider collecting qualitative data. **Qualitative data** consist of written records of observed behavior that are analyzed qualitatively. For example, in a study of client reactions to a new form of psychotherapy, you could collect qualitative data by interviewing clients to determine their perceptions of and attitudes about the new therapy. Unlike the quantitative approach in which you might have clients rate attitude statements on a scale or in which you might count the number of times a certain thing was mentioned (such as the warmth of the experimenter), in the qualitative approach you would review the interview protocols and extract themes that emerged via the interviews (for example, clients' impressions of the language used during the therapy).

Qualitative analysis of qualitative data poses special problems for researchers. Usually there are large amounts of raw data to deal with, and there exist few computerized programs that will analyze qualitative verbal information. This leaves the task of analysis of qualitative data to the ingenuity of the researcher.

In the sections that follow, which introduce various nonexperimental methods, we present a mix of examples representing both quantitative and qualitative approaches.

## NATURALISTIC OBSERVATION

**Naturalistic observation** involves observing your subjects in their natural environments, without making any attempt to control or manipulate variables. For example, you might observe chimpanzees in their African habitat, children in a day care center, shoppers in a mall, or participants in a court proceeding. In all these cases, you would avoid making any changes in the situation that might affect the natural, ongoing behaviors of your subjects.

### Making Unobtrusive Observations

Although you may not intend it, the mere act of observing may disturb the behavior of your subjects. Such disturbances may reduce the internal or external validity of your observations. To prevent this difficulty, you should make *unobtrusive observations*, or observations that do not alter the natural behaviors of your subjects.

Translating this requirement into practice may involve the use of special equipment. When studying the nesting habits of a particular species of birds, for example, you may have to build a blind (an enclosure that shields you from the view of your subjects) from which to make your observations. When studying social interactions among preschool children in a day care center, you may have to make your observations from behind a one-way mirror. In either case, you want to prevent your subjects from knowing that they are being observed.

Unfortunately, it is not always possible to remain hidden. For example, you may need to be closer to your subjects than a blind or observation room allows. In such cases, a widely used technique is to habituate your subjects to your presence (a fancy way of saying "letting your subjects get used to you") before you begin making your observations. Habituating subjects involves gradually introducing yourself to the environment of your subjects. Eventually your subjects will view your presence as normal and ignore you. If you were interested in observing children in a day care center, for example, you might begin by sitting quietly away from the children (perhaps in a far corner of the room) until the children no longer paid attention to you. Gradually you would move closer to the children, allowing them to habituate to your presence at each step before moving closer.

Habituation may be necessary even if you are going to videotape behavior for later analysis. The presence of a television camera in a room will attract attention at first. Allowing your subjects to habituate to the camera before you begin your observations will help reduce the camera's disruptive effects.

You also can make observations unobtrusively by abandoning direct observations of behavior in favor of *indirect measures*. For example, to study recycling behavior, you could look through recycling bins or trash to gauge the extent to which your participants recycle and determine the types of materials they recycle. In this case, participants do not know that their behavior is being observed (that is, unless you get caught snooping through their recycling materials).

## Advantages and Disadvantages of Naturalistic Observation

Naturalistic observation gives you insight into how behavior occurs in the real world. The observations you make are not tainted by an artificial laboratory setting, and you therefore can be reasonably sure your observations are representative of naturally occurring behavior. In other words, properly conducted naturalistic observation has extremely high external validity. However, because naturalistic observation is a purely descriptive technique, you can only speculate about the causes of behavior. You cannot prove that the observed relationships are causal. In addition, naturalistic observation can be time-consuming and expensive. Unlike some types of observation in which subjects in effect record their own data, naturalistic observation requires you to be there, engaged in observation, during the entire data-collecting period, which may last hours, days, or longer. Also, getting to the natural habitat of your subjects may not be easy. In some cases (such as observing chimpanzee behavior in the wild, as Jane Goodall did), naturalistic observation requires traveling great distances to reach the habitat of your subjects.

## ETHNOGRAPHY

In **ethnography** a researcher becomes immersed in the behavioral or social system being studied (Berg, 1998). The technique is used primarily to study and describe the functioning of cultures through a study of social interactions and expressions between people and groups (Berg, 1998). Like an investigative reporter or undercover police officer, you insinuate yourself within a group and study the social structures and interaction patterns of that group from within. Your role as a researcher is to make careful observations and record the social structure of the group you are studying.

Ethnography is a time-tested research technique that has been popular, especially in the field of anthropology. However, it also has been applied to sociological and psychological studies of various behavior systems, in which it has been used to study client and therapist perceptions of marital therapy (Smith, Sells, & Clevenger, 1994), the learning of aggressive behaviors in different cultures (for example, Fry, 1992), the assassination of John F. Kennedy (Trujillo, 1993), the sudden death of loved ones (Ellis, 1993), and even the consumer-based subculture of modern bikers who ride Harley-Davidson motorcycles (Schouten & McAlexander, 1995). In most cases, ethnographic research is conducted in field settings, which makes the ethnographer a field researcher.

As with any research method, ethnography takes a systematic approach to the topics and systems for which it is used. Berg (1998) describes the process of conducting ethnographic research in detail. According to Berg, there are several issues an ethnographer must face with this type of research. We explore these next.

## Observing as a Participant or Nonparticipant

One decision you will have to make early on is whether to conduct your observations using **participant observation**, in which you act as a functioning member of the group, or using **nonparticipant observation**, in which you observe as a nonmember. In addition, you will have to decide whether to conduct your observations overtly (the group members know that you are conducting research on the group) or covertly (unobtrusive observation). When done overtly, both participant and nonparticipant observation carry the possibility of subject reactivity; as we noted in Chapter 5, group members who know they are being observed may behave differently than they otherwise would, thus threatening external validity. This problem becomes more serious with participant observation, in which you interact with your participants.

You can minimize this problem by using participant observers who are trained not to interfere with the natural process of the group being studied or by using observers who are blind to the purposes of the study. Alternatively, if you must use participant observation, you could always become a passive participant. As such, you would keep your contributions to the group to a minimum so that you would not significantly alter the natural flow of behavior. Your main role would be to observe and record what is going on. Finally, if possible, you could become a nonparticipant observer and avoid interacting with the group altogether.

Reactivity can be eliminated by choosing to observe covertly. Nonparticipant covert observation is essentially naturalistic observation. Because your subjects do not know they are being observed, their behavior will be natural. Becoming a covert participant entails joining the group to be observed without disclosing your status as a researcher, so again your subjects will behave naturally in your presence. Additionally, by using covert entry, you may be able to gain access to information that would not be available if an overt entry strategy were used.

When using covert entry, you still need to be concerned about your presence disrupting the normal flow of the social interactions within the group. Your presence as a member/participant may influence how the group functions.

The practice of covertly infiltrating a group carries with it ethical liabilities. Because your subjects are not aware that they are being studied, they cannot give informed consent to participate. As discussed in Chapter 6, such violations may be acceptable if your results promise to make a significant contribution to the understanding of behavior. Thus, before deciding on covert entry, you must weigh the potential benefit of your research against the potential costs to the participants. You should adopt a covert entry strategy only if you and your institutional review board agree that the potential benefits outweigh the potential costs.

## Gaining Access to a Field Setting

Your first task when conducting ethnographic research is to gain access to the group or organization you wish to study. In some cases this would be easy. For example, if you wanted to conduct an ethnographic study of mall shoppers during the Christmas shopping season, you would only need to situate yourself in a mall and record the behaviors and verbalizations of shoppers. Being a public place, the mall offers free and unlimited access. In other cases, settings are more difficult to access. To conduct an ethnographic study of the police subculture, for example, you probably would need to obtain the permission of the police commissioner, various high-ranking police officers, and perhaps the rank-and-file police officers. Only then would you have access to police stations, squad cars, patrols, and so on. Access to the meeting places of elite groups (for example, country clubs) also may be difficult, because such groups often establish barriers and obstacles (such as membership requirements, restrictive guest access) to limit who has access to the facilities (Berg, 1998).

## Gaining Entry into the Group

Gaining access to the research setting often requires gaining entry into the group you plan to study. A popular strategy is "case and approach" (Berg, 1998). In this strategy, you first "case" the group, much as a criminal cases a bank before robbing it. That is, you try to find information about the group, such as its social structure, its hierarchy of authority (if any), and its rituals and routines. Such foreknowledge makes it easier to enter the group and function effectively once inside. Berg suggests starting your search in the local library. Here you may find valuable information in newspapers, magazines, and other information sources. You also might check the Internet; many groups maintain Web sites that provide literature about themselves.

To enter the group, you may have to bargain with the members to establish your role and your boundaries (Berg, 1998). You also may find that you need to get past *gatekeepers* who serve as formal or informal protectors of the group. Getting past gatekeepers may require some negotiation and mediation (Berg, 1998). If you can cast your research in a favorable light, entry into the group may be facilitated. For example, in an ethnographic study of prisoners in a county jail, the gatekeepers are the warden and high-ranking enforcement officials. Your chances of gaining entry into the prison population will be greater if you can convince those officials of the potential benefits of your study.

Another strategy for gaining entry into a group is to use *guides* and *informants* (Berg, 1998). These are members of the group (model inmates, prison guards) who can help convince the gatekeepers that your aims are legitimate and that your study is worthwhile.

Although these techniques for gaining entry into a group are effective, they raise some ethical issues. The targets of your observations may not know that they are being studied. Participants are not able to give informed consent. However, recall from Chapter 6 that under certain conditions an institutional review board (IRB) may approve a study that does not include informed consent. You need to consider the ethical implications of your ethnographic research and justify to an IRB the need to suspend the requirement for informed consent.

## Becoming Invisible

Once inside the group, your presence may alter the behavior of your participants or the operation of the social system being studied. Berg suggests several strategies for making yourself "invisible." If you are using an overt entry strategy, you could join in the routines and rituals of your participants, or you could foster good relations with your participants. You also could choose to enter covertly, masking your role as researcher.

Whichever strategy you use, there are dangers to making yourself invisible (Berg, 1998). For example, if you use covert entry, there is the danger that your identity will be discovered, which would shatter any credibility you may have had.

## Making Observations and Recording Data

The essence of ethnography is to keep a careful record of what transpires within the group being studied. The various "recording" techniques discussed earlier can be applied to ethnography. You could, for example, make copious notes during critical interactions. If you were riding along with police officers, you could make notes of what is said and done during routine traffic stops. When such overt note taking is not possible (especially if you have decided to use covert entry into a group), you could instead keep scraps of paper or index cards and jot down thoughts that will be expanded later (Berg, 1998). You also could use voice-activated tape recorders or other recording devices. Another strategy involves waiting until the end of the day when you are alone to record your observations. One drawback to this latter strategy is that you are relying on your memory for your field notes. Over the course of the day, you may forget details or distort others.

## Analyzing Ethnographic Data

If a purely qualitative approach is taken, data do not take the form of numbers (for example, the number of times a police officer threatens a suspect with arrest) but rather the form of narrative field notes from which themes and ideas are to be extracted. The first step in analyzing ethnographic data is to do an initial reading of your field notes to identify any themes and hypotheses, perhaps with an eye toward identifying themes and hypotheses overlooked (Berg, 1998). You also would systematically extract any major topics, issues, or themes present in your field records (Berg, 1998). The second step in analyzing ethnographic data is to code any systematic patterns in your notes and consider doing an in-depth content analysis (as discussed later in this chapter). Of course, this analysis strategy would be strengthened by using multiple, independent coders and content analyzers.

## Born to Be Wild: An Example of Ethnography

American culture, and Western culture in general, tends to be consumeristic. That is, we tend to buy a lot of stuff. Most of the stuff we buy we enjoy but do not become particularly attached to. There are instances, however, in which consumers become so wedded to the products they buy that an entire subculture develops around the product. One such example is the subculture of consumerism surrounding Harley-Davidson motorcycles. Many individuals who purchase Harley-Davidsons don't just own them; they become psychologically and emotionally immersed in a "biker" subculture. What is this subculture of consumerism like? How does the transformation to a biker occur? What does affiliation with other bikers confer on individuals? These and other questions were addressed in an ethnographic study of the "Harley-Davidson Subculture of Consumerism," or HDSC, conducted by Schouten and McAlexander (1995).

Conducting their ethnographic study of the HDSC over a three-year time span, Schouten and McAlexander first conducted some background research on the behavioral norms of bikers in the HDSC. To this end, they read scholarly literature on biker cultures and popular magazines geared toward this subculture. Next, they gained entry into the HDSC group by obtaining Harley-Davidson motorcycles (a prerequisite for club membership) and attending a meeting of a Harley Owners Group (HOG) chapter. At first they were treated as outsiders, but they were eventually accepted after they stopped to help a member whose motorcycle had broken down. As a consequence, two members took the researchers into their circle of riders.

To help them with their research, Schouten and McAlexander fostered relationships within the group and cultivated informants representing different "types" of Harley owners. The researchers made careful observations of member behavior, keeping copious notes and doing in-depth formal and informal interviews, which they recorded on tape whenever possible. When tape recorders could not be used, skeletal notes were jotted down and fleshed out at the end of the day. Photographs were taken to preserve a visual record of the HDSC. Schouten and McAlexander collected data at HOG chapter meetings, motorcycle rides, swap meets, dealers, bars, restaurants, members' homes, and major motorcycle rallies. They also gained a marketing perspective by interviewing executives of Harley-Davidson Corporation.

As they collected their data, Schouten and McAlexander "amassed, coded, compared and collapsed specific data to form themes or categories" (p. 47). The themes and categories extracted were then synthesized in a "holistic" manner. Themes and categories were verified by triangulating their interview and observational data. This process resulted in four major categories: structure, ethos, transformation of the self, and the role of marketing (p. 47).

By structure, Schouten and McAlexander mean the "structure of the subculture which governs the social interactions within it" (p. 48). Schouten and McAlexander identified a complex social structure involving different subgroups that identify themselves as bikers (with the common thread of owning a Harley-Davidson). For example, there were subgroups for recovering alcoholics, Vietnam Veterans, Born-Again Christians, Rich Urban Bikers (RUBs), and "Mom-and-Pop" bikers. Each of these groups, according to Schouten and McAlexander, maintained its own social hierarchy with officers and subordinates. Those in leadership roles tended to be the most committed (indicated by tattoos, motorcycle customization, club-specific clothing, wearing prestigious rally pins, and so on). The status hierarchy also was manifested in riding positions on group rides, with club officers at the head of the pack. Newer members supported the group economically and by providing social support for dominant members. Harley nonowners, or "aspirants," served as an audience and were important to the group because they often expressed envy, which validated the group's commitment to their Harley-Davidsons (Schouten & McAlexander, 1995).

Schouten and McAlexander described the "ethos" as a core set of values of the HDSC. These were found to include personal freedom, patriotism, machismo, and a nearly religious aspect of the subculture. Aspects of the transformation from nonbiker to biker and how Harley-Davidson markets to the biker ethos also were identified and described.

*Evaluation of the Ethnography of the HDSC*     Schouten and McAlexander's ethnographic analysis of the HDSC is purely qualitative; the various aspects of the HDSC are described in purely verbal terms. Nowhere in our brief description of their study are any numbers, percentages, or other statistics mentioned. For example, Schouten and McAlexander identified several subgroups of Harley-Davidson riders, which were described verbally in detail. However, no data were provided as to the percentage of Harley-Davidson riders that fell into each category. The ethnographic analysis provided is purely *descriptive* in nature. That is, we cannot explain *why* an individual buys into the HDSC, beyond the verbal descriptions of the ethos identified.

Although Schouten and McAlexander made no quantitative analyses of their data, there is nothing about ethnography that precludes at least some quantification (for example, percentage of Harley-Davidson riders who consider themselves bikers). The questions you are interested in addressing should drive your decision concerning the mix of qualitative and quantitative analyses you will use in your study.

## SOCIOMETRY

**Sociometry** involves identifying and measuring interpersonal relationships within a group (Berg, 1998). Sociometry has been applied to the systematic study of friendship patterns among children (for example, Vandell & Hembree, 1994) and peer assessments of teenagers solicited to deal drugs (Weinfurt & Bush, 1995), as well as other social networks and work relationships (Berg, 1998).

To conduct a sociometric study, you have research participants evaluate each other along some dimension. For example, if you were interested in studying friendship patterns among third-grade students, you could have the students identify those in the class who are their friends and those who are not their friends. Similar sociometric ratings could be acquired in a study of relationships among people in a workplace.

Sociometry can be used as the sole research tool to map interpersonal relationships, for example, to map friendship choices among five people in a club. (You might have each of the five people rank the three individuals they like best.) Some hypothetical data are shown in Figure 7–4. The individuals being chosen appear along the top, those doing the choosing along the side. For example, Person A chose Person B as her first choice, Person E as her second, and Person D as her third. Based on the data in Figure 7–4, you could graphically represent the pattern of friendship choices on a **sociogram**. Figure 7–5 displays an example sociogram.

Sociometric ratings can be included within a wider study as one of many measures. For example, you could use the sociometric ratings just presented in a study of whether sociometric status within a group relates to leadership roles. If there is a relationship between friendship choices and leadership roles, you would expect Person B to emerge as a club leader.

### An Example of Sociometry

An example of sociometry as part of a larger study is provided by Vandell and Hembree (1994), who investigated the relationship between peer friendships and a child's social and academic adjustment. They determined a child's status within the peer group using sociometric nominations among the children. Children were provided with a list of children of their own sex and asked to indicate the names of three children they "liked to play with." The children then were given a second list and asked

|  | \ Person chosen A | B | C | D | E |
|---|---|---|---|---|---|
| A |  | 1 |  | 3 | 2 |
| B | 1 |  | 2 |  | 3 |
| C | 1 | 2 |  | 3 |  |
| D |  | 1 | 2 |  | 3 |
| E | 2 | 1 |  | 3 |  |

(Person choosing)

**FIGURE 7–4**   Example of a Sociometric Scoring Sheet.

to circle three names of same-sex children they "did not like to play with." Based on these sociometric nominations, children were classified as either "popular," "neglected," "rejected," or "controversial." The children's social and academic adjustments were assessed via a questionnaire sent to parents, teacher evaluations, report cards, and standardized test scores. Vandell and Hembree (1994) found that popular children tended to fare better in terms of social and academic adjustment, whereas rejected children tended to do more poorly socially and academically.

## THE CASE HISTORY

In some instances, your research needs may require you to study in depth a single case or just a few cases. The **case history** is a descriptive technique in which you observe and report on a single case (or a few cases). A case is the object of study, such as the development of a certain disease in a given individual.

The case history method has a long history in psychology and has many uses. For example, a case history can be used to describe the typical development of a disease or the symptoms of a new disorder. In 1861 Paul Broca reported a case history of a 51-year-old patient who died at the Bicêtre hospital in France. Broca noted that when the patient (whom he called "Tan") was admitted to the hospital at the age of 21, he had already substantially lost his capacity to speak. In fact, he would usually respond to a question with one-syllable answers, most often with the word "tan" (thus, Broca's name for him). Tan was capable of understanding what was said to him, but he could not reply. Other than the speech problem, Tan was relatively healthy. However, over the course of his hospital stay, Tan's health gradually deteriorated to the point where he was losing control over the right side of his body. After Tan died, Broca examined Tan's brain and found a syphilitic lesion in the left frontal lobe of Tan's brain. Broca reported that "the frontal lobe of the *left* hemisphere was soft over a great part of its extent; the convolutions of the orbital region, although atrophied, preserved their shape; most of the other frontal convolutions were entirely destroyed. The result of

**FIGURE 7–5** Example of a Sociogram Based on Data from Figure 7–4.

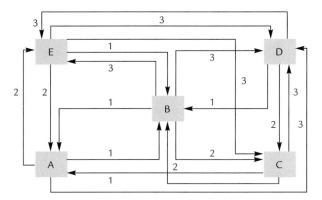

this destruction of the cerebral substance was a large cavity, capable of holding a chicken egg and filled with serous fluid" (Broca, 1861, p. 237).

Broca's case study of Tan became one of the most important findings in physiological psychology. Broca concluded that Tan's speech impairment was due to the lesion in the left frontal lobe and that the progressive damage to his brain eventually caused Tan to lose motor function on the right side of his body. Today we know that the area described by Broca (now called Broca's Area) is essential to the articulation of spoken language.

Although a case history can be useful, it does not qualify as an experimental design. In fact, a case history is a special application of a demonstration (see Chapter 4). Because you do not manipulate independent variables, you cannot determine the causes of the behavior observed in your case history. You can, of course, speculate about such causes. You can even compare theories by interpreting cases from different perspectives, but you cannot state with any certainty which perspective is superior.

## ARCHIVAL RESEARCH

**Archival research** is a nonexperimental strategy that involves studying existing records. These records can be historical accounts of events, census data, court records, police crime reports, published research articles, or any other archived information.

When planning archival research, you should have specific research questions in mind. You may find that the archived material contains an overwhelming amount of information. You need to be able to focus on specific aspects of the material. You can only do so if you know what you are looking for, which depends on having clearly defined and focused research hypotheses. In addition, all the factors pertaining to observational research (developing categories, coding sheets, multiple raters, and so on) apply to archival research.

An important practical matter to consider is your need to gain access to the archived material. This may not be easy. Sometimes the records you are interested in are not available to the general public. You may need to obtain special permission to gain access to the archives. In other cases, archival information may be available in libraries or on a computerized database (the Prosecutor's Management Information System, or PROMIS, for example). Even in these cases, you may have to do some homework to find out how to access them.

Another practical matter is the completeness of the records. After gaining access to the archives, you may find that some of the information you wanted is unavailable. For example, if you were interested in studying court records, you might find that some information, such as background information on the defendant, is confidential and unavailable to you. In short, archived material may not be complete enough for your purposes. You may need to use multiple sources.

Like the case history method, archival research is purely descriptive. You may be able to identify some interesting trends or correlations based on your archival research. However, you cannot establish causal relationships.

## Archival Research: An Example

In Game 3 of the 2003 American League Championship Series between the New York Yankees and the Boston Red Sox, traditional rivals, a brawl erupted. During the game, a Boston pitcher hit a Yankee batter with a pitch that was perceived by the batter as intentional. Later in the game, the Yankees' pitcher threw a pitch that was perceived by the Boston batter as a deliberate attempt to hit him. The Boston batter began walking toward the Yankees' pitcher with bat in hand. A bench-clearing brawl erupted during which a 72-year-old Yankee coach was thrown to the ground by a young Boston player.

Violence in sports has been a topic of great interest in recent years, as has the issue of racism in sports. Is there any connection between a player's race and his or her likelihood of being a victim of sports-related violence? An archival study by Thomas Timmerman (2002) addressed this question.

Timmerman studied interracial sports violence by using baseball's "hit by pitch" statistic. Baseball records are kept on every batter hit by a pitch since 1871. Timmerman used two Major League Baseball statistical archives to test the hypothesis that Black players are more likely to be hit by a pitch than White players: *The Baseball Archive Database* and *Total Baseball*. For the years 1950 to 1997, Timmerman recorded the number of times a batter was hit by a pitch and divided it by the total number of "at bats" (plate appearances) to produce a "rate of being hit by a pitch" measure. He also noted whether the batter was White, Black, or Hispanic. Timmerman found that over the years selected, the average rate of being hit by a pitch was slightly higher for Black (M = .0054) and Hispanic (M = .0053) players than for White players (M = .0045). This relationship held even when other factors (e.g., league affiliation, player ability) were taken into account. However, Timmerman also found that during the 1990s, White and Hispanic players were significantly more likely to be hit by a pitch than were Black players.

## CONTENT ANALYSIS

**Content analysis** is used when you want to analyze a written or spoken record for the occurrence of specific categories or events (such as pauses in a speech), items (such as negative comments), or behavior (such as factual information offered during group discussion). Because it is difficult to content analyze such materials in real time, archival sources are normally used for a content analysis. For example, if you wanted to content analyze the answers given by two political candidates during a debate, it would be nearly impossible to do the analysis while the debate is going on. Instead, you would record the debate and use the resulting footage for your analysis. There are times, however, when content analyses are done in real time. An example is a content analysis of court proceedings. Observers may actually sit in the courtroom and perform the content analysis.

Content analyses have been conducted on a wide range of materials such as mock juror deliberations (Horowitz, 1985), the content of television dramas (Greenberg, 1980), and the content of children's literature (Davis, 1984). In fact, the possible applications of content analysis are limited only by the imagination of the researcher (Holsti, 1969).

Even though a content analysis seems rather simple to do, it can become as complex as any other research technique. Content analysis should be performed within the context of a clearly developed research idea, including specific hypotheses and a sound research design. All the factors that must be considered for observational research (except that of remaining unobtrusive) apply to a content analysis. Response categories must be clearly defined, and a method for quantifying behavior must be developed. In essence, content analysis is an observational technique. However, in content analysis, your unit of analysis is some written, visual, or spoken record rather than the behavior of participants.

## Defining Characteristics of Content Analysis

Holsti (1969) pointed out that proper content analysis entails three defining characteristics. First, your content analysis should be objective. Each step of a content analysis should be guided by an explicit, clear set of rules or procedures. You should decide on the rules by which information will be acquired, categorized, and quantified and then adhere to those rules. You want to eliminate any subjective influence of the analyst. Second, your content analysis should be systematic. Assign information to categories according to whatever rules you developed, and then include as much information as possible in your analysis. For example, if you are doing a content analysis of a body of literature on a particular issue (such as racial attitudes), include articles that are *not* in favor of your position as well as those that are in favor of your position. A content analysis of literature is only as good as the literature search behind it. Third, your content analysis should have generality. That is, your findings should fit within a theoretical, empirical, or applied context. Disconnected facts generated from a content analysis are of little value (Holsti, 1969).

## Performing Content Analysis

To ensure that you acquire valid data for your content analysis, you must carefully define the response categories. According to Holsti (1969, p. 95), your categories should reflect the purposes of the research, be exhaustive, be mutually exclusive, be independent, and be derived from one classification system.

The first requirement is the most important (Holsti, 1969): clear operational definitions of terms. Your categories must be clearly defined and remain focused on the research question outlined in your hypothesis. Unclear or poorly defined categories are difficult to use. The categories should be defined with sufficient precision to allow precise categorization. Yet you do not want your categories to be too narrowly defined. You do not want relevant information to be excluded from a category simply because it does not fit an overly restrictive category definition.

Determining what your categories should be and how you should classify information within them is sometimes difficult. Reviewing related research in which a content analysis was used can help you develop and clearly define your categories. You can then add, delete, or expand categories to fit your specific research needs.

Before you begin to develop categories, read (or listen to) the materials to be analyzed. This will familiarize you with the material, help you develop categories, and help you avoid any surprises. That is, you will be less likely to encounter any information that does not fit into any category. Avoid making up categories as you go along.

After developing your categories, you decide on a unit of analysis. The *recording unit* (Holsti, 1969) is the element of the material that you are going to record. The recording unit can be a word (or words), sentences, phrases, themes, and so on. Your recording unit should be relevant to your research question. Also, Holsti points out that defining a recording unit sometimes may not be enough. For example, if you were analyzing content of a jury deliberation, recording the frequency with which the word "defendant" (the recording unit) was used might not be sufficient. You might also have to note the *context unit*, or context within which the word was used (Holsti, 1969). Such a context unit gives meaning to the recording unit and may help later when you interpret the data. For example, you might record the number of times the word "defendant" was used along with the word "guilty."

Another factor to consider when performing a content analysis is who will do the analysis. Chapter 5 discussed the concept of experimenter bias. If the person performing the content analysis knows the hypotheses of the study or has a particular point of view, your results could be biased. Consequently, you should use a "blind" rater, one who does not know the purpose of your study. Also, avoid using raters who have strong feelings or characteristics that could bias the results. If you use more than one rater (and you should), you must evaluate interrater reliability.

Another important thing to remember about content analysis is that the validity of your results will depend on the materials analyzed. Make every effort to obtain relevant materials, be they books, films, or television shows. In many cases it is not feasible to analyze all materials. For example, a content analysis of all children's books is impossible. In such cases, obtain a sample of materials that is representative of the larger population of materials. A content analysis of a biased sample (for example, only children's books written to be nonsexist) may produce biased results.

The results from a content analysis may be interesting in and of themselves. You may discover something interesting concerning the topic under study. Such was the case with Greenberg's (1980) content analysis of prime-time television shows aired during the fall of 1977. Greenberg found that Blacks were portrayed more often as having low-status jobs and athletic physiques compared with Whites.

### Limitations of Content Analysis

Content analysis can be a useful technique to help you understand behavior. However, keep in mind that content analysis is purely descriptive. It cannot establish causal relationships among variables. Another limitation of content analysis centers on the durability of the findings. In some instances, results from a content analysis are invalidated over time. For example, Greenberg's findings about how Blacks are portrayed on television are probably no longer valid. Presently, Blacks are more likely to be portrayed in higher-status roles (for example, doctors, lawyers, and so on) than in the past. Of course, this prediction could be tested with an updated content analysis!

### Content Analysis: An Example

Violence seems to be all around us. News stories abound concerning school shootings, violent crimes, and interpersonal violence. One possible source of violent behavior is the media. Media critics contend that there are high levels of violence portrayed in the media (television, film, video games). Is this the case? One can answer such a question through content analysis. In fact, a content analysis by Stacy Smith, Ken Lachlan, and Ron Tamborini (2003) looked at the violent content in one media format: video games.

For this content analysis, the researchers analyzed the 20 most popular video games available for major home gaming systems (e.g., Sony Playstation, Nintendo). The games were classified as either for "mature audiences" or for "general audiences." The first 10 minutes of each game were coded for violent content. The researchers defined violence as "any overt depiction of a credible threat of physical force or the actual use of such force intended to harm an animate being or group of beings" (Smith et al., 2003, p. 62). Two measures of violent content were used: the proportion of a video game segment that included violence and the rate of violence per minute. Smith et al. recorded the nature of the perpetrator of violence and the nature of the target.

Smith et al. found that video games intended for mature audiences contained a higher proportion of violence than those intended for the more general audience. Video games targeting mature audiences also were found to have four times as many violent acts per minute as those intended for the general audience. Overall, 68 percent of the video games (regardless of intended audience) had at least one act of violence. Figure 7–6 shows some of Smith et al.'s findings relating to the perpetrators and targets of violence in the video games analyzed. Both the perpetrators and targets of violence were most likely to be White human adult males.

## META-ANALYSIS: A TOOL FOR COMPARING RESULTS ACROSS STUDIES

Imagine that you are a researcher investigating the relationship between attitudes and memory. Specifically, you have been investigating whether or not participants recall more attitude-consistent information than attitude-inconsistent information. After conducting several empirical investigations, you decide that a published literature review is needed to summarize and integrate the findings in the area. Consequently, you decide to conduct a literature review and to write a review article.

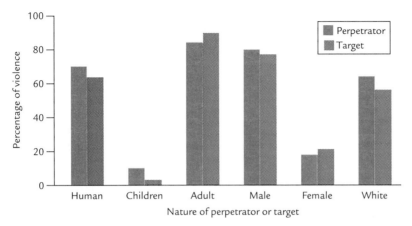

**FIGURE 7–6**    Results from Smith, Lachlan, and Tamborini's (2003) Content Analysis of Violent Video Games.

One strategy for this task is to conduct a traditional literature review. With this strategy, you read the relevant research in your area and then write an article. In your review, you may choose to summarize the major methods used to research the attitude–memory link, report the results of the major studies found, and draw conclusions about the variables that affect the relationship of interest.

In the traditional literature review, you simply summarize what you find and draw conclusions about the state of knowledge in a given area. For example, you might conclude that a certain variable is important (such as the length of a persuasive communication to which an individual is exposed), whereas others are less important (such as incidental versus intentional learning). However, the conclusions you draw are mostly subjective, based on your critical evaluation of the literature. The possibility exists that your subjective conclusion may not accurately reflect the strength of the relationships examined in your review.

You can avoid this possibility by adding a meta-analysis to your traditional review. A **meta-analysis** is a set of statistical procedures that allow you to combine or compare results from different studies. Because you are making use of existing literature, meta-analysis is a form of archival research. When you conduct a meta-analysis, you find and analyze existing research (published and even unpublished) so that you can make statistically guided decisions about the strength of the observed effects of independent variables and the reliability of results across studies.

To conduct a meta-analysis, you must follow three steps: (1) Identify relevant variables, (2) locate relevant research to review, and (3) conduct the meta-analysis proper.

## Step 1: Identifying Relevant Variables

Before you can hope to conduct a meta-analysis, you must identify the variables to be analyzed. This may sound easy enough. However, you will find that, in practice, it is somewhat difficult, especially in a research area in which there is a wide body of research. Generally, the rules that apply to developing testable research questions (see Chapter 2) apply to meta-analysis. It is not enough to say, "I want to do a meta-analysis of the memory literature." Such a broad, general analysis would be extremely difficult to do. The same is true even in less extensive research areas.

To be evaluated, your question must be sufficiently focused to allow for a reasonable meta-analysis. The unit of analysis in a meta-analysis should be the impact of variable X on variable Y (Rosenthal, 1984). Therefore, focus only on those variables that relate to your specific question. For example, you might choose to meta-analyze the impact of imagery on memory. Here you are limiting yourself to a small segment of the memory literature.

After you have narrowed the scope of your analysis, you must decide what variables to record (such as sex of subject, independent variables) as you review each study. Your decision will be driven by your research question. Table 7–4 provides a list of information that might be included in a meta-analysis. For each study to be included in your meta-analysis, you should record the relevant variables, the full reference citation, and the nature of the subject sample and procedure (Rosenthal, 1984). The heart of meta-analysis is the statistical combination of results across studies. Consequently, you also must record information about the findings from the results sections of the papers you review. What information is needed depends on the meta-analytic technique you use. To be safe, record the values of any statistics given (for example, $t$'s, $F$'s) and the associated $p$ values (such as .05, .01). Later these values will be used as the "scores" in your meta-analysis. Data should be collected that help you to evaluate your specific research questions. You do not have to record the results from overall ANOVAs. Focus instead on the results of statistical tests that evaluate the specific relationships among the variables of interest (Rosenthal, 1984).

## Step 2: Locating Relevant Research to Review

One of the most important steps in a meta-analysis is locating relevant research to review. In meta-analysis, you want to draw conclusions about the potency of a set of variables in a particular research area. To accomplish this end, you must thoroughly search the literature. Chapter 3 described how to perform a literature search, so the topic is not examined here.

Recall the previously discussed *file drawer phenomenon,* in which studies that do not achieve statistically reliable findings fail to reach publication (Rosenthal, 1979, 1984). The problem posed by the file drawer phenomenon is potentially serious for meta-analysis because it results in a biased sample. This bias inflates the probability of making a Type I error (concluding that a variable has an effect when it does not). Studies that failed to be published because the investigated variables did not show statistically significant effects are not available to include in the meta-analysis.

There are two ways of dealing with the file drawer phenomenon. First, you can attempt to uncover those studies that never reach print. This can be done by identifying as many researchers as possible in the research area you are covering. You then send each researcher a questionnaire, asking if any unpublished research on the issue of interest exists. You also could do a search of online journals that publish studies that produce null results such as the *Journal of Articles in Support of the Null Hypothesis* (http://www.jasnh.com/). Second, Rosenthal (1979, 1984) suggested estimating the extent of the impact of the file drawer phenomenon on your analysis. This is done by determining the number of studies that must be in the file drawer before

**TABLE 7–4  Sample of Factors to Include When Meta-analyzing Literature**

Full reference citation

Names and addresses of authors

Sex of experimenter

Sex of subjects used in each experiment

Characteristics of subject sample (such as how obtained, number)

Task required of subjects and other details about the dependent variable

Design of the study (including any unusual features)

Control groups and procedures included to reduce confoundings

Results from statistical tests that bear directly on the issue being considered in the meta-analysis (effect sizes, values of inferential statistics, $p$ values)

SOURCE: Adapted from Rosenthal, 1984.

serious biasing takes place (see Rosenthal, 1979; or Rosenthal, 1984, pp. 107–110, for details on how to estimate this). For example, if you determine (based on your analysis) that at least 3,000 studies must be in the file drawer before seriously biasing your results, then you can be reasonably sure that the file drawer phenomenon is not a source of bias.

## Step 3: Doing the Meta-analysis

When you have located relevant literature and collected your data, you are ready to apply one of the many available meta-analytic statistical techniques. Table 7–5 displays meta-analytic techniques that can be applied to the situation in which you have two studies. The first technique shows that you can compare studies. This comparison is made when you want to determine whether two studies produce significantly different effects. Essentially, doing a meta-analysis comparing studies is analogous to conducting an experiment using human or animal subjects. In the case of meta-analysis, each data point represents the results from a study rather than a subject's response. The second technique shows that you also can combine studies to determine the average effect of a variable across studies. Looking at the columns, you can evaluate studies by comparing or combining either the $p$ values from significance testing or effect sizes (Rosenthal, 1984).

Comparing of effect sizes of two studies is more desirable than simply looking at $p$ values (Rosenthal, 1984). This is because effect sizes provide a better indication of the degree of impact of a variable than $p$ values do. (Remember, all the $p$ value tells you is the likelihood of making a Type I error.) Use $p$ values when the information needed to analyze effect sizes is not included in the studies reviewed.

## Drawbacks to Meta-analysis

Meta-analysis can be a powerful tool to evaluate results across studies. Even though many researchers have embraced the concept of meta-analysis, others question its

**TABLE 7-5    Meta-analytic Techniques for Comparing and Combining Two Studies**

| TECHNIQUE | COMMENTS |
|---|---|
| ***Comparing Studies*** | Used to determine if two studies produce significantly different results. |
| Significance testing | Record $p$ values from research and convert them to exact $p$ values (such as a finding reported at $p < .05$ may actually be $p = .036$). Used when information is not available to allow for evaluation of effect sizes. |
| Effect size estimation | Record values of inferential statistics ($F$, $t$, for example) along with associated degrees of freedom. Estimate effect sizes from these statistics. Preferred over significance testing. |
| ***Combining Studies*** | Used when you want to determine the potency of a variable across studies. |
| Significance testing | Can be used after comparing studies to arrive at an overall estimate of the probability of obtaining the two $p$ values under the null hypothesis (there is no causal relationship between the analyzed variables). |
| Effect size estimation | Can be used after comparing studies to evaluate the average impact across studies of an independent variable on the dependent variable. |

Source: Adapted from Rosenthal, 1984.

usefulness on several grounds. This section explores some of the drawbacks to meta-analysis and presents some of the solutions suggested to overcome those drawbacks.

*Assessing the Quality of the Research Reviewed*    Chapter 3 pointed out that not all journals are created equal. The quality of the research found in a journal depends on its editorial policy. Some journals have rigorous publication standards, whereas others have less rigorous standards. This means that the quality of published research may vary considerably from journal to journal.

One problem facing the meta-analyst is how to deal with uneven research quality. For example, should an article published in a nonrefereed journal be given as much weight as an article published in a refereed journal? Unfortunately, there is no simple answer to this question. Rosenthal (1984) suggested weighting articles according to quality.

There is no agreement as to the dimensions along which research should be weighted. The refereed–nonrefereed dimension is one possibility. You should exercise caution with this dimension because whether or not a journal is refereed is not a reliable indicator of the quality of published research. Research in a new area, using new methods, is sometimes rejected from refereed journals even though it is methodologically sound and of high quality. Similarly, publication in a refereed journal helps to ensure that the research is of high quality, but does not guarantee it.

A second dimension along which research could be weighted is according to the soundness of methodology, regardless of journal quality. Rosenthal (1984) suggested having several experts on methodology rate each study for its quality (perhaps on a 0 to 10 scale). Quality ratings would be made twice: once after reading the method section alone and once after reading the method and results sections together (Rosenthal, 1984). The ratings would then be checked for interrater reliability and used to weight the degree of contribution of each study to the meta-analysis.

*Combining and Comparing Studies Using Different Methods*    A frequent criticism of meta-analysis is that it is difficult to understand how studies with widely varying materials, measures, and methods can be compared. This is commonly referred to as the "apples versus oranges argument" (Glass, 1978).

Although common, this criticism of meta-analysis is not valid. Rosenthal (1984) and Glass (1978) suggested that comparing results from different studies is no different from averaging across heterogeneous subjects in an ordinary experiment. If you are willing to accept averaging across subjects, you can also accept averaging across heterogeneous studies (Glass, 1978; Rosenthal, 1984).

The core issue is not whether averaging should be done across heterogeneous studies, but rather whether or not differing methods are related to different effect sizes. In this vein, Rosenthal pointed out that when a subject variable becomes a problem in research, you often "block" on that subject variable to determine how it relates to the differences that emerge. Similarly, if methodological differences appear to be related to the outcome of research, studies in a meta-analysis could be blocked on methodology (Rosenthal, 1984) to determine its effects.

*Practical Problems*    The task facing a meta-analyst is a formidable one. Experiments on the same issue may use widely different methods and statistical techniques. Also, some studies may not provide the necessary information to conduct a meta-analysis. For example, Roberts (1985) was able to include only 38 studies in his meta-analysis of the attitude–memory relationship. Some studies had to be eliminated because sufficient information was not provided. Also, Roberts reported that when an article said that $F$ was less than 1 (as articles often do), he assigned $F$ a value of zero. The problem of insufficient or imprecise information (along with the file drawer problem) may result in a nonrepresentative sample of research being included in your meta-analysis. Admittedly, the bias may be small, but it nevertheless may exist.

*Do the Results of Meta-analysis Differ from Those of Traditional Reviews?*    A valid question is whether or not traditional reviews produce results that differ qualitatively from those of a meta-analysis. To answer this question, Cooper and Rosenthal (1980) directly compared the two methods. Graduate students and professors were randomly assigned to conduct either a meta-analysis or a traditional review of seven articles dealing with the impact of the sex of the subject on persistence on a task. Two of the studies showed that females were more persistent than males, whereas the other five either presented no statistical data or showed no significant effect.

The results of this study showed that participants using the meta-analysis were more likely to conclude that there was an effect of sex on persistence than were participants using the traditional method. Moreover, participants doing the traditional review believed that the effect of sex on persistence was smaller than did those doing the meta-analysis. Overall, 68 percent of the meta-analysts were prepared to conclude that sex had an effect on persistence, whereas only 27 percent of participants using the traditional method were so inclined. In statistical terms, the meta-analysts were more willing than the traditional reviewers to reject the null hypothesis that sex had no effect, so using meta-analysis to evaluate research may lead to a reduction in Type II decision errors (Cooper & Rosenthal, 1980).

Cooper and Rosenthal (1980) also reported that there were no differences between meta-analysis and traditional review groups in their abilities to evaluate the methodology of the studies reviewed. Also, there was no difference between the two groups in their recommendations about future research in the area. Most participants believed research in the area should continue.

Finally, it is worth noting that using the statistical approach inherent in meta-analysis applies the same research strategy as doing statistical analyses of data from traditional experiments. When we obtain results of an experiment, we don't just look at ("eyeball") the data to see if any patterns or relationships exist. Instead, in most instances (there are some exceptions that we discuss in Chapter 11), we apply statistical analyses to evaluate whether relationships exist. By the same token, it can be argued that it is better to apply a statistical analysis to the results of different studies to see if significant relationships exist than to "eyeball" the studies and speculate about possible relationships.

## SUMMARY

In some situations, conducting an experiment may not be possible or desirable. In the early stages of research, or when you are interested in studying naturally occurring behaviors of your subjects, a nonexperimental approach may be best.

Observational research involves observing and recording the behaviors of your subjects. This can be accomplished either in the field or in the lab and can use human or animal participants. Although observational research sounds easy to conduct, as much preparation goes into an observational study as into any other study. Before making observations of behavior, clearly define the behaviors to be observed, develop observation techniques that do not interfere with the behaviors of your subjects, and work out a method of quantifying and recording behavior.

The frequency, duration, and intervals methods are three widely accepted ways to quantify behavior in an observational study. In the frequency method, you count the number of occurrences of a behavior within a specified period of time. In the duration method, you measure how long a behavior lasted. In the intervals method, you break your observation period into small time intervals and record whether or not a behavior occurred within each.

After you have decided how to quantify behavior, you must make some decisions about how to record your observations. Paper-and-pencil data-recording sheets provide a simple and, in most cases, adequate means of recording behavior. In some situations (such as when the behavior being observed is fast paced), you should consider using tape recorders rather than a paper-and-pencil method. Using a tape recorder allows observers to keep their eyes on subjects while making notes about behavior.

In addition to developing a method for quantifying behavior, you also must decide on how and when to make observations. Sometimes it is not possible to watch and record behaviors simultaneously because behavior may occur quickly and be highly complex. In such situations, you could use time sampling or individual sampling or automate your observations by using a video recorder.

In observational research, you should use multiple observers. When multiple observers are used, you must evaluate the degree of interrater reliability. This can be done using either percent agreement, Cohen's Kappa, intraclass correlation, or Pearson $r$. A Cohen's Kappa of .70 or greater or a statistically significant Pearson $r$ of around .90 or greater suggests an acceptable level of interrater reliability.

Nonexperimental techniques include naturalistic observation, ethnography, case study, archival research, and content analysis. In naturalistic observation, you make careful, unobtrusive observations of subjects in their natural environment so that you do not alter their natural behavior. In cases in which you cannot remain unobtrusive, there are steps you can take to habituate your participants to your presence.

Ethnography involves getting immersed in a behavioral or social system to be studied. The technique is best used to study and describe the operation of groups and the social interactions that take place within those groups. An ethnographic study can be run as a participant observation, in which the researcher actually becomes a member of the group, or as nonparticipant observation, in which the researcher is a nonparticipating observer.

Sociometry involves identifying and measuring interpersonal relationships within a group. Research participants evaluate each other along some socially relevant dimension (for example, friendship), and patterns of those ratings are analyzed to characterize the social structure of the group. The results of a sociometric analysis may be plotted on a sociogram, which graphically represents the social connections between participants. Sociometry can be used as a stand-alone research technique or as a measure within a wider study.

When using the case history approach, you analyze an interesting case that illustrates some empirical or theoretical point. Alternatively, you may compare and contrast two or more cases in order to illustrate such points. Archival research makes use of existing records. Those records are examined and data extracted to answer specific research questions.

Content analysis involves analyzing a written or spoken record for the occurrence of specific categories of events or behaviors. As with any observational technique, behavior categories must be developed. During content analysis, recording and context units can be noted and analyzed.

Meta-analysis is a family of statistical techniques that can help you evaluate results from a number of studies in a given research area. In contrast to a traditional literature review (in which subjective evaluations rule), meta-analysis involves statistically combining the results from a number of studies. Meta-analytic techniques tend to be more objective than traditional literature review techniques.

The three steps involved in conducting a meta-analysis are (1) identifying relevant variables to study; (2) locating relevant research to review; and (3) actually doing the meta-analysis (comparing or combining results across studies). Although meta-analysis has advantages over traditional literature reviews, there are some drawbacks. First, it is sometimes difficult to evaluate the quality of the research reviewed. Second, studies in a research area may use vastly different methods, making comparison of results suspect. Third, the information in published articles may be incomplete, eliminating potentially important studies from the analysis.

## REVIEW QUESTIONS

1. What are the defining characteristics of observational research?
2. How do observational techniques apply to experimental and nonexperimental research?
3. How are behavioral categories that are used in observational research developed?
4. What are the techniques used to make behavioral observations in observational research?
5. What is the distinction between recording single acts and behavior sequences?
6. What are the sampling techniques used to handle complexity when making behavioral observations?
7. Why should you evaluate interrater reliability?
8. What are the techniques used to evaluate interrater reliability, and when would each be used?
9. How do you deal with data from multiple observers?
10. What are the sources of bias in observational research, and how can the bias be reduced?
11. What is the difference between quantitative and qualitative data?
12. What are the problems inherent in collecting qualitative data?
13. What are naturalistic observation and unobtrusive observation, and how are they used to study behavior?
14. What are some of the advantages and disadvantages of naturalistic observation?
15. What is ethnography, and what are the issues facing a field ethnographer?
16. How are ethnographic data recorded and analyzed?
17. What is sociometry and when is it used?
18. How are the case history and archival research used?
19. What is content analysis, and what steps are taken when using it?
20. What is meta-analysis, and what steps are involved in using it?
21. What are some of the issues facing you if you decide to do a meta-analysis?

## KEY TERMS

| | |
|---|---|
| behavioral categories | intraclass correlation coefficient ($r_I$) |
| interrater reliability | qualitative data |
| Cohen's Kappa | naturalistic observation |

ethnography

participant observation

nonparticipant observation

sociometry

sociogram

case history

archival research

content analysis

meta-analysis

# Using Survey Research

Gordon Allport (1954) characterized attitude as "probably the most distinctive and indispensable concept in contemporary social psychology" (p. 43). Since Allport's assessment, attitudes have transcended social psychology to become important in our everyday lives. We are surrounded by issues related to attitudes and their measurement. Pollsters and politicians are constantly measuring and trying to change our attitudes about a wide range of issues (abortion, the war on terrorism, and tax cuts, for example).

In the post–September 11th world, understanding attitudes may even be central to survival. Pundits such as Thomas Friedman (2001) have stated in the popular press that negative attitudes toward Americans and America are at the heart of terrorist attacks against Americans and their interests around the world. How do we know that people in other cultures have negative attitudes about Americans? We know because social scientists have conducted surveys of individuals from other countries to evaluate how those individuals view and feel about Americans. Margaret and Melvin DeFleur (2002) conducted one such survey to assess the attitudes of 1,259 high school students (the "next generation") from a variety of countries (e.g., Pakistan, Saudi Arabia, Spain, Italy). Items on the survey measured various attitudes toward Americans and American culture.

The DeFleurs' results are sobering. For the most part, teenagers from other cultures have a quite negative set of attitudes toward Americans and American culture. Figure 8–1 shows some of DeFleur and DeFleur's results combining respondents from all countries. Any bar descending below the zero line indicates a negative attitude. As you can see, foreign teenagers see Americans as materialistic, desiring to dominate others, criminal, and having no respect for others. Ironically, despite the general negative view respondents expressed, foreign teenagers still expressed a fair amount of admiration for Americans and American culture.

Surveys are a widely used research technique. You may have participated in a survey yourself, or (perhaps more likely) you may have been the recipient of survey results. For example, if you have an-

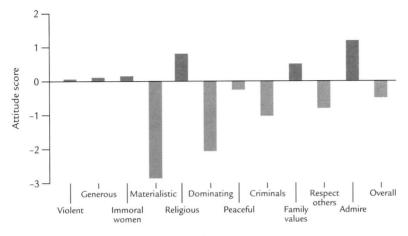

**FIGURE 8–1**   Results from DeFleur and Defleur's (2002) Survey on Attitudes toward Americans (all countries combined).

swered a few questions from a local political party during election time, you have participated in a survey. Even those annoying questions on warranty registration cards that come with most products qualify as a survey of sorts. You are typically asked about your age, income, interests, magazines to which you subscribe, and so on. If you answered those questions and mailed back the card, you took part in a survey.

Even if you rarely participate in surveys, you are still likely to have encountered survey results. Political polls designed to gauge people's attitudes on key issues and candidates come out almost daily during election time, and polls about the President's approval rating come out several times over the course of a year.

Because survey research is highly visible, you should understand the "ins and outs" of this important research technique. If you plan to use a survey technique in your own research, you should know about proper questionnaire construction, administration techniques, sampling techniques, and data analysis. Even if you never use survey techniques, understanding something about them will help you make sense out of the surveys you are exposed to every day.

## SURVEY RESEARCH

Before we discuss survey techniques, note the difference between the *field survey* and the observational techniques described in Chapter 7. In both naturalistic observation and participant observation, you simply observe behaviors and make copious notes about them. You do not administer any measures to your participants. Consequently, you can only speculate about the motives, attitudes, and beliefs underlying the observed behaviors. In a field survey, you directly question your participants about their behavior (past, present, or future) and their underlying attitudes, beliefs, and intentions. From the data collected, you can draw inferences about the factors under-lying behavior.

The inferences you can draw from a field survey are limited by the fact that you do not manipulate independent variables. Instead, you acquire several (perhaps hundreds of) measures of the behaviors of interest. This purely correlational research strategy usually does not permit you to draw causal inferences from your data (see Chapter 4). For example, finding that political conservatism is a good predictor of voter choices does not justify concluding that political conservatism *causes* voter choices.

Instead, you use the field survey to evaluate specific attitudes, such as those con-cerning issues surrounding nuclear disarmament, political candidates, or foreign im-ports. You also can use the field survey to evaluate behaviors. For example, you could design a questionnaire to determine which household products people use.

Surveys also have another important use: predicting behavior. Political polls often seek to predict behavior. Attitudes about political candidates are assessed, and then projections are made about subsequent voter behavior.

When you conduct survey research, you must ensure that your participants are treated ethically. One major ethical issue concerns whether and how you will main-tain the *anonymity* of your participants and the *confidentiality* of their responses. Main-taining anonymity means that you guarantee that there will be no way for the participants' names to be associated with their answers. This might be accomplished by instructing participants to mail back their questionnaires and informed consent forms separately. No coding scheme would be used that would allow you to match up individual participants and their questionnaires. However, sometimes you may wish to code the questionnaires and informed consent forms so that you can match them up later. You might do this, for example, in case a participant has second thoughts about participating after the questionnaire has been returned. If so, and you have promised your participants that their responses will remain anonymous, you must take steps to ensure that only authorized personnel associated with the research project can gain access to the code and only for the stated purpose.

Maintaining confidentiality means that you do not disclose any data in individual form, even if you know which participants filled out which questionnaires. If you promise your participants that their responses will remain confidential, ethical practice dictates that you report only aggregate results.

## DESIGNING YOUR QUESTIONNAIRE

The first step in designing a questionnaire is to clearly define the topic of your study. A clear, concise definition of what you are studying will yield results that can be inter-preted unambiguously. Results from surveys that do not clearly define the topic area may be confusing. It is also important to have clear, precise operational definitions for the attitudes or behaviors being studied. Behaviors and attitudes that are not defined precisely also may yield results that are confusing and difficult to interpret.

Having a clearly defined topic has another important advantage: It keeps your questionnaire focused on the behavior or attitude chosen for study (Moser & Kalton,

1972). You should avoid the temptation to do too much in a single survey. Trying to tackle too much in a single survey leads to an inordinately long questionnaire that may confuse or overburden your participants. It also may make it more difficult for you to summarize and analyze your data (Moser & Kalton, 1972). Your questionnaire should include a broad enough range of questions so that you can thoroughly assess behavior but not so broad as to lose focus and become confusing. Your questionnaire should elicit the responses you are most interested in without much extraneous information.

The type of information gathered in a questionnaire depends on its purpose. However, most questionnaires include items designed to assess the characteristics of the participants, such as age, sex, marital status, occupation, income, and education. Such characteristics are called *demographics*. Demographics are often used as *predictor variables* during analysis of the data to determine whether participant characteristics correlate with or predict responses to other items in the survey. Other, nondemographic items also can be included to provide predictor variables. For example, attitude toward abortion might be used to predict voter preference. In this case, attitude toward abortion would be used as a predictor variable.

In addition to demographics and predictor variables, you also will have items designed to assess the behavior of interest. For example, if you were interested in predicting voter preference, you would include an item or items on your questionnaire to specifically measure voter preference. That item, or a combination of several items, would constitute the *criterion variable*.

The questions to which your participants will respond are the heart of your questionnaire. Take great care to develop questions that are clear, to the point, and relevant to the aims of your research. The time spent in this early phase of your research will pay dividends later. Well-constructed items are easier to summarize, analyze, and interpret than poorly constructed ones. The next section introduces several popular item formats and offers suggestions for writing good questionnaire items.

## Writing Questionnaire Items

Writing effective questionnaire items that elicit the information you want requires care and skill. You cannot simply sit down, write several questions, and use those first-draft questions on your final questionnaire. Writing questionnaire items involves writing and rewriting items until they are clear and succinct. In fact, having written your items and assembled your questionnaire, you should administer it to a pilot group of participants matching your main sample in order to ensure that the items are reliable and valid.

When writing questionnaire items, you may choose among several popular types. Here we discuss the open-ended, restricted, partially open-ended, and rating-scale item types.

*Open-Ended Items*   **Open-ended items** allow the participant to respond in his or her own words. The following example might appear in a survey like that of DeFleur and DeFleur (2002) on the attitudes of foreigners toward Americans and American culture:

**How would you characterize Americans as a group?**

The participant writes an answer to the question in the space provided immediately below. Such information may be more complete and accurate than the information obtained with a restricted item (discussed next). A drawback to the open-ended item is that participants may not understand exactly what you are looking for or may inadvertently omit some answers. Thus, the participants may fail to provide the needed information. Another drawback to the open-ended item is that it can make summarizing your data difficult. When you must interpret what the participants have said, you run the risk of misclassifying their answers.

*Restricted Items*    **Restricted items** (also called *closed-ended items*) provide a limited number of specific response alternatives. A restricted item with ordered alternatives lists these alternatives in a logical order:

**In the past year, how many Americans have you met face to face?**

__ None

__ 1 to 5

__ 6 to 10

__ 11 to 15

__ 16 to 20

__ More than 20

Note how the alternatives for this question go from low frequency (*None, 1 to 5*) to high frequency (*16 to 20, More than 20*). Participants would respond by checking the blank space to the left of the desired answer. However, other methods for recording choices can be used with restricted items. For example, you could use a number to the right of each alternative and have participants circle the numbers corresponding to their choices.

Use unordered alternatives whenever there is no logical basis for choosing a given order:

**The Americans you met face to face in the past year were:**

__ Mostly males

__ Mostly females

__ Both males and females

Because there is no inherent order to the alternatives, other orders would serve just as well.

By offering only specific response alternatives, restricted items control the participant's range of responses. The responses made to restricted items are, therefore, easier to summarize and analyze than the responses made to open-ended items. However, the information you obtain from a restricted item is not as rich as the information from an open-ended item. Participants cannot qualify or otherwise elaborate on their responses. Also, you may fail to include an alternative that correctly describes the participant's opinion, thus forcing the participant to choose an alternative that does not really fit.

*Partially Open-Ended Items*     **Partially open-ended items** resemble restricted items but provide an additional, "other" category and an opportunity to give an answer not listed among the specific alternatives:

**Who introduced you to the American you most recently met face to face?**

\_\_ Family

\_\_ Mutual friend or acquaintance

\_\_ Co-worker

\_\_ Classmate

\_\_ Neighbor

\_\_ Introduced yourself

\_\_ Other (Specify)_____

Dillman (2000) offers several suggestions for formatting restricted and partially open-ended items. He suggests using boldface font for the stem of a question and normal font for response category labels (as we have done in the previous examples). This helps respondents separate the question from the response categories that follow. Make any special instructions intended to clarify a question a part of the question itself. Put check boxes, blank spaces, or numbers in a consistent position throughout your questionnaire (for example, to the left of the response alternatives). Finally, place all alternatives in a single column. Other tips offered by Dillman (2000) for constructing and formatting questionnaire items are summarized in Table 8–1.

*Rating Scales*     A variation on the restricted question uses a rating scale rather than response alternatives. A rating scale provides a graded response to a question:

**How much did you like the last American whom you met face to face?**

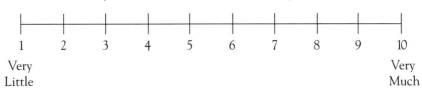

There is no set number of points that a rating scale must have. A rating scale can have as few as 3 and as many as 100 points. However, rating scales commonly do not exceed 10 points. A 10-point scale has enough points to allow a wide range of choice while not overburdening the participant. Scales with fewer than 10 points also are used frequently, but you should not go below 5 points. Many participants may not want to use the extreme values on a scale. Consequently, if you have a 5-point scale and the participant excludes the end points, you really have only three usable points. Scales ranging from 7 to 10 points leave several points for the participants to choose among, even if participants do avoid the extreme values.

TABLE 8–1    **Suggestions for Writing Good Survey Items**

| SUGGESTION | EXAMPLE |
| --- | --- |
| Use simple rather than complex words | Use "work" rather than "employment." |
| Make the stem of a question as short and easy to understand as possible, but use complete sentences | "Would you like to study in America?" |
| Avoid vague questions in favor of more precise ones | Use "How many years have you lived in your current house?" rather than "Years in your house." |
| Avoid asking for too much information. Respondents may not have an answer readily available | Use a list of ordered alternatives rather than an open-ended question when asking how often the respondent does something. |
| Avoid "check all that apply" questions | Instead of "check all that apply," list each item separately and have respondent indicate liking/disliking for each. |
| Avoid questions that ask for more than one thing | Instead of asking "Would you like to study and then live in America?" ask "Would you like to study in America?" and "Would you like to live in America?" separately. |
| Soften the impact of potentially sensitive questions | Instead of asking "Have you ever stolen anything?" ask "Have you ever taken anything without paying for it?" |

Source: After Dillman, 2000.

You also must decide how to label your scale. Figure 8–2 shows three ways you might do this. In the first example, only the end points are labeled. In this case, the participant is told the upper and lower limits of the scale. Such labeled points are called *anchors* because they keep the participant's interpretation of the scale values from drifting.

With only the end points anchored, the participant must interpret the meaning of the rest of the points. In the second example, all the points are labeled. In this case, the participant knows exactly what each point means and may consequently provide more accurate information. In the third example of Figure 8–2, the scale is labeled at the end points and at the midpoint. This scale provides three anchors for the participant. This scale is a reasonable compromise between labeling only the end points and labeling all the points.

You may be wondering whether labeling each point changes the way the participant responds on the scale. The answer seems to be a qualified no. When you develop a measurement scale, you are dealing with (1) the psychological phenomenon under-

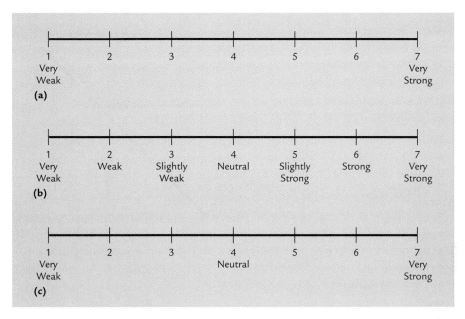

**FIGURE 8–2**   Three ways of Labeling a Rating Scale: (a) end points only, (b) each point labeled, (c) end points and midpoint labeled.

lying the scale and (2) the scale itself. Labeling each point does not change the nature of the psychological phenomenon underlying the scale. You can assume that your scale, labeled at each point, still represents the phenomenon underlying the scale. In fact, researchers have sometimes expressed a misguided concern about such scale transformations (Nunnally, 1967). Minor transformations of a measurement scale (such as labeling each point) probably do not affect its measurement properties or how well it represents the underlying psychological phenomenon being studied.

In the previous examples, participants respond by checking or circling the scale value that best represents their judgments. Alternative ways to format your scale provide participants with more flexibility in their responses. Figure 8–3 shows an example in which the end points are anchored and the participants are instructed to place a check or perpendicular line on the scale to indicate how they feel. To interpret the responses, you simply use a ruler to measure from an end point to the participant's mark. Your scale is then expressed in terms of inches or centimeters, and the resulting numbers are treated just like the numbers on a numbered scale.

Another variation on the rating scale is the *Likert scale*, which is widely used in attitude measurement research. A Likert scale provides a series of statements to which participants can indicate degrees of agreement or disagreement. Figure 8–4 shows two examples of formatting a Likert-scale item. In the first example, the attitude statement is followed by five blank spaces labeled from *Strongly Agree* to *Strongly Disagree*. The participant simply checks the space that best reflects the degree of agreement or disagreement with each statement. The second example provides consecutive numbers rather than blank spaces and descriptive anchors only at the ends.

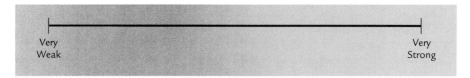

**FIGURE 8–3**   Rating Scale Formatted with No Numbers. End points are labeled, and participants place marks on the line to indicate their responses.

Participants are instructed to circle the number that best reflects how much they agree or disagree with each statement. For further information on Likert scaling, see Edwards (1953).

A final note on rating scales is in order. Although rating scales have been presented in the context of survey research, be aware that rating scales are widely used in experimental research as well. Adapting rating scales to your particular research needs is a relatively simple affair. Anytime your research calls for the use of rating scales, you can apply the suggestions presented here.

## Assembling Your Questionnaire

If your questionnaire is to be effective, its items must be organized into a coherent, visually pleasing format. This process involves paying attention to the order in which the items are included and to the way in which they are presented.

Dillman (2000) and Moser and Kalton (1972) agree that demographic items should *not* be presented first on the questionnaire. These questions, although easy to complete, may lead participants to believe that the questionnaire is boring. Dillman emphasizes the importance of the first question on a questionnaire. A good first question should be interesting and engaging so that the respondent will be motivated to continue. According to Dillman, the first question should apply to everybody completing the questionnaire, be easy so that it takes only a few seconds to complete, and be interesting. Of course, these rules are not carved in stone. If your research needs require a certain question to be presented first, that consideration should take precedence (Dillman, 2000).

Your questionnaire should have continuity; that is, related items should be presented together. This keeps your participant's attention on one issue at a time, rather than jumping from issue to issue. Your questionnaire will have greater continuity if related items are grouped. An organized questionnaire is much easier and more enjoyable for the participant to complete, factors that may increase completion rate. Continuity also means that groups of related questions should be logically ordered. Your questionnaire should read like a book. Avoid the temptation to skip around from topic to topic in an attempt to hold the attention of the participant. Rather, strive to build "cognitive ties" between related groups of items (Dillman, 2000).

The order in which questions are included on a questionnaire has been shown to affect the responses of participants. For example, McFarland (1981) presented questions on a questionnaire ordered in two ways. Some participants answered a general question before specific questions, whereas others answered the specific questions first. McFarland found that participants expressed more interest in politics and religion

The president is doing all he can to reduce the budget deficit.

| Strongly Agree | Agree | Neutral | Disagree | Strongly Disagree |
|:---:|:---:|:---:|:---:|:---:|
| _____ | _____ | _____ | _____ | _____ |

(a)

The president is doing all he can to reduce the budget deficit.

| Strongly Agree | | | | Strongly Disagree |
|:---:|:---:|:---:|:---:|:---:|
| 1 | 2 | 3 | 4 | 5 |

(b)

**FIGURE 8–4**   Samples Showing Likert Scales: (a) a standard Likert item on which the participant places a check in the blank under the statement that best reflects how he or she feels; (b) Likert-type scale using a 5-point scale.

when the specific questions were asked first than when the general questions were asked first. Sigelman (1981) found that question order affected whether or not participants expressed an opinion (about the popularity of the president), but only if the participants were poorly educated. Hence, question order may play a greater role for some participants than for others. Carefully consider your sample and the chosen topic when deciding on the order in which questions are asked.

The placement of items asking for sensitive information (such as sexual preferences or illegal behavior) is an important factor. Dillman suggests placing objectionable questions after less objectionable ones, perhaps even at the end of the questionnaire. Once your participants are committed to answering your questions, they may be more willing to answer some sensitive questions. Additionally, a question may not seem as objectionable after the respondent has answered previous items than if the objectionable item is placed earlier in the questionnaire (Dillman, 2000). You also should pay attention to the way that each page of your questionnaire is set up. There should be a logical "navigational path" (Dillman, 2000) that your respondent can follow. This path should lead the respondent through the questionnaire as if he or she were reading a book. One way to accomplish this is to use appropriate graphics (e.g., arrows and other symbols) to guide respondents through the questionnaire. In fact, Dillman talks about two "languages" of a questionnaire. One language is verbal and relates to how your questions are worded. The other language is graphical and relates to the symbols and graphics used to guide respondents through the items on your questionnaire. Symbols and graphics can be used to separate groups of items, direct respondents where to go in the event of a certain answer (e.g., "If you answered 'No' to item 5, skip to item 7" could be accompanied by an arrow pointing to item 7), or direct respondents to certain pages on the questionnaire. Dillman suggests the following three steps for integrating the verbal and graphical languages into an effective questionnaire:

1. Design a navigational path directing respondents to read all the information on a page.

2. Create effective visual navigational guides to help respondents stay on the navigational path.

3. Develop alternate navigational guides to help with situations where the normal navigational guide will be interrupted (e.g., skipping items or sections).

## ADMINISTERING YOUR QUESTIONNAIRE

After you develop your questionnaire, you must decide how to administer it. You could mail your questionnaire to your participants, deliver your questionnaire via e-mail or post it on the Internet, telephone participants to ask the questions directly, administer your questionnaire to a large group at once, or conduct face-to-face interviews. Each method has advantages and disadvantages and makes its own special demands. The remainder of this section reviews each of these methods and then finishes with a discussion of sampling procedures.

### Mail Surveys

In a **mail survey**, you mail your questionnaire directly to your participants. They complete and return the questionnaire at their leisure. This is a rather convenient method. All you need to do is put your questionnaires into addressed envelopes and mail them. However, a serious problem called **nonresponse bias** occurs when a large proportion of participants fail to complete and return your questionnaire. If the participants who fail to return the questionnaire differ in significant ways from those who do return it, your survey may yield answers that do not represent the opinions of the intended population.

*Combatting Nonresponse Bias*    To avoid nonresponse bias, you should develop strategies to increase your return rate. Dillman (2000) notes that the single most effective strategy for increasing response rate is to make multiple contacts with respondents. Dillman suggests making four contacts via mail. The first consists of a *prenotice letter* sent to the respondent a few days before the questionnaire is sent. The prenotice letter should inform the respondent that an important questionnaire will be coming in the mail in a few days. It also should inform the respondent what the survey is about and why the survey will be useful. The second mailing would deliver the questionnaire itself, accompanied by a cover letter. The cover letter should include the following elements in the order listed (Dillman, 2000): the specific request to complete the questionnaire, why the respondent was selected to receive the survey, the usefulness of the survey, a statement of confidentiality of the respondent's answers, an offer of a token of appreciation (if such an offer is to be made), an offer to answer questions, and a real signature. Figure 8–5 shows a sample cover letter that includes each of these elements.

The third mailing would take the form of a *thank you postcard* sent a few days or a week after the questionnaire was mailed. The postcard should thank the respondent for completing the questionnaire and remind the respondent to complete the questionnaire if not already done. The fourth contact provides a *replacement questionnaire*, sent two to four weeks after the original questionnaire and accompanied by a letter indicating that the original questionnaire had not been received. The letter also should urge the respondent to complete the replacement questionnaire and return it.

You may be able to increase your return rate somewhat by including a small token of your appreciation, such as a pen or pencil that the participant can keep. Some researchers include a small amount of money as an incentive to complete the questionnaire. As a rule, it is better to send the token along with the questionnaire rather than make the token contingent upon returning the questionnaire. One study found that 57 percent of respondents returned a survey questionnaire when promised $50 for its return, whereas 64 percent returned the questionnaire when $1 was included with it (James & Bolstein, 1992).

Ironically, smaller rewards seem to produce better results than larger ones (Johnson & McLaughlin, 1990; Kanuk & Berenson, 1975; Warner, Berman, Weyant, & Ciarlo, 1983). Dillman (2000) suggests that a $1 token is preferred because it is easy to mail and seems to produce the desired results. Finally, monetary incentives work better than tangible rewards (Church, 1993).

A few factors that do *not* significantly affect response rate include questionnaire length, personalization, promise of anonymity, and inclusion of a deadline (Kanuk & Berenson, 1975). (For reviews of the research supporting these findings, see Kanuk & Berenson, 1975, and Warner et al., 1983.)

## Internet Surveys

An increasingly popular method of administering questionnaires is to post them on the Internet. **Internet surveys** can be distributed via e-mail or Listservs, or posted on a Web site. Which method you use depends on the nature and purpose of your survey. E-mail surveys are easy to distribute but do not permit complex navigational designs (Dillman, 2000). Consequently, e-mail surveys are best for relatively short, simple questionnaires. Web-based surveys allow you to create and present more complex questionnaires that incorporate many of the design features discussed previously (Dillman, 2000). To aid you in the task of implementing a Web-based survey, commercial software packages are available that allow you to design sophisticated questionnaires for posting on a Web site.

There is significant advantage to using the Internet to conduct a survey or recruit participants: You can reach a large body of potential participants with relative ease. Data can be collected quickly and easily, resulting in a large data set.

There are disadvantages to Internet surveys as well. As discussed in Chapter 6, a sample of respondents from the Internet may not be representative of the general population. According to a 1999 study by the Department of Labor, only 34.6 percent of

Citizen's State University
Washington, D.C.

5/23/04
Susan Smith
123 Main Street
Union, NJ 07083

Dear Ms. Smith,

Recently, the United States Congress introduced a bill on tax reform. This bill could affect how much of your pay you keep and how much the government keeps. It could also affect the budget deficit and social services. However, Congress does not know how people in the general population feel about the new tax proposal.

You are one in a small group of people that I have contacted to find out about your views on the current tax laws and potential changes in those laws. Since I have only sent out a few questionnaires, it is important that they all be completed and returned. A good return rate will ensure that the results that I report to your congressman are accurate. I would like you to take some time and complete this questionnaire.

Please be assured that all of your responses will remain confidential. Also, at no time will your name be reported along with any of your responses. In fact, do not even put your name on the questionnaire. If you want a copy of the summarized results, complete and mail separately the postcard that is included with the questionnaire.

The results of this survey will be provided to Congress so that it may have an indication about how the people affected by this bill feel about it. We have included a pen for you to use to fill out the questionnaire. You may keep the pen as a token of our appreciation for your time and effort.

If you have any questions, feel free to call me at (999)555-5555 during regular business hours.

Your assistance is greatly appreciated.

Sincerely,
Henry Baker
Henry Baker
Survey Director

**FIGURE 8–5**  Sample Cover Letter for a Mail Survey.
(SOURCE: Adapted from Dillman, 1978.)

households had a computer in 1997. Further, computers were more likely to be owned by individuals with higher levels of education and income. Additionally, computers are more likely to be owned by Asians (49.1 percent) and Whites (36.1 percent) than Blacks (17.9 percent). Another disadvantage is that one must have the resources available to post a survey on the Internet. This requires computer space on a server and the ability to create the necessary Web pages or the resources to pay someone to create your net survey for you.

## Telephone Surveys

In a **telephone survey**, you contact participants by telephone rather than by mail or via the Internet. You can ask some questions more easily over the telephone than you can in written form. Telephone surveys can be done by having an interviewer ask respondents a series of questions or by interactive voice response (IVR). Telephone surveys using live interviewers have lost popularity as new technologies have become available. IVR surveys involve respondents using a touch-tone telephone to respond to a series of prerecorded questions. Modern IVR technologies also allow respondents to provide verbal answers in addition to numeric responses.

Generally, telephone surveys may not be the best way to administer a questionnaire. The plethora of "junk calls" to which the population is exposed has given rise to a backlash against telephone intrusions. Laws have been passed on the state and federal level protecting people from unwanted calls. These, combined with caller ID and answering machines (which allow residents to screen their calls), make the telephone a less attractive medium now than in the past.

## Group-Administered Surveys

Sometimes you may have at your disposal a large group of individuals to whom you can administer your questionnaire. In such a case, you design your questionnaire as you would for a mail survey but administer it to the assembled group. For example, you might distribute to a first-year college class a questionnaire on attitudes toward premarital sex. Using such a captive audience permits you to collect large amounts of data in a relatively short time. You do not have to worry about participants misplacing or forgetting about your questionnaire. You also may be able to reduce any volunteer bias, especially if you administer your questionnaire during a class period. People may participate because very little effort is required.

As usual, this method has some drawbacks. Participants may not treat the questionnaire as seriously when they fill it out as a group as when they fill it out alone. Also, you may not be able to ensure anonymity in the large group if you are asking for sensitive information. Participants may feel that other participants are looking at their answers. (You may be able to overcome this problem by giving adjacently seated participants alternate forms of the questionnaire.) Also, a few participants may express hostility about the questionnaire by purposely providing false information.

A final drawback to group administration concerns the participant's right to decline participation. A participant may feel pressure to participate in your survey. This pressure arises from the participant's observation that just about everyone else is participating. In essence, a conformity effect occurs because completing your survey becomes the norm defined by the behavior of your other participants. Make special efforts to reinforce the understanding that participants should not feel compelled to participate.

## Face-to-Face Interviews

Still another method for obtaining survey data is the **face-to-face interview**. In this method, you talk to each participant directly. This can be done in the participant's home or place of employment, in your office, or in any other suitable place. If you decide to use a face-to-face interview, keep several things in mind. First, decide whether to use a structured interview or an unstructured interview. In a structured interview, you ask prepared questions. This is similar to the telephone survey in that you prepare a questionnaire in advance and simply read the ordered questions to your participants. In the unstructured interview, you have a general idea about the issues to discuss. However, you do not have a predetermined sequence of questions.

An advantage of the structured interview is that all participants are asked the same questions in the same order. This eliminates fluctuations in the data that result from differences in when and how questions are asked. Responses from a structured interview are therefore easier to summarize and analyze. However, the structured interview tends to be inflexible. You may miss some important information by having a highly structured interview. The unstructured interview is superior in this respect. By asking general questions and having participants provide answers in their own words, you may gain more complete (although perhaps less accurate) information. However, responses from an unstructured interview may be more difficult to code and analyze later on. You can gain some advantages of each method by combining them in one interview. For example, begin the interview with a structured format by asking prepared questions; later in the interview, switch to an unstructured format.

Using the face-to-face interview strategy leads to a problem that is not present in mail or Internet surveys but is present to some extent in telephone surveys: The appearance and demeanor of the interviewer may affect the responses of the participants. Experimenter bias and demand characteristics become a problem. Subtle changes in the way in which an interviewer asks a question may elicit different answers. Also, your interviewer may not respond similarly to all participants (for example, an interviewer may react differently to an attractive participant and an unattractive one). This, too, can affect the results.

The best way to combat this problem is to use interviewers who have received extensive training in interview techniques. Interviewers must be trained to ask questions in the same way for each participant. They also must be trained not to emphasize any particular words in the stem of a question or in the response list. The questions should be read in a neutral manner. Also, try to anticipate any questions that participants may have and provide your interviewers with standardized responses. This can be accomplished by running a small pilot version of your survey before running the actual survey. During this pilot study, try out the interview procedure on a small sample of participants. (This can be done with just about anyone, such as friends, colleagues, or students.) Correct any problems that arise.

Another problem with the interview method is that the social context in which the interview takes place may affect a participant's responses. For example, in a survey of sexual attitudes known as the "Sex in America" survey (Michael, Gagnon, Laumann, & Kolata, 1994), some questions were asked during a face-to-face interview. Some participants were interviewed alone, whereas others were interviewed with a spouse or other sex partner present. Having the sex partner present changed the responses to some questions. For example, when asked a question about the number of sex partners one had over the past year, 17 percent of the participants interviewed alone reported two or more. When interviewed with their sex partner present, only 5 percent said they had two or more sex partners. It would be most desirable to conduct the interviews in a standardized fashion with only the participant present.

A final note on survey technique is in order. Although each of the discussed techniques has advantages, the mail survey has been the most popular. The mail survey is able to reach large numbers of participants at a lower cost than either the telephone survey or face-to-face interview (Warner et al., 1983) and produces data that are less affected by *social desirability effects* (answering in a way that seems socially desirable). For these reasons, consider mail surveys first.

After designing your questionnaire and choosing a method of administration, the next step is to assess the reliability and validity of your questionnaire. This is typically done by administering your questionnaire to a small but representative sample of participants. Based on the results, you may have to rework your questionnaire to meet acceptable levels of reliability and validity. In the next sections, we introduce you to the processes of evaluating the reliability and validity of your questionnaire.

## ASSESSING THE RELIABILITY OF YOUR QUESTIONNAIRE

Constructing a questionnaire is typically not a one-shot deal. That is, you don't just sit down and write some questions and magically produce a high-quality questionnaire. Developing a quality questionnaire usually involves designing the questionnaire, administering it, and then evaluating it to see if it does the job.

One dimension you must pay attention to is the reliability of your questionnaire. In Chapter 5, we defined reliability as the ability of a measure to produce the same or highly similar results on repeated administrations. This definition extends to a questionnaire. If, on testing and retesting, your questionnaire produces highly similar results, you have a reliable instrument. In contrast, if the responses vary widely, your instrument is not reliable (Rogers, 1995).

In Chapter 5, we described two ways to assess the reliability of a measure: the test–retest method and the split-half method. In the next sections, we discuss the application of these two methods when assessing the reliability of a questionnaire.

### Assessing Reliability by Repeated Administration

Evaluating test–retest reliability is the oldest and conceptually simplest way of establishing the reliability of your questionnaire. You simply administer your questionnaire, allow some time to elapse, and then administer the questionnaire (or a parallel form of it) again to the same group of participants. Although this method is relatively simple to execute, you need to consider some issues before using it.

First, you must consider how long to wait between administrations of your questionnaire. An intertest interval that is too short may result in participants remembering your questions and the answers they gave. This could lead to an artificially high level of test–retest reliability. If, however, you wait too long, test–retest reliability may be artificially low. According to Tim Rogers (1995), the intertest interval should depend on the nature of the variables being measured, with an interval of a few weeks being sufficient for most applications. Rogers suggests that test–retest methods may be particularly problematic when applied to the following:

1. *Measuring ideas that fluctuate with time.* For example, an instrument to measure attitudes toward universal health care should not be evaluated with the test–retest method because attitudes on this topic seem to shift quickly.

2. *Issues for which individuals are likely to remember their answers on the first testing.*

3. *Questionnaires that are very long and boring.* The problem here is that participants may not be highly motivated to accurately complete an overly long questionnaire and therefore may give answers that reduce reliability.

Some of the problems inherent in using the *same* measure on multiple occasions can be avoided by using alternate or parallel forms of your questionnaire for multiple testing sessions. As noted in Chapter 5, the type of reliability being assessed with this technique is known as parallel-forms reliability (Rogers, 1995).

For the parallel-forms method to work, the two (or more) forms of your questionnaire must be equivalent, so that direct comparison is meaningful. According to Rogers, parallel forms should have the same number of items and the same response format, cover the same issues with different items, be equally difficult, use the same instructions, and have the same time limits. In short, the parallel versions of a test must be as equivalent as possible (Rogers, 1995).

Although the parallel-forms method improves on the test–retest method, it does not solve all the problems associated with multiple testing. Using parallel forms does not eliminate the possibility that rapidly changing attitudes will result in low reliability. As with the test–retest method, such changes make the questionnaire appear less reliable than it actually is. In addition, practice effects may occur even when alternate forms are used (Rogers, 1995). Even though you use different questions on the parallel form, participants may respond similarly on the second test because they are familiar with your question format.

## Assessing Reliability with a Single Administration

Because of the problems associated with repeated testing, you might consider assessing reliability by means of a single administration of your questionnaire. As noted in Chapter 5, this approach involves splitting the questionnaire into equivalent halves and deriving a score for each half; the correlation between scores from the two halves is known as split-half reliability (Rogers, 1995). This technique works best when your survey is limited to a single specific area (for example, sexual behavior) as opposed to multiple areas (sexual behavior and sexual attitudes).

Although the split-half method circumvents the problems associated with repeated testing, it introduces others. First, when you split a questionnaire, each score is based on a limited set of items, which can reduce reliability (Rogers, 1995). Consequently, the split-half method may underestimate reliability. Second, it is not clear how splitting should be done. If you simply do a first-half/second-half split, artificially low reliability may occur if the two halves of the form are not equivalent or if participants are less motivated to answer questions accurately on the second half of your questionnaire and therefore give inconsistent answers to your questions. One remedy for this is to use an odd–even split. In this case, you derive a score for the odd items and a score for the even items.

Perhaps the most desirable way to assess the split-half reliability of your questionnaire is to apply the Kuder–Richardson formula. This formula yields the average of all the split-half reliabilities that could be derived from splitting your questionnaire into two halves in every possible way. The resulting number (designated KR20) will lie between 0 and 1; the higher the number, the greater the reliability of your questionnaire. A KR20 of .75 indicates a "moderate" level of reliability (Rogers, 1995).

In cases in which your questionnaire uses a Likert format, a variation on the Kuder–Richardson formula known as *coefficient alpha* is used (Rogers, 1995). Like KR20, coefficient alpha is a score between 0 and 1, with higher numbers indicating greater reliability. Computation of this formula can be complex. For details, see a text on psychological testing (for example, see Cohen & Swerdlik, 2002; Rogers, 1995).

### Increasing Reliability

Regardless of the method you use to assess the reliability, there are steps you can take to increase the reliability of your questionnaire (Rogers, 1995):

1. Increase the number of items on your questionnaire. Generally, higher reliability is associated with increasing numbers of items. Of course, if your instrument becomes too long, participants may become angry, tired, or bored. You must weigh the benefits of increasing questionnaire length against possible liabilities.

2. Standardize administration procedures. Reliability will be enhanced if you treat all participants alike when administering your questionnaire. Make sure that timing procedures, lighting, ventilation, instructions to participants, and instructions to administrators are kept constant.

3. Score your questionnaire carefully. Scoring errors can reduce reliability.

4. Make sure that the items on your questionnaire are clear, well written, and appropriate for your sample (see our previous discussion on writing items).

## ASSESSING THE VALIDITY OF YOUR QUESTIONNAIRE

In Chapter 5, we discussed the validity of a measure and described several forms of validity that differ in their method of assessment: content validity, criterion-related validity, construct validity, and face validity. As with other measures, a questionnaire must have validity if it is to be useful; that is, it must measure what it is intended to measure. For example, if you are designing a questionnaire to assess political attitudes, the questions on your test should tap into political attitudes and not, say, religious attitudes.

Here we review content validity, construct validity, and criterion-related validity as applied to a questionnaire (Rogers, 1995). In a questionnaire, *content validity* assesses whether the questions cover the range of behaviors normally considered to be part of the dimension you are assessing. To have content validity, your questionnaire on political attitudes should include items relevant to all the major issues relating to such attitudes (for example, abortion, health care, the economy, and defense). The *construct validity* of a questionnaire can be established by showing that the questionnaire's results agree with predictions based on theory.

Establishing the *criterion-related validity* of a questionnaire involves correlating the questionnaire's results with those from another, established measure. There are two ways to do this. First, you can establish *concurrent validity* by correlating your questionnaire's results with those of another measure of the *same* dimension administered at the same time. In the case of your questionnaire on political attitudes, you would correlate its results with those of another, established measure of political attitudes. Second, you can establish *predictive validity* by correlating the questionnaire's results with some behavior that would be expected to occur, given the results. For example, your questionnaire on political attitudes would be shown to have predictive validity if the questionnaire's results correctly predicted election outcomes.

The validity of a questionnaire may be affected by a variety of factors. For example, as noted earlier, how you define the behavior or attitude you are measuring can affect validity. Validity also can be affected by the methods used to gather your data. In the "Sex in America" survey, some respondents were interviewed alone and others with someone else present. One cannot be sure that the responses given with another person present represent an accurate reflection of one's sexual behavior (Stevenson, 1995). Generally, methodological flaws, poor conceptualization, and unclear questions can all contribute to lowered levels of validity.

## ACQUIRING A SAMPLE FOR YOUR SURVEY

In Chapter 6, we distinguished between a population (all individuals in a well-defined group) and a sample (a smaller number of individuals selected from the population). Once you have designed and pretested your questionnaire, you then administer it to a group of participants. It is usually impractical to have everyone in the population (however that may be defined) complete your survey. Instead, you administer your questionnaire to a small sample of that population.

Proper sampling is a crucial aspect of sound survey research methodology. Without proper sampling, you can't generalize your results to your target population (for example, accurately predict voter behavior in an election). Three sampling-related issues you must consider are representativeness, sampling technique, and sample size.

### Representativeness

Regardless of the technique you use to acquire your sample, your sample should be representative of the population of interest. A **representative sample** closely matches the characteristics of the population. Imagine that you have a bag containing 300 golf balls: 100 are white, 100 are orange, and 100 are yellow. Assume you select a sample of 30 golf balls. A representative sample would have 10 balls of each color. A sample having 25 white and 5 orange would not be representative (the ratio of colors does not approximate that of the population) and would constitute a nonrepresentative or **biased sample**.

The importance of representative sampling is shown by the failure of a political poll taken during the 1936 presidential election. In that election, Alf Landon was opposing Franklin Roosevelt. The editors of the *Literary Digest* (a now-defunct magazine) conducted a poll by using telephone directories and vehicle registration lists to draw their sample. The final sample consisted of nearly 10 million people! The results showed that Landon would beat Roosevelt by a landslide. Quite to the contrary, Roosevelt soundly defeated Landon. Why was the poll so wrong?

The problem stemmed from the method used to obtain the sample. Fewer people owned a car or telephone in the 1930s than do today. In fact, very few owned either. Those who did own a telephone or car tended to be relatively wealthy and Republican. Consequently, most of the participants polled favored the Republican candidate. Unfortunately for the *Literary Digest*, this sample did not represent the population of voters, and the prediction failed. How could the editors have been so stupid? In fact, they weren't stupid. Such sampling techniques had been used before and worked. It was only in that particular election (in which people were clearly split along party lines) that the problem emerged (Hooke, 1983).

The *Literary Digest* poll failed because it used a biased source (car registration and telephone listings). Whatever source you choose, you should make an effort to determine whether it includes members from all segments of the population in which you have an interest. A good way to overcome the problem of biased source lists is to use multiple lists. For example, you could use the telephone book *and* vehicle registration *and* voter registration lists to select your sample.

## Sampling Techniques

At the heart of all sampling techniques is the concept of *random sampling*. In random sampling, every member of the population has an equal chance of appearing in your sample. Whether or not a participant is included in your sample is based on chance alone. Sampling is typically done without replacement. Once an individual is chosen for your sample, he or she cannot be chosen a second time for that sample.

Random sampling eliminates the possibility that the sample is biased by the preferences of the person selecting the sample. In addition, random sampling affords some assurance that the sample does not bias itself. As an example of self-biasing, consider the following case. In 1976 Shere Hite published *The Hite Report: A Nationwide Study on Female Sexuality*, which was a survey of women's sexual attitudes and behaviors. Hite's sample was obtained by initially distributing questionnaires through national mailings to women's groups (the National Organization for Women, abortion rights groups, university women's centers, and others). Later, advertisements were placed in several magazines (the *Village Voice*, *Mademoiselle*, *Brides*, and *Ms.*) informing women where they could write for a copy of the questionnaire. Finally, the questionnaire was reprinted in *Oui* magazine in its entirety (253 women returned the questionnaire from *Oui*).

The question you should ask yourself at this point is "Did Hite obtain a random sample of the population of women?" The answer is no. Hite's method had several problems. First, the memberships of the organizations Hite contacted may not represent the population of women. For example, you cannot assume that members of NOW hold similar views, on the average, to those of the population of all women. Second, asking people through magazine ads to write in for questionnaires further biases the sample. Can you figure out why?

If you said that the people who write in for the questionnaires may be somehow different from those who do not, you were correct. Who would write in to obtain a questionnaire on sexuality? Obviously, women who have an interest in such an issue. In fact, Hite indicates that many of her participants expressed such an interest. One woman wrote, "I answered this questionnaire because I think the time is long overdue for women to speak out about their feelings about sex" (Hite, 1976, p. xxxii). As with the members of the women's organizations, you could question whether the women who wrote in for questionnaires are representative of all women. They probably are not.

When a sample is biased, the data obtained may not indicate the attitudes of the population as a whole. Hite concluded from her sample that women in this country were experiencing a "new sexuality." However, that new sexuality was limited to those women whose attitudes were similar to those who answered her questionnaires.

In 1983 Hite published *The Hite Report on Male Sexuality*. The method she used to gather data was similar to the one used in her earlier study of women. In this book, Hite responded to the criticisms of her method. She presented evidence that her sample of men was similar in age, religion, and education to the most recent census data. What was not clear, however, was whether or not the attitudes of the men who responded to her questionnaire were similar to those of the general population. As in the survey of women, the data obtained may not be representative of the population of men. Some evidence suggests they were not. Hite said that 72 percent of married men reported having had an extramarital affair. Is this an accurate estimate of the population or an estimate of a special subsection of the population? Apparently it is the latter. Other surveys have found that about 25 percent of men report having had extramarital affairs.

The lesson of the Hite example is that you should make every effort to obtain a random sample. This may be difficult, especially if you are dealing with a sensitive topic. You could use some of the strategies previously suggested for reducing nonresponse bias (such as including a small reward or using follow-ups). If your sample turns out to be nonrandom and nonrepresentative, temper any conclusions you draw.

Using the proper sampling technique is one way to obtain a representative sample. Several techniques are available to you. Five of them (simple random sampling, stratified sampling, proportionate sampling, systematic sampling, and cluster sampling) are discussed next. These techniques are not mutually exclusive. Often researchers combine them to help ensure a representative sample of the population.

*Simple Random Sampling*    Randomly selecting a certain number of individuals from the population is a technique called **simple random sampling**. Remember the golf ball example? A simple random sample of 50 would involve dipping your hand into the bag 50 times, each time withdrawing a single ball. Figure 8–6 illustrates the simple random sampling strategy. From the population illustrated at the top of the figure, 10 participants are selected at random for inclusion in your survey.

Population

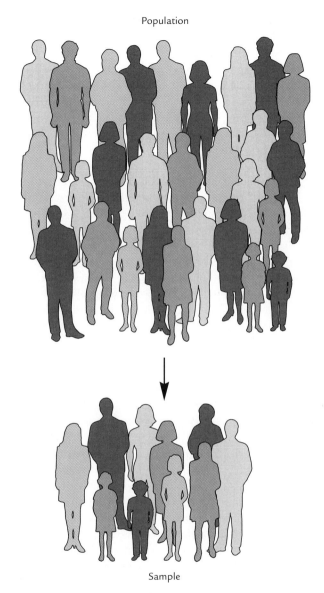

Sample

**FIGURE 8-6**  Example of Simple Random Sampling. The people at the top of the figure represent the population, and the people at the bottom represent the randomly selected sample.

In practice, selecting a random sample for a survey is more involved than pulling golf balls from a bag. Often it involves consulting a table of random numbers. The numbers in such a table have been chosen at random and then subjected to a number of statistical tests to ensure that they have the expected properties of random numbers. You can find a table of random numbers in the Appendix (Table 1A).

As an example of how to use the table of random numbers to select a random sample, imagine you are using the telephone book as a source list. Starting on any page of the random number table, close your eyes and drop your finger on the page. Open your eyes and read the number under your finger. Assume that the number is 235,035. Then go to page 235 in the telephone book and select the 35th name on that page. Repeat this process until you select all the participants constituting the sample.

A variant of random sampling that can be used when conducting a telephone survey is *random digit dialing* (Dillman, 2000). List all the exchanges in a particular area (the first three digits of the phone numbers, not including the area code). You then use the table of random numbers or a computer to select four-digit numbers (for example, 5,891). The exchange plus the four-digit number provides the number to be called. (Any nonworking numbers are discarded.) This technique allows you to reach unlisted as well as listed numbers.

Even though random sampling reduces the possibility of systematic bias in your sample, it does not guarantee a representative sample. You could, quite at random, select participants who represent only a small segment of the population. In the golf ball example, you might select 50 orange golf balls. White and yellow golf balls, even though represented in the population, are not in your sample. One way to combat this problem is to select a large sample (such as 200 rather than just 50 balls). A large sample is more likely to represent all segments of the population than a small one. However, it does not *guarantee* that representation in your sample will be proportionate to representation in the population. You may end up with 90 white, 90 orange, and only 20 yellow golf balls in a sample of 200, although such a result is highly unlikely. In addition, as you increase sample size, you also increase the cost and time needed to complete the survey. Fortunately, more sophisticated techniques provide a random, yet representative, sample without requiring a large number of participants.

*Stratified Sampling*    **Stratified sampling** provides one way to obtain a representative sample. You begin by dividing the population into segments, or *strata* (Kish, 1965). For example, you could divide the population of a particular town into Whites, Blacks, and Hispanics. Next, you select a separate random sample of equal size from each stratum. Because individuals are selected from each stratum, you guarantee that each segment of the population is represented in your sample. Figure 8–7 shows the stratified sampling strategy. Notice that the population has been divided into two segments (dark and light figures). A random sample is then selected from each segment.

*Proportionate Sampling*    Simple stratified sampling ensures a degree of representativeness, but it may lead to a segment of the population being overrepresented in your sample. For example, consider a community of 5,000 that has 500 Hispanics, 1,500 Blacks, and 3,000 Whites. If you used a simple stratification technique in which you randomly selected 400 people from each stratum, Hispanics would be overrepresented in your sample relative to Blacks and Whites, and Blacks would be overrepresented relative to Whites. You could avoid this problem by using a variant of simple stratified sampling called **proportionate sampling**.

In proportionate sampling, the proportions of people in the population are reflected in your sample. In the population example, your sample would consist of

Stratum 1                                  Stratum 2

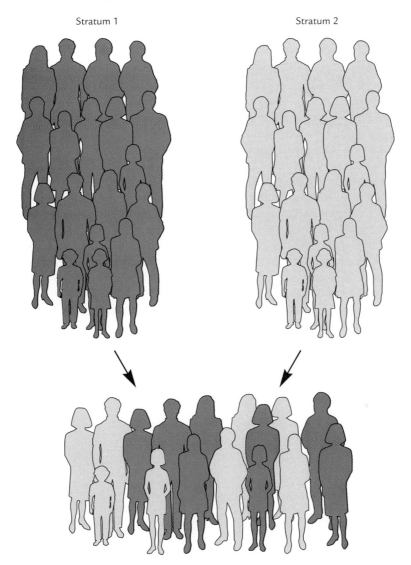

**FIGURE 8–7**  Example of Stratified Sampling. The population is divided into two strata from which independent random samples are drawn.

10 percent Hispanics (500/5,000 = 10 percent), 30 percent Blacks (1,500/5,000 = 30 percent), and 60 percent Whites (3,000/5,000 = 60 percent). So, if you draw a sample of 1,200, you would have 120 Hispanics, 360 Blacks, and 720 Whites. According to Kish (1965), this technique is the most popular method of sampling.

By the way, stratification and proportionate sampling can be done after a sample has been obtained (Kish, 1965). You randomly select from the participants who responded the number from each stratum needed to match the characteristics of the population.

*Systematic Sampling*    **Systematic sampling** is a popular technique that is often used in conjunction with stratified sampling (Kish, 1965). Figure 8–8 illustrates the systematic sampling technique.

According to Kish, this technique involves sampling every *k*th element after a random start. For example, once you have randomly chosen the page of the telephone book from which you are going to sample, you then might pick every fourth item (where *k* = 4). Systematic sampling is much less time-consuming and more cost-effective than simple random sampling. For example, it is much easier to select every fourth item from a page than to select randomly from an entire list.

*Cluster Sampling*    In some cases, populations may be too large to allow cost-effective random sampling—or even systematic sampling. You might be interested in surveying children in a large school district. To make sampling more manageable, you could identify naturally occurring groups of participants (clusters) and randomly select certain clusters. For example, you could randomly select certain departments or classes from which to sample. Once the clusters have been selected, you would then survey all participants within the clusters. **Cluster sampling** differs from the other forms of sampling already discussed in that the basic sampling unit is a group of participants (the cluster) rather than the individual participant (Kish, 1965). Figure 8–9 illustrates cluster sampling. This figure shows how you select four groups from a larger pool of groups.

| | |
|---|---|
| Richardson, E. | 555-6396* |
| Richardson, J. B. | 555-6789 |
| Richardson, L. R. | 555-2311 |
| Richardson, M. | 555-9902 |
| Richardson, V. | 555-7822* |
| Richeson, A. P. | 555-8211 |
| Richeson, T. | 555-3762 |
| Richey, B. B. | 555-9943 |
| Richey, C. L. | 555-1470* |
| Richey, G. J. | 555-8218 |
| Richhart, W. | 555-6539 |
| Richman, A. | 555-8902 |
| Richman, B. I. | 555-0076* |
| Richman, H. H. | 555-9215 |
| Richman, Z. L. | 555-1093 |
| Richmond, A. | 555-7634 |
| Richmond, B. B. | 555-7890* |
| Richmond, C. | 555-2609 |
| Rideman, L. | 555-7245 |
| Ritchey, A. K. | 555-6790 |

Each of the names with a star (*) would be included in your sample.

**FIGURE 8–8**   Example of Systematic Sampling. After a random start, every selected name is included in the sample (indicated with an asterisk).

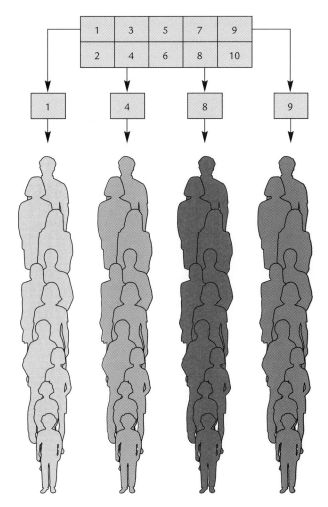

**FIGURE 8–9**  Example of Cluster Sampling. After selecting subgroups of the population, you survey all participants in each subgroup.

An obvious advantage to cluster sampling is that it saves time. It is not always feasible to select random samples that focus on single elements (that is, individuals, families, and so forth). Cluster sampling provides an acceptable, cost-effective method of acquiring a sample. On the negative side, cluster sampling does limit your sample to those participants found in the chosen clusters. If participants within clusters are fairly similar to one another but differ from those in other clusters, the sample will leave out important elements of the population. For example, clusters consisting of geographical areas of the United States (East, Midwest, South, Southwest, West) may differ widely in political opinion. If only East and Midwest are selected for the sample, the opinions collected may not reflect the opinions of the country as a whole. Thus, cluster sampling does have drawbacks.

A variant of cluster sampling is **multistage sampling**. You begin by identifying large clusters and randomly selecting from among them (first stage). From the selected clusters, you then randomly select individual elements (rather than selecting all elements in the cluster). This method can be combined with stratification procedures to ensure a representative sample.

Other sophisticated sampling techniques are available to the survey researcher, but to explore them all would require a whole book. If you are interested in learning about these techniques, read Kish (1965).

### Random and Nonrandom Sampling Revisited

In Chapter 6, we distinguished between random sampling (in which each member of a population has an equal chance of being selected) and nonrandom sampling (in which a limited group of potential participants is tapped). The sampling techniques we have just discussed may be used in the context of random or nonrandom sampling. Ideally, you would want to use random sampling. This is especially true, as noted in Chapter 6, if you want to make specific predictions about specific behaviors. However, as a practical matter, it may not always be possible to use a true random sample. Instead, you may have to administer your questionnaire to a convenience sample, such as students at a particular university, which is a nonrandom sample. Similarly, surveys conducted via the Internet use nonrandom samples, consisting only of those with computers who know how to access the Internet and have the ability to complete the survey. Of course, using a nonrandom sample limits the generality of your results, and making specific predictions about behavior may not be possible. However, a nonrandom sample (as noted in Chapter 6) is perfectly acceptable for most research interests in psychology. If you use nonrandom sampling, you should include a discussion of possible limitations of your results in the discussion section of any report you write.

### Sample Size

One factor you must contend with if you perform a survey is the size of your sample. You should try to select an *economic sample*—one that includes enough participants to ensure a valid survey and no more. You must take into account two factors when considering the size of the sample needed to ensure a valid survey: the amount of acceptable error and the expected magnitude of the population proportions.

The question of acceptable error arises because most samples deviate to some degree from the population. If you conduct a political poll on a sample of 1,500 registered voters and find that 62 percent of the sample favor Smith and 38 percent Jones, you would like to say that 62 percent of the population favor Smith. However, these sample proportions do not exactly match those of the population (the population proportions may be 59 percent and 41 percent). This deviation of sample characteristics from those of the population is called **sampling error**.

When determining sample size, you must decide the acceptable amount of sampling error. Unfortunately, there are no broad rules of thumb as to the acceptable margin of error. It depends in part on the use to which you will put your results

(Moser & Kalton, 1972). If you plan to apply your results to implement changes in behavior, you may want a small margin of error. If you are interested simply in describing a set of characteristics, you may tolerate a larger margin of error. A good way to determine the acceptable margin of error is to look at literature describing similar surveys to see what margin of error was used.

The second component you need to consider when determining sample size is the magnitude of the differences you expect to find. Here again, there is no broad rule of thumb to guide you. Again, you can make use of previous surveys to get an estimate of the magnitude of the differences. Or you can conduct a small pilot survey to gain some insight into the magnitudes.

Once you have determined the acceptable error and the expected magnitude of differences, you can calculate the size of the sample needed. The calculation is relatively easy for simple random sampling. Moser and Kalton (1972) suggested the following formula:

$$n' = \frac{P'(1 - P')}{[SE_P]^2}$$

where $P'$ is the estimate of the proportion of the population that has a particular characteristic and $SE_p$ is the acceptable margin of error. For example, if you expect 62 percent of the population to favor Smith in an election and your acceptable margin of error is 2 percent (0.02), then the formula gives $n' = 589$. Thus, you should have 589 participants in your sample.

When the size of the population is large, you do not need to consider population size when calculating sample size. If the population is small, however, then you must use the *finite population correction (f.p.c.)* when calculating sample size. Crano and Brewer (1986) suggested using the following formula when the sample size is more than 10 percent of the population size:

$$n = N \times n'/(N + n')$$

where $n$ = the corrected sample size, $n'$ = the sample size calculated with the previous formula, and $N$ = the size of the population from which the sample is to be drawn. For example, using the previous numbers and $N = 2,000$, you have

$$n = 2000 \times 589/(2000 + 589) = 455$$

Thus, if the population from which your sample will be drawn consists of only 2,000 participants, you would use a sample size of 455 rather than of 589.

For stratified sampling, determining sample size is more difficult than for simple random sampling. You must take into account the between-strata error (the variability in the scores of participants in different strata) and the within-strata error (the variability in the scores of participants within the same stratum). The formulas for computing sample size with the more sophisticated sampling techniques are complex. If you pursue survey research using these techniques, consult Moser and Kalton (1972) and Kish (1965) for more information.

## SUMMARY

Survey research is used to evaluate the behavior (past, present, and future) and attitudes of your participants. Survey research falls into the category of correlational research. Therefore, you cannot draw causal inferences about behavior from your survey data, no matter how compelling the data look. Surveys are used in a wide variety of situations. They can be used to research the marketability of a new product, to predict voter behavior, or to measure existing attitudes on a variety of issues.

The first step in a survey is to clearly define the goals of your research. Your questionnaire is then designed around those goals. You should have a reasonably focused goal for your survey. A questionnaire that tries to do too much may be confusing and burdensome to your participants. Keep your questionnaire focused on the central issues of your research.

Often a questionnaire is organized so that questions about your participants' characteristics (demographic items) and questions about the behavior or attitude of interest are included. The demographic items can later be used as predictor variables when you look for relationships among the variables that you measured.

Questionnaire items can be of several types. Open-ended questions allow your participants to answer in their own words. A major advantage of this type of question is the richness of the information obtained. A drawback is that responses are difficult to summarize and analyze. A restricted question provides response categories for participants. A variation on the restricted item is a rating scale on which participants circle a number reflecting how they feel. This type of item yields data that are easier to summarize and analyze. However, the responses made to restricted items are not as rich as those obtained with an open-ended item. A partially open-ended item not only provides participants with clearly defined response alternatives but also provides a space for participants to write in their own response category.

Once you have decided what types of items to include on your questionnaire, you must then actually write your questions. When writing items, you should avoid using overly complex words when simpler words will suffice. Your questions should be precise. Vague or overly precise wording yields inconsistent data. In addition, avoid question wording that is biased or judgmental.

A questionnaire is more than just a collection of questions. Questions should be presented in a logical order so that your questionnaire has continuity. Also, it is a good idea to place demographic items at the end. These questions tend to be boring, and participants may be turned off if you have demographic items at the beginning of your questionnaire. Sensitive questions should be placed toward the middle. Your participants may be more willing to answer such questions after answering several other, more innocuous questions. Sensitive items should be carefully worded. Your questionnaire should have a logical "navigational path." This path should lead the respondent through the questionnaire as if he or she were reading a book.

Constructing a questionnaire involves more than sitting down and writing a set of items. Developing a good questionnaire involves several steps, including assessing its reliability, or your questionnaire's ability to produce consistent results. One way to assess reliability is to administer your questionnaire (or parallel forms of the questionnaire) more than once. If the results are highly similar, the questionnaire is reliable. Another way to assess reliability is with a single administration of your questionnaire.

This is known as "establishing internal consistency." The most common way to do this is to use a split-half method by which you divide your questionnaire in half (for example, odd versus even items) and correlate the two halves. Two statistics used to evaluate split-half reliability are the Kuder–Richardson formula and coefficient alpha.

If you find low reliability, you can do several things to increase it. You can increase the number of items on your questionnaire, standardize administration procedures, make sure that you score questions carefully, and ensure that your items are clear, well written, and appropriate for your sample.

In addition to assessing reliability, you should also evaluate the validity of your questionnaire. The term *validity* in this context refers to whether your questionnaire actually measures what you intend it to measure. There are three ways to assess validity. First, you can establish content validity by making sure that items on your questionnaire cover the full range of issues relevant to the phenomenon you are studying. Second, criterion-related validity can be established by correlating the results from your questionnaire with one of established validity. Third, you can establish construct validity by establishing that the results from your questionnaire match well with predictions made by a theory. No one of these methods is best. Perhaps the best approach is to establish validity using more than one of the three methods.

Five ways to administer your questionnaire are the mail survey, Internet survey, telephone survey, group administration, and face-to-face interview. The mail survey is easiest. You simply mail your questionnaires and wait for a response. However, this method is plagued by nonresponse bias. Return rates can be increased with effective cover letters, follow-up reminders tailored to the nature of your participant population, and small rewards. In group administration, you give your questionnaire to a large number of participants at once. The advantage of group administration is that you can collect large amounts of data quickly. Surveys also can be conducted over the telephone. Questionnaires designed for telephone surveys should be relatively short, with clearly worded, short questions. Because your questions will be read to your participants, make sure that the person reading questions speaks clearly and slowly. In an interview, you ask your questions to your participants in a face-to-face session. Interviews can be either structured (questions asked from a prepared questionnaire in a fixed order) or unstructured (each interview is different). Finally, you can conduct your survey on the Internet, which allows you to reach large numbers of potential respondents. Data can be collected quickly and easily via the Internet. However, the sample obtained from the Internet may not be representative, and you must have the equipment, resources, and knowledge necessary to post a questionnaire this way.

One of the most crucial stages of survey research is acquiring a sample of participants. Because you want to make statements about how people think on an issue, be sure your sample represents the population. Biased samples lead to invalid data and ultimately incorrect conclusions. Sampling techniques include simple random sampling (in which every participant has an equal chance of being in your survey) and stratified sampling (in which your population is broken into smaller segments and random samples are then drawn from those smaller segments). Other sampling techniques are proportionate sampling, multistage sampling, and cluster sampling. The sampling technique you use depends on the needs of your survey.

Whichever sampling technique you choose, you must consider the issue of sample size. Your sample should be large enough to be representative of the population,

yet not too large. Try to acquire an economic sample that has just enough participants to adequately assess behavior or attitudes. The size of the most economic sample is determined with a special formula.

## REVIEW QUESTIONS

1. What are some of the applications of survey research?
2. Why is it important to know about survey methods, even if you do not intend
   to conduct surveys?
3. What are the steps involved in designing a questionnaire?
4. How do open-ended and restricted items differ, and what are the advantages
   and disadvantages of each?
5. What are the ways in which questionnaire items can be formatted?
6. What are some of the factors that you should pay attention to when
   constructing questionnaire items?
7. How do you design effective rating scales?
8. Why is the first question on a questionnaire so important?
9. What does it mean that a questionnaire should have continuity? Why is
   continuity important?
10. What is a questionnaire's "navigational path," and why is it important?
11. What are the different ways of administering a questionnaire? What are the
    advantages and disadvantages of each?
12. What can you do to combat nonresponse bias?
13. What techniques are used to assess the reliability of a questionnaire?
14. How can the reliability of a questionnaire be increased?
15. What techniques are used to assess the validity of a questionnaire?
16. Why is it important to have a representative sample for a survey?
17. What are the various sampling techniques used in survey research, and when
    is each used?
18. How do you determine the size of the sample needed for a valid survey?

## KEY TERMS

| | |
|---|---|
| open-ended item | biased sample |
| restricted item | simple random sampling |
| partially open-ended item | stratified sampling |
| mail survey | proportionate sampling |
| nonresponse bias | systematic sampling |
| internet survey | cluster sampling |
| telephone survey | multistage sampling |
| face-to-face interview | sampling error |
| representative sample | |

# 9

C H A P T E R

# Using Between-Subjects and Within-Subjects Experimental Designs

A s we pointed out in Chapters 1 and 3, a major goal of research is to establish clear causal relationships between variables. The correlational research designs discussed in Chapters 7 and 8 identify potential causal relationships and often are used when causal variables cannot or should not be manipulated directly. However, correlational designs are simply not adequate for establishing causal relationships between variables.

When your goal is to establish causal relationships and you can manipulate variables, an experimental research design is used. By manipulating an independent variable while rigidly controlling extraneous factors, you can determine whether this manipulation causes changes in the value of the dependent variable.

## TYPES OF EXPERIMENTAL DESIGN

In Chapter 4, we noted that every true experiment contains an independent variable, which the experimenter manipulates, and a dependent variable, which the experimenter observes and records. To manipulate the independent variable, you set its value to at least two different values or "levels" during the course of the experiment and observe your subjects' performances under each level. You then compare these performances. If you can show that performance differed across the levels of the independent variable and that these differences are reliable, you can conclude that a change in the level of the independent variable *causes* a change in the value of the dependent variable.

There are two ways in which you can manipulate your independent variable. You can vary it quantitatively by changing the amount of the variable to which each group of subjects is exposed. For example, in an experiment testing the effect of different doses of Prozac on memory, you could vary between 10 mg, 20 mg, and 30 mg the amount of Prozac administered to the participants. You also can vary your independent variable qualitatively. For example, in an

*indep. var. - touching vs not touching*

*dep. var - amount of extras or/and sales increase*

261

experiment testing the effects of different antidepressants on memory, you could give participants in your different treatment groups either Prozac, Serzone, or Zoloft.

The simple logic of manipulating an independent variable and observing related changes in behavior is at the heart of every experimental design. However, to deal with the complexities of real-world research problems, researchers have developed a wide variety of experimental designs. We can simplify the situation somewhat by noting that experimental designs can be categorized into three basic types: between-subjects, within-subjects, and single-subject designs. In a **between-subjects design** different groups of subjects are randomly assigned to the levels of your independent variable. In a **within-subjects design**, a single group of subjects is exposed to all levels of your independent variable. In both the between-subjects and within-subjects designs, data from subjects within a given treatment are averaged and analyzed. A **single-subject design** is similar to the within-subjects design in that subjects are exposed to all levels of the independent variable. The main difference from the within-subjects design is that you do not average data across subjects. Instead, you focus on changes in the behavior of a single subject (or a small number of individual subjects) under the different treatment conditions.

In this chapter, we discuss between-subjects and within-subjects designs. (Single-subject designs are discussed in Chapter 11.) The plan of this chapter is to discuss, first, the problem of error variance in experimental design and how it is handled. We then introduce single-factor between-subjects and within-subjects designs, designs that include only one independent variable. Finally, we explore between-subjects and within-subjects designs that include two or more independent variables.

## THE PROBLEM OF ERROR VARIANCE IN BETWEEN-SUBJECTS AND WITHIN-SUBJECTS DESIGNS

**Error variance** is the statistical variability of scores caused by the influence of variables other than your independent variables (extraneous variables or subject-related variables). The problems posed by error variance are common to all three experimental designs. However, each design has its own way of dealing with error variance. In this chapter, we focus on how we deal with error variance in between-subjects and within-subjects designs. In Chapter 11 we discuss how error variance is handled in single-subject designs.

### Sources of Error Variance

In the real world, it is rarely possible to hold constant all the extraneous variables that could affect the value of your dependent variable. Subjects in your experiment differ from one another in innumerable ways that could individually or collectively affect their scores on the dependent measure, the environmental conditions are not absolutely constant, and even the same subject will not be exactly the same from moment to moment. To the extent that these variations affect your dependent variable, they induce fluctuations in scores that have nothing to do with your independent variable. That is, they produce error variance.

An example may help to clarify this concept. In an experiment on the effects of THC (the active ingredient in marijuana) on a simulated air traffic control task, one group is exposed to a dose of THC (the experimental group) and one is not (the control group). Within each group, all participants would have been exposed to the same level of the independent variable. Yet it is unlikely that all participants in a group would turn in the same scores on the dependent measure (number of errors on the simulated air traffic controller task). Participants differ from one another in many ways that affect their performances. Some may be more resistant to fatigue, have better attention skills, or have greater perceptual abilities than others, for example. The variation in scores produced by these uncontrolled variables is the error variance we are discussing.

Table 9–1 shows the scores turned in by participants in this hypothetical experiment. The scores for each group have been averaged and the means are presented at the bottom of the table. Judging from the means, it appears that THC reduced the participants' scores on the dependent variable. However, given the variability in scores evident within each group, it seems plausible to suggest that the difference in the means may reflect nothing more than preexisting participant differences that did not quite balance out across the two conditions of the experiment. The problem is that you cannot tell, simply by looking at the means, which explanation is correct. The problem of error variance is therefore serious. It affects your ability to determine the effectiveness of your independent variable.

## Handling Error Variance

Fortunately, there are ways you can cope with the problem of error variance. You can take steps to reduce error variance, you can take steps to increase the effect of your independent variable, and you can randomize error variance across groups. Let's look at each of these strategies in more detail.

*Reducing Error Variance*   The principal way to reduce error variance is to hold extraneous variables constant by treating subjects within a group as similarly as possible.

| TABLE 9–1   Scores from Hypothetical THC Experiment | |
| --- | --- |
| PERFORMANCE ON DEPENDENT MEASURE | |
| *Control Group* | *Experimental Group* |
| 25 | 13 |
| 24 | 19 |
| 18 | 22 |
| 29 | 18 |
| 19 | 23 |
| Mean    23 | 19 |

For example, you could test participants in an isolated room to eliminate outside distractions and make sure that you read instructions to all participants within a group in the same way. You should also follow the same procedures for all subjects within a group. Error variance also can be reduced by using subjects matched on characteristics that you believe contribute to error variance. For example, you could use participants who are of the same age or educational level. Although this may reduce external validity, you can always relax the restrictions in a later experiment. The first priority is to obtain reliable results. A similar tactic is to match subjects across groups on some characteristic relating to the dependent variable in a matched-groups design or use the same subjects for all levels of your independent variable in a within-subjects design. (We discuss matching and using within-subjects designs later in this chapter.)

*Increasing the Effectiveness of Your Independent Variable*     Another way to deal with error variance is to select the correct levels of your independent variable for your experiment. A weak manipulation may not influence your dependent variable, leaving the effect of your independent variable buried in whatever amount of error variance exists. Of course, it is difficult to know beforehand just how to manipulate your independent variable. You can get some idea about the levels to include from previous research and by conducting a pilot study before you run your actual experiment. You also might consider using a dependent variable that is sensitive enough to detect the effects of your independent variable.

*Randomizing Error Variance across Groups*     Regardless of the steps you take to minimize error variance, you can never eliminate it completely. In between-subjects designs, you can reduce any remaining error variance by randomizing error variance across groups. This is accomplished through *random assignment* of subjects to your treatment conditions. Random assignment means that subjects are assigned to groups on a random basis so that each subject has an equal chance of appearing in any group in your experiment. You could do this by drawing participants' names out of a hat and assigning the first name pulled to Treatment A, the second name to Treatment B, and so on. In an actual experiment, you would probably accomplish random assignment by using a table of random numbers rather than by drawing names out of a hat. In either case, random assignment results in groups of subjects that have been equalized, over the long run, on individual difference factors (for example, intelligence and gender), resulting in error variance being evenly distributed across groups.

*Statistical Analysis*     Although random assignment *tends* to equalize error variance across groups, there is no guarantee that it *will* do so. Similarly, despite your best efforts to eliminate error variance, some will remain. How, then, can you determine whether an effect observed in your data was caused by your manipulation and not by error variance? Although you can never be sure, you can estimate the *probability* with which error variance alone would produce the observed differences between groups. You do this by subjecting your data to a statistical analysis using *inferential statistics* (see Chapter 13). If your results were not likely due to error variance, that result is said to be *statistically significant*, which is another way of saying that your results were most likely due to the manipulation of your independent variable and not error variance.

# BETWEEN-SUBJECTS DESIGNS

The time has come to examine the types of between-subjects designs available to you. In the sections that follow, we introduce you to single-factor designs, in which (as we noted earlier) you manipulate only one independent variable, and we explore the various types of single-factor between-subjects designs.

## The Single-Factor Randomized Groups Design

A commonly used form of the between-subjects design is the *randomized groups design*. When using this design, you randomly assign subjects to the levels of your independent variable to form "groups" of subjects. There are two variants of the randomized groups design: the randomized two-group design and the randomized multigroup design. We explore these designs next.

***The Randomized Two-Group Design***    If you randomly assign your subjects to two groups, expose the two groups to different levels of the independent variable, and take steps to hold extraneous variables constant, you are using a **randomized two-group design**. Figure 9–1 illustrates the basic steps to follow when conducting a randomized two-group experiment. Begin by sampling a group of subjects from the general population (top). Then, randomly assign the participants from this group into your two treatment groups. Next, expose the subjects in each group to their treatments and record their responses. Compare the two means to determine whether they differ. Finally, submit the data to a statistical analysis to assess the reliability of any difference you find.

The randomized two-group design is one of the simplest available, yet it has several advantages over other, more complex designs. First, it is simple to carry out. You need only two levels of your independent variable. Second, everything else being equal, it requires fewer subjects. Usually you need only to select a small group of subjects (perhaps 20 or 30) and randomly assign them to the two groups of the experiment. An experiment with these few subjects is relatively economical in terms of time and materials. Third, no pretesting or categorization of subjects is necessary. The randomized group strategy often is more than adequate to test your hypothesis, obviating the need for a more complex matching strategy (see the section on matched-groups designs later in this chapter). Finally, statistical analysis of the resulting data is relatively simple. Indeed, some electronic calculators have the required statistics built into them, so you need only enter the data and press the appropriate button.

A disadvantage of the randomized two-group design is that it provides a limited amount of information about the effect of the independent variable. You learn only a few things, such as whether the two groups differed (on the average) in their responses to the independent variable under the two levels tested, in what direction, and by how much. You do not learn much about the function relating the independent and dependent variables.

This point can be illustrated with an experiment by Gold (1987). Gold was interested in determining whether glucose (blood sugar) affects memory. In Gold's experiment, rats were individually placed on the white side of a rectangular box that

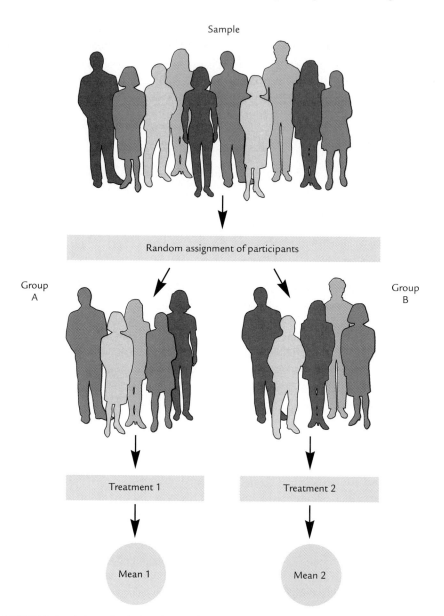

**FIGURE 9–1**    A Completely Randomized Two-Group Experimental Design.

was divided into a well-lit white compartment and a dimly lit black compartment. Because rats tend to prefer darkness over light, they quickly crossed into the black compartment, where they received a mild foot shock. Immediately after this experience, the rats were each injected with glucose. Different groups received different amounts of the glucose. The rats were then returned to their home cages. Twenty-four hours later, the animals were again placed in the white compartment and the amount of time they took to reenter the black compartment was recorded. The rats should have been hesitant to reenter to the extent that they remembered the shock they had received on the previous day. Thus, greater amounts of delay to reenter should have reflected better memory for the shock.

Figure 9–2 shows, in idealized form, the results of Gold's experiment. In Panel (a), the mean number of seconds to reenter the black compartment is plotted against glucose dose. Glucose did affect memory, and in a dose-dependent manner. The function relating glucose dose to reentry time is shaped somewhat like an inverted U, with intermediate doses being more effective than higher or lower doses. Gold concluded that glucose can be used in some cases to improve memory (if it's not overdone).

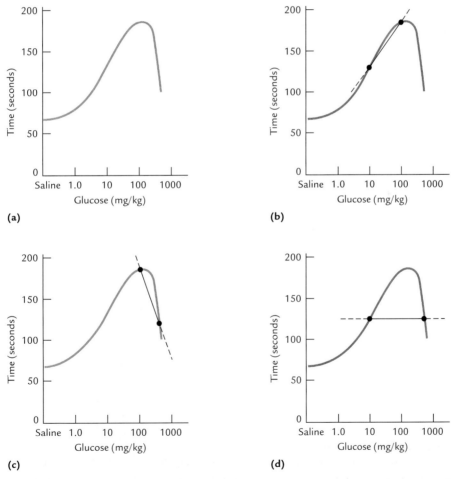

**FIGURE 9–2**   (a) Results of Experiment Relating Glucose Dosage to Memory (as measured by the time required to enter a dark compartment). (b, c, and d) Three Functions Based on Gold's Data, showing lines estimated from various pairs of points.
Source: Panel (a) reprinted from Gold, 1987, with permission.

Although Gold's experiment used several groups, imagine that Gold had used only two. Panel (b) shows what Gold's results would have looked like had he chosen to use glucose doses of 10 and 100 mg/kg of body weight. What would Gold have concluded?

Panel (c) shows what Gold's results would have looked like had he chosen to use 100 and 600 mg/kg doses. What would Gold's conclusion have been in this case?

Finally, Panel (d) shows Gold's results had he chosen 10 and 600 mg/kg doses. What would the conclusion have been now?

If you were unaware of the inverted U-shaped function relating memory to glucose level, it might seem that these three experiments had yielded contradictory results. Furthermore, if you attempted to extrapolate the function beyond the two data points collected in a given experiment—dotted lines in Panels (b), (c), and (d)—you would form an erroneous picture of the relationship.

This problem can be solved by conducting a series of two-group experiments in which different levels of the independent variable are chosen for each experiment. However, more efficient designs for sweeping out a functional relationship are available and will be examined later.

A second limitation of the randomized two-group design concerns its sensitivity to the effect (if any) of the independent variable. In cases in which subjects differ greatly from one another on characteristics that influence their performances on the dependent measure, these variations may make it difficult to detect the effect of the independent variable. In such cases, the randomized two-group design may indicate no effect of the independent variable, although one was actually present. (The solution is to use a matched-pairs design, which we describe later in the chapter.)

Finally, when you are interested in investigating the limits of an effect, two groups are rarely enough. You must include several levels of an independent variable to adequately test the more subtle effects of your independent variable.

*The Randomized Multigroup Design*    One way to expand the randomized two-group design is to add one or more levels of the independent variable. You can, of course, include as many levels of your independent variable as needed to test your hypothesis. As we noted earlier, there are two ways to manipulate your independent variable: quantitatively or qualitatively. When you manipulate your independent variable quantitatively, you are using a **parametric design**. The term *parametric* refers to the systematic variation of the amount of the independent variable. (This use of the term must be distinguished from the use of the word *parametric* to denote a class of inferential statistics.) Manipulating your independent variable qualitatively results in a **nonparametric design**.

A variation on the single-factor multigroup design is one that includes multiple control groups. This design is used when a single control group is not adequate to rule out alternative explanations of your results, and it is known as the **multiple control group design**.

A good illustration is provided by an experiment conducted to test the effect of a drug. It is well known that if a person believes that he or she is under the influence of a drug, then that person's behavior changes even if the drug was not administered. For example, Abrams and Wilson (1983) showed that participants who *believed* they had consumed an alcoholic beverage reported greater sexual arousal and less embarrassment in response to erotic stimuli than if they did not believe they had consumed alcohol. This effect occurred even if the beverage they had consumed was actually nonalcoholic. Participants in this study showed modifications in behavior simply because they believed they were under the influence.

You should include a *placebo control group* to detect such effects. This group receives the same treatment as the subjects who receive the drug. The only difference is that the "drug" they are administered is a *placebo*, or treatment lacking active ingredients. This control group allows you to determine the effect of the drug over and above the effect of the beliefs surrounding the drug.

In any experiment in which the potential exists for confounding from several variables, the multiple control group design is indicated. The additional control groups allow you to evaluate the impact of each potentially confounding factor on the dependent variable.

## Matched-Groups Designs

In some cases, you know or suspect that some subject characteristics correlate significantly with the dependent variable. For example, subjects often differ considerably in their reaction times to simple stimuli. If you were interested in studying the effect of stimulus complexity on reaction time, this large inherent variation in reaction time already present in your subjects could pose a problem. Creating large amounts of error variance could swamp any effect of stimulus complexity, making even large differences in group means statistically unreliable. One way to deal with this problem is to use a matched-groups design.

A **matched-groups design** is one in which matched sets of subjects are distributed at random, one per group, into the groups of the experiment. Figure 9–3 illustrates this process. You begin by obtaining a sample of subjects (group at the top of the figure) from the larger population. Next, you assess the subjects on one or more characteristics that you believe exert an influence on the dependent measure and then group the subjects whose characteristics match. In a reaction time experiment, for example, participants could be pretested for their simple reaction times and then grouped into pairs whose reaction times were similar. These pairs of participants are shown in the middle portion of Figure 9–3.

Having matched your participants, you then distribute them randomly across the experimental groups. In the reaction time experiment, for example, one participant of each pair would be randomly assigned to one of the treatments (perhaps to a high-stimulus-complexity condition); the other participant would then automatically go into the other treatment (in this case, a low-stimulus-complexity condition). This assignment to treatments is shown in the bottom of Figure 9–3.

From here on, the experiment is conducted as in the randomized-groups design. Expose your participants to their respective levels of the independent variable and record the resulting data. Then compare the data from the different groups to determine the effect of the independent variable.

*Logic of the Matched-Groups Design* Because each of the matched subjects goes into a different group, the effect of the characteristic on which the subjects were

Sample

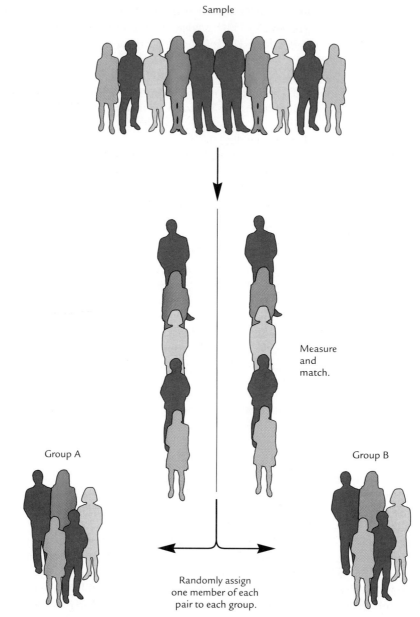

Measure
and
match.

Group A

Group B

Randomly assign
one member of each
pair to each group.

**FIGURE 9–3**   Matched Groups Experimental Design, with Two Groups.

matched is distributed evenly across the treatments. As a result, this characteristic contributes little to the differences between group means. The effect of the error variance contributed by the characteristic has been minimized, making it more likely that any effect of the independent variable will be detected.

*Advantages and Disadvantages of the Matched-Groups Design*     The advantage of matching over random assignment is that it allows you to control subject variables that may otherwise obscure the effect of the independent variable under investigation. Where such variables exist, matching can increase the experiment's sensitivity to the effect of the independent variable (if such an effect is present). This is a potent advantage. You may be able to discover effects that you would otherwise miss. In addition, you may be able to demonstrate a given effect with fewer subjects, thus saving time and money. However, using a matched design is not without risks and disadvantages.

One risk involved in using a matched design concerns what happens if the matched characteristic does *not* have much effect on the dependent variable under the conditions of the study. Matched designs require you to use somewhat modified versions of the inferential statistics you would use in an unmatched, completely randomized design (see Chapter 13). These statistics for matched groups are somewhat less powerful than their unmatched equivalents. This means they are less able to discriminate any effect of the independent variable from the effect of uncontrolled, extraneous variables.

If the matched characteristic has a *large* effect on the dependent variable, eliminating this effect from group differences will more than compensate for the reduced sensitivity of the statistic, resulting in a more sensitive experiment. However (and this is an important "however"), if the matched characteristic has *little or no effect* on the dependent variable, then matching will do no good. Worse, the loss of statistical power will result in a *reduced* ability to detect the effect of the independent variable. For this reason, use matching only when you have good reason to believe that the matched variable has a relatively strong effect on the dependent measure.

When using a matched design, you also must be sure that the instrument used to determine the match is valid and reliable. If you want to match on IQ, for example, be sure that the test you use to measure IQ is valid and reliable. Of course, for some characteristics, such as race, age, or sex, this is usually not a problem.

In other respects, matched-groups designs have the same advantages and disadvantages as randomized groups designs. However, the requirement for pretesting and matching makes the matched design more demanding and time-consuming than the randomized design. In addition, you may require a larger subject pool if you cannot find a match for certain subjects and must discard them from the study. This may be particularly troublesome if you are attempting to match subjects on more than one variable or if the subject pool is limited.

Any of the randomized groups designs described in the previous sections of this chapter could be modified into a matched-groups design. The simplest case, described next, involves the two-group design.

*The Matched-Pairs Design*     The **matched-pairs design** is the matched-groups equivalent to the randomized two-group design. The hypothetical reaction time experiment just described uses a matched-pairs design. As with the randomized two-group design, the need for only two groups makes this approach relatively economical of time and subjects, but does limit the amount of information you can obtain from the experiment.

*Matched-Multigroup Designs*    The same approach used in the matched-pairs design can be extended to other, more complex designs involving multiple levels of a single factor (single-factor, multigroup designs) or multiple factors (factorial designs). You use these matched-groups designs to gain control over subject-related variables that affect your dependent variable and thus tend to obscure any effects of your independent variable.

Using the matching strategy on these multigroup designs requires you to find a matched subject for every treatment group in your experiment. Thus, if your experiment included four treatment groups, you would need to find quadruplets of subjects having similar characteristics on the variables being matched. After matching subjects, you would distribute the subjects from each quadruplet randomly across your experimental groups.

As you might guess, matching becomes unwieldy if your design has more than about three groups, as it becomes increasingly difficult to find three, four, or more subjects with equivalent scores on the variable or variables to be matched. In this case, a better approach might be to use a within-subjects design. The within-subjects design eliminates the need for measuring and matching subject variables, reduces the number of subjects required for the experiment, and yet provides the ultimate degree of matching—in effect, each subject is matched with himself or herself. Unfortunately, situations do occur in which the within-subjects design cannot or should not be used. In such cases, matching may be your best alternative.

## WITHIN-SUBJECTS DESIGNS

In between-subjects designs, you randomly assign subjects to groups and then expose each group to a different, *single* experimental treatment. You measure each subject's performance on the dependent variable, calculate the average score for each group, and then compare the means to determine whether the independent variable or variables had any apparent influence on the dependent variable. You then subject the data to a statistical analysis to assess the reliability of your conclusions.

The within-subjects design follows the same basic strategy as the between-subjects design with one important difference. In the within-subjects design, each subject is exposed to all levels of your independent variable, rather than being randomly assigned to one level. This strategy is shown in Figure 9–4 with a simple two-treatment experiment. Notice that each participant's performance is measured under Treatment A and then again under Treatment B. The design is called "within-subjects" because comparison of the treatment effects involves looking at changes in performance within each participant across treatments. Because participant behavior is measured repeatedly, the within-subjects design is sometimes also called a repeated-measures design.

Within-subjects designs are closely related to the matched-groups designs we discussed in the previous section, in which subjects are first matched into sets on some characteristic (such as IQ score) and then members of each matched set are assigned at random, one to each treatment condition. You might think of a within-subjects design as providing the ultimate in matching, because each participant serves, in effect, as his or her own matched partner across the treatments.

Treatment A          Treatment B

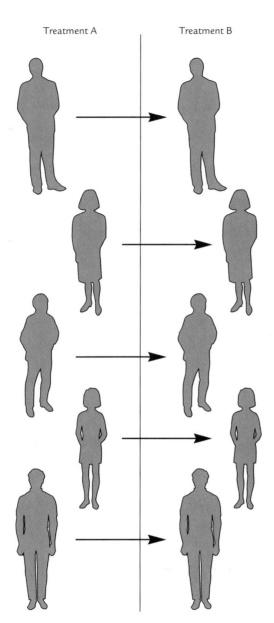

**FIGURE 9–4**   Simple Two-Treatment Within-Subjects Design.

Within-subjects designs offer some powerful advantages over the equivalent between-subjects designs if certain conditions can be met. They also introduce problems whose solution adds complexity to the basic designs, and they present other disadvantages as well. We begin by examining the advantages.

## Advantages of the Within-Subjects Design

Earlier in this chapter, we noted that scores *within* a treatment group differ for reasons having nothing to do with your independent variable. These differences arise from the effects of extraneous variables, which include relatively stable subject-related characteristics, as well as momentary fluctuations that change each subject's performance from moment to moment. Such error variance can be a serious problem because it may mask any effects of your independent variable. Recall that a major strategy for dealing with error variance in the between-subjects design is to randomly assign subjects to treatment groups and to apply statistical analysis to your data to estimate the probability that chance alone could have produced the effect. When subject-related factors are large, they exert a strong influence on performance, resulting in levels of error variance that obscure the effect of your independent variable. Matching can help reduce this important source of error variance.

The within-subjects design pushes the logic of matching to the limit. Each subject is matched with other subjects who are virtual clones of each other, because they are in fact the same subject. All subject-related factors (such as age, weight, IQ, personality, religion, gender) are literally identical across treatments. Thus, any performance differences across treatments cannot be due to error variance arising from such differences, as is the case in the between-subjects design. Because of the reduced error variance, the within-subjects design is more powerful (that is, more sensitive to the effects of your independent variable) than the equivalent between-subjects design. Thus, you are more likely to detect an effect of your independent variable. A second benefit of this increased power is that you can use fewer subjects in your experiment. For example, a four-group between-subjects design with 10 subjects per treatment would require 40 subjects. The equivalent within-subjects experiment would require only 10 subjects, representing a significant savings in time, materials, and money. Of course, you could always use more subjects in a within-subjects design if you needed extra power to detect the effect of a weak independent variable.

## Disadvantages of the Within-Subjects Design

Although the within-subjects design has its advantages, it also has some important disadvantages, which may preclude its use in certain situations. One disadvantage is that a within-subjects design is more demanding on subjects, because each subject must be exposed to every level of the experimental treatment. A complex design involving, for example, nine treatments would require a great deal of time to complete. It may be difficult to find participants willing to take part in such an experiment. Those who do take part may become bored or fatigued after being in an experiment that might be several hours long. You can get around the problem of fatigue and boredom by administering only one or two treatments per session, spreading sessions out over some period of time. However, if you take this approach, you may lose some participants from the experiment because they fail to show up for one or more sessions.

Subject attrition also can occur if you make a mistake while administering one of your treatments (for example, you read the wrong instructions), if you experience equipment failure, or (in the case of animal research) if your subject dies. In each case, you have to throw out the data from the lost subjects and start over.

A second and potentially more serious problem with the within-subjects design is its ability to produce carryover effects. **Carryover effects** occur when a previous treatment alters the behavior observed in a subsequent treatment. The previous treatment changes the subject, and those changes "carry over" into the subsequent treatment, in which they change how the subject performs. This upsets the "perfect match" of subject characteristics that the within-subjects design is supposed to provide.

As an illustration of carryover effects, imagine that you are conducting an experiment to assess the effect of two kinds of practice (simple rehearsal and rehearsal plus imagery) on memory for lists of concrete nouns. Your participants first learn a list of nouns using simple rehearsal and then are tested for retention. Next the participants learn a second list of nouns, using rehearsal plus imagery, and are again tested. You find that participants correctly recall more nouns when they used a rehearsal-plus-imagery technique than when they used rehearsal alone. However, you cannot confidently conclude that the former technique is superior to the latter.

The problem is that the rehearsal-alone treatment gave participants practice memorizing nouns. They may have done better in the rehearsal-plus-imagery treatment simply because they were more practiced at the task, rather than because of any effect of imagery. The previous exposure to the rehearsal-alone treatment may have changed the way participants performed in the subsequent treatment.

Carryover effects can be a serious problem in any within-subjects design. Between-subjects designs do not suffer from carryover effects, simply because there are no previous conditions from which effects can carry over. A matched-groups design may provide a reasonable compromise in those situations in which carryover is a serious problem but in which you want to retain the control over subject variables provided by a within-subjects design.

The problem of carryover in within-subjects designs has received plenty of attention from researchers, who have developed strategies to deal with it. The next section identifies potential sources of carryover. After that, we describe several design options that can help you deal with potential carryover effects.

## Sources of Carryover

Carryover effects can arise from a number of sources, including the following:

- *Learning.* If a subject learns how to perform a task in the first treatment, performance is likely to be better if the same or similar tasks are used in subsequent treatments. For example, rats given alternate sessions of reinforcement and extinction show faster acquisition of lever pressing across successive reinforcement sessions and more rapid return to baseline rates of responding across successive extinction sessions.

- *Fatigue.* If performance in earlier treatments leads to fatigue, then performance in later treatments may deteriorate, regardless of any effect of the independent variable. If measuring your dependent variable involves having participants squeeze against a strong spring device to determine their strength of grip, for example, the participants are likely to tire if repeated testing takes place over a short period of time.

- *Habituation*. Under some conditions, repeated exposure to a stimulus leads to reduced responsiveness to that stimulus because the stimulus is becoming more familiar or expected. This reduction is termed *habituation*. Your subjects may jump the first time you surprise them with a sudden loud noise, but they may not do so after repeated presentations of the noise.

- *Sensitization*. Sometimes exposure to one stimulus can cause subjects to respond more strongly to another stimulus. In a phenomenon called *potentiated startle*, for example, a rat will show an exaggerated startle response to a sudden noise if the rat has recently received a brief foot shock in the same situation.

- *Contrast.* Because of contrast, exposure to one condition may alter the responses of subjects in other conditions. If you pay your participants a relatively large amount for successful performance on one task and then pay them less (or make them work harder for the same amount) in a subsequent task, they may feel underpaid. Consequently, they may work less than they otherwise might have. This change occurs because subjects can compare (contrast) the treatments.

- *Adaptation*. If subjects go through a period of adaptation (becoming adjusted to the dark, for example), then earlier results may differ from later results because of the adaptive changes. Adaptive changes may increase responsiveness to a stimulus (e.g., sight gradually improves while you sit in a darkened theater) or decrease responsiveness (e.g., you readjust to the light as you leave the theater). Adaptation to a drug schedule is a common example. If adaptation to the drug causes reduced response, the change is called *tolerance*.

## Dealing with Carryover Effects

You can deal with carryover effects in three ways: (1) You can use counterbalancing to even out carryover effects across treatments, (2) you can take steps to minimize carryover, and (3) you can separate carryover effects from treatment effects by making treatment order an independent variable.

*Counterbalancing*    In **counterbalancing**, you assign the various treatments of the experiment in a different order for different subjects. The goal is to distribute any carryover equally across treatments so that it does not produce differences in treatment means that could be mistaken for an effect of the independent variable. Two counterbalancing options are complete counterbalancing and partial counterbalancing.

*Complete counterbalancing* provides every possible ordering of treatments and assigns at least one subject to each ordering. Table 9–2 shows an example of a completely counterbalanced single-factor design that includes three treatments. Six subjects are to be tested (identified as subjects $S_1$ through $S_6$), one for each possible ordering of treatments $T_1$, $T_2$, and $T_3$. Note that in a completely counterbalanced design, every treatment follows every other treatment equally often across subjects, and every treatment appears equally often in each position (first, second, and so on).

The minimum number of subjects required for complete counterbalancing is equal to the number of different orderings of the treatments: $k$ treatments have exactly $k!$

**TABLE 9-2   Counterbalanced Single-Factor Design with Three Treatments**

|  | TREATMENTS | | |
|---|---|---|---|
| *Subjects* | $T_1$ | $T_2$ | $T_3$ |
| $S_1$ | 1 | 2 | 3 |
| $S_2$ | 1 | 3 | 2 |
| $S_3$ | 2 | 1 | 3 |
| $S_4$ | 2 | 3 | 1 |
| $S_5$ | 3 | 1 | 2 |
| $S_6$ | 3 | 2 | 1 |

($k$ factorial) orders, where $k! = k(k-1)(k-2) \cdots (1)$. For example, with three treatments (as in our example), the number of treatment orders is $3 \times 2 \times 1 = 6$. If you need to increase the number of subjects in order to improve statistical power, add the same number of additional subjects to each order so that the number of subjects receiving each order remains equal.

Complete counterbalancing is practical for experiments with a small number of treatments, but this approach becomes increasingly burdensome as the number of treatments grows. For an experiment using only four treatments, the $4 \times 3 \times 2 \times 1 = 24$ possible treatment orders require at least 24 subjects to complete the counterbalancing. The economy of subjects that makes a within-subjects approach attractive erodes rapidly.

Fortunately, you can recover some of this economy by switching to partial counterbalancing. *Partial counterbalancing* includes only some of the possible treatment orders. The orders to be retained are chosen randomly from the total set, with the restriction that each treatment appear equally often in each position. Table 9–3 displays all 24 possible orders for a four-treatment experiment, followed by a subset of 8 randomly selected orders that meet this criterion.

When you use partial counterbalancing, you assume that randomly chosen orders will randomly distribute carryover effects among the treatments. Although carryover effects may not balance out under such conditions, they usually will come close to doing so. Furthermore, the likelihood that treatments will differ because of carryover can be evaluated statistically and held to an acceptable level.

If you choose to make the number of treatment orders in your partially counterbalanced design equal to the number of treatments, you can use a *Latin square design* to ensure that each treatment appears an equal number of times in each ordinal position. For more information on how to construct a Latin square design, see Edwards (1985).

Counterbalancing (whether complete or partial) can be counted on to control carryover only if the carryover effects induced by different orders are of the same approximate magnitude. Consider the case of a simple two-treatment experiment shown in Table 9–4. This case has only two possible orders: 1–2 and 2–1. Assume

| TABLE 9-3 | **Twenty-Four Possible Treatment Orders for a Four-Treatment Within-Subjects Design, and a Randomly Selected Subset in Which Each Treatment Appears Equally Often in Each Position** |
|---|---|

| ENTIRE SET OF TREATMENT ORDERS | SELECTED SUBSET |
|---|---|
| 1. ABCD | 1. DABC |
| 2. ABDC | 2. ABCD |
| 3. ACBD | 3. CDAB |
| 4. ACDB | 4. BCDA |
| 5. ADBC | 5. DCBA |
| 6. ADCB | 6. ADCB |
| 7. BACD | 7. BADC |
| 8. BADC | 8. CBAD |
| 9. BCAD | |
| 10. BCDA | |
| 11. BDAC | |
| 12. BDCA | |
| 13. CABD | |
| 14. CADB | |
| 15. CBAD | |
| 16. CBDA | |
| 17. CDAB | |
| 18. CDBA | |
| 19. DABC | |
| 20. DACB | |
| 21. DBAC | |
| 22. DBCA | |
| 23. DCAB | |
| →  24. DCBA | |

that carryover from Treatment 1 to Treatment 2 increases the mean score of Treatment 2 by 10 points, and that carryover from Treatment 2 to Treatment 1 has a similar effect on the mean score of Treatment 1. Table 9–4 shows the result for a completely counterbalanced design. Note that the two carryover effects, being equal, cancel out each other. When carryover effects are equivalent across orders, counterbalancing is effective.

In contrast, when the magnitude of the carryover effect differs for different orders of treatment presentation, counterbalancing may be ineffective. Table 9–5 illustrates this problem, known as *differential carryover effects* (Keppel, 1982). In this example,

TABLE 9–4 **Balancing of Order Effects in a Counterbalanced Two-Treatment Design**

| | TREATMENT | | |
|---|---|---|---|
| | **1** | **2** | |
| Actual treatment effect | 40 | 30 | (difference = 10) |
| Carryover effect (1–2) | | 10 | |
| Carryover effect (2–1) | 10 | | |
| Observed treatment effect | 50 | 40 | (difference = 10) |

the carryover from Treatment 2 to Treatment 1 averages 20 points—twice the carryover from Treatment 1 to Treatment 2. Thus, you have a treatment-by-position interaction. When this occurs, no amount of counterbalancing will eliminate the carryover effects (Keppel, 1982).

The most serious asymmetry in carryover effects occurs when a treatment produces *irreversible changes*. The classic type of irreversible change is that produced by a treatment such as brain lesioning. The effects of the operation, once present, cannot be undone. A somewhat less serious change may occur if subjects learn to perform a task in one treatment and this learning then alters the way in which they perform in a subsequent treatment. It may not be possible to restore subjects to the "naive" state once they have learned the task. In either case, you would want to choose a between-subjects approach.

*Taking Steps to Minimize Carryover* The second way to deal with carryover effects is to try to minimize or eliminate them. Of course, you would want to do this only if the carryover effects were not themselves the object of study. Minimizing carryover effects reduces error variance and increases the power of the design.

Not all sources of carryover can be minimized. For example, permanent changes produced by learning inevitably carry over into subsequent treatments and affect behavior. You cannot return your subjects to the naive state in preparation for a second treatment. However, if you are not interested in the effect of learning per se, you may be able to pretrain your subjects before introducing your experimental treatments. Psychophysical experiments (testing such things as sensory thresholds) and experiments on human decision making often make use of such "practice sessions" to familiarize participants with the experimental tasks. The practice brings their performances up to desired levels, where they stabilize, and effectively eliminates changes caused by practice as a source of carryover.

Adaptation and habituation changes can be dealt with similarly. Before introducing the treatments, allowing time for subjects to adapt or habituate to the experimental conditions can eliminate carryover from these sources.

Another way to deal with habituation (if habituation is short term), adaptation, and fatigue is to allow breaks between the treatments. If sufficiently long, the breaks

**TABLE 9-5    Failure of Order Effects to Balance Out in a Counterbalanced Two-Treatment Design**

|  | TREATMENT | | |
|---|---|---|---|
|  | **1** | **2** |  |
| Actual treatment effect | 40 | 30 | (difference = 10) |
| Carryover effect (1–2) |  | 10 |  |
| Carryover effect (2–1) | 20 |  |  |
| Observed treatment effect | 60 | 40 | (difference = 20) |

allow subjects to recover from any habituation, adaptation, or fatigue induced by the previous treatment.

You can take steps to minimize carryover effects in combination with either of the other two strategies. If you simply want to control carryover, you could take these steps and then use counterbalancing to distribute whatever carryover remains across treatments. Similarly, if you want to determine whether certain variables contribute to carryover, you could take steps to minimize other potential sources of carryover and then treat the variables of interest as independent variables, as described in the following section.

*Making Treatment Order an Independent Variable*    A third way to deal with the problem of carryover is to make treatment order an independent variable. Your experimental design will expose different groups of subjects to different orderings of the treatments, just as in ordinary counterbalancing. However, you include a sufficient number of subjects in each group to permit statistical analysis of treatment order as a separate independent variable. For example, if you were going to conduct a one-factor experiment to compare the effect of two memorization strategies on recall, you could design the experiment to include the order of testing as a second independent variable. Figure 9–5 illustrates the resulting design, which now includes *two* independent variables. Called a *factorial design*, it requires a special type of analysis to separately evaluate the effect of each and is discussed later in this chapter (see "Designs with Two or More Independent Variables"). For now, it is enough to know that this design allows you to separate any carryover effects from the effect of your experimental treatment.

The main advantage of making order of treatments an independent variable is that you can measure the size of any carryover effects that may be present. You can then take these effects into account in future experiments. If you find that carryover is about equal in magnitude regardless of the order of treatments, for example, then you can be confident that counterbalancing will eliminate any carryover-induced bias.

In addition to identifying carryover effects, the strategy of making treatment order an independent variable provides a direct comparison of results obtained in the within-subjects design with those obtained in the logically equivalent between-subjects

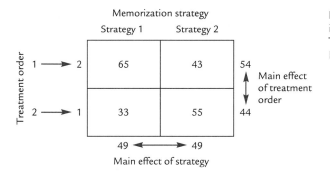

**FIGURE 9–5** A Design in Which Order of Treatments Is Made an Independent Variable.

design. This comparison can be made because every treatment occurs first in at least one of the treatment orders. These "first exposures" provide the data for a purely between-subjects comparison in the absence of carryover effects.

Grice (1966) noted that between-subjects and within-subjects designs applied to the same variables do not always produce the same functional relationships. The reason is that subjects in the within-subjects experiment are able to make comparisons across treatments, whereas those in the supposedly equivalent between-subjects experiment are not. Imagine, for example, a study in which participants must rate the attractiveness of pictures on a five-point scale. In one version of the study, different groups of participants see only one of the pictures. In another version, each participant views all the pictures. A particular picture may rate, say, five on the scale when viewed by itself. However, when seen in the context of the other pictures, the same picture may look better (or worse) in comparison, and thus may produce a different rating. Such changes in response that arise from comparison, termed *contrast effects*, are possible only in the within-subjects version of the study. The presence of such effects in some designs, but not in others, often can explain why studies manipulating the same variables sometimes yield different results.

Although making treatment order a factor in your experiment can provide important information about the size of carryover effects and can pinpoint the source of differences between findings obtained from within-subjects versus between-subjects experiments, the technique does have disadvantages. Every treatment order requires a separate group of subjects. These subjects must be tested under every treatment condition. The result is a complex, demanding experiment that is costly in terms of numbers of subjects and time to test them. Furthermore, these demands escalate rapidly as the number of treatments (and therefore number of treatment orders) increases. This latter problem is the same one encountered when using completely counterbalanced designs. For these reasons, the approach is practical only with a small number of treatments.

## When to Use a Within-Subjects Design

Given the problems created by the potential for carryover effects, the best strategy may be to altogether avoid within-subjects designs. If you decide to do this, you have a lot of company. However, you should not let these difficulties prevent you from adopting the within-subjects design when it is clearly the best approach. There are several situations in which the within-subjects design is best, and others in which it is the *only* approach.

*Subject Variables Correlated with the Dependent Variable*    You should strongly consider using a within-subjects design when subject differences contribute heavily to variation in the dependent variable. As an example, assume you want to assess the effect of display complexity on target detection in a simulated air traffic controller task. Your display simulates the computerized radar screen display seen in actual air traffic control situations, with aircraft (the targets) appearing as blips in motion across the screen. Your independent variable is the amount of information being displayed (the dots alone or dots plus transponder codes, altitude readings, and so on). Because this is a pilot study (no pun intended), you are using college sophomores as participants rather than real air traffic controllers.

Your student participants are likely to differ widely in their native ability to detect targets, regardless of the display complexity. If you were to conduct the experiment using a between-subjects design, this large variation in ability would contribute greatly to within-group error variance. As a consequence, the between-group differences would probably be obscured by these uncontrolled variations.

In this case, you could effectively eliminate the impact of subject differences by adopting a within-subjects design. Each participant is exposed to every level of display complexity. Because each participant's native ability at target detection remains essentially the same across all the treatment levels, the changes (if any) in target detection across treatments would clearly stand out.

Of course, you would have to be reasonably sure that practice at the task does not contribute to success at target detection (or at least that the effect of such practice could be distributed evenly across treatments by using counterbalancing) before you decided to adopt the within-subjects approach. One way to eliminate practice as a source of confounding would be to include several practice sessions in which your participants became proficient enough at the task that little further improvement would be expected.

*Economizing on Subjects*    You also should consider using a within-subjects design when the number of available subjects is limited and carryover effects are absent (or can be minimized). If you were to use actual air traffic controllers in the previous study, for example, you probably would not have a large available group from which to sample. You probably would not be able to obtain enough participants for your study to achieve statistically reliable results using a between-subjects design. Using a within-subjects design would reduce the number of participants required for the study while preserving an acceptable degree of reliability.

*Assessing the Effects of Increasing Exposure on Behavior*    In cases in which you wish to assess changes in performance as a function of increasing exposure to the treatment conditions (measured as number of trials, passage of time, and so on), the within-subjects design is the only option (unless you have enough control to use a single-subject design—see Chapter 11). Designs that repeatedly sample the dependent variable across time or trials are frequently used in psychological research to examine the course of processes such as reinforcement, extinction, fatigue, and habituation. These changes occur as a function of earlier exposure to the experimental conditions and thus represent carryover effects. However, the carryover effects in these designs are the object of study rather than something to be eliminated by measures such as counterbalancing.

Be aware, however, that not all carryover effects can or should be studied within the framework of a within-subjects design. For example, transfer-of-training studies (in which the effects of previous training on later performance of another task are assessed) are not good candidates for a within-subjects approach. This is because the earlier training may have effects on later performance that cannot easily be reversed. For example, if you wanted to compare performance on a mirror-tracing task with and without previous training, subjects first receiving the "previous training" condition probably could not be brought back to the "naive" state prior to being given the "no previous training" condition. In this case, you would have to use separate groups for the training and no-training conditions.

## Within-Subjects versus Matched-Groups Designs

The within-subjects and matched-groups designs both deal with error variance by attempting to control subject-related factors. As we have seen, the two designs go about this in different ways. In the matched-groups design, you measure subject variables and match subjects accordingly, whereas in the within-subjects design you use the same subjects in all treatments. Both designs take advantage of any correlations between subject variables and your dependent variable to improve power, and both use similar statistical analyses to take this correlation into account. However, if the correlation between those subject variables and the dependent variable is weak, a randomized groups design will be more powerful. Thus, if you have reason to believe that the relationship between subject variables and your dependent variable is weak, use a randomized groups design.

A matched-groups design would be a better choice than a within-subjects design if you are concerned that carryover effects will be a serious problem. Although you lose the economy of having fewer subjects, you avoid the possibility of carryover effects while preserving the power advantage made possible by matching.

## Types of Within-Subjects Designs

Just as with the between-subjects design, the within-subjects design is really a family of designs that incorporate the same basic structure. This section discusses several variations on the within-subjects design. These variations include the single-factor, multilevel within-subjects design (in both parametric and nonparametric versions); the multifactor within-subjects design; and multivariate within-subjects designs.

*The Single-Factor Two-Level Design*   The *single-factor two-level design* is the simplest form of within-subjects design and includes just two levels of a single independent variable. All subjects receive both levels of the variable, but half the subjects receive the treatments in one order and half in the opposite order. The scores within each treatment are then averaged (ignoring the order in which the treatments were given) and the two treatment means are compared.

This design is directly comparable to the two-group between-subjects design while offering the general advantages and disadvantages of the within-subjects approach. If order effects are not severe and are approximately equal for both orders, then counterbalancing will control the order effects without introducing excessive error variance. If the dependent variable is strongly affected by subject-related variables, then the two-factor within-subjects design will control this source of variance, and the experiment will more likely detect the effect (if any) of the independent variable. However, if the dependent variable is not strongly affected by subject-related variables, this design will be less effective in detecting the effect of the independent variable than will its two-group between-subjects equivalent.

*Single-Factor Multilevel Designs*    Just as with the between-subjects design, the within-subjects design can include more than two levels of the independent variable. In the *single-factor, multilevel within-subjects design*, a single group of subjects is exposed to three or more levels of a single independent variable. If the independent variable is not a cumulative factor (such as practice), then the order of treatments is counterbalanced to prevent any carryover effects from confounding the effects of the treatments.

Table 9–6 shows the organization of a single-factor within-subjects design with four levels or treatments and eight subjects. In this example, subjects have been randomly assigned to eight different treatment orders, with the restriction that each treatment appears equally often in each ordinal position. Each row indicates the ordinal position of each treatment for a given subject. Treatment orders were determined by constructing two Latin squares, one for each batch of four subjects.

**TABLE 9–6    Structure of a Counterbalanced Single-Factor Within-Subjects Design with Four Treatments**

|  | TREATMENTS | | | |
|---|---|---|---|---|
| *Subjects* | $T_1$ | $T_2$ | $T_3$ | $T_4$ |
| $S_1$ | 4 | 1 | 2 | 3 |
| $S_2$ | 1 | 2 | 3 | 4 |
| $S_3$ | 3 | 4 | 1 | 2 |
| $S_4$ | 2 | 3 | 4 | 1 |
| $S_5$ | 4 | 3 | 2 | 1 |
| $S_6$ | 1 | 4 | 3 | 2 |
| $S_7$ | 2 | 1 | 4 | 3 |
| $S_8$ | 3 | 2 | 1 | 4 |

Earlier we distinguished among several types of single-factor between-subjects design, including parametric, nonparametric, and multiple control group versions. The same distinctions can be applied to within-subjects designs. Because the basic features of these designs have been described before, a separate section is not provided here for each type. Instead, a parametric within-subjects experiment will illustrate the single-factor multilevel within-subjects design.

Peterson and Peterson (1959) conducted a now-classic study of memory processes. This study was designed to determine the effect of retention interval on memory for three-consonant trigrams (such as *JHK*). Retention intervals of 3, 6, 9, 12, 15, and 18 seconds were tested, with each participant receiving all the retention intervals and with order of intervals counterbalanced across participants.

To prevent them from rehearsing the trigram during the retention intervals, the participants were kept busy doing a demanding mental arithmetic task. Figure 9–6 shows the results. Probability of correct recall was found to decline sharply as the retention interval increased. This evidence provided strong support for the existence of short-term memory as a separate entity from long-term memory.

The Petersons' experiment could have been conducted using a between-subjects design. In this case, however, the use of the within-subjects design reduced the time and the number of participants required to complete the study. At the same time, this design prevented the sometimes large individual differences in recall performance from obscuring the effect of retention interval.

The results from a multigroup within-subjects design are interpreted much like the results from a multigroup between-subjects design. If the independent variable is quantitative (that is, measured along an interval or ratio scale), as in the Peterson and Peterson (1959) study or as in designs in which trials or time is the independent variable, then the design is said to be *parametric* (just as with between-subjects designs). In that case, your primary interest in conducting the study may be to determine the form of the function relating the independent and dependent variables. However, if your independent variable represented different categories (such as different types of drugs), then talking about functional relationships would be meaningless. In that case,

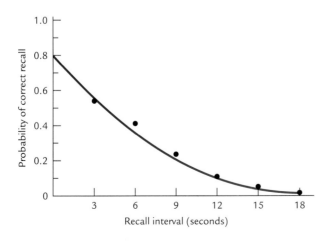

**FIGURE 9–6**  Probability of Correct Recall as a Function of Retention Interval.
SOURCE: Peterson & Peterson, 1959; reprinted with permission.

you would want to compare the effects of the different treatments with each other and with those of any control conditions included in the design.

## DESIGNS WITH TWO OR MORE INDEPENDENT VARIABLES

Thus far, the discussion has assumed that only one independent variable is being manipulated across groups in a given experiment. If you wanted to assess the effects of several independent variables on a given dependent variable, one solution would be to conduct a separate experiment for each independent variable of interest. Although this approach is sometimes used, you may be able to gain more information at less expense by using a design that incorporates two or more independent variables. The most common such design is the **factorial design**. In addition, you may be able to develop special designs when the factorial design is not practical.

### Factorial Designs

A study that illustrates the factorial design was reported by Glass, Singer, and Friedman (1969, Experiment 1). Glass et al. examined the aftereffects of exposure to an irritating noise on several behavioral measures. Of interest here was the tolerance for frustration by the participants, which was assessed by giving participants the opportunity to solve several puzzles. Although the participants did not know it at the time, two of the puzzles were, in fact, insoluble. The dependent measure was the number of attempts the participants made to solve the insoluble puzzles before they became frustrated and gave up.

Glass et al. (1969) wanted to test the effect of two noise-related variables: noise intensity and noise predictability. Participants were to be exposed to one of two levels of noise intensity (loud and soft) and one of two levels of noise predictability (unpredictable and predictable). (There was also a no-noise condition, which is not included in this illustration.) They wanted to vary these two independent variables in such a way as to identify the separate effects of each variable on tolerance for frustration. That is, they wanted to avoid confounding the two variables. Glass et al. achieved this goal by using a factorial design.

In a factorial design, you include a separate group or treatment for each possible combination of the levels of the independent variables. Figure 9–7 shows the resulting groups for the tolerance for frustration study. The two levels of noise intensity are represented by the two columns (labeled across the top). The two levels of predictability are represented by the two rows (labeled along the side). The four boxes represent the four groups that result from each combination of predictability and intensity: Group 1 receives a loud, unpredictable noise; Group 2, a soft, unpredictable noise; Group 3, a loud, predictable noise; and Group 4, a soft, predictable noise.

Participants were assigned at random to the different groups. Participants in this experiment were exposed to the noise while they worked at several tasks. Immediately after this exposure, they were given the puzzles to solve. Figure 9–8 presents the group means for the insoluble puzzles task (the results are for the second insoluble puzzle). On the surface, the experiment appears horribly confounded, because two independent variables have been allowed to vary at once. This is not the case, however. Be-

Noise intensity

|  | Loud | Soft |
|---|---|---|
| Unpredictable | Group 1 | Group 2 |
| Predictable | Group 3 | Group 4 |

Predictability

**FIGURE 9–7**
A 2 × 2 Factorial Design
Investigating Noise
Intensity and Noise
Predictability.
SOURCE: Based on data
provided by Glass et al., 1969.

Noise intensity

|  | Loud | Soft |
|---|---|---|
| Unpredictable | 6.33 | 12.00 |
| Predictable | 26.78 | 25.80 |

Predictability

**FIGURE 9–8**
Organization of a Simple
Two-Factor (2 × 2)
Experimental Design with
Cell Means Filled In.
SOURCE: Based on data
provided by Glass et al., 1969.

cause all possible combinations of the levels of the independent variables are represented, you can statistically separate the effects of the independent variables.

*Main Effects*    The separate effects of each independent variable are termed **main effects**. Here's how you calculate the main effects of your independent variables. First, average the group means in the first column and write the result under the first column. Then do the same for the group means in the second column. These two numbers are your *column means*. Now average the group means across the first row and write the result to the right of the first row. Then do the same for the second row. These two numbers are your *row means*. The result should look like Figure 9–9.

Compare the column means. These represent the main effect of noise intensity, averaged over the two values of noise predictability. They are directly analogous to the two means you would get in a simple two-group design employing these two levels of noise intensity. Now compare the row means. These represent the main effect of noise predictability, averaged over the two values of noise intensity. They are directly analogous to the means of a simple two-group experiment varying noise predictability.

A reliable difference in the column means would indicate an effect of noise intensity, *independent of noise predictability*. Similarly, a reliable difference in the row means would indicate an effect of noise predictability, *independent of noise intensity*.

*Interactions*    Although the main effects of the independent variables are of considerable interest, they are not the only information you can extract from a factorial experiment. You also can test for the presence of interactions among your independent variables. An **interaction** is present when the effect of one independent variable

**FIGURE 9–9**

Two-Factor Design Showing Cell Means and Row and Column Means. SOURCE: Based on data provided by Glass et al., 1969.

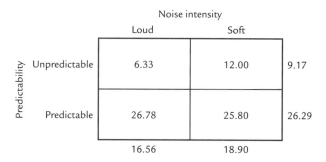

|  | Noise intensity | | |
|---|---|---|---|
|  | Loud | Soft |  |
| Unpredictable | 6.33 | 12.00 | 9.17 |
| Predictable | 26.78 | 25.80 | 26.29 |
|  | 16.56 | 18.90 |  |

changes across the levels of another independent variable. For example, Glass et al. (1969) found that the number of attempts to solve the insoluble puzzle was greater when the noise was soft than when it was loud. However, this relationship held only when the noise was unpredictable. When the noise was predictable, the number of attempts was about 26 *regardless* of noise intensity. Here, changing the noise predictability alters the relationship between noise intensity and attempts to solve. Under these conditions, the noise intensity and noise predictability interact.

Figure 9–10 shows how this relationship looks when graphed. The dashed and solid lines indicate the groups for which noise predictability was the same: unpredictable for the solid line, predictable for the dashed line. Note that, for the groups receiving the unpredictable noise, the number of attempts to solve the puzzles increases from loud noise to soft noise. In contrast, for the groups receiving the predictable noise, the number of attempts to solve the puzzles remains high at both levels of noise intensity.

Each line connecting two of the dots in Figure 9–10 indicates the effect of noise intensity at one specific level of noise predictability (either predictable noise or unpredictable noise). These lines are said to represent the **simple effects** of noise intensity on the number of attempts to solve the insoluble puzzles. In a two-factor design, a simple effect represents the effect of one independent variable at a given level of the other independent variable. In this example, the simple effect of noise intensity under predictable noise conditions (dashed line) shows that noise intensity did not affect the number of attempts to solve puzzles. However, under unpredictable noise conditions (solid line), more attempts were made when the noise was soft than when it was loud.

Interactions can take a variety of forms when graphed. In general, if the lines of the graph representing different levels of an independent variable are *not parallel*, an interaction *may* be present.

The "may" in the preceding statement results from the fact that the lines drawn on the graph may appear to be nonparallel because of random variability in the data. To determine that an interaction exists, you must establish that the apparent nonparallelism of the lines is not likely to have resulted simply from sampling error. Fortunately, statistical tests are available that simultaneously determine the probable reliability of both the main effects and interactions of a particular experiment. (These tests are discussed in Chapter 13.) Incidentally, if the lines on the graph *are* parallel, no interaction exists, and no statistical test will find one.

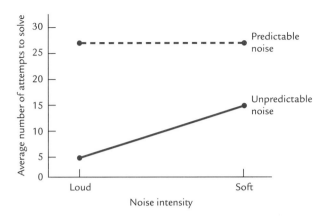

**FIGURE 9–10** Graph Showing an Interaction Between Variables. SOURCE: Data from Glass et al., 1969.

Figure 9–11 illustrates several other ways that a 2 × 2 factorial experiment might come out. In Panel (a), only Factor A has a systematic effect on the dependent variable. In Panel (b), only Factor B has an effect. Panel (c) shows an interaction between Factors A and B but no main effect of either factor, due to the fact that the average value of each factor, collapsed over the other, is the same for each level. Both A and B affect the dependent variable, but their effects in this case show up only in the interaction. Panel (d) shows a main effect of both factors, but no interaction (note the parallel lines).

*Factorial Within-Subjects Designs*    In the factorial within-subjects design, each subject is exposed to every combination of levels of all the factors (independent variables).

An example of the factorial within-subjects design was recently conducted by a research methods class. This experiment was a variant of the Peterson and Peterson (1959) study described previously. In the class's version, the consonant trigrams were presented on the screen of a computer rather than being given verbally as in the original experiment. The students wanted to know whether the display duration of the trigram affected retention and, if so, whether it affected retention more after long retention intervals than after short ones.

To answer these questions, the class decided to test retention after display intervals of 1 second or 5 seconds and retention intervals of 3 seconds or 18 seconds. Combining each display interval with each retention interval resulted in four treatments. Each participant was exposed to each of these treatments in random order until he or she had completed 20 trials at each combination of display interval and retention interval. Figure 9–12 shows the mean numbers of correct recalls.

As you can see in the figure, the number of correct recalls was lower when the retention interval was 18 seconds than when it was 3 seconds, regardless of the display interval. Also, the number of correct recalls was lower when the display interval was 1 second (lower line) than when it was 5 seconds (upper line), regardless of retention interval. The lines connecting treatments having the same display interval appear to be parallel, indicating that the two factors did not interact. A statistical analysis showed a significant effect of display interval, a significant effect of retention interval, and no significant interaction.

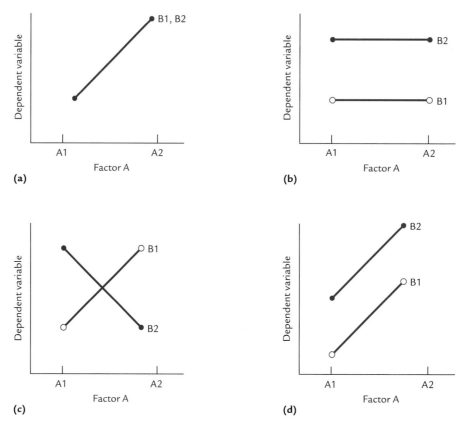

**FIGURE 9–11**    Some Possible Outcomes of a 2 × 2 Factorial Experiment (see text for description).

The research methods class experiment was conducted using just 20 participants (the entire class). To conduct this experiment using a between-subjects design with 10 participants per treatment combination would have required 40 participants to complete. (Each participant in a group would have received 20 retention trials.) As the number of levels of each factor and/or the number of factors increases, the savings in number of participants, time to deliver instructions, materials, and so on, that is achieved by adopting the within-subjects approach becomes considerable.

There is also a dark side to this scenario, however. As the number of levels of each factor and/or number of factors increases, so also does the time required to run each participant through all the required treatments. The number of possible orderings of treatments becomes astronomical with only a few levels per factor and a few factors, thus making complete counterbalancing impractical. Also, unless care is taken, the large demands on participants may lead to fatigue, boredom, inattention, and perhaps outright hostility toward you and your experiment. In other words, the practical limits to the size of a factorial within-subjects experiment are reached more rapidly than with the equivalent between-subjects design.

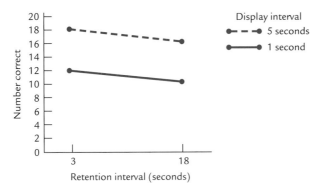

Display interval
• – – • 5 seconds
•——• 1 second

**FIGURE 9–12**   Results of Class Experiment Using a Factorial Design.

To provide a graphic example of how rapidly practical limits can be exceeded, imagine that the class experiment on memory was expanded to include each of Peterson and Peterson's original retention intervals (3, 6, 9, 12, 15, and 18 seconds). With two display intervals, the experiment would have required 12 (6 × 2) treatments, which at 20 trials per treatment would have required each participant to complete 240 trials. If a third variable with two levels were added (say, meaningfulness of the trigram), this number would double to 480 trials.

At an average rate of one trial every 15 seconds, each participant would require two hours to complete the experiment, assuming no breaks. Would the results be comparable to those obtained in the equivalent between-groups experiment, in which each participant would have received only 20 trials, or five minutes of participation?

Despite this limitation, factorial within-subjects designs are often used, especially in areas such as sensory threshold testing, decision making, and perceptual processing. In these areas, the large amount of practice participants get across treatments confers a desirable stability on their performances. To determine whether your research question can best be answered by using a within-subjects design, you need to carefully consider how multiple treatment exposures will affect your participants' responses to the treatments and their willingness to cooperate.

*Higher-Order Factorial Designs*   The simple two-factor, four-cell design can be extended to include any number of levels of a given factor and any number of factors. These are **higher-order factorial designs**. However, practical considerations limit the usefulness of these designs if you try to extend them too far. Two important problems concern the number of subjects required for the design and the complexity of potential interactions.

You should probably use at least five subjects per group for a reasonable ability to detect the effects of the independent variables. The number of required cells can be calculated by multiplying together the number of levels of each factor in the design. In the noise experiment, the two levels of noise intensity and two levels of noise predictability yield four (2 × 2) cells. If you were to repeat this study using 5 participants per group, you would need to recruit 20 participants. Adding a third two-level factor would produce a design that required eight (2 × 2 × 2) groups, or 40 (5 × 8) participants. If each factor had three levels instead of two, you would need 27 (3 × 3 × 3) groups multiplied by five, or 135 participants! And this estimate uses a *minimum* number of participants per group. It would be preferable to use more participants for statistical reliability, but could you afford the time and money required to run such an experiment? As you can see, extended factorial experiments get out of hand quickly.

The second problem with extended factorial designs concerns the number and complexity of the resulting interactions. With three factors, you get three main effects (one for each factor), three *two-way interactions* (Factor A versus Factor B, Factor A versus Factor C, and Factor B versus Factor C), and a *three-way interaction* (Factor A versus Factor B versus Factor C). The two-way interactions are each similar to the simple interaction found in the two-factor design. For example, the A × B interaction represents the interaction of Factors A and B, averaged over the levels of Factor C. However, what is the A × B × C interaction? This interaction occurs when the A × B *interaction* changes depending on the level of Factor C! (Other interpretations are also possible.) Adding a fourth variable to your design adds further interactions, including the dreaded A × B × C × D four-way interaction, which few ordinary mortals can comprehend. Because data resulting from such designs are difficult to analyze and interpret (not to mention expensive because of the large subject requirement), most investigators limit factorial designs to no more than three factors.

In designs with three factors, the simple effects observed at each level of one of the factors consist of two-way interactions of the other two factors. You also could examine the simple effects of each combination of levels of two of the factors. Of course, the same logic can be applied to designs having more than three factors.

If you are willing to give up information about some of the higher-order interactions, you can include a relatively large number of factors and levels within factors while keeping the requirement for subjects within reasonable bounds. Describing the logic behind these designs and the analyses appropriate to them is beyond the scope of this book. If you are interested in looking into such designs, see the discussion of fractional replications of factorial designs in Edwards (1985, pp. 243–245) or Chapter 8 in Winer (1971).

## Other Group-Based Designs

This chapter presents a logical progression from the two-level design through the single-factor multilevel design and finally to the factorial design. This progression might lead you to believe that these are the only ways to conduct experiments. This is far from the truth.

Chapter 4 indicated that you should first develop your research questions and then choose your design. This rule applies when you are deciding how to conduct a between-subjects or within-subjects experiment. Situations occur in which a full factorial design is not the best design to test your hypotheses. After all, in a full factorial design, you examine every possible combination of the levels of your independent variables. In some research situations, this may be neither necessary nor desirable. For example, to address specific questions, you may need to add control groups or treatments to the basic factorial plan. (The Glass et al. 1969 study in fact included such an additional control group—one receiving no noise.) Alternatively, some groups or treatments may not be possible (you may not be able to combine certain drugs, for example).

Designs such as these that do not follow one of the more standard design formats can help you to address special questions or deal with unusual circumstances. However, the data they provide sometimes require special statistical techniques to interpret properly. This may mean extra work in identifying the appropriate techniques and learning to apply them.

In short, the special versions of these designs may pose special problems for you. Nevertheless, you should make the effort. Choose the design that best addresses the questions you want to answer. If your design does not address these questions, you may save some effort, but the effort you do make will be wasted.

## DESIGNS WITH TWO OR MORE DEPENDENT VARIABLES

Just as it is possible to include more than one independent variable in a design, it is also possible to include more than one dependent variable. Indeed, all the designs discussed thus far could be modified to include multiple dependent variables, without changing their essential characters. Designs that include multiple dependent variables are termed *multivariate designs*. Those with single dependent variables (such as previously discussed) are termed *univariate designs*. However, multivariate designs are not limited to experiments. Correlational research that simultaneously measures three or more variables is also termed *multivariate*. Chapter 14 covers multivariate designs in some detail, including experimental, correlational, and mixed strategies.

## CONFOUNDING AND EXPERIMENTAL DESIGN

Chapter 4 defined a confounding variable as one that varies along with your independent variable. The presence of a confounding variable damages the internal validity of your experiment. Consequently, you may not be able to establish a causal relationship between your independent variable (or variables) and your dependent variable. One of the most important aspects of experimental design is to develop an experiment that is free of confounding variables.

Sometimes a source of confounding can be subtle and difficult to detect. Imagine that you are ready to run an experiment on the effect of drugs on discrimination learning. You are using rats as subjects. You order your rats, which are delivered in crates, each housing several animals. You begin to take the rats out of the crates and put them in individual cages in the colony room of your animal research facility. The first rats you catch go in the first row of cages and the remaining rats go in the second row. You decide to assign the rats in the first row to your experimental group and those in the second row to your control group. You run your experiment and find that the rats in the experimental group perform better than those in the control group and conclude that the drug improves performance. Is there another possible explanation? Unfortunately, there is. It could be that the rats in the experimental group were better at discrimination learning to start with. How can this be, you ask?

Remember how you assigned rats to their cages? You caught them and put them in two rows of cages. The rats that went in the top row were caught first. These rats were slower and easier to catch than those in the second row. It may be that these rats are more docile and easier to handle. It is possible that the more docile rats in the experimental group learned faster because they experienced less stress in your experiment than those in your control group. This, and not the drug you administered, may have produced the observed difference. You could have avoided this problem by randomly assigning subjects to treatment conditions so that each subject, regardless of what row it was housed in, had an equal chance of appearing in either of your treatment groups.

Confounding also can occur if you are using human participants in an experiment that will take a long period of time to complete. You should be sure that your experimental treatments are spread out evenly over the entire period of the experiment. That is, be sure not to run all of your participants in one condition at the beginning of a semester and all the participants in another condition at the end. It could be that participants who volunteer for your experiment at the beginning of a semester differ in some important ways from those who volunteer later in a semester. By randomly assigning participants to treatment groups, you can avoid this problem.

Another source of confounding is *experimenter bias*, which we discussed in detail in Chapter 5. For example, if you assigned your participants to groups because you thought that certain participants would perform better in one group than in another, you introduced bias into your experiment as a confounding factor. To avoid this problem it would be best to use a blind or double-blind technique (see Chapter 5).

A major source of confounding occurs when your treatment conditions are not carefully conceived and, as a result, unintended variables are introduced whose values change in lock-step with those of the independent variable. The old "Pepsi Challenge," designed to test Pepsi against Coca-Cola, provides a classic example of this source of confounding. In the original version of the challenge, cups with Pepsi were always marked with an "M," and cups with Coca-Cola with a "Q." The challenge showed that participants preferred Pepsi over Coca-Cola. However, when researchers from Coca-Cola tried to replicate the challenge, they found that participants chose the cup marked with an "M" even if both cups contained Coca-Cola (Huck & Sandler, 1979). Thus, in the original Pepsi Challenge, it is unclear whether participants were choosing based on taste or the letter used to mark the cup.

Avoiding this source of confounding requires paying attention to detail. In the Pepsi Challenge, the cups could have been left unmarked, or the letters could have been counterbalanced. Yet another approach would be to conduct a pilot study to determine whether a preference exists for certain letters over others.

The best way to avoid confounding in an experiment is to plan carefully how your independent variables are to be executed. Ask yourself whether or not there are potential alternative explanations for any effect you may find. Is your independent variable the only factor that could affect the value of your dependent variable? Careful evaluation of your experimental design and variables and a good knowledge of the literature in your area will help you avoid confounding. Remember, results from a confounded experiment cannot be rehabilitated and are generally useless. Therefore, take care during the design stage of your experiment to eliminate confounding variables. This will ensure an experiment with the highest level of internal validity.

# SUMMARY

Experimental designs can be classified as between-subjects, within-subjects, or single-subject designs. Between-subjects designs manipulate the independent variable by administering the different levels of the independent variable to different groups of subjects. Within-subjects designs administer the different levels of the independent variable at different times to a single group of subjects. Single-subject designs manipulate the independent variable as the within-subjects designs do, but focus on the performances of single subjects rather than on the average performances of a group of subjects.

A key problem for any experimental design is the problem of error variance. Error variance consists of fluctuations in scores that have nothing to do with the effect of the independent variable. Error variance tends to obscure any causal relationship that may exist between your independent and dependent variables.

Several steps can be taken to reduce error variance. In any type of design, you can hold extraneous variables as constant as possible and manipulate your independent variable more strongly. In between-subjects designs, you also can randomize error variance across groups by assigning subjects to groups at random, thus tending to equalize the effect of error variance on mean performance across treatments. Alternatively, you can match subjects across treatments on characteristics you believe may strongly affect the dependent variable, which will thus tend to eliminate any average differences in these characteristics across the treatments. In within-subjects designs, you can use the same subjects in each treatment, and thus in effect match each subject with him- or herself and eliminate differences between subjects from the analysis. Whether you have used a randomized groups, matched-groups, or within-subjects design, you can then use inferential statistics to assess the probability with which random error variance by itself (in the absence of any effect of the independent variable) would have produced the observed differences in treatment means. If this probability is small, you can be reasonably confident that your independent variable is effective.

Between-subjects and within-subjects designs can be classified according to the number of levels of a single independent variable (two or more than two), the number of independent variables manipulated (single-factor or multifactor), the way in which subjects are assigned to treatments (random assignment, matching, or same subjects in every treatment), and the number of dependent variables (univariate or multivariate). If an independent variable takes on three or more quantitative values, the manipulation is described as parametric; otherwise, it is said to be nonparametric.

Designs may include multiple control groups or treatments to assess the impact of several potentially confounding factors. These additional conditions can be included in both parametric and nonparametric designs.

When subjects are assigned to groups at random, the design is termed a randomized groups design. Such designs are best when subject characteristics do not contribute greatly to error variance. However, when subject characteristics strongly influence the dependent variable, you can reduce error variance created by these characteristics by using either a matched-groups design or a within-subjects design. This control over error variance can improve your chances of detecting any effects of your independent variable. However, compared with randomized groups designs, matched-groups designs require the extra steps of testing and matching subjects. Both matched-groups and within-subjects designs use somewhat different inferential statistical tests to evaluate the data and may actually be less sensitive to the effects of the independent variable if matching or the use of the same subjects in each treatment does not succeed in reducing error variance. With matched-groups designs, it may be difficult to find enough matching subjects if the design includes several groups. With within-subjects designs, this problem is avoided, but the use of the same subjects in each treatment condition introduces the possibility of carryover, which occurs when exposure to one treatment condition changes how subjects behave in a subsequent treatment condition. Several methods are available for dealing with carryover, including counterbalancing (exposing subjects to treatments in different orders), taking steps to minimize carryover, and using a design that makes any carryover effect into an independent variable.

Two or more independent variables or factors may be manipulated simultaneously in a single experimental design. If each level of each factor is combined once with each level of every other factor, the design is called a factorial design. Each treatment in a factorial design represents a unique combination of the levels of the independent variables, and all possible combinations are represented. Factorial designs make it possible to assess in one experiment the main effect of each independent variable and any interactions among variables. The number of treatment cells required for a factorial design can be computed by multiplying together the number of levels of each factor manipulated.

Some questions are best addressed using designs other than the standard ones. For example, a basic between-subjects factorial design might be expanded to include control groups in order to make comparisons beyond those involving main effects and interactions. Although the statistical analyses required for these designs may be more difficult to define, do not let this difficulty prevent you from choosing the best design for the questions you want to address.

Multivariate experimental designs include two or more dependent variables. These designs provide information about the effect of the independent variable on each dependent variable and on a composite dependent variable formed from a weighted combination of the individual dependent variables.

Confounding occurs when the effects of uncontrolled extraneous variables cannot be separated from those of the intended independent variables. Nonrandom assignment (in between-subjects designs), carryover (in within-subjects designs), experimenter bias, and ill-conceived experimental conditions are sources of confounding. Steps such as random assignment, blind techniques, and careful assessment of experimental conditions and of potential alternative explanations should be taken to avoid potential confounding.

## REVIEW QUESTIONS

1. How do between-subjects, within-subjects, and single-subject experiments differ?
2. How might error variance in a between-subjects design affect your results?
3. What steps can you take to deal with error variance in a between-subjects design?

4. How are statistics used to test the reliability of data from a between-subjects experiment?
5. How does a randomized group design work, and what are some of its advantages and disadvantages?
6. When would you use a matched-groups design?
7. How does a matched-pairs design differ from a randomized two-group design?
8. What are some of the advantages and disadvantages of the matching strategy?
9. What are the advantages and disadvantages of the within-subjects experimental design?
10. What are the sources of carryover effects in a within-subjects design?
11. How do carryover effects influence interpretation of the results from a within-groups experiment?
12. Under what conditions will counterbalancing be effective or ineffective in dealing with carryover effects?
13. When do you use a Latin square design?
14. What strategies can be used to deal with carryover effects?
15. Do between-subjects and within-subjects designs applied to the same variables always produce the same functional relationship (why or why not)?
16. When should you consider using a within-subjects design instead of a between-subjects design?
17. When should you consider using a matched-groups design rather than a within-subjects design?
18. How do single-factor and multiple-factor experimental design differ?
19. What are the advantages to using a multiple-factor experimental design?
20. What is a main effect?
21. What is an interaction, and how does it differ from main effects?
22. How does a confounding variable affect the validity of your results?
23. How can confounding variables be eliminated?

## KEY TERMS

between-subjects design
within-subjects design
single-subject design
error variance
randomized two-group design
parametric design
nonparametric design
multiple control group design
matched-groups design

matched-pairs design
carryover effects
counterbalancing
factorial design
main effects
interaction
simple effects
higher-order factorial designs

# 10

# Using Specialized Research Designs

In Chapters 7 through 9, we introduced you to a variety of research designs appropriate for nonexperimental and experimental research. Although these designs cover a wide range of conventional research situations, there are some research questions that can be adequately addressed only by using a specialized design. In this chapter, we describe several designs in this category. These include combined between-subjects and within-subjects designs, combined experimental and correlational designs, pretest–posttest designs, quasi-experimental designs, and developmental designs.

## COMBINING BETWEEN-SUBJECTS AND WITHIN-SUBJECTS DESIGNS

In Chapter 9, we introduced you to between-subjects and within-subjects designs and described each type's advantages and disadvantages. Both types of design come in versions that allow you to assess simultaneously the effects of two or more independent variables. However, it is also possible (and at times desirable) to combine between-subjects and within-subjects manipulations in a single experiment. This section discusses two designs that combine between-subjects and within-subjects manipulations.

### The Mixed Design

A **mixed design** is sometimes also called a *split-plot design*. The term comes from agricultural research, in which the design was first developed (it referred to a plot of land). In the split-plot design, a field was divided into several plots. Different plots received different levels of a given treatment (different pesticides). Each plot was then split into subplots, and each subplot received a different level of a second treatment (e.g., different fertilizers). Thus, each plot received all the levels of fertilizer, but only one level of pesticide. In psychological research, each "plot" is a group of subjects who all receive the same level of the between-subjects variable. Within a given plot, the subplots represent the different levels of the within-subjects variable to which all members of that group are exposed.

Figure 10–1 depicts a mixed design with one between-subjects variable (Factor X) and one within-subjects variable (Factor Y). Two different groups of subjects are assigned to the two levels of Factor X. Within each group, all subjects receive all four levels of Factor Y.

A mixed design allows you to assess the effects of variables that, because of irreversible effects or carryover, cannot be manipulated effectively within subjects. (These variables are manipulated between subjects.) A mixed design maintains the advantages of the within-subjects design for the remaining variables. An example of this design is provided by a classic experiment on motor learning conducted by Lorge (1930).

Lorge (1930) was interested in determining whether massed practice ("cramming") or distributed practice (spacing the learning out over several sessions) produced faster learning in a mirror-tracing task. Participants learned to trace around a simple geometric figure (such as a star) while looking at the figure through a mirror. Two groups received 20 tracing trials, and the time required to complete the tracing was recorded after each trial. One group completed all 20 trials in one sitting (massed practice), whereas the other group completed its 20 trials at the rate of one trial per day (distributed practice).

Figure 10–2 shows the results of Lorge's (1930) experiment. The upper and lower curves represent the tracing time (in seconds) as a function of trials for the groups receiving massed practice and distributed practice, respectively. What is the within-subjects variable in this study? What is the between-subjects variable? "Trials," of course, is the variable manipulated within subjects, and type of practice ("massed" or "distributed") is the variable manipulated between subjects.

This mixed design included one factor that was manipulated between subjects and one that was manipulated within. More complex mixed designs are possible. Factorial mixed designs with three, four, or more factors in any combination of within-subjects and between-subjects manipulations can be conducted.

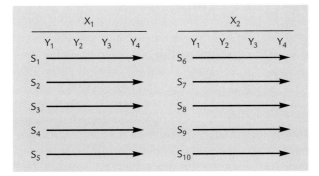

**FIGURE 10–1**   Mixed Between-Within Design. Factor X has two levels that are manipulated between subjects. Factor Y has four levels that are manipulated within subjects.

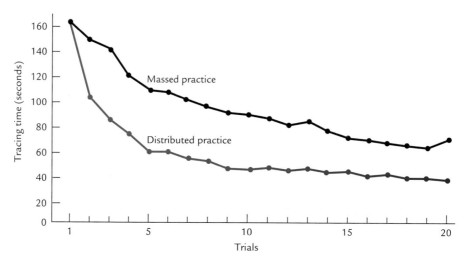

**FIGURE 10–2**    A Mixed Design Combining Within-Subjects and Between-Subjects Designs.

Source: Graph drawn from data provided in Lorge, 1930.

### The Nested Design

Another design that combines within-subjects and between-subjects components is the **nested design.** Figure 10–3 shows an example of a nested design. This example includes three levels of a between-subjects factor ($A_1$, $A_2$, and $A_3$). Under each of the levels of A are "nested" three levels of B. Notice that the levels of B found under different levels of A are *not the same*. For example, $B_1$, $B_2$, and $B_3$ appear under $A_1$, whereas $B_4$, $B_5$, and $B_6$ appear under $A_2$. Each level of Factor A thus includes a within-subjects manipulation of Factor B, although the levels of B included in the manipulation differ with the A level.

Nested designs are more economical than factorial designs, in which each level of a factor is completely crossed with every level of every other factor, but on the negative side, they do not yield as much information as factorial design in that you cannot evaluate certain interactions. However, there are situations in which a factorial design is simply not practical. In such cases, a nested design may give you the information you want. Here we discuss two types of nesting: nesting tasks and nesting groups of subjects.

*Nesting Tasks*    Nested designs are useful when you want to include more than one task under a level of an independent variable. For example, imagine that you are conducting an experiment on the effect of a safety campaign on the number of worker injuries. You want to establish that any positive effect of the campaign is not specific to one industry, so you include several companies in your study, representing different industries. However, each company has a different set of jobs. Company X provides jobs A, B, and C; company Y provides jobs D, E, and F; and company Z provides jobs G, H, and I. Thus, jobs are nested under the different companies. Figure 10–4 shows this design.

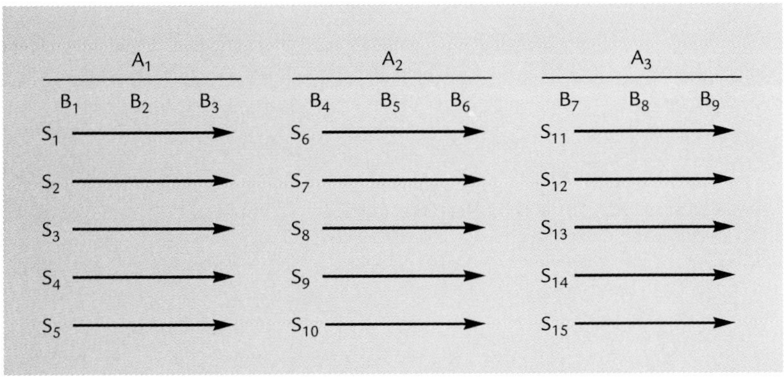

**FIGURE 10–3** A Nested Design That Has a Within-Subjects Component.

The major advantage of a nested design like the one shown in Figure 10–4 is that you increase the generality of your results. By demonstrating the effect of the safety campaign across many types of job within each company, you can be more certain that your effect is not limited to a particular type of job. However, the influences of job type and company (e.g., differences in corporate climate) on the effectiveness of the safety campaign are to some extent confounded in this design, because the jobs nested under different companies are not strictly comparable.

*Nesting Groups of Subjects*    A nested design also can be useful when you must test subjects in large groups rather than individually. For example, you may find it necessary to test participants during their regularly scheduled class hours. If you tested three classes under each of your experimental conditions, you would then have three classes nested under each level of your independent variable. Figure 10–5 illustrates this situation.

In this design, the classes are treated as the "subjects" rather than the participants themselves. These classes would be randomly assigned to the experimental conditions, just as you would randomly assign participants to the experimental conditions in a between-subjects experiment. Random assignment tends to average out any differences between classes, making the experimental groups more nearly equivalent.

Nesting groups of subjects within levels of the independent variable should not be done if you can nest only one group under each level of your independent variable. In this case, your experiment is hopelessly confounded because you have no way of knowing whether the differences between groups of subjects across treatment levels occur because of your independent variable or because of something relating to the nested groups (Keppel, 1982).

Nesting several independent groups under each level of your independent variable is analogous to running individual subjects. When you randomly assign individual subjects to conditions in a between-subjects design, you are essentially nesting subjects within treatments. Each group in a nested design can be viewed as a "subject" nested under a level of your independent variable. As long as you randomly assign groups of subjects to experimental conditions, nesting groups of subjects is legitimate.

| Company X | Company Y | Company Z |
|-----------|-----------|-----------|
| Job$_A$ | Job$_D$ | Job$_G$ |
| Job$_B$ | Job$_E$ | Job$_H$ |
| Job$_C$ | Job$_F$ | Job$_I$ |

**FIGURE 10-4**    A Design with Three Jobs Nested under Each Company. The Jobs Nested under Each Company are Different.

## COMBINING EXPERIMENTAL AND CORRELATIONAL DESIGNS

Experimental designs have the strong advantage of allowing you not only to identify whether relationships exist between variables but also to determine whether the relationships identified are causal ones. The strategy requires that you be able to manipulate the suspected causal variable (the independent variable), hold constant as many extraneous variables as possible, and randomize the effects of any remaining extraneous variables across treatments. Unfortunately, holding variables constant can reduce the generality of your findings (using only males as participants, for example, may yield results that do not generalize to females), whereas randomizing their effects across treatments can produce error variance that obscures the effects of your independent variables.

Fortunately, you often can deal with such problems effectively by using a design that combines experimental and correlational variables. In this section, we explore two ways to combine experimental and correlational variables: including a correlational variable as a covariate in an experimental design and including a quasi-independent variable.

### Including a Covariate in Your Experimental Design

When participants differ on some variable (such as IQ or reaction time), you can statistically control the effects of this variable by measuring the value of the variable for each participant along with the value of the dependent variable. This additional correlational variable is called a **covariate.** The name derives from the fact that you expect the covariate to *covary* with the dependent variable. This will be the case if the covariate has an immediate effect on the dependent variable or if it correlates with some unmeasured variable that has such an effect.

By including a covariate in your experimental design, you can effectively "subtract out" the influence of the covariate (or any variable correlated with it) from the dependent variable and thus reduce error variance and improve the sensitivity of your experiment to the effect of your independent variable.

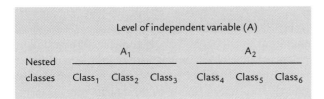

**FIGURE 10–5** Groups of Subjects Nested under Levels of the Independent Variable.

These designs are relatively easy to implement. Simply by collecting additional data on potentially relevant correlational variables, you can convert a standard experimental design into one that examines the impact of those variables on the relationship between the study's independent and dependent variables. For example, in an experiment on jury decision making, you might suspect that a participant's views on the death penalty might be related to his or her willingness to convict a defendant in a case not involving the death penalty. You could measure your participant's attitude toward the death penalty and then use that measure statistically as a covariate when analyzing your data.

Covariates typically take the form of continuous variables or of discrete variables having a relatively large number of levels. If the covariate in question is discrete and has relatively few levels, it may make more sense to treat it as a quasi-independent variable, as described next.

### Including Quasi-Independent Variables in an Experiment

A **quasi-independent variable** is a correlational variable that resembles the independent variable of an experiment. It is created by assigning subjects to groups according to some characteristic they possess (such as age, gender, or IQ), rather than using random assignment. For example, you might be interested in comparing the effectiveness of two types of incentive programs on sales by retail store clerks. You could include gender as a quasi-independent variable to determine whether male and female clerks tend to respond differently to the two programs.

Because subjects come into the "experiment" already "assigned" to their treatment levels, it is always possible that any relationship discovered may be due to the action of some third, unmeasured variable that happens to correlate well with the quasi-independent variable. Even so, the knowledge that a relationship exists may be important. This is especially true when quasi-experimental variables are added to an experimental design.

Such combinations of both experimental and quasi-experimental variables often resemble the factorial designs described in Chapter 9. These combinations yield a main effect for each independent variable, a main effect for each quasi-independent variable, and one or more interactions. The interactions in such designs can be especially illuminating. An example in which this was the case is provided by Schachter (1971) in a study of obesity.

Schachter brought his participants (college students) into a "waiting room" that was equipped with a large wall clock and told the participants that they should wait there until called to participate in an experiment. Actually they were already in the experiment. Bowls of crackers were placed in the room, and participants were invited to help themselves to some crackers if they wished.

The experimental manipulation of Schachter's study concerned the clock on the wall. For one group of participants, the clock ran fast, and soon it seemed that it was nearly dinnertime. For another group, the clock ran slow. For this group, dinnertime really was approaching, but this was not indicated by the clock.

Schachter combined this experimental variable with a correlational one: the weight of the participants. Participants were divided into two groups, one consisting of participants whose weights were considered "normal," the other consisting of participants who were considered "overweight." The dependent variable of the study was the number of crackers eaten.

Participant weight is a correlational variable because participants came to the experiment already having a given weight. They were not assigned randomly to the "normal" or "overweight" conditions. If Schachter had created his two weight classes by force-feeding a randomly chosen half of the participants, then participant weight would have been an experimental variable.

Schachter found that the "normal" participants essentially ignored the clock and consumed more crackers when it was nearly dinnertime than when it was not. "Overweight" participants, in contrast, used the clock to regulate their behavior, eating more crackers when the clock said dinnertime was near than when the clock said dinnertime was still distant. These findings can be summarized by saying that participant weight *interacted* with indicated time.

If you ignore the fact that participant weight is a correlational variable, then Schachter's design looks exactly like a 2 × 2 factorial between-subjects design. This similarity extends even further, as the results of the study would be analyzed exactly as those from the equivalent factorial design as well. What differs is the interpretation.

Any significant effect of the experimental variables in the combined design can be interpreted to mean that the independent variable *caused* changes in the dependent variable. In the Schachter (1971) study, the effect of indicated time on cracker consumption would be interpreted in this way. Any significant effect of the correlational variables in the study *cannot* be legitimately interpreted to indicate a causal relationship. Any correlation between two variables could result from the effect of a third, unmeasured variable that influences both variables. A significant effect of participant weight on cracker consumption would indicate only that consumption is related to weight.

In the case of Schachter's (1971) experiment, the presence of an interaction between indicated time and participant weight complicates the interpretation of the effect of both variables on cracker consumption. The main effect of indicated time lumps together the very different behaviors of "normal" and "overweight" participants. Similarly, the main effect of participant weight combines the very different effects of early time and late time. Indeed, the suspicion that "overweight" participants would react differently to indicated time was what prompted the study in the first place.

To understand what went on in the study, you need to look at the simple effect of indicated time at each level of participant weight. This analysis would show that indicated time affected cracker consumption for "overweight" participants but not for "normal" participants. (See Chapter 13 for a discussion of the analysis of simple effects.)

*Advantages of Including a Quasi-Independent Variable*   Experimental designs that include a quasi-independent variable allow you to test the generality of your findings across the levels of the quasi-independent variable. In the example, Schachter was able to show that altering the clock reading had effects on the participants' eating behavior that did not generalize from normal weight to overweight individuals.

Schachter's results also illustrate a second advantage of including a quasi-independent variable in your design. Had Schachter analyzed the data without regard to the participant's weight, these two effects might have canceled each other out, leading to the false conclusion that clock time had no effect on eating. By including a quasi-independent variable in his design, Schachter was able to reduce error variance by segregating the data into groups of participants who responded in a similar fashion to the manipulation. In this way the effect of the independent variable was made clearly visible.

*Disadvantages of Including a Quasi-Independent Variable*   The main disadvantage of including a quasi-independent variable in your design is that the results are frequently misinterpreted. Although paying lip service to the dictum "Cause cannot be inferred from correlation," researchers too often discuss their results as if they had established causal links between their quasi-independent and dependent variables. This mistake is encouraged by the fact that the correlational variables look exactly like experimental variables in the statistical analysis of the data. In Schachter's (1971) experiment, you may wish to conclude that being overweight causes people's eating behavior to be governed more by the clock than is the case with people of normal weight. However, one could just as well argue that being more sensitive to external cues leads to being overweight. Because weight was not experimentally manipulated, the causal status of this variable remains ambiguous.

Another disadvantage of these designs (although a minor one) is the extra effort sometimes required to obtain subjects differing in the required characteristics. Some quasi-experimental variables (such as anxiety level or IQ) require administration of a questionnaire or test before subjects can be classified. Adding quasi-experimental variables to an experimental design also increases the number of groups of subjects required and adds complexity to the analysis of the data.

# QUASI-EXPERIMENTAL DESIGNS

Pure **quasi-experimental designs** are those that resemble experimental designs but use quasi-independent rather than true independent variables. In this section, we examine several types of quasi-experimental design, including time series designs, the equivalent time samples design, and the nonequivalent control group design.

## Time Series Designs

The basic **time series design** is shown in Figure 10–6. In the time series design (Campbell & Stanley, 1963), you make several observations (O) of behavior over time prior to ($O_1$ to $O_4$) and immediately after ($O_5$ to $O_8$) introducing your treatment. For

$$O_1 \quad O_2 \quad O_3 \quad O_4 \quad \text{Treatment} \quad O_5 \quad O_6 \quad O_7 \quad O_8$$

**FIGURE 10–6** Basic Time Series Design.

example, you might measure children's school performance on a weekly basis for several weeks and then introduce a new teaching technique (the treatment). Following the introduction of the new teaching technique, you again measure school performance on a weekly basis. A contrast is then made between preintervention and postintervention performance.

*Interrupted Time Series Design*    A variation on the basic time series design is the **interrupted time series design**, in which you chart changes in behavior as a function of some naturally occurring event (such as a natural disaster or the introduction of a new law) rather than manipulate an independent variable. In this design, the naturally occurring event is a quasi-independent variable. As with the other time series designs, you make comparisons of behavior prior to and after your subjects were exposed to the treatment.

A study conducted by Berkowitz (1970) provides a good illustration of an interrupted time series design. Berkowitz examined the frequency of violent crime before and after the assassination of President Kennedy. Statistics on the rates of violent crimes for the years before and after the assassination were obtained from FBI crime records. Berkowitz's data showed an increase in the rate of violent crime after the assassination.

*Basic Data for Time Series Studies*    In Chapter 7, we defined archival research as research in which you search existing records for your data. Archival data can be used in a time series design. The Berkowitz (1970) study used crime statistics made available through the FBI. In Berkowitz's study, the inclusion of the quasi-independent variable defined the study as a time series study. Hence, in some cases you may be able to use archival data to investigate possible causal relationships among variables.

You are not limited to archival data when conducting a time series or interrupted time series study. In the example of the impact of a new teaching method on school performance, you could measure ongoing behavior (students' exam scores). In an interrupted time series design, if you know that an event is going to happen (such as the introduction of television to an area in which television is presently unavailable), you can make your observations prior to the introduction of the quasi-independent variable and continue observations afterward.

## Equivalent Time Samples Design

A quasi-experimental strategy related to the time series design is the **equivalent time samples design** (Campbell & Stanley, 1963). In this design, the treatment is administered repeatedly. Figure 10–7 shows this design. Note that the treatment is introduced and then observations (O) are made. Next, observations are made without the treatment, followed by a repeat of this sequence. You could repeat the sequence (in any order appropriate to the research question) as many times as necessary. This de-

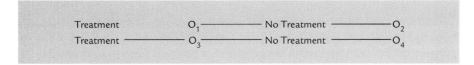

**FIGURE 10–7**  Equivalent Time Samples Design.

sign is most appropriate when the effects of the treatment are temporary or transient (Campbell & Stanley, 1963).

## Advantages and Disadvantages of Quasi-Experiments

One advantage of quasi-experimental designs is that they allow you to evaluate the impact of a quasi-independent variable under naturally occurring conditions. In those cases in which you manipulate the independent variable or even simply take advantage of a naturally occurring event, you may be able to establish clear causal relationships among variables. However, quasi-experimental research does have drawbacks that affect the internal and external validity of your research.

One drawback is that you do not have control over the variables influencing behavior. Another variable that changed along with the variable of interest actually may have caused the observed effect. For example, when the speed limit on the nation's highways was reduced to 55 mph, the accident and death rate noticeably decreased. The temptation is to conclude that driving more slowly caused a reduction in the accident rate.

Although this conclusion is the one that was drawn (and is probably true), other events occurred at the same time. The 55-mph speed limit was instituted during a gasoline shortage. In fact, people drove less and some states instituted "gasless Sundays" on which gasoline was not sold at all. The accident rate could have been reduced because fewer people were on the roads and because those who *were* on the roads drove less after the speed limit reduction than before. Exercise caution when interpreting results from quasi-experiments. Be careful to take into account any changes that may have accompanied changes in the variable of interest.

A second drawback to the quasi-experimental strategy also relates to your degree of control over variables. When you are using naturally occurring events as quasi-independent variables, you have little or no control over when the event will occur. For example, you have no control over when a law is changed or a new service is introduced. A research study of any kind requires significant preparation. In the absence of forewarning about an event, you may be caught off guard and not be able to adequately study the behaviors of interest. In the case of a change in a law or introduction of a new service, keeping in touch with current events will provide you with enough advance warning to design a reasonably good quasi-experiment. However, in other cases you may not have such advance warning.

As an example, if you were interested in conducting a prospective study of the impact of the eruption of Mount St. Helens on the nearby residents, you probably would have had a problem conducting your research. You would have had to predict when the volcano was going to erupt and taken behavioral measures prior to and after the eruption. Unless you were extremely lucky (or knew more about volcanoes than the experts), you probably would not have been prepared to study the impact of such a natural disaster on human behavior with a quasi-experiment. (A more practical design here would make use of available archival data.)

The major problems with the quasi-experiment obviously are related to issues of internal validity. Because the researcher does not completely control the quasi-independent variable and other related variables, confounding variables will probably cloud any causal inferences drawn from the data collected. A partial solution to these problems is to include appropriate control groups in your quasi-experiment. Campbell and Stanley (1963) suggest some quasi-experimental designs that include such control groups to evaluate the internal validity of your study.

## Nonequivalent Control Group Design

In the **nonequivalent control group design**, you include a time series component (that is, $O_1 \ O_2 \ O_3$ Treatment $O_4 \ O_5 \ O_6$) along with a "control group" that is not exposed to the treatment ($O_1 \ O_2 \ O_3 \ O_4 \ O_5 \ O_6$). The essence of the nonequivalent control group design is that a comparable group of subjects is chosen and observed for the same period as the group for which the treatment is introduced. The control group is nonequivalent because it comes from a different community.

A study reported by Fiedler, Bell, Chemers, and Patrick (1984) illustrates a multiple time series design with a nonequivalent control group. Fiedler et al. investigated the impact of a training program on productivity and safety in the silver mining industry. Records of mine safety were examined for three years (1978–1980) prior to the introduction of an "organization development" program at the Lucky Friday mine. The organization development program helped the mining company develop evaluation procedures and promoted mine safety workers to the rank of supervisor. Also, a $25,000 bonus was developed to be distributed to the members of mining shifts with the best safety records. Data on mine safety were collected after the intervention with the organization development program.

The Fiedler et al. (1984) study also included a second mine as a nonequivalent control group. Data were collected on mine safety at the Star mine for the same period during which data were collected at the Lucky Friday mine. The difference between the two mines was that the organization development program was instituted only at the Lucky Friday mine. The frequency of mine accidents at the Lucky Friday mine had been consistently above the frequency for the Star mine before the training program. After intervention, the two mines reversed positions with respect to mine accidents: The Lucky Friday mine now showed fewer accidents than the Star mine.

Although the nonequivalent control group design allows you to make comparisons you ordinarily might not be able to make, there are some drawbacks to the design. First, the validity of the design will be compromised if your two groups differ on some important variable before the study begins (Campbell & Stanley, 1963). For example, if the initially poor safety record at the Lucky Friday mine had led to the firing or deaths of the more unsafe miners there, the subsequent better safety record at the

Lucky Friday mine could be attributed to the greater safety consciousness of those miners who remained. To minimize this problem, your groups must be matched as closely as possible prior to your study. Second, if either group is selected on the basis of extreme scores on the pretest, then any shift of scores from pretest to posttest toward the less extreme values may be due to regression toward the mean rather than to the effect of your treatment (Campbell & Stanley, 1963). For example, if the Lucky Friday mine was selected because it had a very bad safety record, any improvement at the mine might be due to a tendency for extreme scores to drift toward the average (regression to the mean) and not to the safety intervention program.

## PRETEST–POSTTEST DESIGNS

As the name suggests, a **pretest–posttest design** includes a pretest of participants on a dependent measure before the introduction of a treatment, followed by a posttest after the introduction of the treatment. The pretest–posttest design differs from the previously discussed quasi-experimental strategies in that the pretest–posttest design is a true experimental design (Campbell & Stanley, 1963) that resembles a standard within-subjects design. However, it lacks certain important controls for rival hypotheses.

Pretest–posttest designs are used to evaluate the effects of some change in the environment (including interventions such as drug treatment or psychotherapy) on subsequent performance. You might employ a pretest–posttest design to assess the effect of changes in an educational environment (for example, introduction of a new teaching method) or in the work environment (for example, using work teams on an assembly line). By using a pretest–posttest design, you can compare levels of performance before the introduction of your change to levels of performance after the introduction of the change.

Evaluating changes in performance after some change would seem simple: Just measure a behavior, introduce the change, and then measure the behavior again. You should recognize this design as a simple within-subjects experiment with two levels: pretreatment and posttreatment. As with any within-subjects design, carryover effects may confound the effect of the manipulation. Giving your participants the pretest may change the way they perform after you introduce your manipulation; for example, by drawing their attention to the behaviors you are assessing, providing practice on the test, introducing fatigue, and so on. Normally you would control such carryover effects through counterbalancing. Unfortunately, you cannot counterbalance the pretest and posttest administrations (think about it!). Thus, a simple pretest–posttest design leads to problems with internal validity.

To ensure internal validity, you must include control groups. Campbell and Stanley (1963) discuss pretest–posttest designs extensively. According to Campbell and Stanley, the simplest practical pretest–posttest design should take the form of the diagram shown in Figure 10–8.

As shown in Figure 10–8, the design includes two independent groups of participants. Group 1 (the experimental group) receives your treatment (for example, a new teaching method) between the pretest and posttest. Group 2 (the control group) also receives the pretest and posttest but does not receive the treatment. The pretest

| Group 1: | Pretest-Treatment-Posttest | |
| Group 2: | Pretest | Posttest |

**FIGURE 10–8** The Simplest Practical Pretest–Posttest Design: A mixed design with pretest–posttest as the within-subjects factor and with treatment versus no treatment as the between-subjects factor.

and posttest are given to the participants in the experimental and control groups at the same time intervals.

You may have recognized this design from earlier in this chapter: It is simply a mixed design with pretest–posttest as the within-subjects factor and with treatment versus no treatment as the between-subjects factor. As such, you can use the design to determine the main effect of each factor and the interaction between them.

If the pretest affected the performances of participants on the posttest, you would expect to find a difference between pretest and posttest scores *in both groups*. The same could be said for the effects of any other events, unrelated to your treatment, that might occur between the pretest and posttest administrations: They would be expected to affect the two groups similarly. In contrast, if you found a difference between the pretest and posttest scores in the experimental group only, then you would be justified in concluding that your treatment, and not some other factor, produced the observed changes in performance.

An example follows. Imagine you are interested in whether using computers in a second-grade class affects the children's knowledge of scientific principles. You obtain a sample of 100 second graders. You randomly assign 50 of them to a new teaching method involving computer-aided instruction. These participants constitute your experimental group; the remaining participants are your control group. You give a pretest of scientific principles to all 100 students and then provide computer-aided instruction to your experimental group (the control group continues to get the usual instruction). Finally, you give both groups your posttest.

Imagine you find that your experimental participants show an average gain of 20 points from pretest to posttest, whereas your control group shows an average gain of only 2 points. You could then conclude that your new teaching method and not some other factor was responsible for the observed change. Now imagine that both groups had shown the same 20-point gain. Would you reach the same conclusion? Of course not. Now you would have to conclude that the students showed the same rate of improvement regardless of the teaching method used.

Campbell and Stanley (1963) pointed out that in order for this design to qualify as a true experiment, participants must be randomly assigned to your groups. You *could* use naturally formed groups in a pretest–posttest format, but then the between-subjects component would involve a quasi-independent variable, and your conclusions regarding the effect of this variable would be weaker. For example, if you used different classes in your study of computer-aided instruction and found that the class receiving the computers showed a greater increase in performance from pretest to posttest, you could not conclude with any confidence that the computers caused the difference. Perhaps they did, but it is also possible that the teacher of the experimental class simply did a better job of teaching.

Campbell and Stanley also pointed out that although the two-group pretest–posttest design ensures a degree of internal validity, it does not preclude potential problems with external validity. Your results may not generalize beyond the immediate research setting. Although this problem can affect any experiment, a particular problem of this design is that participants may be sensitized by the pretest. Having had the pretest, participants may now perform differently than they would have without the pretest. For example, the experimental group may do better than the control group when both groups receive a pretest but not when the pretests are omitted. Campbell and Stanley suggest two remedies to the problem.

The first remedy is to use a design called the **Solomon four-group design.** This design is illustrated in Figure 10–9. Note that four groups are included in this design. Groups 1 and 2 are identical to those in the two-group design. The additional groups allow you to test for any possible sensitization effects of the pretest. Groups 3 (treatment and then posttest) and 4 (posttest alone) allow you to evaluate the impact of your treatment in the absence of a pretest. By comparing this effect with the impact of your treatment when a pretest is included, you can determine whether inclusion of the pretest alters the effect of your treatment.

Campbell and Stanley's (1963) second remedy to the pretest sensitization problem is to entirely eliminate the pretest. Minus the pretest, this design represents a simple two-group experiment. The decision to eliminate the pretest depends on the question being asked. Situations may exist in which the pretest is needed to completely answer a research question. For example, you may want to know how much students learn in a given course. However, because some students may come into a course already having some background in the subject, good performance on the final exam would not necessarily mean that the students had learned anything new. To eliminate this problem, you might administer a pretest on the first day of class over the same material to be assessed in the final exam. The results of this pretest would provide a baseline against which you could measure any change attributable to the course.

## DEVELOPMENTAL DESIGNS

If you were interested in evaluating changes in behavior that relate to changes in a person's chronological age, you would use one of the specialized *developmental designs* discussed in this section: the cross-sectional design, the longitudinal design, and the cohort-sequential design. These designs represent a special case of quasi-experimental

| Group 1: | Pretest-Treatment-Posttest |
| Group 2: | Pretest                Posttest |
| Group 3: | Treatment-Posttest |
| Group 4: | Posttest |

**FIGURE 10–9**   The Solomon Four-Group Design.

designs, wherein a characteristic of the participant (age) serves as a quasi-independent variable. Because age cannot be assigned to participants randomly, it must be used as a purely correlational variable or a quasi-independent variable. Consequently, interpretations you make from your data should not center on causal relationships between age and behavior change. We also should note that although we are presenting these designs as developmental designs, they often have applications outside of developmental psychology.

## The Cross-Sectional Design

Suppose you were interested in evaluating the changes in intelligence with age. One way to approach the problem is to use a cross-sectional design. In the **cross-sectional design**, you select several participants from each of a number of age groups. Figure 10–10 illustrates the general strategy of the cross-sectional design.

In essence, you are creating groups based on the chronological ages of your participants *at the time of the study*. Different participants form each of the age groups. In a cross-sectional study, you do not measure the same participant at different ages.

Assume that you are interested in investigating the developmental changes in intelligence across the life span (birth to death). Your hypothesis is that intelligence increases steadily during childhood and adolescence, levels off during early and middle adulthood, and declines in late adulthood. To evaluate this hypothesis with a cross-sectional design, you would obtain participants representing the different age groups elaborated in your hypothesis. You would then administer a standardized intelligence test (for example, the Stanford–Binet) to each group and compare results across age groups.

An advantage of the cross-sectional design is that it permits you to obtain useful developmental data in a relatively short period of time. You do not have to follow the same participant for 10 years in order to assess age-related changes in behavior. If you found data consistent with your hypothesis, for example, what would you conclude? The purpose of the study was to draw conclusions about changes in intelligence across the life span. The observed decline in intelligence test scores would seem to indicate that intelligence deteriorates with age after middle adulthood.

Yet a serious problem exists with cross-sectional design that may preclude drawing clear conclusions from the observed differences among intelligence test scores: generation effects. The term *generation effect* refers to the influence of generational differences in experience, which become confounded with the effects of age per se. This confounding threatens the internal validity of cross-sectional studies. Let's say that the participants in your "late adulthood" group were 70 years old and participants in your "early adulthood" group were 20 years old. Assume that your study was done in 2004. Simple subtraction shows that participants in the different groups not only were of different ages but also were born in different decades: the 70-year-olds in 1934 and the 20-year-olds in 1984.

The fact that participants in different age groups were born in different decades may provide an alternative explanation for the observed differences in intelligence scores, thus threatening the internal validity of your study. The educational opportunities available in 1934 could have differed markedly from those available to participants

Age (years)

5          10          15

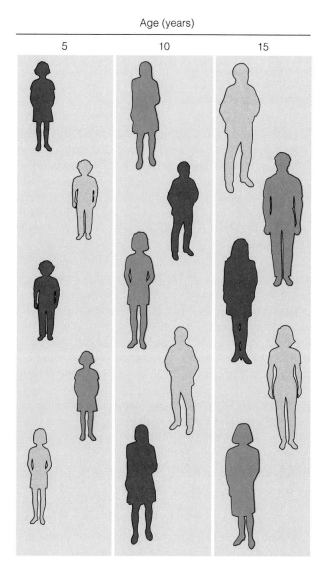

**FIGURE 10–10**   Cross-Sectional Developmental Design.

born in 1984. The observed reduction in intelligence test scores for older participants may be due to poorer educational opportunity rather than chronological age. Research indicates that the reduced intelligence test scores shown by older participants in cross-sectional studies were indeed caused in part by a generation effect (Anastasi, 1976).

Generation effects are a major problem when you use a cross-sectional design to evaluate age-related changes in behavior of participants of quite disparate ages. The design may be more appropriate when the participants are closer in age. For example, you could use the design to evaluate the changes in the ability to solve verbal problems in children ranging in age from two to six. These children would all be of the same generation. In this case, the problem of generation effects may be reduced.

## The Longitudinal Design

An alternative to the cross-sectional design, the **longitudinal design**, is illustrated in Figure 10–11. In this design, a single group of participants is followed over some time period. For example, you could obtain a group of participants and give them intelligence tests at 5-year intervals over a 30-year span.

*Generation Effects in Longitudinal Designs*    In one respect, the longitudinal design circumvents the problem of generation effects that plagues cross-sectional designs. Because you are studying people from the same age group, you need not worry about generational effects when drawing conclusions about *that group*. Even so, generation effects may still be of concern in the longitudinal design. Shaffer (1985) points out that longitudinal research has the problem of *cross-generational effects*. That is, the conclusion drawn from the longitudinal study of a particular generation may not apply to another generation.

Suppose a longitudinal study was begun in 1910 and carried out through 1940. Data were collected on attachment (the special bond between parent and child) and other developmental events. Would the conclusions derived from these data apply to the generation you begin to study in 2000? You cannot be sure. Changing attitudes toward child rearing, day care, breast-feeding, and so forth could invalidate the conclusions drawn from data accumulated during the period from 1910 to 1940. Thus, even though the longitudinal design provides important information about developmental trends, you must be careful when attempting to generalize from one generation to another.

Other problems you should consider when choosing a longitudinal design include participant mortality, testing effects, and the time needed to collect even small amounts of data.

*Subject Mortality*    The term *subject mortality* refers to the loss of participants from the research. Participants may not complete a longitudinal study because they have moved (and don't notify you of their new address), lost interest in the study, find the study offensive, or have died.

The problem of subject mortality relates directly to the external validity of a longitudinal study. If subject mortality is related to factors such as moving or loss of interest, mortality is less problematic than if it is related to the research. Loss of participants due to factors such as changes in address can be considered random in the sense that moving is as likely to happen to one participant as another. If participants drop out of a study because of the nature of the research (for example, the methods are stressful or boring), a biased sample results. Those participants who remain in the study (despite finding it offensive) may have special qualities that differentiate them from participants who quit for this reason. Because the loss of those participants biases the sample, the results may not apply to the general population.

Because subject mortality can bias the results of a longitudinal study, you should make every effort to evaluate why participants do not complete the study. Subject mortality may be more problematic with longitudinal research that spans a long period of time. The longer the time period, the more difficult it is to keep track of participants.

Time of measurement

1945        1955        1965        1975        1985        1995

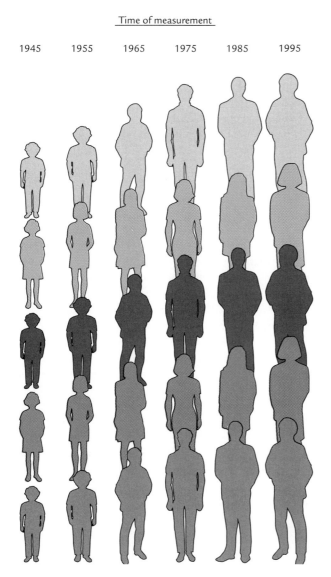

**FIGURE 10-11**    Longitudinal Developmental Design.

*Multiple-Observation Effects*    In a longitudinal design, you make multiple observations of the same participants across time. This very procedure raises problems that may threaten the internal validity of your longitudinal research. Two factors related to multiple observations threaten internal validity.

First, improved performance on the tests over time may be related more to the participants' increasing experience with taking the tests than to changes related to age per se. For example, increases in intelligence scores with age may stem from the fact that participants develop a strategy for taking your test, not from age-related changes in cognitive abilities. Changes in performance due to the effects of repeated testing are referred to as *carryover* (see Chapter 9 for additional information on carryover). The solution to the problem of carryover is relatively simple: (1) Use multiple forms of a test to evaluate behavior at different times, or (2) use different tests that measure the same behavior at different times.

The second problem that results from observing the same participants over time is that other factors tend to arise and become confounded with age (Applebaum & McCall, 1983). For example, if evaluations of behavior are made at five-year intervals, it is not possible to say conclusively whether the changes observed were due to increased age or to some other factor not related to age. Campbell and Stanley (1963) call this a *history effect* that affects internal validity. An example may help to clarify this point.

Suppose you were interested in evaluating the strength of attachment between a parent and child. You choose a longitudinal design and evaluate attachment behaviors at two-year intervals. You notice a change in attachment. Is the change caused by the fact that the child has grown older or by other factors, such as a shift in attitudes toward children or increased use of day care (Applebaum & McCall, 1983)? It is difficult to know.

The longitudinal design suffers from a problem in which the prevailing attitudes at the time of behavior assessment may influence behavior as much as the change in chronological age. This problem is not as easily handled as is the problem of carryover. You might try to deal with it by including a large enough sample so that any effects of attitudes could be statistically controlled while you are evaluating age-related changes in behavior. However, such large samples of people who are willing to make a long-term commitment to a research project may be hard to find. Once found, those people may constitute a biased sample.

*Advantages of the Longitudinal Design*    Despite its disadvantages, the longitudinal design has an attractive quality. It permits you to see developmental changes clearly. You can witness the development of a behavior. This advantage may make the longitudinal design worth the rather large investment of time it takes to collect data.

Returning for the moment to the issue of changes in intelligence with age, longitudinal research indicates that intelligence for the most part changes very little with age. A few areas of intelligence, such as measures requiring reaction time or perceptual skills, do seem to decline with age. However, the large declines seen with the cross-sectional design do not emerge in the longitudinal data.

## The Cohort-Sequential Design

A disadvantage of the cross-sectional and longitudinal designs is their relative inability to determine whether factors other than age are influencing the observed changes in behavior. The **cohort-sequential design**, described by Schaie (1965), combines the two developmental designs and lets you *evaluate* the degree of contribution made by factors such as generation effects. However, the cohort-sequential design does not *eliminate* generation effects. It simply lets you detect them and consider them in interpreting your data.

Figure 10–12 illustrates a cohort-sequential design. Notice that the design embodies the features of both the cross-sectional and longitudinal designs. Along the vertical edge of Figure 10–12 is listed the year of birth. The participants making up one level of this variable (for example, 1980) constitute a *cohort group*. Specifically, a cohort group consists of participants born at a specified time. In our example there

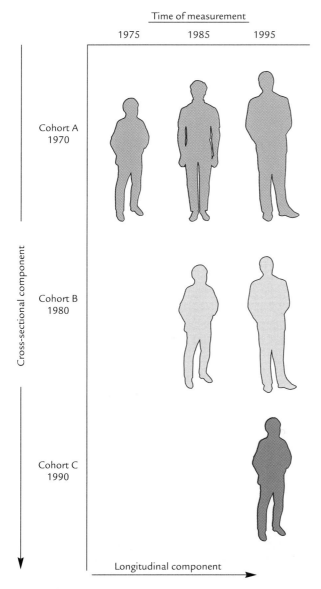

**FIGURE 10–12**  Example of Cohort-Sequential Developmental Design. Comparisons across time of measurement represent the longitudinal component, whereas comparisons across cohort groups represent the cross-sectional component of the design.

are three cohort groups: participants born in 1970 (Cohort A), 1980 (Cohort B), or 1990 (Cohort C). These three cohort groups constitute the cross-sectional component when comparisons are made across cohort groups. Along the horizontal edge of the figure is listed the time of measurement. The different measurement times constitute the longitudinal component when we look at a single cohort group across different times of measurement.

By comparing participants from different cohort groups of the same age (for example, comparing the data from five-year-olds across cohort groups), we can identify potential generation or cohort group effects. This design is thus useful for evaluating developmental changes in behavior while affording the capability to detect potentially important cohort effects. For a more detailed discussion of this and the other developmental research designs, see Applebaum and McCall (1983).

## SUMMARY

In cases in which a conventional nonexperimental or experimental design does not meet your research needs, you can use one of the various specialized designs available. The designs discussed in this chapter provide alternatives to conventional designs for specialized research situations.

The mixed design, also known as the split-plot design, combines a between-subjects and within-subjects design. This design allows you to assess the effects of variables that cannot be manipulated in a within-subjects manner due to irreversible carryover effects.

The nested design also combines the between-subjects and within-subjects designs. There are two ways to implement a nested design. First, you can nest tasks under different levels of a between-subjects variable. This is useful when you want to include more than one task under a level of an independent variable (for example, different lists of words to memorize). Second, you can nest groups of subjects under levels of a between-subjects independent variable. This is useful when you need to run subjects in large groups.

In some research situations, it is desirable to evaluate correlational variables and experimental variables at the same time. There are two ways in which you can add a correlational variable to an experimental design. First, you can include the correlational variable as a covariate. It is measured along with the dependent variable and then used to statistically "subtract out" the effect of the covariate from the dependent variable. Second, you can add the correlational variable as a quasi-independent variable. This variable resembles a true independent variable, but participants come already assigned to their particular level of the variable, rather than being assigned to it at random by the experimenter.

Quasi-experimental designs are useful when true experimental designs do not apply to a research situation. They make use of naturally occurring events (such as a change in law or a disaster) as a quasi-independent variable. You do not randomly assign participants to conditions, and in some cases you may not have appropriate control groups. Typically, the quasi-experiment suffers in the areas of both internal and external validity. You might consider using a quasi-experiment using the nonequivalent control group design to combat the problems of internal and external validity. However, you must take care when selecting groups for inclusion in this design so that validity is preserved.

Pretest–posttest designs are used when you want to evaluate the impact of some environmental change, such as a new company policy, or naturally occurring behavior, such as the productivity of the company's employees. Behavior is measured before and after the change. A major problem with this design is that participants may be sensitized by the pretest. The Solomon four-group design, a variation of the pretest–posttest design, allows you to test for pretest sensitization effects.

Developmental designs are correlational designs that examine changes in behavior that occur as a function of maturation and experience. The basic developmental designs are the longitudinal and cross-sectional designs. In a longitudinal study, a group of participants is followed over a period of time (weeks, months, or years). This design allows you to observe subtle changes in behavior but suffers from cross-generational problems, subject mortality, and high cost. In cross-sectional research, you study participants of different ages at the same time. This approach is less costly than the longitudinal design, but conceptual problems arise when a wide range exists between the youngest and oldest participants in your study. Generation effects may be a problem in this case. The cohort-sequential design, which combines elements of the longitudinal and cross-sectional designs, allows you to test for generation effects.

## REVIEW QUESTIONS

1. What is a mixed design, and when is it used?
2. What is a nested design, and when is it used?
3. What are the various types of nesting that can be done? Why would you use each?
4. When should you consider using a design combining experimental and correlational variables?
5. What is a covariate, and when would you use one?
6. What is a quasi-independent variable, and when would you use one?
7. What are the advantages and disadvantages of including a quasi-independent variable in your research?
8. What are the characteristics of the time series and equivalent time samples designs?
9. What are the advantages and disadvantages of quasi-experimental designs?
10. How are problems of internal validity addressed in quasi-experimental designs?
11. What is a nonequivalent control group design, and when would you use one?
12. What are the defining characteristics of the pretest–posttest design, and what are the design's strengths and weaknesses?
13. What is the Solomon four-group design, and why would you consider using it?
14. What are the defining qualities of the cross-sectional developmental design?
15. What are the advantages and disadvantages of the cross-sectional developmental design?
16. What are the defining qualities of the longitudinal developmental design?

17. What are the advantages and disadvantages of the longitudinal developmental design?
18. What is a cohort-sequential design, and when would you use one?
19. What are the advantages and disadvantages of the cohort-sequential developmental design?

## KEY TERMS

| | |
|---|---|
| mixed design | equivalent time samples design |
| nested design | nonequivalent control group design |
| covariate | pretest–posttest design |
| quasi-independent variable | Solomon four-group design |
| quasi-experimental design | cross-sectional design |
| time series design | longitudinal design |
| interrupted time series design | cohort-sequential design |

# Using Single-Subject Designs

The experimental designs described in the last two chapters require that one or more groups of subjects be exposed to the various treatments of the experiment. The data from each treatment are then averaged. The differences among the means are tested statistically to determine the probability that the observed differences could have arisen by chance through the operation of uncontrolled random factors. If this probability is acceptably low, the investigator concludes that the differences are reliable and attributes these differences to the effect of the independent variable.

This chapter presents a very different approach to conducting experimental research, one that focuses on the behavior of individual subjects. It does not depend on averaging across subjects to control the effects of random factors and, therefore, can be used with few or even only one subject. For this reason, the approach is often called the *single-subject* or *small-*n approach. If you have trouble with inferential statistics, you will be pleased to learn that this approach generally avoids them. This chapter describes the logic of the single-subject approach, indicates conditions under which the single-subject approach is appropriate or inappropriate, and identifies specific single-subject designs.

## A LITTLE HISTORY

A major goal of psychology is to understand human and animal behavior. Understanding a particular behavior means knowing what variables influence the behavior and what functional relationships exist between these variables and the behavior. To be useful to psychologists, this understanding must be applicable to individuals.

This emphasis on developing laws that can be applied to individuals dates back to psychology's beginnings as an experimental discipline in the latter half of the 19th century. The psychophysics of Weber and Fechner, the memory experiments of Ebbinghaus, the investigations of perceptual processes by the early Gestalt psychologists, and Wundt's examinations of "mental chronography," as well as the learning experiments of Thorndike and Pavlov, all focused on the behaviors of individual subjects in an effort to understand psychological processes. An extreme example is provided by Ebbinghaus's research, which employed but a single participant—Ebbinghaus himself.

The pioneering experimentalists managed to identify important psychological phenomena, and the functional relationships they uncovered, by and large, have withstood later scrutiny. This was all accomplished without the benefit of inferential statistics, which had not yet been developed.

From the beginning, these early researchers recognized the problems created by apparently random variations in the behaviors of their subjects. One solution to these problems was to repeat the observations many times under a given set of conditions and then average across observations to provide a stable estimate of the "true" values. Although inferential statistics had not yet been developed, researchers knew that estimates based on means become more stable with increasing numbers of observations.

The focus on individual behavior naturally led investigators to adopt a type of within-subjects approach that differs from that described in Chapter 9. In the traditional within-subjects design outlined there, each subject is exposed once to each level of the independent variable, and then scores are averaged across subjects. The method adopted by the early investigators exposed a single subject repeatedly to the different treatments, and then averaged across exposures within each treatment. The result was a functional relationship between independent and dependent variables that applied (strictly speaking) to the one individual from whom the data were collected. Functional relationships from different individuals were then compared to determine the generality of the relationships.

Despite intersubject variability, the approach worked because of three factors. First, a very large number of observations were collected from a single subject, thus allowing momentary fluctuations to average out. Second, to the extent possible, incidental factors that might contribute unwanted variability were rigidly controlled. For example, Ebbinghaus ate the same meal at the same time each day during the years he studied his own memory processes (Fancher, 1979). Third, the investigators focused their attentions on powerful variables whose effects could easily be detected against the remaining background of uncontrolled variability.

Of course, certain problems could not be attacked with this approach. These problems involved treatments that produced irreversible changes in subject behavior or that exerted very weak effects on the dependent variable or contained dependent variables that could not be stabilized through rigid control of experimental conditions. Such problems required an approach that could extract the relatively weak signal of the independent variable from the noisy background of random variation. Inferential statistics were developed for these cases.

The application of statistical techniques to the study of individual differences was pioneered by Sir Frances Galton (a cousin of Charles Darwin) in the late 1800s. The first correlational statistic was developed by Karl Pearson under the guidance of Galton and laid the groundwork for the application of statistical techniques to other problems in psychology.

The next major step in the evolution of the statistical revolution came in the 1920s and 1930s when Sir Ronald Fisher and other statisticians developed the rationale of inferential statistics to provide some of the first statistical tests. Soon researchers in psychology recognized that these statistical techniques provided powerful tools for dealing with uncontrolled variability. Inferential statistics were adopted, and the single-subject approach waned in popularity. By 1950 it was virtually impossible to publish research in a respectable psychological journal unless the data had been subjected to an appropriate statistical test and were judged to be reliable.

Meanwhile, some die-hard researchers persisted in using the old nonstatistical, single-subject approach. Most prominent among these was B. F. Skinner. Focusing his efforts on the effects of environmental stimuli on the motor behavior of rats, Skinner developed a highly controlled laboratory environment to observe and record selected behaviors of his subjects. Electromechanical equipment (such as clocks, relays, and switches) was used to gain precise control of environmental stimuli, to program the experimental contingencies, and to define and record the behavioral responses. Skinner and his students continued the tradition of observing and analyzing the behavior of individual subjects. In the process, they developed several methodological refinements that extended the power and usefulness of the single-subject approach.

Unfortunately for Skinner and his followers, their unwillingness to use inferential statistics to establish the reliability of their findings made it increasingly difficult for them to get their results published. In 1958 they attacked this problem by establishing their own journal, the *Journal of the Experimental Analysis of Behavior*, or *JEAB*. Eventually researchers using the single-subject approach were able to convince others of the validity of the method. Today the approach is widely accepted, and experiments using it can be published in most reputable psychology journals. Because the method specifically focuses on changes in the behavior of the single subject, it has gained widespread acceptance in applied situations, in which it has been used to assess the effectiveness of behavioral change programs and therapies in the treatment of individuals.

In 1968, the publisher of *JEAB* launched a second journal, the *Journal of Applied Behavior Analysis* (*JABA*), to publish single-subject research on applied problems. This research provides empirical support for the effectiveness of behavioral management techniques employed by practitioners of applied behavior analysis.

As this brief review indicates, single-subject designs have a long and respectable history and have emerged again into acceptance after being temporarily eclipsed by group-based designs.

## BASELINE, DYNAMIC, AND DISCRETE TRIALS DESIGNS

Although single-subject designs come in a variety of forms, all these forms can be categorized into one of three basic types: baseline designs (developed primarily by B. F. Skinner and his followers), what we will call "dynamic" designs, and discrete trials designs (the type used most often by early researchers). Today when researchers refer to "single-subject designs," they usually mean baseline designs. Dynamic designs, which are closely related to baseline designs, are less common but becoming more popular as researchers focus on understanding the dynamics (moment-by-moment changes over time) of behavior. Discrete trials designs are still in use, especially in areas such as psychophysics, in which the emphasis continues to be on the performances of individual subjects.

These three types of single-subject design are sufficiently different from one another to require separate treatment. The next sections describe the logic of baseline designs and indicate how to analyze and interpret the results obtained from such designs. We then focus briefly on dynamic designs. Finally, the last part of the chapter describes the discrete trials approach and examines the issues surrounding the use of statistical techniques with single-subject designs.

## BASELINE DESIGNS

The group-based experimental designs we have discussed in previous chapters depend on averaging to even out across the various treatment conditions the effects of any uncontrolled, extraneous variables on the dependent variable. You perform the experiment and then use inferential statistics to evaluate the significance of any differences in mean performance that do emerge between treatments. The statistical analysis is used to decide whether those differences are *reliable*. If the results are reliable, then you would expect to reproduce essentially the same results if you were to repeat, or *replicate*, the study.

In contrast to group-based designs, **baseline designs** do not rely on averaging to deal with uncontrolled variability. They focus instead on the behavior of a single subject both within and across the experimental treatments. Within a treatment condition, the behavior of interest is sampled repeatedly over time and plotted to create a **behavioral baseline**. This baseline typically changes over time as the effect of the exposure to the treatment condition develops and also in response to the effects of uncontrolled variables. For example, the baseline may rise for a time and then show no further change except for small, unsystematic fluctuations. The subject typically remains under a given experimental treatment until the baseline meets a **stability criterion**, which imposes an objective rule for deciding that the baseline has stabilized. When the behavior has stabilized in this way, the subject is then exposed to the next treatment condition, during which the baseline is again plotted until it becomes stable.

After the subject has been exposed to each experimental treatment, these conditions are then repeated. In the simplest case, the design would involve exposing the subject to two conditions: a **baseline phase**, to assess behavior in the absence of the treatment, and an **intervention phase**, to assess behavior during application of the treatment. The subject would be exposed to each of these phases twice, yielding what is called an **ABAB design**, where A and B represent the two phases. This immediate **intrasubject replication** of each phase allows you to establish the reliability of your observations within each phase. To the extent that your observations are reliable, the level of baseline observed under one exposure to a phase will be recovered during re-exposure to that same phase. In other words, intrasubject replication helps you to establish the *internal validity* of your findings.

When you move from baseline to intervention and then back to baseline, this return to a previous phase is termed a **reversal strategy** and is designed to assess whether any changes in baseline level produced by the intervention are reversible. If so, then you should be able to recover the original baseline.

Despite the name "single-subject design," most studies of this kind include more than one subject to provide what is termed **intersubject replication**. The purpose of intersubject replication is to establish the *external validity* of your findings. To the extent that different subjects show similar changes in baseline levels across the experimental conditions, you demonstrate that your effects are not unique to a particular subject.

Table 11-1 summarizes the characteristics of the single-subject baseline design.

## An Example Baseline Experiment

To illustrate the baseline approach to single-subject design, we describe a typical example, part of a larger experiment that investigated whether rats prefer a schedule of signaled shocks over an equivalent schedule of unsignaled shocks (Badia & Culbertson, 1972). The subjects were tested individually in a small operant conditioning chamber equipped with a response lever, a houselight, and a floor of metal rods that could be electrified to deliver a brief shock to the rat's feet. (The shocks are similar to static electric pokes and do not harm the rat.)

In the baseline phase, each subject received a series of "training" sessions to familiarize the rat with the characteristics of each shock schedule and to establish a behavioral baseline. At times the chamber houselight was off, and at other times it was on. When the light was off, shocks occurred unpredictably according to a random schedule at an average rate of one shock every two minutes (unsignaled schedule). When the light was on, shocks continued to occur on the same schedule, but each shock was immediately preceded by a five-second warning tone (signaled schedule). Each session provided equal experience with the two schedules.

---

**TABLE 11-1    Characteristics of the Single-Subject Baseline**

1. Individual subjects are observed under each of several phases. Multiple responses are recorded in a phase before the next phase begins.

2. Extensive observations are made during the baseline phase to establish a *behavioral baseline* against which any changes due to the independent variable are compared. A behavioral baseline will also be established during the intervention phase.

3. Each subject is observed under all phases, with each treatment phase repeated at least once. This repetition, or *intrasubject replication*, establishes the reliability of the findings.

4. Subjects usually remain in each phase until a *stability criterion* is met.

5. Multiple subjects may be included in the experiment. This *intersubject replication* helps establish the generality of the findings across subjects.

During the baseline phase, responses on the lever had no effect on conditions, but the number of responses during each session was recorded. At the end of each session, the percentage of responses out of the total possible was calculated and plotted to provide the behavioral baseline. The investigators continued to train each rat until three successive points on the baseline remained within a 10 percent range (stability criterion). The subject was then placed in the intervention phase of the experiment.

During the intervention phase, the rat was placed on the unsignaled schedule (identified by darkness). Pressing the lever now "bought" the rat one minute of time on the signaled schedule. The houselight turned on to indicate that the signaled schedule was now in effect, and any shocks that happened to be programmed during the minute were preceded by the warning tone. When this one-minute "changeover period" ended, the houselight was extinguished and the unsignaled schedule was automatically reinstated. At this time the rat could buy another minute in the signaled schedule by again pressing the lever. The number of "changeover responses" on the lever was recorded and, as in the baseline phase, the percentage of responses out of the total possible was calculated and plotted. Intervention-phase sessions continued until the stability criterion (three successive points on the baseline within a 10 percent range) was again met. The baseline phase was then repeated, followed by a second exposure to the intervention phase, to provide an intrasubject replication of each phase.

Note that the two shock schedules were identical except for the signal and that the rat could neither avoid nor escape the shocks. Would the rats nevertheless press the lever to get into the signaled schedule during the intervention phases?

The answer to this question can be found in Figure 11–1, which shows the level of responding during the final three sessions in each phase for each rat.

During the initial baseline phase (during which responses had no programmed consequences), the level of responding of each rat remained low, typically around 10 percent (see the first panel of Figure 11–1). However, note the dramatic changes that occurred when subjects were placed in the intervention phase: Response rates zoomed up to over 85 percent of possible (second panel). The subsequent return to baseline conditions produced an equally dramatic effect as response rates fell back to the low levels obtained during the first baseline phase (third panel). Finally, response rates jumped back to high levels when subjects were returned to the intervention phase (fourth panel).

The fact that response rates were high in the intervention phases would mean little without the comparison provided by responding in the baseline phase, when responses did not produce the signaled schedule. This comparison shows that response rates were high *only* when responses did produce the signaled schedule.

Badia and Culbertson (1972) concluded from this experiment that rats strongly prefer the signaled shock schedule over an equivalent unsignaled schedule, although it was unclear why. Evidently the signaled schedule contains a powerful source of reinforcement that was capable of generating high rates of responding during the intervention phase. The findings, which could not be explained adequately by known principles of conditioning, led to an extensive series of follow-up studies that sought to clarify the sources of reinforcement and their impact on preference responding (reviewed in Badia, Harsh, & Abbott, 1979).

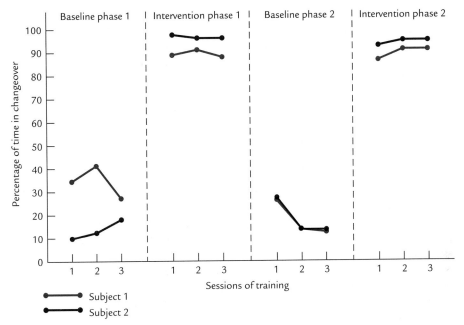

**FIGURE 11–1**    Results of a Single-Subject Experiment on Rat Preference for Scheduled Shock over Unscheduled Shock.
Source: Data from Badia & Culbertson, 1972, table 3.

## Issues Surrounding the Use of Baseline Designs

When using baseline designs, you may have to grapple with a number of issues. These include what stability criterion (if any) to adopt, how to deal with uncontrolled variability (unstable or drifting baselines), and how to cope with irreversible baselines.

*Choosing a Stability Criterion*    Systematic changes such as those due to learning or habituation show up in the behavioral baseline as trends toward increasing or decreasing values. Such trends usually occur immediately after a change to a new phase, when behavior is in transition from one stable level to another. Optimally, your stability criterion should guarantee that your subjects will remain in a given phase only until the baseline shows no further systematic changes, and no longer.

Choosing a good stability criterion is something of an art. If your stability criterion is too stringent, your baseline may never achieve it, and you will not be able to proceed to the next phase. Yet if your stability criterion is too lax, you may proceed to the next phase before your subject's performance has actually stabilized. As a result, your "stable" baseline values will not accurately reflect the effect of your independent variable. Developing a good stability criterion may require some pilot work in which you observe your baseline until it shows no long-term trends. You then attempt to identify a stability criterion that would have allowed you to stop sooner without including transitional data. In the example experiment, experience with the percentage measure used indicated that the baseline was likely to remain stable if the data remained within 10 percent across three successive sessions.

Because only the stable performances truly represent the long-term effect of an independent variable on the dependent variable, you usually report only the data that meet the stability criterion. This was done in the Badia and Culbertson (1972) example: Figure 11–1 omits the transitional data from the plot.

During the experiment, the only way to determine whether your baseline has met the stability criterion is to update your plot after each session and then examine it. If you fail to keep your plot current, you may discover, much to your surprise, that you have run your subject through another session under the previous phase when you should have changed to a new phase. As this is both a waste of time and a violation of experimental procedure, you can appreciate how important it is to keep the baseline up to date when using a baseline design.

*Transitional Behavior and the Stability Criterion*   By imposing a stability criterion, the single-subject baseline approach removes transitional data (when behavior is changing between stable levels) from the analysis. Of course, if the focus of the experiment is on transitional behavior, then using a stability criterion will not reduce the variability in the data of interest. However, it is still useful, as it indicates that the transition is over and you can stop collecting data within that phase.

*Stability Criterion versus Fixed Time or Trials*   The group approach encourages you to design experiments in which all subjects receive the same amount of exposure to each treatment. If some subjects reach stable levels of performance in the allotted time and others do not, then the data from each treatment will reflect varying mixtures of average transition rates and average levels of steady-state performance. Such differences between treatments may turn out to be statistically significant, yet misleading. Employing a stability criterion in such cases helps to ensure that the data will reflect terminal levels of performance for all subjects under a given treatment condition.

There are times, however, when it is important for experimental reasons to keep the amount of exposure to a given treatment constant across subjects prior to introducing the next treatment. In that case, you would probably choose to end the phase according to some criterion other than a stable baseline (e.g., after a certain amount of time in the phase). However, because you continue to monitor the baseline of each subject, you can determine how stable each individual's behavior was in the final stages of exposure to the phase.

## Dealing with Uncontrolled Variability

Within the single-subject approach, extraneous variables produce uncontrolled variability of the baseline within each phase. In the group approach, this variability is handled by averaging data across subjects, but in single-subject designs it is handled instead by tight experimental control. Uncontrolled variability can be reduced only if you can identify its sources. Consequently, the single-subject researcher makes an effort to identify the possible sources of variability. The first step in this process is to graph the data from each subject and look for uncontrolled variability in the baseline, which will be evident when the data points on your graph show moderate to high levels of instability across observation periods.

Of course, it is unreasonable to expect a given subject to show exactly the same pattern of behavior across observational periods, or to expect different subjects to display identical patterns of behavior in a given phase. You must decide how much variation is acceptable. If the observed variation is within acceptable limits, then you (much like the group researcher) consider the observed effects to be reliable. Unlike the group researcher, however, you may still be concerned with uncontrolled variation, despite the emergence of a clear relationship between the independent and dependent variables. In your next experiment, you would then take steps to bring this variation under control.

The difference between the single-subject and group approach is a philosophical one. The group approach assumes that if experimental controls fail to reduce uncontrolled variation, then statistical methods should be used to control it. The single-subject approach assumes that if experimental controls fail to reduce uncontrolled variation, then one should endeavor to identify the extraneous variables responsible for it and bring them under experimental control.

When extraneous variables contribute strongly to variation in the dependent variable, identifying them should help you to better understand the behavior in question. The single-subject approach strongly encourages you to identify these important sources of behavioral influence. The group approach does not do this, because the effects of the sources are hidden from view during the averaging process.

Of course, data collected across replications of a given phase usually will be similar, not identical. How similar do they have to be, and in what ways, before you can say that the results have been replicated? The answer depends on the degree of control you have over the dependent variable within a treatment condition (its stability) and on the questions the experiment was designed to answer.

If you have a relatively high degree of control over your dependent variable within a phase, variation in the baseline across successive observations will be minimal. Any effect of the independent variable will be clearly visible as a shift in performance upward or downward relative to this baseline. If each replication of a given condition produces levels of performance that overlap the levels observed in previous administrations of the same conditions, then the reliability of the data is unquestionable.

If your degree of control over the dependent variable is relatively low, the baseline will be variable and the effect of the independent variable will be more difficult to detect. Variation in baseline levels may occur both within and between replications of the same conditions. Variations between replications can occur both as a result of chance (the data points are varying and happen to be higher or lower during replication) and as a result of carryover. Nevertheless, changes in behavior induced by a particular treatment may be consistent in direction and approximate size.

Figure 11–2 shows an example of such a case. The graph indicates the percentage of study behavior during class for Robbie, a disruptive third grader (Hall, Lund, & Jackson, 1968). During the baseline phase, Robbie's study behavior fluctuated a fair amount but never exceeded 45 percent. When the teacher began to give Robbie special attention for studying (intervention phase), Robbie's study behavior increased dramatically. Withdrawal of the special attention (reversal phase) was ac-

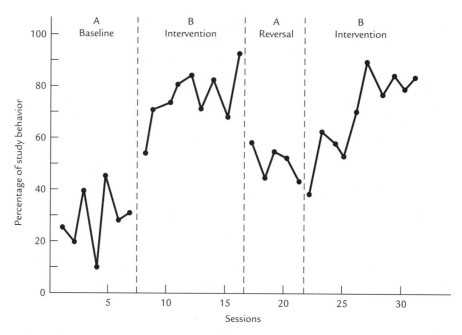

**FIGURE 11–2**    Percentage of Study Behavior during Baseline and Reinforcement Showing Intrasubject Replication.
SOURCE: Hall et al., 1968; reprinted with permission.

companied by a reduction in studying, but the original baseline was not recovered. The return to the intervention phase brought a gradual return to previous reinforcement levels.

In this example, the baseline obtained during the original baseline phase was not recovered during replication. Nevertheless, the change in response rates from the baseline phase to the reinforcement phase is similar on both occasions, and there is little doubt that this change is reliable, even if the amount of change is not.

Whether you would consider the intrasubject replication shown in Figure 11–2 successful would depend on your experimental question. If your question asked whether reinforcement increases the rate of studying, then the answer is yes, and the replication was successful. Studying increased relative to the baseline phase on both occasions. If your question asked by what amount studying increases, however, then the answer differs from first to second administration, and the replication was not successful.

## Determining the Generality of Findings

As previously noted, single-subject baseline designs use intersubject replication (typically with three to six subjects) in order to establish whether the findings generalize across subjects. Intersubject replication does not always succeed.

A classic example of a failure of intersubject replication was provided by Reynolds (1961). In this experiment, two pigeons were trained to peck at a translucent response key. Pecking on the key when it displayed a triangle against a red background led to occasional food reward. Pecking on the key when it displayed a circle against a green background led to nonreward. Both pigeons quickly learned to peck during triangle/red and not during circle/green. They were then tested to see how much they would peck at the key when it displayed each stimulus shape or color separately. One pigeon pecked when the key displayed the triangle but not when it displayed the red color, even though both stimuli had been associated with reward during training. The other pigeon pecked when the key was red but not when the triangle was present.

To explain this failure to obtain intersubject replication, several theorists have suggested that each bird must have attended to different aspects of the original stimuli on which they had been trained. Apparently, one pigeon must have focused on the shapes and the other on the colors. The phenomenon has been termed "overshadowing" and has been used to support theories of selective attention.

Note that although the intersubject replication failed in the Reynolds (1961) experiment, the failure itself revealed a general principle: Learning to discriminate a complex stimulus on the basis of one aspect of it blocks learning about other, equally predictive aspects. The fact that the two birds' key-pecking behaviors came under the influence of different stimuli within the compound stimulus suggests that uncontrolled determining factors were at work. These factors could be the subject of further research. Such factors tend to be hidden by the averaging process when a group approach is used.

Intersubject replication establishes the generality of results across subjects, but establishing the generality of findings across experimental settings requires a different approach. Results are usually double-checked in new experiments. These experiments build on the original findings while extending the range of assessed variables, the types of variables manipulated, and/or the kinds of subjects tested. For example, the patterns of responding generated under various schedules of reinforcement have been replicated by using such varied reinforcers as food, water, chocolate milk, and cigarettes, with such diverse subjects as goldfish, rats, pigeons, cats, dogs, monkeys, dolphins, and humans. Such extensions that incorporate aspects of the original experiment while adding new wrinkles are termed **systematic replications** to distinguish them from exact or **direct replications** (Sidman, 1960).

## Dealing with Problem Baselines

In addition to excessive uncontrolled variability, additional problems you may have to deal with in baseline designs include drifting baselines, unrecoverable baselines, unequal baselines between subjects, and inappropriate baseline levels.

*Drifting Baselines*    In some cases, it may prove impossible to stabilize a baseline against slow, systematic changes (drift). For example, during an experiment in which the dependent measure is basal skin conductance (a psychophysiological measure of arousal), conductance may gradually drift upward or downward as time passes during the experiment. If attempts fail to control this drift, you may be able to deal with the drift by effectively subtracting it out.

Figure 11–3 shows the results from a hypothetical ABAB experiment in which the baseline drifted systematically. Note that the baseline drifted gradually upward

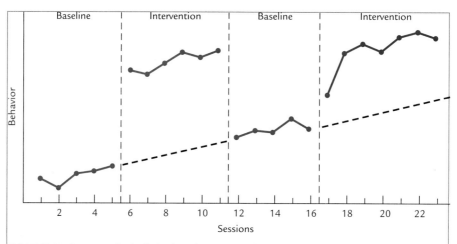

**FIGURE 11–3**   Hypothetical Single-Subject Data Showing a Drifting Baseline.

within each phase. Because the drift was consistent, it is possible to estimate the position (dotted lines) the baseline would have reached at any point during the experiment had the treatment not been introduced. The effect of the treatment is clearly discernible after allowing for the drift.

*Unrecoverable Baselines*     Another, potentially serious problem arises if baseline levels of performance cannot be recovered during reversal. Such changes are considered carryover effects, the familiar problem discussed in Chapter 9 that plagues within-subjects designs. Some carryover effects render the baseline completely unrecoverable (in which case it becomes impossible to conduct a successful intrasubject replication). Special designs are required to deal with such completely irreversible changes. A discussion of these special designs appears later in the chapter. Other carryover effects are less of a problem because they render the baseline at least partially recoverable.

Such partially recoverable baselines frequently occur when learning develops during a treatment condition. In a simple operant conditioning experiment, for example, rats may rarely press a lever during the initial baseline phase (before reinforcement is introduced). During the reinforcement phase, subjects learn that pressing the lever produces food, and the reinforcing effect of this contingency generates high response rates. Return to baseline conditions at this point often fails to produce a return to baseline levels of responding.

Despite the lack of reinforcement for lever pressing, the rats repeatedly approach the lever and press it in a series of widely spaced "bursts" of responding that are characteristic of extinction conditions. As a result, the rate of responding (although considerably lower than that obtained during reinforcement) remains somewhat elevated relative to the initial baseline rate. The rats are no longer naive concerning the potential result of lever pressing.

Partial reversals such as this present few problems for analysis as long as a clear, replicable change remains in the levels of performance across treatments. You may even be able to remove some such carryover effects by taking appropriate steps. For example, if partial reversal results from fatigue or adaptation, you can minimize the effects of these variables by providing rest periods between your experimental treatments.

*Unequal Baselines between Subjects*   In some cases, the baselines of different subjects in an experiment level off at very different values, even though the conditions imposed on the subjects are nominally identical. For example, after the same number of hours of deprivation, one rat may press a lever vigorously to earn a food reward, whereas another may respond in a lackluster fashion. These initial differences in response rates may then produce different rates of learning in the treatment condition and result in apparently different functional relationships, a failure of intersubject replication.

In this case, identical levels of deprivation generate different levels of motivation because physiological differences exist between the subjects. To reduce the differences in motivation, you may increase the level of deprivation of the rat with the lower response rate. A little experimentation may provide a level that produces response rates similar to those of the first rat. With the baseline rates equated, the two subjects may now perform similarly across treatments.

Because the dependent variable is repeatedly measured during the baseline conditions, such steps may be taken to fine-tune the baseline to meet desired characteristics of stability and comparability. If comparable baselines are established across subjects, achieving intersubject replication may become more likely.

*Inappropriate Baseline Levels*   Even if all subjects show similar baseline levels during the baseline phase, the particular levels obtained may not be useful for evaluating the effect of subsequent manipulations. A low baseline is desirable if you expect the treatment to increase the level of responding, but is clearly undesirable if you expect the treatment to *decrease* the level of responding. Studies of the effects of punishment on behavior fall into the latter category. Detecting any suppressive effect of punishment would be difficult if the dependent variable were already near zero before the punishment contingency was introduced. Similarly, you will not be able to detect a facilitating effect of a treatment on behavior if the baseline starts at a value near its ceiling.

The solution to these problems is usually obtained by adjusting the experimental conditions to produce the desired baseline levels. In the punishment experiment, for example, you might increase the baseline response rates by reinforcing responses according to a variable interval schedule. The schedule could then be adjusted to produce any desired level of responding. The same schedule would be maintained in the punishment condition. Thus, you could attribute any changes in the rate of responding to the punishment contingency.

## Types of Single-Subject Baseline Design

As yet, no widely accepted nomenclature exists to describe the wide variety of single-subject designs, although a few descriptive terms have emerged. This section differentiates among designs that manipulate a single independent variable (single-factor designs), those that manipulate two or more independent variables (multifactor designs), and those that measure several dependent variables (multiple baseline designs).

***Single-Factor Designs***    We have focused attention thus far on the ABAB design, which offers a complete intrasubject replication of the baseline (A) and intervention (B) phases of an experiment. Although less common, AB and ABA designs are also used. The AB design presents only a single administration of each condition and thus lacks intrasubject replication. Confounding by time-related factors is a serious problem with this design. The ABA design includes a reversal phase in which baseline conditions are reestablished after exposure to the treatment. This baseline reassessment allows you to determine whether the observed changes in behavior after treatment introduction were caused by the treatment. However, it lacks the final return to the B phase and thus fails to establish the recoverability of the baseline in the intervention phase. AB designs may be necessary if the intervention phase produces irreversible changes or (in an applied setting) if it is desirable to continue a treatment once it has been initiated. ABA designs may be appropriate if it is desirable to return the subject to preexperimental conditions prior to the termination of the study.

These basic procedures can be extended to include multiple levels of the independent variable. As in group designs, if these levels represent quantitative differences, the design is said to be *parametric*.

Using multiple levels of the independent variable presents certain problems for single-subject designs. Because only one or a few subjects are tested, completely counterbalancing the order of treatments across subjects is not usually possible. Instead, each subject may be exposed to the same order of treatments, but treatments will be presented repeatedly in different orders to assess the degree of carryover.

As an example of this counterbalancing strategy, consider a parametric single-factor experiment in which the three levels of the independent variable are A, B, and C. A single subject might be exposed to these treatments in the following order: A, B, A, C, B, C. This order provides transitions between close values of the independent variable (A–B, B–C, C–B), as well as a transition between distant values (A–C). Additional subjects might be tested with different orders. Note that this design provides a single replication of each treatment and thus represents a logical extension of the ABAB design.

If you must test a number of levels of your independent variable and are concerned about possible drift in your baseline, you may want to include a return to the baseline phase after each exposure to a treatment phase. Abbott and Badia (1979) used this technique with rat subjects. The experiment assessed the preference for signaled over unsignaled foot shocks. Signaled shocks were preceded by a warning tone, whereas unsignaled shocks were not. Subjects could choose to receive signaled shocks by pressing a lever. Each response produced one minute in the signaled shock schedule, identified by illumination of a houselight. At other times, unsignaled shocks were delivered.

The independent variable was the length of the signal, which was systematically varied across treatments from 0.5 second to 2.0 seconds (in half-second steps). Baseline response levels were collected during training phases, which also familiarized subjects with the signaled and unsignaled schedules prior to each test phase. Each

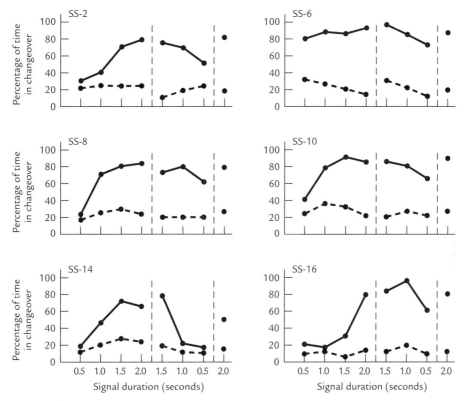

**FIGURE 11–4**  Results of an Experiment in Which Baselines (the dashed lines) Were Repeatedly Assessed. Each graph represents the performances of a single subject.
SOURCE: Abbott & Badia, 1979, p. 413; reprinted with permission.

training phase provided a given signal length and was followed by a test phase at the same length.

Figure 11–4 shows the results of the Abbott and Badia (1979) experiment. The dependent variable (percentage of time in changeover) reflects the number of minutes in the signaled condition "bought" by responses as a percentage of total session time. During training, the responses actually had no effect, but the number of minutes that would have been bought by these responses served to provide the baseline. The average percentage of time in changeover is shown across the final three stable sessions in each condition during the baseline (the black line) and testing (the red line) phases as a function of signal length. Each graph represents the performance of a different subject.

The levels of changeover responding during testing were low (with the exception of one subject) during initial testing at a signal length of 0.5 second. These levels increased as the signals were lengthened across treatments until they reached nearly maximum values. When signals were then shortened, responding tended to decline. These changes were not caused simply by baseline drift. This is shown by the fact that the baselines collected during training phases remained relatively low throughout the experiment.

Also note the failure to recover the original levels of responding on the final return to the 0.5-second signal length in four subjects (all but SS-6 and SS-14). This indicates that some carryover effects were present. Even so, the effect of signal length on changeover responding is clear. Shorter signals supported weaker responding than did longer signals.

*Multifactor Designs*    Single-subject designs can include more than one independent variable. As in factorial group designs, you can assess the main effects of independent variables and their interactions. Sidman (1953) provided an example of this design during an investigation of responding on the free operant avoidance schedule that bears his name. The Sidman avoidance schedule delivers a brief shock at regular intervals (for example, every five seconds) during the shock–shock (or S–S) interval. A response, usually a lever press, terminates the S–S interval and starts another interval, the response–shock (or R–S) interval. If the subject fails to respond during the R–S interval, a shock occurs and a new S–S interval begins. If the subject responds during the R–S interval, no shock is delivered, and the subject is returned to the beginning of the R–S interval. Thus, if the subject always responds during the R–S interval, all scheduled shocks can be avoided.

Sidman investigated the effect of varying the length of both the S–S and R–S intervals. Thus this experiment had two factors: length of the S–S interval and length of the R–S interval. Rats were exposed to several levels of each independent variable in every combination.

Figure 11–5 shows the results from this two-factor single-subject experiment. The figure shows the rates of lever pressing generated under each combination of S–S and R–S intervals. The graph shows portions of each condition in which the stability criterion was met. As you can see, the number of responses per minute was affected by the lengths of both intervals.

Because the data from multifactor single-subject experiments are not submitted to a statistical analysis, omitting some cells of the factorial matrix presents no special analytical problems. If the functional relationships between independent and dependent variables follow regular patterns (as is usually the case), then it is possible to "sweep out" the functions. You can do this by providing data points at well-placed intervals rather than at every possible combination of levels. Each subject must be exposed to every combination of levels for which a point is required. Using less than the full factorial number of combinations can result in considerable savings in the time required to complete the experiment.

*Multiple-Baseline Designs*    Some treatments cause irreversible changes in behavior and a special approach is required to deal with this problem. **Multiple-baseline designs** provide one solution. These designs simultaneously sample several behaviors within the experimental context to provide multiple behavioral baselines.

As an example, imagine you have developed a new technique for eliminating undesirable habits. You expect the changes it produces to be relatively permanent, so a reversal design is clearly inappropriate. You decide to use a multiple-baseline design.

To test your technique, you identify a few individuals who have at least two undesirable habits they wish to kick: smoking and excessive coffee drinking. You begin

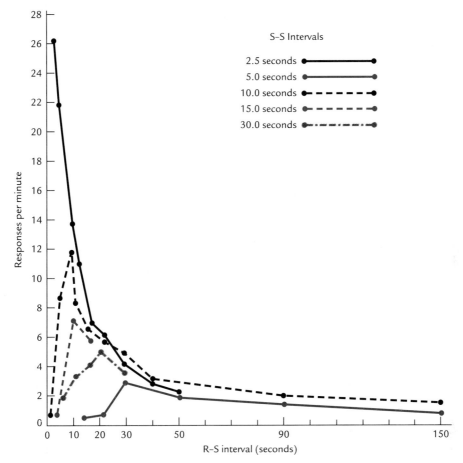

**FIGURE 11–5** Performance of a Single Subject in a Two-Factor Design in Which Both R–S and S–S Intervals Were Manipulated.
SOURCE: Sidman, 1953; reprinted with permission.

your study by simply observing and recording the frequencies of these two behaviors across a number of days to establish a baseline for each behavior. You then introduce your treatment but apply it to only *one* of the behaviors. For one subject you choose to attack smoking; for the other, coffee drinking.

The treatment appears to be successful. The treated behavior soon declines to levels well below the baseline. At the same time, however, the untreated behavior remains at its previous baseline levels. When the new levels of the treated behaviors stabilize, you begin to apply the treatment to the remaining behaviors. These, too, now decline to low levels.

Figure 11–6 shows the data from the hypothetical multiple-baseline study. Note that each behavior changes only after the treatment is introduced for that behavior. Which behavior is treated first apparently makes little difference.

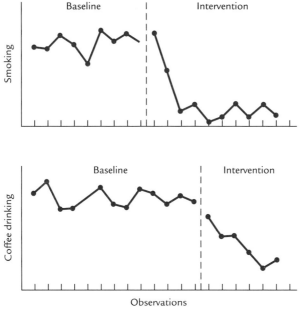

**FIGURE 11–6**    Results of the Hypothetical Multiple-Baseline Study. Both behaviors are collected simultaneously from a single subject.

The multiple-baseline design uses the untreated behavior as a partial control for time-correlated changes that may confound the effect of the independent variable. It is possible that the change in the treated behavior would have happened when it did even if the treatment had not been introduced. However, if this change was not caused by the treatment, the untreated behavior likely would have changed as well. In addition, the untreated behavior most likely would not subsequently change as soon as the treatment was applied to it.

For the multiple-baseline design to be effective, the behaviors chosen for observation should be relatively independent of one another. If the behaviors are correlated, then applying the treatment to one of the behaviors will affect both. Your ability to discriminate treatment-induced changes from changes induced by time-correlated confounding factors will be seriously hampered.

A nice example of a multiple-baseline design was provided by Stephen Camarata (1993), whose study involved working with young children who were having trouble pronouncing certain sounds. Camarata wanted to determine whether "naturalistic conversation training" would improve a child's ability to correctly pronounce these sounds. In this method, the therapist modeled the correct pronunciation following each error a child made during the child's natural conversations, without interrupting the conversation by asking the child to imitate the correct sound. For example, if the child said, "Here's a wope," during training of the "/r/" sound, the therapist might say,

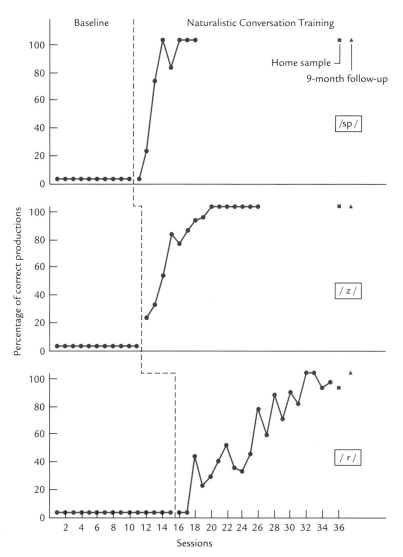

**FIGURE 11–7**   Percentage of Correct Consonant Production within Spontaneous Speech Production for Three Consonants for Participant BH.
SOURCE: Camarata, 1993; reprinted with permission.

"Yes, a rope" (Camarata, 1993). Two children were tested whose difficulties with pronunciation did not arise from hearing or oral motor problems.

Figure 11–7 shows the results for "BH," a boy just under four years of age, during baseline and following introduction of naturalistic conversation training that targeted three specific consonant sounds: "/sp/," "/z/," and "/r/." The data for each sound consist of the percentage of correct productions of the sound during a session, plotted across sessions. As Figure 11–7 shows, the percentage of correct productions was zero for all three sounds during the baseline phase. Training for the "/sp/" sound was initiated on the 11th session (top panel); by the 14th session, correct production had soared to 100 percent. Training for the "/z/" sound was initiated on the 12th session (second panel); correct production of this sound then began an immediate climb, also reaching 100 percent. Training on the "/r/" sound, initiated on the 16th session, produced a slower and more erratic improvement, but performance eventually reached 100 percent, or close to it, for that sound as well. In each case, the improvement began only after naturalistic conversation training had commenced for that sound, so it is unlikely that these changes are due to confounding by time-related factors such as maturation or experience outside the training.

## DYNAMIC DESIGNS

Although baseline designs afford the opportunity to examine moment-to-moment changes in behavior within each baseline or treatment phase, their primary use is to establish how behavior differs from one level of an independent variable to another in the steady state. Adaptation to new conditions may require time and experience; if so, behavior observed immediately after a switch from one treatment to another may not typify the stable pattern that may emerge after more extensive exposure to the new treatment. For this reason, subjects are kept under each treatment condition until behavior shows no sign of further systematic change.

This emphasis on steady-state behavior fosters the use of designs in which independent variables are manipulated in discrete levels, even when the variable itself is continuous. For example, the key-pecking behavior of pigeons may be examined at several widely separated levels of food deprivation (for example, 80 percent, 90 percent, 100 percent of free-feeding body weight). Subjects are maintained at each level of deprivation until their behavior stabilizes and then are moved to the next level. In such designs, behavior immediately following the change in level (described as *transitional* to distinguish it from steady-state behavior) can be observed to determine what has been called "behavioral dynamics"—regular patterns of behavioral change over time. A nice example of this approach is provided by William Palya, Don Walter, Robert Kessel, and Robert Lucke (1996), who investigated behavioral dynamics following an unsignaled step transition from variable-interval reinforcement to extinction in pigeons. To emphasize the regularities in these dynamics, the curves relating response rate to time following the transition were averaged across repeated transitions (but not across subjects). Figure 11–8 depicts the reinforcement rates and response rates as functions of time (in seconds) for four birds. The step transition to extinction occurs at 200 seconds in each graph. Each bird showed a rapid decrease in response rate, which began within seconds of the transition.

Step changes in the level of the independent variable may reveal interesting regularities in transitional behavior, but it may be at least as informative to record behavior during *continuous variation* of the independent variable, so long as the rate of variation is not so fast that the behavioral changes cannot "keep up," and so long as the changes are more or less reversible. Such a design lacks the discrete values of

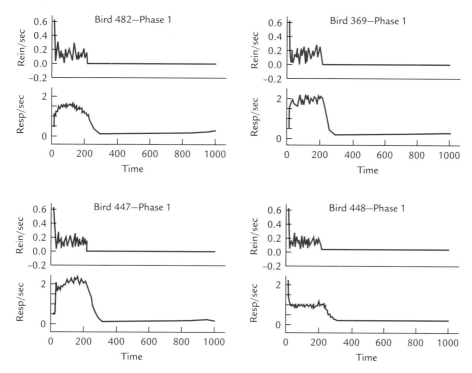

**FIGURE 11–8** Step-Transition Data from Four Pigeons.
Source: Palya, Walter, Kessel, & Lucke, 1996; reprinted with permission.

the independent variable that serve to distinguish the baseline and intervention phases of the baseline design, so, strictly speaking, it may not be appropriate to refer to studies using continuous independent variable variation as baseline designs. For this reason we have chosen to identify designs that include a continuously varying independent variable as **dynamic designs**.

A typical dynamic design was used in a "compensatory tracking" experiment described by Powers (1979). An individual participant was given the task of keeping a cursor (a short, vertical line) aligned with a target (another short, vertical line), which were simultaneously presented on a computer screen. Although the target remained fixed in position on the screen, the cursor could be moved left and right by manipulating a joystick. However, an invisible force or "disturbance" seemed to be acting on the cursor, causing it to drift erratically left and right on its own. To keep the cursor on the target, the participant had to compensate for the cursor's drift by moving the joystick.

The independent variable in this experiment was the disturbance, which varied smoothly and continuously in size and direction over a programmed range of values. The continuously monitored dependent variable was the position of the joystick. Together with the target position, these values were used to compute the moment-by-moment position of the cursor and the error (difference between target and cursor positions).

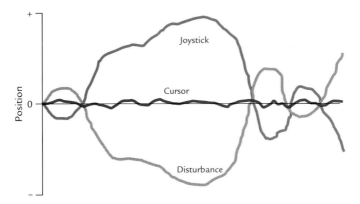

**FIGURE 11–9** Continuous Data from a Dynamic Design That Involved Using a Joystick to Keep a Cursor Horizontally Aligned with a Target Mark at Position Zero over a Period of 60 Seconds (see text). Horizontal scale indicates time; vertical scale indicates vertical distances from target mark.
SOURCE: Adapted from Powers, 1979; reprinted with permission.

Figure 11-9 shows the data from one 60-second experimental run. One line shows the variation in the disturbance (independent variable) over the course of the run. The second line shows the position of the joystick, scaled to screen coordinates. Notice how this line is almost a mirror image of the first. As the cursor moved in one direction, the participant had to move the joystick in the opposite direction in order to cancel out the cursor's movement and keep it over the target. The third line (which varies over a much smaller range than the other two) shows the position of the cursor relative to the target. The fact that cursor excursions were generally small shows that the participant was highly successful in keeping the cursor near the target. The data from such experimental runs were used to evaluate a mathematical model (derived from control theory) that used the moment-by-moment disturbance values to predict the participant's joystick movements. The joystick positions predicted by the model matched the observed positions almost perfectly.

Although we have distinguished between baseline and dynamic designs, it is important to understand the close relation between the two types. The Palya et al. (1996) design described earlier can be thought of as a baseline design involving discrete values of the independent variable. However, it also could be viewed as a dynamic design in which the independent variable changes as a step function, swinging instantly between extreme values. More important than the label you choose to describe the design is the kind of information the study was designed to collect. In the Palya et al. study, the focus was on the dynamics of behavioral change.

The method of continuously varying the independent variable while observing continuous, dynamic changes in the dependent variable has been used infrequently in the behavioral sciences but should become more common as interest in behavioral dynamics increases. In 1992, the *Journal of the Experimental Analysis of Behavior* devoted an entire issue (May) to the topic of behavioral dynamics. There you can find a number of examples of this continuous approach to single-subject research.

## DISCRETE TRIALS DESIGNS

Although baseline and dynamic designs can be powerful tools for discovering causal relationships in the single subject, they will not work in every experimental situation. Imagine, for example, that you are interested in studying the ability of an air traffic controller to detect a radar signal representing a single airplane in trouble (the "signal") against a radar screen full of radar signals from other airplanes (the "noise"). In one condition of your experiment, you present the target radar "blip" embedded within other radar blips ("signal plus noise," in signal detection theory terms). In the second condition, the target blip is absent (only the other radar blips are present— "noise only"). After each trial, your participant indicates whether the target blip was present on the radar screen.

Using the baseline approach, you should first expose all your participants to a series of signal-plus-noise trials. After every 50 trials, you calculate the number of yes responses and plot these numbers to provide the behavioral baseline. You then continue the signal-plus-noise treatment until the baseline stabilizes and then switch over to the noise-only treatment. Can you see any problem with this design?

If you said yes, you're right! During the signal-plus-noise treatment, your participant would soon begin to suspect that the target radar blip (the signal) was present on every trial. Before long you would discover that your baseline had jumped to 100 percent yes responses and would stay there, inducing a ceiling effect. The baseline would not provide a true reflection of your participant's ability to detect the target blip, because on many of the trials the participant would respond yes simply out of habit and not because the signal had actually been detected.

In such cases, the baseline approach must be abandoned in favor of a design that will discourage the participant from establishing a response set, as was the case in the previous example. Fortunately, such a design exists: the **discrete trials design**. Like baseline designs, discrete trials designs focus on the behavior of the individual participant (for example, your air traffic controller) rather than on group behavior.

### Characteristics of the Discrete Trials Design

Both the baseline and discrete trials designs seek to rigidly control extraneous sources of variance, to make the effect of the independent variable readily visible. Unlike the baseline design, however, the discrete trials design does not produce a continuous within-treatment baseline that can be adjusted and fine-tuned. Instead, behavior measured over a series of discrete trials must be averaged to provide relatively stable indices of behavior under the various treatment conditions. The major characteristics of the discrete trials design are shown in Table 11–2.

The single-subject designs commonly used in experimental psychology prior to the 1920s were generally discrete trials. They continue to be used today, especially in psychophysics (which studies the relationship between physical stimuli and the sensations they generate), as well as in some areas of human judgment and decision making.

An example of such a design is provided by an experiment on signal detection reported by Tanner, Swets, and Green (1956). The problem in signal detection is to determine how good a given observer is at detecting a signal that may be almost

---

**TABLE 11-2    Characteristics of the Discrete Trials Design**

1. Individual subjects receive each treatment condition of the experiment dozens (perhaps hundreds) of times. Each exposure to a treatment, or *trial*, produces one data point for each dependent variable measured.
2. Extraneous variables that might introduce unwanted variability in the dependent variable are tightly controlled.
3. If feasible, the order of presenting the treatments is randomized or counter-balanced to control order effects.
4. The behavior of individual subjects undergoing the same treatment may be compared to provide intersubject replication.

---

buried in noise. This is traditionally indexed by the observer's "hit rate," which is the proportion of trials on which the signal was present and the observer reported detecting the signal. However, the hit rate is affected by more than the observer's ability to separate the signal from the noise. It also is determined by the observer's *response bias*, or willingness to decide that a signal was present when he or she is uncertain about that. Observers with a "liberal" response bias will tend to guess "yes," whereas those with a "conservative" response bias will tend to guess "no." Guessing "yes" increases the hit rate, so, everything else being equal, those with a liberal response bias will *seem* to be better at detecting the signal than those with a conservative response bias. Thus, in traditional experiments, ability to detect the signal is confounded by response bias.

The Tanner et al. (1956) experiment was designed to eliminate this confound by separately measuring the observer's response bias and ability to detect the signal. Part of the strategy involved measuring not only the hit rate but also the "false alarm" rate. This is the proportion of trials on which the signal was *not* present and the observer decided that the signal *was* present. Guessing "yes" when uncertain not only increases the hit rate (on trials when the signal was present) but also increases the false alarm rate (on trials when the signal was not present).

In the experiment, two participants were exposed to a series of trials in which an auditory signal was either present or absent against a background of noise. On each trial, the participants were required to respond yes if they thought they heard the signal and no if they did not.

The participants' response biases were manipulated by systematically varying the probability of the signal being present on a trial. When the probability was low, participants would most often be right when guessing if they guessed "no," and therefore adopted a conservative response bias. When the probability was high, participants would most often be right when guessing if they guessed "yes," and therefore adopted a liberal response bias. In the experiment, the probability of signal presentation was systematically varied across days from 0.1 (1 out of 10 trials) to 0.9 (9 out of 10 trials). Participants received 300 trials per day and spent two days at each probability level.

Figure 11–10 shows the results for each participant. The figure depicts the "hit" rate (probability of saying yes when the signal was present) plotted against the "false alarm" rate (probability of saying yes when the signal was absent). The diagonal line represents the points at which hits equal false alarms, a situation that indicates no ability to detect the signal. Points falling above the diagonal indicate cases in which the hit rate exceeded the false alarm rate and thus demonstrate some ability to detect the signal above the noise. All points falling along the same curve indicate the same sensitivity to the signal, and curves lying farther above the diagonal indicate greater sensitivity than those lying closer to the diagonal. The position of a point along a given curve indicates the response bias, ranging from conservative (closer to the lower left) to liberal (closer to the upper right).

## Analysis of Data from Discrete Trials Designs

Analysis of data from discrete trials single-subject experiments usually begins by averaging the responses across the repeated presentations of a particular treatment. A large number of presentations helps to ensure that the resulting mean provides a stable and representative estimate of the population mean (that is, of the mean that would be obtained if an infinite number of trials could be given to the same subject under the treatment conditions). The means obtained from the different treatment conditions may then be compared to determine whether they appear to differ. This comparison may or may not include assessment through inferential statistics to determine whether the observed differences are reliable.

The analysis applied to the data of discrete trials single-subject experiments is usually determined by a theory or model of the behavior being examined. For example, in the area of human judgment and decision making, a lens model analysis has often been applied to data collected from single subjects. Another example is provided by the theory of signal detectability that provided the analytical model for the

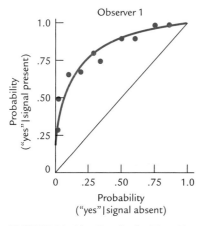
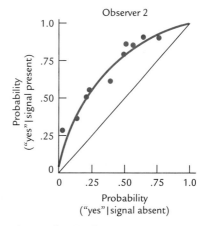

**FIGURE 11–10**   Results for Two Observers in a Signal Detection Study.
SOURCE: Tanner, Swets, & Green, 1956.

signal detection experiment previously described. Often these analyses yield a small number of descriptive statistics, such as the $d'$ (a measure of sensitivity) and $\beta$ (a measure of response bias) in signal detection. If a relatively large number of subjects have been tested, these descriptive measures (although derived from a single-subject analysis) may be used as data for a between-subjects analysis.

Used in this way, inferential statistics are not applied to analyze the data of an individual subject but rather groups of subjects. Recently some investigators have argued for the application of inferential statistics to single-subject data.

## INFERENTIAL STATISTICS AND SINGLE-SUBJECT DESIGNS

Those who advocate the application of inferential statistics to data from single-subject designs would not want to use them as a substitute for control over variables and replication. However, in some cases, they argue that the desired level of control is difficult to achieve (in some clinical situations, for example). For these cases in which the necessary control cannot be obtained, they suggest that inferential statistics may provide a solution.

If you choose to take this route, be aware that the usual statistical procedures developed for group designs cannot be applied to data from single-subject designs without modification, and even then problems may exist (Kazdin, 1976).

The most straightforward approach is to use the multiple observations taken within a treatment to provide an estimate of uncontrolled error variance (in group designs, this estimate is provided by within-treatment observations of multiple subjects). This estimate is then compared with the variance of scores between treatments to give an estimate of the probability that the treatment deviations were the product of chance (Chassan, 1967).

Unfortunately, this approach is upset by the serial dependency across data points. That is, scores from adjacent observations within a treatment are more likely to be similar to each other than to scores from more widely separated observations. This is similar to the problem of correlated scores that appears in within-subjects designs (see Chapter 9). For reasons not discussed here, it is a more serious problem for single-subject designs. Several ways to deal with serial dependency have been proposed, but none is entirely satisfactory. For a discussion of the general problem and a review and assessment of the available options, see Kazdin (1976).

## ADVANTAGES AND DISADVANTAGES OF THE SINGLE-SUBJECT APPROACH

A design that affords advantages in one arena often carries disadvantages in another. This section of the chapter explores some of the major advantages and disadvantages of the single-subject approach.

The main advantage of the single-subject approach is its focus on controlling error variance. By focusing on behavior of individual subjects (as opposed to looking at group means), you may better identify potential sources of error and control them.

On a related note, focusing on individual subjects may lead to a truer estimation of the impact of your independent variable. Individual patterns of behavior often reveal nuances obscured by averaging used in the group approach. (This issue is discussed again in more detail in Chapter 12.)

Single-subject designs in general (and baseline designs in particular) require that a single subject's behavior be followed over a relatively large number of observations. A perhaps extreme example was provided by an experiment conducted by one of the authors of this text (Abbott) in which the same rat subjects were tested in various conditions of the experiment for more than a year. This experiment included two independent variables. Each assessment phase was preceded by a training phase in which baselines were established. About nine days, on the average, were required to reach the stability criterion for the behavior, and each phase had to be replicated.

Of course, not many single-subject designs require this much time to test a subject, but most do require much more time than the equivalent group design would. This intensive investigation of the behavior of a single subject is both a strength and a weakness of the single-subject approach. It is a strength in that the long observational period often reveals nuances of behavior that might be missed in a short-term design. The ability to adjust and fine-tune the baseline over time provides an extended opportunity to identify previously unsuspected important variables. The intensive investigation is a weakness in that the strategy commits the investigator to a relatively long-term project that may be disrupted by uncontrolled factors such as illness or breakdowns of equipment.

On the bright side, even the breakdown of equipment can sometimes lead to new discoveries. Murray Sidman (1960) documented how a sticking relay in his operant conditioning equipment resulted in the accidental delivery of unavoidable shocks to a rat that had been successfully responding to an avoidance schedule. The baseline of responding had been stable, but now began to climb to high rates. The finding was unexpected and generated a whole new direction of research.

Another advantage of single-subject designs is the fact that causal relationships can be established by using as few as one subject. This is particularly important in clinical settings in which the objective of the research may be to identify an effective treatment for the behavioral disorder of a specific client. When more than one subject is used, the single-subject design permits the investigator to compare individual responses to the independent variable. Each subject may be found to exhibit reliable, yet idiosyncratic, responses to the same variable. Comparing subject-related variables may then suggest which differences between the subjects might be responsible for the differential responses. A design with only one subject may provide a good demonstration that a variable has an effect on behavior. However, to elevate the demonstration to the status of a general finding, the results should be replicated with additional subjects.

Another disadvantage of single-subject designs is that the design is inappropriate for many research applications. For example, potential carryover effects may confound the effects of the independent variable. If carryover effects are severe enough to cause irreversible changes, then the single-subject approach may have to be abandoned in favor of the between-subjects approach. In addition, some research questions simply do not lend themselves to a single-subject design. Much of the research in social and developmental psychology could not be run as single-subject designs.

Moreover, the results from single-subject designs sometimes are of limited generality. By tightly controlling the experimental situation to reduce error variance, you may be creating a highly artificial environment within which the behavior of interest is observed. For example, if you study the effects of positive reinforcement on the behavior of autistic children in a tightly controlled laboratory, you cannot be sure that your results will apply to autistic children in a hospital setting. In short, tight experimental control of extraneous variables increases internal validity. However, remember that when you increase internal validity you often reduce external validity.

A final disadvantage of the single-subject approach is that, despite all attempts to control extraneous variables, some variables cannot be easily controlled. Subject variables such as personality and intelligence cannot be controlled by tight experimental design. In research in which a homogeneous strain of rats serves as the subject population, this problem may not be important. However, when you apply single-subject research design to humans (such as in a clinical setting), these variables may come into play, and there is no easy way to eliminate their effects. The only option may be to measure those variables and statistically control their effects.

Consider single-subject research as an alternative to group-based research when appropriate. You should not try to fit every research question into a single-subject design. However, keep this option open when your research question could be best answered with a single-subject approach. Finally, even if you use a group design, you can apply some of the logic of the single-subject approach. Do not ignore individual subject behavior and look only at average performance. In many cases, looking at the scores of individual subjects within your experiment can help you to interpret your data.

## SUMMARY

Single-subject (or small-$n$) designs allow you to establish causal relationships among independent and dependent variables while focusing on the behavior of one or a few subjects. These designs work by collecting large numbers of observations of a subject's behavior within each treatment condition; rigidly controlling extraneous variables that might contribute to unwanted variability in the dependent measure; focusing primarily on relatively powerful independent variables whose effects (given the small amount of uncontrolled variation in the dependent measure) are easily detected by inspection of graphs; and repeating each treatment condition to establish reliability through intrasubject replication.

Single-subject designs dominated psychological research prior to the 1920s but were overshadowed by group-based designs following the development of inferential statistics. Experiments based on single-subject designs were difficult to publish in the past, but today the single-subject approach has regained wide acceptance. This acceptance has arisen especially in applied areas such as clinical psychology in which the primary interest is in assessing the effectiveness of therapeutic procedures on individual clients.

Single-subject designs fall into three broad categories: discrete trials designs, baseline designs, and dynamic designs. Discrete trials designs expose subjects to a series of trials, with each trial providing one exposure to a given treatment and yielding one score for each dependent measure. Each treatment is repeated a large number of times to provide stability to the treatment means. The resulting means may or may not be submitted to an inferential statistical analysis.

Baseline designs repeatedly record the subject's score on the dependent measure within each treatment exposure to plot a baseline for the behavior. Steps are taken to identify and control extraneous variables so that the variability and drift of the baseline are reduced to the minimum level. Usually the baseline must meet a stability criterion before the next treatment condition can be introduced. Each treatment is repeated at least once (intrasubject replication) to determine the reliability of the findings. If more than one subject is tested (intersubject replication), comparison across subjects is performed to establish the generality of results. Generality and reliability are also assessed through systematic replication. This replication examines the same independent and dependent variables under conditions somewhat different from those of the original experiment (for example, different species of subject or different reinforcer).

Baseline designs include single-factor designs (which include one independent variable), multifactor designs (two or more independent variables), and multiple-baseline designs (more than one dependent variable). Single-factor designs may be of the AB, ABA, or ABAB type. The AB type evaluates behavior during a baseline (A) condition and then in a treatment (B) condition. The lack of intrasubject replication makes this design subject to confounding by time-related factors and, therefore, undesirable. The ABA design controls time-related factors by adding a second baseline evaluation after the treatment evaluation. The ABAB design provides a complete intrasubject replication of the experiment. The ABAB design is preferable to the ABA design, especially if it would be unethical to end the experiment after returning the subject's behavior to an undesirable state in the second baseline evaluation. The ABAB design format can be extended for multilevel variables. When such variables are quantitative, the design is said to be parametric.

Multifactor baseline designs require that different combinations of the independent variables be tested across the study. A factorial design may be used (in which every combination is evaluated) or specific combinations of interest may be tested. In either case, each treatment is evaluated at least twice to provide intrasubject replication. These designs can become extremely time-consuming to conduct if the number of variable combinations to be tested is large.

Multiple-baseline designs provide a partial solution to the problem of irreversible treatment effects. Different behaviors are observed and a baseline established for each. The treatment is then introduced separately for each behavior in staggered fashion across time. The treatment is judged effective if the level of each behavior changes only after the treatment is applied to it. The multiple-baseline approach requires that each behavior be relatively independent of the others.

Dynamic designs are similar to baseline designs but employ a continuously varying independent variable. The behavior of interest is monitored continuously to determine the dynamic response of the behavioral system to the ongoing changes in the independent variable. Such designs focus more on transitions of behavior as opposed to the steady state.

Discrete trials designs are used in areas such as psychophysics, human judgment, and decision making, in which the interest focuses on the perceptual or decision-making abilities of individuals. Such designs often follow from a theoretical analysis of the behavior and yield descriptive statistics that are then evaluated in light of the theory. If a relatively large number of subjects are thus tested, the summary statistics from each subject may provide the data for a group-based inferential statistical analysis.

Some interest has recently been expressed in developing inferential statistics that can be applied to single-subject data. These statistics would be employed when the data cannot be stabilized or the independent variables are too weak to produce results that can be visually analyzed. A problem with such analyses is the serial dependency (or correlation) between successive observations of a single subject. Serial dependency seriously biases the traditional statistical tests (such as the *t* test or ANOVA). Despite attempts to deal with serial dependency, the various proposed solutions are controversial and not yet widely accepted.

Single-subject designs have both advantages and disadvantages. Advantages include the ability to obtain functional relationships that apply to a single subject, the avoidance of artifacts that may emerge in group studies because of averaging data across subjects with differing behaviors, the potential identification of new important variables while attempting to stabilize baselines, and the ability to conduct experiments with an extremely limited number of available subjects. Disadvantages include the length of time required to test each subject through all the conditions of the experiment (increasing the possibility of subject loss because of attrition or equipment failure), the inability to detect the effects of weak variables when behavior is not well controlled, the difficulty in assessing the effects of variables that cause irreversible changes, and possibly limited external validity.

## REVIEW QUESTIONS

1. How were single-subject designs used in the early days of behavioral research?
2. What are the major characteristics of the single-subject baseline design?
3. What is a behavioral baseline?
4. Why is it important to establish a behavioral baseline in a single-subject design?
5. What is a stability criterion, and why is it important?
6. What is an ABAB design, and how does it relate to intrasubject replication?
7. What is extrasubject replication, and what does it tell you?
8. What factors affect your decision concerning choosing a stability criterion?
9. How is uncontrolled variability handled in the single-subject approach?
10. How do the single-subject and group approaches differ with respect to handling uncontrolled variability?
11. How is the generality of research findings established in single-subject research?
12. What is a drifting baseline, and how can you deal with one?
13. What is an unrecoverable baseline, and what can you do if you have one?
14. What can you do if you have unequal baselines between subjects?
15. What can you do if you have an inappropriate baseline?
16. What are the characteristics of the single-factor baseline design?
17. What are the characteristics of the multifactor baseline design?
18. What is a multiple baseline design, and when would you use one?

19. What are the characteristics of a dynamic design?
20. What are the major characteristics of the discrete trials design?
21. How are inferential statistics used in single-subject designs?
22. What are the advantages and disadvantages of the single-subject approach?

## KEY TERMS

baseline design

behavioral baseline

stability criterion

baseline phase

intervention phase

ABAB design

intrasubject replication

reversal strategy

intrasubject replication

intersubject replication

systematic replications

direct replications

multiple-baseline design

dynamic design

discrete trials design

# Describing Data

Chapters 1 through 11 have explored how to design and conduct research. Once you have conducted your research, the next step is to organize, summarize, and describe your data. This chapter reviews strategies you can use to effectively organize, summarize, and describe data. The sections on descriptive statistics are intended to provide a brief review of these statistics. Computation is addressed in this chapter only where necessary to explain a particular statistic. If you need more information on these statistics, see one of the many introductory statistics texts available (such as Gravetter & Wallnau, 2004, or Pagano, 2004).

## DESCRIPTIVE STATISTICS
## AND EXPLORATORY DATA ANALYSIS

Although descriptive statistics are commonly used to address the specific questions you had in mind when you designed your study, they also can be employed to help you discover important but perhaps hidden patterns in your data that may shed additional light on the problems you are interested in resolving. The search for such patterns in your data is termed **exploratory data analysis (EDA)**. Over the past 30 years or so, a whole new set of descriptive tools has been developed to aid you in this search, many of which are graphical in nature.

When research has been designed to answer a specific question or set of questions, there is a strong temptation to rush directly to the inferential statistical techniques that will assess the "statistical significance" of the findings and to request only those descriptive statistics related directly to the analysis, such as group means, standard deviations, and standard errors. Resist this temptation. As we explain in Chapter 13, many of the most commonly used inferential statistics make certain crucial assumptions about the populations from which the scores in your data set were drawn. If these assumptions are violated, the results of the statistical analysis may be misleading. Some exploratory techniques help you to spot serious defects in your data that may warrant taking corrective action before you proceed to the inferential analysis. Others help you to determine which summary statistics would be appropriate for a given set of data. Still others may reveal unsuspected influences. In this chapter, we introduce you to a number of descriptive tools (both numerical and graphical) for describing data and revealing secrets that hide within.

## ORGANIZING YOUR DATA

Before you can interpret your data, you must first organize and summarize them. How you organize your data depends on your research design (whether you have conducted a survey, observational study, or experiment), on how many variables were observed and recorded, and on how observations were grouped or subdivided. A few representative examples follow.

For *survey data*, a data summary sheet like that shown in Figure 12–1 would be appropriate. The data are organized into a series of columns, one for numbering the respondents, one for each question asked, and one for each demographic item. To save space, the identifiers over the columns should be kept short. Here, we have simply labeled each question Q1, Q2, and so on. If space permits, you may invent more descriptive labels. Each row gives the data for one respondent. In the example, certain demographic variables have been dummy-coded. **Dummy codes** identify category values as numbers (for example, sex of respondent: 1 = female, 2 = male). If the computer program you are using accepts and can use category names, you need not dummy-code these variables. If it does not, you will have to use dummy coding.

Data sheets like the one shown in Figure 12–1 may go on for pages. A good strategy is to lay out your first data sheet and, before entering any data, copy it. In this way you avoid having to enter the column and row labels by hand on each new page. In addition, you should make out a single "key" or "code sheet" that describes the scale(s) used for the questions, gives a fuller description of the question or variable in each column, and indicates what each dummy code represents. Figure 12–2 shows the code sheet that accompanied the data sheet shown in Figure 12–1. The code sheet shows the Likert-scale codes used in conjunction with each attitude item, the five attitude statements, the three demographic items, and the dummy codes used to represent the category values of sex, marital status, and time of class attendance.

Experimental or quasi-experimental designs break down the dependent variable according to treatments or categories. You can organize data from these designs in two distinct ways. One way (called an *unstacked format*) is to create a separate column for the scores from each treatment. Figure 12–3 shows a simple summary sheet organized in this way for a 2 × 2 within-subjects factorial experiment. The subject numbers appear in the leftmost column. Because each subject was exposed to all the treatments, only one column of subject numbers was needed. Reserve space at the bottom of the data summary sheet for column summary statistics, such as the mean and standard deviation. You can enter these after you have analyzed the data.

The second way to organize your data is to use a *stacked format*. In this format you create one column for the participant IDs, a column for the treatment levels (dummy-coded), and a column for each dependent variable. Figure 12–4 redisplays a

| Resp. | Q1 | Q2 | Q3 | Q4 | Q5 | Sex | Age | Marit. | Time |
|---|---|---|---|---|---|---|---|---|---|
| 1 | 3 | 4 | 4 | 4 | 2 | 2 | 25 | 2 | 1 |
| 2 | 4 | 3 | 5 | 5 | 2 | 1 | 20 | 2 | 3 |
| 3 | 3 | 3 | 4 | 4 | 3 | 1 | * | 1 | 1 |
| 4 | 1 | 4 | 4 | 4 | 2 | 2 | 22 | 2 | 1 |
| 5 | 3 | 4 | 4 | 4 | 2 | 2 | 29 | 1 | 3 |
| 6 | 3 | 3 | 4 | 4 | 3 | 1 | 19 | 2 | 1 |
| 7 | 2 | 4 | 3 | 4 | 1 | 2 | 19 | 2 | 1 |
| 8 | 2 | 4 | 4 | 5 | 4 | 2 | 25 | 2 | 3 |
| 9 | 2 | 3 | 3 | 3 | 3 | 1 | 21 | 2 | 1 |
| 10 | 2 | 3 | 2 | 3 | 3 | 2 | 20 | 2 | 1 |
| 11 | 4 | 3 | 4 | 4 | 3 | 2 | 18 | 2 | 3 |
| 12 | 3 | 4 | 2 | 2 | 3 | 2 | 20 | 2 | 1 |
| 13 | 2 | 2 | 5 | 5 | 2 | 2 | 22 | 2 | 2 |
| 14 | 3 | 3 | 4 | 4 | 2 | 1 | 20 | 2 | 1 |
| 15 | 2 | 5 | 3 | 4 | 2 | 1 | 18 | 6 | 1 |
| 16 | 3 | 4 | 4 | 4 | 2 | 2 | 19 | 2 | 1 |
| 17 | 2 | 3 | 4 | 4 | 1 | 2 | 18 | 2 | 1 |
| 18 | 3 | 3 | 5 | 5 | 3 | 1 | 22 | 1 | 3 |
| 19 | 4 | 4 | 4 | 4 | 2 | 1 | 22 | 2 | 3 |
| 20 | 3 | 4 | 4 | 5 | 3 | 2 | 23 | 2 | 3 |
| 21 | 3 | 4 | 4 | 4 | 3 | 1 | 19 | 2 | 1 |
| 22 | 2 | 4 | 4 | 4 | 2 | 1 | 21 | 2 | 1 |
| 23 | 3 | 3 | 4 | 4 | 1 | 2 | 20 | 2 | 1 |
| 24 | 3 | 4 | 2 | 4 | 2 | 1 | 21 | 2 | 3 |
| 25 | 3 | 3 | 4 | 2 | 2 | 2 | 24 | 2 | 1 |
| 26 | 2 | 3 | 4 | 4 | 3 | 1 | 23 | 2 | 3 |
| 27 | 2 | 4 | 1 | 1 | 3 | 2 | 27 | 1 | 3 |
| 28 | 3 | 4 | 3 | 3 | 3 | 1 | 24 | 1 | 3 |
| 29 | 2 | 3 | 2 | 4 | 3 | 2 | 23 | 2 | 3 |
| 30 | 3 | 3 | 4 | 4 | 3 | 2 | 21 | 2 | 3 |
| 31 | 3 | 4 | 4 | 4 | 3 | 2 | 20 | 2 | 1 |
| 32 | 4 | 4 | 5 | 5 | 2 | 1 | 21 | 2 | 1 |
| 33 | 2 | 4 | 3 | 4 | 2 | 1 | 24 | 1 | 1 |
| 34 | 2 | 3 | 2 | 4 | 3 | 1 | 24 | 2 | 1 |
| 35 | 1 | 2 | 4 | 4 | 4 | 2 | 31 | 3 | 2 |
| 36 | 2 | 4 | 5 | 5 | 3 | 1 | 26 | 2 | 3 |

**FIGURE 12–1**    Example Data Summary Sheet for Survey Data (* = missing data).

portion of the data of Figure 12–3 in this way. The stacked format works better than the unstacked format when your data include multiple independent or dependent variables. These are easily accommodated by including additional columns to indicate the treatment levels or observed values of the additional variables. Also, many

*Sexual Harassment Survey Fall 1994*

*Attitude Items*                                    Likert Scale:
                                                    1. Strongly disagree
                                                    2. Disagree
                                                    3. Neither agree nor disagree
                                                    4. Agree
                                                    5. Strongly agree

1. Sexual harassment is a problem at IPFW.
2. The antiharassment policy at IPFW fills a need.
3. Males are more likely to harass than females are.
4. Women are more often victims of harassment than men are.
5. IPFW's antiharassment policy interferes with my right of
   free speech.

*Demographic Items*

    Sex          1. Female
                 2. Male

    Marital      1. Married
    status       2. Single
                 3. Divorced
                 4. Widowed
                 5. Cohabitating
                 6. Other

    Time         Do you take classes mainly in the
                 1. Daytime
                 2. Evening
                 3. Both

**FIGURE 12–2**    Code Sheet for the Data Summary Sheet of Figure 12-1.

computer statistical analysis packages expect the data to be entered in this format. A disadvantage of the stacked format is that, unlike the unstacked format, it does not provide a simple way to display treatment summary statistics.

More complex designs involving several independent and/or quasi-independent variables can be accommodated within either format. Figure 12–5 displays data in unstacked format from individual subjects for a 2 × 4 between-subjects design in a study by Bordens and Horowitz (1986). Each column provides the data from one treatment. In this two-factor between-subjects design, each treatment represented one level of "Charges Judged" (the first independent variable) combined with one of the four levels

**FIGURE 12–3**  Data Summary Sheet for a
2 × 2 Within-Subjects Factorial Experiment
(unstacked format).

| Subject number | Words/3 sec | Words/18 sec | CCCs/3 sec | CCCs/18 sec |
|---|---|---|---|---|
| 1 | 19 | 19 | 16 | 16 |
| 2 | 18 | 17 | 16 | 06 |
| 3 | 19 | 14 | 20 | 14 |
| 4 | 19 | 16 | 15 | 14 |
| 5 | 19 | 15 | 19 | 13 |
| 6 | 19 | 17 | 13 | 07 |
| 7 | 20 | 20 | 18 | 13 |
| 8 | 19 | 19 | 14 | 06 |
| 9 | 20 | 19 | 17 | 14 |
| 10 | 18 | 13 | 05 | 02 |
| 11 | 19 | 16 | 14 | 11 |
| 12 | 18 | 17 | 08 | 02 |
| 13 | 18 | 13 | 11 | 00 |
| 14 | 16 | 06 | 11 | 03 |
| 15 | 20 | 16 | 13 | 15 |
| 16 | 20 | 17 | 15 | 12 |
| 17 | 20 | 16 | 16 | 10 |
| 18 | 20 | 17 | 14 | 07 |
| 19 | 18 | 15 | 12 | 08 |
| 20 | 20 | 19 | 16 | 07 |
| 21 | 20 | 20 | 18 | 15 |
| 22 | 20 | 16 | 19 | 15 |
| 23 | 19 | 20 | 18 | 19 |
| 24 | 20 | 20 | 19 | 18 |
| 25 | 16 | 10 | 07 | 03 |
| 26 | 20 | 19 | 06 | 06 |
| 27 | 19 | 17 | 18 | 14 |
| 28 | 17 | 19 | 17 | 11 |
| 29 | 19 | 17 | 17 | 11 |
| 30 | 20 | 15 | 14 | 13 |
| 31 | 19 | 19 | 14 | 08 |
| 32 | 20 | 17 | 19 | 17 |
| 33 | 19 | 14 | 07 | 00 |
| 34 | 20 | 14 | 16 | 10 |

of "Charges Filed" (the second independent variable). The bottom two rows display
summary measures (the mean and standard deviation) for each treatment.

A useful data summary sheet must be clearly labeled. Note that the columns of
data in Figure 12–5 are clearly labeled with the levels of the independent variable in
effect for each group. The top headings indicate the two levels of charges judged.
The second level of headings indicates the level of charges filed as appropriate to
each group.

| Subject number | Item type (1 = word, 2 = ccc) | Retention interval (1 = 3s, 2 = 18s) | Number correct |
|---|---|---|---|
| 1 | 1 | 1 | 19 |
| 1 | 1 | 2 | 19 |
| 1 | 2 | 1 | 16 |
| 1 | 2 | 2 | 16 |
| 2 | 1 | 1 | 18 |
| 2 | 1 | 2 | 17 |
| 2 | 2 | 1 | 16 |
| 2 | 2 | 2 | 06 |
| 3 | 1 | 1 | 19 |
| 3 | 1 | 2 | 14 |
| 3 | 2 | 1 | 20 |
| 3 | 2 | 2 | 14 |
| 4 | 1 | 1 | 19 |
| 4 | 1 | 2 | 16 |
| 4 | 2 | 1 | 15 |
| 4 | 2 | 2 | 14 |
| 5 | 1 | 1 | 19 |
| 5 | 1 | 2 | 15 |
| 5 | 2 | 1 | 19 |
| 5 | 2 | 2 | 13 |
| 34 | 1 | 1 | 20 |
| 34 | 1 | 2 | 14 |
| 34 | 2 | 1 | 16 |
| 34 | 2 | 2 | 10 |

**FIGURE 12-4**   Data Summary Sheet for the Same Data as Shown in Figure 12-3, Presented in Stacked Format.

The organization just described works well for a 2 × 4 factorial experiment and can be expanded to handle more levels of each factor or more factors. Other designs may require a different organization.

## Organizing Your Data for Computer Entry

If you are going to submit your data to computer analysis, you should find out how the statistical analysis package you intend to use expects the data to be organized. Many packages require the data to be entered in stacked format, some require the unstacked format, and some will accept either. For example, a popular product called Minitab™ allows you to *enter* data in either format but may require one or the other, depending on the analysis requested. Certain commands allow you to change formats as required.

If you have not already done so on your original data sheets, you may have to code your variables before entering the data into the computer. Most computer programs

| | Charges Judged | | | | | | | |
|---|---|---|---|---|---|---|---|---|
| | One Charge | | | | Two Charges | | | |
| Charges Filed | 1 | 2 | 3 | 4 | 1 | 2 | 3 | 4 |
| | 3 | 5 | 6 | 2 | 6 | 3 | 4 | 5 |
| | 3 | 4 | 3 | 4 | 4 | 5 | 6 | 5 |
| | 3 | 4 | 4 | 5 | 4 | 5 | 4 | 5 |
| | 4 | 4 | 4 | 5 | 5 | 5 | 5 | 6 |
| | 4 | 5 | 5 | 5 | 4 | 4 | 5 | 5 |
| | 3 | 3 | 5 | 5 | 5 | 5 | 4 | 4 |
| | 2 | 3 | 4 | 5 | 5 | 4 | 4 | 5 |
| | 5 | 4 | 5 | 4 | 3 | 5 | 5 | 5 |
| | 6 | 4 | 3 | 6 | 3 | 5 | 5 | 6 |
| | 5 | 5 | 4 | 6 | 5 | 3 | 6 | 6 |
| Mean | 3.8 | 4.1 | 4.3 | 4.7 | 4.4 | 4.4 | 4.8 | 5.2 |
| Standard Deviation | 1.23 | 0.74 | 0.95 | 1.16 | 0.97 | 0.84 | 0.79 | 0.63 |

**FIGURE 12–5**  Data Summary Sheet for a 2 × 4 Between-Subjects Design.
SOURCE: Bordens & Horowitz, 1986.

look for a numeric or alphabetic code to determine the levels or values of your independent and dependent variables. You must decide how to code these variables.

Coding independent variables involves assigning values to corresponding levels. For a quantitative independent variable (for example, number of milligrams of a drug), simply record the number of milligrams administered to subjects in each treatment group (for example, 10, 20, or 30) on your coding sheet. For qualitative independent variables, you must assign an arbitrary number to each level. For example, if your independent variable were the loudness of a tone in an auditory discrimination experiment (low, moderate, and high), you might code the levels as 1 = low, 2 = moderate, 3 = high. As noted, this assignment of numbers to qualitative independent variables is called *dummy coding*.

For quantitative data (for example, if your participants rated the intensity of a sound on a scale ranging from 0 to 10), simply transfer each participant's score to your coding sheet. If, however, your dependent measure were qualitative (yes/no, for example), you must dummy-code your dependent variable. For example, you could code all yes responses as 1 and all no responses as 2.

When coding your dependent variables, transfer the data (numeric or dummy-coded) to your coding sheet exactly as they are. Don't be concerned with creating new variables (for example, by adding together existing ones) or with making special categories. Most computer programs have commands that let you manipulate data in a variety of ways (for example, adding numbers, doing data transformations such as a log transformation, and so on). So don't waste time creating new variables when preparing your data for input.

## Entering Your Data

Compared to the dark ages of computer data analysis, where data entry was a nightmare involving coding data onto punch cards, entering data for computer analysis is relatively easy. Modern PC-based versions of statistical software (such as SPSS) have easy-to-use spreadsheet interfaces that allow you to enter data quickly and make corrections easily. If you don't like the data entry provision in a particular program, many programs allow you to enter your data into a stand-alone spreadsheet program such as Microsoft's *Excel*. The spreadsheet file can then be read into the statistical program's data editor.

You can make data entry easier by organizing your data-coding sheet the way your data editor expects the data to be entered. For example, if your data will be entered one column at a time, organize the data into columns on the sheet. Then simply read down the columns while entering your data.

Errors climb when fatigue sets in, so if you are entering a large amount of data, take frequent breaks. Be sure to save any data you have entered before you leave the keyboard.

Speaking of saving data, nothing can be more frustrating than spending half an hour entering data, only to have them obliterated by an unexpected power failure. You can minimize your losses on such occasions by *frequently saving your data to disk*. Also, don't forget to save your data before you turn off the computer or exit from the data editor. Any data you fail to save will be lost. At this time, you also should make a backup copy of your data on another disk. Then, if your original disk fails, you will still be able to retrieve your data from the backup.

When you save your data to disk, you create a *data file* from which the data will be read when the computer conducts your analysis. When you save the file, the computer will ask you to type in a file name under which the data will be saved. Try to think of a descriptive file name that will uniquely identify the data. When you have several data files on the same disk, using descriptive file names makes it easier to find the correct file.

After you have entered your data, check for errors. Because the computer cannot detect incorrectly entered data, it is up to you to catch any mistakes if you are to avoid invalid results. If you have had someone else enter the data for you, don't assume that the other person has already done the checking.

## Grouped versus Individual Data

After you have organized your data into a coherent format, you must decide on a basic descriptive strategy. In some cases, you may want to summarize your data by averaging scores for each group. In other cases, you may want to focus on the scores of individual subjects. Either strategy is valid, but each has its own advantages and disadvantages.

*Grouped Data*    The major advantage of grouped data is convenience. When you calculate an average, you have one score that characterizes an entire distribution. You then can refer to the performance of subjects in a group by citing the average performance. If your data will be submitted to a statistical analysis based on treat-ment means, you will be treating your data in this way.

Although convenient, the grouped method does have two important limitations. First, the average score may not represent the performance of individual subjects in a group. An average score of 5 can result if all 10 subjects in a group scored 5, or if half scored 0 and half scored 10. In the former case, the average accurately reflects the in-dividual performance of each subject. In the latter case, however, it does not. This idea is examined in more detail during the discussion of the mean.

The second limitation of using grouped data is that a curve resulting from plot-ting averaged data may not reflect the true nature of the psychological phenomenon being studied. In a learning experiment, for example, in which rats must meet a learn-ing criterion (e.g., three consecutive error-free trials), a graph showing how the group average changes across trials might suggest that learning is a gradual process. Inspec-tion of graphs of each individual subject's behavior might tell a different story. It might be that each rat takes a different number of trials to reach the learning cri-terion. However, once the criterion is reached, the rat never makes another error. Such a pattern of data would suggest that learning is an all-or-none proposition resulting in an abrupt shift from not having learned the task to having learned the task perfectly.

*Individual Data*   Examining individual scores makes the most sense when you have repeated measures of the same behavior. Inspecting individual data also can be useful when the phenomenon under study is an either–or proposition (for example, some-thing was learned or not, or a stimulus was detected or not). In some cases, the indi-vidual data may reflect the effect of the independent variable more faithfully than data averaged over the group.

*Using Grouped and Individual Data Together*   Researchers too often fall into the pattern of collecting data and then calculating an average without considering the individual scores constituting the average. A good strategy to adopt is to look at both the grouped and individual data. When you have repeated measures of the same be-havior, examining individual data shows how each subject performed in your study. This may provide insights into the psychological process being studied that are not afforded by grouping data.

When you collect only a single score for each subject, you should still examine the distribution of individual scores. This usually entails plotting the individual scores on a graph and carefully inspecting the graph.

## GRAPHING YOUR DATA

Whether you have chosen a grouped or individual strategy for dealing with your data, you will often find it beneficial to plot your data on a graph. Graphing helps you make sense out of your data by representing them visually. The next sections de-scribe the various types of graphs and indicate their uses. For details on drawing graphs, see Chapter 15.

## Elements of a Graph

A basic graph represents your data in a two-dimensional space. The two dimensions (horizontal and vertical) are defined by two lines intersecting at right angles, called the *axes* of the graph. The horizontal axis is called the *abscissa* or *x-axis* of the graph, and the vertical axis is called the *ordinate* or *y-axis*. (The terms *x-axis* and *y-axis* are used in this discussion.)

When graphing data from an experiment, you normally represent levels of your independent variable along the x-axis and values of the dependent variable along the y-axis. A pair of values (one for the x-axis and one for the y-axis) defines a single *point* within the graph. This point could represent an individual score or a group mean at a particular value of the independent variable.

Data within the two-dimensional space of a graph can be presented as bar graphs, line graphs, scatterplots, or (abandoning the Cartesian x-axis, y-axis geometry) pie charts.

## Bar Graphs

A **bar graph** presents your data as bars extending away from the axis representing your independent variable (usually the x-axis, although this convention is not always followed). The length of each bar is determined by the value of the dependent variable. Figure 12–6 shows group means from a one-factor, three-group experiment plotted as a bar graph. The three bars in Figure 12–6 represent the three levels of the independent variable for which data were collected. The length of each bar along the y-axis represents the score obtained on the dependent variable. Note that each bar straddles the x-axis value it represents. The width of each bar has no meaning and is chosen to provide a pleasing appearance.

You also can use a bar graph to represent data from a multifactor design. Figure 12–7 shows a bar graph of the data from the two-factor joinder experiment discussed earlier. Notice that the four levels of number of charges filed (one to four) are placed along the x-axis. The two levels of charges judged (the second independent variable) are represented within the graph itself. The dark blue bars represent the data from the

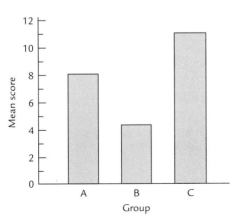

**FIGURE 12–6** Bar Graph of Means from a Hypothetical One-Factor Design.

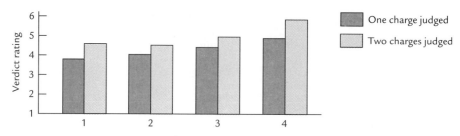

**FIGURE 12-7**    Bar Graph of Means from a Two-Factor Design.

one-charge judged group, whereas the lighter blue shaded bars represent the data from the two-charges judged group.

*Bar graph
qualitative*

A bar graph is the best method of graphing when your independent variable is categorical (such as the type of drug administered). In this case, the distance along the x-axis has no real meaning. A line graph (which visually emphasizes that distance) would be misleading. The bar graph makes the arbitrary ordering of categories apparent, whereas a line graph would inappropriately suggest the presence of trends in these data.

In addition to displaying such statistical values as treatment means, bar graphs may be used to display certain kinds of data distributions, discussed later in the chapter.

## Line Graphs

*Line graph
quantitative*

A **line graph** represents data as a series of points connected by a line. It is most appropriate when your independent variable, represented on the x-axis, is continuous or *quantitative* (e.g., the number of seconds elapsing between learning and recall). This is in contrast to a bar graph, which is most appropriate when your independent variable is categorical or *qualitative* (e.g., categories representing grades on an exam). Line graphs are also appropriate when you want to illustrate functional relationships among variables. A *functional relationship* is one in which the value of the dependent variable varies as a function of the value of the independent variable. Usually the depicted functional relationship is causal.

An illustration of a line graph is shown in Figure 12–8, depicting the means from the single-factor experiment with a continuous independent variable. These data were shown in Figure 12–6 in the form of a bar graph. Notice the difference in how the two types of graphs visually represent the means.

A line graph also can be used to depict the means from multifactor experiments. Figure 12–9 shows such a line graph for the two-factor experiment on joinder of offenses cited earlier. The levels of one factor are represented along the x-axis, just as in a single-factor experiment. The levels of the other factor are represented by using different symbols or line styles. All points collected under the same value of the second factor have the same symbol and are connected by the same line. Chapter 15 discusses how to draw line graphs.

*Shapes of Line Graphs*    Relationships represented on a line graph can take a variety of shapes. Figure 12–10 shows a graph on which the curve is *positively accelerated*.

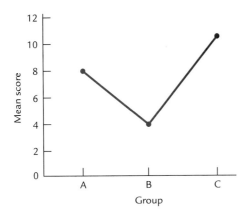

**FIGURE 12–8** Line Graph of Means from a One-Factor Design.

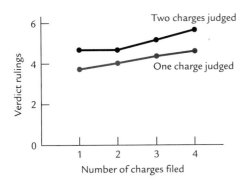

**FIGURE 12–9** Line Graph of Means from a Two-Factor Design.

A positively accelerated curve is relatively flat at first and becomes progressively steeper as it moves along the x-axis. Positive acceleration can occur both in the upward and downward directions along the y-axis.

A curve also may be *negatively accelerated,* as shown in Figure 12–11. Here the curve is steep at first but becomes progressively flatter as it moves along the x-axis. Eventually the curve "levels off" at some maximum or minimum value. The function is said to be *asymptotic* at this value. The *asymptote* of a curve is its theoretical limit, or the point beyond which no further change in the value of the dependent variable is expected. In Figure 12–11 the relationship is asymptotic.

Whether positively or negatively accelerated, any curve also may be characterized as *increasing* or *decreasing*, which refers to whether the values along the y-axis increase or decrease, respectively, as the value along the x-axis increases. For example, a negatively accelerated, increasing function would approach a ceiling value at the asymptote, whereas a negatively accelerated, decreasing function would approach a floor value.

A graph also may vary in complexity. The curves depicted in Figures 12–10 and 12–11 are both *monotonic*. That is, the curve represents a uniformly increasing or decreasing function. A *nonmonotonic* function contains reversals in direction, as illustrated in Figure 12–12. Notice how the curve changes direction twice by starting off low, rising, falling off, and then rising again.

**FIGURE 12–10**   Line Graph of Positively Accelerated Functional Relationship.

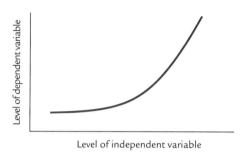

**FIGURE 12–11**   Line Graph of Negatively Accelerated Functional Relationship.

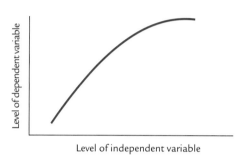

**FIGURE 12–12**   Line Graph of Nonmonotonic Functional Relationship.

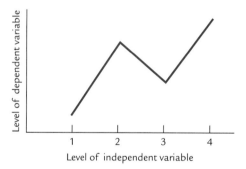

## Scatterplots

In research using a correlational strategy, the data from the two dependent measures are often plotted as a **scatterplot**. On a scatterplot, each pair of scores is represented as a point on the graph. For example, consider the data shown in Table 12–1. To make a scatterplot of these data, you plot the values of Variable A along the x-axis and the values of Variable B along the y-axis (or vice versa, it really does not matter). Then each pair of values is represented by a point within the graph. Figure 12–13 shows a scatterplot of the data in Table 12–1.

## Pie Charts

If your data are in the form of proportions or percentages, then you might find a **pie chart** a good way to represent the value of each category in the analysis. In a pie

| TABLE 12–1 | Bivariate Data for a Scatterplot | |
| --- | --- | --- |
| SUBJECT NUMBER | VARIABLE A | VARIABLE B |
| 1 | 5 | 7 |
| 2 | 4 | 2 |
| 3 | 9 | 8 |
| 4 | 2 | 7 |
| 5 | 6 | 8 |
| 6 | 3 | 9 |

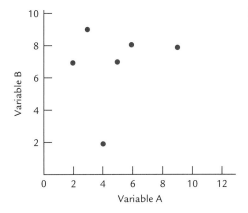

FIGURE 12–13   Scatterplot of the Bivariate Data Presented in Table 12–1.

chart, the data are represented as slices of a circular pie. Figure 12–14 shows two representative pie charts. The pie to the left indicates the proportion of various behaviors observed in rat subjects during a half-hour coding period. The pie to the right displays the same proportions while emphasizing the proportion of time devoted to grooming. This type of display is called an "exploded" pie.

## The Importance of Graphing Data

You can use either tables or graphs to summarize your data. If you organize data in tables, you present the numbers themselves (averages and/or raw score distributions). If you display the data in a graphical format, you lose some of this numerical precision. The value of a point usually can only be approximated by its position along the y-axis of the graph. However, graphing data is important for two major reasons, discussed in the next sections.

*Showing Relationships Clearly*   An old saying, "One picture is worth a thousand words," applies to graphing data from your research. Although summarizing data in a

**FIGURE 12-14**  Pie Chart and Exploded Pie Chart.

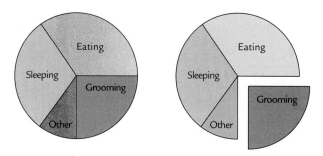

table is fine, proper graphing adds a degree of clarity no table can provide. Consider the data presented in Table 12–2 and the same data graphically presented in Figure 12–9. Although both formats present the data accurately, the graph makes the relationships between the independent variables and dependent variable clearer. The graph brings out subtleties in the relationships that may not be apparent from inspecting a table.

*Choosing Appropriate Statistics*    In addition to making it easier to see relationships in your data, graphs allow you to evaluate your data for the application of an appropriate statistic. Before you apply any statistic to your data, graph your sample distributions and examine their shapes. Your choice of statistic will be affected by the manner in which scores are distributed, as described in the next section.

Graphing your data on a scatterplot is helpful when you intend to calculate a measure of correlation. Inspecting a scatterplot of your data can help you determine which measure of correlation is appropriate for your data. What you would look for and how your findings would affect your decision are taken up during the discussion of correlation measures later in the chapter.

## THE FREQUENCY DISTRIBUTION

One of the first steps to perform when analyzing your data is to create a **frequency distribution** for each dependent variable in an experiment or for each variable in a correlational study. A frequency distribution consists of a set of mutually exclusive categories (*classes*) into which you sort the actual values observed in your data, together with a count of the number of data values falling into each category (*frequencies*). The classes may consist of response categories (for example, for political party affiliation, they might consist of Democrat, Republican, Independent, and Other) or ranges of score values along a quantitative scale (for example, for IQ they might consist of 65–74, 75–84, 85–94, 95–104, 105–114, 115–124, and 125–134).

### Displaying Distributions

Frequency distributions take the form of tables or graphs. Table 12–3 presents a hypothetical frequency distribution of IQ scores using the classes just given. Because IQ scores are quantitative data, the classes are presented in order of value from highest

**TABLE 12-2   Means from the 2 × 4 Joinder Experiment, in Tabular Format**

| NUMBER OF CHARGES JUDGED | NUMBER OF CHARGES FILED | | | |
|---|---|---|---|---|
| | *One* | *Two* | *Three* | *Four* |
| One | 3.8 | 4.1 | 4.3 | 4.7 |
| Two | 4.4 | 4.4 | 4.8 | 5.2 |

**TABLE 12-3   Frequency Distribution Table of Hypothetical IQ Data**

| CLASS | $f$ |
|---|---|
| 125–134 | 5 |
| 115–124 | 12 |
| 105–114 | 22 |
| 95–104 | 25 |
| 85–94 | 26 |
| 75–84 | 7 |
| 65–74 | 3 |
| $\Sigma f$ | 100 |

to lowest. To the right of each class is its frequency, the number of data values falling into that class. Because there were no IQ scores below 65 or above 134, classes beyond these limits are not tabled.

Although a table provides a compact summary of the distribution, it is not particularly easy to extract useful information from it about center, spread, and shape. Much better for this purpose are graphical or semigraphical displays. Here we describe two: the histogram and the stemplot.

*The Histogram*   Figure 12–15 displays our IQ frequency distribution as a **histogram**. Histograms resemble bar graphs, with each bar representing a class. Unlike the bars in a bar graph, those in a histogram are drawn touching to indicate that there are no gaps between adjacent classes. Also, on a histogram, the y-axis represents a frequency: a count of the number of observations falling into a given category (e.g., the number of exam scores falling into the categories of A, B, C, D, or F). On a bar graph, the y-axis typically represents a mean score (e.g., the mean verdict rating shown in Figure 12–7).

The scale on which the variable was measured appears along the x-axis, with the bars positioned appropriately to cover their respective ranges along the scale. The

**FIGURE 12–15**   Hypothetical IQ
Data Displayed as a Histogram.

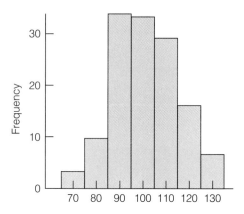

y-axis denotes the frequency; thus, a given bar's length indicates the frequency of
scores falling within its range.

A histogram's appearance changes depending on how wide you make the classes.
Make the classes too narrow, and you produce a flat-looking histogram with many
empty or nearly empty classes. Make the classes too wide, and you produce a tall histogram lacking in detail. The goal is to create a histogram that shows off reasonable
detail without becoming flat and shapeless.

*The Stemplot*   A quick alternative to the histogram you might want to consider using
is the **stemplot** (also known as a stem-and-leaf plot), which was invented by statistician John Tukey (1977) to simplify the job of displaying distributions. To create a stemplot of your data, you simply break each number into two parts: stem and leaf. The
stem part might consist, for example, of the leftmost column or columns and the leaf
part the rightmost column. After finding the lowest and highest stems, make a column
that includes all the numbers in ascending order from lowest to highest stem. Then
draw a vertical line immediately to the right of the stem column. Finally, for each score
in your data, find its stem number and then write its leaf number on the same row immediately to the right of the stem. The result should look something like Figure 12–16,
which replots our IQ data as a stemplot.

Stemplots are easy to construct and display (you can *type* them!) and have the advantage over histograms and tables of preserving all the actual values present in the
data. However, you do not have much freedom to choose the class widths, because
stemplots inherently create class widths of 10 (the span of a stem). Stemplots are not
especially useful for larger data sets because the number of leaves becomes too large.

## Examining Your Distribution

When examining a histogram or stemplot of your data, look for the following important features. First, locate the center of the distribution along the scale of measurement. In the IQ distribution plotted earlier, were the scores centered around 100 IQ
points (an average value for the population as a whole) or somewhere else? The loca-

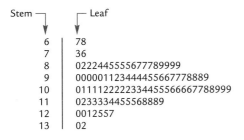

Stem ⌐          ⌐ Leaf

| 6  | 78                            |
| 7  | 36                            |
| 8  | 0222445555677789999           |
| 9  | 00000112344445566777888 9     |
| 10 | 011112222233445556666677889 99 |
| 11 | 0233334455568889              |
| 12 | 0012557                       |
| 13 | 02                            |

**FIGURE 12–16**   Hypothetical IQ Data Displayed as a Stemplot.

tion of the center of a distribution tells you where the scores tended to cluster along the scale of measurement.

Second, note the spread of the scores. Do they tend to bunch up around the center or spread far from it? The spread of the scores indicates how variable they are.

Third, note the overall shape of the distribution. Is it hill-shaped, with a single peak at the center, or does it have more than one peak? If hill-shaped, is it more or less *symmetrical*, or is it skewed? A **skewed distribution** has a long "tail" trailing off in one direction and a short tail extending in the other. Figure 12–17 shows two skewed distributions. A distribution is *positively skewed* if the long tail goes off to the right, upscale (a), or *negatively skewed* if the long tail goes off to the left, downscale (b). Many variables encountered in psychology tend to produce a distribution that follows more or less a mathematical form known as the **normal distribution**, which is symmetrical and hill-shaped—the well-known bell curve. Because many common inferential statistics assume that the data follow a normal distribution, check the distribution of your data to see whether this assumption seems reasonable.

Finally, look for *gaps* or **outliers**. Outliers are scores that lie far from the others, well outside the overall pattern of the data (Moore & McCabe, 2003). Outliers may be perfectly valid (although unusual) scores, but sometimes they represent mistakes made in data collection or transcription. These bogus values can destroy the validity of your analysis. When you find an outlier, examine it carefully to determine whether it represents an error. Correct erroneous values or, if this is not possible, delete them from your analysis.

If you can find no valid reason for removing an outlier, you will have to live with it. However, you can minimize its effects on your analysis by using **resistant measures**, so called because they tend to resist distortion by outliers. We describe some of these measures later in the chapter.

## DESCRIPTIVE STATISTICS: MEASURES OF CENTER AND SPREAD

In many research situations, it is convenient to summarize your data by applying *descriptive statistics*. Descriptive statistics allow you to summarize the properties of an entire distribution of scores with just a few numbers. This section reviews two categories of descriptive statistics: measures of center and measures of spread. The next section describes another category of descriptive statistics, measures of association.

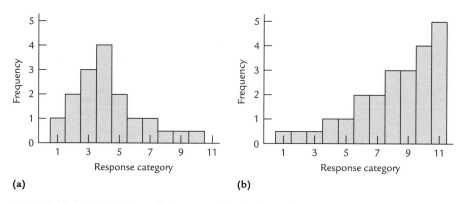

**FIGURE 12–17**    Two Types of Frequency Distribution: (a) positively skewed; (b) negatively skewed.

## Measures of Center

A **measure of center** (also known as a *measure of central tendency*) gives you a single score that represents the general magnitude of scores in a distribution. This score characterizes your distribution by providing information about the score at or near the middle of the distribution. The most common measures of center are the mode, the median, and the mean (also called the *arithmetic average*). Each measure of center has strengths and weaknesses. Also, situations exist in which a given measure of center cannot be used.

*The Mode*    The **mode** is simply the most frequent score in a distribution. To obtain the mode, count the number of scores falling into each response category. The response category with the highest frequency is the mode. The mode of the distribution 1, 2, 4, 6, 4, 3, 4 is 4.

No mode exists for a distribution in which all the scores are different. Some distributions, called *bimodal distributions*, have two modes. Figure 12–18 shows a bimodal distribution.

Although the mode is simple to calculate, it is limited because the values of scores outside of the most frequent score are not represented. The only information yielded by the mode is the most frequent score. The values of other data in the distribution are not taken into account. Under most conditions, take into account the other scores to get an accurate characterization of your data. To illustrate this point, consider the following two distributions of scores: 2, 2, 6, 3, 7, 2, 2, 5, 3, 1 and 2, 2, 21, 43, 78, 22, 33, 72, 12, 8.

In both these distributions, the mode is 2. Looking only at the mode, you might conclude that the two distributions are similar. Obviously, this conclusion is incorrect. It is clear that the second distribution is very different from the first. The mode may not represent a distribution very well and would not be the best measure to use when comparing distributions.

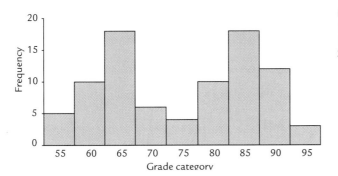

**FIGURE 12–18**
Bimodal Frequency
Distribution of Data
Shown in Table 12–4.

*The Median*   A second measure of center is the **median**. The median is the middle score in an ordered distribution. To calculate the median, follow these steps:

1. Order the scores in your distribution from lowest to highest (or highest to lowest, it does not matter).

2. Count down through the distribution and find the score in the middle of the distribution. This score is the median of the distribution.

What is the median of the following distribution: 7, 5, 2, 9, 4, 8, 1? The correct answer is 5. The ordered distribution is 1, 2, 4, 5, 7, 8, 9, and 5 is the middle score.

You may be wondering what to do if you have an even number of scores in your distribution. In this case, there is no middle score. To calculate a median with an even number of scores, you order the distribution as before, then identify the *two* middle scores. The median is the average of these two scores. For example, with the ordered distribution of 1, 3, 6, 7, 8, 9, the median is 6.5 (6 + 7 = 13; 13/2 = 6.5).

The median takes more information into account than the mode. However, it is still a rather insensitive measure of center because it does not take into account the magnitudes of the scores above and below the median. As with the mode, two distributions can have the same median and yet be very different in character. For this reason, the median is used primarily when the mean is not a good choice.

*The Mean*   The **mean** (denoted as $\overline{X}$) is the most sensitive measure of center because it takes into account all scores in a distribution when it is calculated. It is also the most widely used measure of center. The computational formula for the mean is

$$\overline{X} = \frac{\Sigma X}{n}$$

where $\Sigma X$ is the sum of the scores and $n$ is the number of scores in the distribution. To obtain the mean, simply add together all the scores in the distribution and then divide by the total number of scores.

The major advantage of the mean is that, unlike the mode and the median, its value is directly affected by the magnitude of each score in the distribution. However, this sensitivity to individual score values also makes the mean susceptible to the influence of outliers. One or two such outliers may cause the mean to be artificially high or low. The following two distributions illustrate this point. Assume that Distribution A contains the scores 4, 6, 3, 8, 9, 2, and 3, and Distribution B contains the scores 4, 6, 3, 8, 9, 2, and 43. Although the two distributions differ by only a single score (3 versus 43), they differ greatly in their means (5 versus 10.7, respectively).

The mean of 5 appears to be more representative of the first distribution than the mean of 10.7 is of the second. The median is a better measure of center for the second distribution. The medians of the two distributions are 4 and 6, respectively—not nearly as different from one another as the means. Before you choose a measure of center, carefully evaluate your data for skewness and the presence of deviant, outlying scores. Do not blindly apply the mean just because it is the most sensitive measure of center.

*Choosing a Measure of Center*    Which of the three measures of center you choose depends on two factors: the scale of measurement and the shape of the distribution of the scores. Before you use any measure of center, evaluate these two factors.

Chapter 5 described four measurement scales: nominal (qualitative categories), ordinal (rank orderings), interval (quantities measured from an arbitrary zero point), and ratio (quantities measured from a true zero point). The measurement scale you chose when you designed your experiment will now influence your decision about which measure of center to use.

If your data were measured on a nominal scale, you are limited to using the mode. It makes no sense to calculate a median or mean sex, even if the sex of subjects has been coded as zeros (males) and ones (females).

If your data were measured on an ordinal scale, you could properly use either the mode or the median, but it would be misleading to use the mean as your measure of center. This is because the mean is sensitive to the distance between scores. With an ordinal scale, the actual distance between points is unknown. You cannot assume that scores equally distant in terms of rank order are equally far apart, but you do assume this (in effect) if you use the mean.

The mean can be used if your data are scaled on an interval or ratio scale. On these two scales, the numerical distances between values are meaningful quantities.

Even if your dependent measure were scaled on an interval or ratio scale, the mean may be inappropriate. One of the first things you should do when summarizing your data is to generate a frequency distribution of the scores. Next, plot the frequency distribution as a histogram or stemplot and examine its shape. If your scores are normally distributed (or at least nearly normally distributed), then the mean, median, and mode will fall at the same point in the middle of the distribution, as shown in Figure 12–19. When your scores are normally distributed, use the mean as your measure of center because it is based on the most information.

As your distribution deviates from normality, the mean becomes a less representative measure of center. The two graphs in Figure 12–20 show the relationship between the three measures of center with a positively skewed distribution and a negatively skewed distribution. Notice the relationship between the mean and median for these skewed distributions. In a negatively skewed distribution, the mean underestimates the center. Conversely, in a positively skewed distribution, the mean overestimates the center. Because the median is much less affected by skew, it pro-

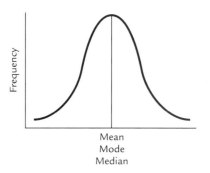

**FIGURE 12-19** Line Graph of Normal Frequency Distribution, Showing Location of Mean, Mode, and Median.

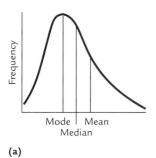 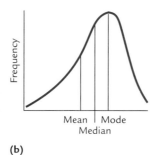

**FIGURE 12-20** Line Graph of Positively (a) and Negatively (b) Skewed Distributions, Showing Relationship between Mean, Mode, and Median.

**(a)**          **(b)**

vides a more representative picture of the distribution's center than does the mean and should be preferred whenever your distribution is strongly skewed.

Deviations from normality also create problems when deciding on an inferential statistic. Chapter 13 discusses inferential statistics and ways to deal with data that are not normally distributed. Neither the mean nor the median will accurately represent the center if your distribution is bimodal. With a bimodal distribution, both measures of center underrepresent one large cluster of scores and overrepresent the other.

Table 12–4 presents hypothetical scores from an introductory psychology exam that generated a bimodal distribution. These scores are shown graphically in Figure 12–18. The mean for these scores is 75.4 and the median is 77, both scores in the "C" category. However, few students actually received a score in this range. The mean and median underrepresent the large cluster of scores in the "B" category and overestimate the large cluster of scores in the "D" category. Thus, neither the mean nor the median would be an appropriate measure of center for the scores in Table 12–4.

To summarize the discussion to this point, the three measures of center are the mean, the median, and the mode. The mean is the most sensitive measure of center because it takes into account the magnitude of each score in the distribution. The mean is also the preferred measure of center. The median is less sensitive to the distribution of scores than the mean but is preferred when your distribution is skewed or the distribution contains serious outliers. Which measure of center you can legitimately use depends on the scale on which the dependent variable was measured and on the manner in which the scores are distributed.

| TABLE 12–4 | Hypothetical Scores on an Exam in an Introductory Psychology Class | | | |
|---|---|---|---|---|
| 54 | 63 | 69 | 82 | 87 |
| 56 | 64 | 69 | 82 | 87 |
| 56 | 64 | 69 | 83 | 87 |
| 56 | 64 | 69 | 83 | 88 |
| 57 | 65 | 72 | 84 | 88 |
| 58 | 65 | 75 | 84 | 88 |
| 59 | 65 | 75 | 84 | 89 |
| 61 | 65 | 75 | 85 | 89 |
| 61 | 65 | 76 | 85 | 89 |
| 62 | 66 | 78 | 86 | 89 |
| 62 | 66 | 78 | 86 | 90 |
| 62 | 66 | 79 | 87 | 90 |
| 62 | 66 | 80 | 87 | 91 |
| 62 | 66 | 81 | 87 | 92 |
| 62 | 67 | 81 | 87 | 92 |
| 62 | 67 | 81 | 87 | 93 |
| 63 | 67 | 81 | 87 | 94 |
| 63 | 68 | 82 | 87 | 95 |

## Measures of Spread

Another important descriptive statistic you should apply to your data is a **measure of spread** (also known as a *measure of variability*). If you look again at some of the sample distributions described thus far (or at the data presented in Table 12–1), you will notice that the scores in the distributions differ from each other. When you conduct an experiment, it is extremely unlikely that your subjects will all produce the same score on your dependent measure. A measure of spread provides information that helps you to interpret your data. Two sets of scores may have highly similar means yet very different distributions, as the following example illustrates.

Imagine you are a scout for a professional baseball team and are considering one of two players for your team. Each player has a .263 batting average over four years of college. The distributions of the two players' averages are as follows: Player 1, .260, .397, .200, .195; Player 2, .263, .267, .259, .263.

Which of these two players would you prefer to have on your team? Most likely, you would pick Player 2 because he is more "consistent" than Player 1. This simple example illustrates an important point about descriptive statistics. When you are evaluating your data, you should take into account both the center *and* the spread of the scores. This section reviews four measures of spread: the range, the interquartile range, the variance, and the standard deviation.

*The Range*   The **range** is the simplest and least informative measure of spread. To calculate the range, you simply subtract the lowest score from the highest score. In the baseball example, the range for Player 1 is .202, whereas the range for Player 2 is .008.

Two problems with the range are that it does not take into account the magnitude of the scores between the extremes and that it is very sensitive to outliers in the distribution. Compare the following two distributions of scores: 1, 2, 3, 4, 5, 6; and 1, 2, 3, 4, 5, 31. The range for the first distribution is 5, whereas the range for the second is 30. The two ranges are highly discrepant despite the fact that the two distributions are nearly identical. For these reasons, the range is rarely used as a measure of spread.

*The Interquartile Range*   The **interquartile range** is another measure of spread that is easy to calculate. To obtain the interquartile range, follow these steps:

1. Order the scores in your distribution.
2. Divide the distribution into four equal parts (quarters).
3. Find the score separating the lower 25 percent of the distribution (Quartile 1 or $Q_1$) and the score separating the top 25 percent from the rest of the distribution ($Q_3$). The interquartile range is equal to $Q_3$ minus $Q_1$.

The interquartile range is less sensitive than the range to the effects of extreme scores. It also takes into account more information, because more than just the highest and lowest scores are used for its calculation. The interquartile range may be preferred over the range in situations in which you want a relatively simple, rough measure of spread that is resistant to the effects of skew and outliers.

*The Variance*   The **variance** ($s^2$) is the average squared deviation from the mean. The defining formula is

$$s^2 = \frac{\Sigma(X - \bar{X})^2}{n - 1}$$

where X is each individual score making up the distribution, $\bar{X}$ is the mean of the distribution, and n is the number of scores. Table 12–5 shows how to use this formula by means of an example worked out for one distribution of scores.

*The Standard Deviation*   Although the variance is frequently used as a measure of spread in certain statistical calculations, it does have the disadvantage of being expressed in units different from those of the summarized data. However, the variance can be easily converted into a measure of spread expressed in the *same* unit of measurement as the original scores: the **standard deviation** (s). To convert from the variance to the standard deviation, simply take the square root of the variance. The standard deviation of the data in Table 12–5 is 2.61 ($\sqrt{6.8}$). The standard deviation is the most popular measure of spread.

TABLE 12–5  **Calculation of a Variance**

| X | $X^2$ | $(X - \bar{X})$ | $(X - \bar{X})^2$ |
|---|---|---|---|
| 3 | 9 | −2 | 4 |
| 5 | 25 | 0 | 0 |
| 2 | 4 | −3 | 9 |
| 7 | 49 | 2 | 4 |
| 9 | 81 | 4 | 16 |
| 4 | 16 | −1 | 1 |
| Σ    30 | 184 | | 34 |

$\bar{X} = 30/6 = 5.0$

$s^2 = 34/5 = 6.8$

*Choosing a Measure of Spread*    The choice of a measure of center is affected by the distribution of the scores, and the same is true for the choice of a measure of spread. Like the mean, the range and standard deviation are sensitive to outliers. In cases in which your distribution has one or more outliers, the interquartile range may provide a better measure of spread.

In addition to noting the presence of outliers, you should note the shape of the distribution (normal or skewed) when selecting a measure of spread. Remember that the mean is not a representative measure of center when your distribution of scores is skewed and that the mean is used to calculate the standard deviation. Consequently, with a skewed distribution, the standard deviation does not provide a representative measure of spread. If your distribution is seriously skewed, use the interquartile range instead.

## Boxplots and the Five-Number Summary

The **five-number summary** provides a useful way to boil down a distribution into just a few easily grasped numbers, several of which are resistant to the effects of skew and outliers and all of which are based on the ranks of the scores. Included in the five-number summary are the following: the minimum, the first quartile, the median (second quartile), the third quartile, and the maximum. The minimum and maximum are simply the smallest and largest scores in the distribution; these are not resistant measures for the simple fact that the most extreme outliers will fall at the ends of the distribution and therefore are likely to *be* the maximum or minimum scores. The three center values (the first quartile, median, and third quartile) are resistant measures. From the five-number summary, you can easily calculate the range (maximum − minimum) and interquartile range ($Q_3 - Q_1$); the latter is, of course, a resistant measure of spread. By examining the five-number summary, you can quickly determine the center, spread, and range of the distribution in question.

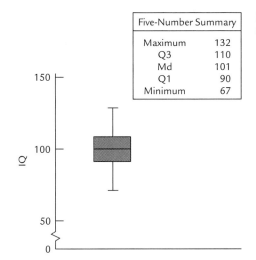

| Five-Number Summary | |
| --- | --- |
| Maximum | 132 |
| Q3 | 110 |
| Md | 101 |
| Q1 | 90 |
| Minimum | 67 |

**FIGURE 12–21**   Five-Number Summary and Boxplot of the IQ Data.

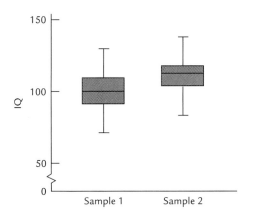

**FIGURE 12–22**   Side-by-Side Boxplots Showing IQ Data from Two Samples.

An even better approach is to display the five-number summary as a **boxplot**. Figure 12–21 shows the five-number summary for our IQ distribution and displays these numbers as a boxplot. The first and third quartiles form the ends of the box, which encloses a line marking the median. The two "whiskers" reach out from the box to mark the minimum and maximum scores.

If you have data from several treatments or samples, you can easily compare the distributions from each using *side-by-side* boxplots, as shown in Figure 12–22. Each box should depict the distribution of the same variable.

You often can discern the general shape of the distribution from the boxplot by noting the position of the median within the box and the relative lengths of the two whiskers. In a symmetrical distribution, the median will fall close to the middle of the box and the two whiskers will be similar in length. In a positively skewed distribution, the median will be pushed toward the left end or bottom of the box (nearer

$Q_1$) and the right or top whisker will usually be longer than the left or bottom one. In a negatively skewed distribution, the reverse pattern will be found.

## MEASURES OF ASSOCIATION, REGRESSION, AND RELATED TOPICS

In some cases, you may want to evaluate the direction and degree of relationship (correlation) between the scores in two distributions. For this purpose, you must use a *measure of association*. This section discusses several measures of association, along with the related topics of linear regression, the correlation matrix, and the coefficient of determination.

### The Pearson Product–Moment Correlation Coefficient

The most widely used measure of association is the **Pearson product–moment correlation coefficient**, or **Pearson r.** It can be used when your dependent measures are scaled on an interval or a ratio scale. The Pearson correlation coefficient provides an index of the direction and magnitude of the relationship between two sets of scores.

The value of the Pearson $r$ can range from +1 through zero to –1. The sign of the coefficient tells you the direction of the relationship. A positive correlation indicates a *direct relationship* (as the values of the scores in one distribution increase, so do the values in the second). A negative correlation indicates an *inverse relationship* (as the value of one score increases, the value of the second decreases). Figure 12–23 illustrates scatterplots of data showing positive, negative, and no correlation.

The magnitude of the correlation coefficient tells you the degree of *linear relationship* (straight line) between your two variables. A correlation of zero indicates that no relationship exists. As the strength of the relationship increases, the value of the correlation coefficient increases toward either +1 or –1. Both +1 and –1 indicate a perfect linear relationship. The sign is unrelated to the magnitude of the relationship and simply indicates the direction of the relationship. Figure 12–24 shows three correlations of differing strengths. Panel (a) shows a correlation of +1, Panel (b) a correlation of about +.8, and Panel (c) a correlation of zero.

*Factors That Affect the Pearson Correlation Coefficient*    Before you use the Pearson correlation coefficient, examine your data much as you do when deciding on a measure of center. Several factors affect the magnitude and sign of the Pearson correlation coefficient.

One factor that affects the Pearson correlation coefficient is the presence of outliers. An outlier can drastically change your correlation coefficient and affect the magnitude of your correlation, its sign, or both. This is especially true if the correlation coefficient is based on a small number of pairs of scores.

Restricting the range over which the variables vary also can affect Pearson $r$. For example, if you were to examine the relationship between IQ and grade point average (GPA) in a group of college students, you would probably find a weaker correlation than if you examined the same two variables using high school students. Because IQ

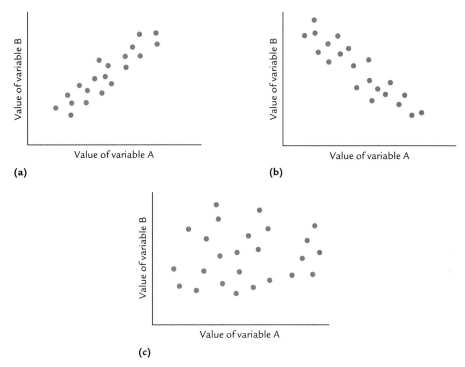

**FIGURE 12–23**   Scatterplots Showing Positive (a), Negative (b), and No Correlation (c).

varies less among college students than among high school students, any variation in GPA that relates to IQ also will tend to vary less. As a result, the impact of extraneous variables such as motivation will be relatively larger, leading to a reduced correlation.

The Pearson correlation coefficient is sensitive not only to the range of the scores but also to the shapes of the score distributions. The formula used to calculate the coefficient uses the standard deviation for each set of scores. Recall that the mean is used to calculate the standard deviation. If the scores are not normally distributed, the mean does not represent the distribution well. Consequently, the standard deviations will not accurately reflect the variability of the distributions, and the correlation coefficient will not provide an accurate index of the relationship between your two sets of scores. Hence you should inspect the frequency distributions of each set of scores to ensure that they are normal (or nearly normal) before using the Pearson coefficient.

Finally, the Pearson coefficient reflects the degree to which the relationship between two variables is linear. Because of this assumption, take steps to determine whether the relationship appears to be linear. You can do this by constructing a scatterplot and then determining whether the points appear to scatter symmetrically around a straight line. Figure 12–25 shows a scatterplot in which the measures have a *curvilinear relationship* (rather than a linear relationship).

When the relationship between variables is nonlinear, the Pearson correlation coefficient underestimates the degree of relationship between the variables. For example, the Pearson correlation between the variables illustrated in Figure 12–25 is

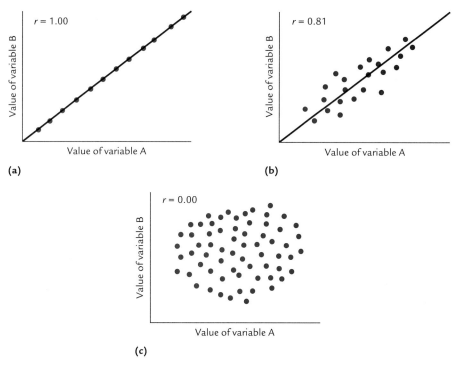

(a)

(b)

(c)

**FIGURE 12-24**   Scatterplots Showing Correlations of Differing Strengths: (a) perfect positive correlation, (b) moderate positive correlation, (c) zero correlation.

zero. However, the two variables are obviously systematically related. There are special correlation techniques for nonlinear data, which are not discussed here.

The Pearson correlation coefficient is used when both of your variables are measured along a continuous scale. You may need to correlate variables when one (or both) of them is not measured along a continuous scale. Special correlation coefficients are designed for these purposes, three of which are discussed in the next sections.

## The Point–Biserial Correlation

You may have one variable measured on an interval scale and the other measured on a nominal scale. For example, perhaps you want to investigate the relationship between self-rated political conservatism (measured on a 10-point scale) and whether or not a referendum was voted for (yes or no). Because one variable is continuous and the other dichotomous (able to take on one of only two values), you would apply the **point–biserial correlation**.

Although there is a special formula for the point–biserial correlation, in practice the formula for the Pearson $r$ is used to compute it. The dichotomous variable is dummy-coded as 0 for one response and 1 for the other. It is easier to use the Pearson formula, especially if you are using a computer program to evaluate your data (assuming the program cannot compute a point–biserial correlation).

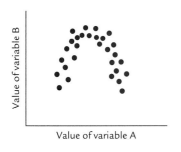

**FIGURE 12–25**   Scatterplot Showing a Curvilinear Relationship.

*Factors That Affect the Point–Biserial Correlation*   You should know a couple of things about the point–biserial correlation. First, its magnitude partly depends on the proportion of participants falling into each of the dichotomous categories. If the number of participants in each category is equal, then the maximum value the point–biserial can attain is plus or minus 1.0 (just as with the Pearson $r$). However, if the number of participants in each category is *not* equal, then the maximum attainable value for the point–biserial correlation is less than plus or minus 1.0. As a consequence, the degree of relationship between the two variables may be underestimated. You should examine the proportion of participants using each category of the dichotomous variable and, if the proportions differ greatly, temper your conclusions accordingly.

The magnitude of the point–biserial correlation also is affected by the limited variation of the dichotomous variable (that is, only two values possible). If the underlying variable is continuous but has been dichotomized for the analysis (for example, anxiety level specified as either low or high), the point–biserial correlation will tend to underestimate the true strength of the relationship.

## The Spearman Rank Order Correlation

The **Spearman rank order correlation**, or *rho* ($\rho$), is used either when your data are scaled on an ordinal scale (or greater) or when you want to determine whether the relationship between variables is monotonic (Gravetter & Wallnau, 2004). The rank order correlation is relatively easy to calculate and can be interpreted in much the same way as a Pearson correlation.

## The Phi Coefficient

The phi coefficient ($\phi$) is used when *both* of the variables being correlated are measured on a dichotomous scale. The phi coefficient can be calculated by means of its own formula. However, like the point–biserial, phi is usually calculated by dummy-coding the responses as 1s and 0s and then plugging the resulting scores into the formula for the Pearson $r$. The same arguments concerning restriction of range that apply to the point–biserial also apply to phi—only doubly so.

## Linear Regression and Prediction

A topic closely related to correlation is **linear regression**. With simple correlational techniques, you can establish the direction and degree of relationship between two variables. With linear regression, you can estimate values of a variable based on knowledge of the values of others. The following section introduces you to simple bivariate (two-variable) regression (also included are some calculations to help you understand regression). Chapter 14 extends bivariate regression to the case in which you want to consider multiple variables together in a single analysis.

*Bivariate Regression*    The idea behind **bivariate linear regression** is to find the straight line that best fits the data plotted on a scatterplot. Consider an example using the data presented in Table 12–6, which shows the scores for each of 10 subjects on two measures (X and Y). Figure 12–26 shows a scatterplot of these data. You want to find the straight line that best describes the linear relationship between X and Y.

The best-fitting straight line is the one that minimizes the sum of the squared distances between each data point and the line, as measured along the y-axis (least squares criterion). This line is called the **least squares regression line**. At any given value for X found in the data, the position of the line indicates the value of Y predicted from the linear relationship between X and Y. You can then compare these predicted values with the values actually obtained. The best-fitting straight line minimizes the squared differences between the predicted and obtained values.

The regression line is described mathematically by the following formula:

$$\hat{Y} = a + bX$$

**TABLE 12–6    Data for Linear Regression Example**

| X | Y | $(X - \bar{X})$ | $(Y - \bar{Y})$ | $(X - \bar{X})(Y - \bar{Y})$ | $(X - \bar{X})^2$ |
|---|---|---|---|---|---|
| 7 | 8 | 1.40 | 1.30 | 1.82 | 1.96 |
| 3 | 4 | −2.60 | −2.70 | 7.02 | 6.76 |
| 2 | 4 | −3.60 | −2.70 | 9.72 | 12.96 |
| 10 | 9 | 4.40 | 2.30 | 10.12 | 19.36 |
| 8 | 9 | 2.40 | 2.30 | 5.52 | 5.76 |
| 7 | 7 | 1.40 | 0.30 | 0.42 | 1.96 |
| 9 | 8 | 3.40 | 1.30 | 4.42 | 11.56 |
| 6 | 8 | 0.40 | 1.30 | 0.52 | 0.16 |
| 3 | 4 | −2.60 | −2.70 | 7.02 | 6.76 |
| 1 | 6 | −4.60 | −0.70 | 3.22 | 21.16 |
| $\bar{X}$ = 5.6 | $\bar{Y}$ = 6.7 | | | SP = 49.80 | $SS_x$ = 88.4 |

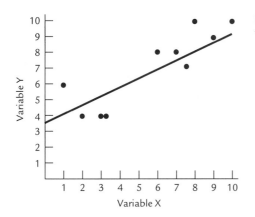

**FIGURE 12–26**   Scatterplot of Data from Table 12–6.

where $\hat{Y}$ (y-hat) is the predicted Y score, b is the slope of the regression line (also called the *regression weight*), X is the value of the X variable, and a is the y-intercept (Pagano, 2004). The constants a and b define a particular regression line. You can use the following formula to determine the value of b for a given set of data points (Gravetter & Wallnau, 2004):

$$b = \frac{SP}{SS_x}$$

where $SP = \Sigma(X - \bar{X})(Y - \bar{Y})$ and $SS_x = \Sigma (X - \bar{X})^2$.
    Using the numbers from Table 12–6, we have

$$b = \frac{49.8}{88.4} = 0.56$$

The formula for the y-intercept (a) is

$$a = \bar{Y} - b(\bar{X})$$

For this example,

$$a = 6.7 - .56(5.6) = 3.56$$

Substituting these values for b and a in the regression equation gives

$$\hat{Y} = 3.56 + .56X$$

This equation allows you to predict the value of Y for any given value of X. For example, if X = 6, then

$$\hat{Y} = 3.56 + .56(6) = 6.92$$

This regression equation was based on raw scores. Its **regression weight** (b) is known as a *raw score regression weight*. Raw score regression weights are difficult to interpret, so an alternative is normally used. If you plug standardized scores rather than raw scores into these equations, you will obtain a different regression equation with a different value for the weight and a zero value for the intercept. The regression weight you obtain from this analysis is called the *standardized regression weight*, or the *beta weight* (β). You would want to use the standardized regression weights when interpreting a regression equation. Chapter 14 discusses how to interpret standardized regression weights.

*Residuals and Errors in Prediction*    After you have computed a regression analysis, you will have a score on one variable (Y) predicted from another variable (X). Because you have the actual values of a variable (Y), as well as the values predicted from the regression equation ($\hat{Y}$), you are in a position to see how accurately your regression equation predicts scores on Y. The difference between the values of Y and $\hat{Y}$ ($Y - \hat{Y}$) is called a *residual*. Residuals will be low when the regression equation generates values of $\hat{Y}$ that are close to the actual values of Y.

When your variables are perfectly correlated, there is no error in prediction (the predicted and actual values of Y will always agree). However, when your correlation is less than perfect, there will be error in predicting Y from X. You can estimate the amount of error in prediction by calculating the **standard error of estimate**, which is a measure of the distance between your data points and your computed regression line (Gravetter & Wallnau, 2004). The following formula is used to compute the standard error of estimate (Gravetter & Wallnau, 2004; *df* stands for "degrees of freedom"):

$$s_{est} = \sqrt{\frac{SS_{error}}{df}} = \sqrt{\frac{\Sigma (Y - \hat{Y})^2}{n - 2}}$$

In the current example, $s_{est}$ = 1.008.

A close, but inverse, relationship exists between the magnitude of $s_{est}$ and the magnitude of the correlation between X and Y. If X and Y are highly correlated, the data points will be clustered tightly around the regression line, and $s_{est}$ will be small. As the strength of the relationship between X and Y decreases, $s_{est}$ increases.

## The Coefficient of Determination

The square of the correlation coefficient (whether Pearson *r*, point–biserial, Spearman rho, or phi) is called the *coefficient of determination*. The coefficient of determination provides a measure of the amount of variance shared by the two variables being tested. It indicates how much of the variability in one of the scores can be "explained" by the variability in the other score. For example, if variation in Score X actually *caused* variations to occur in Score Y, the coefficient of determination would indicate what proportion of the total variation in Score Y was caused by variation in Score X.

As an example, assume that you investigated the relationship between intelligence and school performance and found a correlation of .60. Then the coefficient of determination is .60 × .60, or .36. This means that 36 percent of the variation in school performance can be accounted for by the variation in intelligence.

Of course, you usually don't know if the relationship is truly a causal one or in which direction the causal arrow points. Consequently, you should interpret this statistic with caution. Perhaps the most enlightening use of this statistic is to subtract it from 1.0. The resulting number, called the **coefficient of nondetermination**, gives the proportion of variance in one variable *not accounted for* by variance in the other variable. This is, in effect, *unexplained* variance caused by unmeasured factors. If the coefficient of nondetermination is large, then your measured variables are having little impact on each other relative to these unmeasured factors. If this happens, then perhaps you should try to identify these unmeasured variables and either hold them constant or measure them.

## The Correlation Matrix

If you have computed all the possible correlations among a number of variables, you can make the relationships among the variables easier to comprehend by displaying the correlation coefficients in a table called a **correlation matrix**. Table 12–7 shows a hypothetical correlation matrix for five variables (1–5). The headings along the top and left side of the matrix indicate the variables being correlated. Each number within the matrix is the correlation between the two variables whose row and column intersect at the position of the number. For example, the correlation between Variables 5 and 3 can be found by reading across the row labeled "Variable 5" to the column labeled "Variable 3." The correlation found at that intersection is .06.

Note that the numbers along the diagonal have been omitted from the table. This is because the diagonal positions represent the correlations of each variable with itself, which are necessarily 1.0. The correlations above the diagonal are omitted because they simply duplicate the correlations already given below the diagonal. For example, the correlation of Variable 5 with Variable 3 (below the diagonal) is the same as the correlation of Variable 3 with Variable 5 (which would appear above the diagonal).

## Multivariate Correlational Techniques

The measures of correlation and linear regression discussed in this chapter are all bivariate. Even if you calculate several bivariate correlations and arrange them in a matrix, your conclusions are limited to the relationship between pairs of variables. Bivariate correlation techniques are certainly useful and powerful tools. In many cases, however, you may want to look at three or more variables simultaneously. For example,

### TABLE 12–7 A Correlation Matrix

| | VARIABLES | | | |
|---|---|---|---|---|
| **VARIABLES** | *1* | *2* | *3* | *4* |
| 2 | .54 | | | |
| 3 | .43 | .87 | | |
| 4 | .52 | .31 | .88 | |
| 5 | .77 | .44 | .06 | .39 |

you might want to know what the relationship between two variables is with the effect of a third held constant. Or you might want to know how a set of predictor variables relates to a criterion variable. In these cases and related others, the statistical technique of choice is *multivariate analysis*. Multivariate analysis is a family of statistical techniques that allow you to evaluate complex relationships among three or more variables. Multivariate analyses include multiple regression, discriminant analysis, part and partial correlation, and canonical correlation. Chapter 14 provides an overview of these and other multivariate techniques.

## SUMMARY

When you have finished conducting your research, you begin the task of organizing, summarizing, and describing your data. The first step is to organize your data so you can more easily conduct the relevant analyses. A good way to gain some understanding of your data is to graph the observed relationships. You can do this with a bar graph, line graph, scatterplot, or pie chart, whichever is most appropriate for your data.

A frequency distribution shows how the scores in your data vary along the scale of measurement. Although a frequency distribution can be presented in tabular format, you can grasp its essential features more easily by graphing it as a histogram or by creating a stemplot. When examining these, you should look for several important features: the center, around which the scores tend to vary; the spread, or degree to which the scores tend to vary from the center; the overall shape of the distribution (for example, symmetrical or skewed); and the presence of gaps or outliers—deviant points lying far from the rest. Examine any outliers carefully, and correct or eliminate any that resulted from error. Descriptive statistics are methods for summarizing your data. Descriptive statistics include measures of central tendency, measures of variability, and measures of correlation.

The mode, median, and mean are the three measures of center. The mode is the most frequent score in your distribution. The median is the middle score in an ordered distribution. The mean is the arithmetic average of the scores, obtained by summing the scores and dividing the sum by the total number of scores.

Which of the three measures of center you should use depends both on the scale on which the data were measured and on the shape of the distribution of scores. The mean can be used only with data that are scaled on either a ratio or an interval scale and are normally distributed. In cases in which the data are skewed or bimodal, then the mean does not provide a representative measure of center, and the median or mode should be considered. Ordinally scaled data are best described with the median, whereas nominally scaled data are best described with the mode.

Measures of spread include the range, interquartile range, variance, and standard deviation. The range is simply the difference between the highest and lowest scores in your distribution. Although simple to calculate, the range is rarely used. Serious limitations of the range are that it is strongly affected by extreme scores and takes into account only the highest and lowest scores (thus ignoring the remaining scores in the distribution). The interquartile range takes into account more of the scores in the distribution and is less sensitive than the range to extreme scores. The variance uses all the scores in its calculation but has the disadvantage that its unit of measurement differs from that of the scores from which it derives. This problem can be overcome by taking the square root of the variance. The resulting statistic, the standard deviation, is the most commonly used measure of spread.

Your decision about which of the measures of spread to use is affected by the same two factors that affect your decision about central tendency (scale of measurement and distribution of scores). The standard deviation is a good measure of spread when your scores are normally distributed. As scores deviate from normality, the standard deviation becomes a less representative measure of spread. When your data are skewed, use the interquartile range.

The five-number summary provides a concise view of your distribution by providing the minimum, first quartile, median, third quartile, and maximum. Displaying these five numbers as a boxplot helps to visualize the center, spread, and shape of the distribution. You can quickly compare distributions of the same variable from different treatments or samples by creating side-by-side boxplots.

Measures of correlation provide an index of the direction and degree of relationship between two variables. The most popular measure of correlation is the Pearson product–moment correlation coefficient ($r$). This coefficient can range from $-1$ through 0 to $+1$. A stronger relationship is indicated as the coefficient approaches plus or minus 1. A negative correlation indicates that an increase in the value of one variable is associated with a decrease in the value of the second (inverse relationship). A positive correlation indicates that the two measures increase or decrease together (direct relationship).

The Pearson $r$ is applied to data scaled on either an interval or a ratio scale. Other measures of correlation are available for data measured along other scales. The point–biserial correlation is used if one variable is measured on an interval or ratio scale and the other on a dichotomous nominal scale. Spearman's rho is used if both variables are measured on at least an ordinal scale. The phi coefficient is used if both variables are dichotomous.

Linear regression is a statistical procedure closely related to correlation. With linear regression, you can estimate the value of a criterion variable given the value of a predictor. In linear regression, you calculate a least squares regression line, which is the straight line that best fits the data on a scatterplot. This line minimizes the sum of the squared distances between each data point and the line, as measured along the y-axis (least squares criterion), and minimizes the difference between predicted and obtained values of y. The amount of discrepancy between the values of y predicted with the regression equation and the actual values is provided by the standard error of estimate. The magnitude of the standard error is related to the magnitude of the correlation between your variables. The higher the correlation, the lower the standard error.

By squaring the correlation coefficient, you obtain the coefficient of determination, an index of the amount of variation in one variable that can be accounted for by variation in the other. Subtracting the coefficient of determination from 1.0 gives you the coefficient of nondetermination, the proportion of variance *not* shared by the two variables. The larger this number is, the larger is the effect of unmeasured sources of variance relative to that of the measured variables.

Multivariate statistical techniques are used to evaluate more complex relationships than simple bivariate statistics. With multivariate statistics, you can analyze the degree of relationship between a set of predictor variables and a criterion variable or look at the correlation between two variables with the effect of a third variable held constant.

## REVIEW QUESTIONS

1. Why is it important to scrutinize your data using exploratory data analysis (EDA)?
2. How do you organize your data in preparation for data analysis?
3. What are the problems inherent in entering your data for computer data analysis?
4. What are the advantages and disadvantages of analyzing grouped and individual data?
5. How do various types of graphs differ, and when should each be used?
6. How do negatively accelerated, positively accelerated, and asymptotic functional relationships differ?
7. Why is it important to graph your data and inspect the graphs carefully?
8. How do you graph a frequency distribution as a histogram and as a stemplot?
9. What should you look for when examining the graph of a frequency distribution?
10. What is a measure of center?
11. How do the mode, median, and mean differ, and under what conditions would you use each?
12. What is a measure of spread?
13. What measures of spread are available, and when would you use each?
14. How are the variance and standard deviation related, and why is the standard deviation preferred?
15. What is the five-number summary, and how can you represent it graphically?
16. What do measures of association tell you?
17. What are the measures of association available to you, and when would you use each?
18. What affects the magnitude and direction of a correlation coefficient?
19. What is linear regression, and how is it used to analyze data?
20. How are regression weights and standard error used to interpret the results from a regression analysis?
21. What it the coefficient of nondetermination, and what does it tell you?
22. What is a correlation matrix, and why should you construct and inspect one?
23. How does a multivariate correlational statistic differ from a bivariate correlational statistic?

## KEY TERMS

| | |
|---|---|
| exploratory data analysis (EDA) | frequency distribution |
| dummy code | histogram |
| bar graph | stemplot |
| line graph | skewed distribution |
| scatterplot | normal distribution |
| pie chart | outliers |

resistant measures

measure of center

mode

median

mean

measure of spread

range

interquartile range

variance

standard deviation

five-number summary

boxplot

Pearson product–moment correlation coefficient, or Pearson $r$

point–biserial correlation

Spearman rank order correlation *(rho)*

phi ($\phi$) coefficient

linear regression

bivariate linear regression

least squares regression line

regression weight

standard error of estimate

coefficient of nondetermination

correlation matrix

# 13

# Using Inferential Statistics

Chapter 12 reviewed descriptive statistics that help you characterize and describe your data. However, they do not help you assess the reliability of your findings. A reliable finding is repeatable, whereas an unreliable one may not be. Statistics that assess the reliability of your findings are called **inferential statistics** because they let you infer the characteristics of a population from the characteristics of the samples comprising your data.

This chapter reviews the most widely used inferential statistics. Rather than focusing on how to calculate these statistics, this discussion focuses on issues of application and interpretation. Consequently, computational formulas or worked examples are not presented.

## INFERENTIAL STATISTICS: BASIC CONCEPTS

Before exploring some of the more popular inferential statistics, we present some of the basic concepts underlying these statistics. You should understand these concepts before tackling the discussion on inferential statistics that follows. If you need a more comprehensive refresher on these concepts, consult a good introductory statistics text.

### Sampling Distribution

Chapter 12 introduced the notion of a distribution of scores. Such a distribution results from collecting data across a series of observations and then plotting the frequency of each score or range of scores. It is also possible to create a distribution by repeatedly taking samples of a given size (e.g., $n = 10$ scores) from the population. The means of these samples could be used to form a distribution of sample means. If you could take *every possible* sample of $n$ scores from the population, you would have what is known as the *sampling distribution of the mean*. Statistical theory reveals that this distribution will tend to closely approximate the normal distribution, even when the population of scores from which the samples were drawn is far from normal in shape. Thus you can use the normal distribution as a theoretical model that will allow you to make inferences about the likely value of the population mean, given the mean of a single sample from that population.

The sample mean is not the only statistic for which you can obtain a sampling distribution. In fact, each sample statistic has its own theoretical sampling distribution. For example, the tabled values for the $z$ statistic, Student's $t$, the $F$ ratio, and chi-square represent the sampling distributions of those statistics. Using these sampling distributions, you can determine the probability that a value of a statistic as large as or larger than the obtained value could have occurred by chance. This probability is called the obtained $p$.

## Sampling Error

When you draw a sample from a population of scores, the mean of the sample, $\bar{x}$, will probably differ from the population mean, $\mu$. An estimate of the amount of variability in the expected sample means across a series of such samples is provided by the **standard error of the mean** (or *standard error* for short). It may be calculated from the standard deviation of the sample as follows:

$$s_{\bar{x}} = \frac{s}{\sqrt{n}}$$

where $s$ is the standard deviation of the sample and $n$ is the number of scores in the sample. The standard error is used to estimate the standard deviation of the sampling distribution of the mean for the population from which the sample was drawn.

## Degrees of Freedom

In any distribution of scores with a known mean, a limited number of data points yield independent information. For example, if you have a sample of 10 scores and a known mean (for example, 6.5), only 9 scores are free to vary. That is, once you have selected 9 scores from the population, the value of the 10th must have a particular value that will yield the mean. Thus, the **degrees of freedom (df)** for a single sample are $n - 1$ (where $n$ is the total number of scores in the sample).

Degrees of freedom come into play when you use any inferential statistic. You can extend this logic to the analysis of an experiment. If you have three groups in your experiment with means of 2, 5, and 10, the grand mean (the sum of all the scores divided by $n$) is then 5.7. If you know the grand mean and you know the means from two of your groups, the final mean is set. Hence, the degrees of freedom for a three-group experiment are $k - 1$ (where $k$ is the number of levels of the independent variable). The degrees of freedom are then used to find the appropriate tabled value of a statistic against which the computed value is compared.

## Parametric versus Nonparametric Statistics

Inferential statistics can be classified as either *parametric* or *nonparametric*. A *parameter* in this context is a characteristic of a population, whereas a *statistic* is a characteristic of your sample (Gravetter & Wallnau, 2004). A *parametric statistic* estimates the value of a population parameter from the characteristics of a sample. When you use a parametric statistic, you are making certain assumptions about the population from which your sample was drawn. A key assumption of a parametric test is that your sample was drawn from a normally distributed population.

In contrast to a parametric statistic, a *nonparametric statistic* makes no assumptions about the distribution of scores underlying your sample. Nonparametric statistics are used if your data do not meet the assumptions of a parametric test.

## THE LOGIC BEHIND INFERENTIAL STATISTICS

Whenever you conduct an experiment, you expose subjects to different levels of your independent variable. Although a given experiment may contain several groups, assume for the present discussion that the experiment in question included only two.

The data from each group can be viewed as a sample of the scores obtained if all subjects in the target population were tested under the conditions to which the group was exposed. For example, the treatment group mean represents a population of subjects exposed to your experimental treatment. Each treatment mean is assumed to represent the mean of the underlying population.

In all respects except for treatment, the treatment and control groups were exposed to equivalent conditions. Assume that the treatment had *no effect* on the scores. In that case, each group's scores could be viewed as an independent sample taken from the *same* population. Figure 13–1 illustrates this situation.

Each sample mean provides an independent estimate of the population mean. Each sample standard error provides an independent estimate of the standard deviation of sample means in the sampling distribution of means. Because the two means were drawn from the same population, you would expect them to differ only because of sampling error. You can assume that the distribution of these means is normal (central limit theorem), and you have two estimates of the standard deviation of this distribution (the standard errors). From this information, you can calculate the probability that the two sample means would differ as much as or more than they do simply because of chance factors. This probability is the obtained $p$.

Let's review these points. If the treatment had no effect on the scores, then you would expect the scores from the two groups to provide independent samples from the same population. From these samples you can estimate the characteristics of that population, and from this estimate you can determine the probability that sampling error and sampling error alone would produce a difference at least as large as the observed difference between the two treatment means.

Consider the case in which the treatment *does* affect the scores, perhaps by shifting them upward. Figure 13–2 illustrates this situation. In the upper part of the figure is a population underlying the control group sample distribution and another one underlying the treatment group sample distribution. The population distribution underlying the treatment group is shifted upward and away from the control group population distribution. This shift could be obtained by simply adding a constant to each value in the control group distribution. This new shifted distribution resembles the old, unshifted distribution in standard deviation, but its mean is higher.

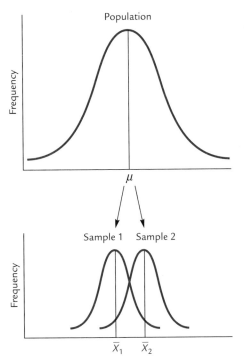

**FIGURE 13–1**    Line Graphs Showing the Relationship between Samples and Population, Assuming That the Treatment Had no Effect on the Dependent Variable ($\bar{X}_1$, mean of sample 1; $\bar{X}_2$, mean of sample 2).

The bottom part of the figure shows two possible sample distributions—one for the control group and one for the treatment group. The scores from the control group still constitute a sample from the unshifted distribution (left-hand upper curve in Figure 13–2), but the scores from the treatment group now constitute a sample from the shifted distribution (right-hand upper curve in Figure 13–2). The two sample means provide estimates of two *different* population means. Because of sampling error, the two sample means might or might not differ, even though a difference exists between the underlying population means.

Your problem (as a researcher) is that you do not know whether the treatment really had an effect on the scores. You must decide this based on your observed sample means (which may differ by a certain amount) and the sample standard deviations. From this information, you must decide whether the two sample means were drawn from the same population (the treatment had no effect on the sample scores) or from two different populations (the treatment shifted the scores relative to scores from the control group). Inferential statistics help you make this decision.

These two possibilities (different or the same populations) can be viewed as statistical hypotheses to be tested. The hypothesis that the means were drawn from the same population (that is, $\mu_1 = \mu_2$) is referred to as the *null hypothesis* ($H_0$). The hypothesis that the means were drawn from different populations ($\mu_1 \neq \mu_2$) is called the *alternative hypothesis* ($H_1$).

Inferential statistics use the characteristics of the two samples to evaluate the validity of the null hypothesis. Put another way, they assess the probability that the means

**FIGURE 13–2** Line Graphs Showing the Relationship between Samples and Population, Assuming the Treatment Had an Effect on the Dependent Variable.

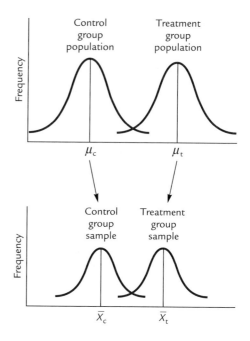

of the two samples would differ by the observed amount or more if they had been drawn from the same population of scores. If this probability is sufficiently small (that is, if it is very unlikely that two samples this different would be drawn by chance from the same population), then the difference between the sample means is said to be *statistically significant*, and the null hypothesis is rejected.

## Statistical Errors

When making a comparison between two sample means, there are two possible states of affairs (the null hypothesis is true or it is false) and two possible decisions you can make (not to reject the null hypothesis or to reject it). In combination, these conditions lead to four possible outcomes, as shown in Table 13–1. The labels across the top of Table 13–1 indicate the two states of affairs, whereas those in the left-hand column indicate the two possible decisions. Each box represents a different combination of the two conditions.

The lower left-hand box represents the situation in which the null hypothesis is true (the independent variable had no effect) and you correctly decide not to reject the null hypothesis. This is a disappointing outcome, but at least you made the right decision.

The upper left-hand box represents a more disturbing outcome. Here the null hypothesis is again true, but you have incorrectly decided to reject the null hypothesis. In other words, you decided that your independent variable had an effect when, in fact, it did not. In statistics this mistake is called a **Type I error**. In signal detection experiments, the same kind of mistake is called a "false alarm" (saying a stimulus was present when actually it was not).

*[handwritten: your decision]*

| TABLE 13-1 **Statistical Errors** | | | |
|---|---|---|---|
| | | TRUE STATE OF AFFAIRS | |
| | | $H_0$ True | $H_0$ False |
| Decision | Reject $H_0$ | Type I error | Correct decision |
| | Do Not Reject $H_0$ | Correct decision | Type II error |

*[handwritten left margin: The data came from the same population]*
*[handwritten: the null hypothesisis true]*
*[handwritten: false]*
*[handwritten left margin: the data belong to different population]*

*[handwritten right margin: $H_0$ = null Hypothesis]*
*[handwritten: Reject Accept]*
*[handwritten: $p = a$    $p = 1 - a$]*
*[handwritten: $p = 1 - \beta$    $p = \beta$]*

*[handwritten: Type I error - saying the treatment works when later its found you were wrong]*
*[handwritten: Type 2 - the treatment may work its the method that doesn't work]*

The lower right-hand box in Table 13–1 represents a second kind of error. In this case, the null hypothesis is false (the independent variable did have an effect) but you have incorrectly decided not to reject the null hypothesis. This is called a **Type II error** and represents the case in which you concluded your independent variable had no effect when it really did have one. In signal detection experiments, such an outcome is called a "miss" (not detecting a stimulus that was present).

Ideally, you would like to minimize the probability of making either a Type I or a Type II error. Unfortunately, some of the things you can do to minimize a Type I error actually increase the probability of a Type II error, and vice versa.

## Statistical Significance

If both samples came from the same population (or from populations having the same mean), then the null hypothesis is true, and any difference between the sample means reflects nothing more than sampling error. The actual difference between your sample means may be just such a chance difference, or it may reflect a real difference between the means of the populations from which the samples were drawn. Which of these is the case? To help you decide, you can compute an inferential statistic to determine the probability of obtaining a difference between sample means as large as or larger than the difference you actually got, under the assumption that the null hypothesis is true. If this probability is low enough, you reject the null hypothesis, as you would be unlikely to have obtained the difference you did simply through sampling error.

To determine this probability, you calculate an *observed value* of your inferential statistic. This observed value is compared to a *critical value* of that statistic (normally found in a statistical table such as those in the appendix, for example, Table 2). Ultimately, you will make your decision about rejecting the null hypothesis based on whether or not the observed value of the statistic meets or exceeds the critical value. As stated, you want to be able to reduce the probability of committing a Type I error. The probability of committing a Type I error depends on the criterion you use to accept or reject the null hypothesis. This criterion, known as the **alpha level** ($\alpha$), represents the probability that a difference at least as large as the observed difference between your sample means could have occurred purely through sampling error. The alpha level you adopt (along with the degrees of freedom) also determines the critical value of the statistic you are using. The smaller the value of alpha, the larger the critical value. Alpha is the probability of a Type I error. The smaller you make alpha, the less likely you are to make a Type I error. In theory, you can reduce the probability of making a Type I error to any desired level. For example, you could average less than one Type I error in one million experiments by choosing an alpha value of .000001. There are good reasons, discussed later, why you do not ordinarily adopt such a conservative alpha level.

By convention, alpha has been set at .05 (5 chances in 100 that sampling error alone could have produced a difference at least as large as the one observed). The particular level of alpha you adopt is called the *significance level*. A difference between means yielding an observed value of a statistic that meets or exceeds the critical value of your inferential statistic is said to be *statistically significant*.

The strategy of looking up the critical value of a statistic in a table and then comparing the obtained value with this critical value was developed in an era when most computations had to be done by hand, making it exceedingly difficult to find the probability with which a value equal to or larger than the obtained value of the test statistic would occur by chance when the null hypothesis is true. These days most statistical analyses are conducted using computerized statistical packages that usually provide the exact probability value $p$ along with the obtained value of the test statistic. You can directly compare this obtained $p$ with your selected alpha level and avoid having to use the relevant table. If the obtained $p$ is less than or equal to alpha, your comparison is statistically significant.

## One-Tailed versus Two-Tailed Tests

The critical values of a statistic depend on such factors as the number of observations per treatment, the number of treatments, and the desired alpha level. They also depend on whether the test is one-tailed or two-tailed.

Figure 13–3 shows two examples of the sampling distribution for the $z$ statistic. This distribution is normal and, therefore, symmetrical about the mean. The left distribution shows the **critical region** (shaded area) for a *one-tailed test*, assuming alpha has been set to .05. This region contains 5 percent of the total area under the curve, representing the 5 percent of cases whose $z$ scores occur by chance with a probability of .05 or less. The $z$ values falling into this critical region are judged to be statistically significant.

The right distribution in Figure 13–3 shows the *two* critical regions for the *two-tailed test*, using the same .05 alpha value. To keep the probability at .05, the total percentage of cases found in the two tails of the distribution must equal 5 percent. Thus, each critical region must contain 2.5 percent of the cases. Consequently, the $z$ scores required to reach statistical significance must be more extreme than was the case for the one-tailed test.

A one-tailed test is conducted if you are interested only in whether the obtained value of the statistic falls in one tail of the sampling distribution for that statistic. This is usually the case when your research hypotheses are directional. For example, you may want to know whether a new therapy is measurably *better* than the standard one. However, if the new therapy is not better, then you really do not care whether it

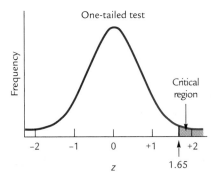
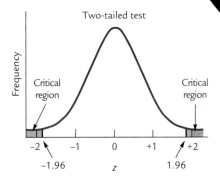

**FIGURE 13–3** Graphs Showing Critical Regions for One-Tailed and Two-Tailed Tests of Statistical Significance.

is simply as good as the standard method or is actually worse. You would not use it in either case.

In contrast, you would conduct a two-tailed test if you wanted to know whether the new therapy was either better *or* worse than the standard method. In that case, you need to check whether your obtained statistic falls into either tail of the distribution.

The major implication of all this is that for a given alpha level, you must obtain a greater difference between the means of your two treatment groups to reach statistical significance if you use a two-tailed test than if you use a one-tailed test. The one-tailed test is, therefore, more likely to detect a real difference if one is present (that is, it is more powerful). However, using the one-tailed test means giving up any information about the reliability of a difference in the other, untested direction.

The use of one-tailed versus two-tailed tests has been a controversial topic among statisticians. Strictly speaking, you must choose which version you will use *before* you see the data. You must base your decision on such factors as practical considerations (as in the therapy example), your hypothesis, or previous knowledge. If you wait until after you have seen the data and then base your decision on the direction of the obtained outcome, your actual probability of falsely rejecting the null hypothesis will be greater than the stated alpha value. You have used information contained in the data to make your decision, but that information may itself be the result of chance processes and unreliable.

If you conduct a two-tailed test and then fail to obtain a statistically significant result, the temptation is to find some excuse why you "should have done" a one-tailed test. You can avoid this temptation if you adopt the following rule of thumb: Always use a two-tailed test unless there are compelling a priori reasons not to.

## PARAMETRIC STATISTICS

Two types of inferential statistics are parametric and nonparametric. The type you apply to your data depends on the scale of measurement used and how your data are distributed. This section discusses parametric inferential statistics.

## Underlying a Parametric Statistic

ons underlie parametric inferential tests (Gravetter & Wallnau,
cores have been sampled randomly from the population, (2) the
ion of the mean is normal, and (3) the within-groups variances are
sumption 3 means the variances of the different groups are highly
al inference, the independent variable is assumed to affect the
variance.

Serious violation of one or more of these assumptions may bias the statistical
test. Such bias will lead you to commit a Type I error either more or less often than
the stated alpha probability and thus undermine the value of the statistic as a guide
to decision making. The effects of violations of these assumptions are examined later
in more detail during a discussion of the statistical technique known as the *analysis of
variance*.

## Inferential Statistics with Two Samples

Imagine you have conducted a two-group experiment on whether "death-qualifying"
a jury (that is, removing any jurors who could not vote for the death penalty) affects
how simulated jurors perceive a criminal defendant. Participants in your experimental group were death-qualified, whereas those in your control group were not. Participants then rated on a scale from 0 to 10 the likelihood that the defendant was guilty
as charged of the crime. You run your experiment and then compute a mean for each
group. You find the two means differ from one another (the experimental group mean
is 7.2 and the control group mean is 4.9).

Your means may represent a single population and differ only because of sampling
error. Or your means may reliably represent two different populations. Your task is to
determine which of these two conditions is true. Is the observed difference between
means reliable, or does it merely reflect sampling error? This question can be answered
by applying the appropriate statistical test, which in this case is a *t* test.

## The *t* Test

The **t test** is used when your experiment includes only two levels of the independent
variable (as in the jury example). Special versions of the *t* test exist for designs involving independent samples (for example, randomized groups) and for those involving
correlated samples (for example, matched-pairs designs, within-subjects designs).

*The t Test for Independent Samples*     You use the **t test for independent samples**
when you have data from two groups of participants who were assigned at random to
the two groups. The test comes in two versions, depending on the error term selected.
The *unpooled* version computes an error term based on the standard error of the mean
provided separately by each sample. The *pooled* version computes an error term based
on the two samples combined, under the assumption that both samples come from
populations having the same variance. The pooled version may be more sensitive to
any effect of the independent variable, but it should be avoided if there are large differences in sample sizes and standard errors. Under these conditions, the probability
estimates provided by the pooled version may be misleading.

*The t Test for Correlated Samples*     When the two means being compared come from samples that are not independent of one another, the formula for the *t* test must be adjusted to take into account any correlation between scores; the adjusted version is called the **t test for correlated samples**. In such cases, the scores from the two samples come in pairs arising from two observations of the same variable on the same participant or from single observations taken on each of a matched pair of participants. Within-subjects and matched-pairs experimental designs and some correlational designs meet this requirement.

The *t* test for correlated samples produces a larger *t* value than the *t* test for independent samples when applied to the same data *if* the scores from the two samples are at least moderately correlated, and this tends to make the correlated samples test more sensitive to any effect of the independent variable. However, this advantage tends to be offset by the correlated sample *t* test's smaller degrees of freedom [equal to $n - 1$, where $n$ is the number of *pairs* of scores, as opposed to the $(n_1 - 1) + (n_2 - 1)$ degrees of freedom of the *t* test for independent samples, where $n_1$ and $n_2$ are the number of scores in the two samples]. When the correlation between samples is zero, the *t* values given by the correlated samples and independent samples *t* tests (pooled version) are identical; with its reduced degrees of freedom, the correlated samples *t* test will then be less able than the independent samples *t* test to detect any effect of the independent variable.

## Contrasting Two Groups: An Example from the Literature

Spinal cord injuries (SCI) represent a major source for physical disabilities (Hess, Marwitz, & Kreutzer, 2003). Spinal cord injuries are often the result of automobile accidents or falls that involve rapid deceleration of the body and may result in "mild traumatic brain injury" (MTBI). Hess et al. note that when a patient with a spinal cord injury is rushed into the emergency room, the possibility that MTBI exists is often overlooked because of the seriousness of spinal cord injuries. Often, patients with SCI show cognitive impairments normally associated with MTBI such as memory loss, attention deficits, and problems with processing information (Hess et al., 2003). The problem is that it is sometimes difficult to determine whether cognitive impairments are the result of MTBI or the emotional trauma associated with SCI.

David Hess, Jennifer Marwitz, and Jeffrey Kreutzer (2003) conducted a study to differentiate between patients with MTBI (without SCI) and patients with SCI. Participants were patients with SCI or MTBI who had been treated at a medical center. Participants' neuropsychological functioning was measured using a battery of tests assessing attention (two tests), motor speed, verbal learning, verbal memory (two tests), visuospatial skills, and word fluency. Mean scores were computed on each measure for patients with SCI and MTBI. Hess et al. used a series of *t* tests to determine if the SCI and MTBI patients differed significantly on any of the neuropsychological tests. They found significant differences between the two groups on 5 of the 10 tests. The results showed that, as a rule, patients with SCI performed better than patients with MTBI. They also found that a high percentage of SCI patients showed significant impairment on several of the cognitive measures (even though they scored better than the MTBI patients). Hess et al. suggest that SCI patients might benefit from a comprehensive rehabilitation program that targets cognitive functioning as well as emotional well-being.

As presented, the data in Table 13–2 do not make much sense. All that you have are means and a $t$ value (with its degrees of freedom) for each measure. You must decide if the $t$ values are large enough to warrant a conclusion that the observed differences are statistically significant.

After calculating a $t$ score, you compare its value with a critical value of $t$ found in Table 2 of the appendix. Before you can evaluate your obtained $t$ value, however, you must obtain the degrees of freedom $(df)$. (For the between-subjects $t$ test, $df$ is $N - 2$, where $N$ is the total number of subjects in the experiment).

Once you have obtained the degrees of freedom (these are shown in the fourth column of Table 13–2 in parentheses), you compare the obtained $t$ score with the tabled critical value, a process requiring two steps. First, read down the column labeled "Degrees of Freedom" and find the number matching your degrees of freedom. Second, find the column corresponding to the desired alpha level (labeled "Alpha Level"). The critical value of $t$ is found at the intersection of the degrees of freedom (row) and alpha level (column) of your test. If your obtained $t$ score is equal to or greater than the tabled $t$ score, then the difference between your sample means is statistically significant at the selected alpha level.

In some instances you may find that the table you have does not include the degrees of freedom you have calculated (for example, 44). If this occurs, you can use the next *lower* degrees of freedom in the table. With 44 degrees of freedom, you would use the entry for 40 degrees of freedom in the table.

If you are conducting your $t$ tests on a computer, most statistical packages will compute the exact $p$ value for the test, given the obtained $t$ and degrees of freedom. In that case, simply compare your obtained $p$ values to your chosen alpha level. If $p$ is less than or equal to alpha, the difference between your groups is statistically significant at the stated alpha level.

### The $z$ Test for the Difference between Two Proportions

In some research, you may have to determine whether two proportions are significantly different. In a jury simulation in which participants return verdicts of guilty or not guilty, for example, your dependent variable might be expressed as the proportion of participants who voted guilty. A relatively easy way to analyze data of this type is to use a **$z$ test for the difference between two proportions**. The logic behind this test is essentially the same as for the $t$ tests. The difference between the two proportions is evaluated against an estimate of error variance.

### Beyond Two Groups: Analysis of Variance (ANOVA)

When your experiment includes more than two groups, the statistical test of choice is **analysis of variance (ANOVA)**. As the name implies, ANOVA is based on the concept of analyzing the variance that appears in the data. For this analysis, the variation in scores is divided, or *partitioned*, according to the factors assumed to be responsible for producing that variation. These factors are referred to as *sources of variance*. The next sections describe how variation is partitioned into sources and how the resulting source variations are used to calculate a statistic called the $F$ ratio. The $F$ ratio is ultimately checked to determine whether the variation among means is statistically significant.

TABLE 13–2    **Means and *t* Values from the Five Significant Differences Found by Hess et al. (2003)**

| TEST | SCI | MTBI | *t (df)* |
|------|-----|------|----------|
| Written attention test | 41.6 | 30.4 | 2.40 (18) |
| Motor speed | 91.4 | 126.1 | –2.20 (31) |
| Verbal learning | 47.1 | 37.9 | 2.4 (34) |
| Verbal memory (immediate recall) | 25.9 | 18.7 | 3.16 (49) |
| Verbal memory (delayed recall) | 21.4 | 10.7 | 4.73 (44) |

*Partitioning Variation*    The value of any particular score obtained in a between-subjects experiment is determined by three factors: (1) characteristics of the subject at the time the score was measured, (2) measurement or recording errors (together called *experimental error*), and (3) the value of the independent variable (assuming the independent variable is effective). Because subjects differ from one another (Factor 1) and because measurement error fluctuates (Factor 2), scores will vary from one another even when all subjects are exposed to the same treatment conditions. Scores will vary even more if subjects are exposed to different treatment conditions and the independent variable is effective.

Figure 13–4 shows how the total variation in the scores from a given experiment can be partitioned into two sources of variability (between-groups variability and within-groups variability). Notice that the example begins with a total amount of variability among scores. Again, this total amount of variability may be attributable to one or more of three factors: your independent variable, individual differences, and experimental error (Gravetter & Wallnau, 2004).

The first component resulting from the partition is the *between-groups variability*. The between-groups variability may be caused by the variation in your independent variable, by individual differences among the different subjects in your groups, by experimental error, or by a combination of these (Gravetter & Wallnau, 2004). The second component, the *within-groups variability*, may be attributed to error. This error can arise from either or both of two sources: individual differences between subjects treated alike within groups and experimental error (Gravetter & Wallnau, 2004). Take note that variability caused by your treatment effects is unique to the between-groups variability.

*The F Ratio*    The statistic used in ANOVA to determine statistical significance is the **F ratio**. The F ratio is simply the ratio of between-groups variability to within-groups variability. Both types of variability that constitute the ratio are expressed as variances. (Chapter 12 described the variance as a measure of spread.) However, statisticians perversely insist on calling the variance the *mean square*, perhaps because the term is more descriptive. Just as with the *t* statistic, once you have obtained your F ratio, you compare it against a table of critical values to determine whether your results are statistically significant.

**FIGURE 13–4**  Partitioning Total
Variation into Between-Groups and
Within-Groups Sources.

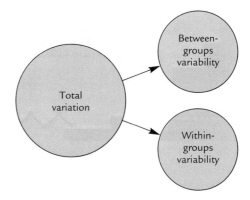

## The One-Factor Between-Subjects ANOVA

The one-factor between-subjects ANOVA is used when your experiment includes only one factor (with two or more levels) and has different subjects in each experimental condition. As an example, imagine you have conducted an experiment on how well participants can detect a signal against a background of noise. Participants were exposed to different levels of background noise (no noise, 20 decibels, or 40 decibels) and asked to indicate whether or not they heard a tone. The number of times the participant correctly stated that a tone was present represented your dependent variable. You found participants in the no-noise group detected more of the tones (36.4) than participants in either the 20-decibel (23.8) or 40-decibel (16.0) groups. Table 13–3 shows the distributions for the three groups.

Submitting your data to a one-factor between-subjects ANOVA, you obtain an $F$ ratio of 48.91. This $F$ ratio is now compared with the appropriate critical value of $F$ in Tables 3A and B in the appendix. To find the critical value, you need to use the degrees of freedom for both the numerator ($k - 1$, where $k$ is the number of groups) *and* denominator [$k(s - 1)$, where $s$ is the number of subjects in each group] of your $F$ ratio. In this case the degrees of freedom for the numerator and denominator are 2 and 12, respectively.

To identify the appropriate critical value for $F$ (at $\alpha = .05$), first locate the appropriate degrees of freedom for the numerator across the top of Table 3A. Then read down the left-hand column to find the degrees of freedom for the denominator. In this example, the critical value for $F(2,12)$ at $\alpha = .05$ is 3.89. Because your obtained $F$ ratio is greater than the tabled value, you have an effect significant at $p < .05$. In fact, if you look at the critical value for $F(2,12)$ at $\alpha = .01$ (found in Table 3B), you will find your obtained $F$ ratio is also significant at $p < .01$.

When you report a significant effect, typically you express it in terms of a $p$ **value**. *Alpha* refers to the cutoff point you adopt. In contrast, the $p$ value refers to the actual probability of making a Type I error given that the null hypothesis is true. Hence, for this example, you would report that your finding was significant at $p < .05$ or $p < .01$. The discussion in the following sections assumes the "$p <$" notation.

Sometimes the table of the critical values of $F$ does not list the exact degrees of freedom for your denominator. If this happens, you can approximate the critical value

TABLE 13-3    **Data from Hypothetical Signal Detection Study**

|  | NO NOISE | 20 DECIBELS | 40 DECIBELS |
|---|---|---|---|
|  | 33 | 22 | 17 |
|  | 39 | 24 | 14 |
|  | 41 | 25 | 19 |
|  | 32 | 21 | 11 |
|  | 37 | 27 | 19 |
| $\Sigma X$ | 182 | 119 | 80 |
| $\Sigma X^2$ | 6,684 | 2,855 | 1,328 |
| $\bar{X}$ | 36.4 | 23.8 | 16.0 |

of $F$ by choosing the next lower degrees of freedom for the denominator in the table. Choosing this lower value provides a more conservative test of your $F$ ratio.

*Interpreting Your F Ratio*    A significant $F$ ratio tells you that at least some of the differences among your means are probably not caused by chance but rather by variation in your independent variable. The only problem, at this point, is that the $F$ ratio fails to tell you where among the possible comparisons the reliable differences actually occur. To isolate which means differ significantly, you must conduct specific comparisons between pairs of means. These comparisons can be either planned or unplanned.

*Planned Comparisons*    **Planned comparisons** (also known as *a priori* comparisons) are used when you have specific preexperimental hypotheses. For example, you may have hypothesized that the no-noise group would differ from the 40-decibel group but not from the 20-decibel group. In this case, you would compare the no-noise and 40-decibel groups and then the no-noise and 20-decibel groups. These comparisons are made using information from your overall ANOVA (see Keppel, 1982). Separate $F$ ratios (each having one degree of freedom) or $t$ tests are computed for each pair of means. The resulting $F$ ratios are then compared with the critical values of $F$ in Tables 3A and 3B.

You can conduct as many of these planned comparisons as necessary. However, a limited number of such comparisons yield unique information. For example, if you found that the no-noise and 20-decibel groups did not differ significantly and that the 40- and 20-decibel groups did, you have no reason to compare the no-noise and 40-decibel groups. You can logically infer that the no-noise and 40-decibel groups differ significantly. Those comparisons that yield new information are known as *orthogonal comparisons*. Any set of means has $(k - 1)$ orthogonal comparisons, where $k$ is the number of treatments.

Planned comparisons can be used in lieu of an overall ANOVA if you have highly specific preexperimental hypotheses. In this case, you would not have the information required to use the given formula for planned comparisons. A simple alternative is to conduct multiple *t* tests. You should not perform too many of these comparisons, even if the relationships were predicted before you conducted your experiment. Performing multiple tests on the same data increases the probability of making a Type I error across comparisons through a process called *probability pyramiding* (discussed immediately following).

*Unplanned Comparisons*    If you do not have a specific preexperimental hypothesis concerning your results, you must conduct **unplanned comparisons** (also known as *post hoc* comparisons). Unplanned comparisons are often "fishing expeditions" in which you are simply looking for any differences that might emerge. In experiments with many levels of an independent variable, you may be required to perform a fairly large number of unplanned comparisons to fully analyze the data.

Two types of error must be considered when many comparisons are made: **per-comparison error** and **familywise error**. Per-comparison error is the alpha for each comparison between means. If you set an alpha level of .05, the per-comparison error rate is .05. The familywise error rate (Keppel, 1982) takes into account the increasing probability of making at least one Type I error as the number of comparisons increases (that is, probability pyramiding). Familywise error can be computed with the following formula:

$$\alpha_{FW} = (1 - \alpha)^c$$

where *c* is the number of comparisons made and $\alpha$ is your per-comparison error rate. For example, if you are making four comparisons ($c = 4$) and $\alpha = .05$, then $\alpha_{FW} = 1 - (1 - .05)^4 = 1 - .95^4 = 1 - .815 = .185$.

Special tests can be applied to control familywise error, but it is beyond the scope of this chapter to discuss each of them individually. Table 13–4 lists the tests most often used to control familywise error and gives a brief description of each. For more information about these tests, see Keppel (1982, chap. 8).

*Sample Size*    You can still use an ANOVA if your groups contain unequal numbers of subjects, but you must use adjusted computational formulas. The adjustments can take one of two forms, depending on the reasons for unequal within-cell sample sizes.

Unequal sample sizes may simply be a by-product of the way you conducted your experiment. If you conducted your experiment by randomly distributing your materials to a large group, for example, you would not be able to keep the sample sizes equal. In such cases, unequal sample sizes do not result from the properties of your treatment conditions.

Unequal sample sizes also may result from the effects of your treatments. If one of your treatments is painful or stressful, participants may drop out of your experiment because of the aversive nature of that treatment. Death of animals in a group receiving highly stressful conditions is another example of subject loss related to the experimental manipulations that result in unequal sample sizes.

*Unweighted Means Analysis*    If you end up with unequal sample sizes for reasons *not* related to the effects of your treatments, one solution is to equalize the groups by

**TABLE 13–4  Post Hoc Tests**

| TEST | USE | COMMENTS[a] |
|---|---|---|
| Scheffé test | To keep familywise error rate constant regardless of the number of comparisons to be made | Very conservative test; Scheffé correction factor corrects for all possible comparisons, even if not all are made |
| Dunnett test | To contrast several experimental groups with a single control group | Not as conservative as the Scheffé test because only the number of comparisons made is considered in the familywise error rate correction |
| Tukey-a HSD test | To hold the familywise error rate constant over an entire set of two-group comparisons | Not as conservative as the Scheffé test for comparisons between pairs of means; less powerful than the Scheffé for more complex comparisons |
| Tukey-b WSD test | Alternative Tukey test | Not as conservative as Tukey's HSD test, but more conservative than the Newman–Keuls test |
| Newman–Keuls test | To compare all possible pairs of means and control per-comparison error rate | Less conservative than the Tukey test; critical value varies according to the number of comparisons made |
| Ryan's Test (REGWQ) | Modified Newman–Keuls test in which critical values decrease as the range between the highest and lowest means decreases | Controls familywise error better than the Newman–Keuls test but is less powerful than the Newman–Keuls test |
| Duncan test | To compare all possible pairs of means | Computed in the same way as the Newman–Keuls test; with more than two means to be compared, it is less conservative than the Newman–Keuls |
| Fisher test | To compare all possible combinations of means | Powerful test that does not overcompensate to control familywise error rate; no special correction factor used; significant overall F ratio justifies comparisons |

[a]A conservative test is one with which it is more difficult to achieve statistical significance than with a less conservative test. "Power" refers to the ability of a test to reject the null hypothesis when the null hypothesis is false.

Source: Information in this table was summarized from Keppel, 1982, pp. 153–159; Pagano, 2004; Winer, 1971; and information found at http://www2.chass.ncsu.edu/garson/pa765/anova.htm.

randomly discarding the excess data from the larger groups. Even then, discarding data may not be a good idea, especially if the sample sizes are small to begin with. The loss of data inevitably reduces the power of your statistical tests.

Rather than dropping data, you could use an *unweighted means analysis* that involves a minor correction to the ANOVA. This analysis gives each group in your design equal weight in the analysis, despite unequal group sizes.

*Weighted Means Analysis*    If the inequality in sample sizes was planned or reflects actual differences in the population, you should use a *weighted means analysis* (Keppel, 1973). In a weighted means analysis, each group mean is weighted according to the number of subjects in the group. As a result, means with higher weightings (those from larger groups) contribute more to the analysis than do means with lower weights. See Keppel (1973, 1982) or Gravetter and Wallnau (2004) for more information about unequal sample size in ANOVA.

## The One-Factor Within-Subjects ANOVA

If you used a multilevel within-subjects design in your experiment, the statistical test to use is the *one-factor within-subjects* ANOVA. As in a between-subjects analysis, the between-treatments sum of squares can be affected by the level of the independent variable and by experimental error (Gravetter & Wallnau, 2004). However, unlike the between-subjects case, individual differences no longer contribute to the between-treatments sum of squares because the same subjects are in each experimental treatment group. The within-subjects source of variance(s) also can be partitioned into two factors: variability within a particular treatment (that is, different subjects reacting differently to the same treatment) and experimental error.

The contribution of individual differences is estimated by treating subjects as a factor in the analysis (S). You then subtract S from the usual within-groups variance. This subtraction reduces the amount of error in the denominator of the F ratio, thus making the F ratio more sensitive to the effects of the independent variable—a major advantage.

*The Latin Square ANOVA*    Latin square designs are used to counterbalance the order in which subjects receive treatments in within-subjects experiments (see Chapter 9). The carryover effects contained in the Latin square design tend to inflate the error term used to calculate your F ratio. Consequently, they must be removed before you calculate F. This is done by treating practice effects as a factor in the analysis and removing their effects from the error term. For more information on the Latin square ANOVA, see Keppel (1982, pp. 385–391).

*Interpreting Your F Ratio*    A significant overall F ratio tells you that significant differences exist among your means, but, as usual, it does not tell you where these significant differences occur. To determine which means differ, you must further analyze your data. The tests used to compare your means are similar to those used in the between-subjects analysis. Once again, they can be either planned or unplanned.

## The Two-Factor Between-Subjects ANOVA

Chapter 9 discussed the two-factor between-subjects design. In this design, you include two independent variables and randomly assign different subjects to each condition. In addition, you combine independent variables across groups so that you can extract the independent effect of each factor (the main effects) and the combined effect of the two factors (interaction) on the dependent variable. (If you are unclear about the meanings of these terms, review Chapter 9.) The analysis appropriate to data from this design is the *two-factor between-subjects* ANOVA. This ANOVA is necessarily more complicated than a one-factor ANOVA because it must determine the statistical significance of both main effects and their interaction as well.

*Main Effects and Interactions* If you find both significant main effects and interactions in your experiment, you must be careful about interpreting the main effects. When you interpret a main effect, you are suggesting that your independent variable has an effect on the dependent variable, regardless of the level of your other independent variable. The presence of an interaction provides evidence to the contrary. The interaction shows that neither of your independent variables has a simple, independent effect. Consequently, you should avoid interpreting main effects when an interaction is present.

Another fact to be aware of when dealing with interactions is that certain kinds of interaction can cancel out the main effects. The independent variables may have been effective, and yet the statistical analysis will fail to reveal statistically significant main effects for these factors. To see how this can happen, imagine you have conducted a two-factor experiment with two levels of each factor. Figure 13–5 shows the cell means for this hypothetical experiment.

The diagonal lines depict the functional relationship between Factor A and the dependent variable at the two levels of Factor B. The fact that the lines form an X indicates the presence of an interaction. Notice that Factor A strongly affects the level of the dependent variable at *both* levels of Factor B but that these effects run in opposite directions.

The dotted line in Figure 13–5 represents the main effect of Factor A, computed by averaging the upper and lower points to collapse across the levels of Factor B. This dotted line is horizontal, indicating that there is no change in the dependent variable across the two levels of Factor A (collapsed over Factor B). Although Factor A has strong effects on the dependent variable at each level of Factor B, its average (main) effect is zero.

Logically, if the interaction of two variables is significant, then the two variables themselves have reliable effects. Consequently, if you have a significant interaction, ignore the main effects. The factors involved in the interaction are reliable whether or not the main effects are statistically significant.

Finally, most of the time you are more interested in the significant interaction than in main effects, even before your experiment is conducted. Hypothesized relationships among variables are often stated in terms of interactions. Interactions tend to be inherently more interesting than main effects. They show how changes in one variable alter the effects on behavior of other variables.

**FIGURE 13–5**   Graph Showing a Two-Way Interaction That Masks Main Effects.

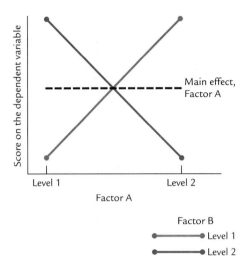

Sample Size   Just as with a one-factor ANOVA, you can compute a multifactor ANOVA with unequal sample sizes. The unweighted means analysis can be conducted on a design with two or more factors (the logic is the same). For details on modifications to the basic two-factor ANOVA formulas for weighted means and unweighted means analyses, see Keppel (1973, 1982).

*ANOVA for a Two-Factor Between-Subjects Design: An Example*   An experiment conducted by Doris Chang and Stanley Sue (2003) provides an excellent example of the application of ANOVA to the analysis of data from a two-factor experiment. Chang and Sue were interested in investigating how the race of a student affected a teacher's assessments of the student's behavior and whether those assessments were specific to certain types of issues. Teachers (163 female and 34 male) completed a survey on which they were asked to evaluate the behavior of three hypothetical children. Each survey included a photograph of either an Asian-American, an African-American or a Caucasian child. The survey also included a short description of the child's behavior. The child's behavior was depicted as falling into one of three "problem" types: (1) "overcontrolled" (anxious to please and afraid of making mistakes), (2) "undercontrolled" (disobedient, disruptive, and easily frustrated), or (3) "normal" (generally follows rules, fidgets only occasionally, etc.). These two variables comprise the two independent variables in a 3 (race of child) × 3 (problem type) factorial design. The survey also included several measures on which teachers evaluated the child's behavior (e.g., seriousness, how typical the behavior was, attributions for the causes of the behavior, and academic performance).

We limit our discussion of the results to one of the dependent variables: typicality of the behavior. The data were analyzed with a two-factor ANOVA. The results showed a significant main effect of problem type, $F(2, 368) = 46.19, p < .0001$. Normal behavior ($\bar{X} = 6.10$) was seen as more typical than either undercontrolled ($\bar{X} = 4.08$) or overcontrolled ($\bar{X} = 4.34$) behavior. The ANOVA also showed a statistically significant race × problem-type interaction, $F(4, 368) = 7.37, p < .0001$.

*Interpreting the Results*    This example shows how to interpret the results from a two-factor ANOVA. First, consider the two main effects. There was a significant effect of problem type on typicality ratings. Normal behavior was rated as more typical than overcontrolled or undercontrolled behavior. If this were the only significant effect, you could then conclude that race of the child had no effect on typicality ratings because the main effect of race was not statistically significant. However, this conclusion is not warranted, because of the presence of a significant interaction between race of learner and problem type.

The presence of a significant interaction suggests that the relationship between the two independent variables and your dependent variable is complex. Figure 13–6 shows the data contributing to the significant interaction in the Chang and Sue experiment. Analyzing a significant interaction like this one involves making comparisons among the means involved.

Because Chang and Sue predicted the interaction, they used planned comparisons (*t* tests) to contrast the relevant means. The results showed that the typicality of the Asian-American child's behavior was evaluated very differently from that of the Caucasian child and African-American child. Teachers saw the normal behavior of the Asian-American child as less typical than the normal behavior of either the Caucasian or African-American child. Teachers saw the overcontrolled behavior by the Asian-American child as more typical than the same behavior attributed to the African-American or Caucasian child. The undercontrolled behavior was seen as less typical for the Asian-American child than for the African-American and Caucasian children, respectively. So the race of the child did affect how participants rated the typicality of a behavior, but the nature of that effect depended on the type of behavior attributed to the child.

## The Two-Factor Within-Subjects ANOVA

All subjects in a within-subjects design with two factors are exposed to every possible combination of levels of your two independent variables. These designs are analyzed

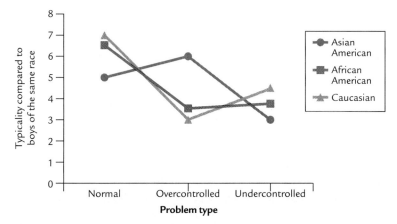

**FIGURE 13–6**    Results from Chang and Sue's (2003) Experiment Showing an Interaction between Race and Problem Type. Reprinted with permission.

using a *two-factor within-subjects* ANOVA. This analysis applies the same logic developed for the one-factor within-subjects ANOVA. As in the one-factor case, subjects are treated as a factor along with your manipulated independent variables.

The major difference between the one- and two-factor within-subject ANOVA is that you must consider the interaction between each of your independent variables and the subjects factor (A × S and B × S), in addition to the interaction between your independent variables (A × B). Because the basic logic and interpretation of results from a within-subjects ANOVA are essentially the same as for the between-subjects ANOVA, a complete example is not given here. A complete example of the two-factor within-subjects ANOVA can be found in Keppel (1973).

## Mixed Designs

In some situations, your research may call for a design mixing between-subjects and within-subjects components. This design was discussed briefly in Chapter 10. If you use such a design (known as a *mixed* or *split-plot* design), you can analyze your data with an ANOVA. The computations involve calculating sums of squares for the between factor and for the within factor.

The most complex part of the analysis is the selection of an error term to calculate the *F* ratios. The within-groups mean square is used to calculate the between-subjects *F*, whereas the interaction of the within factor with the within-groups variance is used to evaluate both the within-subjects factor and the interaction between the within-subjects and between-subjects factors. Keppel (1973, 1982) provides an excellent discussion of this analysis and a complete worked example.

## Higher-Order and Special-Case ANOVAs

There are variations of ANOVA for just about any design used in research. For example, you can include three or four factors in a single experiment and analyze the data with a *higher-order* ANOVA. In a three-factor ANOVA, for example, you can test three main effects (A, B, and C), three two-way interactions (AB, AC, and BC), and a three-way interaction (ABC). As you add factors, however, the computations become more complex and probably should not be done by hand. In addition, as discussed in Chapter 9, it may be difficult to interpret the higher-order interactions with more than four factors.

A special ANOVA is used when you have included a continuous correlational variable in your experiment (such as age). This type of ANOVA, called the **analysis of covariance (ANCOVA),** allows you to examine the relationship between experimentally manipulated variables while controlling another variable that may be correlated with them. Keppel (1973, 1982) provides clear discussions of these analyses and other issues relating to ANCOVA.

To summarize, ANOVA is a powerful parametric statistic used to analyze one-factor experiments (either within-subjects or between-subjects) with more than two treatments and to analyze multifactor experiments. It is intended for use when your dependent variable is scaled on at least an interval scale. The assumptions that apply to the use of parametric statistics in general (such as homogeneity of variance and normally distributed sampling distribution) apply to ANOVA.

ANOVA involves forming a ratio between the variance caused by your independent variable plus experimental error and the variance (mean square) caused by experimental error alone. The resulting score is called an $F$ ratio. A significant $F$ ratio tells you that at least one of your means differs from the other means. Once a significant effect is found, you then perform more detailed analyses of the means contributing to the significant effect in order to determine where the significant differences occur. These tests become more complicated as the design of your experiment becomes more complex.

## NONPARAMETRIC STATISTICS

Thus far, this discussion has centered on parametric statistical tests. In some situations, however, you may not be able to use a parametric test. When your data do not meet the assumptions of a parametric test, or when your dependent variable was scaled on a nominal or ordinal scale, consider a nonparametric test. This section discusses three nonparametric tests: chi-square, the Mann–Whitney $U$ test, and the Wilcoxon signed ranks test. You might consider using many other nonparametric tests. For a complete description of these, see Siegel and Castellan (1988). Table 13–5 summarizes some information on these and other nonparametric tests.

### Chi-Square

When your dependent variable is a dichotomous decision (such as yes–no or guilty–not guilty) or a frequency count (such as how many people voted for Candidate A and how many for Candidate B), the statistic of choice is **chi-square ($\chi^2$)**. Versions of chi-square exist for studies with one and two variables. This discussion is limited to the two-variable case. For further information on the one-variable analysis, see either Siegel and Castellan (1988) or Roscoe (1975).

*Chi-Square for Contingency Tables*    Chi-square for contingency tables (also called the chi-square test for independence) is designed for frequency data in which the relationship, or contingency, between two variables is to be determined. In a voter preference study, for example, you might have measured sex of respondent in addition to candidate preference. You may want to know whether the two variables are related or independent. The chi-square test for contingency tables compares your *observed cell frequencies* (those you obtained in your study) with the *expected cell frequencies* (those you would expect to find if chance alone were operating).

A study reported by Harari, Harari, and White (1985) provided an excellent example of the application of the chi-square test to the analysis of frequency data. Harari et al. investigated whether male participants would help the victim of a simulated rape. Previous research on helping behavior suggested that individuals are less likely to help someone in distress if they are with others than if they are alone. Harari et al. conducted a field investigation of this effect. Participants (either walking alone or in noninteracting groups) were exposed to a mock rape (a male confederate of the

**TABLE 13–5    Nonparametric Tests**

| TEST | MINIMUM SCALE OF MEASUREMENT | COMMENTS |
|------|------------------------------|----------|
| *One-Sample Tests* | | |
| Binomial | Nominal | |
| Chi-square | Nominal | |
| Kolmogorov–Smirnov | Ordinal | Can be used as a more powerful alternative to chi-square |
| *Two Independent Samples* | | |
| Chi-square | Nominal | |
| Fisher exact probability | Nominal | Alternative to chi-square when expected frequencies are small |
| Kolmogorov–Smirnov | Ordinal | More powerful than the Mann–Whitney $U$ test |
| Wald–Wolfowitz runs | Ordinal | |
| Moses test of extreme reactions | Ordinal | Less powerful than Mann–Whitney $U$ test |
| Randomization test | Interval | Tests the difference between means without assuming normality of data or homogeneity of variance |
| Mann–Whitney $U$ | Ordinal or above | Good alternative to $t$ test when assumptions violated |
| *Two Related Samples* | | |
| McNemar | Nominal | Good test when you have a before–after hypothesis |
| Sign | Ordinal | Good when quantitative measures are not possible, but you can rank data |
| Wilcoxon matched pairs | Ordinal | Good alternative to $t$ test when normality assumption is violated |
| Walsh test | Interval | Good nonparametric alternative to the $t$ test; data must be distributed symmetrically |
| Randomization test for matched pairs | Interval | |

*continues*

**TABLE 13–5    Nonparametric Tests    *(continued)***

| TEST | MINIMUM SCALE OF MEASUREMENT | COMMENTS |
|------|------------------------------|----------|
| *More Than Two Related Samples* | | |
| Cochran Q test | Nominal | Most useful when data fall into natural dichotomous categories |
| Friedman two-way ANOVA | Ordinal | |
| *More Than Two Independent Samples* | | |
| Chi-square | Nominal | |
| Kruskal–Wallis one-way ANOVA | Ordinal | Good alternative to a one-factor ANOVA when assumptions are violated |

SOURCE: Data from Roscoe, 1975, and Siegel & Castellan, 1988.

experimenters grabs a female confederate and drags her into some bushes). Observers recorded how many participants helped the female rape victim. Table 13–6 shows the frequencies of participants helping under the two conditions. The results from a chi-square test performed on these data showed a significant relationship between the decision to offer help and whether participants were alone or in groups. Participants in groups were actually more likely to help than those who were alone.

*Limitations of Chi-Square*    A problem arises if any of your expected cell frequencies is less than five. In such cases, the value of chi-square may be artificially inflated (Gravetter & Wallnau, 2004). You have three options to deal with this problem. First, you could include more subjects to increase your sample size. Second, you could combine cells (if it is logical to do so). For example, you could categorize subjects into three categories rather than five. Third, you could consider a different test. The Fisher exact probability test (see Roscoe, 1975, or Siegel & Castellan, 1988) is an alternative to chi-square when you have small expected frequencies and a $2 \times 2$ contingency table (Roscoe, 1975).

A significant chi-square tells you that your two variables are significantly related. In the previous example, all you know is that group size and helping are related. As with ANOVA, however, chi-square does not tell you where the significant differences occur when more than two categories of each variable exist. To determine the locus of the significant effects, you can conduct separate chi-square tests on specific cells of the contingency table.

TABLE 13–6    **Number of Participants Helping Mock Rape Victim, in Two Conditions**

|  | INTERVENED | DID NOT INTERVENE |  |
|---|---|---|---|
| PARTICIPANTS IN GROUPS | 34 | 6 | 40 |
| PARTICIPANTS ALONE | 26 | 14 | 40 |
|  | 60 | 20 |  |

SOURCE: Data from Hatari, Hatari, & White, 1985.

### The Mann–Whitney U Test

Another powerful nonparametric test is the **Mann–Whitney U test**. The Mann–Whitney U test can be used when your dependent variable is scaled on at least an ordinal scale. It is also a good alternative to the t test when your data do not meet the assumptions of the t test (such as when the scores are not normally distributed, when the variances are heterogeneous, or when you have small sample sizes).

Calculation of the Mann–Whitney U test is fairly simple. The first step is to combine the data from your two groups. Scores are ranked (from highest to lowest) and labeled according to the group to which they belong. If there is a difference between your groups, then the ranks for the scores in one group should be consistently above the ranks from the other group, rather than being randomly distributed. A U score is calculated for each group in your experiment. The lower of the two U scores obtained is then evaluated against critical values of U. If the lower of the two U scores is *smaller* than the tabled U value, you then conclude your two groups differ significantly.

### The Wilcoxon Signed Ranks Test

If you conducted a single-factor experiment using a correlated-samples (related) or matched-pairs design, the **Wilcoxon signed ranks test** would be a good statistic to analyze your data. For this test, a difference score is calculated for each pair of scores for each subject. The resulting difference scores are then ranked (disregarding the sign of the difference score) from smallest to largest. Next, each rank is assigned a positive or negative sign, depending on whether the difference score was positive or negative. The positive and negative ranks are then summed. If the null hypothesis is true, then the two sums should be equal or very close to being equal. However, if the sums of the positive and negative ranks are very different, then the null hypothesis can be rejected. For more information on the Wilcoxon signed ranks test, see Siegel and Castellan (1988).

### Parametric versus Nonparametric Statistics

Nonparametric statistics are useful when your data do not meet the assumptions of parametric statistics. If you have a choice, choose a parametric statistic over a nonparametric one because parametric statistics are generally more powerful. That is, the parametric statistic usually provides a more sensitive test of the null hypothesis than does an equivalent nonparametric statistic.

A second problem with nonparametric statistics is that appropriate versions are not always available for complex designs. Consequently, when designing your study, you should try to scale your dependent measures so an ANOVA or other suitable parametric statistic can be used.

## SPECIAL TOPICS IN INFERENTIAL STATISTICS

The application of the appropriate inferential statistic may appear simple and straight-forward. However, several factors must be considered, beyond whether to apply a parametric or nonparametric statistic, when using any inferential statistic. This section discusses some special topics to consider when deciding on a strategy to statistically evaluate data.

### Power of a Statistical Test

Inferential statistics are designed to help you determine the validity of the null hypothesis. Consequently, you want your statistics to detect differences in your data that are inconsistent with the null hypothesis. The **power** of a statistical test is its ability to detect these differences. Put in statistical terms, power is a statistic's ability to correctly reject the null hypothesis (Gravetter & Wallnau, 2004). A powerful statistic is more sensitive to differences in your data than a less powerful one.

The issue of the power of your statistical test is an important one. Rejection of the null hypothesis implies that your independent variable affected your dependent variable. Failure to reject the null hypothesis may lead you to abandon a potentially fruitful line of research. Consequently, you want to be reasonably sure your failure to reject the null hypothesis is not caused by a lack of power in your statistical test.

The power of your statistical test is affected by your chosen alpha level, the size of your sample, whether you use a one-tailed or two-tailed test, and the size of the effect produced by your independent variable.

*Alpha Level*    As you reduce your alpha level (for example, from .05 to .01), you reduce the probability of making a Type I error. Adopting a more conservative alpha level makes it more difficult to reject the null hypothesis. Unfortunately, it also reduces power. Given a constant error variance, a larger difference between means is required to obtain statistical significance with a more conservative alpha level.

*Sample Size*    The power of your statistical test increases with the size of your sample because larger samples provide more stable estimates of population parameters. In particular, the standard errors of the means from your treatments will be lower, so the likely positions of the population means fall within narrower bounds. Consequently, it is easier to detect small differences in population means and thus to reject the null hypothesis when it is false.

*One-Tailed versus Two-Tailed Tests*    A two-tailed test is less powerful than a one-tailed test. This can be easily demonstrated by looking at the critical values of *t* found in Table 2 in the appendix. At 20 degrees of freedom, the critical value at $\alpha = .05$ for a one-tailed test is 1.73. For a two-tailed test, the critical value is 2.09. It is thus easier to reject the null hypothesis with the one-tailed test than with the two-tailed test.

See
table
c.7

*Effect Size*    The degree to which the manipulation of your independent variable changes the value of the dependent variable is termed the **effect size**. To facilitate comparison across variables and experiments, effect size is usually reported as a proportion of the variation in scores *within* the treatments under comparison; for example, the effect size for the difference between two treatment means might be reported as $(X_2 - X_1)/s$, where *s* is the pooled sample standard deviation (Cohen, 1988). Measured in this way, effect size estimates the amount of overlap between the two population distributions from which the samples were drawn. Large effect sizes indicate relatively little overlap: The mean of Population 2 lies far into one tail of the distribution of Population 1, so that a real difference in population means is likely to be detected in the inferential test (good power). Small effect sizes indicate great overlap in the population distributions and, thus, everything else being equal, relatively little power. However, because inferential tests rely on the sampling distribution of the test statistic rather than the population distributions, you may be able to improve power in such cases by, for example, increasing the sample size.

*Determining Power*    Because the business of inferential statistics is to allow you to decide whether or not to reject the null hypothesis, the issue of power is important. You want to be reasonably sure that your decision is correct. Failure to achieve statistical significance in your experiment (thus not rejecting the null hypothesis) can be caused by many factors. Your independent variable actually may have no effect, or your experiment may have been carried out so poorly that the effect was buried in error variance. Or maybe your statistic simply was not powerful enough to detect the difference, or you did not use enough subjects.

Although alpha (the probability of rejecting the null hypothesis when it is true) can be set directly, it is not so easy to determine what the power of your analysis will be. However, you can work backward from a desired amount of power to estimate the sample sizes required for a study. To calculate these estimates, you must be willing to state the amount of power required, the magnitude of the difference you expect to find in your experiment, and the expected error variance.

The expected difference between means and the expected error variance can be estimated from pilot research, from theory, or from previous research in your area. For example, if previous research has found a small effect of your independent variable (for example, two points), you can use this as an estimate of the size of your effect.

Unfortunately, the proper amount of power is not easy to establish. There is no agreed-on acceptable or desirable level of power (Keppel, 1982). If you are willing and able to specify the values mentioned, however, you can estimate the size of the sample needed to detect differences of a given magnitude in your research. (See Gravetter & Wallnau, 2004, or Keppel, 1982, for a discussion on how to calculate sample size.)

Too much power can be as bad as too little. If you ran enough subjects, you could conceivably find statistical significance in even the most minute and trivial of differences. Similarly, when you use a correlation, you can achieve statistical significance if you include enough subjects. Consequently, your sample should be large enough to be sensitive to differences between treatments, but not so large as to produce significant but trivial results.

The possibility of your results being statistically significant and yet trivial may seem strange to you. If so, the next section may clarify this concept.

## Statistical versus Practical Significance

To say results are significant (statistically speaking) merely indicates that the observed differences between sample means are probably reliable, not the result of chance. Confusion arises when you give the word *significant* its more common meaning. Something "significant" in this more common sense is important or worthy of note.

The fact that the treatment means of your experiment differ significantly may or may not be important. If the difference is predicted by a particular theory and not by others, then the finding may be important because it supports the theory over the others. The finding also may be important if it shows that one variable strongly affects another. Such findings may have practical implications by demonstrating, for example, the superiority of a new therapeutic technique. In such cases, a statistically significant (that is, reliable) finding also may have *practical significance*.

Advertisers sometimes purposely blur the distinction between statistical and practical significance. A few years ago, Bayer aspirin announced the results of a "hospital study on pain other than headache." Evidently, groups of hospital patients were treated with Bayer aspirin and with several other brands. The advertisement glossed over the details of the study, but apparently the patients were asked to rate the severity of their pain at some point after taking Bayer or Brand X (the identities of both brands were probably concealed). According to the ad, "the results were significant—Bayer was better." However, the ad did not say in what way the results were significant. Evidently, the results were statistically significant and thus probably not caused by chance. Without any information about the pain ratings, however, you do not know if this finding has any practical significance. It may be that the Bayer and Brand X group ratings differed by less than 1 point on a 10-point scale. Although this average difference may have been reliable, it also may be the case that no individual could tell the difference between two pains so close together on the scale. In that case, the statistically significant difference would have no practical significance and would provide no reason for choosing Bayer over other brands of aspirin.

## The Meaning of the Level of Significance

In the behavioral sciences, an alpha level of .05 (or 1 chance in 20) is usually considered the maximum acceptable rate for Type I errors. This level provides reasonable protection against Type I errors while also maintaining a reasonable level of power for most analyses. Of course, if you want to guard more strongly against Type I errors, you can adopt a more stringent alpha level, such as the .01 level (1 chance in 100).

Whatever alpha level you determine is reasonable for your purposes, remember this number does nothing more than provide a criterion for deciding whether the differences you have obtained are reliable. A difference is either reliable or it is not. If your results are significant at the .0001 level, they are not any more reliable than if they were significant at the .05 level. It does not mean your results are "more significant" or "more reliable" than significant results obtained at the .05 level. If the results are statistically significant at your chosen alpha level, it simply means you are willing to believe that the differences are real. However, lower alpha levels (moving from .05 to .01) allow you greater confidence in your decision about your results.

The importance of Type I errors may vary depending on the type of research and the purposes to which the information may be put. For example, applied research may be better evaluated at a less conservative alpha level (for example, $p < .10$). If you were testing the effectiveness of a new form of judicial instruction on the reduction of bias against Black defendants, a Type II error might be more serious than a Type I error. If you retain the null hypothesis when it is false, more Black defendants may be convicted as a result.

Ultimately, it is up to you to decide on an appropriate balance between Type I and Type II errors. Unfortunately, most journals will not publish a finding unless it is significant at least at the $p < .05$ level. Chapter 3 examined this issue in the discussion of publication practices.

## Data Transformations

Sometimes you may find it necessary to transform your data with the appropriate **data transformation**. Transforming data means converting your original data to a new scale. For example, a simple transformation can be accomplished by adding or subtracting a constant to or from your data. You might do this if the original numbers are very large. When you compute some statistics, large numbers make the computations difficult. Subtracting a constant from each score can make the numbers manageable without affecting the relationships within the data. Conversely, adding a constant to each score might remove negative numbers.

When you add or subtract a constant, the shape of the original frequency distribution does not change. The mean of the distribution changes, but its standard deviation does not. When you multiply or divide by a constant, both the mean and standard deviation change. Such transformations, called *linear transformations*, simply change the magnitude of the numbers representing your data, but they do not change the scale of measurement.

Certain statistics can be used only if your data meet certain assumptions. If your data do not meet these assumptions, you could choose a different statistic. Unfortunately, this is not always desirable or possible. A nonparametric statistic that can be substituted for a parametric statistic may not exist for your experimental situation. Another solution is to consider using a data transformation that will tend to correct the problem (for example, by changing a skewed distribution of scores into a normal one or by removing inhomogeneities in variance). Different problems with the data require different transformations to correct them. Table 13–7 lists some of the more popular data transformations and the conditions under which each might be used.

Data transformations to make data conform to the assumptions of a statistic are being used less and less frequently (Keppel, 1973). ANOVA, perhaps the most commonly used inferential statistic, appears to be very robust against even moderately serious violations of its assumptions underlying the test. For example, Winer (1971) has

**TABLE 13-7    Data Transformations and Uses**

| TRANSFORMATION | FORMULA | USE |
|---|---|---|
| *Square root* | $X' = \sqrt{X}$<br>or<br>$X' = \sqrt{X + 1}$ [a] | When cell means and variances are related, this transformation makes variances more homogeneous; also, if data show a moderate positive skew |
| *Arcsin* | $X' = 2\arcsin\sqrt{X}$<br>or<br>$X' = 2\arcsin\sqrt{X \pm (1/2n)}$ [b] | When basic observations are proportions and have a binomial distribution |
| *Log* | $X' = \log X$<br>or<br>$X' = \log(X + 1)$ [c] | Normalizes data with severe positive skew |

[a]Formula used if basic observations are frequencies or if values of $X$ are small.
[b]Formula used if values of $X$ are close to 0 or 1.
[c]Formula used if value of $X$ is equal to or near 0.

SOURCE: Information summarized from Tabachnick & Fidell, 2001, and Winer, 1971.

demonstrated that even if the within-cell variances vary by a 3:1 ratio, the $F$ test is not seriously biased. Transformations of the data may not be necessary in these cases. Also, when you transform your data, your conclusions must be based on the transformed scale and not the original. In most cases, this is not a problem. However, Keppel (1973) provides an example in which a square-root transformation changed significantly the relationship between two means. Prior to transformation, the mean for group 1 was lower than the mean for group 2. The opposite was true after transformation.

Use data transformations only when absolutely necessary, because they can be tricky. Sometimes transformations of data correct one aspect of the data (such as restoring normality) but induce new violations of assumptions (such as heterogeneity of variance). If you must use a data transformation, before going forward with your analysis, check to be sure that the transformation had the intended effect.

## Alternatives to Inferential Statistics

Inferential statistics are tools to help you make a decision about the null hypothesis. Essentially, inferential statistics provide you with a way to test the reliability of a single experiment. When you reject the null hypothesis at $p < .05$, it means a difference (as large as or larger than the one obtained) resulting by chance would occur only once (on the average) in 20 replications of the experiment.

Because such chance differences are relatively rare, you conclude that the difference you obtained was probably not due to chance but rather to the effect of the independent variable. If, in fact, the independent variable was the cause of the observed differences, then you would expect to obtain similar results on replication of the experiment. In other words, you would expect your findings to be reliable.

Inferential statistics cannot always be applied to assess the reliability of your results. You may have too few subjects (such as in single-subject or small-n research designs). Or you may have data that badly violate the assumptions of parametric tests with no appropriate nonparametric statistic to use instead. In these cases, you may test the reliability of your data by replication.

*Replication* means that you repeat your experiment. If your data are reliable, you should find a highly similar pattern of results after each replication. Replication does not mean that you have to conduct exactly the same experiment each time. Often a subsequent experiment in a series will include conditions that replicate those of the original experiment. The subsequent experiment may include conditions designed to test the effects of changing some parameters within the original context. The new experiment will provide a check on the original findings while providing new information.

Keep in mind that replication is not limited to small-n designs or situations in which violations of assumptions occur. You can include an element of replication in just about any study. Moreover, you need not limit yourself to replicating your own findings. If previous research shows a certain effect, you may wish to replicate that finding in your own research before extending your observations to new situations. Indeed, such replications are the heart of the scientific method. When successful, they demonstrate the reliability of findings both within the original context and across experimenters, subjects, and laboratories. When unsuccessful, they point to potentially important variables that may limit the generality of findings to particular situations and parameters. Either result can be important for the advancement of scientific knowledge.

Inferential statistics were developed to assess the reliability of findings within the confines of a single set of observations. By providing an index of probable reliability, they reduce the need for direct replication and thus save time and money by reducing the requirement for subjects. Nevertheless, they should not be viewed as a substitute for replication. Probably no finding in psychology has been accepted on the basis of a single experiment that was statistically significant at some alpha level. The value of inferential statistics is found not so much in the elimination of replication as in their warning that the effects apparent in research data may result from nothing more than random factors. Human beings are extremely good at recognizing patterns, even when such patterns are simply the result of "noise." Inferential statistics can control the human tendency to interpret every apparent trend or difference in the data as if it were meaningful.

Inferential statistics sometimes may lack sufficient power and therefore may fail to detect effects that are clearly shown by replication. A case in point is provided by a series of experiments conducted by one of the authors of this text (Abbott) to test the effect of predictable versus unpredictable stress schedules on pain sensitivity. In each experiment, three groups of eight rats were exposed to a schedule of predictable stress, unpredictable stress, or no stress. The subjects were then tested in the same apparatus for pain sensitivity by means of the "tail flick" test. In the tail flick test, a hot beam of light was focused on the rat's tail. The length of time elapsing until the rat flicked its tail out of the beam (a protective reflex) indicated the degree of pain sensitivity.

The results of the first experiment indicated that the two groups exposed to stress were less sensitive to the heat than the group exposed to no stress, replicating a well-established finding. In addition, the group exposed to unpredictable stress seemed less sensitive than the group exposed to predictable stress. However, this effect was not statistically significant ($p > .05$).

Parameters of the experiment were twice altered in ways that were expected to increase the size of the predictability effect (if it existed), and the experiment was replicated. However, each replication produced virtually the identical result. On each occasion, the unpredictable stress group demonstrated less sensitivity to pain than the predictable stress group, and each time this difference was not statistically significant.

The problem could be dealt with by taking measures to increase the power of the statistical test (such as increasing sample sizes or going to a matched groups design). However, to do so would appear to be a waste of resources. In this case, the reliability of the finding was already established through replication, even though the statistical analysis itself indicated that the results were probably not reliable.

Inferential statistics are simply a guide to decision making and are not the goal of the research project. As such, you should not design and conduct your research in a particular way simply because a particular inferential statistic is available to analyze such a design. Much like designing your experiment before developing hypotheses, choosing a statistical test before designing a study can place unwanted restrictions on your research. For example, you may not be able to manipulate your independent variable the way you would like and may miss some important relationships. Instead, design your study to answer your research questions in the clearest way possible, and then select the method of analysis (whether inferential statistic or replication) that works best for that design.

## SUMMARY

This chapter has reviewed some of the basics of inferential statistics. Inferential statistics go beyond simple description of results. They allow you to determine whether the differences observed in your sample are reliable. Inferential statistics allow you to make a decision about the viability of the null hypothesis (which states that there is no difference among treatments) while controlling the probability of rejecting the null hypothesis when it is, in fact, true (Type I error). The two types of inferential statistics are parametric and nonparametric. Parametric tests (such as the $t$ test and ANOVA) make assumptions about the populations underlying your samples. For example, these tests assume that the sampling distribution of means is normal and that there is homogeneity of within-cell variances. Parametric statistics are designed for use when your data are scaled on at least an interval scale. If your data seriously violate the assumptions of a parametric test, or your data are scaled on a nominal or ordinal scale, a nonparametric statistic can be used (such as chi-square or the Mann–Whitney $U$ test). These tests are usually easier to compute than parametric tests. However, they are less powerful and more limited in application. Nonparametric statistics may not be available for higher-order factorial designs.

Statistical significance indicates that the difference between your means was unlikely if only chance were at work. It suggests that your independent variable had an effect. Two factors contribute to a statistically significant effect: the size of the difference between means and the variability among the scores. You can have a large difference between means, but if the variability is high, you may not find statistical significance. Conversely, you may have a very small difference and find a significant effect if the variability is low.

Consider the power of your statistical test when evaluating your results. If you do not find statistical significance, perhaps no differences exist. Or it could mean that your test was not sensitive enough to pick up small differences that do exist. Sample size is an important contributor to power. Generally, the larger the sample, the more powerful the statistic. This is because larger samples are more representative of the underlying populations than are small samples. Use a sample that is large enough to be sensitive to differences but not so large as to be oversensitive. There are methods for determining optimal sample sizes for a given level of power. However, you must be willing and able to specify an expected magnitude of the treatment effect, an estimate of error variance, and the desired power. The first two can be estimated from pilot data or previous research. Unfortunately, there is no agreed-on acceptable level of power.

An alpha level of .05 is the largest generally acceptable level for Type I errors. This value has been chosen because it represents a reasonable compromise between Type I and Type II errors. In some cases (such as in applied research), the .05 level may be too conservative. However, journals probably will not publish results that fail to reach the conventional level of significance

Data transformations are available for those situations in which your data are in some way abnormal. You may transform data if the numbers are large and unmanageable or if your data do not meet the assumptions of a statistical test. The transformation of data to meet assumptions of a test, however, is being done less frequently because inferential statistics tend to be robust against the effects of even moderately severe violations of assumptions. Transformations should be used sparingly, because they change the nature of the variables of your study.

## REVIEW QUESTIONS

1. Why are sampling distributions important in inferential statistics?
2. What is sampling error, and why is it important to know about?
3. What are degrees of freedom, and how do they relate to inferential statistics?
4. How do parametric and nonparametric statistics differ?
5. What is the general logic behind inferential statistics?
6. How are Type I and Type II errors related?
7. What does statistical significance mean?
8. When should you use a one-tailed or a two-tailed test?
9. What are the assumptions underlying parametric statistics?

10. Which parametric statistics would you use to analyze data from a experiment with two groups? Identify which statistic would be used for a particular type of design or data.
11. Which parametric statistic is most appropriate for designs with more than one level of a single independent variable?
12. When would you do a planned versus an unplanned comparison and why?
13. What is the difference between weighted and unweighted means analysis, and when would you use each?
14. What are a main effect and an interaction, and how are they analyzed?
15. Under what conditions would you use a nonparametric statistic?
16. What is meant by the power of a statistical test, and what factors can affect it?
17. Does a statistically significant finding always have practical significance? Why or why not?
18. When are data transformations used, and what should you consider when using one?
19. What are the alternatives to inferential statistics for evaluating the reliability of data?

## KEY TERMS

inferential statistics

standard error of the mean

degrees of freedom (df)

Type I error

Type II error

alpha level ($\alpha$)

critical region

t test

t test for independent samples

t test for correlated samples

z test for the difference between two proportions

analysis of variance (ANOVA)

F ratio

p value

planned comparisons

unplanned comparisons

per-comparison error

familywise error

analysis of covariance (ANCOVA)

chi-square ($\chi^2$)

Mann–Whitney U test

Wilcoxon signed ranks test

power

effect size

data transformation

# 14

# Using Multivariate Design and Analysis

During discussions of experimental and nonexperimental design, previous chapters assumed that only one dependent variable was included in a design, or that multiple dependent variables were treated separately in any statistical tests. This approach to analysis is called a **univariate strategy**. Although many research questions can be addressed with a univariate strategy, others are best addressed by considering variables together in a single analysis. When you include two or more dependent measures in a single analysis, you are using a **multivariate strategy**.

This chapter introduces the major multivariate analysis techniques. Keep in mind that providing an in-depth introduction to these techniques in the confines of one chapter is impossible. Such a task is better suited to an entire book. Also, the complex and laborious calculations needed to compute multivariate statistics are better left to computers. Consequently, this chapter does not discuss the mathematics behind these statistical tests, except for those cases in which some mathematical analysis is required to understand the issues. Instead, this chapter focuses on practical issues: applications of the various statistics, the assumptions that must be met, and interpretation of results. If you want to use any of the statistics discussed in this chapter, read *Using Multivariate Statistics* (Tabachnick & Fidell, 2001) or one of the many monographs published by Sage Publications (such as Asher, 1976, or Levine, 1977).

## CORRELATIONAL AND EXPERIMENTAL MULTIVARIATE DESIGNS

A **multivariate design** is a research design in which multiple dependent or multiple predictor variables are included. Analysis of data from such designs requires special statistical procedures. Multivariate design and analysis apply to both experimental and correlational research studies. The following sections describe some of the available multivariate statistical tests.

## Correlational Multivariate Design

If you include multiple measures in a correlational study, one strategy you could use to evaluate the degree of relationship among dependent measures is to calculate bivariate correlations (for example, Pearson correlations) for all possible pairs of measures. Or you might choose a *multivariate correlational analysis* in which you include all your measures in a single analysis.

Several analyses are designed to assess complex correlational relationships among multiple dependent variables. For example, the goal of **multiple regression** is to explain the variation in one variable (the dependent or *criterion variable*) based on variation in a set of others (the *predictor variables*). You measure several variables, one of which serves as the criterion variable in the analysis and the others as predictors. Precisely what constitutes a "predictor variable" and what constitutes a "criterion variable" is not related to anything inherent in the variable itself. Rather, you decide which variables to use as predictors based on your research question. Relevant previous research, theory, or practical experience should guide your decision about which variables should be measured and what role each variable should play in your analysis.

Two other multivariate techniques used to evaluate relationships in a correlational study are **discriminant analysis** and **canonical correlation**. Discriminant analysis is a variation of multiple regression in which your criterion variable is measured nominally (for example, yes–no). Canonical correlation allows you to evaluate the relationship between two *sets* of variables, one of which may be identified as a predictor set and the other as the criterion variable set.

In some research situations (questionnaire and test construction, for example), you may reduce a large set of variables to smaller sets that consist of variables relating to one another. **Factor analysis** is used for this purpose. In this analysis, several dependent variables are analyzed to find out if any of them constitute common underlying dimensions called *factors*. You examine the dependent variables that make up the factors to identify the dimension that those variables represent.

*Advantages of the Correlational Multivariate Strategy*   Single multivariate analysis has two major advantages over separate bivariate analyses. First, if you conduct a large number of independent bivariate correlation analyses, you increase your risk of finding relationships that occur merely by chance. Multivariate statistics allow you to look at complex relationships while controlling such statistical errors. Second, independent univariate analyses allow you to evaluate relationships only between *pairs* of variables. You may discover that Variable X correlates highly with Variable Y. However, what you do not know is whether this high correlation will persist when you consider a third variable, Z. It may be that X is correlated with Y only because Z is highly correlated with X. Multivariate statistics provide the information needed to evaluate the importance of a predictor variable for explaining variability in the criterion variable, given the effects of other predictor variables.

## Experimental Multivariate Design

The logic of univariate experimental design applies to multivariate design. That is, you manipulate one or more independent variable(s) and look for changes in the values of your dependent variables. The major difference between a univariate experimental strategy and a multivariate experimental strategy is how dependent variables are handled. When you use a univariate strategy, multiple dependent measures are analyzed separately with multiple statistical tests. In contrast, when you use a multivariate strategy, multiple dependent variables are combined statistically (based on the correlations among them) and analyzed with a single statistical test.

Implied in your choice of a multivariate design over a univariate design is that your dependent measures are correlated. Typically, you include multiple dependent measures because you have some reason to believe that those measures are important to the phenomenon under study and that those measures relate in some way to one another. Multivariate statistical techniques take into account the correlations among your dependent measures and, in most cases, use them to your advantage.

*Multivariate Statistical Tests*    The two multivariate statistics most widely used to analyze multiple dependent variables in an experimental design are **multivariate analysis of variance (MANOVA)** and *multivariate analysis of covariance (MANCOVA)*. As with univariate statistics, these tests help you to evaluate the reliability of the relationship between your independent variable (or variables) and your dependent variables.

*Advantages of the Experimental Multivariate Strategy*    A multivariate experimental strategy has several advantages over a univariate strategy. First, collecting several dependent measures and treating them as a correlated set may reveal relationships that might be missed if a traditional univariate approach were taken. Because multivariate statistical tests consider the correlations among dependent variables, they tend to be more powerful than separate univariate tests of those same dependent variables. Second, because all your dependent variables are handled in a single analysis, complex relationships among variables can be studied with less chance of making a Type I error than when using multiple univariate tests (Bray & Maxwell, 1982).

A third advantage of the multivariate strategy is realized when you have used a within-subjects design. A fairly restrictive set of assumptions underlies the univariate within-subjects ANOVA that are often difficult to satisfy. Using MANOVA allows you to analyze your data with less concern over these restrictive assumptions.

## Causal Inference

Multivariate techniques allow you to draw some *tentative* causal inferences from your correlational data. At the least, when properly applied, they allow you to have greater confidence in possible causal connections among variables. However, remember that you are still using correlational data, so any causal inferences you draw must be discussed with caution.

Path analysis, which applies multiple regression analysis to the investigation of possible causal relationships among variables, begins with a theory or model specifying a causal chain of events involving several variables and a behavior. For example, a model may suggest that a consumer's buying behavior will not occur until the consumer first finds out about a product, then generates positive ideas about the product, and finally forms an intention to buy the product. You could obtain measures on the degree to which the consumer was familiar with the product, had positive ideas about it, and intended to buy it. You could then enter the measures into a series of multiple regression analyses. Based on the results, you could test the validity of your theory or model and begin to form some tentative conclusions about possible causal relationships among your variables.

To summarize, multivariate analysis is a family of analytic techniques designed to analyze research in which multiple dependent measures are used. These analytic techniques can be used with experiments or correlational studies that have multiple dependent measures. All the multivariate statistical tests make use of the correlations among your dependent measures. In most cases, using a multivariate analysis is more informative than using several univariate analyses.

## ASSUMPTIONS AND REQUIREMENTS OF MULTIVARIATE STATISTICS

Before using multivariate statistics, you must check to see that your data meet the assumptions and requirements underlying the statistic to be used. These assumptions include linearity, normality, and homoscedasticity. In addition, you must evaluate your data for the presence of outliers, measurement error, and sample size.

### Linearity

An assumption underlying bivariate correlational statistics is that the relationship between continuously measured variables is linear (see Chapter 12 for a more complete discussion). Violation of this assumption leads to an underestimation of the degree of relationship between variables. Multivariate statistics, which are all based on correlations (even MANOVA), also assume that the relationships among continuously measured variables are linear. You check for linearity by visually inspecting scatterplots of pairs of variables. If your data are linear, then all the points should follow a straight line. Nonlinear data, in contrast, will show a horseshoe-shaped function (Tabachnick & Fidell, 2001).

Whereas mild deviations from linearity probably will not lead to a serious underestimation of a relationship by multivariate statistics, moderate to serious deviations may. If your data are nonlinear, you may be able to correct the problem by transforming your data. You may have to transform both offending variables in order to restore linearity. After any transformation, you should again inspect the scatterplots to see if the transformation had its intended effect.

### Outliers

Bivariate correlational statistics work by fitting the best straight line to the data. This *regression line* minimizes the distance of the data points from the line according to some statistical criterion (usually a least squares criterion). If your data set has extreme scores or *outliers*, how the regression line fits the data may not represent the trend shown by the majority of scores. Outliers change the slope of the regression line calculated from your data. They also affect both the magnitude and sign of the calculated correlation. (See Chapter 12 for a more complete discussion.)

*Identifying Outliers*    Two types of outliers that must be considered in multivariate statistics are *univariate outliers* and *multivariate outliers*. A univariate outlier is a deviant score on one measure from a given source (for example, from a single subject), whereas a multivariate outlier is a deviant score on a combination of variables from a single source.

Univariate outliers may be detected by converting raw scores to $z$ scores. If the $z$ score is very deviant (such as ±3), then that raw score is considered to be a univariate outlier, especially with a large sample (Tabachnick & Fidell, 2001). Another way to look for outliers is to evaluate the amount of skewness in your data. If your data are skewed, then outliers probably exist. However, note that measures of skewness (see Chapter 12) detect skewness if outliers exist only in one tail of your distribution.

Detecting multivariate outliers is more difficult than detecting univariate outliers. Multivariate outliers can be detected either statistically or graphically (Tabachnick & Fidell, 2001). Using the statistical method, you obtain a statistic called the *Mahalanobis Distance* from a statistical program such as SPSS. The Mahalanobis Distance represents the distance between a particular case and the centroid (the point created by the means of all the variables in the analysis) of remaining cases. The statistical program also calculates a discriminant analysis that tells you which case separates from the other cases in the analysis (Tabachnick & Fidell, 2001). A multivariate outlier with an unusual combination of scores will be weighted heavily in the discriminant function equation, yielding a significant Mahalanobis Distance of the outlier from other cases. There are other statistical techniques that you can use to detect multivariate outliers (see, for example, Tabachnick and Fidell, 2001, pp. 68–70). You also can detect multivariate outliers by inspecting plots of residuals provided by multiple regression programs. Any point on the plot that is distant from other points is a multivariate outlier. Screening for multivariate outliers should be done again after the data are cleaned up, because some outliers may "hide" behind others (Tabachnick & Fidell, 2001).

*Dealing with Outliers*    You can use several strategies to deal with outliers if you discover them in your data. To normalize the distribution, Tabachnick and Fidell (2001) suggested using one of several transformations on the data from the offending variable. Data with a moderate positive skew should be transformed with a square root transformation. You should use a logarithmic transformation if your data have a more serious positive skew. Again, transformations such as these reduce the impact of outliers if they are found only in one tail of your distribution. If outliers exist in both tails, transformations may not help (Tabachnick & Fidell, 2001).

If your data are negatively skewed, you use a *reflecting strategy*. The first step in reflecting is to transform your data so that they are positively skewed. You accomplish this by subtracting each score from the highest score in the distribution and adding 1. The resulting positively skewed data are then transformed with either a square root or log transformation, depending on the degree of skewness.

Another way to deal with outliers is to delete from the analysis either all data from the subject with the outlying scores or the entire variable. The disadvantage to this procedure is that you lose data. If you start with a relatively small sample, the loss of data may preclude using multivariate statistics.

Finally, you should check for transcription and other data entry errors. Sometimes outliers are caused by entering the wrong numbers or by telling the computer to look for data in the wrong positions. Any erroneous data should be corrected.

Of all the requirements of multivariate statistics, detecting outliers is probably the most important. The presence of just a single multivariate outlier can change the results of your analysis and affect your conclusions. Consequently, you should check and correct for both univariate and multivariate outliers.

## Normality and Homoscedasticity

As is the case with bivariate statistics, multivariate statistics assume that the population distribution underlying your sample distribution is normal. This is the assumption of *normality*. Transform skewed data with one of the indicated transformations, in order to normalize the distributions, before using any multivariate statistic.

*Homoscedasticity* is related to normality and is the assumption that "the variability in scores on one variable is roughly the same at all values of the other variable" (Tabachnick & Fidell, 2001, p. 79). Figure 14–1 shows two scatterplots of two hypothetical variables. Panel (a) shows the pattern of data indicating homoscedasticity. Notice that the shape of the scatterplot created by the data points is elliptical. If both variables are normally distributed, homoscedasticity results.

Contrast the scatterplot shown in Panel (b) of Figure 14–1 with the one shown in Panel (a). Notice how the shape of the scatterplot has changed from elliptical to conical. The conical pattern of data points indicates that *heteroscedasticity* is present. Heteroscedasticity usually occurs because the distribution of one or more variable(s) included in the analysis is skewed. To eliminate heteroscedasticity, apply one of the data transformations previously discussed.

## Multicollinearity

*Multicollinearity* results when variables in your analysis are highly correlated (Tabachnick & Fidell, 2001). The impact of multicollinearity is complex and beyond the scope of this chapter. If two variables are highly correlated, one of them should be eliminated from the analysis. The high correlation means the two variables are measuring essentially the same thing, so little is lost by eliminating one of them.

## Error of Measurement

The heart of the research process is identifying important variables to study, measuring those variables, establishing relationships among variables, and drawing conclusions about behavior based on those relationships. Drawing valid conclusions about the behavior under study requires that your variables be accurately measured. Inaccurate measurement may lead to an inordinate number of Type II errors. For example, you may conclude that a theoretical model is invalid when, in fact, the reason for rejecting the model was an inaccurate measurement of variables.

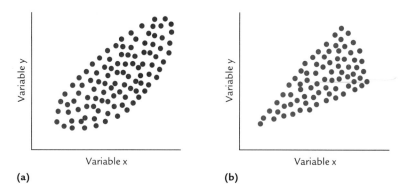

**FIGURE 14–1**    Homoscedasticity and Heteroscedasticity:
(a) homoscedasticity between two variables; (b) heteroscedasticity
between two variables.

In a perfectly ordered world with perfect measuring devices, you could obtain the *true value* of your dependent variable. Unfortunately, we do not live in a perfectly ordered world, nor do we have perfect measuring devices. Consequently, the best you can do is to *estimate* the true value of a variable by obtaining an *observed value*. The difference between the true value of a variable and your observed value is the *error of measurement*. Figure 14–2 shows the relationship between a variable's true value, observed value, and measurement error. Notice that the observed value is a function of both the true value of the variable and the measurement error (Asher, 1976).

Error of measurement is a problem for both multivariate and univariate research. It is particularly troublesome when you adopt a multivariate strategy because it leads to an underestimation of the correlations among variables that are used to compute the various multivariate statistics (Asher, 1976; Hunter, 1987). This leads to Type II errors.

Measurement error can arise from many sources, including incomplete, inaccurate, or biased sources of information. For example, if you were interested in studying the relationship between three predictor variables (sex, socioeconomic status, and education level) and crime rate, you need a good source for each of these four variables. Consider the crime rate. You could obtain records of crimes reported to the police, but this source may not be complete because many crimes go unreported. The best way to avoid this source of measurement error is to use multiple sources of information.

Another source of measurement error is inaccurate or invalid measurement devices. Defects in mechanical recording devices, poorly designed rating scales, and the like all contribute to measurement error. To avoid this source of error, be sure that your equipment is in working order and that you have adequately pretested your measures.

## Sample Size

Fairly large sample sizes are needed for multivariate analyses. The large sample size is necessary because the correlations used to calculate these statistics are not very stable when based on small samples. A multivariate analysis that uses a small sample may result in an unacceptable Type II error rate. This occurs because unstable correla-

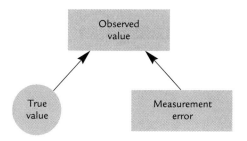

**FIGURE 14–2** The observed value of any variable (top) is a function of the true value of that variable and the measurement error (bottom).

tions tend to provide less reliable estimates of the degree of relationship among your variables.

Tabachnik and Fidell (2001, p. 117) offer the following formula for computing the sample size required for a multiple regression analysis:

$$N \geq 50 + 8m$$

where $m$ = the number of predictor variables. So, if you have five predictor variables, you would need a minimum of 90 participants in your sample. Larger samples may be needed if your data are skewed, there is substantial measurement error, or you antici-pate weak relationships among variables (Tabachnick & Fidell, 2001). Tabachnick and Fidell also caution that you can have *too large* a sample. With overly large sam-ples, very weak relationships that may have neither theoretical nor practical value can achieve statistical significance.

To summarize, several factors should be considered before using multivariate sta-tistics. Make sure that your data meet the assumptions of the test you are going to use (that is, normality, linearity, and homoscedasticity); that you have removed any out-liers or minimized their effects through transformation; that you have considered error of measurement; and that you have gathered a sufficiently large sample. If you violate the assumptions of the test or fail to take into account the other important factors, the results you obtain may not be valid.

## MULTIVARIATE STATISTICAL TESTS

Now that you are familiar with the general logic behind multivariate statistics and understand the assumptions and requirements of these tests, you can explore some of the more popular multivariate data analysis techniques. This discussion begins with an examination of factor analysis, then examines the techniques commonly applied to correlational designs, and finally discusses MANOVA.

### Factor Analysis

Imagine that you are interested in measuring the degree to which males conform to male social norms. Before you conduct your study, you need to find a way to define just what those norms are. While reviewing the literature, you discover that there are several male social norms that are relevant to male social behavior. You decide to design a questionnaire including 100 items to measure male social norms and administer it to a sample of male participants.

After running all your participants, you now face the task of determining the underlying nature of male social norms. One question that interests you is whether all the questions on your questionnaire measure a single dimension (such as aggressiveness) or several dimensions (such as aggressiveness, competitiveness, and dominance). Your search for the dimensions underlying male social norms lends itself perfectly to factor analysis.

Factor analysis operates by extracting as many significant factors from your data as possible, based on the bivariate correlations between your measures. A *factor* is a dimension that consists of any number of variables. In your study of male social norms, for example, you may find that your 100 questions actually measure three underlying dimensions (for example, aggressiveness, competitiveness, and dominance). Factor analysis involves extracting one factor (such as aggressiveness) and then evaluating your data for the existence of additional factors.

The successive factors extracted in factor analysis are not of equal strength. Each successive factor accounts for less and less variance. Typically, the first two or three factors will be the strongest (that is, account for the most variance). The strength of a factor is indicated by its *eigenvalue* (for a more complete discussion of eigenvalues, see Tatsuoka, 1971, or Tabachnick & Fidell, 2001). Factors with eigenvalues less than 1.0 usually are not interpreted.

*Factor Loadings*    In order to determine the dependent variables constituting a common factor, *factor loadings* are computed (usually with a computer because the calculations are laborious, even for only a few measures). Each factor loading is the correlation between a measure and the underlying factor. A positive factor loading means that a variable positively correlates with the underlying dimension extracted, whereas a negative loading means that a negative correlation exists. By convention, loadings are interpreted only if they are equal to or exceed plus or minus .30.

*Rotation of Factors*    After you have obtained your factor loadings, you must interpret them. The factor loadings computed initially are often difficult to interpret because they are somewhat ambiguous. *Factor rotation* is used to make the factors distinct. Figure 14–3 shows a plot of some factor loadings. The factor loadings for each variable are used as coordinates on the graph. Panel (a) of Figure 14–3 shows the plot of the unrotated factor loadings. Rotation means that the axes of the graph are rotated so that they better represent the points on the graph. Panel (b) of Figure 14–3 shows the axes after rotation.

Two types of rotation are *orthogonal rotation* and *oblique rotation*. In orthogonal rotation, the axes remain perpendicular. In oblique rotation, the angle between the axes, as well as the orientation of the axes in space, may change. Figure 14–4 illustrates the difference between the two rotation strategies. Panel (a) shows orthogonal rotation, whereas Panel (b) shows oblique rotation. Generally, orthogonal rotation is preferred over oblique rotation because the results are easier to interpret. The most popular orthogonal rotation method is varimax. This type of rotation maximizes the variance of loadings on each factor and simplifies factors (Tabachnick & Fidell, 2001).

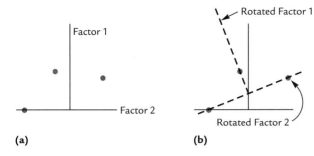

**FIGURE 14–3**  Factor Rotation: (a) factor loadings, represented by large dots before rotation; (b) the same loadings after rotation of the axis.

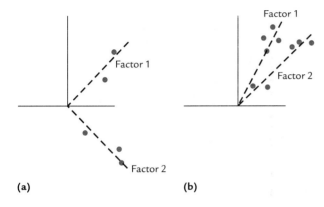

**FIGURE 14–4** Orthogonal and Oblique Factor Rotation. In orthogonal rotation (a), the rotated axes remain at right angles. In oblique rotation (b), the angle of the axes changes.

*Principal Components and Principal Factors Analysis*   Two types of factor analysis are principal components analysis and principal factors analysis. Panel (a) of Table 14–1 shows a standard three-variable correlation matrix. Remember, such correlations are used to calculate factor loadings. Panel (b) shows the same correlation matrix completed by filling in the correlations missing from the matrix in Panel (a). Notice that the values on the diagonal of the matrix are all ones. In principal components analysis, the diagonal of the completed correlation matrix is filled with ones. In contrast, principal factors analysis completes the correlation matrix by entering *communalities* along the diagonal. Essentially, a communality is a measure of a variable's reliability and is fairly easy to obtain after factor analysis. In practice, however, you need these values before analysis. Various techniques have been proposed for estimating communalities (see Bennett & Bowers, 1976), none of which is much better than any other.

Your choice between principal components and factor analysis rests on the goals of the analysis. If your goal is to reduce a large number of variables down to a smaller set and to obtain an empirical summary of the data, then principle components analysis is most appropriate. If your research is driven by empirical or theoretical predictions, then principal factors analysis is best (Tabachnick & Fidell, 2001). In the absence of any clear information on which technique is best, you should probably use principal components in those situations in which you do not have any empirical or theoretical guidance on the values of the communalities.

TABLE 14–1    **Two Correlation Matrices for Three Variables**

**(A) HYPOTHETICAL CORRELATION MATRIX**

|  | Variable 1 | Variable 2 | Variable 3 |
|---|---|---|---|
| Variable 1 |  |  |  |
| Variable 2 | .71 |  |  |
| Variable 3 | .61 | .74 |  |

**(B) COMPLETED CORRELATION MATRIX**

|  | Variable 1 | Variable 2 | Variable 3 |
|---|---|---|---|
| Variable 1 | 1.00 | .71 | .61 |
| Variable 2 | .71 | 1.00 | .74 |
| Variable 3 | .61 | .74 | 1.00 |

*Exploratory versus Confirmatory Factor Analysis*    A distinction also is made between *exploratory factor analysis* and *confirmatory factor analysis* (Tabachnick & Fidell, 2001). Exploratory factor analysis is used when you have a large set of variables that you want to describe in simpler terms and you have no *a priori* ideas about which variables will cluster together. Exploratory factor analysis is often used in the early stages of research to identify the variables that cluster together. From such an analysis, research hypotheses can be generated and tested (Tabachnick & Fidell, 2001). Confirmatory factor analysis is used in later stages of research where you can specify how variables might relate given some underlying psychological process (Tabachnick & Fidell, 2001).

*An Example of Factor Analysis*    Consider the previous example of investigating the dimensions underlying male gender-role stereotypes. Such an investigation was actually carried out by James Mahalik, Benjamin Locke, Harry Ludlow, Matthew Diemer, Ryan Scott, Michael Gottfried, and Gary Freitas (2003). Mahalik et al. had 752 men complete the *Conformity to Male Norms Inventory (CMNI)*. The CMNI consists of 144 items designed to tap into 12 male norms. The responses collected from the 752 participants were analyzed with factor analysis using oblique factor rotation. The analysis revealed 11 separate factors. These are shown in Table 14–2 along with their respective eigenvalues and the percentage of variance accounted for by each factor. As you can see, the factor labeled "winning" (a strong desire to win) by the researchers was the strongest factor, with "emotional control" being the second strongest factor. Notice how the eigenvalues and percent of variance accounted for become progressively smaller with each factor extracted. For example, "power over women" and "disdain for homosexuals" emerge as relatively weak factors.

TABLE 14–2   **Eleven Factors Identified on the CMNI**

| FACTOR NAME | EIGENVALUE | PERCENT VARIANCE |
|---|---|---|
| Winning | 17.19 | 13.02 |
| Emotional control | 7.88 | 5.97 |
| Risk taking | 5.92 | 4.48 |
| Violence | 5.08 | 3.85 |
| Dominance | 4.88 | 3.70 |
| Playboy | 3.55 | 2.69 |
| Self-reliance | 3.17 | 2.40 |
| Primacy of work | 2.98 | 2.26 |
| Power over women | 2.71 | 2.05 |
| Disdain for homosexuals | 2.44 | 1.85 |
| Pursuit of status | 2.33 | 1.77 |

## Partial and Part Correlations

Sometimes two variables are both influenced by a third variable. If this third variable was not held constant when the data were collected, it can affect the apparent relationship between the two variables of interest. However, if you have recorded the values of the third variable along with the other two, you can statistically evaluate the impact of the third variable. Partial correlation and part correlation (also called the *semipartial correlation*) are two statistics that determine the correlation between two variables while statistically controlling for the effect of a third.

*Partial Correlation*   **Partial correlation** allows you to examine the relationship between two variables with the effect of a third variable *removed* from both of these variables. For example, suppose you are interested in the factors relating to performance on the Scholastic Assessment Test (SAT). You obtain the SAT scores from 500 high school seniors, as well as their grade point averages (GPA). You also collect data on the parents' educational level (PE) in the belief that it may affect SAT scores. Specifically, you are interested in the relationship between GPA and SAT scores but are concerned that parental education may confound the relationship between GPA and SAT. You want to look at the relationship between GPA and SAT with any effect of PE removed. This problem calls for a partial correlation.

Imagine that a causal relationship exists between parental education and grade point average. In that case, variations in parental education would induce variations in GPA. Imagine that a causal relationship also exists between parental education and SAT scores. In that case, variations in parental education also would induce variations in SAT scores. If these were both direct relationships, then SAT scores and GPA would tend to rise and fall together as parental education rose and fell. In other words, SAT scores and GPA would be positively correlated. This positive correlation would emerge even if there were no direct causal connection between SAT scores and GPA.

Would a correlation remain if you could somehow remove the common influence parental education has on SAT scores and GPA? This is what partial correlation attempts to determine, as shown in Figure 14–5. Panel (a) shows a scatterplot of the relationship between PE and GPA. The straight line through the points represents the trend relating changes in GPA to changes in PE. If you could remove this trend, the GPA scores would show less variability, and they would show no systematic change as PE changed.

In fact, you *can* remove this trend statistically by calculating a *residual score* for each data point. This residual score is the distance from the point to the line, measured (in this case) in terms of GPA. Panel (b) in Figure 14–5 plots the residual scores as a function of PE. Note that the trend relating PE to GPA is now flat. The changes in GPA induced by changes in PE have been statistically removed. The same process

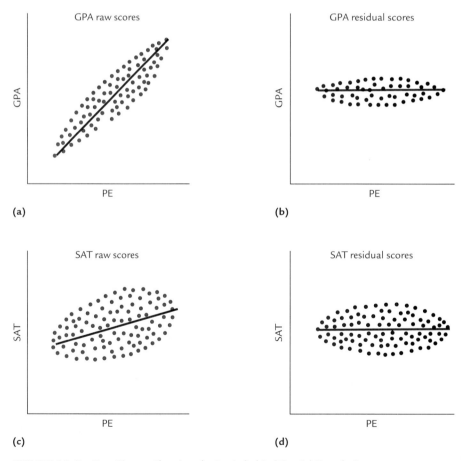

(a)    (b)    (c)    (d)

**FIGURE 14–5**  Four Figures Showing the Logic behind Partial Correlation.

of statistically removing the effect of PE is also applied to the SAT scores. Panels (c) and (d) of Figure 14–5 show the relationship before and after this removal. The partial correlation is then determined by correlating the residual GPA scores, Panel (b), with the residual SAT scores, Panel (d). This is the correlation of GPA and SAT with the effect of PE removed from both.

Fortunately, there is an easier way to compute the partial correlation than by graphing and subtracting. First, you find the simple correlations between your three variables. Then these correlation coefficients are entered into a special partial correlation formula.

Partial correlation is not limited to three-variable cases. You can examine the relationship between two variables with the effects of several others removed. You can learn more about these more complex partial correlations in Thorndike (1978).

**Part Correlation**    In some cases, you may want to examine the relationship between two variables when the influence of a third is removed from only *one* of these variables. The **part correlation** (also known as semipartial correlation) is used in this situation.

Conceptually, the part correlation is similar to the partial correlation. As with the partial correlation, the relationship between one variable (such as SAT) and the variable to be removed (such as PE) is determined and residual scores are calculated. This yields an SAT score for each participant with the effect of parental education held constant (Thorndike, 1978). These residual scores are then correlated with the *raw* scores of the other variable (GPA) to yield the part correlation coefficient (Thorndike, 1978).

In practice, the part correlation is computed by using a formula similar to that used for the partial correlation.

## Multiple Regression

Assume you are interested in studying the variables correlating with college students' attitudes toward seeking counseling for personal problems. You are interested in investigating those variables that relate to a student having either a positive or negative attitude toward seeking professional counseling. Multiple regression analysis is the best statistic to address such an issue. You will have a single measure of attitude toward counseling (the criterion or dependent variable) and several measures that might relate to that attitude (predictor variables).

**The Multiple Regression Equation**    Chapter 12 discussed bivariate linear regression and provided the linear equation for that analysis. The logic developed for the bivariate case can be easily extended to the multivariate case. The linear equation for multiple regression is

$$y' = B_1X_1 + B_2X_2 + B_3X_3 + B_4X_4 + B_5X_5 + constant$$

where $y'$ is the predicted criterion score; $B_1$, $B_2$, $B_3$, $B_4$, and $B_5$ are the regression weights associated with the predictors; $X_1$, $X_2$, $X_3$, $X_4$, and $X_5$ are the values of the predictors; and *constant* is the y-intercept.

*Types of Regression Analysis*    The several types of regression analysis include *simple*, *hierarchical*, and *stepwise* analyses. The major difference between these types is how your predictor variables are entered into the regression equation, which may affect the regression solution.

In *simple regression analysis* (the type used in the example to follow), all variables are entered together. Each predictor variable is assessed as if it had been entered after each of the other predictors had been entered (Tabachnick & Fidell, 2001). In *hierarchical regression*, you specify the order in which your variables are entered into the regression equation. You use hierarchical regression if you have a well-developed theory or model suggesting a certain causal order. In *stepwise regression*, the order in which variables are entered is based on a statistical decision, not on a theory.

When you enter variables into a stepwise regression analysis, the order in which predictors are entered is determined by the qualities of the sample data. The first variable entered is the one accounting for the most variance in the dependent measure. The next variable entered is the one that adds most to the ability of the regression equation to account for the variance in the dependent variable (that is, increases *R*-square the most). Variables are entered one at a time until none of the remaining variables add significantly to *R*-square.

Your choice of regression strategies should be based on your research questions or underlying theory. If you have a theoretical model suggesting a particular order of entry, use hierarchical regression. In the absence of any well-specified theory, you should usually choose simple regression. Stepwise regression is used infrequently because it tends to capitalize on chance. Sampling and measurement error tend to make unstable correlations among variables in stepwise regression. Thus, the statistical decisions used to determine order of entry may vary considerably from sample to sample. The resulting regression equation may be unique to a particular sample.

*Multiple R and R-Square*    **Multiple R** is the correlation between the predicted values of Y (Y′) and the observed values of Y. **R-square** is simply the square of multiple *R* and provides an index of the amount of variability in the dependent variable accounted for by the predictor variables (Roscoe, 1975). There is a problem with *R*-square. Because of sampling error, *R*-square tends to overestimate the variance accounted for, especially with small samples (Tabachnick & Fidell, 2001). Adjusted *R*-square compensates for this overestimation. You should use the adjusted *R*-square as a measure of variance accounted for rather than the unadjusted *R*-square. You also should pay attention to the standard error. The standard error gives you an indication of how much variability there is around the calculated regression line. The lower the value, the better.

*Regression Weights*    Regression weights are used to interpret the results from a multiple regression analysis. There are two types of regression weights: raw and standardized. A raw regression weight (*B*) is calculated based on the raw scores entered into the regression analysis. A standardized regression weight is calculated after your raw scores have been transformed to standard scores. The standardized regression weights are known as **beta weights** (abbreviated with the Greek symbol $\beta$). When you use a computer program (such as SPSS) to conduct a regression analysis, a *t* value for each regression weight should be provided. The $t$ value tells you whether the regression weight is statistically significant.

For most applications in psychological research, you should use the standardized regression weights (beta weights) because they can be directly compared, even if the variables to which they apply were measured on very different scales. For example, the beta weights given to variables such as intelligence, grade point average, and socioeconomic status (which are all measured on different, nonequivalent scales) can be directly compared, whereas the $B$ weights cannot. Only when your variables are measured on the same standard scale should you use the raw score regression weights.

*Interpretation of Regression Weights*    If your regression analysis is significant, you may want to know how much of the variability in the criterion variable can be accounted for by variation in each predictor. Avoid using the beta weights for this. A beta weight is not an index of the *unique* contribution of a given predictor to variability in the dependent variable.

A beta weight for a given predictor variable may be high either because the predictor *directly* produces most of the variance in the dependent variable or because it is merely *correlated* with another, effective predictor variable (Tabachnick & Fidell, 2001). Similarly, a beta weight for a given predictor variable may be low, and yet the predictor may have a strong causal influence on the dependent variable. This situation can occur when other predictor variables in the analysis correlate with the effective variable. The analysis may then mistakenly assign weight to the correlated variables instead of to the effective one. In such cases, the correlated variables are termed "suppressor variables" because they mask (or suppress) the effect of the effective variable.

An alternative to using beta weights to determine the unique contribution of each predictor is the *squared semipartial correlation* (Tabachnick & Fidell, 2001). Simply square the part correlation for each variable to obtain the squared semipartial correlation. These numbers represent the amount of variability accounted for by each variable.

The squared semipartial correlations need not sum to $R$-square. If the sum of the semipartial correlations is less than $R$-square, then the difference between the two numbers represents the shared variance (Tabachnick & Fidell, 2001). In some cases, the sum of squared semipartial correlations can be larger than $R$-square.

*An Example of Multiple Regression*    Recall the previously mentioned study of the factors correlating with a student's attitude toward seeking counseling for personal problems. A study was actually conducted to investigate the factors that relate to this attitude (Vogel & Wester, 2003). David Vogel and Stephen Wester had 209 college students (143 male and 66 female) complete a measure of their attitude toward seeking counseling. They also completed measures concerning their willingness to disclose personal information about themselves, how risky they felt such disclosures were, and whether they had sought counseling in the past. These latter measures, along with participant gender, yielded five predictor variables for a multiple regression analysis: willingness to self-disclose personal information, risk of disclosing emotional information, utility of disclosing emotional information, gender, and previous counseling.

The results showed a significant regression analysis, $F(5, 190) = 25, p < .001$. The $R^2$ was .40 and the adjusted $R^2$ was .39, indicating that 39 percent of the variance was accounted for by the regression analysis. Table 14–3 shows how each predictor variable related to the dependent variable and whether each predictor variable contributed significantly to the regression analysis. The second column shows the raw score regression weights. Remember, we don't use them to interpret a regression analysis. The third column shows the standard error of the regression weights. The beta weights (standardized regression weights) are shown in the fourth column. These are the ones we use to interpret the regression analysis.

As you can see, the strongest predictor of attitude toward seeking counseling is a person's willingness to disclose distressing information. The positive regression weight tells us that individuals who are more willing to self-disclose are more likely to have a positive attitude toward seeking counseling. Another strong predictor is the anticipated utility of self-disclosing emotional information ($\beta = .24$), indicating that individuals who see emotional self-disclosure as useful have a more positive attitude toward seeking help. Notice that the anticipated risk of emotional self-disclosure is negative related to help-seeking attitude ($\beta = -.18$), indicating that those who see emotional self-disclosure as risky have a more negative attitude toward seeking help.

## Discriminant Analysis

Discriminant analysis is a special case of multiple regression. It is used when your dependent variable is categorical (for example, male–female or Democrat–Republican–Independent) and you have several predictor variables. Discriminant analysis allows you to predict membership in a group (one of the discrete categories of your dependent variable) based on knowledge of a set of predictor variables. You can use discriminant analysis to identify a simple rule for classifying participants into groups or to determine which of your predictor variables contributes most heavily to the separation of groups. The analysis works by forming *discriminant functions*. For each dependent variable group, a discriminant function score is calculated according to the following formula (Tabachnick & Fidell, 2001):

$$D_i = d_{i1}z_1 + d_{i2}z_2 + \cdots + d_{in}z_n$$

where $D_i$ is the discriminant function score calculated for each participant, $d_i$ is the regression weight, and $z_i$ is the standardized raw score on a particular predictor. In discriminant analysis, a new variable ($D_i$) is calculated for each participant. This variable is the best linear combination of predictor variables, just as in multiple regression. When the discriminant function scores have been calculated for each group, a *centroid* can then be determined. The centroid is simply the average of the discriminant function scores within a group.

More than one discriminant function can link your predictors with your dependent variable. However, the number of functions is limited to the number of predictors or to the number of levels of the dependent variable minus 1, whichever is smaller. For example, if you had seven predictors and three levels of the dependent variable, the number of possible functions is 2 (or 3 − 1). Each discriminant function

TABLE 14–3    **Results from Vogel and Wester's (2003)
Multiple Regression Analysis**

| CRITERION VARIABLE | B | $SE_b$ | β | t | p |
|---|---|---|---|---|---|
| Self-disclosure of distressing information | 4.1 | .84 | .29 | 4.8 | <.001 |
| Anticipated risk of emotional self-disclosure | –1.9 | .63 | –.18 | –3.1 | <.01 |
| Anticipated utility of emotional self-disclosure | 2.9 | .69 | .24 | 4.1 | <.001 |
| Participant gender | 7.5 | 1.7 | .27 | 4.5 | <.001 |
| Previous counseling | –5.4 | 1.6 | –.2 | –3.4 | <.01 |

Reprinted with permission.

represents a different linkage between the predictors and dependent variable. The first one calculated maximizes the separation between levels of the dependent variable. Subsequent functions represent progressively weaker linkages between the predictors and the dependent variable.

Because the computations needed to perform a discriminant analysis are complex, you will probably use a computer program to conduct a discriminant analysis. SPSS conducts a discriminant analysis within its Analyze subprogram. (This and subsequent illustrations are based on SPSS Version 12.0 for Windows.) The output of the SPSS analysis gives you several important pieces of information. First, the output will indicate the number of discriminant functions extracted, along with tests of statistical significance. Second, you can request several other statistics needed to interpret your results. These include the standardized discriminant function coefficients (analogous to beta weights) and pooled within-groups correlations between the discriminant functions and predictor variables (structure correlations).

You can use a discriminant analysis in two ways. First, you can evaluate the amount of variability accounted for by each function. You would do this by conducting a dimension reduction analysis that provides a canonical correlation coefficient and significance tests for each function. The squared canonical correlation coefficient gives a measure of the amount of variability accounted for by a specific function. By looking at the dimension reduction analysis, you can determine the significance of each function and the amount of variability accounted for by each function.

The second way you can use the discriminant analysis is to evaluate the degree of contribution of each predictor (within a function) to the separation of groups. One strategy is to look at the standardized discriminant function coefficients. However, these weights (like beta weights) do not reveal how much each individual predictor contributes to variation in the dependent variable. Another strategy is to look at the structure correlations, which can be interpreted much like factor loadings. By convention, you typically consider those structure correlations that exceed .30. The structure correlations can help you determine what each discriminant function represents. However, they are not good indicators of the predictor's degree of unique contribution to discriminating among dependent variable groups (Tabachnick & Fidell, 2001).

Rather than looking at beta weights or structure correlations, you could conduct a set of specific contrasts in which each dependent variable group is contrasted with all others. You then look for which predictor variables separate a particular group from the rest (Tabachnick & Fidell, 2001). This procedure is too complex to fully describe here. (See Tabachnick & Fidell, 2001.)

## Canonical Correlation

Multiple regression determines the relationship between a set of variables (predictors) and a *single* dependent variable. To determine the relationship between a set of predictors and a *set* of dependent variables, you use canonical correlation. Canonical correlation works by creating two new variables for each subject, called *canonical variates*. A canonical variate is computed both for the dependent and predictor sets. The canonical variate is simply the score predicted from a regression equation based on the variables within a set. The correlation between the two canonical variates is the *canonical correlation*.

Canonical correlation does not appear much in published psychological literature because, at this point in its development, it is a purely descriptive strategy (Tabachnick & Fidell, 2001). It can be used to describe the relationship between two sets of variables, but it cannot be used to infer causal relationships. Consequently, this technique is not discussed further. If you want to know more about the technique, see Tabachnick and Fidell (2001) and Levine (1977).

## Multivariate Analysis of Variance

Assume that you are required to conduct an experiment for a senior thesis. Your major area of interest is in the development of a concept of death among school-aged children. You have reviewed the literature and have found most of the current research to be correlational. You decide there is room for some experimental work in the area, but you also decide to draw on the existing correlational research to help you develop your measures. You find that the previous research suggests that several important measures should be applied to assessing children's concepts of death. So you decide to include three measures in your experiment.

The existing literature suggests that a child's concept of death can be accelerated by exposure to experience with the concept of death. So you decide to conduct a single-factor experiment with three groups. The first group is simply exposed to a film about a character who dies. The second group role-plays a dying animal. The third group, a control group, receives no special treatment.

After running your experiment, you are faced with the problem of how to analyze your three dependent measures. Of course, you could simply conduct three separate one-factor ANOVAs. You are uncomfortable with this strategy because the existing literature indicates that your three chosen measures are correlated. You might miss some important relationships among your variables if you simply use a series of univariate tests. In this situation, a viable alternative is to use a MANOVA to analyze your data. Like canonical correlation and discriminant analysis, MANOVA operates by forming a new linear combination of dependent variables for each effect in your design. For example, for a two-factor between-subjects design, a different linear combination of scores is formed for each of the two main effects and for the interaction.

*An Example of MANOVA*    Suppose you conducted the one-factor experiment looking at the effect of a training program on children's concepts of death. Your measure of the concept of death consisted of a questionnaire containing several important questions concerning death (for example, "What happens when you die?" "What can you do to bring something dead back to life?" and "Do dead people feel pain?"). Children simply answered the questions. Independent raters then indicated how mature the concept of death was in each response. Because your measures were related to the same concept, you decide to use a MANOVA rather than separate ANOVAs to analyze the data.

Table 14–4 shows some hypothetical data that might be generated from such a study. Table 14–5 shows part of the output from an SPSS MANOVA analysis of these data. The top part of Table 14–5 shows the multivariate tests of significance. Although the results from a number of such tests are shown, you decide to use the Wilks's test (the reasons why you choose one test over another are not important here because, in most cases, there will be little difference among them). The Wilks's test indicates that the effect of the treatment was significant, $F(6, 20) = 13.14, p < .001$. This tells you that your independent variable reliably affected the value of the linear dependent variable created in the MANOVA.

When you conduct a single-factor MANOVA, you get essentially the same analysis as a canonical correlation analysis. As in canonical correlation, SPSS MANOVA extracts as many discriminant functions as possible (two in this case). The second section of Table 14–5 shows the statistics relevant to the discriminant functions extracted. Here, the canonical correlations are presented ("Canon Cor.") along with the percentage of variance accounted for ("Pct.") and the associated

TABLE 14–4    **Data from Hypothetical Experiment on Developing a Concept of Death**

| | FILM | | | ROLE PLAYING | | | CONTROL | | |
|---|---|---|---|---|---|---|---|---|---|
| Subject | $X_1$ | $X_2$ | $X_3$ | $X_1$ | $X_2$ | $X_3$ | $X_1$ | $X_2$ | $X_3$ |
| 1 | 6 | 3 | 5 | 8 | 7 | 9 | 1 | 2 | 1 |
| 2 | 5 | 5 | 3 | 7 | 9 | 5 | 2 | 2 | 4 |
| 3 | 6 | 4 | 2 | 9 | 9 | 7 | 1 | 1 | 2 |
| 4 | 4 | 2 | 2 | 6 | 8 | 8 | 3 | 3 | 3 |
| 5 | 3 | 2 | 6 | 7 | 8 | 9 | 4 | 1 | 2 |

Note: $X_1, X_2,$ and $X_3$ refer to the three dependent measures listed in the text.

TABLE 14–5    **Partial SPSS-PC Output for Hypothetical Experiment on Developing a Concept of Death**

## MULTIVARIATE TESTS OF SIGNIFICANCE (S = 2, M = 0, N = 4)

| Test Name | Value | Approx. F | Hypoth. df | Error df | Sig. of F |
|---|---|---|---|---|---|
| Pillai's | 1.21442 | 5.66832 | 6.00 | 22.00 | .001 |
| Hotelling's | 17.82643 | 26.73964 | 6.00 | 18.00 | .000 |
| Wilks's | .03962 | 13.41251 | 6.00 | 20.00 | .000 |
| Roy's | .94583 | | | | |

Note: F statistic for Wilks's Lambda is exact.

## EIGENVALUES AND CANONICAL CORRELATIONS

| Root No. | Eigenvalue | Pct. | Cum. Pct. | Canon Cor. |
|---|---|---|---|---|
| 1 | 17.459 | 97.940 | 97.940 | .973 |
| 2 | .367 | 2.060 | 100.000 | .518 |

## DIMENSION REDUCTION ANALYSIS

| Roots | Wilks's L | F Hypoth. | df | Error df | Sig. of F |
|---|---|---|---|---|---|
| 1 TO 2 | .03962 | 13.41251 | 6.00 | 20.00 | .000 |
| 2 TO 2 | .73140 | 2.01981 | 2.00 | 11.00 | .179 |

## ROY–BARGMAN STEPDOWN F TESTS

| Variable | Hypoth. MS | Error MS | Stepdown | F Hypoth. df | Error df | Sig. of F |
|---|---|---|---|---|---|---|
| DIE | 33.80000 | 1.56667 | 21.57447 | 2 | 12 | .000 |
| LIFE | 13.73684 | 1.06132 | 12.94322 | 2 | 11 | .001 |
| FEEL | 7.89738 | 2.47695 | 3.18835 | 2 | 10 | .085 |

## CORRELATIONS BETWEEN DEPENDENT AND CANONICAL VARIABLES

| | Canonical Variable | |
|---|---|---|
| VARIABLE | 1 | 2 |
| DIE | −.436 | .870 |
| LIFE | −.735 | −.198 |
| FEEL | −.376 | −.025 |

eigenvalues. Eigenvalues are not discussed here. See Tabachnick and Fidell (2001) for a discussion of these values.

The third section of Table 14–5 presents the results of a dimension reduction analysis. This analysis reveals that only the first function was significant ($p < .001$).

The significant $F$ ratio in the multivariate test indicates a reliable effect of the training program on concepts of death. As a next step, you assess each dependent variable's contribution to this significant effect. There are several ways to do this. You could simply look at the univariate $F$ tests produced by SPSS. This strategy has limitations, especially if your dependent variables are correlated with one another (Tabachnick & Fidell, 2001). An alternative strategy is to examine the *Roy–Bargman stepdown analysis* shown in the fourth section of Table 14–5.

In the Roy–Bargman stepdown analysis, the first dependent variable is entered and tested for significance. Then the second variable is entered, and the first variable is treated as a covariate. This test tells you whether each dependent variable explains variability over and above the variability already explained by those previously entered (Tabachnick & Fidell, 2001). The Roy–Bargman stepdown analysis is similar in concept to hierarchical regression. The main drawback to this analysis is that it can be used only when you can specify the order in which variables are entered. In the absence of a theoretically or empirically based order of entry, the Roy–Bargman test should not be used.

We should note that you cannot obtain the Roy–Bargman stepdown analysis directly from SPSS's pull-down menu system. Instead, you will have to use the syntax editor and enter a series of commands in the old SPSS-X format (the mainframe version of SPSS). To do this, you will need to know the appropriate commands. It would be extremely helpful to have a copy of the SPSS-X manual. In any event, the commands needed to produce the Roy–Bargman stepdown analysis are as follows:

```
manova happens backlife feelpain by conditio(1,3)
/PRINT SIGNIF(STEPDOWN DIMENR)
/PRINT DISCRIM(STAN COR).
```

These commands will produce the entire output shown in Table 14–5, along with the stepdown analysis.

Finally, you also could look at the structure correlations shown at the bottom of Table 14–5 (labeled "Correlations between Dependent and Canonical Variables"). The structure correlations are similar to factor loadings and can be interpreted as such.

In addition to these analyses, you might want to conduct some post hoc analyses to determine the specific effect of the independent variable on the dependent variables. These tests are similar to those used in univariate ANOVA, but more complex.

*Using MANOVA for Within-Subjects Designs*    Chapters 9 and 13 discussed within-subjects designs and analyses. Each subject in a within-subjects design is exposed to all levels of your independent variable. Chapter 13 indicated that a repeated measures ANOVA can be used to analyze data from this design. Data from within-subjects (and mixed) designs also can be analyzed with MANOVA.

The within-subjects ANOVA assumes homogeneity of both within-cell variances and within-cell covariances. The first assumption states that variance should be homogeneous across treatments. This assumption is common between the between-subjects and within-subjects analyses. However, the assumption of homogeneity of covariance is special to the within-subjects ANOVA. The following example illustrates the idea of homogeneity of covariances.

Figure 14–6 shows a simple one-factor within-subjects design. Notice that the behavior of each subject is evaluated under each level of the independent variable. This being the case, you can form pairs of conditions and subtract the scores associated with each subject within those two conditions (Keppel, 1982). You can then obtain variances based on the resulting difference scores. This variance is called *covariance*. In the design illustrated in Figure 14–6, you can form three pairs of conditions ($C_1$ with $C_2$, $C_2$ with $C_3$, and $C_1$ with $C_3$) and three concomitant covariances. If the covariances are not homogeneous, then the homogeneity-of-covariance assumption has been violated.

In a between-subjects ANOVA, mild to moderate violations of the homogeneity assumption do not significantly affect the validity of the statistical test. In a within-subjects ANOVA, however, violations of the homogeneity assumption lead to a serious positive bias: rejecting the null hypothesis more often than you should at a given alpha level. Thus, you are making more Type I errors than are acceptable.

Another problem with the univariate within-subjects analysis is that when you add a second independent variable, the analysis becomes somewhat controversial. The controversy surrounds selecting an error term appropriate to test the main effects and interactions. You can select a "pooled" error term and use this same term for all the within-subjects factors, or you can use separate error terms for each. Unfortunately, the two choices may lead to different outcomes of the statistical analysis, and there is little agreement on which choice is best.

Because MANOVA circumvents the problems with the homogeneity assumptions and error-term selection, it has been suggested as an alternative to a standard within-subjects ANOVA (O'Brien & Kaiser, 1985; Tabachnick & Fidell, 2001). In the MANOVA, the repeated measures taken on each subject are treated as correlated dependent variables and analyzed accordingly. Rather than assuming homogeneity of covariance, MANOVA takes into account the covariances actually present in the data. For information on using MANOVA to analyze within-subjects designs, see O'Brien and Kaiser (1985).

## Multiway Frequency Analysis

Most of the powerful inferential statistics discussed in this chapter and in Chapter 13 require that your variables be measured along at least an interval scale. However, there are research situations in which you may want to measure or manipulate categorical variables (for example, sex of subject). Statistics such as ANOVA, MANOVA, and multiple regression are not appropriate to analyze such data. For these cases, **multiway frequency analysis** is an alternative. A specific type of multiway frequency analysis used for categorical or qualitative variables is **loglinear analysis**.

Loglinear analysis is analogous to chi-square (see Chapter 13) in that you use observed and expected frequencies to evaluate the statistical significance of your

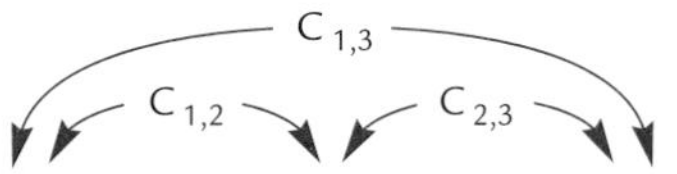

| Subject | Level 1 | Level 2 | Level 3 |
|---------|---------|---------|---------|
| 1 | $X_{1,1}$ | $X_{2,1}$ | $X_{3,1}$ |
| 2 | $X_{1,2}$ | $X_{2,2}$ | $X_{3,2}$ |
| 3 | $X_{1,3}$ | $X_{2,3}$ | $X_{3,3}$ |
| 4 | $X_{1,4}$ | $X_{2,4}$ | $X_{3,4}$ |
| 5 | $X_{1,5}$ | $X_{2,5}$ | $X_{3,5}$ |

Note: $X_{i,j}$ represents a subject's score, where $i$ = the level of the independent variable and $j$ = the subject number. $C_{i,j}$ indicates the covariances that could be calculated, where $i$ and $j$ are the levels of the independent variable.

**FIGURE 14–6** Three-Treatment Within-Subjects Design Showing Covariances.

data. An important difference between chi-square and loglinear analysis is that loglinear analysis can be easily applied to experimental research designs that include more than two independent variables, whereas chi-square is normally limited to the two-variable case.

*Applications of Loglinear Analysis* Loglinear analysis has a wide range of applications. You can use loglinear analysis if you conducted a correlational study with several categorical variables. Loglinear analysis is well suited to this task. You also can use loglinear analysis if you conducted an experiment including a categorical dependent variable (for example, guilty–not guilty), even if your independent variables were quantitative.

Loglinear analysis is also a useful tool for testing and building theoretical models. In this application, you specify how variables should be entered into the analysis for the models you wish to test. Loglinear analysis is then used to test the relative adequacy of each model.

Finally, because loglinear analysis is a nonparametric statistic, you can use it if your data violate the assumptions of parametric statistics (such as ANOVA). In this instance, you can use loglinear analysis even if your dependent variable was measured along an interval or ordinal scale (Tabachnick & Fidell, 2001). However, one important requirement must still be met.

Like chi-square, loglinear analysis uses observed and expected cell frequencies to compute your test statistic. In order to obtain valid results, your cell expected frequencies must be relatively large. Tabachnick and Fidell (2001) recommend having five times as many subjects as cells to ensure adequate expected frequencies. So, for example, if you have a $2 \times 2 \times 2$ design you should have $2 \times 2 \times 2 \times 5$ (= 40) subjects to ensure sufficiently large expected cell frequencies.

You should inspect all expected frequencies to ensure that they are all larger than one and that no more than 20 percent of them fall below five (Tabachnick & Fidell, 2001). If you find small expected frequencies, Tabachnick and Fidell suggest several remedies. First, you could accept and live with the reduced power of the analysis caused by low expected frequencies. Second, categories can be collapsed or combined to increase frequencies within each category. Third, you could delete variables to reduce the number of categories in your analysis. This latter strategy should be done with caution, and you should not delete variables that are correlated with other variables in the analysis (Tabachnick & Fidell, 2001).

*How Loglinear Analysis Works*    When you use ANOVA or multiple regression to analyze your data, your analysis uses group means as a basis for analysis. When you have categorical data, however, you must deal with proportions instead of means. For example, if you used a three-factor design with a categorical dependent variable (yes–no), you would summarize your data according to the proportion of subjects falling into each category.

In a standard analysis of proportional data from a two-factor experiment, in which you are interested in a single relationship between two variables, chi-square is used to evaluate that relationship. However, when evaluating more than one relationship (that is, two main effects and an interaction), chi-square is not the best test statistic because the component chi-squares do not sum to the total chi-square (Tabachnick & Fidell, 2001). In this case, a likelihood ratio ($G^2$) is used in place of chi-square. Although similar to chi-square (in that cell expected and observed frequencies are compared), $G^2$ involves taking the natural log (ln) of the ratio of observed cell frequency to the expected cell frequency, according to the following formula (Tabachnick & Fidell, 2001):

$$G^2 = 2(f_o) \ln(f_o/f_e)$$

where $f_o$ is the observed cell frequency and $f_e$ is the expected cell frequency. A $G^2$ is computed for each main effect and interaction in your design and is interpreted in the same way as chi-square (using the chi-square tables to establish statistical significance).

Space limitations here preclude a detailed description of all the applications of loglinear analysis or how loglinear analysis is used. If you need to use loglinear analysis, detailed discussions can be found in Agresti and Finlay (1986) and Tabachnick and Fidell (2001).

## Path Analysis

**Path analysis** applies multiple regression techniques to causal modeling. For example, suppose you are interested in determining how attitudes and behaviors relate to one another. You have reviewed the literature and have come across the "theory of reasoned action" by Fishbein and Ajzen (1975). This theory postulates that attitudes are evaluative dimensions that, along with subjective norms (such as knowing what your friends are going to do), mediate between other variables (such as sex) and behavioral intentions (that is, what you specifically intend to do). According to the theory, behavioral intentions, in turn, determine behavior.

You decide to test the limits of the Fishbein and Ajzen theory by measuring each of the important components of the theory with a questionnaire. The topic you have chosen is the relationship between attitudes toward college and actual college attendance. In order to test the theory, you collect data on attitudes toward attending college, subjective norms about college, a specific intention to attend college, and actual college attendance behavior.

After you have collected your data, you now face the task of analyzing them. Whereas you could simply compute bivariate correlation coefficients between all variables, the disadvantages of this approach have been discussed. Besides, simple correlational analyses will not allow you to evaluate possible causal relationships among your variables. As an alternative, consider using path analysis.

Unlike the other analytic techniques already discussed, path analysis is not a statistical procedure in and of itself. Rather, it is an application of multiple regression techniques to the testing of causal models. Path analysis allows you to test a model specifying the causal links among variables by applying simple multiple regression techniques.

Always remember that path analysis is designed to test causal models, not to sift through data for interesting relationships among variables. Developing a clearly articulated causal model is crucial in path analysis. The model should not rest on flimsy ideas and unsupported conjecture. Instead, the causal relationships proposed in the model should rest on a strong theoretical or empirical base.

Translating theoretical propositions into a clearly defined path model can be tricky. You always are tempted to determine how to measure your variables first and then derive the model. This method may not be the best. It may limit the possible causal relationships within your model and consequently may not allow you to adequately test your theory. Instead, first develop a list of the causal links among variables as suggested by your theory (Hunter & Gerbing, 1982). Then show these links among variables in a *path diagram*. After developing the path model and diagram, you can then decide how to measure your variables.

*Causal Relationships*     The heart of path analysis is developing a causal model and identifying causal relationships. Causal relationships among variables can take many forms. The simplest of these is shown in Panel (a) of Figure 14–7, where Variable A (independent variable) causes changes in Variable B (dependent variable).

Another possible causal relationship is shown in Panel (b). Here, two variables impinge on Variable B. This model suggests that variation in the dependent variable has multiple causes. These causal variables can be uncorrelated, as shown in Panel (b). Panel (c) shows a situation in which two variables believed to cause changes in the dependent variable are correlated. In Figure 14–7 (and in path analysis, in general), straight arrows denote causal relationships and are called *paths*. Curved, double-headed arrows denote correlational relationships.

The simple causal relationships just described can be combined to form more complex causal models. One such model is the *causal chain*, in which a sequence of events leads ultimately to variation in the dependent variable. To illustrate a simple causal chain, consider a modification of a previous example in which you were trying to determine what variables correlated with SAT scores.

**FIGURE 14-7**   Three
Possible Causal Relation-
ships: (a) Variable A
causes changes in B;
(b) uncorrelated Variables
A and C contribute to
changes in the value of B;
(c) correlated Variables
A and C cause changes in
the value of B.

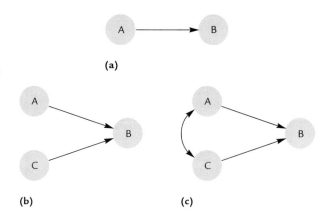

Suppose you believe parental education (PE) and student motivation (SM) relate to variation in SAT scores. You have reason to believe a causal relationship exists. So you develop a causal model like the one illustrated in Panel (a) of Figure 14–8. Your model suggests PE causes changes in SM, which then causes changes in SAT scores. Notice you are proposing that PE does not directly cause changes in SAT but rather operates through SM.

When developing simple causal chains (and more complex causal models), keep in mind that the validity of your causal model depends on how well you have done your homework and conceptualized your model. Perhaps SM does not directly cause changes in SAT scores as conjectured but rather operates through yet another variable, such as working hard (WH) in class. Panel (b) of Figure 14–8 shows a causal chain including WH. If you excluded WH from your model, the causal relationships and the model you develop may not be valid.

You can progress from simple causal chains to more complex models quite easily. Figure 14–9 shows three examples of more complex causal models. In Panel (a), the causal model suggests Variables A and B are correlated (indicated with the curved arrow). Variable A is believed to exert a causal influence on Variable C, and B on D. Variable D is hypothesized to cause changes in C, and both D and C are believed to cause changes in E.

*Types of Variables and Causal Models*    Variables A and B in Panel (a) of Figure 14–9 are called *exogenous variables*. Exogenous variables begin the causal sequence. Notice that no causal paths lead to Variable A or B. All the other variables in the model shown in Panel (a) are *endogenous variables*. These variables are internal to the model, and changes in them are believed to be caused by other variables. Variables C, D, and E are all endogenous variables. Panel (b) of Figure 14–9 shows essentially the same model as Panel (a), except that the two exogenous variables are not correlated in Panel (b).

The models in Panels (a) and (b) are both known as *recursive models*. Notice that there are no loops of variables. That is, causal relationships run in only one direction (for example, D causes C, but C does not cause D). In contrast, Panel (c) of Figure 14–9 shows a *nonrecursive model*, which has a causal loop. In this case, Vari-

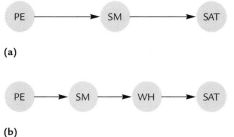

**FIGURE 14–8** Three-Variable Causal Chain (a) and a Four-Variable Causal Chain (b).

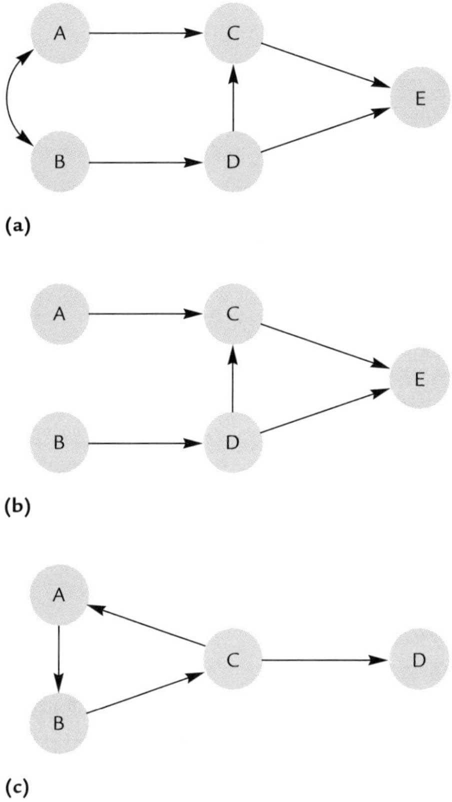

**(a)**

**(b)**

**FIGURE 14–9** Three Complex Causal Models.

**(a)**

**(b)**

**(c)**

able A is believed to be a cause of C (operating through B), but C also can cause A. In general, recursive models are much easier to deal with conceptually and statistically (Asher, 1976).

*Estimating the Degree of Causality* After you have developed your causal models and measured your variables, you then obtain estimates of the causal relationships among your variables. These estimates are called *path coefficients*. Figure 14–10 shows a causal model with the path coefficients indicated for each causal path.

**FIGURE 14–10**   Path Diagram Showing
Path Coefficients.

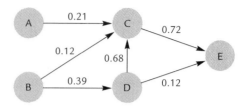

Path coefficients are determined by using a series of multiple regression analyses. Each endogenous variable is used as a dependent variable in the regression analysis. All the variables in the model that are assumed to impinge on the dependent variable are used as predictors. For example, the path coefficients for A–C and D–C in Figure 14–10 are obtained by using C as the dependent variable and A, B, and D as predictors. The path coefficients are the standardized regression weights (beta weights) from these analyses.

***Interpreting Path Analysis***   Path analysis is used to test the validity of a presumed causal model. To that end, you look at the path coefficients and determine whether the pattern expected by the model has emerged. In addition to looking at the path coefficients (which give you estimates of the direct effects of variables on other variables), you also decompose the paths into indirect effects. Decomposition can be done according to *Wright's rules* (cited in Asher, 1976).

Wright's rules state that the correlation between any two variables can be broken down into simple and compound paths. The compound path is the product of the simple paths that it comprises (Asher, 1976). The simple path is the direct link between the two variables, and the compound path consists of all indirect routes from one variable to another. The following are three general instructions given by Wright to guide the decomposition of a path (Asher, 1976, p. 33):

1. No path may pass through the same variable more than once.

2. No path may go backward on (against the direction of) an arrow after the path has gone forward on a different arrow.

3. No path may pass through a double-headed curved arrow . . . more than once in any single path.

In Figure 14–10, the relationship between Variables B and C consists of the simple path linking B with C, plus the product of the path coefficients linking B, D, and C. Table 14–6 shows the decomposition of the model shown in Figure 14–10.

Interpretation of the path coefficients themselves can be tricky. In most cases, the beta weights cannot be interpreted as representing the unique contribution of one variable to variance in another. Remember that a beta weight not only has components of the degree of relationship between two variables but also includes components of any other predictors. For example, in Figure 14–10, the path coefficient linking Variables C and E does not represent the unique contribution of C to E. Rather, Variables A, B, and D also contribute to E, and these contributions may be reflected in the C to E path coefficient.

| TABLE 14-6 | Decomposition of Path Model Shown in Figure 14-10 | |
|---|---|---|
| PATCH | DIRECT EFFECT | INDIRECT EFFECT |
| B → E | None | 0.32 |
| A → E | None | 0.15 |
| B → C | 0.12 | 0.27 |
| A → C | 0.21 | None |

There is no easy way around this conceptual difficulty. One possible solution is to use semipartial correlation coefficients in place of beta weights. As we indicated, these can be obtained from SPSS or calculated easily by hand. These semipartial correlations provide a better estimate of the degree of impact of one variable on another (with others held constant) than do the beta weights.

## MULTIVARIATE ANALYSIS: A CAUTIONARY NOTE

The bare-bones overview of the major multivariate techniques in this chapter could not provide a detailed discussion of the controversies surrounding the use of these tests. Although some researchers characterize multivariate statistics such as MANOVA as "a powerful and rich methodology to characterize group difference" (Bray & Maxwell, 1982), others advocate extreme caution in applying multivariate statistics (Hunter, 1987). In our experience, caution is called for when multivariate statistics are used.

The computer can analyze multivariate data quickly and efficiently. In fact, the computer has made multivariate statistical techniques readily available to most researchers. With such easy access inevitably comes misapplication. The computer can grind out pages and pages of output in an amazingly short period of time. It cannot interpret the results for you, however. Much of the controversy over the use of multivariate statistics lies in the area of interpretation.

In multiple regression, for example, is it really better to use the standardized regression weights or the unstandardized weights to interpret the data? Or should you heed the advice of Tabachnick and Fidell (2001) to calculate semipartial correlations? In discriminant analysis, should you use the standardized coefficients or the structure correlations? In factor analysis, should you use orthogonal or oblique rotation? Unfortunately, there are no universally agreed-on answers to these and other major questions concerning multivariate analyses.

This chapter has discussed some of the advantages of multivariate statistics over univariate statistics. Unfortunately, multivariate statistics are not simple substitutions for univariate statistics. In a univariate ANOVA, for example, the effect of an independent variable on a dependent variable is evaluated by determining if the observed means change as a function of changes in the independent variable. Fine-grained analyses are then conducted to determine which means differ significantly. MANOVA, however, produces results that are more difficult to interpret. Instead of performing simple fine-grained analyses to localize significant effects, you set up contrasts with discriminant analyses. In short, interpreting results from a MANOVA is more complex than interpreting results from univariate ANOVAs.

The most prudent thing you can do at this point is to spend some time learning about the intricacies of these tests so you can identify and avoid these hidden traps. Thoroughly familiarize yourself with the assumptions of multivariate statistics and with how these statistics operate before attempting to use them.

Also, pay close attention to how you design your study. In many cases, failure to uncover relationships with a multivariate test is caused by faulty logic more during the design phase than during the analysis phase (Asher, 1976). Multivariate statistics cannot make sense out of poorly conceptualized and measured variables. There is no substitute for a carefully designed multivariate study that has a sound theoretical or empirical base and a well-defined measurement model.

## SUMMARY

Whenever you include several related measures in the same study, you are using a multivariate design. Analysis of your data is then done with one of the many multivariate statistical tests. There are multivariate tests for experiments with multiple dependent measures (MANOVA and MANCOVA) and tests for correlational designs (multiple regression, canonical correlation, discriminant analysis, and factor analysis). These tests allow you to identify complex relationships while controlling statistical errors.

Like univariate and bivariate statistics, multivariate statistics make assumptions that must be met. Your variables must be linearly related and normally distributed. Violations of these assumptions may lead to invalid conclusions. In addition, you must identify and deal with both univariate and multivariate outliers, because outliers can drastically affect the correlations used to compute multivariate statistics. Outliers can be handled either by deleting cases or variables or by using an appropriate data transformation. Also, make an effort to develop a sound measurement model to avoid the problem of error of measurement. Error of measurement can lead to an unacceptable number of Type II errors.

Factor analysis is used either to reduce a large set of variables to a smaller set or to confirm that certain variables measure the same underlying factor. Two types of factor analysis are principal components and principal factors. The difference between the two is found in the values placed on the diagonal of the correlation matrix used to extract factors. In principal components analysis, ones are placed on the diagonal. In principal factors analysis, communalities are placed on the diagonal. These communalities are difficult to derive before factor analysis. Principal components analysis is therefore more popular.

Factor analysis extracts as many significant factors as possible. For each factor, a variable will have a certain loading. These loadings are the correlations between the original variable and the factor extracted. You should rotate the factors before interpreting the loadings. The most popular rotation method is varimax.

Partial and part correlation analyses are used when you want to evaluate the relationship between two variables while controlling for a third. Partial correlation evaluates the relationship between two variables with the effect of a third variable removed from both of the variables being correlated. A part correlation (also known as a *semipartial correlation*) evaluates the relationship between two variables with the effect of a third removed from only one of them.

Multiple regression is used when you have identified a single, continuously measured dependent variable and several predictor variables. The analysis operates by determining regression weights based on the correlations among your variables. Two types of regression weights are raw and standardized weights. In general, you should use the standardized weights to help interpret your results. Unfortunately, the standardized weights do not tell you how much each variable contributes to explaining variability in your dependent variable. To do this, you should calculate the squared semipartial correlations. These correlations can then be used to determine the degree to which each variable independently contributes to variation in the dependent variable.

Discriminant analysis is an extension of canonical correlation. It is used when your dependent variable is categorical. Essentially, you are trying to predict group membership based on knowledge of your predictor variables. Interpretation is made by examining the amount of variability accounted for by each of the extracted discriminant functions and by setting up contrasts between your dependent variable groups. The former tells you how important each function is, and the latter how important each variable is to the solution.

In situations in which you have two sets of variables, the analysis of choice is canonical correlation. One set of variables may be identified as the dependent variable set and the other the predictor variable set. Canonical correlation computes for each set a new variable called a *canonical variate*. The correlation between the canonical variates is the canonical correlation. Interpretation of a canonical analysis can be made by looking at the structure correlations. These can be interpreted much like factor loadings in factor analysis.

MANOVA is used when you have an experiment with several related dependent measures. The analysis is essentially an extension of discriminant analysis to experimental data. Interpretation is based on the significance of the discriminant functions extracted for each effect, the Roy–Bargman stepdown test, and the structure correlations.

MANOVA also can be used to analyze data from a within-subjects design. Because of the restrictive assumptions of the univariate within-subjects ANOVA and the controversy surrounding error term selection for that analysis, MANOVA should be considered as an alternative. In MANOVA, the repeated measures taken from each subject are treated as correlated dependent variables. Using MANOVA in this capacity circumvents many of the problems associated with the traditional within-subjects ANOVA.

Multiway frequency analysis is a nonparametric multivariate statistic with a variety of applications. It can be used to analyze categorical data from an experiment or categorical variables from a correlational study. It also can be used on interval or ratio data in instances in which your data do not meet the assumptions of the analysis of variance. One form of multiway frequency analysis commonly used is loglinear analysis.

Path analysis is used to test a clearly specified causal model. Using a theory, you develop a causal model, measure your variables, and then use a series of simple multiple regression analyses to derive path coefficients. The path coefficients are used as estimates of the magnitude of causal relationships among variables. Interpretation is facilitated by looking at both direct and indirect effects of variables. Causal models can be of several types. Simple causal chains propose that there is a linear path from one variable to another. More complex models can involve complex path linkages. Models can be either recursive (which contain no causal loops) or nonrecursive (which contain causal loops). Conceptually, recursive models are easier to analyze and interpret.

Finally, multivariate analyses are complex and tricky to use. Don't try to use them until you have a sound understanding of how they work, what assumptions they make, and how results can be interpreted.

## REVIEW QUESTIONS

1. What statistics are used to evaluate correlational and experimental multivariate relationships?
2. What are the key assumptions and requirements of multivariate statistics?
3. How do various violations of the assumptions underlying multivariate statistics affect your data analysis?
4. What are outliers, why should you look for them, and how are they handled? What are the different types of outliers?
5. When is factor analysis used?
6. Why are factors rotated in factor analysis?
7. What do partial and part correlations tell you?
8. For what research applications would you use the various types of multiple regression analysis?
9. How are multiple $R$, $R^2$, and adjusted $R^2$ used to interpret the results from a multiple regression analysis?
10. What is the difference between the raw and standardized regression weights, and why are the standardized weights used when interpreting the results from a regression analysis?
11. What is the squared semipartial correlation, and when is it used?
12. What is discriminant analysis, and when is it used?
13. What is canonical correlation, and when is it used?
14. When would you use a multivariate analysis of variance to analyze your data?
15. How are the results of a multivariate analysis of variance interpreted?
16. Why would you use a multivariate analysis of variance to analyze data from a within-subjects design?
17. What is multiway frequency analysis, and when is it used?
18. What is path analysis, and how is it used in the research process?
19. Why is it important to develop a causal model when using path analysis?
20. What are the different types of variables used in a path analysis?

21. How are path coefficients used to interpret a path analysis?
22. What is meant by decomposition of a path model, and what rules are used to do it?

## KEY TERMS

univariate strategy

multivariate strategy

multivariate design

multiple regression

discriminant analysis

canonical correlation

factor analysis

multivariate analysis of variance
(MANOVA)

partial correlation

part correlation

multiple $R$

$R$-square

beta weight

multiway frequency analysis

loglinear analysis

path analysis

# 15

CHAPTER

# Reporting Your Research Results

Your journey through the world of research has taken you through the steps involved in choosing a research question, developing hypotheses, choosing a general strategy and specific design to test your hypotheses, and describing and analyzing your data. The final step in this process is to tell the world what you did and what you found.

Reporting your research results is perhaps the most important step because it is only by this reporting that science progresses. Other scientists working in the field need to know what you have done: the questions you have asked, the methods you have used to address them, and the answers you have found. Not only is this step essential for progress, it is required to assess the reliability of your findings and the soundness of your conclusions. Only when your research has been reported can others attempt to replicate and extend your findings.

To effectively communicate the results of your research, you need to know what must be said and how to communicate it clearly and in the proper format. This chapter discusses how to organize and present your research findings.

Even if you are not planning to pursue a career in psychological research, you will find that much of the information contained in this chapter is valuable. Many occupations—especially those at a managerial or technical level—require you to organize facts, to draw conclusions, and to present the facts and conclusions clearly and logically in a written report. Although the format and contents of your reports are likely to differ from those of the scientific report described here, the general principles of organization and composition will be the same.

## APA WRITING STYLE

Scientific journals in all disciplines specify the format, or *writing style*, that articles submitted to the journal are to follow. This writing style determines what subsections will be present in the report, how figures and tables will be presented, what rules are to be followed in typing the manuscript, and other such details.

In psychology, most journals follow the style established by the American Psychological Association (APA) in the *Publication Manual of the American Psychological Association* (5th ed., 2001). We refer to this manual simply as the APA publication manual. When you follow the manual, your manuscript conforms to APA style.

Sometimes you may come across a journal that does not completely follow APA style. For example, *Learning & Behavior* follows the style of the American Institute of Physics in abbreviating physical units, rather than the style specified by the APA. Nevertheless, these journals usually follow APA style closely, with only a few minor exceptions. (These exceptions are usually indicated on or near an inside cover of each journal issue under a heading such as "Notes to Authors.") Therefore, most of what you learn about APA style will apply even to non-APA psychology journals. The following discussion briefly describes how to write a research report in APA style. A comprehensive review cannot be presented in the space available here. (For additional details, consult the APA publication manual.) In this chapter, we also discuss how to avoid some common errors of composition and grammar and how to prepare a paper presentation.

## WRITING AN APA-STYLE RESEARCH REPORT

There are seven main sections in an APA-style research report manuscript: the title page, abstract, introduction, method, results, discussion, and references. When you are preparing an APA-style manuscript, many guidelines must be followed. For example, specific instructions govern margins, line spacing, what to cover in each section, and how to present information in tables and figures. In this section, we discuss some of the basic guidelines for preparing an APA-style manuscript.

### Getting Ready to Write

For this discussion, we assume that you will be creating your manuscript by using word processing software (such as *Microsoft Word* or *Corel WordPerfect*). Before you begin to type, make sure that the settings of your word processor conform to the requirements of an APA-style manuscript. In most cases, you can use the default settings, but there may be exceptions that will require a change. In particular, you should pay attention to the settings for paper size, font (typeface and size), margins, line spacing, hyphenation, and justification.

To create an APA-style manuscript, select the 8.5- × 11-inch paper size (usually the default). As for typeface, APA recommends choosing either Times New Roman or Courier. A *serif* typeface such as these is preferred for the body of the manuscript (i.e., typeface that has lines extending from the beginnings and ends of letters) because it is easier to read. A *sans serif* (without the lines) is preferred for figures because this typeface gives a very clean, clear look. Set the font size to 12 points.

Use double-spacing throughout your manuscript. This goes for the spaces between lines of text, between lines in the title, and after headings, footnotes, quotations, references, figure captions, and all elements of a table (APA, 2001, p. 286).

Be sure that right justification is turned off so that the last words of the lines on a page form a ragged right edge. Also, check to be sure that automatic hyphenation is turned off. APA style requires that a word too long to fit on a given line be moved in its entirety to the next line. This will happen only if automatic hyphenation is off.

All margins for an APA-style manuscript must be at least 1 inch all around (top, bottom, left, and right). With most word processors, 1-inch margins are usually the default. If they are not, consult your manual to find out how to change the margins. The length of a typed line has a maximum of 6½ inches.

Print the completed manuscript on 8.5- × 11-inch heavy white bond paper. Use a high-quality printer (e.g., inkjet or laser printer) and check to be sure that the manuscript is free of defects such as light printing.

*Formatting a Page*   Each page of an APA manuscript (excluding figures) includes a **manuscript page header** and a page number. Use your word processor's page header option to create the text and set up automatic page numbering so that the header and page number appear on every page of your manuscript. The manuscript page header consists of the first two or three words of the title of your manuscript. The editorial staff uses it to identify pages that may become separated from your manuscript during handling. Figure 15–1 shows the proper placement of the manuscript page header and page number. The page number can appear five spaces to the right of the header text and flush with the right margin, or on a separate line immediately below the text. In the latter case, right-justify both text and page number.

Type no more than 27 lines per page (assuming a 1-inch margin all around), not including the manuscript page header and page number. The first line of every paragraph and footnote must be indented (with the exception of the abstract, block quotes, titles and headings, table titles, notes, and figure captions). Set the tabs on your word processor to give an indent of from five to seven spaces. Finally, leave a *single space* after punctuation marks (including periods and colons).

*Heading Structure*   Headings within a manuscript identify different sections and subsections. In an APA-style manuscript you can have anywhere from one to five levels of headings. The structure for these five levels is as follows (APA, 2001, p. 113):

CENTERED UPPERCASE HEADING (Level 5)

Centered Uppercase and Lowercase Heading (Level 1)

*Centered, Italicized, Uppercase and Lowercase Heading* (Level 2)

*Flush Left, Italicized, Upper and Lowercase Side Heading* (Level 3)

  *Indented, italicized, lowercase paragraph heading ending with a period.* (Level 4)

You may have noticed that the highest-level heading is perversely identified by the lowest-level label (Level 5). It is rarely used, so the heading most commonly used to designate the top level gets the "Level 1" label. Each heading occupies its own line with the exception of the Level 4 (paragraph) heading. Start the text following a Level 4 heading on the same line as the heading, just as if it were following a sentence.

In most cases you will use only Levels 1, 3, and 4. A three-level heading structure looks like this:

Method (Level 1)

*Participants* (Level 3)

    *Participants not meeting requirements.* (Level 4)

For manuscripts requiring more than three levels of headings, consult the APA publication manual (2001, p. 114).

## The Title Page

The title page includes (in order) the manuscript page header, page number, running head, title of your paper, author name, and institutional affiliation. Place the title, author, and institutional affiliation information on the top half of the title page, below the manuscript page header and centered between the left and right margins. Figure 15–1 shows how to format a title page for multiple authors from different institutions. To see how to format a title page for other types of authorship, consult the APA publication manual (2001, pp. 296–298).

*Title*    When researchers looking for relevant articles on a particular topic scan the table of contents of a journal or an abstract in *PsychINFO*, the title of an article first captures attention. If the title fails to communicate clearly what the paper is about, readers may skip the paper.

    A paper that isn't read is useless. To avoid this fate for your paper, make your title concise, yet informative. Avoid using words that add little to the meaningfulness of

The Effects of   1

Running head: JURY SIZE

The Effects of Jury Size, Evidence Complexity, and Note Taking<br>
on Jury Process and Performance in a Civil Trial<br>
Irwin A. Horowitz<br>
Oregon State University<br>
Kenneth S. Bordens<br>
Indiana University-Purdue University Fort Wayne

**FIGURE 15–1**    Sample Title Page.

your title (for example, "An Experimental Investigation of . . . ," "A Correlational Field Study of . . ."). Keep your title short enough to avoid confusion about your research, but not so short that it fails to convey the topic of your paper. The recommended length for a title is 10 to 12 words.

Taking our cue from the story of "Goldilocks and the Three Bears," we present the following examples showing a title that is too long, a title that is too short, and one that is just right:

*Too long*:     An Experimental Study of the Effect of Delay of Reinforcement on Discrimination Learning in White Rats

*Too short*:    The Effect of Reinforcement on Learning

*Just right*:   Effect of Delay of Reinforcement on Discrimination Learning in Rats

In the first example, the words "An Experimental Study of" and "White" add extraneous words to your title. The second title is too general. A potential reader has only a vague idea about the focus of your study. The third example concisely conveys the essence of your study.

Type your title in the specified position on the title page. If multiple lines are required, double-space them just as you do other text. Capitalize the first letter of the first word and of all subsequent words (except for articles, prepositions, and conjunctions).

*Author Name(s) and Affiliation(s)*    If you are the sole author of the paper, your name goes one double-spaced line beneath the title. Include your given name, middle initial(s), and last name (in that order), centered between the margins. Do not include any titles (such as Mr., Ms., Dr.) or degrees (B.A., M.A., Ph.D., M.D., and so on).

Your affiliation is the organization that provided the local facilities and/or support for your research (usually a university or college). Its name appears one double-spaced line below yours on the title page, centered between the margins.

If there are two or more authors, how you organize the information depends on whether everyone has the same affiliation. Consult the APA publication manual for details. In cases of multiple authorship, the APA publication manual directs that multiple authors must be listed in order of their degree of contribution to the paper. If all authors contributed equally, they should work out some method for listing (e.g., alphabetically). If this is done, it should be noted in the manuscript in an "author note."

*Running Head*    The **running head** is a shortened version of your title having no more than 50 characters (including punctuation and spaces). The running head is typed flush left at the top of the title page, but below the manuscript page header and page number. Type "Running head:" followed by your running head typed in all capital letters (see Figure 15–1).

The running head is *not* the same as the manuscript page header we discussed earlier. The latter consists of the first three words of the full title (whether these are meaningful or not), whereas the running head should suggest the topic of the article (see Figure 15–1).

## The Abstract

The **abstract** is a concise summary of your paper and should not exceed 120 words. The length and content of your abstract will depend on the nature of your paper. In the abstract for an empirical study, include the following information (APA, 2001, p. 14):

1. Information on the problem under study (preferably in one sentence).

2. The nature of the subject sample (for example, age, sex, and so on).

3. A description of the methods used, including equipment, procedures for gathering data, names of tests, and so on.

4. A statement of the findings, including information on levels of statistical significance reached.

5. A statement of the conclusions drawn and any implications or applications of your results.

Although short, the abstract is important. Abstracts of papers are printed at the beginning of the final journal article, in *Psychological Abstracts*, and in *PsycINFO* entries. A potential reader will use your abstract to determine whether your paper is one that he or she should read as part of a literature search. If your abstract is poorly written, readers may fail to understand the significance of your work and may pass it by. Thus, you should put effort into writing a clear, concise abstract.

The Effects of   2

### Abstract

Jury-eligible men and women (N=567) participated in an experiment on the effects of jury size (6- v. 12-person), note taking, and number of plaintiffs on juror and jury decisions. Participants saw a videotape of a civil trial that featured either one plaintiff or four, while taking or not taking notes. Six-person note-taking juries gave higher compensation awards with four plaintiffs than non-note-taking 6-person juries. No difference between note-taking and non-note-taking 6-person juries was found with one plaintiff. Six-person juries were polarized more than 12-person juries and rendered more extreme punitive awards than the jurors who composed the 12-person groups. Twelve-person juries deliberated longer and recalled more case-relevant information than 6-person juries.

**FIGURE 15–2**   Sample Abstract Page.

Your abstract is the first substantive section of your paper. However, you typically write it *after* you have written the rest of your paper. Preparing a summary of your paper is much easier after you have written the paper, when you will have a clearer idea about what must be included in the abstract.

Here are a few general guidelines you should follow when preparing your abstract. First, make sure that the information in your abstract reflects what is in the body of your paper. Do not include any information in the abstract that does not appear in your paper. Second, your abstract should be self-contained. You must define all abbreviations that must be explained in the body of your paper, spell out all names, and define unique terms (APA, 2001). Third, avoid using direct quotes in your abstract; paraphrase instead. Fourth, make your abstract as concise as possible. Include only the most important information and write in concise sentences. Remember, you have a maximum of 120 words. Fifth, use your abstract to report what is in your paper, not to comment on or evaluate what is in your paper (APA, 2001). Sixth, avoid including reference citations in your abstract.

***Formatting the Abstract***    Your abstract is typed on a separate page, immediately after your title page. Type the word "Abstract" as a Level 1 heading (centered and not italicized). On the next line, begin your abstract. Do not indent the first line of the abstract (see Figure 15–2).

## The Introduction

The text of the paper begins with the introduction. The primary function of the **introduction** is to justify the study described in the report. To help the reader understand why the particular study was conducted, the introduction usually contains the following parts:

1. An introduction to the topic under study.
2. A brief review of the research findings and theories related to the topic.
3. A statement of the problem to be addressed by the research (identifying an area in which knowledge is incomplete).
4. A statement of the purpose of the research (always to solve the problem identified, but perhaps only a specific aspect of it).
5. A brief description of the research strategy, intended to establish the relationship between the question being addressed and the method used to address it.
6. A description of any predictions about the outcome and of the hypotheses used to generate those predictions.

The APA publication manual suggests that a good introduction should address the following questions in a paragraph or two (APA, 2001, p. 16):

1. Why is the problem studied important?
2. How do the hypotheses and the methodology relate to the problem under study?

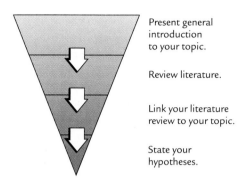

Present general
introduction
to your topic.

Review literature.

Link your literature
review to your topic.

State your
hypotheses.

**FIGURE 15–3**    General-to-Specific
Organization of an APA-Style
Introduction.

3. What, if any, are the theoretical implications of the research, and how does the study relate to previous research in the area?

4. What, if any, theoretical views are tested, and how were those views developed?

To provide this information in a comprehensible way, the structure of the introduction proceeds from the general to the specific. The inverted triangle shown in Figure 15–3 illustrates this structure. In the opening paragraph of your introduction, discuss (in general terms) the issue you have chosen to study. Next, develop the underlying logic and rationale for your study in more specific terms by reviewing relevant research and integrating its findings. Then identify the problem addressed by your research and state the purpose of your study. Finally, show how your study addresses the question and state your specific hypotheses.

If your introduction includes information of a controversial nature, that information should be presented in a fair and balanced manner. You should avoid expressing strong opinions on one side or another of the controversial issue. If you must express a personal opinion in the introduction, it should be offered without hostility and without making personal attacks on those with whom you disagree. When using citations to support your view or your research, you must present the research fairly and not out of context (APA, 2001).

Students often have difficulty determining what should go into the review of previous findings. Should it include a comprehensive review of *all* relevant research or be limited to a few papers that relate specifically to your research? The answer: "Try for something between these extremes."

You can assume your reader has some knowledge of the basic psychological concepts that underlie your study. Your job is to bring your reader up to date on the literature that most directly relates to your study. For example, if you investigated the effect of amount of reinforcement on behavior modification of developmentally delayed children, you need not review all research on operant conditioning and reinforcement. You can assume your reader has some knowledge of the basic concepts of operant conditioning. Instead, focus on the important issues relating directly to using operant conditioning to modify the behavior of developmentally delayed persons.

Assume you have decided to focus your introduction on the important issues. You then head to the library and, to your shock and horror, you find 200 articles that relate in some way to your research topic. Just how many of these must be included in your literature review? Of course, you cannot hope to review them all.

In fact, such a comprehensive literature review is inappropriate for a research paper. Your review should focus on those issues that are most important for establishing the rationale of your study. Therefore, you should identify all of the papers most directly relevant to the issues raised by your introduction. Within this narrower area, you can cite all relevant papers.

*Formatting the Introduction*     To follow APA style, you begin the introduction on a fresh page. Center the title of the paper at the top of the page and start the introduction immediately below the title. Do *not* type the heading "Introduction." Also, neither your name nor your affiliation appears on the first page of the introduction. Figure 15–4 shows a sample introduction. Notice how the authors followed the general-to-specific structure suggested in Figure 15–3 by beginning with a statement of the problem to study, followed by a review of relevant literature. It ends with a statement of the hypothesis to be tested (not shown).

## The Method Section

After you have established the rationale of your study and stated your hypotheses in the introduction, you then must tell your reader exactly how your study was conducted. This is done in the **method section**, which describes in detail the characteristics of your subjects, materials, and apparatus used, as well as the procedures followed. The level of detail should be sufficient to allow another researcher to replicate your study. If your paper uses a methodology described before, you may give a brief summary of the methods used and refer the reader to the more detailed published account.

The method section is usually divided into subsections to improve organization and readability. APA style permits considerable flexibility in how the divisions are made and labeled. The most commonly used format contains the following subsections: *participants* (or *subjects* if animals were used), *apparatus* (or *materials*, if this descriptor is more appropriate), and *procedure*. If you consider it necessary, you also may include a *design* section in which you specify the design of your study. A design section should only be included when your study uses an unconventional or complex design. You also can combine sections if this improves the clarity of the report. A description of each subsection follows.

*Participants or Subjects*     If humans participated as subjects in your study, describe them in a **participants subsection**. In this section, you specify the nature and size of the sample used in your study. Specify the number of participants and provide information on relevant demographic variables (such as sex, age, race, ethnicity), the procedures used for selection of participants and their assignment to treatments, any special agreements made with participants (such as payment for their participation), and information on personal characteristics of the participants (for example, IQ, personality). Also report any special characteristics of your participants, such as mental retardation, psychopathology, or special abilities.

The Effects of    3

The Effects of Jury Size, Evidence Complexity, and Note Taking on Jury Process

and Performance in a Civil Trial

In 1970, the United States Supreme Court held that juries of 6 members in criminal cases were constitutional (*Williams v. Florida*, 1970). Justice White, writing for the majority in *Williams*, concluded that the traditional 12-member jury was a historical accident without significance ". . . unnecessary to effect the purposes of the jury system and wholly without significance 'except to mystics'" (*Williams v. Florida*, 1970, p. 102). The Court soon thereafter held that the Seventh Amendment did not require 12-member juries in civil cases (*Colgrove v. Battin*, 1973).

These decisions flew in the face of 600 years of tradition and legal scholarship (Arnold, 1993). As Ellsworth (1999) has noted, social scientists were distressed that the Court could draw far-reaching conclusions about jury behavior without any empirical evidence that substantiated the assumption stated in the majority opinion that smaller juries would function much like larger juries. The Court made the empirical claim that "the reliability of the jury as a fact-finder hardly seems likely to be a function of its size" (*Williams v. Florida*, 1970, p. 102).

It may very well be that 12 was a historical accident. Why 12 jurors? The evidence is scant here. Rembar (1980) notes that 12 was not impractical, large enough to reach consensus but not so large as to be unwieldy. However, things less rational seem to have fixed the size of the jury. The number 12 has a numerological pedigree that anointed it with more than just utilitarian advantage. Various legal scholars have noted the mystic quality attached to the number 12, as encompassed in the 12 tribes of Israel and the 12 patriarchs, as well as the fact that Solomon's officers numbered 12 (Arnold, 1993; Holthoff, 1996).

**FIGURE 15–4**   Sample Introduction.

If your subjects were animals, then describe them in a **subjects subsection**. Describe the genus, species, strain, and any other important relevant information (such as the supplier). Also, give the number of animals used in the study and their sex, age, weight, and physical condition. Provide details of the care and housing of the animals (for example, whether they were housed individually or in groups, whether they were given free access to food and water, and the scheduling of light and darkness in the colony room). In this section, you also specify the number of subjects assigned to each condition in your experiment and any other information (such as special handling) that your reader needs to know in order to replicate your study.

Finally, in either subsection, indicate that your participants or subjects were treated in accordance with APA ethical codes.

*Apparatus or Materials*    The equipment or any materials used to measure behavior are described here. If you used primarily "equipment" (such as slide projectors, operant chambers, computers), describe that equipment in an **apparatus subsection**. If you used primarily written materials (such as a questionnaire, summaries of criminal cases, or rating scales), describe them in a **materials subsection** (APA, 2001, p. 308). In either case, the level of detail necessary in your description depends on the nature of the equipment or materials used.

If you used a commercial piece of laboratory equipment (for example, an operant chamber or a computer), you do not have to detail its characteristics. Instead, simply provide the name of the manufacturer and the model number of the equipment. Similarly, if you used a standardized test (such as the Stanford–Binet or the Bem Sex Roles Inventory), simply name the test (and the version, if relevant) and describe how it was obtained.

If you designed special equipment or developed a new measure, you must describe the equipment or measure in detail. If you designed a special operant chamber, for example, give its dimensions, materials of construction, and the types, characteristics, and locations of attached equipment (such as feeders, houselights, response levers, and sound sources). In short, provide any information your reader would need to reproduce your chamber in its essential details. Similarly, describe any measures you developed (for example, questionnaires).

Although you should provide enough information that another researcher could replicate your study, it is not feasible to reproduce extensive materials (such as a 250-item questionnaire or lengthy instructions) in your method section. If you used such materials, simply inform your reader where and how the materials can be obtained. Some journals may allow you to place such materials in an appendix.

*Procedure*    In the **procedure subsection**, tell your reader precisely what procedure was followed throughout the course of the study. Describe the conditions to which subjects were exposed or under which they were observed, what behaviors were recorded, how the behaviors were measured or scored, when the measures were taken, and any debriefing procedures. Provide enough information about the procedure that another researcher could reproduce its essential details.

If animal subjects were used, describe how the animals were handled, the length of the experimental sessions, any special deprivation schedules, and to what manipulations the subjects were exposed. If humans were used, include details about the instructions they received (if you cannot reproduce them, describe them in detail), informed consent procedures, procedures for assigning subjects to conditions, and how the experimental manipulations were introduced.

*Formatting the Method Section*    The method section begins immediately after the end of the introduction (do not necessarily start a new page). Center the word "Method" (Level 1 heading). On the next double-spaced line, type the word "Participants" beginning at the left margin, and italicize it (Level 3 heading). Again, move down a double-spaced line, indent, and start the first paragraph of the participants (or subjects) subsection. Follow the same format you used with the participants subsection for the apparatus (or materials) and procedure subsections. Figure 15–5 shows an

The Effects of   14

## Method

*Participants*

Participants were 576 jury-eligible individuals recruited from jury rolls and newspaper ads. Three hundred and fifty were women and 226 were men. Participants ranged in age from 21 to 64. Participants were informed that the research was aimed at examining how jurors decide civil cases and were paid a nominal $15.00 for their time.

*Materials*

The materials for this experiment included a videotaped civil trial involving plaintiffs suing a railroad company for repetitive motion injuries allegedly sustained on the job, an informed consent form, and several dependent measures.

*The trial.* The trial, produced on videotape, involved claims by railroad workers of repetitive stress injuries, specifically carpal tunnel syndrome (CTS) allegedly caused by repetitive actions across a number of different tasks. Carpal tunnel syndrome comprises a set of symptoms, including pain and weakness in the arms and hands, limited range of motion, swelling, and feelings of cold, numbing, or tingling. CTS usually appears in the hands and wrist. Many people who complain of CTS have jobs that require them to perform repetitive motions or to hold their bodies for extended periods of time in static positions.

Pretesting the strength of evidence for each plaintiff was done employing 35 third-year law students as evaluators. Previous research confirmed that no one plaintiff was deemed more worthy than any other plaintiff (Horowitz & Bordens, 2000). The original videotaped trial was also edited so that the evidence was calibrated to favor the plaintiffs because our primary interest was in having the juries deal with the damage awards.

*Procedure*

Mock jurors participated in the experiment in a room resembling a moot courtroom. Groups ranged from a minimum of 6 individuals to a maximum of 36. There was a total of 64 mock juries, 8 in each experimental condition. After all

**FIGURE 15–5**   First Page of a Methods Section.

example method section, with participants, materials, and procedure subsections. Note how each subsection contributes to your understanding of the described experiment.

## The Results Section

The purpose of your **results section** is to report your findings. All relevant data and analyses should be presented. As a rule, do not present raw (unanalyzed) or individual data unless the focus of the study was on the behavior of individual subjects (e.g., case history or single-subject design). If your analysis is complex, you may want to provide an overview of your strategy for data analysis in the opening paragraph. Outline for the reader which statistical tests you applied, and in what order.

Your results section should be primarily a narrative where you describe what you found. Make this narrative the driving force behind your results section. The results of descriptive and inferential statistics also will appear in your results section. However, these statistics should support the narrative statements you make. Too often, students allow statistics to drive the discourse in the results section, throwing in everything but the kitchen sink. What results is a compilation of numbers with little coherence.

If you are using statistical tests that are not generally available, indicate to your reader where the test was found and how information about it can be obtained. Next, report the results of any tests used to establish that your data met the requirements of the applied statistical tests (for example, homogeneity of variance, normality). Report any data transformations you applied to your data.

After you have presented this preliminary information, you can report your results. Include values of any descriptive and inferential statistics you calculated, along with the relevant $p$ values. Do not interpret or discuss your findings in the results section (APA, 2001); that is done in the next section of your paper.

*Formatting the Results Section* The results section begins immediately after the method section, on the same page as the end of the method section, if there is room. The results section should be a continuation of your paper. Center the heading "Results" (Level 1 heading), double space, and indent to start the first paragraph of your new section. Figure 15–6 shows the first page of an example results section.

The results section is where you discuss any tables or figures that present data from your study. Although these will appear in the body of the *published* text, they do *not* appear in the body of the manuscript. Instead you make reference to the figure at the appropriate place. However, when referring to a figure or table, do not make reference to its position. For example, *do not* say, "Figure 1, shown above, illustrates . . ." This is dangerous because, in the published article, the figure may not be placed where you expected to find it. Simply refer to the figure by number in your manuscript: "Figure 1 shows the relationship between . . ."

Presenting the results of a statistical test is a bit tricky but not difficult once you get the hang of it. You usually report the results of a statistical test in sentence format. The sentence states the effect being evaluated, whether or not the difference between treatment levels was statistically significant, the critical statistic used, the degrees of freedom, the value obtained for the statistic, and the level of significance achieved. Next we provide examples of how the results from an analysis of variance are reported in the body of your paper. Table 15–1 presents examples of how other statistics are reported. In cases in which your analysis is very complex, you could present the results of your statistical tests in a table.

When reporting the results from an inferential statistical analysis, you should begin by stating the alpha used to evaluate statistical significance (APA, 2001). For example, you might say,

The Effects of     16

## Results

### Analysis Strategy

The dependent variables were analyzed with independent factorial analyses of variance (ANOVA). For all comparisons p < .05 was adopted as the criterion for establishing statistical significance. Pearson correlation coefficients were used to explore relationships between dependent variables. All statistical analyses were performed with SPSS Version 10.0. Missing data were deleted casewise.

### Predeliberation Individual Measures

Analysis of the compensation data showed a significant main effect of note taking on compensation, $F(1, 52) = 10.84$, $p = .002$ ($\eta^2 = .172$). Note takers awarded lower compensation ($M = 20.64$, $SD = 9.23$) than non-note-takers ($M = 29.02$, $SD = 11.59$). The two-way interaction between information load and note taking was also statistically significant, $F(1, 52) = 4.89$, $p = .031$ ($\eta^2 = .086$). The three-way interaction between load, note taking, and jury size was also statistically significant, $F(1, 52) = 5.83$, $p = .019$ ($\eta^2 = .101$).

Analysis of the three-way interaction showed a simple interaction between load and note taking for the 6-person jury, $F(1, 52) = 11.07$, $p < .01$, but not for the 12-person jury. Analytical analyses of the simple two-way interaction at the 6-person jury condition showed a simple main effect of load when notes were not taken, $F(1, 52) = 10.52$, $p < .01$. In the high load condition, more compensation was awarded ($M = 40.75$, $SD = 12.27$) than in the low load condition ($M = 25.38$, $SD = 7.59$). There was no simple main effect of load when notes were taken.

**FIGURE 15–6**   First Page of a Results Section.

All statistical tests employed an alpha level of .05.

Alternatively, you can indicate the alpha level when you report the results of your statistical analysis:

At the .05 alpha level, the main effect of stimulus complexity was statistically significant, $F(2, 35) = 12.45$, $p = .03$.

If you do not have $p$ (the exact probability value obtained in the test), you can substitute the alpha level as follows:

The main effect of stimulus complexity was statistically significant, $F(2, 35) = 12.45$, $p < .05$.

| TABLE 15–1    Commonly Used Statistical Citations | |
|---|---|
| STATISTICAL TEST | FORMAT |
| Analysis of Variance | $F(1, 85) = 5.96, p < .01$ |
| Chi-square | $\chi^2 (3, N = 100) = 11.34, p < .01$ |
| t Test | $t(56) = 4.78, p < .01$ |
| z Test | $z = 2.04, p < .05$ |
| Pearson correlation coefficient | $r = .87$ or $r = -.87$ |

Note: Numbers in parentheses are the degrees of freedom. For the analysis of variance, the first number in the parentheses is the degrees of freedom for the numerator and the second number the degrees of freedom for the denominator (error).

Here, the "less than" symbol indicates that the value to follow is the alpha level rather than the obtained probability, and that $p$ was less than alpha. When an effect was *not* statistically significant, use the "greater than" symbol:

> The main effect of stimulus complexity was not statistically significant, $F(2, 35) = 1.46, p > .05$.

As you can see from these examples, APA style follows a consistent format for reporting results of statistical inference tests. For statistical symbols, use the normal typeface for Greek letters and for acronyms (e.g., ANOVA) but italicize all other symbols that use standard alphabetical characters (e.g., *F*, *df*, *p*). Table 15–2 displays the format for reporting results of several commonly used statistical tests.

## The Discussion Section

In the **discussion section**, you interpret your results, draw conclusions, and relate your findings to previous research or theory. The structure of your discussion section, as shown in Figure 15–7, reverses that of the introduction; rather than moving from general to specific, it moves from specific research findings to general implications.

Begin your discussion section with a brief restatement of your hypotheses. Next, briefly indicate whether your data were consistent with your preexperimental hypotheses. Use the remainder of the discussion section to integrate your findings with previous research and theory. Discuss how consistent your findings are with previous work in the area.

If your study yielded results that are discrepant from previous work, you should speculate on why the discrepancies emerged. Also, point out any problems encountered during the course of your research that might temper any conclusions drawn from your study. Often, methodological problems become evident only when you actually run your study, and these should be communicated to your reader. Finally, indicate what implications your research has for future research in the area. Point out any specific areas that need to be investigated further.

TABLE 15–2   **Abbreviations for Statistical Symbols**

| ABBREVIATION | MEANING |
|---|---|
| $df$ | Degrees of freedom |
| $F$ | $F$ ratio |
| $M$ | Arithmetic average (mean) |
| $N$ | Number of subjects in entire sample |
| $n$ | Number of subjects in limited portion of a sample |
| $p$ | $p$ value |
| $SD$ | Standard deviation |
| $t$ | $t$ statistic |
| $z$ | Results from $z$ test or a $z$ score |
| $\mu$ | Population mean (mu) |
| $\alpha$ | Alpha level |
| $\beta$ | Beta |

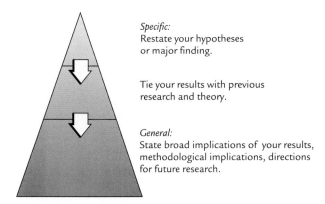

*Specific:*
Restate your hypotheses
or major finding.

Tie your results with previous
research and theory.

*General:*
State broad implications of your results,
methodological implications, directions
for future research.

**FIGURE 15–7**   Specific-to-General Organization of an APA-Style Discussion Section.

In the discussion section, you have license to speculate on the importance of your findings. Nevertheless, avoid the temptation to overstep the bounds of that license. Your interpretations must be based on your data, data from previous research, and/or established theory. Avoid the temptation to make unsubstantiated interpretations, even if they make intuitive sense to you.

Figure 15–8 shows an example of the first page of a discussion section. The authors of this paper followed the specific-to-general organization shown in Figure 15–7. Notice that the authors begin with a brief statement of what was found and follow by integrating their findings with those of other research in the area.

The Effects of    22

Discussion

The present experiment examined the effects of group size, number of plaintiffs judged, and note taking on simulated civil jury decisions. It was hypothesized that 6-person juries would award higher punitive damage awards than 12-person juries and that 12-person juries would polarize less than 6-person juries. Both of these hypotheses were supported.

Previous research on the relationship between jury size and awards has been inconclusive. Saks and Marti (1997) found no significant effect of jury size on civil jury decisions. Davis et al. (1997) found that 6-person juries award lower damages than 12-person juries. Conversely, Munsterman et al. (1990) suggest, tentatively, that smaller juries award more in compensatory damages than larger ones.

In the present study we had mock jurors provide both compensatory and punitive damage awards. When juries confronted punitive damages, 6-person juries gave significantly higher awards than 12-person juries. More specifically, when 6-person juries were permitted to take notes, they awarded more punitive damages than if not permitted to take notes. This result suggests that even in the light of the qualifying interaction between jury size and note taking, smaller juries tend to award larger punitive damages than larger juries. Because, as a general rule, most juries do not take notes, it is important to note the difference in damages awarded by smaller and larger juries.

Group polarization was evaluated by comparing predeliberation individual damage awards with group awards. Six-person juries showed a marked tendency to polarize. That is, they, as a group, awarded higher damages than the individual damages indicated before deliberation. Put another way, we found

**FIGURE 15–8**    First Page of a Discussion Section.

## The Reference Section

The **reference section** provides a list of the bibliographical references cited in the report. Any articles or books you cited in the body of your paper *must* be listed in the reference section. Conversely, any references listed in the reference section *must* be cited in the paper. If you read hundreds of papers but only cited three of them, your reference section should contain only the three papers actually cited. Figure 15–9 shows how a reference section is formatted in APA style.

Use a hanging indent when typing each APA-style reference, as shown in Figure 15–9. Your word processor should allow you to do this easily. For a journal reference, italicize the title of the journal, volume number, and associated punctuation marks. Do not italicize the page numbers, however. A specific reference would look like this:

The Effects of 29

References

Arnold, R. S. (1993). Trial by jury: The constitutional right to a jury of
    twelve in civil trials. *Hofstra Law Review, 22,* 5–38.

Ballew v. Georgia, 435 U.S. 223, 226 (1978).

Cather, C., Greene, E., & Durham, R. (1996). Plaintiff injury and defendant
    reprehensibility: Implications for compensatory and punitive damages.
    *Law and Human Behavior, 20,* 189–205.

Colgrove v. Battin, 413 U.S. 149 (1973).

Daniels, S., & Martin, J. (1995). *Civil juries and the politics of reform.* Evanston,
    IL: Northwestern Press.

Davis, J. H., Stasson, M. F., Parks, C. D., Hulbert, L., Kameda, T., Zimmerman,
    S. K., & Ono, K. (1993). Quantitative decisions by groups and individuals:
    Voting procedures and monetary awards by mock civil juries. *Journal of*
    *Experimental Social Psychology, 29,* 326–346.

Davis, J. H., Wing, T. A., Hulbert, L., Chen, X-P., & Zarnoth, P. (1997). Effects of
    group size and procedural influence on consensual judgments of quality:
    The example of damage awards and mock civil juries. *Journal of*
    *Personality and Social Psychology, 73,* 703–719.

Ellsworth, P. C. (1999). Introduction: Jury reform at the end of the century:
    Real agreement, real changes. *University of Michigan Journal of Legal*
    *Reform, 32,* 213–227.

ForsterLee, L., & Horowitz, I. A. (1997). Enhancing juror competence in a
    complex trial. *Applied Cognitive Psychology, 11,* 1–15.

ForsterLee, L., Horowitz, I. A., & Bourgeois, M. (1994). Effects of notetaking on
    verdicts and evidence processing in a civil trial. *Law and Human*
    *Behavior, 18,* 567–578.

**FIGURE 15–9**   First Page of a Reference Section.

Otto, A. L., Penrod, S. D., & Dexter, H. R. (1994). The biasing impact of pretrial
    publicity on juror judgments. *Law and Human Behavior, 18,* 453–469.

Table 15–3 provides examples of reference formats for the more commonly cited reference types. If you encounter a reference of a type not covered in the table, consult the APA publication manual.

Entries in your reference section are listed alphabetically according to the last name of the first author. If there are two articles by the same author from different years, list them in order from oldest to newest. So, Smith (2001) is listed before Smith (2003). If you have two (or more) references by the same author published in the same year, list them alphabetically according to the title (excluding prepositions such as "a" or "the"). Lowercase letters are placed immediately after each date, which will correspond to letters assigned to in-text citations for these entries. For example:

**TABLE 15–3    Reference Entry Formats**

## JOURNAL ARTICLE

Bandura, A. (1977). Toward a unifying theory of behavioral change. *Psychological Bulletin, 84,* 191–215.

Storms, M. D., & Nisbett, R. E. (1970). Insomnia and the attribution process. *Journal of Personality and Social Psychology, 16,* 319–328.

Tulving, E., McNulty, J. A., & Ozier, M. (1965). Vividness of words and learning to learn in free recall learning. *Canadian Journal of Psychology, 19,* 242–252.

## MAGAZINE ARTICLE

Finkel, L. H., & Sadja, P. (1994, May/June). Constructing visual perception. *American Scientist, 82,* 224–237.

## BOOKS

Lifton, R. J. (1986). *The Nazi doctors: Medical killing and the psychology of genocide.* New York: Basic Books.

Tabachnick, B. G., & Fidell, L. S. (1989). *Using multivariate statistics* (2nd ed.). New York: Harper & Row.

## ARTICLE IN AN EDITED BOOK

Austin, W. G. (1986). Justice in intergroup conflict. In S. Worchel & W. G. Austin (Eds.), *Psychology of intergroup relations* (pp. 153–176). Chicago: Nelson-Hall.

## PAPER PRESENTED AT A MEETING

Rosch, J. (1984, June). *Processing criminal cases in Japan: Implications for debate about plea bargaining in the U.S.* Paper presented at the meeting of the Law and Society Association, Boston, MA.

## LEGAL CASE DECISION

Nix v. Williams, 81. L. Ed. 2d 377 (U.S. 1984).

Smith, A. B. (2004a). Control mechanisms in . . .
Smith, A. B. (2004b). A replication of . . .

One-author entries come before multiple-author entries in which the first author is the same as the single author. So, for example:

Adams, J. K. (2004) . . .
Adams, J. K., & Smith, B. D. (2001) . . .

Entries with more than two authors are alphabetized by the last name of the first author, then by the second author, and then by the third author and so on. For example,

Adams, J. K., Charles, S. L., & Smith, B. D. (2003) . . .
Adams, J. K., Smith, B. D., & Charles, S. L. (2003) . . .

There are other rules for ordering reference entries. For more information see the APA manual (2001, pp. 220–222).

It is increasingly common to find resources published in an electronic medium such as the Internet or compact disc (CD-ROM). If you use materials from these sources, there are special reference formats for them. Table 15–4 shows how to format reference citations for information obtained from an Internet source. By the way, if you are citing an entire Web site, an in-text citation is all that is needed. For example, you might say: "The information just presented was found using a link on the Research Design and Methods Web site (www.mhhe.com/bordens6)." Formats for other electronic media can be found in the APA publication manual and on the APA Web site (http://www.apa.org/ journals/webref.html#Specific Documents).

## Additional Material

In addition to the formal sections of a manuscript just described, there is other, optional information that you might include in your manuscript. Such information includes an author note, footnotes, tables, figure captions, and figures. Although these appear in the body of a published research report, each is normally placed on a separate page at the end of your manuscript. An exception to this placement rule applies to the author note, discussed next.

---

**TABLE 15–4  Format for Electronic Sources**

*Internet Article Based on a Print Source*

Burke, B. L., Arkowitz, H., & Menchola, M. (2003). The efficacy of motivational interviewing: A meta-analysis of controlled clinical trials [Electronic version]. *Journal of Consulting and Clinical Psychology, 71,* 843–861.

*Article in an Internet-Only Journal*

Altemeyer, B. (2003). What happens when authoritarians inherit the Earth? A simulation. *Analyses of Social Issues and Public Policy, 3.* Retrieved November 13, 2003, from http://www.asap-spssi.org/

*Report from a Private Organization from Its Web Site*

Alan Guttmacher Institute (2003, September/October). *Services for men at publicly funded family planning agencies, 1998–1999.* Retrieved November 13, 2003, from http://www.agi-usa.org/pubs/journals/3520203.html

*U.S. Government Report from a Web Site*

United States Department of Justice. *Terrorism in the United States 1999.* Retrieved November 13, 2003, from http://www.fbi.gov/publications/terror/terror99.pdf

***Author Note***    Published APA-style journal articles include a small footnote at the bottom of the first page to identify each author's departmental affiliation, provide acknowledgments, state disclaimers or conflicts of interest, and indicate how readers can contact the authors.

The author note itself is arranged in four paragraphs. The first paragraph identifies the author's affiliation at the time the study was conducted. The second paragraph lists any changes in author affiliation since the study was conducted. The third paragraph includes acknowledgments such as grants that supported the research or the names of those who made special contributions to the research (such as informal review, assistance with the research design, or statistical analysis). It also indicates any special circumstances concerning the paper (such as that the study was a replication of an earlier one or that the study was done as a requirement for a degree). The fourth paragraph presents the "point of contact." Here you provide a complete mailing address (including, if desired, an e-mail address at the end of the paragraph) where readers can contact you.

Placement of the author note in your manuscript depends on whether your paper will undergo masked review, in which the reviewers will not know who wrote the paper, or nonmasked review. If your paper is to undergo masked review, type the author note on the title page. If not, place it on a separate manuscript page after your reference section. Figure 15–10 shows an example of an author note typed on a separate page. Individual entries are not numbered.

The Effects of   41

Author Note

    Irwin A. Horowitz, Department of Psychology, Oregon State University; Kenneth S. Bordens, Department of Psychology, Indiana University-Purdue University Fort Wayne.

    Everyone is still at the same place. However, if an author had taken a new position it would be disclosed in this second paragraph.

    We thank Bruce B. Abbott for his advice on the design of the present experiment and data analysis.

    Correspondence concerning this article should be addressed to Irwin A. Horowitz, Department of Psychology, Oregon State University, hisemail@osu.edu.

**FIGURE 15–10**    Sample Author Note Page.

*Footnotes*  APA writing style specifies two types of footnote. A *content footnote* is used to clarify a point made in the text of the paper or to provide additional details that would detract from the flow of your discussion at that point. The other type of footnote, the *copyright permission footnote,* is used to acknowledge the source of copyrighted quoted material, figures, or tables.

In the body of your paper, you number content and copyright footnotes consecutively. At the point in the text at which the reader should consult the footnote, simply place a superscript number (beginning with 1 for the first footnote), as in the following example:

The trial, used previously (Horowitz & Bordens, 1988), consisted of a 4-hour audiotape.[1]

The actual footnotes appear on a separate page entitled "Footnotes." Figure 15–11 shows how each footnote is numbered and presented.

*Tables*  Tables are used to present complex information that cannot be easily summarized in the body of your paper. For example, they can illustrate the design of your study or present summary data (e.g., tables of means and standard errors, correlation matrices). Tables are somewhat time-consuming to make and expensive to reproduce. Use a table only when it is impractical to fully describe information in the text of your paper.

The Effects of   42

Footnotes

[1]A more complete description of the trial may be found in Horowitz and Bordens (1988).

[2]This trial was adapted from an actual case (*Wilhoite v. Olin Corp.*, 1985). While the names of the various participants and locations were fictitious, the trial scenario in this study was taken from the above case.

**FIGURE 15–11**  Sample Footnotes Page.

The Effects of    45

Table 1

*Mean Juror Compensation Awards*

| | Group Size | | | |
| | Twelve | | Six | |
| Plaintiffs | Four | One | Four | One |
| Notes | | | | |
| Yes | 22.50 | 19.00 | 17.25 | 24.57 |
| | 9.94 | 8.96 | 8.13 | 10.06 |
| No | 25.75 | 23.50 | 40.75 | 25.37 |
| | 9.36 | 8.71 | 12.26 | 7.59 |

*Note:* Mean compensation scores denote thousands of dollars. The second number in each cell is the standard deviation.

**FIGURE 15–12** • Sample Table.

Tables prepared according to APA specifications include a title, a number, headings, a body, and, if necessary, notes. Create a separate page for each table, which should appear as shown in Figure 15–12. Place the title and number of the table at the top of the page, as illustrated. The headings of your table should clearly tell your reader what information is included in your table. In the body of the table, include the information you want your reader to see. Finally, as shown in Figure 15–12, use notes to explain the meaning of symbols in the table or to provide information not included in the table itself.

*Figure Captions*    Figure captions, unlike table captions, appear on a page separate from the figures to which they refer. Center the words "Figure Captions" at the top of the page. Underneath, beginning at the left margin, type "*Figure 1.*" and leave a single space; then type the caption for Figure 1. Follow the same format for each subsequent figure. Figure 15–13 shows a sample figure captions page.

*Figures*    Like tables, *figures* are used in your paper to provide graphic illustrations of complex material or relationships that cannot be adequately described in text. Although they appear most often in the results section of your paper, they also can appear in any other section. For example, a figure may be used in the method section to illustrate the materials used in your study or in the introduction to show an important theoretical relationship. Because figures are difficult to prepare and are expensive to reproduce in journals, use them sparingly.

The Effect of  47

Figure Captions

*Figure 1.* Mean jury compensation as a function of jury size, information load, and note taking.

*Figure 2.* Mean nonprobative facts recalled as a function of jury size, information load, and note taking.

**FIGURE 15-13**   Sample Figure Captions Page.

Graphs, drawings, and photographs are three commonly used types of figures. Use graphs to illustrate complex relationships among variables. Use drawings and photographs to illustrate equipment, materials, or stimuli that were used in a study. Photographs also might be used to convey aspects of results that cannot be adequately described in the text of your paper. For example, articles about physiological psychology may present photographs of histological sections to show the location of a lesion or stimulating electrode in the brain.

A simple rule to follow when preparing graphs is to make them simple and accurate. A visually confusing graph adds little to your paper. An improperly drawn graph can confuse your reader or make small, albeit statistically significant, effects look unnaturally large. Carefully plan and draw your graphs.

Figure 15-14 illustrates how the scaling of an axis on a graph can influence the reader's impression of the size of an effect. Participants scanned a one-page document for typographical errors under dim, medium, and bright lighting. The document contained five errors. Panel (a) displays the average number of errors found (vertical axis) as a function of lighting intensity (horizontal axis). A cursory look at this graph conveys the impression that lighting intensity had a large influence on the number of errors detected. However, the examination of the scale along the vertical axis reveals that the entire range of values varies only between zero and three errors. A more accurate impression of the influence of lighting intensity on number of errors detected is conveyed by the graph shown in Panel (b). Here the scale of errors presented along the horizontal axis covers the entire range of possible values (0 to 5). The small differences among means are represented fairly, and your reader is not misled.

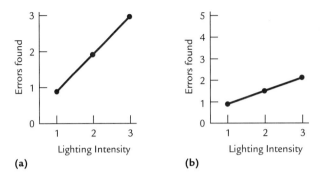

(a)                                    (b)

**FIGURE 15–14**    (a) Graph That Exaggerates the Size
of a Relationship. (b) Graph That Accurately Depicts
a Relationship.

In some cases you may find it necessary to break an axis to fit all your data on a graph. For example, if values of the dependent variable can range from 0 to 50, but participants used only numbers between 0 and 3 and between 32 and 40, you may want to show the data on a graph similar to the one shown in Figure 15–15. Notice that the y-axis is broken by slash marks. This shows your reader that a range of values along the y-axis has been skipped over. You should also break any lines within the graph that cross the broken part of an axis, as shown in the figure.

Some graphs require a *legend* to identify the meanings of the symbols or line styles used in the graph. Look again at Figure 15–15. The legend at the bottom of the graph tells the reader that the black line represents data from Level 1 of $IV_2$, whereas the colored line represents data from Level 2 of $IV_2$.

## Citing References in Your Report

In some writing styles, citations in the body of your paper are indicated with footnotes. In APA style, however, citations are made by providing the name(s) of the author(s), the publication date of the source, and (when needed) specific pages within the source.

The format of a citation within the text of your manuscript depends on how you choose to write a sentence that includes the citation. If the citation is included as an integral part of the sentence, you give the last name(s) of the author(s) and, in parentheses, the year in which the work was published. Here is an example with two authors:

> According to Smith and Jones (2004), memory for meaningful information is much better than memory for meaningless material.

If the citation is "tacked on" to the sentence, enclose the entire citation in parentheses, as follows:

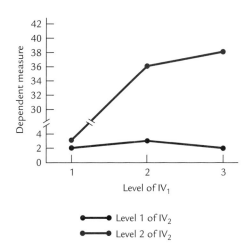

**FIGURE 15–15** Graph Showing a Broken Axis.

Memory for meaningful information tends to be much better than memory for meaningless information (Smith & Jones, 2004).

The two examples just provided are *multiple author citations*. Notice that when you cite the names of two authors in the sentence itself (the first example), you use the word *and* to connect the authors' names. When the names are used in parentheses (as in the second example), you use an ampersand (&) to connect them.

When you have more than two authors, the citation takes the following form:

According to Smith, Jones, and Harris (2004), memory for meaningful information is better than memory for meaningless information.

or

Memory for meaningful information is better than memory for meaningless information (Smith, Jones, & Harris, 2004).

When a citation is from a source with only two authors, *always* provide the names of both authors each time you cite the source. However, if you must cite an article with three or more authors several times in your paper, writing each name repeatedly becomes tedious. In this case, provide all of the authors' names the first time you cite the source (e.g., Smith, Jones, & Harris). Thereafter, you can provide only the first author's name followed by "et al." (Latin for "and others"). Here is an example:

Memory for meaningful information is much better than memory for meaningless information (Smith, Jones, Harris, Baker, & Thomas, 2004) . . . Smith et al. also point out that . . .

If you cite a source with more than six authors, use the "et al." device for the first citation and all subsequent citations. In the reference section, you would provide the last names and initials for the first six authors and et al. for the remaining authors.

What happens if you have two citations from the same authors in different orders from the same year (e.g., Smith, Jones, Harris, & Baker, 2003, and Smith, Harris,

Jones, & Baker, 2003)? Using the et al. device would be confusing because your reader would not know to which source you are referring. In this case you provide as many author names as needed to distinguish between the two sources (e.g., Smith, Jones, et al., 2003, and Smith, Harris, et al., 2003).

Finally, several special in-text citations are sometimes used. These are summarized in Table 15–5.

*Citing Quoted Material*    Whenever you directly quote or paraphrase a source, you must acknowledge the source in a citation. As with reference citations, the form to follow depends on the sentence structure. For example,

> Although research does suggest that television has the potential to aid in the socialization of children, there is still reason to be cautious. In fact, according to Liebert, Sprafkin, and Davidson (1982, p. 209), "Although most studies suggest that prosocial television can have desired effects, our ability to magnify these effects and minimize undesirable ones is in its infancy."

or

> Even though research does suggest that television has the potential to aid in the socialization of children, "our ability to magnify these effects and minimize undesirable ones is in its infancy" (Liebert, Sprafkin, & Davidson, 1982, p. 209).

These examples cited a direct quotation. Even when you simply paraphrase the ideas of Liebert et al., however, you still cite the source. This issue is discussed in greater detail later in this chapter in the section on plagiarism.

## Using Numbers in the Text

As a general rule, numbers lower than 10 are spelled out, whereas numbers 10 and above are expressed numerically. A few exceptions to this rule are as follows (APA, 2001). Numerals are used in these cases:

1. All numbers are expressed numerically if they are grouped for comparison (for example, 5 of 40 subjects). This exception does not apply if items are not directly compared (for example, 12 demographic items on each of five questionnaires).

2. Use numerals when a number immediately precedes a unit of measurement (for example, a 5-mg dose).

3. Use numerals when representing statistical or mathematical functions, percentages, ratios, percentiles, and quartiles (for example, multiplied by 4, the 2nd percentile).

4. Numerals are used when representing time, dates, ages, sample or population sizes, specific numbers of subjects in an experiment, scores and points on a scale, sums of money, and numerals as numerals (for example, the longitudinal study took 4 years, numbers on the scale ranged from 0 to 10).

**TABLE 15–5  APA-Style, In-Text Citations**

| APPLICATION | CITATION FORMAT |
|---|---|
| *Single Author* | |
| AUTHOR NAMED IN SENTENCE | |
| One article: | Jones (2001) |
| Two articles (same year): | Jones (2001a, 2001b) |
| Two articles (different years): | Jones (2000, 2001) |
| Personal communication: | Smith (personal communication, July 15, 2001)[a] |
| AUTHOR NAMED IN PARENTHESES | |
| One article: | (Jones, 2001) |
| Two articles (same year): | (Jones, 2001a, 2001b) |
| Two articles (different years): | (Jones, 2000, 2001) |
| Personal communication: | (Smith, personal communication, July 15, 2001)[a] |
| *Multiple Authors*[b] | |
| AUTHORS NAMED IN SENTENCE | |
| Two authors: | Smith and Jones (1998) |
| More than two authors: | Smith, Jones, and Key (1982) |
| AUTHORS NAMED IN PARENTHESES | |
| Two authors: | (Smith & Jones, 1998) |
| More than two authors: | (Smith, Jones, & Key, 1982) |
| Multiple citation for same idea: | (Harris, 1998; Jones, 2001; Smith & Jones, 1992) |
| *Special Citations* | |
| LEGAL CITATIONS | |
| Litigants named in sentence: | *Ballew v. Georgia* (1976) |
| Litigants named in parentheses | (*Ballew v. Georgia*, 1976) |

[a]Personal communication items are *not* placed in the reference list.
[b]Format for multiple articles follows that for single authors.
SOURCE: Information compiled from American Psychological Association, 2001.

5. Use numerals when discussing a specific place in an ordered series, parts of books, and each number in a list of four or more numbers (for example, Grade 2, Trial 1).

6. All numbers that appear in the abstract of a paper.

Numbers are expressed in words in the following cases (APA, 2001):

1. Numbers below 10 that do not represent precise measurements and are grouped for comparison with numbers below 10 are expressed in words (for example, five of the remaining seven trials, a two-dimensional figure).

2. Write out the numbers *zero* and *one* when that would be easier to understand than if numerals were used (for example, one-word answer, only one response was considered correct).

3. Any number that begins a sentence, title, or heading is written out (for example, Twenty subjects were assigned, Three subjects were dropped from the analysis, leaving 58 subjects). However, consider rewriting sentences or headings that begin with numbers so that they do not begin with a number.

4. Write out numbers that denote common fractions (a two-thirds majority) or universally accepted language (the Fourth of July).

5. Words and numerals are combined to express numbers when rounding large numbers beginning in the millions (the cost of the program was over $5 million) or when back-to-back modifiers are used (three 5-point Likert scales, 2 three-way interactions).

Additional rules for using numbers in APA style are too lengthy to cover here. See the APA publication manual (2001, pp. 128–136).

## Avoiding Biased Language

Sometimes in our writing we inadvertently use language that presupposes that one group is preferred over another or that might be offensive to a group of people. For example, by using the male pronoun *he* to express ideas generically, we are falling into the trap of biased writing. The APA publication manual gives three guidelines to follow to avoid biased language. First, provide descriptions at the appropriate level of specificity. For example, when describing ethnic groups, avoid using general terms such as *Asian* or *Hispanic*. Instead, be specific. If your participants were Chinese or Puerto Rican, use those more specific terms. Second, be aware of labeling. For example, the label "the elderly" categorizes people as if they were objects (APA, 2001). The term *elderly people* is preferred (APA, 2001). Also in this category of bias is writing that elevates one's own group above others. For example, the phrase "men and wives" implies that males are the standard by which women are to be judged (APA, 2001). In this case "men and women" would be better. Third, refer to individuals who participate in your research in a way that acknowledges their participation. For example, rather than saying, "Participants were run in groups of four," say, "Participants completed the experiment in groups of four." The latter sentence conveys that the *participants* were active in the experiment, which they were.

Space does not allow us to discuss in detail how to avoid biased language. The APA publication manual (2001, pp. 61–76) provides an extended discussion of the three guidelines just outlined, as well as discussions of specific areas of concern (for example, racial and ethnic identity, gender, sexual preference, and disabilities). You should consult the APA publication manual (2001) for further information on how to avoid biased language. One thing to keep in mind, however, is that avoiding biased language should not come at the expense of precision and accuracy. An attempt to avoid offending anybody can cloud important information. The American Psychological Association urges that good judgment be used, rather than a set of rigid rules concerning what is acceptable writing.

## EXPRESSION, ORGANIZATION, AND STYLE

The previous sections explained the general conventions to be followed when writing an APA-style paper. Unfortunately, merely knowing about subsections and citation formats does not guarantee that you will write a quality paper. You also must know how to present your ideas in a clear and organized way. Although this chapter cannot teach you to be a good writer, it can help you to avoid some of the common pitfalls. This section points out some of the flaws commonly found in student papers.

Perhaps the most common flaws in student papers are poorly expressed ideas, unorganized presentation of ideas, and sloppy presentation style. You can have a good handle on your research topic, procedures, and results but still be unable to communicate them well to your readers. Unclear writing and a disorganized presentation obscure important points.

### Expressing Your Ideas Clearly

In your writing, you should express your ideas clearly and concisely to your readers. We explore three elements of clear expression in the sections that follow: grammatical correctness, proper word choice, and economy of expression (APA, 2001).

*Grammatical Correctness*     Students often do not pay close enough attention to the grammatical structure of their sentences. A good illustration is the following ambiguous sentence:

> The experimenter recorded how fast each rat ran the maze with a stopwatch.

In this example, the intention was to say that the experimenter used a stopwatch to time the rat's running speed. Instead, you get the image of a rat running the maze while holding a stopwatch! The problem here is that the modifier "with a stopwatch" is misplaced in such a way that it refers to the rat, not to the experimenter. The following sentence is unambiguous, and consequently much clearer:

> Using a stopwatch, the experimenter timed each rat's running speed.

Here, the modifier is properly attached to the experimenter.

Another common grammatical error is disagreement between subject and verb. In the following incorrect sentence, the verb goes with the word "records" and not "one":

Only one of the subject's *records were* included in the analysis.

This sentence should be corrected as follows:

Only *one* of the subject's records *was* included in the analysis.

This chapter cannot explore all the common grammatical errors. Make an effort to reduce grammatical errors in your writing. Some good guides that may help you are Crews (1980); Hall (1979); Leggett, Mead, and Charvat (1978); Strunk and White (1979); and Chapter 2 of the APA publication manual (2001). A grammar checker, now included with most word processors, can also help.

*Proper Word Choice*    Proper word choice is the second aspect of clear writing. Make sure that your selected words convey your ideas as intended. For example, in general writing, the words *feel* and *believe* are used interchangeably. In scientific writing, however, they may mean very different things (APA, 2001). Choose the word that most accurately conveys your meaning. If you mean *believe*, then say *believe*.

Unnecessary qualifiers also tend to reduce clarity of expression. Phrases such as "approximately equal" and "particularly strong" are imprecise and may be interpreted differently by different readers. Be specific when referring to quantity estimates. And be careful about using pronouns in place of nouns, especially in long sentences. Following the meaning of a sentence that has many "they's," "it's," and so on is difficult.

Avoid using complex words when a simple word would suffice. For example, don't say *masticate* when you mean *chew*, or *cogitate* when you mean *think* (Hall, 1979, p. 84). And never utilize the word *utilize*—use *use* instead. Constant use of fancy words becomes tedious to read. Base your choice on how well a word conveys your meaning, not on how intelligent you think it makes you seem. If a complex word best conveys your meaning (for example, *clandestine* implies much more than *secret*), by all means use it. In other cases, use the preferred simple word.

*Economy of Expression*    You should express your ideas in a concise, frugal manner (APA, 2001). Two major flaws in writing threaten economy of expression: the use of jargon and wordiness (APA, 2001).

*Jargon* refers to the use of technical vocabulary even when that vocabulary is not relevant. Not all readers will know what you mean by these terms, so it is best to avoid them if possible. For example, using the term *voir dire* throughout an article may confuse readers who are not familiar with legal terminology. It would be better to use the term *jury selection*. Jargon is also the substitution of euphemistic phrases for familiar terms, another practice you should avoid (APA, 2001, p. 35). For example, using the term *electrically oriented aversive stimulation* for the term *electric shock* adds to confusion and detracts from clear expression.

Wordiness refers to using more words than necessary to express an idea clearly. Consider the following examples:

*Wordy*:      There were several participants who required additional assistance.

*Better*:      Several participants required additional assistance.

The currently popular phrase "the exact same" is not only grammatically suspect ("exactly the same" would be better); it uses three words when one will do: "identical."

Two other factors that contribute to unclear writing are *redundancy* and *unit length* (APA, 2001). Redundancy occurs when words duplicate a meaning already conveyed by other words. In the following example, the word "past" is redundant: "The participant's past history was examined." Unit length concerns the length of sentences within a paragraph. Using too many short sentences creates a choppy, boring style. Using excessively involved, long sentences can be confusing. Vary the length of the sentences within a paragraph to establish and maintain the interest of your reader. Attention to unit length also extends to the length of paragraphs (APA, 2001), a topic we discuss in the next section.

## Organization

Whereas clarity of expression relates most closely to the structure of sentences, organization relates to how those sentences are organized into paragraphs and how paragraphs are woven into an entire paper. You can write the most beautiful, grammatically correct sentences, yet fail to clearly convey your ideas. A paragraph is more than a collection of grammatically correct sentences. Those sentences must be woven into a coherent, unified entity that clearly conveys information to your readers.

Paragraphs can include four types of sentences (Crews, 1980). These are *theme sentences, support sentences, limiting sentences,* and *transitional sentences.* The theme sentence, which is usually the first sentence in a paragraph, conveys to your reader the topic of the paragraph. Support sentences follow the theme sentence and support and elaborate the theme. Limiting sentences point out possible limits to the assertion made in the theme sentence. Finally, transitional sentences are used to shift smoothly from one idea to another within a paragraph. These four types of sentences should be combined to achieve unity.

Crews (1980) suggests four general rules to help you attain unity within paragraphs:

1. Make only one major point within a paragraph.

2. Make your theme sentence the most general sentence within a paragraph. All subsequent sentences should focus on the theme stated in the theme sentence.

3. Stick to the theme stated at the outset of the paragraph. Unity is disrupted when you stray from the point.

4. Use complete sequences of limiting or supporting sentences. That is, if you have something positive to say about a topic, list all the positive elements before turning to the negative.

The following paragraph exemplifies these points:

Piaget's view of the development of object permanence was based on rather informal tests with infants. In a typical test, Piaget hid an object and the infant was required to engage in a visual or manual search for it. From the results of such tests, Piaget concluded that infants do not demonstrate object permanence until they are six months old, and do not achieve a full understanding that objects continue to exist when out of sight until the end of the sensorimotor stage. However, later research suggests that infants may acquire the concept of object permanence long before Piaget suggested they do.

The first sentence in the paragraph is the theme sentence, because it tells the reader that the paragraph is about Piaget's views on object permanence. The subsequent sentences discuss issues relevant to the theme sentence. The next two support the theme sentence, whereas the last one limits it.

In addition to unity, a paragraph should have coherence. Coherence is disrupted when sentences that relate only tangentially to a topic are included in a paragraph (Hall, 1979, p. 193). Two problematic sentences are underlined in the following paragraph. The first disrupts unity, and the second disrupts coherence.

> Methodological problems were apparent in the Jones and Smith (2001) experiment. Smith was only a graduate student at the time of the study. The methodological problems stemmed from use of outdated equipment. Some of the equipment was so old that it could hardly be kept working. This equipment did not have the sensitivity to accurately record the subtle changes in the subjects' behavior.

The first underlined sentence is irrelevant to the topic introduced at the beginning of the paragraph. The second underlined sentence, although tangentially related, is not necessary. It serves only to break up the important points in the previous and subsequent sentences (points that should be linked directly). The two underlined sentences together add little to the discussion and disrupt the unity of the paragraph.

Without these two unnecessary statements, the paragraph still conveys the important idea that the Jones and Smith study was flawed because of archaic equipment:

> Methodological problems were apparent in the Jones and Smith (2001) experiment. The methodological problems stemmed from use of outdated equipment. This equipment did not have the sensitivity to accurately record the subtle changes in the subjects' behavior.

Paragraphs can become confusing when they become too long. If a paragraph runs longer than one double-spaced manuscript page, look for places to break the paragraph into shorter ones (APA, 2001). Breaking long paragraphs into shorter ones provides pauses for your readers and is preferable to a single, overly long paragraph. Weave together paragraphs to create a unified and consistent narrative that will hold your readers' interest. Avoid confusing your readers with too much information packed into too little space.

On a similar note, you also should avoid using a sequence of overly short paragraphs. Overusing one- or two-sentence paragraphs breaks up the flow of your writing and makes it abrupt and difficult to read (APA, 2001). If you find you have many short paragraphs, see if you can reorganize your ideas to create fewer but longer paragraphs.

Each section of your paper should be organized into units. For example, your introduction might be organized into three subsections (even if they are not labeled as such). In the first subsection, you introduce your topic (using perhaps two paragraphs).

In the second subsection, you might review relevant literature (five paragraphs). Finally, in the third subsection, you might summarize the research you reviewed and state your hypotheses (three paragraphs). Information in your method, results, and discussion sections should be organized in a similar fashion.

The best way to avoid disorganization is to make an outline of your paper before you begin writing and then stick to the outline. Indicate the main sections (introduction, method, and so forth), and identify the subtopics to be handled within the major sections.

## Style

Your final paper is a reflection of you, as well as of your work. A paper can be well organized and clearly written, yet still make a negative impression on your reader because of sloppy presentation. Frequent misspellings, misused words, and typographical errors detract significantly from your paper. Work to eliminate them.

Misspellings can best be avoided by using a dictionary (we recommend *Webster's 10th edition* or *Webster's Third International Edition*). If you have difficulty with spelling (as many of us do), have your paper read by a good speller. The spelling checker that comes with your word processing program also can help to identify any spelling errors. However, it will not catch errors involving "sound-alike" words (such as using "witch" when you meant "which") or the wrong grammatical form (e.g., typing "our" when you meant "your"). In addition, it may not recognize certain technical terms even when these are spelled correctly. For those you will need to keep your dictionary handy.

Misused words also detract from your paper. For example, "affect" and "effect" are commonly confused. As a verb, "affect" means "to act on" and "effect" means "to bring about" (see Table 15–6 for a list of commonly misused words). Avoiding these errors involves acquiring a good vocabulary. If you have trouble in this area, have your paper read by someone who has a good vocabulary. Also, your word processor probably includes a facility that flags possible grammatical errors and suggests alternative constructions. Although these are not always accurate, they do help you to spot potential trouble spots. Frequent typographical errors (including crossed-out words, penciled-in words, and mistyping) also detract from your work. Careful proofreading is essential. Correct any errors you find before you submit your work. These corrections should be made on your word processor, not penciled in on the manuscript.

Today's word processors are invaluable for making corrections. They allow you to insert, delete, or move words or even whole paragraphs quickly and easily. You can fix errors, make stylistic changes, or improve organization without retyping sections of the manuscript.

## Making It Work

A goal you should strive to achieve is to produce a well-written report of your results that is clear, organized, and visually pleasing. Most writers, even professionals, cannot produce a "finished product" after only a single writing. The best way to approach writing a paper (especially in the early stages of your writing career) is to prepare a rough draft and then make careful revisions.

**TABLE 15–6    Commonly Misused Words**

| WORDS | TRUE MEANINGS AND COMMENTS |
|---|---|
| affect/effect | *affect:* to influence<br>*effect:* the result of; to implement |
| accept/except | *accept:* to take willingly<br>*except:* excluding; to exclude |
| among/between | *among:* used when you refer to more than two<br>*between:* used when you refer to only two |
| amount/number | *amount:* refers to quantity<br>*number:* refers to countable elements |
| analysis/analyses | *analysis:* singular form<br>*analyses:* plural form |
| cite/site | *cite:* make reference to<br>*site:* location |
| datum/data | *datum:* singular form<br>*data:* plural form |
| every one/everyone | *every one:* each one<br>*everyone:* everybody |
| few/little | *few:* refers to number<br>*little:* refers to amount |
| its/it's | *its:* possessive pronoun<br>*it's:* contraction of "it is" |
| many/much | *many:* refers to countable elements<br>*much:* refers to quantity |
| principle/principal | *principle:* strongly held belief<br>*principal:* foremost |
| than/then | *than:* conjunction used when making a comparison<br>*then:* refers to the past in time |
| that/which | *that:* used to specify a crucial aspect of something: "the study that was conducted by Smith (1984)"<br>*which:* used to offer a qualification that is not crucial to something: "the study, which was published in 1984"<br>(*which* is always preceded by a comma; *that* takes no comma) |
| there/their/they're | *there:* refers to a place<br>*their:* possessive pronoun<br>*they're:* contraction of "they are" |
| whose/who's | *whose:* the possessive of "who"<br>*who's:* contraction of "who is" |
| your/you're | *your:* possessive pronoun<br>*you're:* contraction of "you are" |

SOURCE: Compiled from Crews, 1980; Hall, 1979; Leggett, Mead, & Charvat, 1978; and Strunk & White, 1979.

During the revision process, look for three major things. First, read through your paper, paragraph by paragraph, and check for unity, coherence, and proper word usage. Second, read your paper for organization between paragraphs and sections. Finally, carefully comb your paper for typographical errors, misused words, and other stylistic errors. Only after you have completed several cycles of writing and revising should you submit your paper to your instructor or to a journal.

## Avoiding Plagiarism and Lazy Writing

Reference citations must be included in your paper to give credit to another person or persons who have published or presented ideas. If you use someone else's words or ideas without proper citation, you are guilty of **plagiarism**, which is at best unethical, and at worst illegal. Penalties for plagiarism can range from a failing grade on an assignment to civil litigation (if plagiarized work is published).

A broad rule of thumb to avoid plagiarism is to provide a citation whenever another person's work influenced your thinking. Of course, this means citing more than direct quotations and paraphrases of someone else's writing. If an idea you present in your paper is not originally yours, then you must cite the source.

A writing deficiency closely related to plagiarism is **lazy writing** (Rosnow & Rosnow, 1986). In lazy writing, an individual simply lifts paragraph after paragraph out of one or more sources and presents them as a paper. The difference between plagiarism and lazy writing is that in lazy writing, the individual properly cites the source of the material.

Although lazy writing is technically not plagiarism, few instructors will accept a paper that relies heavily on quoted material. Keep the following rules of thumb in mind when writing a paper:

1. Always properly cite the source of words and ideas that are not your own.

2. Always paraphrase information from another source and provide a proper citation.

3. Enclose directly quoted material in quotation marks or set longer passages off in a block paragraph style and provide the proper citation, which includes the page number(s) where the material can be found in the original source.

4. Use quoted material sparingly and *only* to support something you have written *in your own words*.

5. Make sure that any written assignment you turn in is written in your own words. *Never* turn in a paper that consists of large amounts of material taken from other sources with little of your own writing. This is true even if you made some minor, cosmetic changes to the original material and properly cited the original source.

For further information on lazy writing, go to the Web site supporting this text. There you will find extended examples of plagiarism and lazy writing as well as advice on how to avoid these two writing flaws. You also will find links to a number of Web sites that deal with plagiarism.

## TELLING THE WORLD ABOUT YOUR RESULTS

If you decide to pursue a career as a psychologist, you will probably need to submit your research to a journal for publication. Once you have prepared your APA-style paper, you must make a few decisions about how to disseminate your results, or make your results known, to the scientific community. You have several options, which are not necessarily mutually exclusive. You may present your results at a local, regional, or national convention (for example, the Annual Meeting of the Midwestern Psychological Association), an option we discuss below. You also may decide to have your results published in a scientific journal, or you could publish your results on a Web site on the Internet.

### Publishing Your Results

Before submitting your paper to a scientific journal for possible publication, you have to make a couple of preliminary decisions. One decision is where to send your paper. If your paper has a highly specific focus (such as treating abnormal behavior), you should consider sending your paper to a specialized journal (for this example, perhaps the *Journal of Abnormal Psychology*). If your paper is more broadly focused, you might send it to a less specialized journal. For example, if you conducted a study of the attributions made by schizophrenic patients, you might send your paper to the *Journal of Personality and Social Psychology*. Refer to Chapter 3 for a list of some of the major psychological journals.

A second decision is whether to send your paper to a refereed or nonrefereed journal. As stated in Chapter 3, papers sent to a refereed journal are reviewed before publication, but those sent to a nonrefereed journal are not reviewed. Select a refereed journal because work published in a refereed journal usually receives more serious attention by the scientific community.

*The Publication Process*    After your paper has been submitted to a refereed journal, it goes through a standard procedure for review and publication. First, your paper is sent out for review. After the initial review, you receive a decision about acceptance or rejection. The editor of the journal may unconditionally accept or reject your paper. In many cases, however, papers are given a *provisional acceptance*. The editor then asks you to revise and resubmit your paper. After resubmission, the paper may be sent out for another review if the revisions are extensive.

Once accepted, your paper goes to a *copy editor*, who makes sure the paper conforms to the style and requirements of the journal. In most cases, the copyedited manuscript will be returned to you so you can review it. At this point, you may still make limited changes to the manuscript. Once you have reviewed the manuscript and corrected any errors, you then return the copyedited manuscript to the editor. Many journals allow you to electronically return your manuscript to the publisher for production. However, doing this requires that you make a few changes to your manuscript file. For a complete list of these changes, see the APA publication manual (2001, p. 385).

When your manuscript has been typeset by the publisher, you receive *proofs*, which are copies of your paper as it will appear in the journal. You read these proofs to be sure they agree with your manuscript and that there are no errors. Errors may be of two types: printer errors and author errors. A printer error occurs when the text in the proofs does not match the manuscript. You would indicate these errors and identify them as printer errors. Author errors are things you did not catch in the previous rounds of editing. For example, you may have discovered that you reported a statistic incorrectly. These can be fixed at the proof stage, but they must be marked as author errors. (Journals usually charge the author for the cost of these author alterations.) Having reviewed the proofs and corrected any errors, you return them to the publisher.

The cycle of submission–review–revision and resubmission–acceptance–publication is a relatively long one. After your initial submission to a refereed journal, two months or more may pass before you receive your first feedback. After revision, another two months or more may pass (depending on whether your paper was sent out for a second review). The entire process (from submission to publication) may take a year or more. Chapter 3 discusses this and other publication-related issues in greater detail.

## Paper Presentations

In addition to publication, you can communicate your research results through a paper presentation. Paper presentations can range from class presentations to more formal seminars to presentations at professional meetings. Two methods of presenting the results of your research are used at professional meetings. You can deliver a talk, or an *oral presentation*, before an audience, or you can present your findings in a *poster session*.

*Oral Presentations*    For an *oral presentation*, you are usually given a limited amount of time to present your information. At paper sessions at professional meetings, for example, you are given 15 minutes. In that brief period of time, you must communicate to your audience the rationale behind your study, your methods, results, and conclusions. Because your time is extremely limited, it is helpful to your audience if you have a written summary of your paper (including figures and tables) to distribute at a paper session. Some conferences may require that you do this. Even if they do not, you should prepare handouts.

When preparing for an oral presentation, follow a few general rules. First, organize your talk. Do not go before a room full of professionals (or even other students) and try to "wing it." Instead, develop an outline of your talk and stick to it. Second, do not read your paper. Store what you want to say in your head. Use your notes only as a guide. Third, use appropriate visual aids whenever possible. Computerized slide shows, overhead projector transparencies, and printed handouts provide quick, easy ways to present complex methods and results. Rather than waste precious time describing methods and complex results, refer to your visual aids and restrict your discussion to the most important aspects of your research. Fourth, take some time to practice your presentation, perhaps in front of some colleagues. This will allow you to tell whether the length of your presentation is appropriate, whether you are communicating clearly, and whether there are any elements you left out. Feedback from your colleagues during a practice session can be valuable in identifying the strong points and weak points of your presentation.

A common mistake during oral presentations is giving an overly detailed account of the methods and procedures. These complexities are not well communicated verbally. Listeners can retain only so much information and may become lost if you try to give too much. Try to boil down a complex method to its essential elements. To understand your study, listeners may need to know that you tested rats in an operant chamber. They may become lost in the details if you try to explain that the rats were Long–Evans females weighing between 250 and 350 grams and housed individually in 7- × 7- × 14-inch wire cages, and that the chamber was 25 × 25 × 30 cm, constructed from aluminum sheet, and fitted with a floor consisting of 0.8-cm-diameter stainless steel bars spaced 1.2 cm apart. If your procedure is complicated, diagram it and present it on a slide or handout rather than attempting to explain it all verbally.

A final rule to follow is to avoid being pedantic and pompous. Some presenters are so consumed with self-importance that they consider it necessary to bore the audience with unnecessary details of their lives and research. Pomposity is manifested when the presenter is 13 minutes into his or her presentation and has yet to say anything about the methods and results of the study. Your audience will appreciate your presentation more and get more out of it if you focus your presentation on central issues of the research being reported.

*Poster Sessions*    In a *poster session*, you prepare a poster that outlines the rationale behind your study and your hypotheses, method, results, and conclusions. Unlike the oral presentation, you are not limited to 15 minutes. Poster sessions may last as long as an hour or more. Many related papers are presented within each session.

The main advantage of a poster session is that you can engage in meaningful conversations with other people who are doing research in your area. During oral presentations, interaction with the audience may be limited to a few questions immediately following your presentation or a few minutes after the paper session. In a poster session, an interested person can take time to read your poster and perhaps formulate more meaningful questions and input.

Poster sessions usually require more time and effort on your part than do oral presentations. Posters may be time-consuming to make and difficult to transport, although new technologies such as vinyl posters are cutting down on these logistical problems. Despite the difficulties, in some ways the poster format is superior to the oral presentation. It allows you greater freedom of presentation, more time for discussion, and less superficial interactions with other researchers in your area.

Conferences differ in the guidelines you must follow to format your poster (for example, what elements must be included, placement of sections, typeface style and size). If you are planning to present a poster, you should obtain a copy of the guidelines used at the conference at which you will be presenting. Also, as was the case for the oral presentation, you should prepare a written version of your poster to distribute to interested individuals.

## The Ethics of Reporting or Publishing Your Results

Your decision to report or publish your results in a public forum carries with it some important responsibilities. Concern over protection of participants and adherence to ethical guidelines does not stop at the publication stage. These ethical considerations include avoiding plagiarism, giving proper publication credit (for example, granting authorship status and deciding on an order of authorship), not publishing previously published results, and sharing data with qualified scientists who might want to reanalyze the data.

## SUMMARY

After you have designed and conducted a study and have analyzed your data, you then prepare a report of your results. Two ways of reporting your results are the written report and presentation. The written report establishes a permanent record of your results that is less susceptible to misunderstanding and misinterpretation than is a presentation. The presentation format gives a forum to disseminate results quickly.

Psychological research is reported using APA style (or a close variant of it), which specifies how a paper must be prepared. An APA-style paper consists of a title page, an abstract, an introduction, a method section, a results section, a discussion section, and a reference list, plus additional pages for author notes, footnotes, tables, and figures.

The title page of your paper includes the title of your paper, your name, institutional affiliation, and a short running head. The abstract is a brief, but concise, summary of your research and is the last part of your paper that you write. The introduction of your paper introduces your topic, reviews relevant research, and states your hypotheses. It begins with a general discussion of issues and then moves to a specific discussion of your research. Its major purpose is to provide a logical justification for the study being reported.

The method section describes exactly how your study was conducted. Separate subsections provide information about subjects, apparatus or materials, and procedures. The goal of the method section is to provide enough information that another researcher could replicate your study in all its essential details.

Your results are presented in the results section, which provides a detailed report of the findings (illustrated if necessary with tables and figures) and the results of any statistical analyses of the data.

The results are discussed in the discussion section. The section usually begins with a brief summary of the results about to be discussed and a restatement of any hypotheses bearing on these results. The discussion indicates whether these hypotheses were supported by the results. The findings are then related to previous knowledge in the field and conclusions are drawn.

Figures and tables are used to communicate complex information about methods or results that cannot be adequately described verbally. Graphs of relationships must be carefully drawn to avoid misleading the reader. Graphs that make small, albeit statistically significant, effects look large should not be drawn. Clear legends and captions, listed on a separate figure captions page, also must be included. Tables, like figures, can help summarize complex information. Each table consists of a number, a title, a body, and (if needed) notes describing the table. Because figures and tables are time-consuming to prepare and expensive to reproduce in journals, they should only be used to illustrate complex materials or relationships.

Certain conventions are followed when you prepare an APA-style paper. References in the body of your paper are not footnoted. Instead, the author(s) of a reference is included in the text, along with the date of publication of the reference. Each reference cited in the body of your paper should be listed in expanded format in your reference section.

In a well-prepared paper, ideas must be clearly expressed, organized, and presented in a visually pleasing way. Clarity of expression requires grammatically correct sentences, properly chosen words, and economical expression. Ideas can be obscured by poorly constructed sentences (that is, ambiguous sentences), poorly chosen words, and wordy sentences. Poor organization, like unclear expression, can obscure important points in your paper. Organization can be enhanced by developing and sticking to an outline.

Finally, a paper can be well written and organized, yet still make a bad impression on the reader. Frequent misspellings, typographical errors, and improper word usage make your paper appear poor to your reader. Have someone proofread your paper to identify spelling and grammatical errors. Make corrections professionally by retyping, rather than penciling in or crossing out, information.

Plagiarism is using the words or ideas of another person without giving credit to the source. Plagiarism is considered unethical and, in a published work, may result in legal action against you. Lazy writing is writing that consists primarily of quoted (although properly cited) material. Although lazy writing is not as serious a problem as plagiarism, it is still inappropriate. To avoid both, make sure your paper consists mainly of your own writing and ideas. Use quoted material and reference citations to support your ideas, not to present them.

After you have prepared your APA-style paper, you may want to submit it to a journal for publication. If you submit your paper to a refereed journal, it will be reviewed by outside reviewers. The editor of the journal can decide (based on the reviews) either to unconditionally accept or reject a paper or to ask you to revise and resubmit your paper. If you revise and resubmit your paper, it may be sent out for a second review. Typically, the entire cycle of initial review, second review, acceptance, and publication takes almost a year.

You also can communicate your research findings through a presentation. In an oral presentation, you stand before an audience and present your results. In a poster session, you prepare a poster and answer questions about your work. The poster session affords more time and deeper communication with others in your field than does an oral presentation.

Finally, concern over ethics does not end with the completion of your research project. Ethical practice dictates that you give proper credit to the ideas and findings of others presented in your research report, properly order the authors' names to reflect the relative importance of their contributions to the research, avoid submitting for publication findings that have already been published elsewhere, and make your data available to fellow researchers who request them.

## REVIEW QUESTIONS

1. How do you set up a paper using APA writing style?
2. What is the heading structure used in an APA-style manuscript?
3. What information is included on the title page, and in what order would you find that information (from the top of the page to the bottom of the page)?

4. What are the differences between a running head and a manuscript page header?
5. Where does the page number go on a page, and on which page does numbering start?
6. What is an abstract, and why is it so important?
7. What information goes into an abstract, and how long should an abstract be?
8. What information is included in the introduction to an APA-style paper? How is the introduction organized?
9. What information would you expect to find in the method section? Describe the various subsections of the method section.
10. What would you expect to find in the results section of a manuscript?
11. How is the results section formatted, and how are statistics reported?
12. How is the discussion organized, and what would you expect to find in the discussion section?
13. When do you include author notes and footnotes in an APA-style manuscript? Where should they be placed?
14. How are the tables used in an APA-style manuscript formatted? When are tables used?
15. How is a page containing a figure set up? When are figures used?
16. What is included in the reference list of an APA-style manuscript? Describe how a typical journal reference is formatted.
17. What are the general rules for using numbers in the text of a manuscript?
18. What is biased language, and how can you avoid using it?
19. Why are clarity of expression, organization, and style so important to consider when preparing a manuscript? What does each comprise?
20. What are plagiarism and lazy writing, and how can you avoid them?
21. What is typically the sequence of events involved in submitting a paper for publication?
22. What is an oral presentation and a poster session, and how do they differ?
23. What are the ethical obligations involved in reporting or publishing your results?

## KEY TERMS

manuscript page header

running head

abstract

introduction

method section

participants subsection

subjects subsection

apparatus subsection

materials subsection

procedure subsection

results section

discussion section

reference section

plagiarism

lazy writing

# APPENDIX: STATISTICAL TABLES

## TABLE 1A   1,000 Six-Digit Random Numbers (first 500)

| 1 | 2 | 3 | 4 | 5 | 6 | 7 | 8 | 9 | 10 |
|---|---|---|---|---|---|---|---|---|---|
| 192805 | 905642 | 577821 | 582703 | 418793 | 921234 | 423676 | 926116 | 359852 | 611072 |
| 696843 | 580817 | 915407 | 920290 | 587586 | 090028 | 592469 | 094911 | 428558 | 679779 |
| 459327 | 255992 | 252995 | 257878 | 756380 | 258822 | 761262 | 263704 | 528645 | 779865 |
| 706608 | 962545 | 590582 | 595465 | 925173 | 427615 | 930056 | 432498 | 597352 | 848572 |
| 603541 | 637720 | 928169 | 933052 | 093968 | 596408 | 098850 | 601291 | 697438 | 948659 |
| 469093 | 312895 | 265757 | 270640 | 262761 | 765202 | 267644 | 770085 | 766145 | 017367 |
| 283598 | 988069 | 634724 | 639607 | 431554 | 933995 | 436437 | 938878 | 866232 | 117453 |
| 716374 | 663244 | 972311 | 977194 | 600348 | 102790 | 605231 | 107673 | 934939 | 186160 |
| 180530 | 338419 | 309899 | 314782 | 769141 | 271583 | 774024 | 276466 | 035026 | 286247 |
| 613306 | 044973 | 647486 | 652369 | 937935 | 440377 | 942818 | 445260 | 103733 | 354954 |
| 046083 | 720147 | 985073 | 989956 | 106729 | 609170 | 116612 | 614053 | 203820 | 455040 |
| 478858 | 395322 | 322661 | 327543 | 275523 | 777964 | 280406 | 782847 | 272527 | 523747 |
| 561285 | 070497 | 660248 | 665130 | 475696 | 978137 | 480579 | 983020 | 372613 | 623834 |
| 293364 | 745671 | 997834 | 002718 | 644490 | 146932 | 649372 | 151814 | 441320 | 692541 |
| 025442 | 420846 | 335422 | 340305 | 813283 | 315725 | 818166 | 320608 | 541407 | 792627 |
| 726139 | 127400 | 673009 | 677892 | 982077 | 484518 | 986959 | 489401 | 610114 | 861334 |
| 458218 | 802574 | 010597 | 015480 | 150871 | 653312 | 155754 | 658195 | 710200 | 961421 |
| 190296 | 477749 | 348184 | 353067 | 319664 | 822105 | 324547 | 826988 | 778907 | 030218 |
| 890993 | 152924 | 717151 | 722034 | 488458 | 990899 | 493341 | 995782 | 878994 | 130215 |
| 623072 | 828098 | 054739 | 059622 | 657251 | 159693 | 662134 | 164576 | 947700 | 198922 |
| 323770 | 503273 | 392326 | 397209 | 826045 | 328487 | 830928 | 333370 | 047788 | 299009 |
| 055848 | 209827 | 729913 | 734796 | 994838 | 497280 | 999721 | 502163 | 116495 | 367715 |
| 787926 | 885001 | 067501 | 072383 | 163633 | 666074 | 168516 | 670956 | 216582 | 467802 |
| 488624 | 560176 | 405088 | 409970 | 332426 | 834867 | 337309 | 839750 | 285288 | 536509 |
| 220702 | 235351 | 742675 | 747557 | 501220 | 003662 | 506103 | 008544 | 385375 | 636596 |
| 571051 | 910525 | 080262 | 085145 | 670013 | 172455 | 674896 | 177338 | 485462 | 736682 |
| 952780 | 585700 | 417849 | 422732 | 838807 | 341249 | 843689 | 346131 | 554169 | 805389 |
| 303129 | 260874 | 755436 | 760319 | 007601 | 510042 | 012484 | 514925 | 654255 | 905476 |
| 653478 | 967428 | 093024 | 097907 | 176395 | 678835 | 181277 | 683718 | 722962 | 974182 |
| 035208 | 642603 | 430611 | 435494 | 345188 | 847629 | 350071 | 852512 | 823049 | 074270 |
| 385556 | 317778 | 768198 | 773081 | 513981 | 016423 | 518864 | 021306 | 891755 | 142977 |
| 735905 | 992952 | 137166 | 142049 | 682775 | 185217 | 687658 | 190100 | 991842 | 243064 |
| 117635 | 668127 | 474753 | 479636 | 851568 | 354010 | 856451 | 358893 | 060550 | 311770 |
| 467983 | 343301 | 812340 | 817223 | 020363 | 522804 | 025246 | 527687 | 160637 | 411857 |
| 818332 | 049856 | 149928 | 154810 | 189156 | 691597 | 194039 | 696480 | 229343 | 480564 |
| 200062 | 725030 | 487515 | 492397 | 357950 | 860391 | 362833 | 865273 | 329430 | 580651 |
| 550410 | 400205 | 825102 | 829984 | 562743 | 029185 | 531626 | 034068 | 398137 | 649357 |
| 900759 | 075380 | 162689 | 167572 | 726917 | 229359 | 731799 | 234241 | 498224 | 749444 |
| 251109 | 750554 | 500276 | 505159 | 895710 | 398152 | 900593 | 403035 | 566930 | 818151 |
| 632837 | 425728 | 837863 | 842746 | 064505 | 566945 | 069387 | 571828 | 667017 | 918237 |
| 983186 | 132283 | 175451 | 180334 | 233298 | 735739 | 238181 | 740622 | 735724 | 986944 |
| 333536 | 807457 | 513038 | 517921 | 402091 | 904532 | 406974 | 909415 | 835810 | 087032 |
| 715264 | 482632 | 850625 | 855508 | 570885 | 073327 | 575768 | 078210 | 904517 | 155739 |
| 065614 | 157807 | 219593 | 224476 | 739678 | 242120 | 744561 | 247003 | 004605 | 255825 |
| 415963 | 832980 | 557180 | 562063 | 908472 | 410914 | 913355 | 415797 | 073312 | 324532 |
| 797691 | 508155 | 894767 | 899650 | 077266 | 579707 | 082149 | 584590 | 173398 | 424619 |
| 148041 | 214710 | 232355 | 237237 | 246060 | 748501 | 250943 | 753383 | 242105 | 493326 |
| 498390 | 889884 | 569942 | 574824 | 414853 | 917294 | 419736 | 922177 | 342192 | 593412 |
| 880118 | 565059 | 907529 | 912411 | 583647 | 086089 | 588529 | 090971 | 410899 | 662119 |
| 230468 | 240234 | 245116 | 249999 | 752440 | 254882 | 757323 | 259765 | 510985 | 762206 |

**TABLE 1A    1,000 Six-Digit Random Numbers (second 500)**

| 1 | 2 | 3 | 4 | 5 | 6 | 7 | 8 | 9 | 10 |
|---|---|---|---|---|---|---|---|---|---|
| 869354 | 895876 | 568055 | 572938 | 409027 | 911468 | 413910 | 916351 | 350086 | 601306 |
| 687077 | 571051 | 905642 | 910525 | 577821 | 080262 | 582703 | 085145 | 418793 | 670013 |
| 449562 | 246226 | 243230 | 248113 | 746614 | 249056 | 751497 | 253939 | 518879 | 770100 |
| 696843 | 952780 | 580817 | 585700 | 915407 | 417849 | 920290 | 422732 | 587586 | 838807 |
| 593775 | 627955 | 918404 | 923286 | 084202 | 586643 | 089085 | 591526 | 687673 | 938893 |
| 459327 | 303129 | 255992 | 260874 | 252995 | 755436 | 457878 | 760319 | 756380 | 007601 |
| 273833 | 978303 | 624958 | 629841 | 421789 | 924230 | 426672 | 929113 | 856466 | 107688 |
| 706608 | 653478 | 962545 | 967428 | 590582 | 093024 | 595465 | 097907 | 925173 | 176395 |
| 170765 | 328653 | 300133 | 305016 | 759376 | 261818 | 764259 | 266701 | 025261 | 276481 |
| 603541 | 035208 | 637720 | 642603 | 928169 | 430611 | 933052 | 435494 | 093968 | 345188 |
| 036317 | 710382 | 975307 | 980190 | 096964 | 599405 | 101847 | 604287 | 194054 | 445275 |
| 469093 | 385556 | 312895 | 317778 | 265757 | 768198 | 270640 | 773081 | 262761 | 513981 |
| 551520 | 060731 | 650482 | 655365 | 465931 | 968371 | 470813 | 973254 | 362848 | 614068 |
| 283598 | 735905 | 988069 | 992952 | 634724 | 137166 | 639607 | 142049 | 431554 | 682775 |
| 015676 | 411080 | 325657 | 330540 | 803517 | 305959 | 808400 | 310842 | 531641 | 782862 |
| 716374 | 117635 | 663244 | 668127 | 972311 | 474753 | 977194 | 470636 | 600348 | 851568 |
| 448452 | 792809 | 000832 | 005714 | 141105 | 643546 | 145988 | 648429 | 700435 | 951655 |
| 180530 | 467983 | 338419 | 343301 | 309899 | 812340 | 314782 | 817223 | 769141 | 020363 |
| 881228 | 143158 | 707385 | 712268 | 478692 | 981133 | 483575 | 986016 | 869228 | 120450 |
| 613306 | 818332 | 044973 | 049856 | 647486 | 149928 | 652369 | 154810 | 937935 | 189156 |
| 314005 | 493507 | 382560 | 387443 | 816279 | 318721 | 821162 | 323604 | 038023 | 289243 |
| 046083 | 200062 | 720147 | 725030 | 985073 | 487515 | 989956 | 492397 | 106729 | 357950 |
| 778160 | 875236 | 057735 | 062618 | 153867 | 656308 | 158750 | 611191 | 206816 | 458036 |
| 478858 | 550410 | 395322 | 400205 | 322661 | 825102 | 327543 | 829984 | 275523 | 526743 |
| 210937 | 225585 | 732909 | 737792 | 491454 | 993895 | 496337 | 998778 | 375609 | 626830 |
| 561285 | 900759 | 070497 | 075380 | 660248 | 162689 | 665130 | 167572 | 475696 | 726917 |
| 943014 | 575934 | 408084 | 412967 | 829041 | 331483 | 833924 | 336366 | 544403 | 795623 |
| 293364 | 251109 | 745671 | 750554 | 997834 | 500276 | 002718 | 505159 | 644490 | 895710 |
| 643712 | 957663 | 083259 | 088141 | 166629 | 669070 | 171512 | 673953 | 713196 | 964417 |
| 025442 | 632837 | 420846 | 425728 | 335422 | 837863 | 340305 | 842746 | 813283 | 064505 |
| 375791 | 308012 | 758432 | 763315 | 504216 | 006658 | 509099 | 011541 | 881990 | 133211 |
| 726139 | 983186 | 127400 | 132283 | 673009 | 175451 | 677892 | 180334 | 982077 | 233298 |
| 107869 | 658361 | 464987 | 469870 | 841803 | 344245 | 846686 | 349127 | 050784 | 302005 |
| 458218 | 333536 | 802574 | 807457 | 010597 | 513038 | 015480 | 517921 | 150871 | 402091 |
| 808566 | 040090 | 140162 | 145045 | 179391 | 681832 | 184274 | 686714 | 219578 | 470798 |
| 190296 | 715264 | 477749 | 482632 | 348184 | 850625 | 353067 | 855508 | 319664 | 570885 |
| 540645 | 390439 | 815336 | 820219 | 516978 | 019420 | 521860 | 024302 | 388371 | 639592 |
| 890993 | 065614 | 152924 | 157807 | 717151 | 219593 | 722034 | 224476 | 488458 | 739678 |
| 241343 | 740788 | 490511 | 495394 | 855944 | 388386 | 890827 | 393269 | 557165 | 808385 |
| 623072 | 415963 | 828098 | 832980 | 054739 | 557180 | 059622 | 562063 | 657251 | 908472 |
| 973420 | 122517 | 165686 | 170568 | 223532 | 725973 | 228415 | 730856 | 725958 | 977179 |
| 323770 | 797691 | 503273 | 508155 | 392326 | 894767 | 397209 | 899650 | 826045 | 077266 |
| 705499 | 472866 | 840559 | 845742 | 561119 | 063561 | 566002 | 068444 | 894752 | 145973 |
| 055848 | 148041 | 209827 | 214710 | 729913 | 232355 | 734796 | 237237 | 994838 | 246060 |
| 406197 | 823215 | 547414 | 552297 | 898706 | 401148 | 903589 | 406031 | 063546 | 314767 |
| 787926 | 498390 | 885001 | 889884 | 067501 | 569942 | 072383 | 574824 | 163633 | 414853 |
| 138275 | 204944 | 222589 | 227472 | 236294 | 738735 | 241177 | 743618 | 232340 | 483560 |
| 488624 | 880118 | 560176 | 565059 | 405088 | 907529 | 409970 | 912411 | 332426 | 583647 |
| 870353 | 555293 | 897763 | 902646 | 573881 | 076323 | 578764 | 081206 | 401133 | 652353 |
| 220702 | 230468 | 235351 | 240234 | 742675 | 245116 | 747557 | 249999 | 501220 | 752440 |

NOTE: This table was generated with a computer program written in BASIC.

## TABLE 1B   Random Orderings of the Numbers 1–30

| 1 | 2 | 3 | 4 | 5 | 6 | 7 | 8 | 9 | 10 | 11 | 12 | 13 | 14 | 15 | 16 | 17 | 18 | 19 | 20 |
|---|---|---|---|---|---|---|---|---|----|----|----|----|----|----|----|----|----|----|----|
| 25 | 15 | 25 | 30 | 20 | 14 | 25 | 3 | 21 | 2 | 20 | 27 | 19 | 26 | 17 | 30 | 22 | 4 | 6 | 10 |
| 14 | 26 | 17 | 7 | 2 | 9 | 14 | 13 | 6 | 20 | 29 | 16 | 13 | 19 | 9 | 17 | 14 | 16 | 22 | 20 |
| 17 | 11 | 2 | 17 | 21 | 13 | 3 | 24 | 23 | 21 | 12 | 24 | 24 | 2 | 3 | 25 | 6 | 17 | 25 | 29 |
| 5 | 4 | 18 | 18 | 23 | 20 | 16 | 20 | 26 | 14 | 1 | 7 | 26 | 21 | 22 | 9 | 26 | 13 | 27 | 22 |
| 3 | 16 | 12 | 19 | 16 | 22 | 10 | 7 | 13 | 7 | 21 | 20 | 29 | 11 | 24 | 20 | 27 | 8 | 12 | 15 |
| 19 | 20 | 5 | 11 | 11 | 26 | 6 | 21 | 16 | 22 | 23 | 21 | 20 | 7 | 16 | 22 | 20 | 22 | 17 | 25 |
| 22 | 6 | 23 | 21 | 24 | 17 | 19 | 22 | 29 | 25 | 10 | 4 | 6 | 22 | 13 | 5 | 19 | 24 | 29 | 26 |
| 10 | 22 | 24 | 24 | 18 | 1 | 21 | 23 | 19 | 23 | 24 | 23 | 22 | 25 | 26 | 23 | 30 | 26 | 20 | 19 |
| 23 | 23 | 16 | 14 | 17 | 19 | 11 | 16 | 2 | 15 | 27 | 9 | 3 | 16 | 27 | 15 | 21 | 28 | 1 | 28 |
| 24 | 13 | 28 | 25 | 30 | 5 | 26 | 26 | 20 | 26 | 16 | 25 | 23 | 27 | 21 | 28 | 2 | 3 | 23 | 21 |
| 16 | 28 | 27 | 28 | 19 | 21 | 15 | 28 | 3 | 28 | 30 | 26 | 11 | 28 | 2 | 27 | 23 | 21 | 3 | 3 |
| 27 | 29 | 1 | 2 | 5 | 10 | 2 | 30 | 22 | 29 | 22 | 18 | 25 | 30 | 4 | 19 | 10 | 5 | 24 | 4 |
| 28 | 3 | 21 | 5 | 9 | 23 | 4 | 1 | 10 | 30 | 4 | 28 | 16 | 4 | 23 | 29 | 25 | 23 | 10 | 23 |
| 29 | 21 | 4 | 22 | 22 | 25 | 20 | 6 | 24 | 4 | 6 | 29 | 27 | 24 | 5 | 2 | 15 | 10 | 26 | 11 |
| 30 | 5 | 7 | 9 | 14 | 16 | 9 | 25 | 15 | 10 | 25 | 30 | 28 | 10 | 25 | 7 | 28 | 27 | 16 | 27 |
| 4 | 10 | 26 | 26 | 25 | 27 | 24 | 12 | 27 | 27 | 14 | 1 | 2 | 15 | 15 | 26 | 1 | 14 | 30 | 16 |
| 8 | 27 | 13 | 15 | 1 | 30 | 13 | 27 | 1 | 19 | 28 | 5 | 5 | 29 | 28 | 12 | 3 | 29 | 2 | 1 |
| 13 | 14 | 29 | 1 | 3 | 3 | 27 | 17 | 4 | 1 | 18 | 13 | 9 | 18 | 30 | 16 | 9 | 30 | 4 | 7 |
| 2 | 30 | 30 | 4 | 7 | 6 | 30 | 2 | 8 | 3 | 2 | 17 | 15 | 5 | 19 | 4 | 11 | 20 | 8 | 8 |
| 21 | 19 | 20 | 8 | 13 | 12 | 17 | 4 | 11 | 8 | 7 | 2 | 1 | 8 | 7 | 6 | 29 | 6 | 28 | 14 |
| 6 | 9 | 6 | 12 | 15 | 15 | 7 | 9 | 28 | 12 | 13 | 6 | 4 | 14 | 11 | 10 | 18 | 11 | 13 | 2 |
| 11 | 12 | 9 | 29 | 4 | 4 | 22 | 15 | 17 | 18 | 17 | 11 | 8 | 1 | 1 | 13 | 4 | 1 | 21 | 5 |
| 1 | 2 | 14 | 16 | 8 | 7 | 23 | 19 | 5 | 5 | 5 | 14 | 12 | 20 | 20 | 3 | 8 | 19 | 5 | 9 |
| 20 | 17 | 3 | 6 | 12 | 24 | 1 | 5 | 9 | 9 | 8 | 3 | 30 | 9 | 6 | 21 | 12 | 7 | 9 | 12 |
| 7 | 7 | 22 | 23 | 26 | 2 | 18 | 10 | 12 | 11 | 11 | 22 | 18 | 12 | 10 | 11 | 16 | 12 | 14 | 30 |
| 12 | 24 | 10 | 13 | 28 | 18 | 8 | 14 | 30 | 16 | 15 | 10 | 21 | 17 | 14 | 14 | 5 | 15 | 19 | 18 |
| 15 | 1 | 15 | 3 | 29 | 8 | 12 | 18 | 18 | 6 | 19 | 15 | 10 | 6 | 18 | 18 | 24 | 18 | 7 | 6 |
| 18 | 18 | 19 | 20 | 6 | 11 | 28 | 8 | 7 | 24 | 9 | 19 | 14 | 23 | 8 | 8 | 13 | 9 | 11 | 24 |
| 9 | 8 | 8 | 10 | 10 | 28 | 29 | 11 | 25 | 13 | 26 | 8 | 17 | 13 | 12 | 24 | 17 | 25 | 15 | 13 |
| 26 | 25 | 11 | 27 | 27 | 29 | 5 | 29 | 14 | 17 | 3 | 12 | 7 | 3 | 29 | 1 | 7 | 2 | 18 | 17 |

## TABLE 1B  Random Orderings of the Numbers 1–30  *continued*

| 21 | 22 | 23 | 24 | 25 | 26 | 27 | 28 | 29 | 30 | 31 | 32 | 33 | 34 | 35 | 36 | 37 | 38 | 39 | 40 |
|----|----|----|----|----|----|----|----|----|----|----|----|----|----|----|----|----|----|----|----|
| 19 | 19 | 29 | 5  | 19 | 15 | 15 | 21 | 18 | 8  | 11 | 6  | 6  | 11 | 30 | 25 | 16 | 20 | 19 | 11 |
| 26 | 12 | 21 | 17 | 30 | 11 | 8  | 9  | 7  | 14 | 3  | 17 | 18 | 24 | 16 | 13 | 23 | 26 | 15 | 12 |
| 11 | 21 | 5  | 24 | 11 | 24 | 20 | 22 | 16 | 23 | 15 | 19 | 13 | 21 | 6  | 18 | 28 | 8  | 26 | 27 |
| 8  | 24 | 24 | 19 | 4  | 28 | 25 | 25 | 24 | 28 | 20 | 10 | 11 | 15 | 20 | 1  | 20 | 3  | 30 | 22 |
| 21 | 27 | 17 | 8  | 24 | 17 | 27 | 19 | 26 | 17 | 19 | 15 | 21 | 2  | 22 | 4  | 13 | 24 | 22 | 17 |
| 17 | 30 | 10 | 22 | 22 | 22 | 28 | 16 | 20 | 20 | 6  | 20 | 25 | 16 | 12 | 21 | 2  | 16 | 23 | 1  |
| 13 | 22 | 25 | 16 | 9  | 4  | 22 | 27 | 19 | 3  | 26 | 23 | 27 | 5  | 23 | 22 | 21 | 15 | 5  | 20 |
| 28 | 5  | 27 | 12 | 27 | 21 | 1  | 29 | 6  | 18 | 24 | 25 | 28 | 19 | 26 | 8  | 5  | 27 | 24 | 3  |
| 29 | 23 | 19 | 25 | 25 | 6  | 23 | 20 | 22 | 7  | 25 | 27 | 1  | 20 | 18 | 23 | 22 | 30 | 9  | 21 |
| 18 | 15 | 30 | 28 | 17 | 23 | 4  | 3  | 13 | 21 | 18 | 3  | 22 | 8  | 27 | 24 | 10 | 29 | 25 | 7  |
| 2  | 25 | 23 | 30 | 28 | 12 | 24 | 5  | 23 | 11 | 28 | 22 | 3  | 23 | 28 | 15 | 25 | 21 | 18 | 23 |
| 6  | 18 | 2  | 1  | 1  | 25 | 12 | 23 | 17 | 24 | 29 | 7  | 24 | 13 | 2  | 27 | 27 | 23 | 27 | 24 |
| 22 | 28 | 9  | 3  | 23 | 27 | 26 | 12 | 25 | 27 | 30 | 24 | 8  | 26 | 4  | 28 | 19 | 7  | 28 | 15 |
| 10 | 29 | 26 | 23 | 2  | 16 | 17 | 26 | 2  | 15 | 5  | 14 | 26 | 29 | 25 | 30 | 29 | 11 | 2  | 29 |
| 27 | 2  | 14 | 7  | 6  | 29 | 29 | 17 | 3  | 29 | 9  | 26 | 17 | 1  | 9  | 2  | 30 | 28 | 4  | 30 |
| 15 | 7  | 28 | 26 | 26 | 30 | 30 | 28 | 21 | 30 | 27 | 16 | 30 | 4  | 13 | 6  | 4  | 19 | 8  | 2  |
| 30 | 11 | 18 | 15 | 15 | 5  | 2  | 1  | 10 | 5  | 16 | 4  | 2  | 7  | 29 | 11 | 7  | 1  | 13 | 4  |
| 3  | 16 | 3  | 29 | 29 | 7  | 6  | 7  | 14 | 10 | 1  | 9  | 4  | 25 | 19 | 29 | 12 | 4  | 1  | 9  |
| 5  | 1  | 7  | 18 | 21 | 14 | 11 | 11 | 1  | 13 | 22 | 13 | 9  | 12 | 5  | 17 | 15 | 9  | 3  | 28 |
| 9  | 4  | 13 | 6  | 3  | 1  | 16 | 15 | 4  | 1  | 8  | 1  | 29 | 30 | 10 | 3  | 3  | 14 | 6  | 14 |
| 12 | 9  | 1  | 9  | 7  | 19 | 3  | 2  | 9  | 4  | 12 | 5  | 16 | 17 | 15 | 5  | 6  | 2  | 11 | 19 |
| 16 | 13 | 20 | 13 | 12 | 9  | 5  | 6  | 11 | 22 | 2  | 21 | 20 | 6  | 3  | 10 | 11 | 5  | 29 | 6  |
| 7  | 17 | 8  | 2  | 18 | 13 | 9  | 10 | 15 | 12 | 21 | 11 | 7  | 9  | 21 | 14 | 14 | 25 | 16 | 10 |
| 23 | 6  | 11 | 20 | 5  | 3  | 13 | 13 | 5  | 2  | 10 | 2  | 10 | 27 | 11 | 20 | 17 | 12 | 21 | 13 |
| 25 | 8  | 15 | 11 | 8  | 18 | 19 | 30 | 8  | 19 | 13 | 18 | 14 | 28 | 14 | 7  | 8  | 18 | 7  | 18 |
| 14 | 26 | 4  | 14 | 13 | 8  | 7  | 18 | 12 | 9  | 17 | 8  | 5  | 3  | 17 | 12 | 24 | 6  | 12 | 8  |
| 4  | 3  | 22 | 4  | 16 | 26 | 10 | 8  | 27 | 25 | 7  | 12 | 23 | 22 | 8  | 16 | 1  | 10 | 17 | 25 |
| 20 | 20 | 12 | 21 | 20 | 2  | 14 | 24 | 28 | 26 | 23 | 28 | 12 | 10 | 24 | 19 | 18 | 13 | 20 | 26 |
| 24 | 10 | 16 | 10 | 10 | 20 | 18 | 14 | 29 | 16 | 14 | 29 | 15 | 14 | 1  | 9  | 9  | 17 | 10 | 16 |
| 1  | 14 | 6  | 27 | 14 | 10 | 21 | 4  | 30 | 6  | 4  | 30 | 19 | 18 | 7  | 26 | 26 | 22 | 14 | 5  |

*continues*

## TABLE 1B  Random Orderings of the Numbers 1–30 *continued*

| 41 | 42 | 43 | 44 | 45 | 46 | 47 | 48 | 49 | 50 |
|----|----|----|----|----|----|----|----|----|----|
| 20 | 15 | 25 | 25 | 12 | 7 | 16 | 17 | 7 | 1 |
| 16 | 19 | 21 | 20 | 30 | 27 | 8 | 30 | 15 | 17 |
| 9 | 3 | 1 | 3 | 17 | 15 | 25 | 20 | 28 | 18 |
| 26 | 11 | 22 | 21 | 7 | 23 | 28 | 23 | 25 | 14 |
| 23 | 21 | 13 | 13 | 19 | 3 | 23 | 9 | 16 | 3 |
| 24 | 23 | 9 | 7 | 22 | 18 | 20 | 26 | 3 | 20 |
| 18 | 18 | 23 | 22 | 11 | 21 | 1 | 24 | 19 | 10 |
| 28 | 17 | 24 | 23 | 24 | 5 | 21 | 13 | 22 | 11 |
| 29 | 24 | 18 | 16 | 25 | 22 | 5 | 29 | 5 | 21 |
| 22 | 26 | 26 | 26 | 16 | 12 | 24 | 28 | 24 | 24 |
| 4 | 30 | 28 | 28 | 28 | 24 | 13 | 19 | 11 | 27 |
| 7 | 6 | 29 | 30 | 18 | 25 | 26 | 21 | 26 | 28 |
| 25 | 22 | 30 | 1 | 1 | 17 | 27 | 3 | 27 | 2 |
| 14 | 10 | 3 | 6 | 5 | 28 | 18 | 6 | 18 | 4 |
| 27 | 14 | 5 | 24 | 8 | 29 | 29 | 11 | 29 | 22 |
| 19 | 27 | 27 | 12 | 26 | 30 | 30 | 27 | 30 | 7 |
| 2 | 1 | 14 | 27 | 15 | 4 | 2 | 18 | 4 | 26 |
| 5 | 4 | 20 | 17 | 29 | 11 | 6 | 1 | 10 | 13 |
| 11 | 7 | 2 | 2 | 3 | 14 | 10 | 8 | 14 | 29 |
| 15 | 12 | 6 | 4 | 21 | 1 | 17 | 10 | 1 | 30 |
| 3 | 28 | 10 | 9 | 9 | 19 | 3 | 16 | 21 | 19 |
| 6 | 16 | 17 | 15 | 13 | 8 | 7 | 2 | 8 | 9 |
| 10 | 5 | 4 | 19 | 2 | 13 | 11 | 7 | 12 | 12 |
| 13 | 8 | 7 | 5 | 6 | 16 | 14 | 25 | 2 | 16 |
| 30 | 25 | 11 | 10 | 23 | 6 | 4 | 14 | 20 | 5 |
| 17 | 2 | 15 | 14 | 14 | 9 | 22 | 5 | 9 | 8 |
| 21 | 20 | 19 | 18 | 4 | 26 | 12 | 22 | 13 | 25 |
| 12 | 9 | 8 | 8 | 20 | 2 | 15 | 12 | 17 | 15 |
| 1 | 13 | 12 | 11 | 10 | 20 | 19 | 15 | 6 | 6 |
| 8 | 29 | 16 | 29 | 27 | 10 | 9 | 4 | 23 | 23 |

NOTE: These random orders were derived with a computer program written in BASIC.

**TABLE 2 Critical Values of *t***

| | ALPHA LEVEL (TWO-TAILED TEST) | | | | | | | | | |
|---|---|---|---|---|---|---|---|---|---|---|
| Degrees of Freedom | *.8* | *.5* | *.2* | *.1* | *.05* | *.02* | *.01* | *.005* | *.002* | *.001* |
| 1 | 0.325 | 1.00 | 3.078 | 6.314 | 12.706 | 31.821 | 63.657 | 127.32 | 318.31 | 636.62 |
| 2 | .289 | 0.816 | 1.886 | 2.920 | 4.303 | 6.965 | 9.925 | 14.089 | 22.327 | 31.598 |
| 3 | .277 | .765 | 1.638 | 2.353 | 3.182 | 4.541 | 5.841 | 7.453 | 10.214 | 12.924 |
| 4 | .271 | .741 | 1.533 | 2.132 | 2.776 | 3.747 | 4.604 | 5.598 | 7.173 | 8.610 |
| 5 | 0.267 | 0.727 | 1.476 | 2.015 | 2.571 | 3.365 | 4.032 | 4.773 | 5.893 | 6.869 |
| 6 | .265 | .718 | 1.440 | 1.943 | 2.447 | 3.143 | 3.707 | 4.317 | 5.208 | 5.959 |
| 7 | .263 | .711 | 1.415 | 1.895 | 2.365 | 2.998 | 3.499 | 4.029 | 4.785 | 5.408 |
| 8 | .262 | .706 | 1.397 | 1.860 | 2.306 | 2.896 | 3.355 | 3.833 | 4.501 | 5.041 |
| 9 | .261 | .703 | 1.383 | 1.833 | 2.262 | 2.821 | 3.250 | 3.690 | 4.297 | 4.781 |
| 10 | 0.260 | 0.700 | 1.372 | 1.812 | 2.228 | 2.764 | 3.169 | 3.581 | 4.144 | 4.587 |
| 11 | .260 | .697 | 1.363 | 1.796 | 2.201 | 2.718 | 3.106 | 3.497 | 4.025 | 4.437 |
| 12 | .259 | .695 | 1.356 | 1.782 | 2.179 | 2.681 | 3.055 | 3.428 | 3.930 | 4.318 |
| 13 | .259 | .694 | 1.350 | 1.771 | 2.160 | 2.650 | 3.012 | 3.372 | 3.852 | 4.221 |
| 14 | .258 | .692 | 1.345 | 1.761 | 2.145 | 2.624 | 2.977 | 3.326 | 3.787 | 4.140 |
| 15 | 0.258 | 0.691 | 1.341 | 1.753 | 2.131 | 2.602 | 2.947 | 3.286 | 3.733 | 4.073 |
| 16 | .258 | .690 | 1.337 | 1.746 | 2.120 | 2.583 | 2.921 | 3.252 | 3.686 | 4.015 |
| 17 | .257 | .689 | 1.333 | 1.740 | 2.110 | 2.567 | 2.898 | 3.222 | 3.646 | 3.965 |
| 18 | .257 | .688 | 1.330 | 1.734 | 2.101 | 2.552 | 2.878 | 3.197 | 3.610 | 3.922 |
| 19 | .257 | .688 | 1.328 | 1.729 | 2.093 | 2.539 | 2.861 | 3.174 | 3.579 | 3.883 |
| 20 | 0.257 | 0.687 | 1.325 | 1.725 | 2.086 | 2.528 | 2.845 | 3.153 | 3.552 | 3.850 |
| 21 | .257 | .686 | 1.323 | 1.721 | 2.080 | 2.518 | 2.831 | 3.135 | 3.527 | 3.819 |
| 22 | .256 | .686 | 1.321 | 1.717 | 2.074 | 2.508 | 2.819 | 3.119 | 3.505 | 3.792 |
| 23 | .256 | .685 | 1.319 | 1.714 | 2.069 | 2.500 | 2.807 | 3.104 | 3.485 | 3.767 |
| 24 | .256 | .685 | 1.318 | 1.711 | 2.064 | 2.492 | 2.797 | 3.091 | 3.467 | 3.745 |
| 25 | 0.256 | 0.684 | 1.316 | 1.708 | 2.060 | 2.485 | 2.787 | 3.078 | 3.450 | 3.725 |
| 26 | .256 | .684 | 1.315 | 1.706 | 2.056 | 2.479 | 2.779 | 3.067 | 3.435 | 3.707 |
| 27 | .256 | .684 | 1.314 | 1.703 | 2.052 | 2.473 | 2.771 | 3.057 | 3.421 | 3.690 |
| 28 | .256 | .683 | 1.313 | 1.701 | 2.048 | 2.467 | 2.763 | 3.047 | 3.408 | 3.674 |
| 29 | .256 | .683 | 1.311 | 1.699 | 2.045 | 2.462 | 2.756 | 3.038 | 3.396 | 3.659 |
| 30 | 0.256 | 0.683 | 1.310 | 1.697 | 2.042 | 2.457 | 2.750 | 3.030 | 3.385 | 3.646 |
| 40 | .255 | .681 | 1.303 | 1.684 | 2.021 | 2.423 | 2.704 | 2.971 | 3.307 | 3.551 |
| 60 | .254 | .679 | 1.296 | 1.671 | 2.000 | 2.390 | 2.660 | 2.915 | 3.232 | 3.460 |
| 120 | .254 | .677 | 1.289 | 1.658 | 1.980 | 2.358 | 2.617 | 2.860 | 3.160 | 3.373 |
| ∞ | .253 | .674 | 1.282 | 1.645 | 1.960 | 2.326 | 2.576 | 2.807 | 3.090 | 3.291 |

NOTE: To obtain one-tailed alpha levels, simply divide the two-tailed alpha by 2 (for example, $p < .05$ for a one-tailed test is $1/2 = .05$).

SOURCE: Adapted from Table 12, *Biometrika: Tables for Statisticians* (Vol. 1, 3rd ed.), 1966, by E. S. Pearson & H. O. Hartley; reprinted with permission.

A-8    Appendix

**TABLE 3A   Critical Values of F (p < .05)**

| | | DEGREES OF FREEDOM IN THE NUMERATOR | | | | | | | |
|---|---|---|---|---|---|---|---|---|---|
| | 1 | 2 | 3 | 4 | 5 | 6 | 7 | 8 | 9 |
| 1 | 161.4 | 199.5 | 215.7 | 224.6 | 230.2 | 234.0 | 236.8 | 238.9 | 240.5 |
| 2 | 18.51 | 19.00 | 19.16 | 19.25 | 19.30 | 19.33 | 19.35 | 19.37 | 19.38 |
| 3 | 10.13 | 9.55 | 9.28 | 9.12 | 9.01 | 8.94 | 8.89 | 8.85 | 8.81 |
| 4 | 7.71 | 6.94 | 6.59 | 6.39 | 6.26 | 6.16 | 6.09 | 6.04 | 6.00 |
| 5 | 6.61 | 5.79 | 5.41 | 5.19 | 5.05 | 4.95 | 4.88 | 4.82 | 4.77 |
| 6 | 5.99 | 5.14 | 4.76 | 4.53 | 4.39 | 4.28 | 4.21 | 4.15 | 4.10 |
| 7 | 5.59 | 4.74 | 4.35 | 4.12 | 3.97 | 3.87 | 3.79 | 3.73 | 3.68 |
| 8 | 5.32 | 4.46 | 4.07 | 3.84 | 3.69 | 3.58 | 3.50 | 3.44 | 3.39 |
| 9 | 5.12 | 4.26 | 3.86 | 3.63 | 3.48 | 3.37 | 3.29 | 3.23 | 3.18 |
| 10 | 4.96 | 4.10 | 3.71 | 3.48 | 3.33 | 3.22 | 3.14 | 3.07 | 3.02 |
| 11 | 4.84 | 3.98 | 3.59 | 3.36 | 3.20 | 3.09 | 3.01 | 2.95 | 2.90 |
| 12 | 4.75 | 3.89 | 3.49 | 3.26 | 3.11 | 3.00 | 2.91 | 2.85 | 2.80 |
| 13 | 4.67 | 3.81 | 3.41 | 3.18 | 3.03 | 2.92 | 2.83 | 2.77 | 2.71 |
| 14 | 4.60 | 3.74 | 3.34 | 3.11 | 2.96 | 2.85 | 2.76 | 2.70 | 2.65 |
| 15 | 4.54 | 3.68 | 3.29 | 3.06 | 2.90 | 2.79 | 2.71 | 2.64 | 2.59 |
| 16 | 4.49 | 3.63 | 3.24 | 3.01 | 2.85 | 2.74 | 2.66 | 2.59 | 2.54 |
| 17 | 4.45 | 3.59 | 3.20 | 2.96 | 2.81 | 2.70 | 2.61 | 2.55 | 2.49 |
| 18 | 4.41 | 3.55 | 3.16 | 2.93 | 2.77 | 2.66 | 2.58 | 2.51 | 2.46 |
| 19 | 4.38 | 3.52 | 3.13 | 2.90 | 2.74 | 2.63 | 2.54 | 2.48 | 2.42 |
| 20 | 4.35 | 3.49 | 3.10 | 2.87 | 2.71 | 2.60 | 2.51 | 2.45 | 2.39 |
| 21 | 4.32 | 3.47 | 3.07 | 2.84 | 2.68 | 2.57 | 2.49 | 2.42 | 2.37 |
| 22 | 4.30 | 3.44 | 3.05 | 2.82 | 2.66 | 2.55 | 2.46 | 2.40 | 2.34 |
| 23 | 4.28 | 3.42 | 3.03 | 2.80 | 2.64 | 2.53 | 2.44 | 2.37 | 2.32 |
| 24 | 4.26 | 3.40 | 3.01 | 2.78 | 2.62 | 2.51 | 2.42 | 2.36 | 2.30 |
| 25 | 4.24 | 3.39 | 2.99 | 2.76 | 2.60 | 2.49 | 2.40 | 2.34 | 2.28 |
| 26 | 4.23 | 3.37 | 2.98 | 2.74 | 2.59 | 2.47 | 2.39 | 2.32 | 2.27 |
| 27 | 4.21 | 3.35 | 2.96 | 2.73 | 2.57 | 2.46 | 2.37 | 2.31 | 2.25 |
| 28 | 4.20 | 3.34 | 2.95 | 2.71 | 2.56 | 2.45 | 2.36 | 2.29 | 2.24 |
| 29 | 4.18 | 3.33 | 2.93 | 2.70 | 2.55 | 2.43 | 2.35 | 2.28 | 2.22 |
| 30 | 4.17 | 3.32 | 2.92 | 2.69 | 2.53 | 2.42 | 2.33 | 2.27 | 2.21 |
| 40 | 4.08 | 3.23 | 2.84 | 2.61 | 2.45 | 2.34 | 2.25 | 2.18 | 2.12 |
| 60 | 4.00 | 3.15 | 2.76 | 2.53 | 2.37 | 2.25 | 2.17 | 2.10 | 2.04 |
| 120 | 3.92 | 3.07 | 2.68 | 2.45 | 2.29 | 2.17 | 2.09 | 2.02 | 1.96 |
| ∞ | 3.84 | 3.00 | 2.60 | 2.37 | 2.21 | 2.10 | 2.01 | 1.94 | 1.88 |

Degrees of Freedom in the Denominator

SOURCE: Adapted from Table 18, *Biometrika: Tables for Statisticians* (Vol. 1, 3rd ed.), 1966, by E. S. Pearson & H. O. Hartley; reprinted with permission.

**TABLE 3A   Critical Values of $F$ ($p < .05$)   *continued***

| | DEGREES OF FREEDOM IN THE NUMERATOR | | | | | | | | | |
|---|---|---|---|---|---|---|---|---|---|---|
| | *10* | *12* | *15* | *20* | *24* | *30* | *40* | *60* | *120* | *∞* |
| 1 | 241.9 | 243.9 | 245.9 | 248.0 | 249.1 | 250.1 | 251.1 | 252.2 | 253.3 | 254.3 |
| 2 | 19.40 | 19.41 | 19.43 | 19.45 | 19.45 | 19.46 | 19.47 | 19.48 | 19.49 | 19.50 |
| 3 | 8.79 | 8.74 | 8.70 | 8.66 | 8.64 | 8.62 | 8.59 | 8.57 | 8.55 | 8.53 |
| 4 | 5.96 | 5.91 | 5.86 | 5.80 | 5.77 | 5.75 | 5.72 | 5.69 | 5.66 | 5.63 |
| 5 | 4.74 | 4.68 | 4.62 | 4.56 | 4.53 | 4.50 | 4.46 | 4.43 | 4.40 | 4.36 |
| 6 | 4.06 | 4.00 | 3.94 | 3.87 | 3.84 | 3.81 | 3.77 | 3.74 | 3.70 | 3.67 |
| 7 | 3.64 | 3.57 | 3.51 | 3.44 | 3.41 | 3.38 | 3.34 | 3.30 | 3.27 | 3.23 |
| 8 | 3.35 | 3.28 | 3.22 | 3.15 | 3.12 | 3.08 | 3.04 | 3.01 | 2.97 | 2.93 |
| 9 | 3.14 | 3.07 | 3.01 | 2.94 | 2.90 | 2.86 | 2.83 | 2.79 | 2.75 | 2.71 |
| 10 | 2.98 | 2.91 | 2.85 | 2.77 | 2.74 | 2.70 | 2.66 | 2.62 | 2.58 | 2.54 |
| 11 | 2.85 | 2.79 | 2.72 | 2.65 | 2.61 | 2.57 | 2.53 | 2.49 | 2.45 | 2.40 |
| 12 | 2.75 | 2.69 | 2.62 | 2.54 | 2.51 | 2.47 | 2.43 | 2.38 | 2.34 | 2.30 |
| 13 | 2.67 | 2.60 | 2.53 | 2.46 | 2.42 | 2.38 | 2.34 | 2.30 | 2.25 | 2.21 |
| 14 | 2.60 | 2.53 | 2.46 | 2.39 | 2.35 | 2.31 | 2.27 | 2.22 | 2.18 | 2.13 |
| 15 | 2.54 | 2.48 | 2.40 | 2.33 | 2.29 | 2.25 | 2.20 | 2.16 | 2.11 | 2.07 |
| 16 | 2.49 | 2.42 | 2.35 | 2.28 | 2.24 | 2.19 | 2.15 | 2.11 | 2.06 | 2.01 |
| 17 | 2.45 | 2.38 | 2.31 | 2.23 | 2.19 | 2.15 | 2.10 | 2.06 | 2.01 | 1.96 |
| 18 | 2.41 | 2.34 | 2.27 | 2.19 | 2.15 | 2.11 | 2.06 | 2.02 | 1.97 | 1.92 |
| 19 | 2.38 | 2.31 | 2.23 | 2.16 | 2.11 | 2.07 | 2.03 | 1.98 | 1.93 | 1.88 |
| 20 | 2.35 | 2.28 | 2.20 | 2.12 | 2.08 | 2.04 | 1.99 | 1.95 | 1.90 | 1.84 |
| 21 | 2.32 | 2.25 | 2.18 | 2.10 | 2.05 | 2.01 | 1.96 | 1.92 | 1.87 | 1.81 |
| 22 | 2.30 | 2.23 | 2.15 | 2.07 | 2.03 | 1.98 | 1.94 | 1.89 | 1.84 | 1.78 |
| 23 | 2.27 | 2.20 | 2.13 | 2.05 | 2.01 | 1.96 | 1.91 | 1.86 | 1.81 | 1.76 |
| 24 | 2.25 | 2.18 | 2.11 | 2.03 | 1.98 | 1.94 | 1.89 | 1.84 | 1.79 | 1.73 |
| 25 | 2.24 | 2.16 | 2.09 | 2.01 | 1.96 | 1.92 | 1.87 | 1.82 | 1.77 | 1.71 |
| 26 | 2.22 | 2.15 | 2.07 | 1.99 | 1.95 | 1.90 | 1.85 | 1.80 | 1.75 | 1.69 |
| 27 | 2.20 | 2.13 | 2.06 | 1.97 | 1.93 | 1.88 | 1.84 | 1.79 | 1.73 | 1.67 |
| 28 | 2.19 | 2.12 | 2.04 | 1.96 | 1.91 | 1.87 | 1.82 | 1.77 | 1.71 | 1.65 |
| 29 | 2.18 | 2.10 | 2.03 | 1.94 | 1.90 | 1.85 | 1.81 | 1.75 | 1.70 | 1.64 |
| 30 | 2.16 | 2.09 | 2.01 | 1.93 | 1.89 | 1.84 | 1.79 | 1.74 | 1.68 | 1.62 |
| 40 | 2.08 | 2.00 | 1.92 | 1.84 | 1.79 | 1.74 | 1.69 | 1.64 | 1.58 | 1.51 |
| 60 | 1.99 | 1.92 | 1.84 | 1.75 | 1.70 | 1.65 | 1.59 | 1.53 | 1.47 | 1.39 |
| 120 | 1.91 | 1.83 | 1.75 | 1.66 | 1.61 | 1.55 | 1.50 | 1.43 | 1.35 | 1.25 |
| ∞ | 1.83 | 1.75 | 1.67 | 1.57 | 1.52 | 1.46 | 1.39 | 1.32 | 1.22 | 1.00 |

Degrees of Freedom in the Denominator

**TABLE 3B    Critical Values of *F* (*p* < .01)**

| | | \multicolumn{9}{c}{DEGREES OF FREEDOM IN THE NUMERATOR} | | | | | | | | |
|---|---|---|---|---|---|---|---|---|---|---|
| | | *1* | *2* | *3* | *4* | *5* | *6* | *7* | *8* | *9* |
| | 1 | 4,052 | 4,999.5 | 5,403 | 5,625 | 5,764 | 5,859 | 5,928 | 5,981 | 6,022 |
| | 2 | 98.50 | 99.00 | 99.17 | 99.25 | 99.30 | 99.33 | 99.36 | 99.37 | 99.39 |
| | 3 | 34.12 | 30.82 | 29.46 | 28.71 | 28.24 | 27.91 | 27.67 | 27.49 | 27.35 |
| | 4 | 21.20 | 18.00 | 16.69 | 15.98 | 15.52 | 15.21 | 14.98 | 14.80 | 14.66 |
| | 5 | 16.26 | 13.27 | 12.06 | 11.39 | 10.97 | 10.67 | 10.46 | 10.29 | 10.16 |
| | 6 | 13.75 | 10.92 | 9.78 | 9.15 | 8.75 | 8.47 | 8.26 | 8.10 | 7.98 |
| | 7 | 12.25 | 9.55 | 8.45 | 7.85 | 7.46 | 7.19 | 6.99 | 6.84 | 6.72 |
| | 8 | 11.26 | 8.65 | 7.59 | 7.01 | 6.63 | 6.37 | 6.18 | 6.03 | 5.91 |
| | 9 | 10.56 | 8.02 | 6.99 | 6.42 | 6.06 | 5.80 | 5.61 | 5.47 | 5.35 |
| | 10 | 10.04 | 7.56 | 6.55 | 5.99 | 5.64 | 5.39 | 5.20 | 5.06 | 4.94 |
| | 11 | 9.65 | 7.21 | 6.22 | 5.67 | 5.32 | 5.07 | 4.89 | 4.74 | 4.63 |
| | 12 | 9.33 | 6.93 | 5.95 | 5.41 | 5.06 | 4.82 | 4.64 | 4.50 | 4.39 |
| | 13 | 9.07 | 6.70 | 5.74 | 5.21 | 4.86 | 4.62 | 4.44 | 4.30 | 4.19 |
| | 14 | 8.86 | 6.51 | 5.56 | 5.04 | 4.69 | 4.46 | 4.28 | 4.14 | 4.03 |
| | 15 | 8.68 | 6.36 | 5.42 | 4.89 | 4.56 | 4.32 | 4.14 | 4.00 | 3.89 |
| | 16 | 8.53 | 6.23 | 5.29 | 4.77 | 4.44 | 4.20 | 4.03 | 3.89 | 3.78 |
| | 17 | 8.40 | 6.11 | 5.18 | 4.67 | 4.34 | 4.10 | 3.93 | 3.79 | 3.68 |
| | 18 | 8.29 | 6.01 | 5.09 | 4.58 | 4.25 | 4.01 | 3.84 | 3.71 | 3.60 |
| | 19 | 8.18 | 5.93 | 5.01 | 4.50 | 4.17 | 3.94 | 3.77 | 3.63 | 3.52 |
| | 20 | 8.10 | 5.85 | 4.94 | 4.43 | 4.10 | 3.87 | 3.70 | 3.56 | 3.46 |
| | 21 | 8.02 | 5.78 | 4.87 | 4.37 | 4.04 | 3.81 | 3.64 | 3.51 | 3.40 |
| | 22 | 7.95 | 5.72 | 4.82 | 4.31 | 3.99 | 3.76 | 3.59 | 3.45 | 3.35 |
| | 23 | 7.88 | 5.66 | 4.76 | 4.26 | 3.94 | 3.71 | 3.54 | 3.41 | 3.30 |
| | 24 | 7.82 | 5.61 | 4.72 | 4.22 | 3.90 | 3.67 | 3.50 | 3.36 | 3.26 |
| | 25 | 7.77 | 5.57 | 4.68 | 4.18 | 3.85 | 3.63 | 3.46 | 3.32 | 3.22 |
| | 26 | 7.72 | 5.53 | 5.64 | 4.14 | 3.82 | 3.59 | 3.42 | 3.29 | 3.18 |
| | 27 | 7.68 | 5.49 | 4.60 | 4.11 | 3.78 | 3.56 | 3.39 | 3.26 | 3.15 |
| | 28 | 7.64 | 5.45 | 4.57 | 4.07 | 3.75 | 3.53 | 3.36 | 3.23 | 3.12 |
| | 29 | 7.60 | 5.42 | 4.54 | 4.04 | 3.73 | 3.50 | 3.33 | 3.20 | 3.09 |
| | 30 | 7.56 | 5.39 | 4.51 | 4.02 | 3.70 | 3.47 | 3.30 | 3.17 | 3.07 |
| | 40 | 7.31 | 5.18 | 4.31 | 3.83 | 3.51 | 3.29 | 3.12 | 2.99 | 2.89 |
| | 60 | 7.08 | 4.98 | 4.13 | 3.65 | 3.34 | 3.12 | 2.95 | 2.82 | 2.72 |
| | 120 | 6.85 | 4.79 | 3.95 | 3.48 | 3.17 | 2.96 | 2.79 | 2.66 | 2.56 |
| | ∞ | 6.63 | 4.61 | 3.78 | 3.32 | 3.02 | 2.80 | 2.64 | 2.51 | 2.41 |

*Degrees of Freedom in the Denominator*

SOURCE: Adapted from Table 18, *Biometrika: Tables for Statisticians* (Vol. 1, 3rd ed.), 1966, by E. S. Pearson & H. O. Hartley; reprinted with permission.

**TABLE 3B**   **Critical Values of *F* (*p* < .01)**   *continued*

| | | | DEGREES OF FREEDOM IN THE NUMERATOR | | | | | | | |
|---|---|---|---|---|---|---|---|---|---|---|
| | 10 | 12 | 15 | 20 | 24 | 30 | 40 | 60 | 120 | ∞ |
| 1 | 6,056 | 6,106 | 6,157 | 6,209 | 6,235 | 6,261 | 6,287 | 6,313 | 6,339 | 6,366 |
| 2 | 99.40 | 99.42 | 99.43 | 99.45 | 99.46 | 99.47 | 99.47 | 99.48 | 99.49 | 99.50 |
| 3 | 27.23 | 27.05 | 26.87 | 26.69 | 26.60 | 26.50 | 26.41 | 26.32 | 26.22 | 26.13 |
| 4 | 14.55 | 14.37 | 14.20 | 14.02 | 13.93 | 13.84 | 13.75 | 13.65 | 13.56 | 13.46 |
| 5 | 10.05 | 9.89 | 9.72 | 9.55 | 9.47 | 9.38 | 9.29 | 9.20 | 9.11 | 9.02 |
| 6 | 7.87 | 7.72 | 7.56 | 7.40 | 7.31 | 7.23 | 7.14 | 7.06 | 6.97 | 6.88 |
| 7 | 6.62 | 6.47 | 6.31 | 6.16 | 6.07 | 5.99 | 5.91 | 5.82 | 5.74 | 5.65 |
| 8 | 5.81 | 5.67 | 5.52 | 5.36 | 5.28 | 5.20 | 5.12 | 5.03 | 4.95 | 4.86 |
| 9 | 5.26 | 5.11 | 4.96 | 4.81 | 4.73 | 4.65 | 4.57 | 4.48 | 4.40 | 4.31 |
| 10 | 4.85 | 4.71 | 4.56 | 4.41 | 4.33 | 4.25 | 4.17 | 4.08 | 4.00 | 3.91 |
| 11 | 4.54 | 4.40 | 4.25 | 4.10 | 4.02 | 3.94 | 3.86 | 3.78 | 3.69 | 3.60 |
| 12 | 4.30 | 4.16 | 4.01 | 3.86 | 3.78 | 3.70 | 3.62 | 3.54 | 3.45 | 3.36 |
| 13 | 4.10 | 3.96 | 3.82 | 3.66 | 3.59 | 3.51 | 3.43 | 3.34 | 3.25 | 3.17 |
| 14 | 3.94 | 3.80 | 3.66 | 3.51 | 3.43 | 3.35 | 3.27 | 3.18 | 3.09 | 3.00 |
| 15 | 3.80 | 3.67 | 3.52 | 3.37 | 3.29 | 3.21 | 3.13 | 3.05 | 2.96 | 2.87 |
| 16 | 3.69 | 3.55 | 3.41 | 3.26 | 3.18 | 3.10 | 3.02 | 2.93 | 2.84 | 2.75 |
| 17 | 3.59 | 3.46 | 3.31 | 3.16 | 3.08 | 3.00 | 2.92 | 2.83 | 2.75 | 2.65 |
| 18 | 3.51 | 3.37 | 3.23 | 3.08 | 3.00 | 2.92 | 2.84 | 2.75 | 2.66 | 2.57 |
| 19 | 3.43 | 3.30 | 3.15 | 3.00 | 2.92 | 2.84 | 2.76 | 2.67 | 2.58 | 2.49 |
| 20 | 3.37 | 3.23 | 3.09 | 2.94 | 2.86 | 2.78 | 2.69 | 2.61 | 2.52 | 2.42 |
| 21 | 3.31 | 3.17 | 3.03 | 2.88 | 2.80 | 2.72 | 2.64 | 2.55 | 2.46 | 2.36 |
| 22 | 3.26 | 3.12 | 2.98 | 2.83 | 2.75 | 2.67 | 2.58 | 2.50 | 2.40 | 2.31 |
| 23 | 3.21 | 3.07 | 2.93 | 2.78 | 2.70 | 2.62 | 2.54 | 2.45 | 2.35 | 2.26 |
| 24 | 3.17 | 3.03 | 2.89 | 2.74 | 2.66 | 2.58 | 2.49 | 2.40 | 2.31 | 2.21 |
| 25 | 3.13 | 2.99 | 2.85 | 2.70 | 2.62 | 2.54 | 2.45 | 2.36 | 2.27 | 2.17 |
| 26 | 3.09 | 2.96 | 2.81 | 2.66 | 2.58 | 2.50 | 2.42 | 2.33 | 2.23 | 2.13 |
| 27 | 3.06 | 2.93 | 2.78 | 2.63 | 2.55 | 2.47 | 2.38 | 2.29 | 2.20 | 2.10 |
| 28 | 3.03 | 2.90 | 2.75 | 2.60 | 2.52 | 2.44 | 2.35 | 2.26 | 2.17 | 2.06 |
| 29 | 3.00 | 2.87 | 2.73 | 2.57 | 2.49 | 2.41 | 2.33 | 2.23 | 2.14 | 2.03 |
| 30 | 2.98 | 2.84 | 2.70 | 2.55 | 2.47 | 2.39 | 2.30 | 2.21 | 2.11 | 2.01 |
| 40 | 2.80 | 2.66 | 2.52 | 2.37 | 2.29 | 2.20 | 2.11 | 2.02 | 1.92 | 1.80 |
| 60 | 2.63 | 2.50 | 2.35 | 2.20 | 2.12 | 2.03 | 1.94 | 1.84 | 1.73 | 1.60 |
| 120 | 2.47 | 2.34 | 2.19 | 2.03 | 1.95 | 1.86 | 1.76 | 1.66 | 1.53 | 1.38 |
| ∞ | 2.32 | 2.18 | 2.04 | 1.88 | 1.79 | 1.70 | 1.59 | 1.47 | 1.32 | 1.00 |

Degrees of Freedom in the Denominator

**TABLE 4A    Critical Values of the Mann–Whitney $U$ Test**

| | $p < .05$ (TWO-TAILED TEST) | | | | | | | | | | | | | | | | | | | |
|---|---|---|---|---|---|---|---|---|---|---|---|---|---|---|---|---|---|---|---|---|
| | $n$ | | | | | | | | | | | | | | | | | | | |
| $m$ | 1 | 2 | 3 | 4 | 5 | 6 | 7 | 8 | 9 | 10 | 11 | 12 | 13 | 14 | 15 | 16 | 17 | 18 | 19 | 20 |
| 1 | — | | | | | | | | | | | | | | | | | | | |
| 2 | — | — | | | | | | | | | | | | | | | | | | |
| 3 | — | — | — | | | | | | | | | | | | | | | | | |
| 4 | — | — | — | 0 | | | | | | | | | | | | | | | | |
| 5 | — | — | 0 | 1 | 2 | | | | | | | | | | | | | | | |
| 6 | — | — | 1 | 2 | 3 | 5 | | | | | | | | | | | | | | |
| 7 | — | — | 1 | 3 | 5 | 6 | 8 | | | | | | | | | | | | | |
| 8 | — | 0 | 2 | 4 | 6 | 8 | 10 | 13 | | | | | | | | | | | | |
| 9 | — | 0 | 2 | 4 | 7 | 10 | 12 | 15 | 17 | | | | | | | | | | | |
| 10 | — | 0 | 3 | 5 | 8 | 11 | 14 | 17 | 20 | 23 | | | | | | | | | | |
| 11 | — | 0 | 3 | 6 | 9 | 13 | 16 | 19 | 23 | 26 | 30 | | | | | | | | | |
| 12 | — | 1 | 4 | 7 | 11 | 14 | 18 | 22 | 26 | 29 | 33 | 37 | | | | | | | | |
| 13 | — | 1 | 4 | 8 | 12 | 16 | 20 | 24 | 28 | 33 | 37 | 41 | 45 | | | | | | | |
| 14 | — | 1 | 5 | 9 | 13 | 17 | 22 | 26 | 31 | 36 | 40 | 45 | 50 | 55 | | | | | | |
| 15 | — | 1 | 5 | 10 | 14 | 19 | 24 | 29 | 34 | 39 | 44 | 49 | 54 | 59 | 64 | | | | | |
| 16 | — | 1 | 6 | 11 | 15 | 21 | 26 | 31 | 37 | 42 | 47 | 53 | 59 | 64 | 70 | 75 | | | | |
| 17 | — | 2 | 6 | 11 | 17 | 22 | 28 | 34 | 39 | 45 | 51 | 57 | 63 | 69 | 75 | 81 | 87 | | | |
| 18 | — | 2 | 7 | 12 | 18 | 24 | 30 | 36 | 42 | 48 | 55 | 61 | 67 | 74 | 80 | 86 | 93 | 99 | | |
| 19 | — | 2 | 7 | 13 | 19 | 25 | 32 | 38 | 45 | 52 | 58 | 65 | 72 | 78 | 85 | 92 | 99 | 106 | 113 | |
| 20 | — | 2 | 8 | 14 | 20 | 27 | 34 | 41 | 48 | 55 | 62 | 69 | 76 | 83 | 90 | 98 | 105 | 112 | 119 | 127 |
| 21 | — | 3 | 8 | 15 | 22 | 29 | 36 | 43 | 50 | 58 | 65 | 73 | 80 | 88 | 96 | 103 | 111 | 119 | 126 | 134 |
| 22 | — | 3 | 9 | 16 | 23 | 30 | 38 | 45 | 53 | 61 | 69 | 77 | 85 | 93 | 101 | 109 | 117 | 125 | 133 | 141 |
| 23 | — | 3 | 9 | 17 | 24 | 32 | 40 | 48 | 56 | 64 | 73 | 81 | 89 | 98 | 106 | 115 | 123 | 132 | 140 | 149 |
| 24 | — | 3 | 10 | 17 | 25 | 33 | 42 | 50 | 59 | 67 | 76 | 85 | 94 | 102 | 111 | 120 | 129 | 138 | 147 | 156 |
| 25 | — | 3 | 10 | 18 | 27 | 35 | 44 | 53 | 62 | 71 | 80 | 89 | 98 | 107 | 117 | 126 | 135 | 145 | 154 | 163 |
| 26 | — | 4 | 11 | 19 | 28 | 37 | 46 | 55 | 64 | 74 | 83 | 93 | 102 | 112 | 122 | 132 | 141 | 151 | 161 | 171 |
| 27 | — | 4 | 11 | 20 | 29 | 38 | 48 | 57 | 67 | 77 | 87 | 97 | 107 | 117 | 127 | 137 | 147 | 158 | 168 | 178 |
| 28 | — | 4 | 12 | 21 | 30 | 40 | 50 | 60 | 70 | 80 | 90 | 101 | 111 | 122 | 132 | 143 | 154 | 164 | 175 | 186 |
| 29 | — | 4 | 13 | 22 | 32 | 42 | 52 | 62 | 73 | 83 | 94 | 105 | 116 | 127 | 138 | 149 | 160 | 171 | 182 | 193 |
| 30 | — | 5 | 13 | 23 | 33 | 43 | 54 | 65 | 76 | 87 | 98 | 109 | 120 | 131 | 143 | 154 | 166 | 177 | 189 | 200 |
| 31 | — | 5 | 14 | 24 | 34 | 45 | 56 | 67 | 78 | 90 | 101 | 113 | 125 | 136 | 148 | 160 | 172 | 184 | 196 | 208 |
| 32 | — | 5 | 14 | 24 | 35 | 46 | 58 | 69 | 81 | 93 | 105 | 117 | 129 | 141 | 153 | 166 | 178 | 190 | 203 | 215 |
| 33 | — | 5 | 15 | 25 | 37 | 48 | 60 | 72 | 84 | 96 | 108 | 121 | 133 | 146 | 159 | 171 | 184 | 197 | 210 | 222 |
| 34 | — | 5 | 15 | 26 | 38 | 50 | 62 | 74 | 87 | 99 | 112 | 125 | 138 | 151 | 164 | 177 | 190 | 203 | 217 | 230 |
| 35 | — | 6 | 16 | 27 | 39 | 51 | 64 | 77 | 89 | 103 | 116 | 129 | 142 | 156 | 169 | 183 | 196 | 210 | 224 | 237 |
| 36 | — | 6 | 16 | 28 | 40 | 53 | 66 | 79 | 92 | 106 | 119 | 133 | 147 | 161 | 174 | 188 | 202 | 216 | 231 | 245 |
| 37 | — | 6 | 17 | 29 | 41 | 55 | 68 | 81 | 95 | 109 | 123 | 137 | 151 | 165 | 180 | 194 | 209 | 223 | 238 | 252 |
| 38 | — | 6 | 17 | 30 | 43 | 56 | 70 | 84 | 98 | 112 | 127 | 141 | 156 | 170 | 185 | 200 | 215 | 230 | 245 | 259 |
| 39 | 0 | 7 | 18 | 31 | 44 | 58 | 72 | 86 | 101 | 115 | 130 | 145 | 160 | 175 | 190 | 206 | 221 | 236 | 252 | 267 |
| 40 | 0 | 7 | 18 | 31 | 45 | 59 | 74 | 89 | 103 | 119 | 134 | 149 | 165 | 180 | 196 | 211 | 227 | 243 | 258 | 274 |

SOURCE: Reprinted from R. C. Milton (1964), An extended table of critical values for the Mann–Whitney (Wilcoxon) two-sample statistic, *Journal of the American Statistical Association, 59,* 925–934.

## TABLE 4B   Critical Values of the Mann–Whitney *U* Test

### $p < .01$ (TWO-TAILED TEST)

| m | n=1 | 2 | 3 | 4 | 5 | 6 | 7 | 8 | 9 | 10 | 11 | 12 | 13 | 14 | 15 | 16 | 17 | 18 | 19 | 20 |
|---|---|---|---|---|---|---|---|---|---|---|---|---|---|---|---|---|---|---|---|---|
| 1 | — | | | | | | | | | | | | | | | | | | | |
| 2 | — | — | | | | | | | | | | | | | | | | | | |
| 3 | — | — | — | | | | | | | | | | | | | | | | | |
| 4 | — | — | — | — | | | | | | | | | | | | | | | | |
| 5 | — | — | — | — | 0 | | | | | | | | | | | | | | | |
| 6 | — | — | — | 0 | 1 | 2 | | | | | | | | | | | | | | |
| 7 | — | — | — | 0 | 1 | 2 | 4 | | | | | | | | | | | | | |
| 8 | — | — | — | 1 | 2 | 4 | 6 | 7 | | | | | | | | | | | | |
| 9 | — | — | 0 | 1 | 3 | 5 | 7 | 9 | 11 | | | | | | | | | | | |
| 10 | — | — | 0 | 2 | 4 | 6 | 9 | 11 | 13 | 16 | | | | | | | | | | |
| 11 | — | — | 0 | 2 | 5 | 7 | 10 | 13 | 16 | 18 | 21 | | | | | | | | | |
| 12 | — | — | 1 | 3 | 6 | 9 | 12 | 15 | 18 | 21 | 24 | 27 | | | | | | | | |
| 13 | — | — | 1 | 3 | 7 | 10 | 13 | 17 | 20 | 24 | 27 | 31 | 34 | | | | | | | |
| 14 | — | — | 1 | 4 | 7 | 11 | 15 | 18 | 22 | 26 | 30 | 34 | 38 | 42 | | | | | | |
| 15 | — | — | 2 | 5 | 8 | 12 | 16 | 20 | 24 | 29 | 33 | 37 | 42 | 46 | 51 | | | | | |
| 16 | — | — | 2 | 5 | 9 | 13 | 18 | 22 | 27 | 31 | 36 | 41 | 45 | 50 | 55 | 60 | | | | |
| 17 | — | — | 2 | 6 | 10 | 15 | 19 | 24 | 29 | 34 | 39 | 44 | 49 | 54 | 60 | 65 | 70 | | | |
| 18 | — | — | 2 | 6 | 11 | 16 | 21 | 26 | 31 | 37 | 42 | 47 | 53 | 58 | 64 | 70 | 75 | 81 | | |
| 19 | — | 0 | 3 | 7 | 12 | 17 | 22 | 28 | 33 | 39 | 45 | 51 | 57 | 63 | 69 | 74 | 81 | 87 | 93 | |
| 20 | — | 0 | 3 | 8 | 13 | 18 | 24 | 30 | 36 | 42 | 48 | 54 | 60 | 67 | 73 | 79 | 86 | 92 | 99 | 105 |
| 21 | — | 0 | 3 | 8 | 14 | 19 | 25 | 32 | 38 | 44 | 51 | 58 | 64 | 71 | 78 | 84 | 91 | 98 | 105 | 112 |
| 22 | — | 0 | 4 | 9 | 14 | 21 | 27 | 34 | 40 | 47 | 54 | 61 | 68 | 75 | 82 | 89 | 96 | 104 | 111 | 118 |
| 23 | — | 0 | 4 | 9 | 15 | 22 | 29 | 35 | 43 | 50 | 57 | 64 | 72 | 79 | 87 | 94 | 102 | 109 | 117 | 125 |
| 24 | — | 0 | 4 | 10 | 16 | 23 | 30 | 37 | 45 | 52 | 60 | 68 | 75 | 83 | 91 | 99 | 107 | 115 | 123 | 131 |
| 25 | — | 0 | 5 | 10 | 17 | 24 | 32 | 39 | 47 | 55 | 63 | 71 | 79 | 87 | 96 | 104 | 112 | 121 | 129 | 138 |
| 26 | — | 0 | 5 | 11 | 18 | 25 | 33 | 41 | 49 | 58 | 66 | 74 | 83 | 92 | 100 | 109 | 118 | 127 | 135 | 144 |
| 27 | — | 1 | 5 | 12 | 19 | 27 | 35 | 43 | 52 | 60 | 69 | 78 | 87 | 96 | 105 | 114 | 123 | 132 | 142 | 151 |
| 28 | — | 1 | 5 | 12 | 20 | 28 | 36 | 45 | 54 | 63 | 72 | 81 | 91 | 100 | 109 | 119 | 128 | 138 | 148 | 157 |
| 29 | — | 1 | 6 | 13 | 21 | 29 | 38 | 47 | 56 | 66 | 75 | 85 | 94 | 104 | 114 | 124 | 134 | 144 | 154 | 164 |
| 30 | — | 1 | 6 | 13 | 22 | 30 | 40 | 49 | 58 | 68 | 78 | 88 | 98 | 108 | 119 | 129 | 139 | 150 | 160 | 170 |
| 31 | — | 1 | 6 | 14 | 22 | 32 | 41 | 51 | 61 | 71 | 81 | 92 | 102 | 113 | 123 | 134 | 145 | 155 | 166 | 177 |
| 32 | — | 1 | 7 | 14 | 23 | 33 | 43 | 53 | 63 | 74 | 84 | 95 | 106 | 117 | 128 | 139 | 150 | 161 | 172 | 184 |
| 33 | — | 1 | 7 | 15 | 24 | 34 | 44 | 55 | 65 | 76 | 87 | 98 | 110 | 121 | 132 | 144 | 155 | 167 | 179 | 190 |
| 34 | — | 1 | 7 | 16 | 25 | 35 | 46 | 57 | 68 | 79 | 90 | 102 | 113 | 125 | 137 | 149 | 161 | 173 | 185 | 197 |
| 35 | — | 1 | 8 | 16 | 26 | 37 | 47 | 59 | 70 | 82 | 93 | 105 | 117 | 129 | 142 | 154 | 166 | 179 | 191 | 203 |
| 36 | — | 1 | 8 | 17 | 27 | 38 | 49 | 60 | 72 | 84 | 96 | 109 | 121 | 134 | 146 | 159 | 172 | 184 | 197 | 210 |
| 37 | — | 1 | 8 | 17 | 28 | 39 | 51 | 62 | 75 | 87 | 99 | 112 | 125 | 138 | 151 | 164 | 177 | 190 | 203 | 217 |
| 38 | — | 1 | 9 | 18 | 29 | 40 | 52 | 64 | 77 | 90 | 102 | 116 | 129 | 142 | 155 | 169 | 182 | 196 | 210 | 223 |
| 39 | — | 2 | 9 | 19 | 30 | 41 | 54 | 66 | 79 | 92 | 106 | 119 | 133 | 146 | 160 | 174 | 188 | 202 | 216 | 230 |
| 40 | — | 2 | 9 | 19 | 31 | 43 | 55 | 68 | 81 | 95 | 109 | 122 | 136 | 150 | 165 | 179 | 193 | 208 | 222 | 237 |

SOURCE: Reprinted from R. C. Milton (1964), An extended table of critical values for the Mann–Whitney (Wilcoxon) two-sample statistic, *Journal of the American Statistical Association, 59,* 925–934.

**TABLE 5 Areas under the Normal Curve**

| | HUNDREDTHS VALUE OF *z* | | | | | | | | | |
|---|---|---|---|---|---|---|---|---|---|---|
| *z* (Ones and Tenths Value of *z*) | .00 | .01 | .02 | .03 | .04 | .05 | .06 | .07 | .08 | .09 |
| 0.0 | .0000 | .0040 | .0080 | .0120 | .0160 | .0199 | .0239 | .0279 | .0319 | .0359 |
| 0.1 | .0398 | .0438 | .0478 | .0517 | .0557 | .0596 | .0636 | .0675 | .0714 | .0753 |
| 0.2 | .0793 | .0832 | .0871 | .0910 | .0948 | .0987 | .1026 | .1064 | .1103 | .1141 |
| 0.3 | .1179 | .1217 | .1255 | .1293 | .1331 | .1368 | .1406 | .1443 | .1480 | .1517 |
| 0.4 | .1554 | .1591 | .1628 | .1664 | .1700 | .1736 | .1772 | .1808 | .1844 | .1879 |
| 0.5 | .1915 | .1950 | .1985 | .2019 | .2054 | .2088 | .2123 | .2157 | .2190 | .2224 |
| 0.6 | .2257 | .2291 | .2324 | .2357 | .2389 | .2422 | .2454 | .2486 | .2517 | .2549 |
| 0.7 | .2580 | .2611 | .2624 | .2673 | .2704 | .2734 | .2764 | .2794 | .2823 | .2852 |
| 0.8 | .2881 | .2910 | .2939 | .2967 | .2995 | .3023 | .3051 | .3078 | .3106 | .3133 |
| 0.9 | .3159 | .3186 | .3212 | .3238 | .3264 | .3289 | .3315 | .3340 | .3365 | .3389 |
| 1.0 | .3413 | .3438 | .3461 | .3485 | .3508 | .3531 | .3554 | .3577 | .3599 | .3621 |
| 1.1 | .3643 | .3665 | .3686 | .3708 | .3729 | .3749 | .3770 | .3790 | .3810 | .3830 |
| 1.2 | .3849 | .3869 | .3888 | .3907 | .3925 | .3944 | .3962 | .3980 | .3997 | .4015 |
| 1.3 | .4032 | .4049 | .4066 | .4082 | .4099 | .4115 | .4131 | .4147 | .4162 | .4177 |
| 1.4 | .4192 | .4207 | .4222 | .4236 | .4251 | .4265 | .4279 | .4292 | .4306 | .4319 |
| 1.5 | .4332 | .4345 | .4357 | .4370 | .4382 | .4394 | .4406 | .4418 | .4429 | .4441 |
| 1.6 | .4452 | .4463 | .4474 | .4484 | .4495 | .4505 | .4515 | .4525 | .4535 | .4545 |
| 1.7 | .4554 | .4564 | .4573 | .4582 | .4591 | .4599 | .4608 | .4616 | .4625 | .4633 |
| 1.8 | .4641 | .4649 | .4656 | .4664 | .4671 | .4678 | .4686 | .4693 | .4699 | .4706 |
| 1.9 | .4713 | .4719 | .4726 | .4732 | .4738 | .4744 | .4750 | .4756 | .4761 | .4767 |
| 2.0 | .4772 | .4778 | .4783 | .4788 | .4793 | .4798 | .4803 | .4808 | .4812 | .4817 |
| 2.1 | .4821 | .4826 | .4830 | .4834 | .4838 | .4842 | .4846 | .4850 | .4854 | .4857 |
| 2.2 | .4861 | .4864 | .4868 | .4871 | .4875 | .4878 | .4881 | .4884 | .4887 | .4890 |
| 2.3 | .4893 | .4896 | .4898 | .4901 | .4904 | .4906 | .4909 | .4911 | .4913 | .4916 |
| 2.4 | .4918 | .4920 | .4922 | .4925 | .4927 | .4929 | .4931 | .4932 | .4934 | .4936 |
| 2.5 | .4938 | .4940 | .4941 | .4943 | .4945 | .4946 | .4948 | .4949 | .4951 | .4952 |
| 2.6 | .4953 | .4955 | .4956 | .4957 | .4959 | .4960 | .4961 | .4962 | .4963 | .4964 |
| 2.7 | .4965 | .4966 | .4967 | .4968 | .4969 | .4970 | .4971 | .4972 | .4973 | .4974 |
| 2.8 | .4974 | .4975 | .4976 | .4977 | .4977 | .4978 | .4979 | .4979 | .4980 | .4981 |
| 2.9 | .4981 | .4982 | .4982 | .4983 | .4984 | .4984 | .4985 | .4985 | .4986 | .4986 |
| 3.0 | .4987 | .4987 | .4987 | .4988 | .4988 | .4989 | .4989 | .4989 | .4990 | .4990 |
| 3.1 | .49903 | | | | | | | | | |
| 3.2 | .49931 | | | | | | | | | |
| 3.3 | .49952 | | | | | | | | | |
| 3.4 | .49966 | | | | | | | | | |
| 3.5 | .49977 | | | | | | | | | |
| 3.6 | .49984 | | | | | | | | | |
| 3.7 | .49989 | | | | | | | | | |
| 3.8 | .49993 | | | | | | | | | |
| 3.9 | .49995 | | | | | | | | | |
| 4.0 | .50000 | | | | | | | | | |

SOURCE: Reprinted with permission from *Computational Handbook of Statistics,* by J. L. Bruning & B. L. Kintz. Copyright © 1987, 1977, 1968 by Scott, Foresman & Company.

TABLE 6   **Critical Values of Chi-Square**

| | | | | p VALUE | | | |
|---|---|---|---|---|---|---|---|
| | **.25** | **.10** | **.05** | **.025** | **.01** | **.005** | **.001** |
| 1 | 1.32330 | 2.70554 | 3.84146 | 5.02389 | 6.63490 | 7.87944 | 10.828 |
| 2 | 2.77259 | 4.60517 | 5.99146 | 7.37776 | 9.21034 | 10.5966 | 13.816 |
| 3 | 4.10834 | 6.25139 | 7.81473 | 9.34840 | 11.3449 | 12.8382 | 16.266 |
| 4 | 5.38527 | 7.77944 | 9.48773 | 11.1433 | 13.2767 | 14.8603 | 18.467 |
| 5 | 6.62568 | 9.23636 | 11.0705 | 12.8325 | 15.0863 | 16.7496 | 20.515 |
| 6 | 7.84080 | 10.6446 | 12.5916 | 14.4494 | 16.8119 | 18.5476 | 22.458 |
| 7 | 9.03715 | 12.0170 | 14.0671 | 16.0128 | 18.4753 | 20.2777 | 24.322 |
| 8 | 10.2189 | 13.3616 | 15.5073 | 17.5345 | 20.0902 | 21.9550 | 26.125 |
| 9 | 11.3888 | 14.6837 | 16.9190 | 19.0228 | 21.6660 | 23.5894 | 27.877 |
| 10 | 12.5489 | 15.9872 | 18.3070 | 20.4832 | 23.2093 | 25.1882 | 29.588 |
| 11 | 13.7007 | 17.2750 | 19.6751 | 21.9200 | 24.7250 | 26.7568 | 31.264 |
| 12 | 14.8454 | 18.5493 | 21.0261 | 23.3367 | 26.2170 | 28.2995 | 32.909 |
| 13 | 15.9839 | 19.8119 | 22.3620 | 24.7356 | 27.6882 | 29.8195 | 34.528 |
| 14 | 17.1169 | 21.0641 | 23.6848 | 26.1189 | 29.1412 | 31.3194 | 36.123 |
| 15 | 18.2451 | 22.3071 | 24.9958 | 27.4884 | 30.5779 | 32.8013 | 37.697 |
| 16 | 19.3689 | 23.5418 | 26.2962 | 28.8454 | 31.9999 | 34.2672 | 39.252 |
| 17 | 20.4887 | 24.7690 | 27.5871 | 30.1910 | 33.4087 | 35.7185 | 40.790 |
| 18 | 21.6049 | 25.9894 | 28.8693 | 31.5264 | 34.8053 | 37.1565 | 42.312 |
| 19 | 22.7178 | 27.2036 | 30.1435 | 32.8523 | 36.1909 | 38.5823 | 43.820 |
| 20 | 23.8277 | 28.4120 | 31.4104 | 34.1696 | 37.5662 | 39.9968 | 45.315 |
| 21 | 24.9348 | 29.6151 | 32.6706 | 35.4789 | 38.9322 | 41.4011 | 46.797 |
| 22 | 26.0393 | 30.8133 | 33.9244 | 36.7807 | 40.2894 | 42.7957 | 48.268 |
| 23 | 27.1413 | 32.0069 | 35.1725 | 38.0756 | 41.6384 | 44.1813 | 49.728 |
| 24 | 28.2412 | 33.1962 | 36.4150 | 39.3641 | 42.9798 | 45.5585 | 51.179 |
| 25 | 29.3389 | 34.3816 | 37.6525 | 40.6465 | 44.3141 | 46.9279 | 52.618 |
| 26 | 30.4346 | 35.5632 | 38.8851 | 41.9232 | 45.6417 | 48.2899 | 54.052 |
| 27 | 31.5284 | 36.7412 | 40.1133 | 43.1945 | 46.9629 | 49.6449 | 55.476 |
| 28 | 32.6205 | 37.9159 | 41.3371 | 44.4608 | 48.2782 | 50.9934 | 56.892 |
| 29 | 33.7109 | 39.0875 | 42.5570 | 45.7223 | 49.5879 | 52.3356 | 58.301 |
| 30 | 34.7997 | 40.2560 | 43.7730 | 46.9792 | 50.8922 | 53.6720 | 59.703 |
| 40 | 45.6160 | 51.8051 | 55.7585 | 59.3417 | 63.6907 | 66.7660 | 73.402 |
| 50 | 56.3336 | 63.1671 | 67.5048 | 71.4202 | 76.1539 | 79.4900 | 86.661 |
| 60 | 66.9815 | 74.3970 | 79.0819 | 83.2977 | 88.3794 | 91.9517 | 99.607 |
| 70 | 77.5767 | 85.5270 | 90.5312 | 95.0232 | 100.425 | 104.215 | 112.317 |
| 80 | 88.1303 | 96.5782 | 101.879 | 106.629 | 112.329 | 116.321 | 124.839 |
| 90 | 98.6499 | 107.565 | 113.145 | 118.136 | 124.116 | 218.299 | 137.208 |
| 100 | 109.141 | 118.498 | 124.342 | 129.561 | 135.807 | 140.169 | 149.449 |

Degrees of Freedom

SOURCE: Adapted from Table 8, *Biometrika: Tables for Statisticians* (Vol. 1, 3rd ed.), 1966, by E. S. Pearson & H. O. Hartley; reprinted with permission.

A-16    Appendix

## TABLE 7    Conversion of *r* to *z*

| r | z | r | z | r | z | r | z | r | z |
|---|---|---|---|---|---|---|---|---|---|
| .000 | .000 | .200 | .203 | .400 | .424 | .600 | .693 | .800 | 1.099 |
| .005 | .005 | .205 | .208 | .405 | .430 | .605 | .701 | .805 | 1.113 |
| .010 | .010 | .210 | .213 | .410 | .436 | .610 | .709 | .810 | 1.127 |
| .015 | .015 | .215 | .218 | .415 | .442 | .615 | .717 | .815 | 1.142 |
| .020 | .020 | .220 | .224 | .420 | .448 | .620 | .725 | .820 | 1.157 |
| .025 | .025 | .225 | .229 | .425 | .454 | .625 | .733 | .825 | 1.172 |
| .030 | .030 | .230 | .234 | .430 | .460 | .630 | .741 | .830 | 1.188 |
| .035 | .035 | .235 | .239 | .435 | .466 | .635 | .750 | .835 | 1.204 |
| .040 | .040 | .240 | .245 | .440 | .472 | .640 | .758 | .840 | 1.221 |
| .045 | .045 | .245 | .250 | .445 | .478 | .645 | .767 | .845 | 1.238 |
| .050 | .050 | .250 | .255 | .450 | .485 | .650 | .775 | .850 | 1.256 |
| .055 | .055 | .255 | .261 | .455 | .491 | .655 | .784 | .855 | 1.274 |
| .060 | .060 | .260 | .266 | .460 | .497 | .660 | .793 | .860 | 1.293 |
| .065 | .065 | .265 | .271 | .465 | .504 | .665 | .802 | .865 | 1.313 |
| .070 | .070 | .270 | .277 | .470 | .510 | .670 | .811 | .870 | 1.333 |
| .075 | .075 | .275 | .282 | .475 | .517 | .675 | .820 | .875 | 1.354 |
| .080 | .080 | .280 | .288 | .480 | .523 | .680 | .829 | .880 | 1.376 |
| .085 | .085 | .285 | .293 | .485 | .530 | .685 | .838 | .885 | 1.398 |
| .090 | .090 | .290 | .299 | .490 | .536 | .690 | .848 | .890 | 1.422 |
| .095 | .095 | .295 | .304 | .495 | .543 | .695 | .858 | .895 | 1.447 |
| .100 | .100 | .300 | .310 | .500 | .549 | .700 | .867 | .900 | 1.472 |
| .105 | .105 | .305 | .315 | .505 | .556 | .705 | .877 | .905 | 1.499 |
| .110 | .110 | .310 | .321 | .510 | .563 | .710 | .887 | .910 | 1.528 |
| .115 | .116 | .315 | .326 | .515 | .570 | .715 | .897 | .915 | 1.557 |
| .120 | .121 | .320 | .332 | .520 | .576 | .720 | .908 | .920 | 1.589 |
| .125 | .126 | .325 | .337 | .525 | .583 | .725 | .918 | .925 | 1.623 |
| .130 | .131 | .330 | .343 | .530 | .590 | .730 | .929 | .930 | 1.658 |
| .135 | .136 | .335 | .348 | .535 | .597 | .735 | .940 | .935 | 1.697 |
| .140 | .141 | .340 | .354 | .540 | .604 | .740 | .950 | .940 | 1.738 |
| .145 | .146 | .345 | .360 | .545 | .611 | .745 | .962 | .945 | 1.783 |
| .150 | .151 | .350 | .365 | .550 | .618 | .750 | .973 | .950 | 1.832 |
| .155 | .156 | .355 | .371 | .555 | .626 | .755 | .984 | .955 | 1.886 |
| .160 | .161 | .360 | .377 | .560 | .633 | .760 | .996 | .960 | 1.946 |
| .165 | .167 | .365 | .383 | .565 | .640 | .765 | 1.008 | .965 | 2.014 |
| .170 | .172 | .370 | .388 | .570 | .648 | .770 | 1.020 | .970 | 2.092 |
| .175 | .177 | .375 | .394 | .575 | .655 | .775 | 1.033 | .975 | 2.185 |
| .180 | .182 | .380 | .400 | .580 | .662 | .780 | 1.045 | .980 | 2.298 |
| .185 | .187 | .385 | .406 | .585 | .670 | .785 | 1.058 | .985 | 2.443 |
| .190 | .192 | .390 | .412 | .590 | .678 | .790 | 1.071 | .990 | 2.647 |
| .195 | .198 | .395 | .418 | .595 | .685 | .795 | 1.085 | .995 | 2.994 |

SOURCE: Reprinted with permission from A. L. Edwards (1985), *Experimental Design in Psychological Research* (5th ed.).

# GLOSSARY

**ABAB design**  In a single-subject baseline design, the baseline (A) and intervention (B) phases are each repeated to provide an immediate intrasubject replication.

**ABA design**  In a single-subject baseline design, the baseline phase (A) is run before and after the intervention phase (B).

**abstract**  A concise (50–150 words) summary of an APA-style manuscript that includes a brief description of the rationale for the study, methods, results, and conclusions.

**accuracy**  Agreement of a measurement with a known standard.

**alpha level ($\alpha$)**  The probability of obtaining a difference at least as large as the one actually obtained, given that the difference occurred purely as a result of chance factors. By convention, the maximum acceptable alpha level is .05 (5 chances in 100 or 1 chance in 20).

**analogical theory**  A theory that explains a relationship through analogy to a well-understood model.

**analysis of covariance (ANCOVA)**  Variant of the analysis of variance used to analyze data from experiments that include a correlational variable (covariate).

**analysis of variance (ANOVA)**  An inferential statistic used to evaluate data from experiments with more than two levels of an independent variable or data from multifactor experiments. Versions are available for between-subjects and within-subjects designs.

**apparatus subsection**  Subsection of the method section of an APA-style manuscript in which any equipment, materials, and measures are described in detail. Sometimes called the *materials* subsection.

**applied research**  Research carried out to investigate a real-world problem.

**archival research**  A nonexperimental research strategy in which you make use of existing records as your basic source for data.

**bar graph**  A graph on which data from groups of subjects are represented by bars of differing heights tied to the value of the dependent variable for the group.

**baseline design**  A single-subject experimental design in which subjects are observed under each of several treatment conditions. Observations made during baseline periods (no treatment) are compared with observations made during intervention periods (treatment introduced).

**baseline phase**  Phase of a single-subject, baseline design in which you establish the level of performance on the dependent measure before introducing the treatment.

**basic research**  Research carried out primarily to test a theory or empirical issues.

**behavioral baseline**  Level of behavior under the baseline and intervention phases of a single-subject, baseline design. It is used to determine the amount of uncontrolled variability in the data.

**behavioral categories**  The general and specific classes of behavior to be observed in an observational study.

**behavioral measure**  A measure of a subject's activity in a situation; for example, the number of times a rat presses a lever (frequency of responding).

**belief-based explanation**  An explanation for behavior that is accepted without evidence because it comes from a trusted source or fits within a larger framework of belief.

**beta weight (β)**    Standardized regression weight used to interpret the results of a linear regression analysis. A beta weight can be interpreted as a partial correlation coefficient.

**between-subjects design**    An experimental design in which different groups of subjects are exposed to the various levels of the independent variable.

**biased sample**    A sample that is not representative of the population it is supposed to represent.

**bivariate linear regression**    A statistical technique for fitting a straight line to a set of data points representing the paired values of two variables.

**boxplot**    A graphical display of the values of the five-number summary of a distribution.

**canonical correlation**    Multivariate statistical techniques used to correlate two sets of variables.

**carryover effects**    A problem associated with within-subjects designs in which exposure to one level of the independent variable alters the behavior observed under subsequent levels.

**case history**    A nonexperimental research technique in which an individual case is studied intensively to uncover its history (for example, a patient in therapy).

**causal relationship**    A relationship in which changes in the value of one variable cause changes in the value of another.

**chi-square ($\chi^2$)**    Nonparametric inferential statistic used to evaluate the relationship between variables measured on a nominal scale.

**circular explanation (or tautology)**    An explanation of behavior that refers to factors whose only proof of existence is the behavior they are being called on to explain.

**cluster sampling**    A sampling technique in which naturally occurring groups (such as students in an elementary school class) are randomly selected for inclusion in a sample.

**coefficient of nondetermination**    Statistic indicating the proportion of variance in one variable not accounted for by variation in a second variable.

**Cohen's Kappa**    A popular statistic used to assess interrater reliability. It compares the observed proportion of agreement to the proportion of agreement that would be expected if agreement occurred purely by chance.

**cohort-sequential design**    A developmental design including cross-sectional and longitudinal components.

**commonsense explanations**    Loose explanations for behavior that are based on what we believe to be true about the world.

**concurrent validity**    The validity of a test established by showing that its results can be used to infer an individual's value on some other, accepted test administered at the same time.

**confirmational strategy**    A strategy for testing a theory that involves finding evidence that confirms the predictions made by the theory.

**confirmation bias**    The human tendency to seek out information that confirms what is already believed.

**confounding**    Two variables that vary together in such a way that the effects of one cannot be separated from the effects of the other.

**confounding variable**    A variable that systematically varies along with the independent variable.

**construct validity**    Validity that applies when a test is designed to measure a "construct" or variable "constructed" to describe or explain behavior on the basis of theory (for example, intelligence). A test has construct validity if the measured values of the construct predict behavior as expected from the theory (for example, those with higher intelligence scores achieve higher grades in school).

**content analysis**    A nonexperimental research technique that is used to analyze a written or spoken record for the occurrence of specific categories of events.

**content validity**    Validity of a test established by judging how adequately the test samples behavior representative of the universe of behaviors the test was designed to sample.

**control group**    A group of subjects in an experiment that does not receive the experimental treatment. The data from the control group are used as a baseline against which data from the experimental group are compared.

**correlational relationship**    A relationship in which the value of one variable changes systematically with the value of a second variable.

**correlational research**    Research in which no independent variables are manipulated. Instead, two or more dependent variables are measured to identify possible correlational relationships.

**correlation matrix**   A matrix giving the set of all possible bivariate correlations among three or more variables.

**counterbalancing**   A technique used to combat carryover effects in within-subjects designs. Counterbalancing involves assigning the various treatments of an experiment in a different order for different subjects.

**covariate**   A correlational variable (usually a characteristic of the subject) included in an experiment to help reduce the error variance in statistical tests.

**criterion-related validity**   The ability of a measure to produce results similar to those provided by other, established measures of the same variable.

**critical region**   Portion of the sampling distribution of a statistic within which observed values of the statistic are considered to be statistically significant. Usually the 5 percent of cases found in the upper and/or lower tail(s) of the distribution.

**cross-sectional design**   A developmental design in which participants from two or more age groups are measured at about the same time. Comparisons are made across age groups to investigate age-related changes in behavior.

**data transformation**   Mathematical operation applied to raw data, such as taking the square root or arcsine of the original scores in a distribution. Often applied to data that violate the assumptions of parametric statistical tests, to help them meet those assumptions.

**debriefing**   A session, conducted after an experimental session, in which participants are informed of any deception used and the reasons for the deception.

**deception**   A research technique in which participants are misinformed about the true nature and purpose of a study. Deception is ethical if the researcher can demonstrate that important results cannot be obtained in any other way.

**deductive reasoning**   Reasoning that goes from the general to the specific. Forms the foundation of the rational method of inquiry.

**degrees of freedom (*df*)**   The number of scores that are free to vary in a distribution of a given size having a known mean.

**demand characteristics**   Cues inadvertently provided by the researcher or research context concerning the purposes of a study or the behavior expected from participants.

**demonstration**   A nonexperimental technique in which some phenomenon is demonstrated. No control group is used.

**dependent variable**   The variable measured in a study. Its value is determined by the behavior of the subject and may depend on the value of the independent variable.

**descriptive theory**   A theory that simply describes the relationship among variables without attempting to explain the relationship.

**directionality problem**   A problem that interferes with drawing causal inferences from correlational results that involves not being able to clearly specify the direction of causality between variables.

**direct replication**   Exactly replicating an experiment. No new variables are included in the replication.

**disconfirmational strategy**   A method of testing a theory that involves conducting research to provide evidence that disconfirms the predictions made by the theory.

**discrete trials design**   A single-subject experimental design in which subjects receive each treatment condition dozens or hundreds of times. Each trial (exposure to a treatment) produces one data point, and data points are averaged across trials to provide stable estimates of behavior.

**discriminant analysis**   Multivariate statistical technique used when you have multiple predictor variables and a categorical criterion variable.

**discussion section**   The section of an APA style manuscript that includes the author's interpretation of the findings of a study and conclusions drawn from the data.

**domain**   The range of situations to which a theory applies. Also called the *scope* of a theory.

**double-blind technique**   Neither the participants in a study nor the person carrying out the study know at the time of testing which treatment the participant is receiving.

**dummy code**    In a data file, numbers used to stand for category values; for example, 0 = male, 1 = female.

**dynamic design**    An experimental design in which the independent variable is varied continuously over time while monitoring the response of the dependent variable.

**effect size**    The amount by which a given experimental manipulation changes the value of the dependent variable in the population, expressed in standard deviation units.

**empirical question**    A question that can be answered through objective observation.

**equivalent time samples design**    A variation of the time series design in which a treatment is administered repeatedly, with each administration followed by an observation period.

**error variance**    Variability in the value of the dependent variable that is related to extraneous variables and not to the variability in the independent variable.

**ethnography**    A nonquantitative technique used to study and describe the functioning of cultures through a study of social interactions and expressions between people and groups.

**expectancy effect**    When a researcher's preconceived ideas about how subjects should behave are subtly communicated to subjects and, in turn, affect the subjects' behavior.

**experimental group**    A group of subjects in an experiment that receives a nonzero level of the independent variable.

**experimental research**    Research in which independent variables are manipulated and behavior is measured while extraneous variables are controlled.

**experimenter bias**    When the behavior of the researcher influences the results of a study. Experimenter bias stems from two sources: expectancy effects and uneven treatment of subjects across treatments.

**exploratory data analysis (EDA)**    Examining data for potentially important patterns and relationships, especially through the use of simple graphical techniques and numerical summaries.

**external validity**    The extent to which the results of a study extend beyond the limited sample used in the study.

**extraneous variable**    Any variable that is not systematically manipulated in an experiment but that still may affect the behavior being observed.

**face-to-face interview**    Method of administering a questionnaire that involves face-to-face interaction with the participant. Two types are the structured and unstructured interview.

**face validity**    How well a test appears to measure (judging by its contents) what it was designed to measure. Example: A measure of mathematical ability would have face validity if it contained math problems.

**factor analysis**    Multivariate statistical technique that uses correlations between variables to determine the underlying dimensions (factors) represented by the variables.

**factorial design**    An experimental design in which every level of one independent variable is combined with every level of every other independent variable.

**familywise error**    The likelihood of making at least one Type I error across a number of comparisons.

**file drawer phenomenon**    A problem associated with publication practices and meta-analysis that occurs because results that fail to achieve statistical significance often fail to be published (that is, get relegated to the researcher's file drawer).

**five-number summary**    A set of five numbers used to summarize the characteristics of a distribution: the minimum, first quartile, median, third quartile, and maximum.

**F ratio**    The test statistic computed when using an analysis of variance. It is the ratio of the between-groups variance to within-groups variance.

**frequency**    The number of times a particular value or range of values of a variable occurs in a set of data.

**frequency distribution**    A graph or table displaying a set of values or range of values of a variable, together with the frequency of each.

**functional explanation**    An explanation for a phenomenon given in terms of its function, that is, what it accomplishes.

**fundamental theory**    A theory that proposes a new structure or underlying process to explain how variables and constants relate.

**generalization**    Applying a finding beyond the limited situation in which it was observed.

**higher-order factorial design**   Experimental design that includes more than two independent variables (factors).

**histogram**   A graph depicting a frequency distribution in which the frequencies of class intervals are represented by adjacent bars along the scale of measurement.

**hypothesis**   A tentative statement, subject to empirical test, about the expected relationship between variables.

**independent variable**   The variable that is manipulated in an experiment. Its value is determined by the experimenter, not by the subject.

**inferential statistics**   Statistical procedures used to infer a characteristic of a population based on certain properties of a sample drawn from that population.

**institutional animal care and use committee (IACUC)**   A committee that screens proposals for research using animal subjects and monitors institutional animal-care facilities to ensure compliance with all local, state, and federal laws governing animal care and use.

**institutional review board (IRB)**   A committee that screens proposals for research using human participants for adherence to ethical standards.

**interaction**   When the effect of one independent variable on the dependent variable in a factorial design changes over the levels of another independent variable.

**internal validity**   The extent to which a study evaluates the intended hypotheses.

**Internet survey**   Survey conducted on the Internet, typically by having participants fill out a Web-based questionnaire. Such surveys are subject to potential respondent bias as only those having access to the Internet can respond.

**interquartile range**   A measure of spread in which an ordered distribution of scores is divided into four groups. The score separating the lower 25 percent is subtracted from the score separating the upper 25 percent. The resulting difference is divided by 2.

**interrater reliability**   The degree to which multiple observers agree in their classification or quantification of behavior.

**interrupted time series design**   A variation of the time series design in which changes in behavior are charted as a function of time before and after some naturally occurring event.

**intersubject replication**   The behaviors of multiple subjects used in a single-subject design are compared to establish the reliability of results.

**interval scale**   A measurement scale in which the spacing between values along the scale is known. The zero point of an interval scale is arbitrary.

**intervention phase**   Phase of a single-subject, baseline design in which the treatment is introduced and the dependent measure evaluated.

**interview**   See **face-to-face interview.**

**intraclass correlation coefficient ($r_I$)**   A measure of agreement between observers that can be used when your observations are scaled on an interval or ratio scale of measurement.

**intrasubject replication**   In a single-subject experiment, each treatment is repeated at least once for each subject and behavior is measured. This helps establish the reliability of the results obtained from a single-subject experiment.

**introduction**   The first substantive section of an APA-style manuscript, which includes the rationale for the study, a literature review, and usually a statement of the hypothesis to be tested.

**Latin square design**   A counterbalanced design ensuring that each treatment appears an equal number of times at each ordinal position across subjects.

**law**   A relationship that has been substantially verified through empirical test.

**lazy writing**   Flaw in writing, closely related to plagiarism, that involves using too much quoted (albeit properly cited) material in a manuscript.

**least squares regression line**   Straight line, fit to data, that minimizes the sum of the squared distances between each data point and the line.

**linear regression**   Statistical technique used to determine the straight line that best fits a set of data.

**line graph**   A graph on which data relating the variables are plotted as points connected by lines.

**literature review**   A review of relevant research and theory conducted during the early stages of the research process to identify important variables and accepted methods and to establish a rationale for research hypotheses.

**loglinear analysis**   A nonparametric, multivariate statistical technique used primarily to evaluate data from multifactor research with a nominal dependent variable. It can also be used on interval or ratio data that violate the assumptions of the analysis of variance.

**longitudinal design**   A developmental design in which a single group of subjects is followed over a specified period of time and measured at regular intervals.

**mail survey**   Method of administering a survey that involves mailing questionnaires to participants. Nonresponse bias may be a problem.

**main effect**   The independent effect of one independent variable in a factorial design on the dependent variable. There are as many main effects as there are independent variables.

**manipulation checks**   Measures included in an experiment to test the effectiveness of the independent variables.

**Mann–Whitney U test**   Nonparametric inferential statistic used to evaluate data from a two-group experiment in which the dependent variable was measured along at least an ordinal scale. It can also be used on interval or ratio data if the data do not meet the assumptions of the *t* test for independent samples.

**manuscript page header**   The first two or three words of the title of a manuscript that is typed flush right at the top of the pages of an APA-style manuscript.

**matched groups design**   Between-subjects experimental design in which matched sets of subjects are distributed, at random, one per group across groups of the experiment.

**matched pairs design**   A two-group matched groups design.

**materials subsection**   A subsection of the method section of an APA-style manuscript in which primarily written materials used in a study (for example, questionnaires) are described.

**mean**   The arithmetic average of the scores in a distribution. The most frequently reported measure of central tendency.

**measure of center**   A single score, computed from a data set, that represents the general magnitude of the scores in the distribution.

**measure of spread**   A single score, computed from a data set, that represents the amount of variability of the scores in the distribution (i.e., how spread out they are).

**mechanistic explanation**   An explanation for a phenomenon given in terms of a mechanism that is assumed to produce it through an explicit chain of cause and effect.

**median**   The middle score in an ordered distribution.

**meta-analysis**   A statistics-based method of reviewing literature in a field that involves comparing or combining the results of related studies. See also **traditional literature review.**

**method of authority**   Relying on authoritative sources (for example, books, journals, scholars) for information.

**method section**   The section of an APA-style manuscript in which the methods used in a study are described in detail.

**mixed design**   An experimental design that includes between-subjects as well as within-subjects factors. Also called a **split-plot design.**

**mode**   The most frequent score in a distribution. The least informative measure of center.

**model**   Specific application of a general theoretical view. The term *model* is sometimes used as a synonym for *theory.*

**multiple-baseline design**   Simultaneously sampling several behaviors in a single-subject, baseline design to provide multiple baselines of behavior. Used if your independent variable produces irreversible changes in the dependent variable.

**multiple control group design**   Single-factor, experimental design that includes two or more control groups.

**multiple R**   The correlation between the best linear combination of predictor variables entered into a multiple regression analysis and the dependent variable.

**multiple regression**   Multivariate linear regression analysis used when you have a single criterion variable and multiple predictor variables.

**multistage sampling**   A variant of cluster sampling in which naturally occurring groups of subjects are identified and randomly sampled.

Individual subjects are then randomly sampled from the groups chosen.

**multivariate analysis of variance (MANOVA)** Multivariate analog to the analysis of variance used to analyze data from an experimental design with multiple dependent variables.

**multivariate design** A research design in which multiple dependent or predictor variables are included.

**multivariate strategy** A data analysis strategy in which multiple dependent measures are analyzed with a single, multivariate statistical test.

**multiway frequency analysis** A class of alternatives to ANOVA, MANOVA, or regression analysis for use when you want to measure or manipulate categorical variables.

**naturalistic observation** Observational research technique in which subjects are observed in their natural environments. The observers remain unobtrusive so that they do not interfere with the natural behaviors of the subjects being observed.

**nested design** An experimental design with a within-subjects factor in which different levels of one independent variable are included under each level of a between-subjects factor.

**nominal scale** A measurement scale that involves categorizing cases into two or more distinct categories. This scale yields the least information.

**nonequivalent control group design** A time series experiment that includes a control group that is not exposed to the experimental treatment.

**nonparametric design** Experimental research design in which levels of the independent variable are represented by different categories rather than differing amounts.

**nonparametric statistic** A statistic that makes no assumptions about the population underlying a sample.

**nonparticipant observation** An observational research technique in which the observer attends group functions and records observations without participating in the group's activities.

**nonrandom sample** A specialized sample of subjects used in a study who are not randomly chosen from a population.

**nonrefereed journal** A journal in which articles do not undergo prepublication editorial review.

**nonresponse bias** A problem associated with survey research, caused by some participants not returning a questionnaire, resulting in a biased sample.

**normal distribution** A specific type of frequency distribution in which most scores fall around the middle category. Scores become less frequent as you move from the middle category. Also referred to as a *bell-shaped curve*.

**open-ended item** Questionnaire item that allows the subject to fill in a response rather than selecting a response from provided alternatives.

**operational definition** A definition of a variable in terms of the operations used to measure it.

**ordinal scale** A measurement scale in which cases are ordered along some dimension (for example, large, medium, or small). The distances between scale values are unknown.

**outliers** Values of a variable in a set of data that lie far from the other values.

**paper session** or **presentation** A meeting at a scientific convention at which the most up-to-date research results are presented. A paper session may involve disseminating data by reading a paper or presenting a poster.

**parallel-forms reliability** Establishing the reliability of a questionnaire by administering parallel (alternate) forms of the questionnaire repeatedly.

**parametric design** An experimental design in which the amount of the independent variable is systematically varied across several levels.

**parametric statistic** A statistic that makes assumptions about the nature of an underlying population (for example, that scores are normally distributed).

**parsimonious explanation** An explanation or theory that explains a relationship using relatively few assumptions.

**part correlation (semipartial correlation)** Multivariate correlational statistic used to examine the relationship between two variables with the effects of a third variable removed from only one of them.

**partial correlation** Multivariate correlational statistic used to examine the relationship between two variables with the effect of a third variable removed from both of them.

**partially open-ended item**    Questionnaire item that provides participants with response categories but includes an "other" response category with a space for participants to define the category.

**participant observation**    An observational research technique in which a researcher insinuates him- or herself into a group to be studied.

**participants subsection**    A subsection of the method section of an APA-style manuscript used when humans are employed in a study and describing the nature of the sample.

**path analysis**    An application of multiple regression used to develop and test causal models using correlational data.

**Pearson *r* (Pearson product-moment correlation)**    The most popular measure of correlation. Indicates the magnitude and direction of a correlational relationship between variables.

**peer review**    Process of editorial review used by refereed journals. Manuscripts are usually sent out to at least two reviewers who screen the research for quality and importance.

**per-comparison error**    The alpha level for each of any multiple comparisons made among means.

**personal communication**    Information obtained privately from another researcher (for example, by letter or phone).

**phi (φ) coefficient**    Measure of correlation used when both variables can take on only two values.

**physiological measure**    A measure of a bodily function of subjects in a study (for example, heart rate).

**pie chart**    Type of graph in which a circle is divided into segments. Each segment represents the proportion or percentage of responses falling in a given category of the dependent variable.

**pilot study**    A small, scaled-down version of a study used to test the validity of experimental procedures and measures.

**plagiarism**    A serious flaw in writing that involves using another person's words or ideas without properly citing the source. See also **lazy writing.**

**planned comparisons**    Hypothesis-directed statistical tests made after finding statistical significance with an overall statistical test (such as ANOVA).

**point-biserial correlation**    A variation of the Pearson correlation used when one variable can take on only two values.

**population**    All possible individuals making up a group of interest in a study. For example, all U.S. women constitute a population. A small proportion of the population is selected for inclusion in a study (see **sample**).

**power**    The ability of an experimental design or inferential statistic to detect an effect of a variable when one is present.

**predictive validity**    The ability of a measure to predict some future behavior.

**pretest–posttest design**    A research design that involves measuring a dependent variable (pretest), then introducing the treatment, and then measuring the dependent variable a second time (posttest).

**primary source**    A reference source that contains the original, full report of a study. It includes all the details needed to replicate and interpret the study.

**procedure subsection**    The subsection of the method section of an APA-style manuscript that provides a detailed description of the procedures used in a study.

**proportionate sampling**    A variation of stratified sampling in which the proportion of subjects sampled from each stratum is matched to the proportion of subjects in each stratum in the population.

**pseudoexplanation**    An explanation proposed for a phenomenon that simply relabels the phenomenon without really explaining it.

***PsycARTICLES***    A computerized source of articles, downloadable in PDF format, that were published in the journals of the American Psychological Association.

***Psychological Abstracts***    A noncomputerized index of publications in psychological journals.

***PsycINFO***    A computerized database system that indexes journals and book chapters relevant to psychology and related fields.

***p* value**    In a statistical test, the probability, estimated from the data, that an observed difference in sample values arose through sampling error. $p$ must be less than or equal to the chosen alpha level for the difference to be statistically significant.

**Q-sort methodology**    A qualitative measurement technique that involves establishing evaluative categories and sorting items into those categories.

**qualitative data**    Data in which the values of a variable differ in kind (quality) rather than in amount.

**qualitative theory**    A theory in which terms are expressed verbally rather than mathematically.

**quantitative theory**    A theory in which terms are expressed mathematically rather than verbally.

**quasi-experimental design**    A design resembling an experimental design but using quasi-independent rather than true independent variables.

**quasi-independent variable**    A variable resembling the independent variable in an experiment, but whose levels are not assigned to subjects at random (the subject's age, for example).

**randomized two-group design**    A between-subjects design in which subjects are assigned to groups randomly.

**random sample**    A sample drawn from the population such that every member of the population has an equal opportunity to be included in the sample.

**range**    The least informative measure of spread; the difference between the lowest and highest scores in a distribution.

**range effects**    A problem in which a variable being observed reaches an upper limit (ceiling effect) or lower limit (floor effect).

**rational method**    Developing explanations through a process of deductive reasoning.

**ratio scale**    Highest scale of measurement; it has all of the characteristics of an interval scale plus an absolute zero point.

**refereed journal**    A journal whose articles have undergone prepublication editorial review by a panel of experts in the relevant field.

**reference section**    The section of an APA-style manuscript in which all citations used in the manuscript are listed alphabetically.

**regression weight**    Value computed in a linear regression analysis that provides the slope of the least squares regression line. See also **beta weight.**

**reliability**    Whether a questionnaire produces the same or similar responses with multiple administrations of the same or similar instrument.

**replication**    Repeating a study in order to determine whether its results are reproducible.

**representative sample**    A sample of subjects in which the characteristics of the population are adequately represented.

**research**    The principal method for acquiring knowledge and uncovering the causes for behavior.

**resistant measures**    Statistics that are not strongly affected by the presence of outliers or skewness in the data.

**restricted item**    Questionnaire item that provides participants with response alternatives from which the participant selects an answer.

**results section**    The section of an APA-style manuscript that contains a description of the findings of a study. The section normally reports the values of descriptive and inferential statistics obtained.

**reversal strategy**    Running a second baseline phase after the intervention phase in a single-subject, baseline design.

**role attitude cues**    Unintended cues in an experiment that suggest to the participants how they are expected to behave.

**role playing**    Alternative to deceptive research that involves having participants act as though they had been exposed to a certain treatment.

**R-square**    The square of the multiple $R$ in a multiple regression analysis. Provides a measure of the amount of variability in the dependent measure accounted for by the best linear combination of predictor variables.

**running head**    A shortened version of the title to a manuscript (no more than 50 characters) that appears on the title page.

**sample**    A relatively small number of individuals drawn from a population for inclusion in a study. See also **population.**

**sampling error**    The deviation between the characteristics of a sample and a population.

**scatterplot**   A plot used to display correlational data from two measures. Each point represents the two scores provided by each subject, one for each measure, plotted against one another.

**scientific explanation**   A tentative explanation for a phenomenon, based on objective observation and logic, and subject to empirical test.

**scientific method**   The method of inquiry preferred by scientists. It involves observing phenomena, developing hypotheses, empirically testing the hypotheses, and refining and revising hypotheses.

**scientific theory**   A theory that goes beyond simple hypothesis, deals with verifiable phenomena, and is highly ordered and structured.

**secondary source**   A reference source that summarizes information from a primary source and includes research reviews and theoretical articles.

**self-report measure**   A measure that requires participants to report on their past, present, or future behavior.

**semipartial correlation**   See **part correlation.**

**simple effects**   In a factorial analysis of variance (ANOVA), the effect of one factor at a given level (or combination of levels) of another factor (or factors).

**simple random sampling**   A sampling technique in which every member of a population has an equal chance of being selected for a sample and in which the sampling is done on a purely random basis.

**simulation**   A laboratory research technique in which you attempt to re-create as closely as possible a real-world phenomenon.

**single-blind technique**   The person testing subjects in a study is kept unaware of the hypotheses being tested.

**single-subject design**   An experimental design that focuses on the behavior of an individual subject rather than groups of subjects.

**skewed distribution**   A frequency distribution in which most scores fall into categories above or below the middle category.

**sociogram**   A graphical representation of the pattern of friendship choices.

**sociometry**   A nonexperimental research technique involving identifying and measuring interpersonal relationships within a group.

**Solomon four-group design**   An expansion of the pretest–posttest design that includes control groups to evaluate the effects of administering a pretest on your experimental treatment.

**Spearman rank order correlation (rho)**   A measure of correlation used when variables are measured on at least an ordinal scale.

**split-half reliability**   A method of assessing reliability of a questionnaire using a single administration of the instrument. The questionnaire is split into two parts, and responses from the two parts are correlated.

**stability criterion**   Criterion used to establish when a baseline in a single-subject, baseline design no longer shows any systematic trends. Once the criterion is reached, the subject is placed in the next phase of the experiment.

**standard deviation**   The most frequently reported measure of spread. The square root of the variance.

**standard error of estimate**   A measure of the accuracy of prediction in a linear regression analysis. It is a measure of the distance between the observed data points and the least squares regression line.

**standard error of the mean**   An estimate of the amount of variability in expected sample means across a series of samples. It provides an estimate of the deviation between a sample mean and the underlying population mean.

**stemplot**   A graphical display of a distribution of scores consisting of a column of values (the stems) representing the leftmost digit or digits of the scores and, aligned with each stem, a row of values representing the rightmost digit of each score having that particular stem value.

**stratified sampling**   A sampling technique designed to ensure a representative sample that involves dividing the population into segments (strata) and randomly sampling from each stratum.

**strong inference**   A strategy for testing a theory in which a sequence of research studies is systematically carried out to rule out alternative explanations for a phenomenon.

**subjects subsection**   A subsection of the method section of an APA-style manuscript in which the nature of the subject sample employed is described. This section is called *subjects* if animals were employed in a study.

**systematic replication**   Conducting a replication of an experiment while adding new variables for investigation.

**systematic sampling**   A sampling technique in which every $k$th element is sampled after a randomly determined start.

**systematic variance**   Variability in the value of the dependent variable that is caused by variation in the independent variable.

**tautology**   See **circular explanation.**

**telephone survey**   Method of conducting a survey that involves calling participants on the telephone and asking them questions from a prepared questionnaire.

**test–retest reliability**   A method of assessing the reliability of a questionnaire by administering repeatedly the same or parallel form of a test.

**theory**   A set of assumptions about the causes for behavior and the rules that specify how the causes operate. A theory is subjected to empirical test and retained, modified, or rejected.

***Thesaurus of Psychological Index Terms***   A thesaurus available in hard copy or in computerized form that is used to help narrow or broaden a search of the psychological literature.

**third-variable problem**   A problem that interferes with drawing causal inferences from correlational results. A third, unmeasured variable affects both measured variables, causing the latter to appear correlated even though neither variable influences the other.

**time series design**   A research design in which behavior of subjects in naturally occurring groups is measured periodically both before and after introduction of a treatment.

**traditional literature review**   A literature review that involves reading, summarizing, and interpreting research in a given field. See also **meta-analysis.**

**treatment**   A level of an independent variable applied during an experiment. In multifactor designs, a specific combination of the levels of each factor.

***t* test**   An inferential statistic used to evaluate the reliability of a difference between two means. Versions exist for between-subjects and within-subjects designs and for evaluating a difference between a sample mean and a population mean.

***t* test for correlated samples**   A parametric inferential statistic used to compare the means of two samples in a matched-pairs or a within-subjects design in order to assess the probability that the two samples came from populations having the same mean.

***t* test for independent samples**   A parametric inferential statistic used to compare the means of two independent, random samples in order to assess the probability that the two samples came from populations having the same mean.

**Type I error**   Deciding to reject the null hypothesis when, in fact, the null hypothesis is true. Also referred to as an *alpha error.*

**Type II error**   Deciding not to reject the null hypothesis when, in fact, the null hypothesis is false. Also referred to as a *beta error.*

**univariate strategy**   A data analysis strategy in which multiple dependent measures are analyzed independently with separate statistical tests.

**unplanned comparison**   Comparison between means that is not directed by your hypothesis and is made after finding statistical significance with an overall statistical test (such as ANOVA).

**validity**   The extent to which a measuring instrument measures what it was designed to measure.

**valid measure**   A measure that actually measures what it is intended to measure.

**variable**   Any quantity or quality that can take on a range of values.

**variance**   A measure of spread. The averaged square deviation from the mean.

**volunteer bias**   Bias in a sample that results from using volunteer participants exclusively.

**Wilcoxon signed ranks test**   A nonparametric statistical test that can be used when the assumptions of the *t* test for correlated samples are seriously violated.

**within-subjects design**   An experimental design in which each subject is exposed to all levels of an independent variable.

***z* test for the difference between two proportions**   A parametric inferential statistic used to determine the probability that two independent, random samples came from populations having the same proportion of "successes" (for example, persons favoring a particular candidate).

# REFERENCES

Abbott, B., & Badia, P. (1979). Choice for signaled over unsignaled shock as a function of signal length. *Journal of the Experimental Analysis of Behavior, 32*, 409–417.

Abrams, D. B., & Wilson, G. T. (1983). Alcohol, sexual arousal, and self-control. *Journal of Personality and Social Psychology, 45*, 188–198.

Adair, J. G. (1973). *The human subject: The social psychology of the psychological experiment.* Boston: Little, Brown.

Agresti, A., & Finlay, B. (1986). *Statistical methods for the social sciences.* San Francisco: Dullen.

Allport, G. W. (1954). Historical background of modern social psychology. In G. Lindzey (Ed.), *Handbook of social psychology* (Vol. 1, pp. 3–56). Cambridge, MA: Addison-Wesley.

Allport, G. W., & Postman, L. (1945). The basic psychology of rumor. *Transactions of the New York Academy of Sciences, 11*, 61–81.

American Psychological Association [APA]. (1973). *Ethical principles in the conduct of research with human participants.* Washington, DC: American Psychological Association.

American Psychological Association [APA]. (1992). Ethical principles of psychologists. *American Psychologist, 45*, 1597–1611.

American Psychological Association [APA]. (2001). *Publication manual FAQ.* Washington, DC: Author. Retrieved March 1, 2001, from http://www.apa.org/journals/ faq.html

American Psychological Association [APA]. (2001). *Publication manual of the American Psychological Association* (5th ed.).Washington, DC: American Psychological Association.

American Psychological Association [APA]. (2002). *Ethical principles of psychologists and code of conduct.* Retrieved April 1, 2004, from http://www.apa.org/ethics/code2002.html

Anastasi, A. (1976). Psychological testing (4th ed.). New York: Macmillan.

Anderson, C. A., & Dill, K. E. (2000). Video games and aggressive thoughts, feelings, and behavior in the laboratory and in life. *Journal of Personality and Social Psychology, 78*, 772–790.

Anderson, N. (1968). A simple model for information integration. In R. P. Abelson, E. Aronson, W. J. McGuire, T. M. Newcomb, M. J. Rosenberg, & P. Tannenbaum (Eds.), *Theories of cognitive consistency: A sourcebook* (pp. 731–743). Chicago: Rand McNally.

Applebaum, M. I., & McCall, R. B. (1983). Design and analysis in developmental psychology. In P. H. Mussen & W. Kessen (Eds.), *Handbook of child psychology: Vol. 1. History, theory, and methods* (pp. 415–476). New York: Wiley.

Arnett, B., & Rikli, R. (1981). Effects of method of subject selection and treatment variable on motor performance. *Research Quarterly for Exercise and Sport, 52*, 433–440.

Aronson, E., & Carlsmith, J. M. (1968). Experimentation in social psychology. In G. Lindzey & E. Aronson (Eds.), *Handbook of social psychology* (Vol. 1, pp. 1–79). Reading, MA: Addison-Wesley.

Asher, H. B. (1976). Causal modeling. *Sage University Paper Series on Quantitative Applications in the Social Sciences* (Series No. 07-003). Beverly Hills, CA: Sage.

Badia, P., & Abbott, B. B. (1984). Preference for signaled over unsignaled shock schedules: Ruling out asymmetry and response fixation as factors. *Journal of the Experimental Analysis of Behavior, 41,* 45–52.

Badia, P., & Culbertson, S. (1972). The relative aversiveness of signalled vs. unsignalled escapable and inescapable shock. *Journal of the Experimental Analysis of Behavior, 17,* 463–471.

Badia, P., Harsh, J., & Abbott, B. (1979). Choosing between predictable and unpredictable shock conditions: Data and theory. *Psychological Bulletin, 86,* 1107–1131.

Badia, P., & Runyon, R. P. (1982). Fundamentals of behavioral research. Reading, MA: Addison-Wesley.

Bakeman, R., & Gottman, J. M. (1989). *Observing interaction: An introduction to sequential analysis.* Cambridge, England: Cambridge University Press.

Baumrind, D. (1964). Some thoughts on the ethics of research: After reading Milgram's "Behavioral study of obedience." *American Psychologist, 26,* 887–896.

Bell, R. (1992). *Impure science: Fraud, compromise and political influence in scientific research.* New York: Wiley.

Bem, D. J. (1972). Self-perception theory. In L. Berkowitz (Ed.), *Advances in experimental social psychology* (Vol. 6, pp. 1–62). New York: Academic Press.

Bennett, S., & Bowers, D. (1976). *An introduction to multivariate techniques for social and behavioral sciences.* New York:Wiley.

Berg, B. L. (1998). *Qualitative research methods for the social sciences.* Boston: Allyn and Bacon.

Berkowitz, L. (1970). The contagion of violence: An S-R mediational analysis of some effects of observed aggression. *Nebraska Symposium on Motivation, 18,* 95–136.

Bolt, M., & Myers, D. G. (1983). *Teacher's resource and test manual to accompany* Social Psychology. New York: McGraw-Hill.

Bordens, K. S. (1984). The effects of likelihood of conviction, threatened punishment, and assumed role on mock plea bargain decisions. *Basic and Applied Social Psychology, 5,* 59–74.

Bordens, K. S., & Horowitz, I. A. (1986). Prejudicial joinder of multiple offenses: The relative effects of cognitive processing and criminal schemata. *Basic and Applied Social Psychology, 7,* 243–258.

Braithwaite, R. B. (1953). *Scientific explanation.* New York: Harper & Row.

Bray, J. H., & Maxwell, S. E. (1982). Analyzing and interpreting significant MANOVAs. *Review of Educational Research, 52,* 340–367.

Broad, W., & Wade, N. (1983). *Betrayers of the truth.* New York: Simon & Schuster.

Broca, P. P. (1861). Loss of speech, chronic softening and partial destruction of the anterior left lobe of the brain. Retrieved May 20, 2004, from http://psychclassics.yorku.ca/Broca/perte-e.htm

Brody, J. L., Gluck, J. P., & Aragon, A. S. (2000). Participants' understanding of the process of psychological research: Debriefing. *Ethics and Behavior, 10,* 13–25.

Brown, R. (1965). *Social psychology.* New York: Free Press.

Brown, S. R. (1996). Q methodology and qualitative research. *Qualitative Health Research, 6,* 561–567. Retrieved on December 17, 2003, from http://www.rz.unibw-muenchen.de/~p41bsmk/qmethod/srbqhc.htm

Bruning, J. L., & Kintz, B. L. (1987). *Computational handbook of statistics* (3rd ed.). Glenview, IL: Scott, Foresman.

Butler, B. E., & Petrulis, J. (1999). Some further observations concerning Cyril Burt. *British Journal of Psychology, 90,* 155–160.

Camarata, S. (1993). The application of naturalistic conversation training to speech production in children with speech disorders. *Journal of Applied Behavior Analysis, 26,* 173–182.

Campbell, D. T. (1969). Prospective: Artifact and control. In R. Rosenthal and R. L. Rosnow (Eds.), *Artifact in behavioral research* (pp. 351–382). New York: Academic Press.

Campbell, D. T., & Stanley, J. C. (1963). *Experimental and quasi-experimental designs for research.* Chicago: Rand McNally.

CDC (2000). HIV/AIDS among US women: Minority and young women at continuing risk. Retrieved May 20, 2004, from http://www.cdc.gov/hiv/pubs/facts/women.htm

Ceci, S. J., Bruck, M., & Loftus, E. F. (1998). On the ethics of memory implantation research. *Applied Cognitive Psychology, 12,* 230–240.

Chang, D. F., & Sue, S. (2003). The effects of race and problem type on teachers' assessments of student behavior. *Journal of Consulting and Clinical Psychology, 71,* 235–242.

Chassan, J. B. (1967). *Research design in clinical psychology and psychiatry.* New York: Appleton-Century-Crofts.

Chomsky, N. (1965). *Aspects of a theory of syntax.* Cambridge, MA: MIT Press.

Church, A. H. (1993). Estimating the effects of incentives on mail survey return rates: A meta-analysis. *Public Opinion Quarterly, 57,* 62–79.

Cialdini, R. B. (1994). A full-cycle approach to social psychology. In G. G. Brannigan & M. R. Merrens (Eds.), *The social psychologists: Research adventures* (pp. 52–72). New York: McGraw-Hill.

Cohen, J. (1988). *Statistical power analysis for the behavioral sciences* (2nd ed.). Hillsdale, NJ: Erlbaum.

Cohen, R. J., & Swerdlik, M. E. (2002). *Psychological testing and assessment: An introduction to tests and measures* (5th Ed.). Boston: McGraw-Hill.

Conrad, E., & Maul, T. (1981). *Introduction to experimental psychology.* New York: Wiley.

Cooper, H. M., & Rosenthal, R. (1980). Statistical versus traditional methods for summarizing research findings. *Psychological Bulletin, 87,* 442–449.

Cooperman, E. (1980). Voluntary subjects' participation in research: Cognitive style as a possible biasing factor. *Perceptual and Motor Skills, 50,* 542.

Cornell University Library. (2000). *Distinguishing scholarly journals from other periodicals.* Retrieved October 16, 2000, from http://www.library.cornell.edu/okuref/research/skill20.html#scholarly

Crano, W. D., & Brewer, M. B. (1986). *Principles and methods of social research.* Boston: Allyn and Bacon.

Crews, F. (1980). *The Random House handbook* (3rd ed.). New York: Random House.

Davis, A. J. (1984). Sex-differentiated bias in nonsexist picture books. *Sex Roles: A Journal of Research, 11,* 1–16.

DeFleur, M. J., & DeFleur, M. L. (2002). The next generation's image of Americans: Attitudes and beliefs held by teen-agers in twelve countries, a preliminary report. Retrieved August 12, 2003, from http://www.bu.edu/news/releases/2002/defleur/report.pdf

Dewsbury, D. A. (1978). *Comparative animal behavior.* New York: McGraw-Hill.

Dillman, D. A. (1978). *Mail and telephone surveys: The total design method.* New York: Wiley.

Dillman, D. A. (2000). *Mail and Internet surveys: The tailored design method* (2nd ed.). New York: Wiley.

Ebbinghaus, H. E. (1964). *Memory: A contribution to experimental psychology.* New York: Dover. (Original work published 1885)

Edwards, A. L. (1953). *Techniques of attitude scale construction.* New York: Appleton-Century-Crofts.

Edwards, A. L. (1985). *Experimental design in psychological research* (5th ed.). New York: Harper & Row.

Ellis, C. (1993). "There are survivors": Telling a story of sudden death. *Sociological Quarterly, 34,* 711–730.

Epley, N., & Huff, C. (1998). Suspicion, affective response, and educational benefit as a result of deception in psychology research. *Personality and Social Psychology Bulletin, 24,* 759–768.

Fancher, R. E. (1979). *Pioneers of psychology.* New York: Norton.

Fancher, R. E. (1985). *The intelligence men: Makers of the IQ controversy.* New York: Norton.

Feild, H. S., & Barnett, N. J. (1978). Students vs. "real" people as jurors. *Journal of Social Psychology, 104,* 287–293.

Festinger, L. (1957). *A theory of cognitive dissonance.* Stanford, CA: Stanford University Press.

Fiedler, F. E., Bell, C. H., Chemers, M. M., & Patrick, D. (1984). Increasing mine productivity and safety through management training and organization development: A comparative study. *Basic and Applied Social Psychology, 5,* 1–18.

Fischer, H., Anderson, J. L. R., Furmark, T., Wik, G., & Fredrikson, M. (2002). Right-sided human prefrontal brain activation during acquisition of conditioned fear. *Emotion,* 233–241.

Fishbein, M., & Ajzen, I. (1975). *Belief, attitude, intention and behavior: An introduction to theory and research.* Reading, MA: Addison-Wesley.

Fiske, D. W., & Fogg, L. (1990). But the reviewers are making different criticisms of my paper! *American Psychologist, 45,* 591–598.

Florian, V., Mikalmcez, M., & Harschberger, H. (2002). The anxiety-buffering function of close relationships: Evidence that relationship commitment acts as a terror management mechanism. *Journal of Personality and Social Psychology, 82,* 527–542.

Forscher, B. K. (1963). Chaos in the brickyard. *Science, 42,* 339.

Freedman, J. L. (1969). Role playing: Psychology by consensus. *Journal of Personality and Social Psychology, 13,* 107–114.

Friedman, T. L. (2001). *Longitudes and attitudes: Exploring the world after September 11.* New York: Farrar, Straus and Giroux.

Friedrich, L. K., & Stein, A. H. (1973). Aggressive and prosocial television programs and the natural behavior of preschool children. *Monographs for the Society for Research on Child Development, 38.*

Fry, D. P. (1992). "Respect for the rights of others is peace": Learning aggression versus nonaggression among the Zapotec. *American Anthropologist, 94,* 621–639.

Gamson, W. A., Fireman, B., & Rytina, S. (1982). *Encounters with unjust authority.* Homewood, IL: Dorsey Press.

Garcia, J., & Koelling, R. A. (1966). Relation of cue to consequences in avoidance learning. *Psychonomic Science, 4,* 123–124.

Gibbon, J. (1977). Scalar expectancy theory and Weber's law in animal timing. *Psychological Review, 84,* 279–325.

Glass, D. C., Singer, J. E., & Friedman, L. N. (1969). Psychic cost of adaptation to an environmental stressor. *Journal of Personality and Social Psychology, 12,* 200–210.

Glass, G. V. (1978). In defense of generalization. *The Behavioral and Brain Sciences, 1*(3), 394–395.

Gold, P. E. (1987). Sweet memories. *American Scientist, 75,* 151–155.

Goldiamond, I. (1965). Stuttering and fluency as manipulable operant response classes. In L. Krasner & L. P. Ullman (Eds.), *Research in behavior modification* (pp. 106–156). New York: Holt, Rinehart & Winston.

Goldstein, J. H., Rosnow, R. L., Goodstadt, B. E., & Suls, J. E. (1972). The good subject in verbal operant conditioning research. *Journal of Experimental Research in Personality, 28,* 29–33.

Gravetter, F. J., & Wallnau, L. B. (2004). *Statistics for the behavioral sciences* (6th ed.). Belmont, CA: Wadsworth.

Greenberg, B. S. (1980). *Life on television: Current analyses of U.S. TV drama.* Norwood, NJ: Ablex.

Greene, E., & Loftus, E. F. (1984). What's in the news? The influence of well-publicized news events on psychological research and courtroom trials. *Basic and Applied Social Psychology, 5,* 211–221.

Grice, G. R. (1966). Dependence of empirical laws upon the source of experimental variation. *Psychological Bulletin, 66,* 488–498.

Hall, D. (1979). *Writing well.* Boston: Little, Brown.

Hall, R. V., Lund, D., & Jackson, D. (1968). Effects of teacher attention on study behavior. *Journal of Applied Behavior Analysis, 1,* 1–12.

Haney, C., Banks, C., & Zimbardo, P. (1973). Interpersonal dynamics in a simulated prison. *International Journal of Criminology and Penology, 1,* 69–87.

Harari, H., Harari, O., & White, R. V. (1985). The reaction to rape by American male bystanders. *Journal of Social Psychology, 125,* 653.

Helmstetter, F. J., & Fanselow, M. S. (1987). Strain differences in reversal of conditional analgesia by opioid antagonists. *Behavioral Neuroscience, 101,* 735–737.

Hempel, C. G. (1966). *Philosophy of natural science.* Englewood Cliffs, NJ: Prentice Hall.

Herrmann, D., & Yoder, C. (1998). The potential effects of the implanted memory paradigm on child subjects. *Applied Cognitive Psychology, 12,* 198–206.

Hess, D. W., Marwitz, J., & Kreutzer, J. (2003). Neuropsychological impairments in SCI . *Rehabilitation Psychology, 48*(3).

Higbee, K. L., Millard, R. J., & Folkman, J. R. (1982). Social psychology research during the 1970s: Predominance of experimentation on college students. *Personality and Social Psychology Bulletin, 8,* 182–183.

Hite, S. (1976). *The Hite report: A nationwide study on female sexuality.* New York: Macmillan.

Hite, S. (1983). *The Hite report on male sexuality*. New York: Ballantine Books.

Holmes, D. S. (1976a). Debriefing after psychological experiments I: Effectiveness of postdeception dehoaxing. *American Psychologist, 31,* 858–867.

Holmes, D. S. (1976b). Debriefing after psychological experiments II: Effectiveness of postdeception desensitizing. *American Psychologist, 31,* 868–875.

Holsti, O. R. (1969). *Content analysis for the social sciences and humanities.* Reading, MA: Addison-Wesley.

Hooke, R. (1983). *How to tell the liars from the statisticians.* New York: Dekker.

Horowitz, I. A. (1969). The effects of volunteering, fear arousal, and number of communications on attitude change. *Journal of Personality and Social Psychology, 11,* 34–37.

Horowitz, I. A. (1985). The effects of jury nullification instructions on verdicts and jury functioning in criminal trials. *Law and Human Behavior, 9,* 25–36.

Horowitz, I. A., & Bordens, K. S. (1988). The effects of outlier presence, plaintiff population size, and aggregation of plaintiffs on simulated jury decisions. *Law and Human Behavior, 13,* 209–229.

Horowitz, I. A., & Bordens, K. S. (2001). *The effects of jury size, evidence complexity, and note-taking on jury process and performance in a civil trial.* Unpublished manuscript, Oregon State University.

Horowitz, I. A., Bordens, K. S., & Feldman, M. S. (1980). A comparison of verdicts obtained in severed and joined criminal trials. *Journal of Applied Social Psychology, 10,* 444–456.

Horowitz, I. A., & Rothschild, B. H. (1970). Conformity as a function of deception and role playing. *Journal of Personality and Social Psychology, 14,* 224–226.

Huck, S. W., & Sandler, H. M. (1979). *Rival hypotheses: Alternative explanations of data based conclusions.* New York: Harper & Row.

Hunter, J. E. (1987). Multiple dependent variables in program evaluation. In M. M. Mark & R. L. Shotland (Eds.), *Multiple methods.* San Francisco: Jossey-Bass.

Hunter, J. E., & Gerbing, D. W. (1982). Unidimensional measurement, second-order factor analysis and causal models. *Research in Organizational Behavior, 4,* 267–320.

Institute for Scientific Information. (1988). SSCI journal citation reports: A bibliometric analysis of social science journals in the ISI data base. *Social Sciences Citation Index, 6.*

James, J. M., & Bolstein, R. (1990). The effect of monetary incentives and follow-up mailings on the response rate and response quality in mail surveys. *Public Opinion Quarterly, 54,* 346–361.

Janis, I., & Mann, L. (1965). Effectiveness of emotional role playing in modifying smoking habits and attitudes. *Journal of Experimental Research in Personality, 1,* 84–90.

Joynson, R. B. (1989). *The Burt affair.* London: Routledge.

Kalichman, M., & Friedman, P. (1992). A pilot study of biomedical trainees perceptions concerning research ethics. *Academic Medicine, 67,* 769–775.

Kanuk, L., & Berenson, C. (1975). Mail surveys and response rates: A literature review. *Journal of Marketing Research, 12,* 440–453.

Katz, J. (1972). Experimentation with human beings. New York: Russell Sage Foundation.

Kazdin, A. E. (1976). Statistical analyses for single-case experimental designs. In M. Hersen & D. H. Barlow (Eds.), *Single-case experimental designs: Strategies for studying behavior change* (pp. 265–316). New York: Pergamon Press.

Kelly, G. (1963). *A theory of personality: The psychology of personal constructs.* New York: Norton.

Kelman, H. C. (1967). The use of human subjects: The problem of deception in social psychological experiments. *Psychological Bulletin, 67,* 1–11.

Keppel, G. (1973). *Design and analysis: A researcher's handbook.* Englewood Cliffs, NJ: Prentice Hall.

Keppel, G. (1982). *Design and analysis: A researcher's handbook* (2nd ed.). Englewood Cliffs, NJ: Prentice Hall.

Key, W. B. (1973). *Subliminal seduction.* New York: Signet.

Kish, L. (1965). *Survey sampling.* New York: Wiley.

Krantz, J. H., & Dalal, R. (2000). Validity of Web-based research. In M. H. Birnbaum

(Ed.). *Psychological experiments on the Internet* (pp. 35–57). San Diego, CA: Academic Press.

**Kuhn, T. S. (1970).** *The structure of scientific revolutions* (2nd ed.). Chicago: University of Chicago Press.

**Kunda, Z. (1990).** The case for motivated reasoning. *Psychological Bulletin, 108,* 480–498.

**Landy, E., & Aronson, E. (1969).** The influence of the character of the criminal and his victim on the decisions of simulated jurors. *Journal of Experimental Social Psychology, 5,* 141–152.

**Latané, B. (1981).** The psychology of social impact. *American Psychologist, 36,* 343–356.

**Leaton, R. N., & Borszcz, G. S. (1985).** Potentiated startle: Its relation to freezing and shock intensity in rats. *Journal of Experimental Psychology: Animal Behavior Processes, 11,* 421–428.

**Leggett, G., Mead, C. D., & Charvat, W. (1978).** *Prentice Hall handbook for writers* (7th ed.). Englewood Cliffs, NJ: Prentice Hall.

**Levine, M. S. (1977).** Canonical analysis and factor comparison. *Sage University Paper Series on Quantitative Applications in the Social Sciences* (Series No. 07-006). Beverly Hills, CA: Sage.

**Lindsey, D. (1978).** *The scientific publication system in social science.* San Francisco: Jossey-Bass.

**Loftus, E. F. (1979).** *Eyewitness testimony.* Cambridge, MA: Harvard University Press.

**Longino, H. E. (1990).** *Science as social knowledge.* Princeton, NJ: Princeton University Press.

**Lord, F. M. (1953).** On the statistical treatment of football numbers. *American Psychologist, 8,* 750–751.

**Lorenz, K. (1950).** The comparative method in studying innate behavior patterns. *Symposium of the Society for Experimental Biology, 4,* 221–268.

**Lorge, I. (1930).** Influence of regularly interpolated time intervals on subsequent learning. *College Contributions to Education, 438,* 1–57.

**Macaulay, D. (1979).** *Motel of the mysteries.* Boston: Houghton Mifflin.

**Mahalik, J. R., Locke, B. D., Ludlow, L. H., Diemer, M. A., Scott, R. P. J., Gottfried, M., & Freitas, G. (2003).** Development of the conformity to masculine norms inventory. *Psychology of Men and Masculinity, 4,* 3–25.

**Mahoney, M. J. (1977).** Publication prejudices: An experimental study of confirmatory bias in the peer review system. *Cognitive Therapy and Research, 1,* 161–175.

**Martin, E. (1985).** *Doing psychology experiments* (2nd ed.). Monterey, CA: Brooks/Cole.

**Mayo, C., & LaFrance, M. (1977).** *Evaluating research in social psychology.* Monterey, CA: Brooks/Cole.

**McFarland, S. (1981).** Effects of question order on survey responses. *Public Opinion Quarterly, 48,* 208–215.

**McGraw, K. O., & Wong, S. P. (1996).** Forming inferences about some intraclass correlation coefficients. *Psychological Methods, 1,* 30–46.

**McNemar, Q. (1946).** Opinion-attitude methodology. *Psychological Bulletin, 43,* 289–374.

**Michael, R. T., Gagnon, J. H., Laumann, E. O., & Kolata, G. (1994).** *Sex in America: A definitive survey.* Boston: Little, Brown.

**Milgram, S. (1963).** Behavioral study of obedience. *Journal of Abnormal and Social Psychology, 67,* 371–378.

**Milgram, S. (1974).** *Obedience to authority.* New York: Harper & Row.

**Milton, R. C. (1964).** Extended tables for the Mann–Whitney (Wilcoxon) two-sample test. *Journal of the American Statistical Association, 59,* 925–934.

**Mitchell, S. K. (1979).** Interobserver agreement, reliability, and generalizability of data collected in observational studies. *Psychological Bulletin, 86,* 376–390.

**Montee, B. B., Miltenberger, R. G., & Wittrock, D. (1995).** An experimental analysis of facilitated communication. *Journal of Applied Behavior Analysis, 28,* 189–200.

**Mook, D. G. (1983).** In defense of external validity. *American Psychologist, 38,* 379–387.

**Moore, D. S., & McCabe, G. P. (2003).** *Introduction to the practice of statistics* (4th ed.). New York: Freeman.

**Moser, C. A., & Kalton, G. (1972).** *Survey methods in social investigation.* New York: Basic Books.

**Mosteller, F., & Tukey, J. W. (1977).** *Data analysis and regression.* New York: Addison-Wesley.

Myers, D. G. (1999). *Social psychology* (6th ed.). New York: McGraw-Hill.

National Research Council. (1996). *Guide for the care and use of laboratory animals.* Washington, DC: National Academy Press.

Neisser, U. (1976). *Cognition and reality: Principles and implications for cognitive psychology.* San Francisco: Freeman.

Nerb, J., & Spada, H. (2001). Evaluation of environmental problems: A coherence model of cognition and emotion. *Cognition and Emotion, 15,* 521–551.

Nunnally, J. C. (1967). *Psychometric theory.* New York: McGraw-Hill.

O'Brien, R. G., & Kaiser, M. K. (1985). MANOVA method for analyzing repeated measures designs: An extensive primer. *Psychological Bulletin, 97,* 316–333.

Ogloff, J. R. P., & Vidmar, N. (1994). The impact of pretrial publicity on jurors: A study to compare the relative effects of television and print media in a child sex abuse case. *Law and Human Behavior, 18,* 507–525.

Orne, M. T. (1962). On the social psychology of the psychological experiment with particular reference to demand characteristics and their implications. *American Psychologist, 17,* 776–783.

Ornstein, P. A., & Gordon, B. N. (1998). Risk versus rewards of applied research with children: Comments on "The potential effects of the implanted memory paradigm on child participants" by Douglas Herrmann and Carol Yoder. *Applied Cognitive Psychology, 12,* 241–244.

Pagano, R. R. (2004). *Understanding statistics in the behavioral sciences* (7th ed.). Belmont, CA: Wadsworth.

Palya, W. L., Walter, D., Kessel, R., & Lucke, R. (1996). Investigating behavioral dynamics with a fixed-time extinction schedule and linear analysis. *Journal of the Experimental Analysis of Behavior, 66,* 391–409.

Pearson, E. S., & Hartley, H. O. (Eds.). (1966). *Biometrika: Tables for statisticians* (Vol. 1, 3rd ed.). London: Cambridge University Press.

Peplau, L. A., & Conrad, E. (1989). Beyond nonsexist research: The perils of feminist methods in psychology. *Psychology of Women Quarterly, 13,* 379–400.

Peters, D. P., & Ceci, S. J. (1982). Peer-review practices of psychological journals: The fate of published articles submitted again. *The Behavioral and Brain Sciences, 5,* 187–255.

Peterson, L. R., & Peterson, M. J. (1959). Short-term retention of individual verbal items. *Journal of Experimental Psychology, 58,* 193–198.

Piaget, J. (1952). *The origins of intelligence in children.* New York: Norton.

Platt, J. R. (1964). Strong inference. *Science, 146,* 347–353.

Plous, S. (1996). Attitudes toward the use of animals in psychological research and education: Results from a national survey of psychologists. *American Psychologist, 51,* 1167–1180.

Plous, S. (1998). Signs of change within the animal rights movement: Results from a follow-up survey of activists. *Journal of Comparative Psychology, 112,* 48–54.

Powers, W. T. (1978). Quantitative analysis of purposive systems: Some spadework at the foundations of scientific psychology. *Psychological Review, 85,* 417–435.

Prato-Previde, E., Custance, D. M, Spiezio, C., & Sabatini, F. (2003). Is the dog–human relationship an attachment bond? An observational study using Ainsworth's strange situation. *Behavior, 140,* 225–254.

Rescorla, R. A., & Wagner, A. R. (1972). A theory of Pavlovian conditioning: Variations in the effectiveness of reinforcement and nonreinforcement. In A. H. Black & W. F. Prokosy (Eds.), *Classical conditioning II: Current research and theory* (pp. 64–99). New York: Appleton-Century-Crofts.

Resnick, J. H., & Schwartz, T. (1973). Ethical standards as an independent variable in psychological research. *American Psychologist, 28,* 134–139.

Reynolds, G. S. (1961). Attention in the pigeon. *Journal of the Experimental Analysis of Behavior, 4,* 203–208.

Rhodes, J. C., Kjerulff, K. H., Langenberg, P. W., & Guzinski, G. M. (1999). Hysterectomy and sexual functioning. *Journal of the American Medical Association, 282,* 1934–1941.

Riva, G., Teruzzi, T., & Anolli, L. (2003). The use of the Internet in psychological research: Comparison of online and offline questionnaires. *CyberPsychology and Behavior*, 6, 73–80.

Roberts, J. V. (1985). The attitude–memory relationship after 40 years: A meta-analysis of the literature. *Basic and Applied Social Psychology*, 6, 221–242.

Rogers, T. B. (1995). *The psychological testing enterprise: An introduction*. Pacific Grove, CA: Brooks/Cole.

Roscoe, J. T. (1975). *Fundamental statistics for the behavioral sciences* (2nd ed.). New York: Holt, Rinehart & Winston.

Rosenthal, R. (1976). *Experimenter effects in behavioral research* (Enlarged ed.). New York: Irvington.

Rosenthal, R. (1979). The "file drawer problem" and tolerance for null results. *Psychological Bulletin*, 86, 638–641.

Rosenthal, R. (1984). Meta-analytic procedures for social research. *Applied Social Research Methods* (Vol. 6). Beverly Hills, CA: Sage.

Rosenthal, R., & Rosnow, R. L. (1975). *The volunteer subject*. New York: Wiley.

Rosnow, R. L., & Rosnow, M. (1986). *Writing psychology papers*. Monterey, CA: Brooks/Cole.

Ross, L., Lepper, M. R., & Hubbard, M. (1975). Perseverance in self-perception and social perception: Biased attributional processes in debriefing paradigms. *Journal of Personality and Social Psychology*, 32, 880–892.

Sagar, H. A., & Schofield, J. W. (1980). Racial and behavioral cues in black and white children's perceptions of ambiguously aggressive acts. *Journal of Personality and Social Psychology*, 19, 590–598.

Saini, J., Kuczynski, E., Gretz, H. F., III, & Sills, E. S. (2002). Supracervical hysterectomy versus total abdominal hysterectomy: Perceived effects on sexual function. *BMC Womens Health*, 1. Retrieved November 1, 2003, from http://www.pubmedcentral.nih.gov/articlerender.fcgi?artid=65528

Saunders, D. R. (1980). Definition of Stroop interference in volunteers and non-volunteers. *Perceptual and Motor Skills*, 51, 343–354.

Schachter, S. (1971). *Emotion, obesity, and crime*. New York: Academic Press.

Schaie, K. W. (1965). A general model for the study of developmental problems. *Psychological Bulletin*, 64, 92–107.

Schmitt, B. H., Dube, L., & Leclerc, F. (1992). Intrusions into waiting lines: Does the queue constitute a social system? *Journal of Personality and Social Psychology*, 63, 806–815.

Schouten, J. W., & McAlexander, J. H. (1995). Subcultures of consumption: An ethnography of the new bikers. *Journal of Consumer Research*, 22, 43–61.

Schuler, H. (1982). *Ethical problems in psychological research*. New York: Academic Press.

Seligman, M. E. P. (1970). On the generality of the laws of learning. *Psychological Review*, 77, 406–418.

Seligman, M. E. P., & Hager, J. L. (1972). *Biological boundaries of learning*. New York: Appleton-Century-Crofts.

Shaffer, D. (1985). *Developmental psychology: Theory, research, and applications*. Monterey, CA: Brooks/Cole.

Sheridan, C. E. (1979). *Methods of experimental psychology*. New York: Holt, Rinehart & Winston.

Shrout, P. E., & Fleiss, J. L. (1979). Intraclass correlations: Uses in assessing rater reliability. *Psychological Bulletin*, 86, 420–428.

Sidman, M. (1953). Two temporal parameters of the maintenance of avoidance behavior by the white rat. *Journal of Comparative and Physiological Psychology*, 46, 253–261.

Sidman, M. (1960). *Tactics of scientific research: Evaluating experimental data in psychology*. New York: Basic Books.

Sieber, J. E., Iannuzzo, R., & Rodriguez, B. (1995). Deception methods in psychology: Have they changed in 23 years? *Ethics & Behavior*, 5, 67–85.

Siegel, S., & Castellan, N. J. (1988). *Nonparametric statistics for the behavioral sciences* (2nd ed.). New York: McGraw-Hill.

Sigelman, L. (1981). Question order effects on presidential popularity. *Public Opinion Quarterly*, 45, 199–207.

Silverman, I., Shulman, A. D., & Weisenthal, D. L. (1970). Effects of deceiving and debriefing psychological subjects on performance in later experiments. *Journal of Personality and Social Psychology, 14,* 203–212.

Singer, P. (1975). *Animal liberation: A new ethics for our treatment of animals.* New York: Avon Books.

Singer, P. (1990). *Animal liberation* (Rev. ed.) New York: Avon Books.

Skinner, B. F. (1949). Are theories of learning necessary? *Psychological Review, 57,* 193–216.

Slovic, P., & Fischoff, B. (1977). On the psychology of experimental surprise. *Journal of Experimental Psychology: Human Perception and Performance, 3,* 544–551.

Smith, S. L., Lachlan, K., & Tabmorini, R. (2003). Popular video games: Quanitifying the presentation of violence and its context. *Journal of Broadcast & Electronic Media, 47,* 58–76.

Smith, S. S., & Richardson, D. (1983). Amelioration of deception and harm in psychological research: The important role of debriefing. *Journal of Personality and Social Psychology, 44,* 1075–1082.

Smith, T. E., Sells, S. P., & Clevenger, T. (1994). Ethnographic content analysis of couple and therapist perceptions in a reflecting team setting. *Journal of Marital and Family Therapy, 20,* 267–286.

Snowdon, C. T. (1983). Ethology, comparative psychology, and animal behavior. *Annual Review of Psychology, 34,* 63–94.

Solomon, S., Greenberg, J., & Pyszczynski, T. (1991). A terror management theory of social behavior: The psychological functions of self-esteem and cultural worldviews. In L. Berkowitz (Ed.), *Advances in experimental social psychology* (Vol. 24, pp. 93–159). New York: Academic Press.

Stanovich, K. E. (1986). *How to think straight about psychology.* Glenview, IL: Scott Foresman.

Steinberg, J. A. (2002). Misconduct of others: Prevention techniques for researchers. *American Psychological Society Observer.* Retrieved March 31, 2004, from http://www.psychological science.org/observer/0102/misconduct.html

Stevens, S. S. (1946). On the theory of scales of measurement. *Science, 103,* 677–680.

Stevenson, M. R. (1995). Is this the definitive sex survey? *Journal of Sex Research, 32,* 77–91.

Strunk, W., & White, E. B. (1979). *The elements of style* (3rd ed.). New York: Macmillan.

Tabachnick, B. G., & Fidell, L. S. (2001). *Using multivariate statistics* (4th ed.). Boston: Allyn and Bacon.

Tanford, S. L. (1984). *Decision making processes in joined criminal trials.* Unpublished doctoral dissertation, University of Wisconsin, Madison.

Tanner, W. P., Jr., Swets, J. A., & Green, D. M. (1956). *Some general properties of the hearing mechanism* (Tech. Rep. No. 30). Ann Arbor: University of Michigan, Electronic Defense Group.

Tatsuoka, M. M. (1971). *Multivariate analysis: Techniques for educational and psychological research.* New York: Wiley.

Taylor, S. E. (1989). *Positive illusions: Creative self-deception and the healthy mind.* New York: Basic Books.

Thompson, S. C., Kyle, D., Swan, J., Thomas, C., & Vrungos, S. (2002). Increasing condom use by undermining perceived invulnerability to HIV. *AIDS Education and Prevention, 14,* 505–514.

Thorndike, R. M. (1978). *Correlational procedures for research.* New York: Gardner Press.

Timmerman, T. A. (2002). Violence and race in professional baseball. *Aggressive Behavior, 28,* 109–116.

Tinbergen, N. (1951). *The study of instinct.* Oxford: Clarendon Press.

Treadway, M., & McCloskey, M. (1987). Cite unseen: Distortions of Allport and Postman's rumor study in the eyewitness testimony literature. *Law and Human Behavior, 11,* 19–26.

Trujillo, N. (1993). Interpreting November 22: A critical ethnography of an assassination site. *Quarterly Journal of Speech, 79,* 447–466.

Tucker, W. H. (1997). Re-reconsidering Burt: Beyond a reasonable doubt. *Journal of the History of the Behavioral Sciences, 33,* 145–162.

Tukey, J. W. (1977). *Exploratory data analysis.* Reading, MA: Addison-Wesley.

Ullman, D., & Jackson, T. (1982). Researchers' ethical concerns: Debriefing from 1960–1980. *American Psychologist, 37,* 972–973.

Unger, R. K. (1983). Through the looking glass: No wonderland yet. *Psychology of Women Quarterly, 8,* 9–32.

Unger, R., & Crawford, M. (1992). *Women and gender: A feminist psychology.* New York: McGraw-Hill.

U.S. Department of Health and Human Services (1991). *Code of Federal Regulations, Title 45, public welfare, Part 46, protection of human subjects.* Retrieved February 2, 2001, from http://ohrp.osophs.dhhs.gov/humansubjects/guidance/45cfr46.htm

U.S. Department of Health and Human Services. (1991). *Protection of human subjects* (HHS Document 4, 108:45, Pt. 46). Washington, DC: Author.

U. S. Department of Labor: Bureau of Labor Statistics (1999). *Issues in labor statistics: Computer ownership up sharply in the 1990s.* Retrieved November 5, 2003, from http://www.bls.gov/opub/ils/pdf/opbils31.pdf

U. S. Office of Research Integrity (2003). Handling misconduct: Whistleblowers. Retrieved May 20, 2004, from http://ori.dhhs.gov/html/misconduct/ whistleblowers.asp

Vandell, D. L., & Hembree, S. E. (1994). Peer social status and friendship: Independent contributors to children's social and academic adjustment. *Merrill-Palmer Quarterly, 40,* 461–477.

Velleman, P. F., & Wilkinson, L. (1993). Nominal, ordinal, interval, and ratio typologies are misleading. *American Statistician, 47,* 65–72.

Vinacke, W. E. (1954). Deceiving experimental subjects. *American Psychologist, 9,* 155.

Vogel, D., & Wester, S. (2003). To seek help, or not to seek help: The risks of self-disclosure. *Journal of Counseling Psychology, 50,* 351–361.

Wadsworth, B. J. (1971). *Piaget's theory of cognitive development.* New York: McKay.

Walster, E., Berscheid, E., Abrahams, D. B., & Aronson, E. (1967). Effectiveness of debriefing after deception experiments. *Journal of Personality and Social Psychology, 6,* 371–380.

Walster, E., Walster, G. W., & Berscheid, E. (1978). *Equity theory and research.* Boston: Allyn and Bacon.

Warner, J. L., Berman, J. J., Weyant, J. M., & Ciarlo, J. A. (1983). Assessing mental health program effectiveness: A comparison of three client follow-up methods. *Evaluation Review, 7,* 635–658.

Weinfurt, K. P., & Bush, P. J. (1995). Peer assessment of early adolescents solicited to participate in drug trafficking: A longitudinal analysis. *Journal of Applied Social Psychology, 25,* 2141–2157.

Williams, C. D. (1959). The elimination of tantrum behavior by extinction procedures. *Journal of Abnormal and Social Psychology, 59,* 269.

Wilson, D. W., & Donnerstein, E. (1977). Guilty or not guilty? A look at the simulated jury paradigm. *Journal of Applied Social Psychology, 7,* 175–190.

Winer, B. J. (1971). *Statistical principles in experimental design* (2nd ed.). New York: McGraw-Hill.

Winkel, G. H., & Sasanoff, R. (1970). An approach to objective analysis of behavior in architectural space. In H. M. Proshansky, W. H. Ittelson, & L. G. Rivlin (Eds.), *Environmental psychology: Man and his environment* (pp. 619–630). New York: Holt, Rinehart & Winston.

Wong, D., and Baker, C. (1988). Pain in children: Comparison of assessment scales. *Pediatric Nursing, 14,* 9–17.

Wood, C. (1979). The I-knew-it-all-along effect. *Journal of Experimental Psychology: Human Perception and Performance, 43,* 345–353.

Wozniak, R. H. (1999). Oskar Pfungst: *Clever Hans (The horse of Mr. von Osten)* (1907; English 1911). Retrieved May 20, 2004, from http://www.thoemmes.com/psych/pfungst.htm

Yaremko, R. M., Harari, H., Harrison, R. C., & Lynn, E. (1982). *Reference handbook of research and statistical methods.* New York: Harper & Row.

# CREDITS

**Page 45**   Fig. 2-2 reprinted with permission from J. Lorenz, "The Comparative Method in Studying Innate Behavior Patterns," *Symposium of the Society for Experimental Biology*, 4; adapted from Fig. 2.4 in D. A. Dewsbury, *Comparative Animal Behavior*. Copyright © 1950, 1978 by Cambridge University Press and McGraw-Hill Company respectively.

**Page 72**   Fig. 3-2 reprinted with permission of the American Psychological Association, publisher of the PsycINFO and PsycARTICLES databases. Copyright © 1999–2004 by the American Psychological Association. All rights reserved. For more information, contact *psycinfo@apa.org*.

**Page 103**   Fig. 4-2 reprinted with permission from Tinbergen, N. (1948). "Dierkundles in het meeuwenduin." *Der Levende Natuur*, 51, 49–56.

**Page 138**   Fig. 5-2 reprinted with permission from D. Wong and C. Baker, "Pain in Children: Comparison of Assessment Scales," *Pediatric Nursing*, 14, 9–17. Copyright © 1988 by Pediatric Nursing.

**Page 188**   Fig. 6-5 reprinted from C. D. Williams, "The Elimination of Tantrum Behavior by Extinction Procedures," *Journal of Abnormal and Social Psychology*, 59, 269. Copyright © 1959 by the American Psychological Association. Reprinted with permission of the author.

**Page 267**   Fig. 9-2 reprinted with permission from P. E. Gold, "Sweet Memories," *American Scientist*, p. 153. Copyright © 1987 by Sigma Xi, the Scientific Society, Inc.

**Page 285**   Fig. 9-6 reprinted from L. P. Peterson and M. J. Peterson, "Short-term Retention of Individual Verbal Items," *Journal of Experimental Psychology*, 58, 193–198. Copyright © 1959 by the American Psychological Association. Reprinted with permission of the author.

**Page 330**   Fig. 11-2 reprinted with permission from R. V. Hall, D. Lund, and J. Jackson, "Effects of Teacher Attention on Study Behavior," *Journal of Applied Behavior Analysis*, 1, 1–12. Copyright © 1968 by the Society for the Experimental Analysis of Behavior.

**Page 335**   Fig. 11-4 reprinted with permission from B. Abbott and P. Badia, "Choice for Signaled Over Unsignaled Shock as a Function of Signal Length, *Journal of the Experimental Analysis of Behavior*, 32, 409–417. Copyright © 1979 by the Society for the Experimental Analysis of Behavior.

**Page 337**   Fig. 11-5 reprinted from H. Sidman, "Two Temporal Parameters of the Maintenance of Avoidance Behavior by the White Rat," *Journal of Comparative and Physiological Psychology*, 46, 253–261. Copyright © 1953 by the American Psychological Association. Reprinted with permission of the author.

**Page 339**   Fig. 11-7 reprinted with permission from S. Camarata, "Application of Naturalistic Conversation Training to Speech Production in Children with Speech Disorders," *Journal of Applied Behavior Analysis*, 26, 173–182. Copyright © 1993 by the Society for the Experimental Analysis of Behavior.

**Page 341**   Fig. 11-8 reprinted with permission from W. L. Palya, D. Walter, R. Kessel, and R. Lucke, "Investigating Behavioral Dynamics with a Fixed-Time Extinction Schedule and Linear Analysis," *Journal of the Experimental Analysis of Behavior*, 66, 391–409.

# NAME INDEX

# SUBJECT INDEX